D0511546

338.984 (411)

THE DEVELOPMENT OF
INDUSTRIAL SOCIETY
IN IRELAND

IRISH MANAGEMENT INSTITUTE LIBRARY

2

PROCEEDINGS OF THE BRITISH ACADEMY · 79

THE DEVELOPMENT OF INDUSTRIAL SOCIETY IN IRELAND

The Third Joint Meeting of
the Royal Irish Academy and the British Academy

Edited by
J. H. GOLDTHORPE
&
C. T. WHELAN

Published for THE BRITISH ACADEMY
by OXFORD UNIVERSITY PRESS

Oxford University Press, Walton Street, Oxford OX2 6DP
Oxford New York Toronto
Delhi Bombay Calcutta Madras Karachi
Kuala Lumpur Singapore Hong Kong Tokyo
Nairobi Dar es Salaam Cape Town
Melbourne Auckland Madrid
and associated companies in
Berlin Ibadan

Published in the United States
by Oxford University Press Inc, New York

© The British Academy, 1992

First published 1992
Paperback edition 1994

All rights reserved. No part of this publication may be reproduced,
stored in a retrieval system, or transmitted, in any form or by any means,
electronic, mechanical, photocopying, recording, or otherwise, without
the prior permission of The British Academy

British Library Cataloguing in Publication Data
Data available

ISBN 0-19-726141-8
ISSN 0068-1202

Typeset by J&L Composition Ltd, Filey, North Yorkshire
Printed in Great Britain by
Bookcraft (Bath) Limited
Midsomer Norton, Avon

CONTENTS

Proceedings of the British Academy, **79**, 1–3

Introduction

JOHN H. GOLDTHORPE* & CHRISTOPHER T. WHELAN†
* Nuffield College, Oxford; Fellow of the British Academy
† Economic and Social Research Institute, Dublin

THE PAPERS collected in this volume were (apart from the last) initially prepared for a conference held at Nuffield College, Oxford, in December 1990. This conference itself had its origins in ties built up over two decades between Nuffield and the Economic and Social Research Institute, Dublin. These ties were first formed by Irish students who came to Nuffield, with support from ESRI, in order to undertake graduate work, and who were then instrumental in bringing into contact other social scientists in the two institutions whose interests were in important respects complementary.

At ESRI sociologists and applied economists were concerned to develop an understanding of contemporary Irish society that was both theoretically informed and of relevance to policy issues. At Nuffield there was a long-standing interest in current theories of industrial society and in the possibility of testing these theories through systematic comparative research. It readily became apparent that the Irish experience of industrialisation offered a valuable opportunity for extending such research, while the critique emerging from Nuffield of both standard liberal and Marxist theories of modern industrialism proved illuminating in the Irish case.

It was, then, in order to further collaboration on these lines that the 1990 conference was arranged. A majority of those who participated had affiliations with ESRI or Nuffield (or both) but the opportunity was taken to involve others, in particular, sociologists of religion and political scientists, who were able to widen the range of issues addressed.

No attempt was made to impose a uniformity of approach on those invited to prepare papers, apart from the request that they should, implicitly if not explicitly, situate their treatment of whatever aspect of the Irish case they dealt with in the larger context of debates on the nature and development of industrial society in general. This request was readily

January 1992. © The British Academy 1992.

complied with, but, as will be apparent from the pages that follow, in a variety of styles. Thus, some authors base their arguments on wide-ranging reviews of the relevant literature, while others concentrate on the more detailed analysis of findings from their own research. One consequence of this is that papers differ in the demands they make on readers' technical capabilities. We recognise that, for some, regression analysis and loglinear modelling, not to mention Voronoi tessellations, may appear as rather alien and forbidding notions. However, general readers should find sufficient explanation provided to enable them to grasp the main purposes of these techniques and the significance of the results to which they lead, while students of the social sciences should by now be prepared to acquire an understanding of such techniques as essential tools of their trade.

At the same time, we may add that one feature is common to the papers here collected to a greater degree than we had initially dared hope: that is, the presentation and discussion of Irish data in a comparative context, as the result of authors' awareness of, or indeed participation in, major cross-national research enterprises. Thus, for example, the CASMIN (Comparative Analysis of Social Mobility in Industrial Nations) Project, the Luxembourg Income Study, the DUES (Development of Unions in European Societies) Project, the European Value Systems Study and the European Parliament Election Study are all drawn on to good effect. Such interest and involvement in comparative research provides, in our view, the best means of ensuring both that the study of Irish society continues to be conducted to a high standard and that it attracts the attention that it merits within the international community of social scientists.

Finally as regards the scope of the papers, we should make it clear that it was from the start understood that attention was to focus on the Republic of Ireland, since the experience of the Republic and of the North, in their industrial development as in other respects, appeared too divergent to make a joint treatment feasible within a single volume. It would of course still be unrealistic to leave the North entirely out of account, and authors have not attempted to do so. However, where the name 'Ireland' appears in the text, it is to be taken as applying to the Republic, other than where it is indicated, or the context makes abundantly clear, that the reference is to the island as a whole.

It remains here for us to acknowledge the extensive support and assistance that we have received in preparing this collection. First of all, we must, on our own behalf and that of all contributors, thank the British Academy and the Royal Irish Academy for allowing the conference at Nuffield to be held under their auspices and for their financial backing. Valuable additional support, financial and in kind, was provided by both Nuffield and ESRI. In organising the conference, we were greatly reliant on the energy and efficiency of Mairead Reidy, and Brendan Halpin and Niamh Hardiman also gave timely help.

The success of the conference was of crucial importance in motivating the authors of papers to produce the new versions here presented; and, in this connection, we should emphasise the significant input made by other participants, especially those who acted as 'prepared discussants': John Geary, Brian Girvin, Anthony Heath, Joseph Lee, Dorren McMahon, Tony McCashin, Lars Mjøset, Michael O'Higgins and Mairead Reidy.

We are further grateful to the British Academy for undertaking publication of this volume and for the assistance given to us by the Academy's Publications Officer, James Rivington, and his colleague, Hilary Kent. In carrying out our editorial duties, we have also received unfailing help from our staff of our own institutions, and we would in particular wish to thank Mary Cleary, Pat Hopkins, Peter Murray and Maura Rohan at ESRI and Audrey Skeats at Nuffield.

Proceedings of the British Academy, **79**, 5–29

The Context of Economic Development

KIERAN A. KENNEDY

Economic and Social Research Institute, Dublin; Member of the Royal Irish Academy

Introduction

IN THE LAST FIVE YEARS or so there has been a spate of studies on Irish economic development over the longer term (notably Crotty, 1986; Kennedy *et al.*, 1988; Lee, 1989; Girvin, 1989; O'Malley, 1989; Breen *et al.*, 1990)—to mention only those that cover the broad canvas.[1] The studies have involved a wide range of disciplinary perspectives—economic, historical, political and sociological. In this paper I shall not attempt a balanced survey, let alone a synthesis, of these studies and other relevant work. Instead I will draw selectively on them to try to give a picture of the more important things we know, and do not know, about economic development in Ireland since independence.

The first section outlines the aggregate economic growth record since independence in a comparative European perspective. The thorny issue of performance in relation to potential is then considered, in the course of which some of the major structural changes in the Irish economy are documented. Explanations of the Irish performance are next discussed. We then turn to the question of how well or how badly Ireland is placed as a result of its past development to face future prospects in an ever more integrated Europe. The final section points to major gaps in our knowledge where further research and reflection are needed.

The Economic Growth Record Since Independence

Table 1 shows the growth rates of total real product, population and product per capita in the Republic for various periods from the mid-1920s

Read 7 December 1990. © The British Academy 1992.

[1] Reference should also be made to the studies of Johnson (1985) and L. Kennedy (1988) in the pamphlet series of the Economic and Social History Society of Ireland. Significant recent works on the development of the Northern Ireland economy include L. Kennedy and Ollerenshaw (1985) and Harris *et al.* (1990).

Table 1. Average annual growth rates (%) of total and per capita real product in Ireland and the United Kingdom, 1926–1985.

	Total real product			Population			Real product per capita		
	Republic	Northern Ireland	United Kingdom	Republic	Northern Ireland	United Kingdom	Republic	Northern Ireland	United Kingdom
1926–38[a]	1.3	0.7	2.4	−0.1	0.2	0.4	1.4	0.6	2.0
1938–50	1.1	4.0	1.4	0.1	0.5	0.4	1.0	3.5	0.9
1950–60	1.7	2.6	2.5	−0.5	0.4	0.4	2.2	2.2	2.1
1960–73	4.4	3.7	3.1	0.6	0.6	0.5	3.8	3.1	2.6
1973–85	1.7	1.1	1.2	1.2	0.1	0.1	0.5	1.0	1.1
1926–85[a]	2.1	2.4	2.1	0.3	0.4	0.4	1.8	2.0	1.7

[a] For Northern Ireland, the starting year is 1924.

Source: Kennedy, Giblin and McHugh (1988: Table 6.1)

to the mid-1980s, with corresponding figures for Northern Ireland and the UK. The most striking feature of the table is how close the figures are for the three areas over the period as a whole—and particularly for the Republic and the UK—despite differences in sub-periods. In view of the close ties between the Republic and the UK, the similarity in their long-term growth rates is hardly coincidental and I shall return to the point later.

How satisfactory is it merely to have kept pace with Britain? Obviously it means that there has been little in the way of catching-up or convergence, so that Ireland's living standards remain well below the UK. This in itself, though disappointing, would not matter so much perhaps if the UK had been a star performer in this period. But, in fact, as Table 2 shows, the UK had the worst record in Europe over the period in terms of the growth both of output and output per capita—a conclusion that is generally

Table 2. Comparative long-term growth rates and levels of total product per capita in Western Europe.

European countries (ranked in descending order of product per capita in 1913 in in col. 3)	Average Annual Growth Rates (%) 1913–87		Level of Real Product Per Capita relative to UK (UK = 100)	
	(1) Real Product	(2) Real Product per Capita	(3) 1913	(4) 1987
1. United Kingdom	1.9	1.5	100	100
2. Switzerland	2.9	2.1	81	130
3. Belgium	2.1	1.8	78	96
4. Netherlands	3.0	1.8	78	100
5. Denmark	2.8	2.0	73	108
6. Austria	2.2	2.0	65	96
7. France	2.6	2.2	63	103
8. West Germany	2.8	2.3	62	109
9. Sweden	2.9	2.4	58	113
10. Italy	2.9	2.2	58	98
11. **Ireland**	**1.9**	**1.7**	**53**	**60**
12. Norway	3.5	2.7	51	127
13. Spain	2.8	1.9	51	71
14. Finland	3.4	2.7	42	104
15. Portugal	3.1	2.4	27	51
16. Greece	3.3	2.4	26	51
Mean	2.7	2.1	61	95

Source: Derived from Maddison (1989) and OECD *National Accounts 1960–1989: Main Aggregates, Vol. 1*. The product per capita levels relate to GDP per head using purchasing power parities based on 1980 relative prices.

regarded as robust even with due allowance for the fragility of estimates
of long-term economic growth. Just prior to the First World War, Ireland's
income per capita at between one-half and three-fifths of the UK level—
then the highest in Europe—stood at quite a respectable relative level,
close to the mean of the other countries of western Europe. Today, still
standing at about three-fifths of the British level, Ireland has one of the
lowest living standards in western Europe, with less than two-thirds of the
mean level and only Portugal and Greece below it.

Reverting to Table 1 for a moment, it will be noted that Ireland's
record did improve considerably in the 1960s when its growth rate
substantially outpaced that of the UK and came into line with the average
for continental Western Europe. Even in this period, however, as may be
seen from Table 3, the Irish growth rate was still well below that of the
other low income countries of Europe, which were then experiencing a
strong convergence towards the levels of the richer countries. Moreover, the improvement in Ireland's record was not soundly maintained
subsequently after the first oil crisis in 1973.[2]

Table 3. Growth rate of real GDP in poorer Western European countries 1960–1973
(% p.a.).

Ireland	Finland	Italy	Portugal	Spain	Greece
4.4	5.0	5.3	6.9	7.3	7.7

Source: OECD *Historical Statistics*.

An alternative basis of comparison is to look at the growth record in
the seventy years since independence in relation to the seventy years
previously. Briefly, the picture is that, while the growth of output was
undoubtedly higher after independence and population decline was eventually arrested, the growth of per capita income, surprisingly, was probably
not significantly higher. In the public mind, however, the most demoral-
ising feature of Ireland's economic experience after independence was the
failure for so long to arrest population decline which continued up to 1961,
involving net emigration in that period of over one million persons. Indeed
if one wished to stick rigidly to Kuznets's definition of economic growth as
involving a sustained rise both in population and in product per capita
(Kuznets, 1965: 6), Ireland experienced economic growth only for a
small proportion of the last one hundred and fifty years. Moreover,

---

[2] Since 1973, GDP is not a good measure of Ireland's performance since its growth depended
so heavily on government spending and inward foreign investment. These gave rise to
offsetting outflows of interest on foreign debt and profit repatriations, which substantially
reduced GNP relative to GDP.

notwithstanding the substantial population exodus, Ireland failed to provide enough jobs for those who remained: the unemployment rate has been high throughout and never fell below about 5 per cent even when rates of 2 per cent or less were commonplace in the rest of Europe.

Ireland's unfavourable demographic and labour force experience makes it unique, and I shall return later to the cause and effect relationship with economic development. Here I would only like to add that this experience, in a purely accounting sense, 'explains' a not insignificant part of the gap in the level and growth of income per capita *vis-à-vis* other European countries. In 1986, only 30.5 per cent of the Irish population were employed, a figure well below the EC average of 38.7 per cent. The low figure for Ireland is not simply due to the much higher unemployment rate in Ireland—though that indeed is the major factor. It arises also because of the higher proportion of the population in the dependent age groups, and the lower than average participation rate. These variables interact in complex ways with each other and with other demographic or labour force variables—such as Ireland's birth rate which only began to fall in the 1980s, or the selective character of Irish emigration which has always been heavily concentrated in the young active age groups.

Compared, for instance, to Finland in 1986, Ireland's income per capita amounted only to 59 per cent, but had Ireland had the same proportion of the population at work (50 per cent in Finland), the difference in income per capita would be almost entirely eliminated. Or to put the matter another way, the productivity of those at work in Ireland in 1986 was nearly as high as in Finland: the difference in living standards was due, arithmetically, to the fact that so few were at work in Ireland.[3] Likewise, over time, the growth of GDP per worker in Ireland relative to other countries has been better than the growth of GDP per capita. This is because the proportion of the population actually employed fell by 26 per cent between 1926 and 1986 (from 41.4 per cent to 30.5 per cent)—a much bigger decline than in other European countries, in some of which (notably the Scandinavian countries) the proportion rose.

Performance in Relation to Potential

The Irish growth record since independence can be described, at best, as mediocre. But the question immediately arises as to whether this poor

[3] This statement is designed only to illustrate the order of magnitude of Ireland's exceptionally low employment/population ratio, and not to assert causality. Clearly if Ireland had had the same proportion of the population in employment as Finland, the Irish productivity level would not have been the same unless other things also had changed (e.g. the capital stock).

record might not be due to Ireland having a smaller potential for growth
than other countries—due for example to disadvantages that applied
uniquely to Ireland. It is not inconceivable that Ireland performed as well
in relation to potential as other European countries, and that its mediocre
record arose simply from its poor potential.

In the present state of knowledge, there is no precise way to determine
a country's potential for long-term growth. The prevailing measures of
potential output used by economists relate essentially to the short run.
They take as given existing structures, institutions, attitudes etc. whereas
the process of long-run development involves major changes in such
variables. An even more fundamental difficulty in specifying a country's
potential arises from the importance of the human dimension—both as a
direct input and as embodied in institutions and culture. This factor is
evident from the rapid progress made by some countries in the face of
considerable material and locational disadvantages. Indeed, virtually all
countries which have developed rapidly have demonstrated an ability to
overcome constraints and disadvantages through human ingenuity. A
feature of the human dimension that does not apply to the other factors
of production is that, because it can react consciously to its environment,
its contribution may sometimes be stimulated and enhanced by the very
existence of difficulties. Thus, it is possible to point to examples where
difficulties were instrumental in evoking human ingenuity that might
otherwise have lain dormant—a truth enshrined in the motto 'necessity is
the mother of invention'. But one can also point readily to cases where
necessity proved to be crushing when the human response was inadequate,
and we are very far from understanding which forces and conditions are
most likely to stimulate a creative human response either at the individual
or at the social level.

Perhaps what can usefully be done is to try to assess the significance of
some major constraints applying in the Irish situation, leaving open for the
moment whether these were greater or less than those that applied to other
countries.

The UK connection

At independence over 90 per cent of Irish exports went to the UK (Table
4). In addition the financial, labour market, institutional and other links
were extremely close. This is not surprising given that Ireland was for so
long a region of the UK. Nor would it necessarily have been a disadvantage
if the UK had been a dynamic economy. But there is strong, if not decisive,
theoretical and empirical support for the view that peripheral low income
areas find it difficult to catch up when the core is stagnant or growing slowly.

Table 4. Composition of Irish merchandise exports (%).

	1929	1950	1988
Destination			
UK	92	88	35
Other EC	3	7	39
US	2	2	9
Other	3	3	17
Total	100	100	100
Commodity			
Food and drink	86	80	26
Manufactures	} 14	7	66
Other		13	8
Total	100	100	100
Ratio Exports: GNP (factor cost)	29	20	66

Source: *Statistical Abstract of Ireland.*

In this regard the contrasting experience of the poorer member states of the EC (Greece, Spain, Portugal and Ireland) before and after 1973 is striking (Table 5). Prior to 1973, when the whole western world experienced rapid growth, there was strong convergence in all except for Ireland. Even Ireland is not an outright exception since during 1960–73 its living standards were converging rapidly in relation to the UK, the market on which it was still largely dependent. From 1973 to the mid-1980s convergence ceased with the general slow-down in growth.[4] There are plausible reasons for attributing the causation to growth. When growth generally is buoyant and the strong centres are pressing on the limits of capacity, forces enter in which enable the periphery to outpace the core. The core areas begin to experience labour and skill shortages, congestion intensifies, house prices soar—thereby enhancing the attractions of the periphery as a location for new investment. On the other hand, when there is slack everywhere the centralising tendencies in economic activity tend to dominate.[5]

[4] The suggestion in Table 5 of a slight convergence for Ireland from 1973 to 1987 is more apparent than real, due to the limitations of the GDP measure in this period pointed out in n. 2, above.
[5] Eoin O'Malley had drawn my attention to another argument derived from traditional trade theory pointing in the same direction, namely, that the law of comparative advantage presupposes full employment and that when such conditions apply at the centre the less developed areas are likely to enjoy greater scope to exploit their comparative advantage.

Table 5. Relative GDP per capita in poorer EC countries 1960, 1973 and 1987 (Euro 12 = 100).

	1960	1973	1987
Greece	39	57	54
Ireland	62	60	63
Portugal	38	55	54
Spain	59	77	74
Four poorest combined	52	70	67
Ratio 4 poorest: 4 richest	42	63	60

Source: EC Commission *Annual Economic Report 1988–89*, Statistical Annex, Table A.4.

No other European country was as dependent on one market as Ireland was on the UK. No matter how hard Ireland tried, it was going to take time to reduce this dependence. The 1930s and 1940s were not auspicious times for diversifying the destination of trade, even if Irish policy had been directed more effectively towards that goal. Indeed as late as 1950 the degree of trade dependence on the UK was virtually unaltered. The postwar period was much more favourable to diversifying the destination and commodity composition of Irish trade, and it is surely no accident that Ireland began to outpace Britain as that process intensified. Yet the fact that even by 1960 Ireland still sent 75 per cent of its exports to the UK goes at least some way towards accounting for the fact, shown in Table 3, that Ireland grew more slowly from 1960 to 1973 than the other low-income countries of Europe. During this period the volume of imports of goods and services rose annually by 5 per cent in the UK compared with 8.5 for OECD Europe, so that it is not surprising that Ireland, with its heavy UK dependence, had a much lower export growth than any of the other countries in Table 3 (except Finland).

Inherited economic structure

The partition of Ireland, with Northern Ireland remaining in the UK, deprived the new state of the only region with substantial industrial development. Independent Ireland was heavily reliant on agriculture in relation both to trade (Table 4) and employment (Table 6), with only a minuscule manufacturing sector.

One must be careful here to avoid special pleading, since the high share of agriculture in the 1920s was not dissimilar to what prevailed in many European countries 50 years earlier (see Maddison, 1982: Table C5). It might therefore be said to portray simply Ireland's latecomer status rather

Table 6.   Structure of employment in Ireland 1926 and 1986.

	1926		1986	
	No. (000)	Share (%)	No. (000)	Share (%)
Agriculture	653	54	168	16
Industry	162	13	307	28
Manufacturing	(120)	(10)	(211)	(20)
Services	406	33	606	56
Total	1,220	100	1,081	100

Source: Kennedy, Giblin and McHugh (1988: Table 7.2).

than a constraint on future development. Nevertheless, even without necessarily accepting O'Malley's (1989) thesis about the difficulties of late industrialisation, it can be argued that the structure of activity which Ireland inherited at independence was not conducive to rapid development in the prevailing conditions. The real agricultural price declined drastically from 1919 to the mid-1930s, and thereafter the long-term trend was downwards. The widespread resort to agricultural protectionism in the 1930s restricted market access almost exclusively to the UK, where the indigenous farmers were subsidised in a way that kept prices low. Ireland made matters worse for its own agriculture in the 1930s on the UK market —both in terms of price and market access—as a result of the Economic War. But even without that, conditions were never for long conducive to a strong agricultural performance until Ireland joined the European Community; and even then the prosperous conditions were short-lived. Furthermore, on the supply side, the inherited structure of land tenure— resulting from the settlement of the land question in favour of small scale owner occupation—was ill-adapted to a dynamic expansion of agriculture.

The absence of any widespread manufacturing tradition may be seen from the fact that two-thirds of the tiny manufacturing sector in the 1920s comprised processing of food and drink. Maddison's figures, referred to earlier, show that even fifty years earlier, few of the sixteen developed countries in his sample had quite so small an industrial base, while the figures in Flora (1987) for about the 1920s suggest that, apart from Finland, Ireland was the least developed industrially among thirteen west European countries in terms of the share of the labour force in that sector. Inevitably, it would take time to build this base, and in the prevailing conditions— the widespread protectionism of the 1930s and the absence of a strong flow of mobile, export-oriented foreign enterprise—it would have been very difficult then to build an export-oriented industry even if Ireland had tried to do so.

Cultural legacy

A number of writers have drawn attention to the inhibitions on Irish
economic development at independence resulting from attitudes, institutions etc. inherited from the country's turbulent past. Meenan (1970) has
argued cogently that the conceptions about the economy engendered
during the nationalist struggle, and which were potent in mobilising
support for that struggle, were ill-adapted to the task of economic
regeneration. The major preconceptions which, he claims, were widely
held and took long to unlearn were fourfold: that Irish economic
development had been retarded by British misgovernment; that economic
development depended on the policies followed by the state; that self-
government would quickly bring prosperity; and that the future of the
economy would be determined by what happens in Ireland.

Likewise, a central thesis of Lee (1989) is that the insecurity of
nineteenth century life in Ireland engendered—quite rationally in the
conditions of the time—a 'possession' mentality which carried over into
the twentieth century and stifled the emergence of a 'performance' ethic
so vital for progress in the economy as well as in other areas. In regard to
Olson's (1982) thesis about the inhibiting effect of established interest
groups, it may be noted that the character of the Irish revolution was such
that it did not involve any shake-up of such interests. Crotty's (1986)
theory about the problems of former capitalist colonies can also be
included in the catalogue of arguments suggesting that Ireland's development potential was constrained by its prior history. Finally the incomplete
settlement of the national question at independence had lasting repercussions. Fanning (1990) has argued that 'the Treaty split and the civil war
ensured that, after the Union as under the Union, the dynamic of Irish
politics drew its energy from the conflict of opinion about the legitimacy
of the British connection' so that 'the struggle for political power hinged
on the shape and form of Irish independence, not on the economic policies
best suited to a newly independent state'. Later, since the end of the 1960s,
the Northern Ireland conflict has absorbed much government time as well
as involving substantial security and other costs.

Assessment

Whether the foregoing constraints were greater or less than those facing
other European countries is not a question that can be precisely answered,
at least not in the present state of knowledge. For one thing, there simply
has not been enough quantitative comparative work on the subject. It must
also be taken into account that Ireland at independence had many

advantages not possessed in the same degree by some of the countries that have since outpaced it. Ireland then could no longer be said to be overpopulated, having a relatively low population density; it had no national debt and substantial external capital reserves; there was an extensive rail network; the banking system was widely spread; communications were satisfactory by contemporary standards; and education levels were not inferior to those generally prevailing.

Furthermore, the constraints mentioned above have more force in accounting for Ireland's slow initial progress rather than for the sustained mediocrity of its record. While they might reasonably indicate a low potential in the first thirty years of independence, they are less cogent in explaining why Ireland had not prepared itself better to take early advantage of the great postwar recovery of Europe—so that even in the 1960s it did not catch up as rapidly as the other less developed states of Europe—or why in the late 1970s it created such enormous problems for itself in the 1980s.

The studies mentioned at the start take the view that Ireland's poor record was not chiefly a reflection of a low potential but derived from Ireland's poor performance. By this I take them to mean either that Ireland was not noticeably disadvantaged *vis-à-vis* other European countries *or*, to the extent that it was, these disadvantages were capable of being overcome by feasible policies and actions (not always specified!). While the verdict is unanimous, and is shared by this author, it may not be beyond reasonable doubt: certainly it should be interpreted as an informed opinion rather than an established fact.

There is another possible defence against the charge of poor performance, namely that Ireland simply did not place as high a value on economic development as other countries did. A nation may be conceived of as pursuing many objectives with different degrees of intensity and the fact that it scores poorly on one objective might reflect the low priority attached to the achievement of that objective. It is probable that every country falls short of realising its full economic potential because other goals temper, in varying degree, the urgency with which development is pursued. If the Irish preferred large families to higher per capita income, or chose a quiet life in favour of the disruptions accompanying rapid economic growth, then who is to say they have performed badly? The Irish, so this argument would run, failed to hit the target of economic development, not because they were bad shots but because they were aiming at a different target.

The only author to address this issue (Lee, 1989) dismisses it scornfully in less than a page, arguing that the Irish were not lacking in concern for material gain, though they may have been 'inefficient materialists'. One can sympathise with this dismissive attitude, given that the argument is liable to be invoked to excuse even the most inept performance. Nevertheless, the issue probably deserves a more extensive treatment. Ireland's large religious missionary effort absorbed the energies of many highly motivated and enterprising people. De Valera articulated a vision of Ireland, which had at least wide sentimental appeal, as 'the home of a people who valued material wealth only as the basis of right living, of a people who were satisfied with frugal comfort and devoted their leisure to the things of the spirit' (Moynihan, 1980). Yet, even if it were demonstrated that the Irish attached an exceptionally high priority to spiritual values to the detriment of economic development, this would still raise large questions about the nature of that spirituality. The inadequate rate of economic development imposed severe hardship on many of the weakest classes who were forced to emigrate or remain poor, unemployed and often celibate for life. Hence, even if it were true that Ireland valued economic development less than other countries in the interest of spiritual values, one would still be left to explain *why* it accorded so little priority to an objective that could affect so profoundly what many would now regard as a central spiritual value, namely, the welfare of its most vulnerable people.

Explanations

Economic development is studied not only from different perspectives but also with different objectives. Some are interested in exploring the processes manifested in the course of economic development, others in its causes, and others still in its consequences for various aspects of society which are the ultimate focus of their attention. Of course these objectives are not entirely separable. A fuller knowledge of the 'how' of economic development is indispensable for throwing light on the 'why' questions, while the consequences of economic development in any period may have feedback effects which determine the subsequent course of economic development. Even in the case of those primarily interested in the explanation of economic development, the different disciplinary perspectives they bring to bear will inevitably influence the character of the explanations they provide. Furthermore, explanations may be offered at different levels: some may concentrate on the more proximate causes, while others may wish to explore the deeper forces underlying the proximate causes.

The range of recent interpretations of Irish economic development in the studies mentioned at the start of the paper exemplify this diversity.

Before attempting to generalise about them as a body of literature, it may be helpful to the reader not familiar with them to give a brief individual outline of the approach adopted in each study, taking them in order of date of publication.

Crotty (1986) focuses on the failure of Ireland to provide a livelihood for all its people at acceptable living standards, as exemplified by the long history of emigration and unemployment. In seeking to explain this failure, he rejects detailed comparison with the other countries of Europe. Ireland is altogether unique among European countries in being the only one that was 'capitalist colonised'. Although possessing distinctive features, it is more appropriately analysed in the context of third world underdevelopment. According to Crotty, all former capitalist colonies have not only failed to develop but have 'undeveloped'. The basic reason is that capitalist colonisation imposed a social structure for the profit of the colonial power which was inimical to indigenous development. Independence has not remedied the situation, since independence was generally gained by local elites benefiting from colonisation, who worked to preserve the inherited structures and institutions so as to safeguard their privileged position. The state itself, therefore, became a major barrier to development in all such countries. Undevelopment can only be reversed by 'countering the effects of western culture on non-western societies' (p. 111), involving a major reduction in the power of the State, and Crotty advances a set of radical proposals along those lines for Ireland.

Kennedy et al. (1988) explicitly take the record of economic growth in European countries as an appropriate standard against which to evaluate the Irish record of economic development in the twentieth century. The Irish record emerges as 'mediocre', and the authors argue that it cannot be fully excused by disadvantages applying particularly to Ireland. The analysis of Ireland's performance centres on conventional economic variables such as human and physical capital, foreign trade etc., but the explanation they offer, which is summarised later at the end of this section, invokes more deep-rooted strategic weaknesses.

Although Lee's (1989) book is a general history of Ireland, it concentrates heavily on Irish economic development and, indeed, more than any of the other studies, has been influential in drawing the attention of the wider public to Ireland's poor record over the longer-term. Like Kennedy et al. (1988), but unlike Crotty (1986), Lee views Ireland within a European framework and reaches similar, but more trenchant, conclusions on Ireland's performance. Lee's explanation is contained in a detailed historical discussion of four factors: institutions, intellect, character and identity. The discussion, though always fascinating, is rather diffuse and not easily summarised. The chief organising principle running through the discussion is the 'possession–performance' dichotomy already referred to. Though the social processes through which the possession mentality, developed in the nineteenth century, is transmitted from generation to generation and continues to triumph over a performance ethic, are not explicitly addressed, Lee obviously attaches considerable importance to emigration in this regard. The Irish socio-economic system was one 'that decreed mass emigration and natural population decline as prerequisites for the comfort of the survivors' (p. 644). Lee also has much to say about the failure of elite groups, notably the public administration and social science practitioners, to generate and make use of the knowledge that could transform society.

Girvin's (1989) characterisation of Ireland is given by the title of his book, *Between Two Worlds*, the world of the liberal democratic industrialised states and the underdeveloped, and often undemocratic, states of the Third World. Ireland is placed between these two poles, and does not fit readily into either. In fact it is a hybrid, combining a politically sophisticated society with an underdeveloped economy. Ireland's failure to attain industrial maturity lies at the heart of many of its economic difficulties, and the book provides an in-depth account, drawing heavily on departmental files, of the changing industrial policies pursued in the first forty years or so of independence up to the mid-1960s.

O'Malley's (1989) book also focuses on the inadequate development of industry. This is examined in the context of a general theory about the problems of late industrialisation for all developing countries. The theory emphasises the major barriers to entry and expansion facing indigenous firms in such circumstances, arising from the superior competitive position of larger and longer-established rivals in advanced countries. The barriers exist 'in the wide range of industries which are characterised by factors such as economies of scale, large capital requirements, product differentiation, advanced technology, specialised skills or dependence on external economies inherent in large advanced industrial centres' (p. 259). It is claimed that these barriers would exclude indigenous firms in late industrialising countries from developing many internationally traded industries without active and selective state support in surmounting the barriers. The attraction of foreign enterprises would not suffice to fill the gap since 'they would generally have no decisive secondary effects in stimulating local industry through technology transfer or the development of skills or linkages' (p. 260). Irish industrial experience is investigated in this framework and is interpreted as conforming to it.

The work of Breen *et al.* (1990) examines the transformation of the Irish economy and society since the late 1950s and the consequences of this transformation. It takes social class as the key to explaining social change, but since the class structure in Ireland has been profoundly affected by the State, the central focus of the book is on the impact of State policies on the Irish class structure. The study concludes that the state 'has been monumentally unsuccessful either in ensuring sustained economic growth or in moderating inegalitarian tendencies in the class system' (p. 209). How is this explained? The explanation concentrates heavily on the degree of independence enjoyed by the State in setting its goals ('autonomy') and its ability to achieve these goals ('capacity'). The autonomy of the State has become increasingly circumscribed by, above all, the kind of industrial policy pursued which required ever increasing public expenditure and left the supply of enterprise, which was chiefly foreign, dependent on the vagaries of world economic conditions. The capacity of the State was always limited and has not been enhanced despite the vast increase in the scope of State intervention and expenditure. The catch-all nature of the two main political parties led to a situation where successive governments sought to placate all sectional interests, so that distributional issues were obfuscated rather than resolved. In such circumstances politics were dominated by short-term expediency, so that systematic attempts at long-term planning proved abortive or were not even tried at all. In short, the essence of the problem for these authors is that 'the State has tended to give in rather than develop an overall strategy of development' (p. 218).

It is clear from this brief sketch of the different studies that, while there is overlap in some of the explanations, no unified common explanation emerges. Nevertheless, there are a number of generalisations that are worth making about this range of studies.

First, although some of the authors are either practising economists, or received training in economics, none has attempted to offer an explanation solely in terms of mainstream neoclassical economics. Presumably none of them was convinced that this framework was adequate, and the many Irish economists who profess faith in the application of this paradigm have not sought to confront it with Ireland's long-term development experience. I regard this as a pity since, although not personally convinced that a neoclassical analysis can provide a satisfactory explanation, I believe it could enhance our knowledge, as I shall suggest below. Moreover, such an exercise would, I believe, lead to a clearer identification of where the neoclassical framework breaks down, with the possibility of positive feedback to the development of an enriched neoclassical paradigm.

Second, and partly related to the foregoing point, most of the authors, though in varying degree, emphasise the presence of market failures which could not have been overcome by private individuals or organisations, but which they see as capable of being remedied by government, if only it adopted the right policies.[6] I think this underlies the strong public policy focus in most of the studies as the key to why Ireland did not do better. To overstate the point somewhat, the reader of these studies might reasonably draw the conclusion that Ireland's failure since independence ultimately lay in the fact that government and the public administration lacked either the will or the competence to find and implement the correct policies—though this mythical reader might well be perplexed by the fact that there are often wide divergences among the authors on what they would see as the correct policies! Perhaps some, if not all, of the authors, might have directed more attention to two other possible reasons for policy impotence even when there is no lack of discernment or will: first, not all market failures can be remedied even by a government with unlimited political power; and, second, the political power of government may be severely constrained by the unwillingness of the electorate to support necessary remedies. I do not say that any of the authors was unaware of these points, only that the points might often have figured more prominently. In this regard, an explicit application of the developing body of literature on the economic analysis of democratic choice might yield useful insights.

Third, although some of the studies made extensive use of quantitative data for descriptive purposes, the explanations are all qualitative in nature. None of them attempts an explicit quantification of the various explanatory factors identified. No doubt it might be premature to expect anything better at this stage, but the absence of such quantification makes it hard for others to weigh the significance of different forces either from the viewpoint of evaluating their plausibility or of drawing out a concrete policy programme (see Barry, 1988).

Fourth, the explanations can be divided broadly into those which regard Ireland as an illustration of a more general theory, and those which emphasise special features in the Irish situation. Crotty's (1986) capitalist colonisation and O'Malley's (1989) late development theses fall clearly into the former category, while the explanations offered in Kennedy *et al.* (1988), Lee (1989), Girvin (1989) and Breen *et al.* (1990) fit mainly into the second category.

Finally, it may be noted that the explanations, where different, are not necessarily in conflict since they often operate at different levels. Perhaps I might illustrate this by outlining the basis of the explanation put forward in my own study along with two other ESRI colleagues. Having detailed

---

[6] Crotty is an exception in that for him the State itself is an inevitable impediment and its power must be drastically reduced if development is to take place. He fails to demonstrate convincingly, however, how this could be accomplished and by whom.

the achievements and failures of Ireland's development efforts, we then asked whether there were important common weaknesses attaching to the various efforts. We believed we could identify three such weaknesses: failure to grasp the implications of small size of country, absence of long-term perspective, and neglect of the human resource dimension.

One or more of these weaknesses seemed to be operative in all major areas of policy throughout the period and, as the poor performance of indigenous industry shows, they were just as evident in the private, as in the public, sector. To illustrate in the case of industrial development, all three weaknesses prevailed even when widely different strategies were attempted. Successful industrial expansion in a small economy calls for a high degree of selectivity, since such an economy cannot hope to produce efficiently across as wide a range of activities as a larger country. Yet the methods used in implementing both of the major industrial strategies followed since independence—the protectionist and the outward-looking —failed to grasp this imperative, at least until recently. Both of these strategies made sense in the long-term only on the basis of some variant of the infant industry argument, according to which the infants would eventually grow up and prosper without continuing state protection or subvention. Yet neither of the two strategies had any long-term vision as to how that process would come about, so that further expansion came to depend on increased doses of the same medicine rather than a reduction of the dosage. As to the human resource dimension, it is now widely agreed that deficiencies in personal skills—management, marketing, technological competence etc.—constitute a greater impediment to indigenous industrial development than scarcity of physical capital or finance. Yet it is only in the last decade or so that steps have been taken to redirect incentives and policies to address the human deficiencies.

I would readily concede that these weaknesses themselves require further explanation. They are clearly symptoms of something deeper, the more fundamental explanation of which may lie in the culture, political framework, distribution of power and resources, and various forces on which other authors have focused. What then is the point of the more proximate explanation which we advanced? I would claim two merits. If we are correct in identifying these major weaknesses, then they provide a useful framework within which (i) to explore a deeper understanding, and (ii) to design better strategies for the future. The second of these was uppermost in our minds, and I might draw an analogy between our approach and the prevailing treatment of psychiatric illnesses. Many such illnesses are now treated as arising from a chemical imbalance which can be restored to order by the administration of a variety of drugs. I doubt if anyone regards such an explanation as more than a proximate one, but if the practice of psychiatry had to await ultimate explanations before applying remedies, then it might have to wait a long time. Similarly the formulation of economic strategies cannot wait until the ultimate explanations arrive—if they ever do—but must proceed on the basis of interim but, hopefully, intelligent judgements.

Future Prospects

In a paper on the Irish experience of economic development, it may seem odd to discuss future prospects when there is so much we do not know about the past. Nevertheless, a brief forward look can be justified for two reasons. First, an assessment of future prospects may give greater perspective to our present view of the past. In this connection it should be noted that the research for the studies mentioned above took place in the middle of the 1980s, a time when the Irish economy fared particularly badly and pessimism and demoralisation abounded. It is conceivable that this could have coloured the perspective of some or all of the authors, so that a forward look in the light of the improvement at the end of the decade may provide a useful corrective. Second, if it emerges that Ireland has established a firm basis for future progress, this would take some of the sting out of its poor record up to now.

In many important respects Ireland is now structurally better adapted to develop economically in the future than it was in the 1920s. No longer is it totally dependent on one slowly-growing market (the UK) and on one slowly-growing product (food). Managerial and industrial skills have been improved and are more widely dispersed among the labour force. A much smaller proportion of the labour force is located in activities (agriculture and domestic service) subject to inevitable decline. There is a more sensible awareness of the constraints and opportunities facing Ireland, and a considerable body of experience on which to draw. The EC connection is forcing Ireland to learn from other models besides the UK. The financial collapse that threatened a few years ago, as a result of the inexorable growth of national debt, has been averted by the Programme for National Recovery and associated policies.

The deterioration in the world economy that became evident from the onset of the Iraqi crisis in the autumn of 1990 has led to a marked reduction in growth in 1991. Even more worrying it has led to record unemployment levels as emigration dropped off with the rising unemployment in Britain: by July 1991 the number on the Live Register had reached an all-time high of 261,000. Yet the ESRI *Medium Term Review 1991–1996*, published in June 1991, took a moderately optimistic view of the medium-term outlook.

Following what it saw as a temporary slow-down in 1991, it projected a resumption of steady growth of GNP up to 1996 at an average rate of 3.5 per cent per annum. Inflation would remain low, the balance of payments in surplus, and the ratio of national debt to GNP would continue declining to a level of 93 per cent in 1996 compared with 137 per cent in 1987.

Even with this relatively rosy outlook, however, the prospects for the labour market remain bleak. While the *Medium-Term Review* projected an increase in total employment of about 50,000 over the five-year period (or somewhat less than 1 per cent per annum), this would be quite inadequate to bring down unemployment or prevent a resumption in emigration once the UK labour market improves. Ireland is faced with a situation in which the natural flow into the labour force will continue at a high rate (over 20,000 per annum) until near the end of the decade, since the birth rate began to fall only after 1980. Consequently, Ireland's most intractable problem seems set to persist up to the end of the century, at least. Neither is it clear that Ireland is on the way to developing a strong indigenous manufacturing sector, while the outlook for its agricultural sector is uncertain as a result of the impending reform of the EC Common Agricultural Policy.

In seeking to strengthen its development base in the 1990s to cope with the major problems of labour surplus and low living standards, Ireland will be operating as a member of the European Community which is on the way to becoming ever more closely integrated. While economists are not unanimous on the subject, the weight of opinion favours the view that economic integration in itself will not bring about convergence of the less developed regions, particularly those on the periphery, and indeed there are reasons why it might lead to greater divergence. (Padao-Schioppa, 1987; NESC, 1989). The dilemma posed for Ireland is that, while closer economic union limits the range of development policies that can be applied at national level, there is as yet no indication that adequate regional policies will be implemented at Community level. The next ten years, during which Ireland retains considerable freedom of action to lift itself, will obviously be critical in shaping the course of the economy well into the next century. It is encouraging that this is recognised by the Irish Congress of Trade Unions which, in its proposals for a new programme to follow the Programme for National Recovery, argued the need for the social partners to agree on a ten-year development strategy, noting that Ireland's fundamental structural problems 'owe much to our failure, as a nation, to lay down a long-term strategy for development' (ICTU, 1990). The latter conclusion is one with which I think all of the authors of the recent studies on Irish economic development would agree, though it should be added that Hardiman (1988) showed that absence of long-term perspective was in the past as prevalent in the trade union movement as elsewhere in Ireland.

My own book concluded with the following sentence: 'Provided Ireland can recognise its past failings, and begin to learn to overcome them, then its potential for future development is considerable'. I stand by that sentence, but would also add that the future outlook is not so encouraging as to make any of the authors want to revise significantly what they had to say about the past.

Major Gaps

I have tried to give a brief sketch of where, on the basis of recent studies, we stand in terms of our understanding of Irish economic development. It only remains for me to indicate some of the key gaps in our understanding. Some of these emerge from the recent interpretations, while others have not been dealt with at all in these perspectives.

Major data deficiencies

Official national income estimates begin only from 1938 and the available estimates prior to then badly need to be re-examined. There are many puzzles about the course of the economy in the 1920s and 1930s which cannot be explored satisfactorily until annual national income estimates are made for this period. This is a feasible, though laborious, research task. Indeed it would be possible to provide national income estimates going back to about the middle of the nineteenth century that would be of comparable quality to those widely used for several other European countries. The availability of such estimates, apart from facilitating existing researchers, would have the additional merit of attracting other labourers to the vineyard. Scholars like Maddison, interested in long-term comparative studies, are anxious to include as many countries as possible in their sample. The reason why Ireland is omitted from, and Finland included in, so many such studies is mainly because Ireland has not generated the required long-term estimates—thereby impoverishing research on Ireland.

Another major deficiency in economic statistics is the limited availability of capital stock estimates. The recent study by Henry (1989) has made a valiant effort to repair this deficiency for the period since the Second World War by providing estimates for all sectors, whereas previously estimates were available only for industry. Henry's estimates avowedly leave room for improvement, but, like all statistics, they will be improved best by use. The derivation of capital stock estimates prior to the Second World War would only become a feasible project following the provision of data on investment as part of the compilation of national income estimates referred to above.

Establishing the state of the economy at independence

One of the first difficulties facing anyone investigating Irish economic development since independence is getting a good fix on the starting point. The difficulty stems not only from the poor quality of the data but also from the paucity of research on how Ireland reached that position. As previously mentioned, available estimates suggest that Ireland at independence had a surprisingly high average level of income per capita in a European context. Yet only about seventy years earlier, prior to the Great Famine of 1845–47, it had been widely perceived as having one of the lowest average living standards in Europe.[7] Clearly these two positions are reconcilable only if Ireland had a relatively rapid growth in average income per capita in the seventy years or so prior to independence. Yet most outside commentators have assumed that it grew more slowly than the UK, and although economic historians in Ireland have been aware that this assumption is not well founded, they have not taken the trouble to document the overall position. This gap has arisen partly because systematic aggregate estimates have not been made, and partly because the prime focus of many Irish economic historians is on 'micro' and local developments.

There is a fascinating story here waiting to be documented, which is not only of innate interest but undoubtedly has profound implications for the subsequent course of events after independence. What seems to have happened is that Ireland did indeed have a relatively rapid rise in average income per capita despite having a very low growth in total real output. This came about not only because of the massive fall in population but also because real income was augmented by favourable terms of trade, which encouraged specialisation in favourably priced livestock production and in turn intensified population decline. In addition real disposable income was probably boosted further by increased emigrants' remittances, a reversal of net factor income outflows (interest on capital and rent), and possibly greater government net transfers. Moreover, there must have been enormous changes in the distribution of income since the decline in

---

[7] Louis Cullen has pointed out to me that this perception may have been formed incorrectly from the gross inequality in income distribution and resulting extreme poverty, so that we cannot be certain that overall average income was exceptionally low in Ireland by the European standards of the time.

population predominantly affected the poorest element: among other things, this factor produces the statistical quirk of raising average income without any necessary improvement for the remaining population. In short, the broad picture seems to be that Ireland achieved a respectable standard of living without experiencing a corresponding real development —a very unusual situation.

The anomaly is compounded by the fact that the crude estimates we have for the 1920s suggest that the average income level in Northern Ireland was not much greater than in the rest of the country. This is surprising given that the North is generally thought of as more prosperous at the time of the Famine, and that subsequently the North experienced considerable industrialisation whereas the South, if anything, experienced de-industrialisation.

Neoclassical framework

Earlier, I mentioned the absence of a systematic quantitative analysis of Irish economic development along mainstream neoclassical lines. A standard growth accounting methodology, derived from neoclassical analysis and pioneered in the 1960s by Edward Denison for the US, has now been applied to a wide range of countries.[8] This methodology does not provide a fundamental explanation of economic growth: rather it 'accounts for' growth in the sense of quantifying the contribution of all the various inputs that can be identified, relying basically on neoclassical assumptions to justify the use of distributive shares in national income as weights. Nevertheless, the availability of such an analysis for Ireland would greatly sharpen the focus of thinking about Irish economic development.[9] The body of data now available makes this a feasible exercise at least for the period since the Second World War.

Neoclassical economics also attaches great importance to the deleterious effects of such factors as price distortions, the possibility of the exchange rate having been overvalued, tax disincentives, restrictive practices, employment protection legislation etc. Yet there has been little attempt over the long-term to identify these systematically and to quantify their effects in order to assess how far they might go to explaining Ireland's mediocre record. This would be particularly interesting in regard to the

[8] The application of this methodology formed the core of the major study of UK economic growth from 1856 to 1973 by Matthews *et al.* (1982), who then used the results as a foundation for exploring more fundamental causes.

[9] An application of this approach to Ireland as one of a group of countries was made by Balassa and Bertrand (1970) but the application was limited to manufacturing industry.

allocation of entrepreneurial effort in view of the central importance attached by all writers to Ireland's unimpressive record in developing indigenous industry. Baumol (1990) has argued recently that differences between countries in the allocation of entrepreneurial talent among different activities are of far more consequence than differences in the total supply of entrepreneurs. Moreover, the reward structure profoundly influences the allocation of enterprise between productive and nonproductive activities, and 'the prevailing rules that affect the allocation of entrepreneurial activity can be observed, described, and, with luck, modified and improved . . .' Such an analysis would not necessarily conflict with that of O'Malley if it emerged that the relative reward structure applying to different activities is strongly influenced by late development.

Cross-country and cross-regional comparisons

It is surprising how little interest scholars in the South and North of Ireland, with some exceptions, have shown in studying each others' economy since partition. Both have tended to look more towards the UK than towards each other. Even less work has been done by way of comparing the Republic with other regions of the UK. Such comparisons would often prove more enlightening than comparison with the UK as a whole. They would, for instance, help us to address more meaningfully the question of how much independence mattered to the Republic, distinguishing the degree to which political independence was accompanied by economic freedom from the uses made of that freedom.

Systematic attempts to learn from the experience of other small European countries are only at the beginning stage, but offer the prospect of rich insights. In particular, once the quantifiable differences in such variables as natural resource endowments, growth of factor inputs and productivity, access to external markets etc. have been systematically isolated, such comparative studies could help to provide a more definite assessment of the importance of the political, social and cultural influences that are not readily quantifiable. Such comparative work is essential to examine various hypotheses needing further investigation, such as the nature of national institutions conducive to innovation, the significance of consensus and corporatist arrangements, and the possibility of virtuous or vicious cycles of development. A major study commissioned by the National Economic and Social Council and recently completed explores such issues for Ireland in companion with a number of other small European countries (Mjøset, 1992).

Consequences of emigration

The most unique features of Irish economic experience lie in the demographic area, and in particular in the scale and character of emigration. There is general agreement that emigration is a consequence of poor economic development, but no similar agreement about the feedback impact of emigration on subsequent development. Plausible arguments can be made that emigration relieved pressures that would otherwise have led to immiserisation of the population. The recent NESC report (Sexton *et al.*, 1991), for instance, concluded that there was no firm evidence that high emigration leads to lower economic growth, and even went so far as to say that 'there is evidence that the rise in population that would have followed the cessation of emigration would have had adverse repercussions on living standards' (p. 235). But it is also possible to take an alternative view, and plausible arguments can be made that, while the short-term impact of emigration was to improve living standards for those remaining, its longer-term consequences were corrosive. Proponents of this view, such as Kennedy *et al.* (1988) and Lee (1989), emphasise the long-run impact of emigration in limiting the scale of the home market and in removing pressures to reform a conservative and conformist social structure, the institutions of which were ill-adapted to innovation. In this view emigration is seen as a major cause, as well as a consequence, of Ireland's poor rate of development, and it would figure as a key link in any interpretation of Ireland's experience as a vicious circle in contrast with the virtuous circles in other small European countries.

Any research contributing to a resolution of this issue would be of wider interest now in an EC context, given the differing views on the degree to which emigration might provide an avenue towards convergence for the peripheral low income areas of the Community.

The services sector

It is now platitudinous to bemoan the paucity of attention to the services sector, given that in most modern economies the sector now accounts for about 60 per cent or more of the labour force. Nevertheless the point is worth repeating for Ireland since even at independence the services sector was substantial. The share of the labour force then engaged in services (33 per cent) was higher than in many other countries at a similar stage of their development—the share in Finland, for instance, at about the same time was probably less than 15 per cent—while, as a proportion of non-agricultural employment, the services sector was quite exceptionally dominant in Ireland, accounting for almost three-quarters of the total.

A major reason for the widespread neglect of services is the belief that its growth, unlike industry, is a consequence rather than a cause of development. Even if that is true, there are still important reasons for concentrating greater attention on this sector. For example, Irish economists have been considerably exercised by the fact that state policy subsidised capital when there was a perennial labour surplus, but the main focus of their attack has been on the manufacturing sector. In fact, however, in the ten years 1974–84 manufacturing accounted for only one-fifth of gross fixed investment (and much less earlier on) whereas services absorbed over one-third and dwellings a further one-quarter—and in both these areas capital was often priced well below its social opportunity cost. If, therefore, the subsidisation of capital was a major factor explaining the the non-absorption of surplus labour, then the services sector deserves at least as close an examination as the manufacturing sector.

There are of course many other issues worthy of study in relation to the role of services, such as the adequacy of the part played by the financial sector in encouraging productive development, or the degree to which considerations of security and status led parents to push the brightest children towards safe jobs in the public service and the professions. More attention to the services sector, apart from its direct importance, might throw light on some of Ireland's more obvious failures in economic development, such as the poor performance of indigenous industry.

I hope, therefore, that in this paper I have managed to show that while the recent spate of studies on Irish economic development have left many unanswered questions, they have opened up the subject in a way that will give lasting and productive employment to an enlarged group of scholars!

Acknowledgements. I would like to thank Frank Barry of University College Dublin, Louis Cullen and Dermot McAleese of Trinity College Dublin, my ESRI colleagues, Terry Baker, Richard Breen, John Fitz Gerald and Eoin O'Malley, and the joint editors of this volume for valuable comments on an earlier draft.

Proceedings of the British Academy, **79**, 31–52

Problems of Industrialisation in Ireland

EOIN O'MALLEY

Economic and Social Research Institute, Dublin

Introduction

WHEN THE IRISH FREE STATE was established in the early 1920s, it had a very small industrial sector. In 1926, only 13 per cent of the labour force was engaged in industry, broadly defined,[1] and only 10 per cent of the labour force was in manufacturing (O'Mahony, 1967: 19). By comparison, about 25 per cent or more of the labour force was engaged in manufacturing in other small European economies such as Denmark, Sweden, Belgium and the Netherlands at around that time, although the situation in Finland was more comparable to Ireland.

Since then, Irish manufacturing has grown considerably, with output growth averaging 4.5 per cent per annum in the six decades 1926–86 and manufacturing employment growth averaging 1.9 per cent per annum in the same period (Kennedy, Giblin and McHugh, 1988: 228). By the early 1980s, 21 per cent of the labour force was in manufacturing with 31 per cent in all of industry, and this proportion in total industrial employment was similar to, or even higher than in Denmark, the Netherlands and Sweden.

In some important respects, however, the nature of Ireland's relatively late industrialisation has been rather different to that of earlier developers and the structure of industry in Ireland today differs from that of more advanced economies. There are also certain similarities to the experience of developing countries or newly industrialising countries.

Phases of Industrial Growth

During the 1920s there was very limited industrial growth in Ireland and there was no very strong government policy to promote industrialisation.

Read 7 December 1990. © The British Academy 1992.

[1] This includes building, electricity, gas and other non-manufacturing 'industrial' activities, as well as manufacturing.

The first phase of substantial industrial growth occurred in the 1930s and 1940s, following the introduction of strong protection against imports which encouraged import-substitution. This growth virtually came to a halt in the 1950s, however, and the second main phase of industrialisation in the 1960s and 1970s followed the introduction of new 'outward-looking', export-promoting policies. There were then further significant difficulties in the 1980s, which saw the greatest and longest sustained decline in industrial employment since the foundation of the state. In the past few years, however, since about the end of 1987, growth of industrial employment has picked up again.

In the first phase of industrialisation in the 1930s and 1940s which followed the introduction of protection, industry grew quite rapidly apart from a temporary halt caused by the difficulty of obtaining materials and fuel imports during the Second World War. Manufacturing employment more than doubled in the period 1931–51 according to the Census of Industrial Production.[2] This experience of considerable industrial growth beginning during the international depression of the 1930s was obviously quite anomalous among western European countries. But it corresponds quite well with the contemporary experience of some of the less-developed countries (e.g., Argentina, Brazil, Chile and Mexico) which were independent at the time and resorted to protection during the depression, thereby facilitating import-substituting industrialisation.

By 1951, 22 per cent of the Irish labour force was working in all of industry with 15 per cent in manufacturing alone. This was distinctly higher than in the 1920s but was still little more than half the level of many western European countries, although it was comparable to some Latin American countries such as Mexico and Brazil (Furtado, 1976: ch. 11). The main emphasis in industrial expansion had been on consumer goods and certain technically mature intermediate products, with only a very limited range of capital goods or technically advanced industries in general. The pattern of industrial growth had been fairly typical of what is commonly called the 'easy' stage of import-substitution in developing countries. It appears that protection helped to overcome the difficulties faced by new or small firms in competing with larger and stronger established foreign competitors, in the home market at least, in the more technically mature and less complex types of industry. But there was little progress in developing the more technologically demanding or highly skill-intensive activities.

---

[2] This source exaggerates the rate of growth to some extent, however, since the coverage of the Census of Industrial Production was extended during the period. It is clear, nevertheless, that there was considerable industrial growth in the 1930s and 1940s.

There was also very little development of industrial exports as the protected industries relied very heavily on the home market. By 1951, just 16 per cent of manufactured output was exported and, if Food, Drink and Tobacco are excluded, the figure was just 6 per cent for the rest of manufacturing. Thus little progress had been made in breaking into open competition with advanced industrial countries.

The phase of protectionist industrial growth ended in the 1950s and there was virtually no increase in manufacturing employment between 1951 and 1958. The difficulties of the 1950s were basically due to the emergence of a chronic balance of payments constraint. This arose partly from the near exhaustion of the 'easy' stage of import-substituting industrialisation, which meant that there was little further replacement of imports by new domestic production. At the same time, imports of goods which had *not* been replaced by domestic production, including many capital goods and material inputs, had to continue to grow as long as the economy was growing. Thus the bill for imports of goods which had not been substituted by domestic production eventually grew to exceed the cost of imports before the process of import-substitution began. Since there was a continuing failure to achieve significant growth of exports, serious balance of trade deficits became inevitable, leading to a chronic balance of payments crisis and an inability to pay for the increased imports which would have been needed to accompany further growth.

Thus, the Republic of Ireland in the 1950s experienced a fairly typical conclusion to a process of import-substituting industrialisation, where rather indiscriminate protectionism was the main policy instrument used. Other developing countries using the same approach commonly ran into a similar problem eventually with a balance of payments constraint on further growth, although many of them went through the sequence rather later than Ireland since they only acquired the independence necessary to adopt protection in the 1950s or 1960s.

In view of the difficulties experienced in Ireland in the 1950s, a number of related and quite fundamental changes in policy were introduced. From the late 1950s, the emphasis shifted to developing industrial exports, and new tax concessions and grants were introduced to encourage and assist firms to develop production for export markets. In addition, active steps began to be taken to seek out and attract foreign firms to produce in Ireland for export markets. And finally, the protectionist measures against imports were gradually dismantled, opening up the home market to more direct foreign competition. This latter process began in earnest with a free trade agreement with the United Kingdom in the mid-1960s and it was taken further when Ireland entered into free trade with the EC after joining the Community in 1973.

Such a switch from an 'inward-looking' to an 'outward-looking' strategy for industrialisation has since been at least partially followed by quite a large number of developing countries which ran into problems similar to those experienced by Ireland in the 1950s. However, while many of them have adopted the goal of export promotion, and have sought to attract foreign firms as one means of achieving that aim, not many have gone as far as Ireland has in entering into full free trade arrangements with major advanced industrial countries. Ireland was one of the earliest of relatively late-industrialising countries to switch from an inward-looking to an outward-looking strategy and, in the matter of dropping protection at least, it has so far gone further than most of them.

Under the new outward-looking strategy, industrial growth picked up considerably in the 1960s and 1970s compared with the 1950s. Whereas manufacturing output grew by just 1.7 per cent per annum in 1951–58, it increased to 6.7 per cent per annum in 1958–73 and 5.1 per cent per annum in 1973–79. The average annual rate of growth of manufacturing employment increased from just 0.2 per cent in 1951–58 to 2.4 per cent in 1958–73 and 0.8 per cent in 1973–79.[3]

This phase of industrialisation was characterised by particularly rapid growth of exports. Whereas just 16 per cent of manufactured output was exported in 1951, this rose to 41 per cent in 1978 and further to 64 per cent by 1988. Naturally this trend helped to ease the balance of payments difficulties which had caused such problems in the 1950s and thus it facilitated overall growth of the economy.

In the 1980s, however, worrying new trends emerged, even though the indicators appeared somewhat ambiguous at first sight. Manufacturing employment reached its peak level in 1979 and then declined for eight consecutive years until 1987, falling by as much as one-fifth in that period. But then, for most of this period, industrial output continued to grow quite strongly, often at about the highest rate of any OECD country. The roots of these apparently paradoxical developments lie in the major structural changes which had been occurring in Irish industry and in the differing experience and performance of Irish indigenous and foreign-owned multinational firms.

Irish Indigenous Industry

Following the introduction of outward-looking policies from the late 1950s onwards, new investment by foreign-owned multinational companies made

---

[3] The source for these data is the *Census of Industrial Production*.

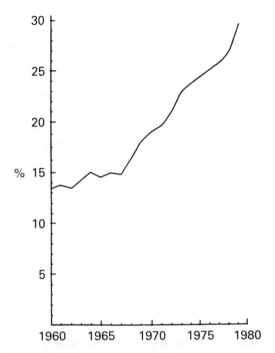

Figure 1. Competing imports' share of home consumption. Source: O'Malley (1989: ch. 6).

the major contribution to the growth of manufacturing employment, output and exports. Native Irish-owned or indigenous industry did not prosper greatly. Indigenous industry was apparently not able to take much advantage of the new incentives and opportunities to export, while at the same time it was losing market share in the home market as the protectionist measures were dismantled.

While foreign investment in new export-oriented industries began to create jobs from the late 1950s, employment also grew in the rest of industry (which was mostly Irish-owned), up to 1966. When the removal of protection began in earnest in the mid-1960s, however, competing imports began to take a continuously increasing share of the home market (see Figure 1). There was no further employment growth in indigenous manufacturing from the mid-1960s to the end of the 1970s and then in the 1980s its employment fell sharply. Essentially what happened was that Irish firms were losing home market shares while making little or no gains in export market shares. Since they were selling very largely to the domestic market, they could just about maintain their overall employment level while domestic demand was growing sufficiently strongly, thereby compensating for the loss of market share, in the late 1960s and the 1970s. But when domestic demand weakened considerably in the 1980s for a variety of reasons, their employment slumped, falling by 27 per cent in just seven years. It is very likely that the level of employment in indigenous manufacturing by 1985 was lower than at any time since the 1940s.[4]

Within indigenous manufacturing, there were some structural changes which are worth noting. First, some sectors fared relatively well and these mostly involved either basic processing of local primary products such as food, or else sheltered or 'non-traded' activities which have a significant degree of natural protection against distant competitors and do not usually enter much into international trade. Such activities can be sheltered in the local market because of high transport costs for products of low value in relation to their weight (e.g., concrete products, cement, packaging materials). Or others can be similarly sheltered because of a need for local knowledge or close contact with customers (e.g., printing and publishing, and engineering or other activities involving an element of on-site installation or construction). While indigenous firms in activities such as these were able to grow and to increase in relative importance, other more internationally traded activities declined.

A second structural change within indigenous industry was a particularly rapid decline among the larger firms in the more internationally traded activities, while there were generally increasing numbers of small firms. It seems that the larger firms were generally engaged in activities in which there are significant economies of scale (hence their own relatively large size, by Irish standards). But they were generally not large enough to match still larger and longer established foreign competitors under free trade, so that they were at a disadvantage due to inferior economies of scale and this hastened their decline.

For smaller firms, which would generally have been in activities in which economies of scale are less important, this problem did not really arise and small indigenous firms increased in numbers. In fact, the rate of establishment of new small native industrial firms in the 1970s, in relation to the size of indigenous industry, was similar to the USA and Canada in the 1950s and 1960s, and about 40 per cent greater than in the United Kingdom in the late 1960s and early 1970s (O'Farrell and Crouchley, 1984). Nevertheless, total indigenous manufacturing employment scarcely changed in the 1970s due to the simultaneous decline of larger firms. And, again, the establishment of new small firms meant that the total number of indigenous manufacturing companies changed little during the substantial fall in employment of 1980–87 when there were many closures of existing firms.

---

[4] See O'Malley (1989: ch. 6) for details on these and other developments discussed in this section.

Irish indigenous industry today is relatively lacking in large-scale enterprises, and there is generally relatively little indigenous activity in those sectors in which economies of scale are most important and which are consequently dominated by large firms in more advanced European economies. For example, there are seven (NACE 2-digit) sectors in each of which large firms employing over 500 people account for more than 70 per cent of the sector's employment in West Germany, France, the UK and Italy.[5] These seven sectors account for 40 per cent of manufacturing employment in the EC (EUR 9), but they account for only 12 per cent of employment in Irish indigenous manufacturing.

The existence of significant economies of scale, and the consequent presence of large established firms in a range of important industries in the advanced industrial economies, can be seen as presenting a significant barrier to the development of such industries by new or small indigenous firms in a relatively late-developing country which trades freely with the advanced countries. For they generally lack the resources that would be required to enter into open competition on a competitive scale of production or to survive a period of initial loss-making while building up to an adequate market share to support a competitive scale of production. Of course, a basic purpose of protection was to make it possible for Irish industries to get established, by shutting out overwhelming competition from larger and stronger firms already existing elsewhere. This succeeded to some degree but in many cases, with a rather small protected market, the Irish firms did not attain a scale of operation that was adequate to match foreign competitors following the return to free trade.

While the existence of economies of scale and large established competitors presents a barrier to the development of Irish indigenous industry in a range of important sectors, there are also some other significant types of barriers arising from the strength of established competitors elsewhere. For example, it can be very difficult for new or small indigenous firms in a late-industrialising country to match the technological strength already developed by advanced economies in sectors where technology is of key importance. Similarly, if strong marketing is a key requirement for an industry, the established marketing strength of existing firms presents an important entry barrier for new or small firms.

---

[5] The seven sectors concerned are Motor Vehicles, Other Means of Transport, Chemical Industry, Man-Made Fibres Industry, Production and Preliminary Processing of Metals, Office & Data Processing Machinery and Electrical Engineering. The source of data on industry size structures is Eurostat, *Structure and Activity of Industry: Data by Size of Enterprises—1984.*

Such entry barriers which confront new or small indigenous firms in a late-industrialising country such as Ireland must comprise a large part of the explanation for the relatively poor performance of Irish indigenous industry. For most other potential explanations do not appear to be very convincing. For example, the record of start-ups of many new small firms suggests that there has not been a marked lack of a spirit of entrepreneurial initiative; it is rather the restriction of new start-up industries to generally small-scale activities, while larger firms declined, that has been the nub of the problem. Also, as is outlined below, many foreign multinational companies have found the Irish economic environment attractive and have operated successfully in it. This suggests that there can scarcely have been crippling defects in factors such as the quality of the labour force, labour costs, the infrastructure, producer services, the tax system or the political and bureaucratic system.

It is possible that the general quality of native managerial skills may leave something to be desired but it seems clear, nevertheless, that there has been a certain amount of good quality managerial talent available. For most of the foreign-owned multinational companies in Ireland have been content to recruit their local management from within the country. Also, many of the larger Irish firms, which are often in naturally sheltered or 'non-traded' types of business, have engaged successfully in international markets in the form of taking over foreign firms and becoming multinational companies.

Foreign-owned Industries in Ireland

The main source of growth of industry in Ireland after the end of the 1950s was new investment by foreign-owned multinational companies which chose Ireland as a site in which to produce for export markets.

At first, until about the end of the 1960s, new foreign investment was largely in technologically mature and often labour-intensive industries such as clothing, footwear, textiles, plastics and light engineering. As Vernon (1966) suggested, such mature industries were most capable of locating in industrially undeveloped countries because they no longer required close contacts with the specialised technologists, skills, suppliers and services found in advanced industrial centres. And since they were generally quite labour-intensive they had a motivation to move to relatively low-wage locations once they were sufficiently free from the need for such close contacts with advanced industrial areas. The international dispersal of such industries occurred quite early in relatively low-income countries on the periphery of the developed world, such as Puerto Rico and Ireland. Then, from about the mid-1960s, such mobile multinational industries increasingly went to poorer, less-developed countries with much lower wages. Grants and tax concessions which were often introduced in the host countries (including Ireland) added to the attraction of low labour costs.

From about the late 1960s, foreign investment in Ireland increasingly involved newer, more technologically advanced products, such as electrical and electronic products, machinery, pharmaceuticals, and medical instruments and equipment. Typically, these industries have involved only certain *stages* of production which are usually not the most demanding on local technological inputs, skills and high-quality suppliers. Again, there is some parallel here with the type of mobile industry which has been able to go to less-developed countries since the late 1960s (e.g. see Helleiner, 1973). But the industries going to Ireland include some more highly skilled activities, particularly in electronics and pharmaceuticals, even if they have usually lacked the key technological and business functions of the firm. Most foreign investment in Ireland since the early 1970s has been undertaken by US-owned companies aiming to produce primarily for European markets. As Ireland has been a member of the EC since 1973, they have selected Ireland as a relatively low-wage, virtually tax-free[6] site which is suitable as a base for penetrating EC markets. Thus Ireland's main competitors in attracting such industries would usually be other European countries.

The new export-oriented foreign-owned firms contributed substantially to industrial growth, particularly in the 1960s and 1970s. By 1988, foreign firms accounted for 44 per cent of total manufacturing employment, 55 per cent of manufacturing output and 75 per cent of manufactured exports.[7] However, while employment in foreign-owned manufacturing grew almost continuously in the 1960s and 1970s, it reached a peak at 88,400 in 1980 and then fell continuously to 78,700 by 1987. While this was a distinctly lower rate of decline than in the indigenous sector, it still amounted to a cumulative decline of 11 per cent over seven consecutive years.

The output of foreign-owned firms continued to grow quite strongly, even while their employment was declining, for much of the 1980s. But a problem as regards the contribution of such growth to the Irish economy was that most of the growth occurred at very high rates in a small number of predominantly foreign-owned sectors which had particularly low levels

---

[6] From 1958 to 1980 there was no tax on profits arising from new manufactured exports. Since 1981, the maximum tax rate on *all* manufacturing profits has been 10 per cent, and companies established before that date still paid no tax on profits arising from manufactured exports until 1990. Combined with a number of tax allowances, these measures meant very low taxation of manufacturing profits, particularly those arising from exports.

[7] Data from *Census of Industrial Production, 1988.*

of linkages with the local economy. Thus virtually all of the growth of industrial output in the period 1980–87 can be attributed to five sectors— Pharmaceuticals, Office and Data Processing Machinery, Electrical Engineering, Instrument Engineering and 'Other Foods'—while all other sectors combined had virtually no growth (Baker, 1988). These sectors import a high proportion of their inputs and expatriate very substantial profits, so that data on their output give a rather misleading impression of their contribution to the economy.

What matters from the point of view of the Irish economy is not the value of output of foreign firms, but rather how much of that value is retained in Ireland, in the form of payments of wages and taxes and purchases of Irish-made goods and services as inputs. It has been found that such 'Irish economy expenditures' are a considerably lower proportion of the value of output in foreign-owned industry than in indigenous industry, and this is especially true of the five high-growth sectors of the 1980s mentioned above.[8] Thus, although there was quite high growth of output in foreign-owned industry in 1980–87, this does not reverse the impression, arising from its falling employment, that its contribution to domestic economic development weakened in that period compared with the 1960s and 1970s.

Part of the reason for this weaker performance of foreign-owned industry in most of the 1980s was a reduction of inflows of new foreign investment after 1981.[9] This, in turn, partly reflected the fact that new US investment in Europe was declining or stagnating for much of the 1980s. This was due both to recession or relatively slow growth in Europe in much of this period and probably also to the fact that the marked surge of US investment in the European Community which followed the integration of substantial markets since the 1960s was slowing down. In addition to these trends, there was increasingly intense competition from other European countries which were trying more actively to attract mobile industries because they were experiencing persistent unemployment.

Apart from the slowing down of new foreign investment in Ireland in the early 1980s, it had also emerged that the longer established foreign firms already in Ireland tended to decline in employment eventually, after an initial period of employment growth. This pattern was already

---

[8] Data on this have been collected annually since 1983 by the Industrial Development Authority in its Irish economy expenditures survey. Irish economy expenditures of foreign-owned non-food manufacturing grew at just two-thirds of the rate of growth of its gross output in 1983–87, because of the fact that nearly all of the growth of its output occurred in sectors with particularly low levels of Irish economy expenditures in relation to sales.

[9] See O'Malley (1989: ch. 7) for details on this and other developments discussed in this section.

established during the 1970s; for example, employment in foreign-owned manufacturing firms established before 1969 fell by 12 per cent between 1973 and 1980 while overall industrial employment was increasing at the fastest rate of any EEC country. This meant that overall growth of employment in foreign industry was being sustained only by the continuing inflow of new first-time foreign investors.

With the passage of time, the overall trend of employment in foreign-owned industry was being increasingly affected by the large stock of relatively old plants with declining employment, so that an ever greater inflow of new first-time investors would have been needed to maintain a given growth rate. By the early 1980s, when new foreign investment was reduced, the result was employment decline in most branches of foreign-owned industry and in the foreign sector as a whole.

Already in the early 1980s, the Telesis (1982) report to the National Economic and Social Council had made a number of criticisms of the practice of relying so heavily on foreign investment. This point was largely taken on board by the NESC itself, and the events which followed tended to give weight to the view that more had to be done to develop a stronger indigenous sector since heavy reliance on foreign industry was not producing acceptable results. In this context, there has been a good deal of debate and a number of quite significant changes in industrial policy, which are briefly outlined below.

Location of Industries

First, however, it is worth noting how the changing structure of industry in Ireland has been reflected in a marked change in its geographical concentration. Table 1 shows the location of manufacturing employment in 1961 and 1981, and it can be seen from the table that there was considerable decentralisation in the location pattern of industry between those years.

While total manufacturing employment increased by 32.7 per cent in 1961–81, it actually fell by 9.6 per cent in the Dublin area and Dublin's share of the total dropped from 47 per cent to 32 per cent. In the other three main urban areas, manufacturing employment increased by 23 per cent, but this meant a small decline in their share of the total. In the rest of the country manufacturing employment rose by 80.7 per cent and so the smaller towns and rural areas generally increased their share of the total quite significantly.

Labour Force Survey data show that industrial employment was also hit harder in Dublin than in the rest of the country in the 1980s. Dublin's

Table 1. Location of manufacturing employment, 1961 and 1981.

Location	Manufacturing employment		% of manufacturing employment	
	1961	1981	1961	1981
Main Urban Areas				
Dublin City and County	83,915	75,836	46.8	31.8
Cork, Limerick, Waterford Cities	17,904	22,065	10.0	9.3
Other Areas				
Rest of Leinster	32,807	57,270	18.3	24.0
Rest of Munster	28,460	47,951	15.9	20.1
Connaught	8,723	21,212	4.9	8.9
Ulster (3 counties)	7,627	13,810	4.3	5.8
Total	179,436	238,144	100	100

Source: Census of Population

share of employment in 'production industries' (excluding building and construction) fell from 30.8 per cent in 1983 to 27.5 per cent in 1988, thus continuing the decline in Dublin's share of industry.

This changing pattern of geographical location of industry was largely a reflection of the combination of decline among the older formerly protected firms, which had been quite heavily concentrated in the main urban areas, together with the rise of new foreign-owned industries, many of which were induced to go to smaller towns and rural areas. O'Farrell (1980) found that as much as 59 per cent of the new foreign industrial firms established in the period 1960–73 were set up in the less-developed 'Designated Areas' in the West. Similarly, four of the more peripheral western regions accounted for 31 per cent of employment in new foreign firms established in the period 1973–81, compared with 19 per cent of employment in new indigenous projects in the same period (derived from O'Farrell, 1984).

One reason for this location pattern among new foreign owned firms was that higher government grants were on offer for those which went to the less-developed regions. In addition, labour costs were often somewhat lower in those regions and the traditions of labour organisation or unionisation were relatively weak compared with the main urban areas.

But apart from these considerations, Ireland as a whole is less industrially developed than most of Europe and this was even more obviously the case in the 1960s. Consequently, multinational companies planning new investment projects would have been slow to consider any location in Ireland if they particularly required a site with ease of access to the concentrations of specialist skills, suppliers and services found in major industrial areas. This means that the foreign projects going to Ireland would have been disproportionately composed of the more 'mobile' types of operation, which are relatively free to choose locations outside the more industrialised areas. This being the case, many of them would have been relatively open to considering a location in a less developed area within Ireland, in order to take advantage of the higher grant incentives and lower labour costs.

Whatever the reason for the industrial location pattern which emerged, it meant that industrialisation since the late 1950s did not involve the development of large concentrated centres of industry. The larger towns, particularly Dublin, did grow, but this was mainly for other reasons, while the process of industrialisation itself was quite dispersed geographically.

Some Recent Developments

From the early 1980s, as was mentioned above, there was growing support for the view that more had to be done to develop a stronger indigenous manufacturing sector, particularly since heavy reliance on foreign industry was no longer producing the sort of results that it had for the previous two decades. This view was supported by the National Economic and Social Council (1982), and a subsequent government white paper, *Industrial Policy* (1984), stated that the future direction of industrial policy would 'entail the concentration of resources on internationally traded manufacturing and services, particularly Irish-owned firms'. This did not mean an end to the policy of attracting foreign investment by any means, but rather it indicated a shift in emphasis towards promoting indigenous firms and in practice this change materialised rather slowly.

The new emphasis was reflected in a reorganisation of the Industrial Development Authority (IDA) so as to give separate divisions responsibility for overseas and Irish firms, thereby recognising the distinction and ensuring that part of the organisation would give its full attention to the indigenous sector. A policy statement from the IDA in 1988 said that the proportion of its resources devoted to domestic industry was to increase from 40 to 50 per cent over the following few years.

Giving some substance to the expressed concern to focus more on indigenous industry, a number of new policy measures were introduced in the 1980s to cope with weaknesses which would be most typical of Irish rather than foreign firms, particularly as regards management, export marketing and technology acquisition. Grants are now available to help pay for costs associated with acquiring foreign technology, market research, development of export marketing and general management development.

Since the mid-1980s, an increasing proportion of the state's expenditure on promoting industrial development has gone to support marketing and technological development, particularly in indigenous industry.

In addition, policy towards indigenous industry has become somewhat more 'active' and 'selective' in certain respects, rather than just passively offering grants and tax concessions to any company and waiting for them to take advantage of the incentives. Examples of this are the Company Development Programme and the National Linkage Programme, which involve state development agencies with a variety of expertise working with selected relatively strong Irish companies on identifying and implementing strategic development initiatives. The role of the state agencies in this is to act as catalysts, sharing opinions, acting as information brokers and making suggestions on how they can assist a company's development through their range of grants and services.

There have also been signs of greater selectivity in the sense of focusing attention more on certain sectors which seem relatively promising for indigenous development. For example, the IDA prepared a plan for the Food and Drink sector, *A Future in Food* (1987), which contained some quite specific details about what types of products would be eligible or not eligible for grant assistance. In addition, the *Programme for National Recovery* (1987) identified a number of specific sectors which were regarded as being promising for indigenous development, including tool-making, automotive components, mechanical engineering, electronics and clothing. Sectoral studies and strategic development plans were drawn up for some of these selected industries, such as the Department of Industry and Commerce's (1989) strategy document on the indigenous electronics industry.

In these more selective and/or active measures, industrial policy for indigenous development has begun to attempt to identify and build on the relative strengths of indigenous industry and to take advantage of apparent opportunities arising in the market. There seems to be a recognition in this that indigenous industry is weak by international standards, and that consequently there is some need to focus the rather limited available resources on developing those companies and sectors which have the best prospects of succeeding in international competition. Given the barriers to development for new or small indigenous firms in many sectors in a late-industrialising country such as Ireland, which were discussed earlier, this line of thinking makes sense, and indeed it probably needs to be acted on further if very significant progress is to be achieved.

Although manufacturing employment fell steeply for much of the 1980s, the lowest point was reached at the end of 1987 and since then it has grown again. And rather than occurring only in foreign-owned industries, employment growth has occurred in the indigenous sector as well, which was a distinct change from previous experience.

The return to growth of manufacturing employment would have been partly due to an improved general economic environment in 1987–90 but there were also some more specific factors having a bearing on industry. One such factor was an increased inflow of new foreign industrial investment, in the context of a general increase of American investment in Europe after 1987, which was encouraged by the perceived market opportunities arising from plans to create a single integrated EC market by 1992.

As regards indigenous industry, it seems likely that the new policy initiatives of the 1980s have begun to have favourable effects. This can be seen from the fact that, while the new emphasis of policy was on developing indigenous industry, the employment record of indigenous firms which were assisted by industrial grants has improved by more than that of grant-assisted foreign industry, although both were operating in the same economic environment, thus reversing a long-standing pattern whereby the grant-assisted foreign-owned firms used to contribute most to employment growth. This seems to show the differential impact of policy measures focusing more on indigenous development in recent years.

The focus of indsustrial policy for indigenous industry has also been on selectively developing stronger firms which would be internationally competitive and capable of exporting successfully. And in fact there has been a marked growth of exports from indigenous industry and a significant increase in the proportion of its output going to export markets since 1986, to a degree which was unprecedented for decades previously. A general improvement in the economic environment would no doubt have helped to bring about this result. But since there must have been periods in the past when general economic conditions were similarly favourable without causing such a result, it is likely that the changed emphasis in industrial policy was responsible to a significant degree.

After many years of domestic market shares being lost to competing imports following the removal of protection, which resulted in a major shake-out of weaker companies, it is reasonable to suppose that most of the indigenous firms existing now are better able to survive in conditions of international competition than was the case ten or twenty years ago. For these firms are either the survivors of many years of intensifying competition or else they are relatively young companies which were established in a competitive environment. If Irish firms are now typically more competitive than formerly, there was, of course, a heavy price paid in arriving at that situation. But it may well mean that the worst is over and that further major decline like that seen in 1980–87 is unlikely.

Indigenous industry still sells most of its output to the home market but, by 1988, 36 per cent of its output was exported, which was up from 27 per cent only two years previously in 1986 and from less than 19 per cent in 1960.[10] Thus Irish companies now are typically more engaged in competing in export markets than they used to be. Furthermore, quite a significant minority of indigenous industry could not be expected to export much because it is engaged in naturally sheltered 'non-traded' types of activity, and the presence of these activities reduces the overall level of export-orientation. Among the more highly traded sectors of industry which are mainly Irish-owned, it is not uncommon to find sectors which now export half or more of their output, for example, metals, meat processing, dairy products, leather and footwear, clothing, and transport equipment other than motor vehicles.

Future Prospects

The recent increase in new foreign investment has brought about renewed growth of employment in the foreign-owned sector and this could continue for some years. It seems to be, to an important degree, a response to the completion of the EC internal market by 1992. The removal of non-tariff barriers to trade between EC countries should have the effect of making it more attractive for non-EC companies to invest in production within the EC for this large integrated market. At the same time, it should make it more feasible for both EC and non-EC firms to select a small peripheral EC country such as Ireland as a site in which to produce for the major EC markets, since there will be fewer impediments to intra-EC trade. Such an effect on Ireland could last for some time, but it should not be seen as continuing indefinitely. For most of the 1980s, until about 1988, it seemed that the phase of industrialisation relying heavily on foreign investment was running out of dynamism. Such a situation could well return eventually, when multinational companies have completed their adjustment to the new conditions of the single EC market.

Thus, the problem of how to develop a stronger indigenous industrial sector continues to be an issue of critical importance. Indigenous industry now seems to be less vulnerable than it was for a long time past. Also, the further freeing of intra-EC trade which will result from the single

---

[10] Data on exports of indigenous industry *per se* are available from the *Census of Industrial Production* since 1986. The 19 per cent figure for 1960 refers to all of industry, which at that time included a small number of highly export-oriented foreign firms, so that the true figure for indigenous industry would have been a little less than 19 per cent.

European market probably does not pose a major new competitive threat to most Irish firms, either because they are not much engaged in the types of industry where there are very significant non-tariff barriers which will be removed or else because they are reasonably strong in such sectors (O'Malley, 1990). But if the future outlook seems rather less threatening than past experience, there has, as yet, been only fairly limited progress in promoting the expansion of indigenous industry.

It seems likely that the policy changes of the 1980s are by now having a favourable effect in developing Irish companies. There is now, at least, a consciousness of the need to focus attention on the issue of indigenous development. And some aspects of industrial policy are concerned with identifying the relative strengths of Irish-owned industry and building on these in a concentrated manner. This approach could still be taken further, however, and it does seem to make sense given that much of indigenous industry is relatively weak and small in scale by international standards and therefore companies require focused support in order to expand in competition with larger and longer established firms in more advanced economies.

It could be argued that there remains a need for state development agencies or state enterprises to take the lead more in committing direct investment to starting up or developing major projects, whether alone or in co-operation with private companies. As it is, no new state industrial enterprises have been established since the 1960s. The potential of present policies for indigenous development is still largely limited to what Ireland's relatively small private firms can be encouraged or persuaded to do, with assistance from the state which is generally limited to some proportion of investment costs incurred by such firms. Compared with what should be possible with a greater degree of state initiative and participation, this must impose limits on the type of industrial projects which can be seriously considered, that is, limits in terms of the scale of investment or the time horizon required for attaining profitability.

There is also the significant difficulty that, over the past decade in particular, many of the larger and more successful Irish firms have been inclined to expand by taking over foreign companies, rather than by expanding their activity within the country. Such companies cannot be compelled to concentrate on expansion in Ireland, whereas state enterprises can be instructed to do so, subject to maintaining commercial viability.

Lessons of Ireland's Experience

Before concluding, it is of interest to consider what general lessons are suggested by Ireland's experience of industrialisation. Ireland began as an independent state with very little industry in the 1920s and, in that respect, it was comparable to many other less-developed countries which have aimed to develop industry in this century starting from a very small or non-existent base. Since Ireland tried different industrialisation strategies in different periods, its experience should be of some relevance for the general issue of industrial development policy in less-developed or newly-industrialising countries.

ᕁ Much of the discussion on this issue has concerned the advantages and disadvantages of an 'inward-looking' strategy of import-substituting indus-trialisation (ISI) as compared to an 'outward-looking' strategy of export-led industrialisation (ELI). Ireland has attempted a version of both of these, so the results should be instructive.

Ireland's experience with the inward-looking ISI strategy in the 1930s–1950s was ultimately unsatisfactory, since it culminated in almost a decade of virtual stagnation. The key failure was the lack of development of exports since the policy of protection did not result in development of internationally competitive industries. This experience was fairly typical of that of many less-developed countries which have tried a similar approach and it appears that protection, on its own at least, is not an adequate policy.

It should be noted, however, that before introducing protection in the early 1930s Ireland had previous long experience of a free trade *laissez-faire* approach, both as part of the United Kingdom and in the first decade of its own independence. This approach had not fostered industrialisation, and in fact the early progress which had been made in developing industry in the late eighteenth and early nineteenth centuries had turned into a process of industrial decline (O'Malley, 1989: ch. 3). Against this back-. ground, it can be seen that the protectionist policy was not the original *cause* of industrial stagnation which overtook the country in the 1950s, as might be thought by those who argue for the benefits of free market forces. Rather protection was a temporarily useful but ultimately unsatisfactory response to a long-standing difficulty in fostering industrialisation.

The 'outward-looking' or ELI strategy which was introduced during and after the late 1950s was in general accordance with the prescriptions for industrial development which are put forward by neo-classical econ-omists, or by proponents of modernisation theory in sociology. Thus, Ireland sought to promote export growth and to encourage foreign direct investment in the country for that purpose, while it also dismantled protective barriers against imports and opened the economy to inter-national market forces. Foreign-owned companies were also free to withdraw their profits from the country as they wished and to purchase input requirements freely from abroad.

While quite a large number of less-developed countries have adopted some elements of this strategy, such as the objective of export promotion and incentives to attract foreign firms as one means of attaining that objective, few of them have gone as far as Ireland did in entering into full free trade with advanced industrial countries. For this reason, Ireland is quite an important test case for the full outward-looking free market strategy.

Under that strategy, Ireland had an increase in industrial growth rates compared with the 1950s and its growth of industrial output often compared favourably with other EC countries in the 1970s and 1980s. However, a distinctive feature of this performance was that it relied very heavily on foreign-owned industry. Up to 1987 at least, the strategy could only be considered a failure as regards the performance of indigenous industry.

Thus, Ireland's fairly strong industrial growth in the 1960s to 1980s was basically due to the fact that an exceptionally large proportion of the available mobile export-oriented foreign investment was attracted to a rather small country. Since such internationally mobile investment occurs on only a limited scale worldwide, relative to the size of all the less-developed or newly-industrialising countries, this was an *exceptional* experience which could not be readily repeated by many other such countries. Thus Ireland's experience offers no general support for recommending this type of strategy. Indeed the experience of its indigenous industry serves as a general warning of the risks involved for a developing country which could not realistically expect to obtain a disproportionately large share of internationally mobile foreign direct investment.

It is also worth noting that unemployment and/or emigration persisted in Ireland in the period since the 1950s despite the degree of success which was achieved in attracting a relatively large share of such investment. Thus, even for Ireland, the results of the outward-looking free market strategy were never really satisfactory.

It might be argued, however, that the strategy was basically sound and that unsatisfactory outcomes were due to defects in the Irish economic environment, for example, a poor infrastructure, low quality labour force or a misguided tax system. In reply to this, it can be pointed out that numerous foreign multinational firms have found the Irish economic environment reasonably attractive and they have found it possible to operate successfully in many parts of the country. This indicates the existence of at least fairly suitable conditions in the physical infrastructure, the political and bureaucratic environment, the tax system, financial and professional services, and in the attitudes and productivity of the labour force. Such conditions could, no doubt, be improved on, but the performance of foreign industry in Ireland suggests that they do not represent major constraints which would explain the markedly poorer performance of indigenous industry in the same environment.

It might also be argued that the outward-looking free market strategy was the right one and that, if Irish indigenous industry did not prosper in conditions which suited foreign multinational companies, this was because of deficiencies in native Irish entrepreneurship. However, there was no great lack of indigenous entrepreneurship in the sense of a scarcity of people who were willing to start up and run industrial companies. It was mentioned above that the rate of establishment of new indigenous manu-facturing companies was comparable to that of the USA and Canada and greater than in the UK. The problem was that new indigenous firms generally remained small while larger existing firms tended to decline.

It seems reasonable to conclude that the outward-looking free market strategy proved inadequate as a means of developing indigenous industry, despite the existence of general economic conditions which were not seriously unfavourable. This can be explained, as was suggested above, by the prevalence in many industries of barriers to entry, arising from the strengths of established competitors, which confront new or small indigenous firms in a late-industrialising country such as Ireland. Free market policies which do not recognise the resulting inherent competitive disadvantages of the latecomer are inadequate in this situation.

A recent analysis of Ireland's experience by O'Hearn (1989), which is highly critical of the country's outward-looking free market strategy, suggests that the strategy was rather worse than merely inadequate. O'Hearn describes Ireland as a 'classic case of "dependent" relations: slow growth and inequality caused by foreign penetration'. His argument is that Ireland had slow overall economic growth and this occurred partly because 'radical free trade . . . allowed domestic industry to atrophy', and partly because the very liberal policy towards foreign industries allowed them to import most of their input requirements and to repatriate substantial profits which meant a loss of foreign exchange.

It may be agreed that the free trade, free market policy, for a long time at least, 'allowed domestic industry to atrophy', and that foreign industry imports many inputs and withdraws large profits. But it seems clear, despite this, that foreign industry in Ireland has not in itself done positive damage by causing a net loss of foreign exchange. Foreign-owned industry in Ireland has consistently exported a very high proportion of its output, with 85 per cent of the value of its total sales being exported in 1989, and it also imports most of its inputs and withdraws substantial profits from the country. Nevertheless, foreign-owned industry does spend a certain amount in Ireland on wages and locally produced materials and services.

In 1989, according to the Industrial Development Authority's annual survey, these expenditures in the Irish economy amounted to 40 per cent of the value of its sales. This left a maximum outflow from the country equal to 60 per cent of the value of its sales, in the form of payments for imported inputs and withdrawals of profits. With 85 per cent of the value of sales being exported, this means that foreign-owned industry had net foreign exchange earnings for Ireland equal to at least 25 per cent of the value of its sales, which was very much less than the value of its exports but was nevertheless positive. Even if all of the wages of employees in foreign industry were spent on imports, there would still have been positive net foreign exchange earnings equal to 12 per cent of the value of sales after allowing for this. In addition, foreign investment, when it initially occurs, involves some inflow of foreign capital which adds to the positive foreign exchange effect.[11]

Thus while O'Hearn (1989) argues that Ireland's *overall* ELI strategy had detrimental effects, it is worth clarifying the point that it was the unsuitability or inadequacy of the free trade, free market approach for indigenous industry that was the main problem, rather than positive damage being done by the growth of foreign-owned industry. The key issue in aiming to improve matters, therefore, is to improve the performance of indigenous industry, rather than laying blame for deficiencies in the overall performance on detrimental effects of the foreign-owned sector.

While much of the discussion concerning industrialisation strategy for developing countries has been couched in terms of general strategies such as ISI or ELI, in practice there can be significant variations on these general approaches. Thus the full outward-looking free market strategy, which some call ELI, involves export promotion, freedom for foreign direct investment, free trade and an absence of selective intervention by the state in the operation of market forces. Ireland's approach from the end of the 1950s until recent years was close to this. However, it is possible to envisage export-led industrialisation without much reliance on foreign direct investment, or to envisage export-led industrialisation with a good deal of foreign investment but without free trade and with a significant

---

[11] It should be noted that O'Hearn (1989) does not necessarily argue that foreign industry actually has caused a *net* loss of foreign exchange. His argument seems to be that Ireland's ELI strategy, as a package incorporating free trade with resulting import penetration together with growth of foreign-owned industry (which has either very low positive, or perhaps negative, net foreign exchange earnings), led to overall negative foreign exchange effects on balance. While this may be so, it is worth clarifying that foreign-owned industry *per se* has had positive foreign exchange effects; if the ELI package as a whole had negative foreign exchange effects, this must have been due to increased import penetration resulting from free trade.

amount of selective state intervention. In practice such variations are often lumped together and described as ELI or outward-looking strategies. This practice is unhelpful since it obscures important distinctions.

Ireland, as noted above, had each of the major elements of the outward-looking free market strategy and largely failed to develop its indigenous industry. Some other countries which have had greater success in indigenous development, notably South Korea and Taiwan, are often cited as examples of the success of the ELI or outward-looking strategy but in reality their strategy was different, and the differences may well be crucial. As O'Hearn (1989) notes, these countries relied a good deal less than Ireland on foreign direct investment, and they were characterised by a good deal of selective state intervention, widespread use of selective protection rather than free trade, and a definite favouring of indigenous industry (see also O'Malley, 1989: ch. 8). Their strategies were 'outward-looking' mainly in the limited sense of aiming to develop exports from internationally competitive industries, without heavy reliance on foreign investment, free trade or unaided market forces to achieve this.

It is arguable that, since about the mid-1980s, Ireland's strategy for industrial development has been gradually evolving into a further variant with significant differences from its approach in the previous twenty-five years. While retaining an emphasis on export promotion, a liberal and generally encouraging approach to foreign direct investment, and free trade (in the context of commitment to EC membership), the present Irish approach involves concentrating greater efforts, in quite an active and selective manner, on developing internationally competitive indigenous industries. This approach to indigenous development involves selective intervention in the operation of market forces, not with the intention of resisting those forces indefinitely, but rather with the aim of ultimately providing indigenous industries with the characteristics and strengths required to survive and grow in a competitive environment.

Since about 1987, the results have been quite encouraging and the performance of indigenous industry has improved considerably. This is a very short period on which to judge the effectiveness of an industrial development strategy, but it may well be of some general interest in the future to see if the newly evolving Irish policy meets with longer term success.

Acknowledgements. I would like to thank participants in the conference on the Development of Industrial Society in Ireland held at Nuffield College, Oxford, in December 1990, for comments on an earlier draft of this article. In particular, I am grateful for comments from Brian Girvin, Kieran Kennedy, Lars Mjøset and the editors of this book.

Proceedings of the British Academy, **79**, 53–77

The Demographic Transition in Ireland in International Context

D. A. COLEMAN
University of Oxford

Introduction

THE DEMOGRAPHY OF IRELAND has been unique in Europe since the nineteenth century. Its demographic transition is still incomplete. But rapid convergence is now taking place which is bringing the Irish demographic regime closely in line with that of the rest of Europe. Mortality is already about the EC average. In 1991, for the first year ever, Irish fertility fell to replacement level. The peculiarities of the past, the delayed inception of changes, and its subsequent rapid pace, are all difficult to explain. Ireland's demography challenges demographic theory. It cannot adequately account for Irish exceptionalism; it did not forecast the timing of its convergence with modern demographic regimes. Now, at the end of the twentieth century, Irish population is rejoining the mainstream. This demographic change is but an outward sign of inward changes in Irish society itself. This paper cannot account for Ireland's demography. That would require substantial empirical comparative analysis, with appropriate modelling. The aims of this paper are modest. It compares Ireland's recent demography with its neighbours, and considers some hypotheses that might explain observed trends.

Data

Demographic data on Ireland are poor. As far as population size is concerned, contemporary estimates began with William Petty in 1697. The first census was held in 1821, but censuses were not considered to be reliable until that of 1841, the first to be based on a household canvass.

Read 7 December 1990. © The British Academy 1992

D. A. Coleman

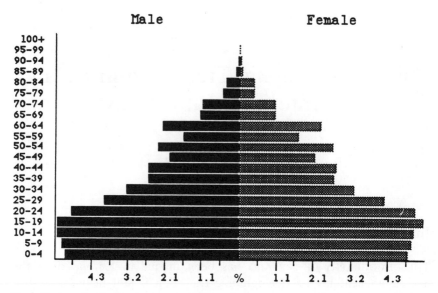

Figure 1. Age distribution of the population of Ireland, per cent, 1901. Source: Census of Ireland (1901) Part II General report, table 15.

Even so, characteristic digit preference errors (favouring years ending in 0) are clearly evident even in the 1901 population (Figure 1). These and other data formed the basis for the major analysis of Irish historical demography by Connell (1950). More recent research has revised his pre-1841 population figures but, it seems, in doing so reinforced his model of pre-famine Irish population as one where high rates of increase were driven by early marriage and high fertility (Clarkson, 1981).

The parish registers of baptisms, burials and marriages, so useful to historical demographers elsewhere since Henry's technical innovations, scarcely exist in usable form in Ireland. Civil registration of births, marriages and deaths did not begin until 1851 and the returns are incomplete. There are also serious difficulties, up to the end of the nineteenth century, in relating aggregate vital events (births, marriages and deaths) to the local populations at risk (Teitelbaum, 1984). In the twentieth century both census and vital registration have been much improved. But there was no census in 1921 and since then two series of data, for the Irish Republic and for Northern Ireland, have complicated study. However, they have also created a natural experiment for testing hypotheses about similar populations which differ in known ways. Official demographic data routinely published for the Republic and for Northern Ireland are very limited compared to those available for most Western countries. For example, annual fertility data for Northern Ireland are not

Table 1. Demographic comparison of Ireland with 36 industrial countries.

		36 Industrial countries *c.* 1987			
Variable	Ireland	Mean	Coeff. of variation *100	Median	N
Population (millions)	3.6	35.3	177.8	12.7	36
Density (per sq kilometre)	52.0	416.8	267.0	116.5	34
Population growth rate /000	–0.9	6.2	73.0	5.2	36
Natural increase /000	8.1	4.7	86.0	3.8	36
Proportion < age 15 /000	289.0	215.9	15.7	213.0	36
Proportion ≥ age 65 /000	109.0	116.6	26.2	122.0	36
Total Fertility Rate	234.0	179.0	16.3	173.5	36
Completed Family Size	265.0	197.1	8.8	192.0	15
Age at first birth	25.8	25.6	4.4	25.8	19
Proportion 1st births /000	313.0	430.9	8.6	438.5	28
Proportion 2nd births /000	258.0	353.5	6.5	357.0	28
Proportion 3rd births /000	185.0	142.5	17.0	137.0	28
Proportion 4th+ births /000	243.0	66.5	34.8	64.5	28
Illegitimacy ratio	126.0	176.7	83.7	133.0	25
Age at first marriage bachelors	27.9	27.0	4.5	27.0	17
Age at first marriage spinsters	25.8	24.7	5.2	24.6	25
Births to mothers aged >30 /000	458.0	275.9	34.4	262.5	12
Abortion ratio /000 live births	69.0	281.8	66.0	221.0	16
Divorces /10000 married	0.0	82.8	52.0	85.0	17
Infant Mortality Rate /000	7.8	11.2	53.8	9.0	36
expectation of life at birth (m)	70.1	71.0	3.8	71.5	35
expectation of life at birth (f)	75.6	77.3	3.1	77.6	35
expectation of life age 65 (m)	12.6	14.1	7.4	14.3	27
expectation of life age 65 (f)	15.7	17.7	7.4	17.6	27

Sources: CSO Dublin (1990a), Eurostat (1989), Council of Europe (1989)

related to a population at risk by age. There is no published long series of mean age at marriage for the Republic before 1960; its most recent life table dates from 1980–82. The first comprehensive fertility survey in Northern Ireland, which compensated for the absent fertility questions in the 1981 census, was not held until 1983 (Compton and Coward, 1989).

Ireland and the Rest of the Industrial World

Let us begin by seeing the extent to which Ireland stood out in comparison with the unweighted averages and range of variation of various demographic parameters in 36 other industrial countries around 1987 (Table 1). Ireland had the highest natural increase, which is more than balanced by the highest proportional rate of out-migration. Some other countries already have birth rates which exceed their death rates; Ireland is still the only developed country which is losing population through emigration, despite a healthy natural increase. Irish fertility, whether measured by the total period fertility rate (TFR or TPFR) or by the completed fertility of the cohorts born in the mid-1950s (see Sardon, 1990) was the highest of any developed country in 1987, with the exception of the USSR and Albania. Cyprus (TFR = 2.32) Romania (2.30) and Poland (2.20) are the only close rivals; apart from the USA and Sweden, the rest are all below 2.0. Elsewhere in the industrial world, first births comprise up to 45 per cent of all births. Ireland has the lowest proportion of first births and by far the highest proportion of fourth and higher order births (almost four times the industrial average). Age at first marriage and age at first birth are now close to the European average, having at one time been much higher. Prolonged childbearing means that almost half of all births are to mothers over age 30, compared with an average of little more than a quarter. As a consequence of high fertility, the Irish population is the most youthful in the industrial world (Figure 2) with 29 per cent of the population under age 15. Ireland is unique in having no divorce and in Europe shares with Belgium the distinction of not permitting abortion for any purpose. However, abortions on Irish residents in the UK bring this figure up to a minimum ratio of 69 per 1000 live births (see OPCS, 1990a).

Mortality figures are now unexceptional. Infant mortality is below average, although expectation of life is slightly inferior to the European

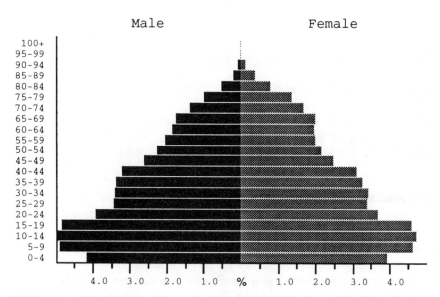

Figure 2. Age distribution of the population of Ireland, per cent, 1990. Source: Eurostat (1991: table B-5).

average (but most European data in Table 1 relate to the late 1980s while the latest Irish life table is based on 1980–82). Some countries are not internally homogeneous; when subdivided into their provinces or regions, especially those which are religiously or ethnically distinct, it is possible to find more substantial demographic variation. But Irish exceptionalism cannot be matched on any comparable demographic scale by any sub-division of a larger Western European country except Northern Ireland. Some of the nations within the former European USSR and Yugoslavia are similarly distinctive but they are hardly appropriate comparisons, being either economically backward or with substantial Muslim minorities. The only similar discontinuity at sub-national level was in Quebec up to the 1970s (Henripin, 1978) and the state of Utah in the USA.

The History and Survival of the Irish Demographic Regime

The components of Ireland's demographic regime were formed by the early nineteenth century. These were: exceptionally late marriage with low levels of illegitimacy or cohabitation; 'natural' high fertility within marriage; corresponding relatively low levels of overall fertility compared with other nineteenth century natural fertility populations which married earlier. By this time, and possibly much earlier, the nuclear family was the most common household type. Before and after the famine, mortality was probably moderate by contemporary standards, possibly because of the low level of urbanisation and the avoidance of subsequent subsistence crises through emigration.

The whole system was overshadowed, and its peculiar features made possible, by the institutionalization of very high rates of emigration. This enabled high rates of natural increase to continue for over a century without feeding back on population size (Figure 3). After the famine, Irish population fell throughout the nineteenth century; a feature unique in Europe. There was therefore no demographic incentive for a reduction in marital fertility. Irish emigration was also peculiar in that it included a higher proportion of females than males. Since the death rate was also unfavourable to females, Ireland acquired an unusual sex ratio (which it has only recently lost) with more males than females. Among other things, this depressed the marriage chances of bachelors relative to those of spinsters, giving some substance to its depiction as 'a nation of elderly bachelors'.

Little is known about marriage and fertility in Ireland before the 1840s. But marriage seems to have been relatively early and may have become even earlier and more universal through the subdivision of farms, the use

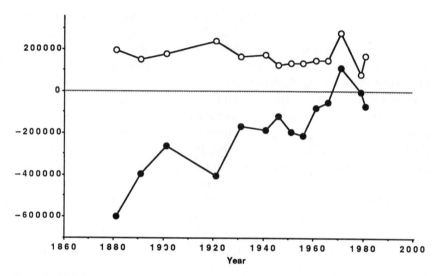

Figure 3. Irish Republic 1881–1986, intercensal natural increase (○) and net migration (●). Source: CSO (1989).

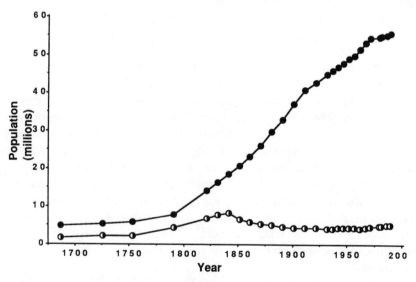

Figure 4. Population trends, all Ireland (◗) and Great Britain (●). Sources: OPCS (1990b), CSO (1989), Clarkson (1981), Wrigley and Schofield (1981). GB data before 1801 refer to England only.

of new land and the cultivation of the potato. The argument that the traditional restraints against early marriage had been eroded by the ease of supporting a family through potato cultivation seems to have stood the test of time. Mortality may have fallen, partly because the potato increased the subsistence base. Smallpox may have been checked by inoculation in the eighteenth century. According to recent revisions of pre-census estimates of population (Clarkson, 1981), Ireland's population actually grew faster than that of late eighteenth century England or anywhere else in Europe (Figure 4). But Ireland failed to go through the agricultural revolution, so important to England's later economic success and which enabled it to sustain a large population with a growing standard of living. Without such developments, the catastrophe of the famine forced the population into a completely new regime in order to survive desperate new circumstances.

Ireland and the Demographic Transition

Ireland's post-1841 demographic regime has been put into European perspective by the Princeton group's international demographic project (Coale and Watkins, 1986). This charts the evolution of the European demographic transition at the level of 431 provinces from the mid-nineteenth century to 1961. To ensure the effective comparison of inter-national data, fertility and marriage data are standardised with indices developed for the purpose (Coale, Hill and Trussell, 1975). These indices relate the fertility and marriage patterns of the European provinces with the benchmark of the high natural fertility of the Hutterite religious enclaves of the rural United States. The Hutterites show the upper limits of high fertility which a healthy and well-nourished population can achieve in the absence of deliberate parity-specific birth control. These measures of indirect standardisation enable the relative contribution to fertility reduction of changes in marriage, and of the adoption of contraception within marriage, to be estimated. From the 1870s most European countries began to adopt family planning within marriage. Ireland did not.

Four indices have been developed. I_f is an index of overall fertility based on all women of childbearing age in a population, irrespective of their marital status. On a scale of 0–1.0 it shows the ratio of the real fertility of those women compared with that which they would have had with Hutterite levels of childbearing. Thus a level of 0.4 (high for modern Europe) indicates that the birth rate of the population in question was equivalent to 40 per cent of the level it would have had with Hutterite fertility rates. Departures from the Hutterite level of 1.0 are due in the first instance to the intervention of a number of 'proximate' determinants; delayed marriage, contraception, abortion, breast-feeding (which increases birth intervals) and differences in fecundity (the physiological capacity to conceive). The next index permits the relative importance of delayed marriage or permanent celibacy to be inferred. I_g relates only to the fertility of women who are married, and typically yields figures of up to 0.8 in populations not practising birth control. A departure of that magnitude from 1.0 can readily be due to non-contraceptive factors, but a wider gap suggests deliberate family limitation. A population with a low or moderate I_f, but a high I_g, like Ireland in the recent past, is one where fertility is being limited almost entirely by late marriage or high proportions remaining permanently unmarried or both. A population with low I_f and low I_g is one almost certainly practising birth control within marriage. Modern European populations typically have I_g indices of 0.2 or even less. I_h relates only to illegitimate fertility. It is typically low in the period in question: between 0.05 and 0.10. Finally I_m is the index of proportions married (Western European women were less prone to marry, and married later than the Hutterites). This index is based on the proportions married among the Hutterites weighted by their natural fertility at each age. The relationship of these indices can be summed up as:

$$I_f = I_g.I_m + (1 - I_m) I_h$$

These indices have been applied to an analysis of the trends in fertility and marriage in Ireland and Great Britain (Teitelbaum, 1984). It is immediately obvious that overall Irish fertility (I_f, Figure 5a) was distinctive in the nineteenth century because it was so low. Then, by changing much less than that of other countries, it came to appear distinctively high sometime in the 1920s, exposed to view by the receding tide of fertility almost everywhere else. The trend of I_g (marital fertility) from 1871 to 1911 shows no trend at all in the Irish case, whereas it fell amost everywhere else. For any given age at marriage, Irish fertility was about the same as that of Scotland or England and Wales (Figure 5b). But Ireland did not join the substantial decline in marital fertility in Scotland and England after the 1870s which followed the adoption of family limitation in marriage by most couples. This reduced British I_g to 0.25 by 1961 when in Ireland it remained at 0.60 (after some decline which will be discussed later). Instead, the trend of I_m (Figure 5c) shows that in Ireland, but not in England or Scotland, there was a substantial further reduction in nuptiality, thus increasing age at marriage still further and reducing the proportions ever-marrying. This is usually interpreted as a primitive and partial response through marriage to those pressures which in England and Scotland had led to the general adoption of family planning.

However, other comparisons of fertility of women married around the turn of the century, based on birth-order (parity) distributions rather than age-specific fertility, show that marital fertility control had been spreading quite fast among urban women in Ireland. This conclusion comes from analysis of the 1911 Census, the first to ask retrospective questions on fertility. Urban women tended to marry earlier than rural women. The adoption of fertility control by some urban women brought their fertility back in line with that of the traditionally later-marrying rural population (David and Sanderson, 1988). Different parts of Ireland were already diverging in fertility patterns. Marital fertility even rose somewhat in rural Galway (Figure 6a) while it fell consistently from 1871 to 1936 in Antrim, Down and Belfast (unified here because of boundary difficulties). Nuptiality, however, originally lower in Antrim than in Galway, increased with time, moderating the overall difference in fertility (Figure 6b). This may reflect the partial replacement of older forms of fertility control (marriage) by more modern ones (contraception).

Throughout this period the proportion of births outside marriage remained very low. Illegitimacy fell throughout Europe in the nineteenth century. Those at risk of having illegitimate children would have been the most avid customers of the new knowledge of contraception. No such decline is evident in Ireland, although illegitimate births may have suffered particularly from under-registration.

Changes in the Twentieth Century

Irish fertility declined slowly in the first three quarters of the twentieth century. Since 1900 the rest of Europe has left Irish fertility patterns behind as an increasingly anomalous example of persistent high fertility. We saw above how the fertility levels of England and Ireland parted company in the 1920s. By then the fertility difference between the Protestant and Catholic populations of Northern Ireland had also become apparent, although Protestant fertility remained higher than on the British mainland. After the second world war, Irish fertility was only matched in Europe by that of Iceland and the Netherlands, and further abroad by Quebec. By the 1960s Irish fertility was uniquely high in Europe. The TFR in 1975 was about what it had been in 1950—around 3.2 (Figure 7). In the baby boom which began in the 1950s the TFR rose to a peak of 4.1 in 1964, only matched by New Zealand among countries in the western cultural sphere. The timing of the Irish baby boom was almost identical with that of Great Britain and many other European countries, presumably a response to the same economic and social changes which were driving up fertility throughout the western world.

D. A. Coleman

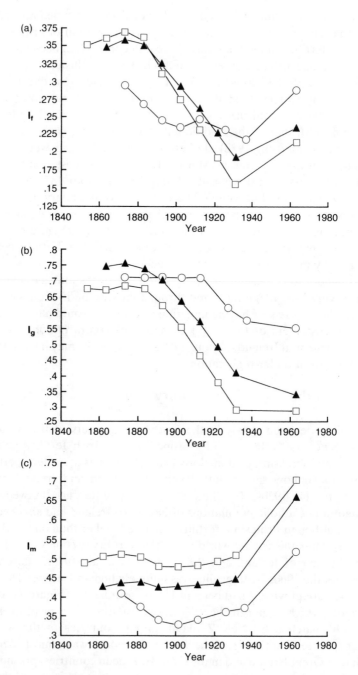

Figure 5. Trends of (a) I_f, (b) I_g, (c) I_m, 1851–1961, in Ireland (○), Scotland (▲), England and Wales (□). Source: Coale and Watkins (1986).

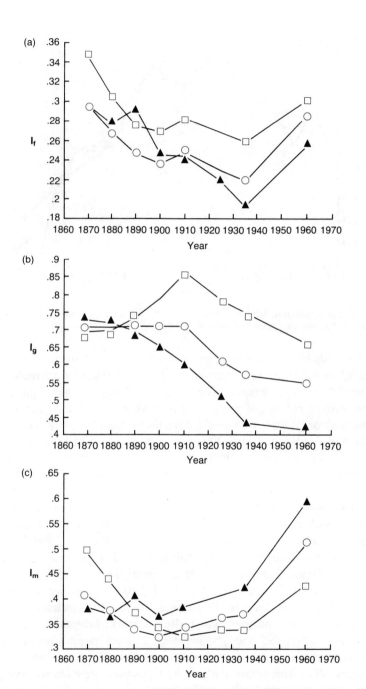

Figure 6. Trends of (a) I_f, (b) I_g, (c) I_m, 1871–1961, in Galway (□), and in Antrim, Down and Belfast (▲). Ireland (○). Source: Coale and Watkins (1986).

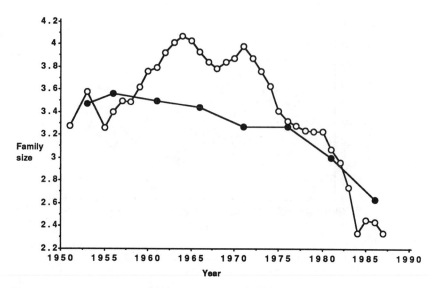

Figure 7. Fertility trends, Irish Republic, 1950–1989: TFR (○), completed family size (●). Sources: CSO (1990a), Council of Europe (1989).

The Irish baby boom was, as in most western countries, primarily a result of changes in the timing of births rather than an increase in the number of births per woman. The completed family sizes in Figure 7 refer to the birth of cohorts of women born 30 years before the year indicated on the horizontal axis, who would have been about half way through their family building by that time. The most recent data in the graph are based on projection (see Sardon, 1990). There is no increase in completed family sise. Instead a gradual decline from a peak around the mid 1950s (births to mothers born in the mid-1930s) is evident. Both completed family size and TFR show marked declines from the late 1970s onwards, a point to which we will return. Irish fertility does show a small recovery in the late 1970s and early 1980s, a pattern not shared either by Great Britain or by any of the countries which Ireland's fertility pattern most closely resembles. Figure 8 shows the TFR trends of the western countries most strongly correlated with that of Ireland (≥0.95) together with that of England and Wales. Irish fertility trends are poorly correlated with those of most European countries, which show a marked depression of fertility before and after the baby boom period. Irish period fertility trends have most in common with other Roman Catholic, Southern European countries, all of which started a fertility transition late from relatively high beginnings (especially Spain and Portugal).

The timing of births accelerated because the Irish gave up their unique

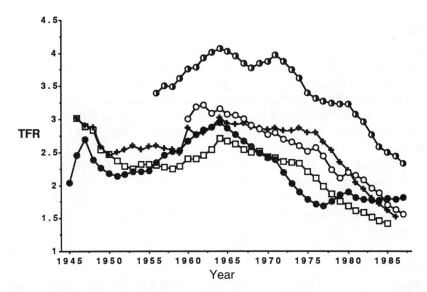

Figure 8. TFR trends 1945–1987, selected countries: Ireland (◑), Italy (□), Spain (+), Portugal (○), UK (●). Sources: Eurostat (1989), OPCS (1990b), CSO (1990a), and other national statistical yearbooks.

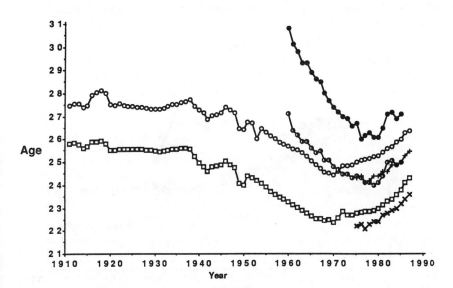

Figure 9. Mean age at marriage, bachelors and spinsters: England and Wales, bachelors (○), spinsters (□); S. Ireland, bachelors (●), spinsters (◑); N. Ireland, bachelors (+), spinsters (×). Sources: Eurostat (1989), OPCS (1990b), Registrar-General Northern Ireland (1989).

pattern of very late marriage during the 1950s (see Kennedy, 1989). In the late 1950s mean age at first marriage was still 31 for bachelors and 27 for spinsters; by 1977 women were marrying at average age 24. Illegitimate fertility nonetheless remained very low. Other European countries had moved away from a less extreme form of the old West European pattern of delayed marriage by the late 1930s (e.g. England and Wales, see Figure 9). But the change occurred later in Ireland and involved a greater proportional decline. Even so, mean age at marriage in 1980 was almost two years older than the lowest point reached in 1972 in England and Wales.

The Irish baby boom was also unusual in another way. Although the birth rate went up, the number of births did not rise in proportion. Therefore it did not produce the very characteristic 'bulge' of a baby-boom age structure (Figure 10). This was because the maternal generations producing the babies were relatively few in number. Figure 10 shows the birth totals, indexed to 100 in 1950, from a selection of countries. The typical baby boom pattern is that of England and Wales with a bulge centred around 1964, and surrounding troughs in the yearly output of births which become fixed in the age-structure. Ireland does not show this at all; rather, an uneven increase to an absolute peak in 1980, followed by a sharp decline.

The decline of large families is also evident in fewer high order births after 1960 (Figure 11). The proportion of fourth and higher order births

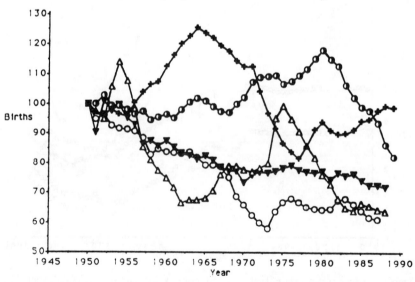

Figure 10. Birth totals, 1950–1988, selected countries: Finland (○), Yugoslavia (▼), Hungary (△), Ireland (◐), England and Wales (+). 1950 = 100. Source: Eurostat (1989).

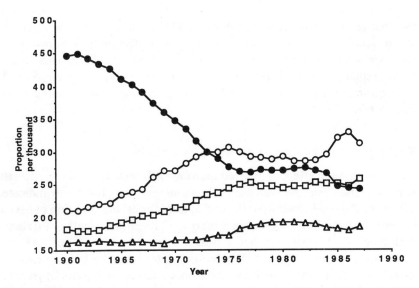

Figure 11. Births by birth order, Irish Republic, 1960–1988: first (O), second (□), third (△), fourth and higher (●). Sources: Eurostat (1989), CSO (1990a).

to mothers in Ireland fell from just under half to just over a quarter by the late 1970s. Correspondingly, first births increased from about a fifth to almost a third. This proportion was still substantially behind other western societies, however, where at least 40 per cent of births were first births by this time. From about 1977 to 1984 these trends halted. The temporary recovery of the TFR in the 'mini-boom' mentioned above corresponded with an Irish economic recovery sufficiently strong to provoke a powerful return migration. This reversed for several years the loss of population through migration (Figure 3).

The end of the transition?

Most recently, the fertility decline has resumed (Figure 11). Fourth and higher order births have fallen further, to little more than a fifth of the total. First births have risen to about 35 per cent. At the rates of decline current through most of the 1980s, the Irish TFR would have fallen below the replacement level of 2.1 in 1990 for the first time in history. A small increase in births in that year (mostly outside marriage) kept it just above this level. This decline in fertility can partly be attributed to the delay of childbearing, just as the earlier increase in TFR followed a fall in the average age at marriage in the 1950s. Mean age at marriage has increased by over a year since 1980. But completed family size has also fallen. This is apparent from the completed family size of recent birth cohorts and from the changes in birth order distribution. This decline should be regarded as an accelerated continuation of an earlier decline which had been interrupted by the temporary economic growth around 1980. That faded, to be replaced with 17 per cent unemployment and a resumption of emigration at a level sufficient to bring back the population decline of the early 1950s.

Illegitimacy and the 'second demographic transition'

The demographic effect of delayed marriage is somewhat offset by the rise in cohabitation and the increase in illegitimate births. The latter indicates a startling change in attitudes; the end of a centuries' old tradition of sexual restraint before even long-delayed marriage. Illegitimacy rates in Ireland, both North and South, reached a post-war low of under 25 per 1000 live births around 1960 (Figure 12), somewhat later than the English nadir in about 1955. Since then illegitimacy has increased in both parts of Ireland, particularly since 1980. This trend is shared with many other European countries (Figure 12). Ireland, with 126 illegitimate births per 1000 live births in 1989 (the 'illegitimacy ratio') is a long way behind England and

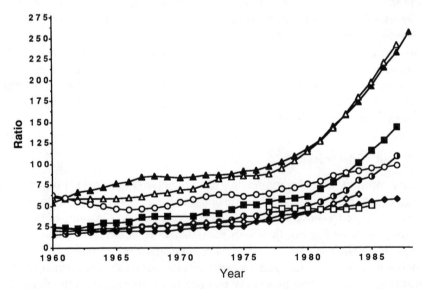

Figure 12. Illegitimacy ratio per 1000 live births, 1960–1988, selected countries: Ireland (◑), N. Ireland (■), England and Wales (▲), Belgium (◇), France (△), FRG (○), Italy (◆), Poland (□). Sources: Registrar-General Northern Ireland (1989), CSO (1990a), OPCS (1990b), and other national statistical yearbooks.

France, not to mention Sweden and Denmark. But there is a fivefold increase on earlier levels. Ireland's illegitimacy ratio is no longer the lowest in Europe, having overtaken Belgium, the Federal Republic of Germany, Italy and Poland. In this respect the social changes which are accelerating the belated completion of the first Irish demographic transition are, at the same time, ushering in the second, of more sexual freedom and of a plurality of family forms (van de Kaa, 1987; Cliquet, 1991). However, this is a complex, pluralistic kind of sexual revolution, coexisting as it does with a reaffirmation in 1986 of the 1937 constitutional ban on divorce which had the support of 63 per cent of those voting, and the incorporation into the constitution of the prohibition of abortion. No other European country forbids divorce, and the prohibition of abortion is shared only by Belgium and (since 1990) Poland. Access to British abortion facilities brings the Irish abortion rate up to at least 59 per 1000 live births, judging from the number of abortions carried out in Britain on Irish residents (OPCS, 1990a). Separation, annulment and desertion, and divorce abroad, substitute to some extent for the absence of domestic divorce arrangements. In 1986 there were 37,245 separated persons in Ireland (in proportional terms, a larger number than in England).

The mortality transition

Early this century, Ireland was unique in Europe in that women lived shorter lives than men. Such a pattern is found today only in the Third World, especially in the northern parts of the Indian sub-continent. There, up to 1977 at least, males enjoyed better survival than females up to age 50, and particularly in early childhood and younger adult life (Ruzicka, 1989). This is attributed to the systematically disadvantaged position of females in such societies, not just to maternal mortality. It was a pattern more common in the past. Between 1840 and 1910, in about 60 per cent of western countries and 70–90 per cent of other countries female mortality exceeded that of males around age 10, while in about 30 per cent of western, and 60 per cent of other countries, female mortality was higher than male around age 30, the peak age of childbearing (Stolnitz, 1956). By the 1930s, this pattern had become rare in the West and Ireland remained alone in the West in having higher male survival rates than female at any age.

Within the last thirty years almost all trace of this pattern has been lost, and the female advantage in life-expectation in Ireland (5.5 years measured from birth) is little less than the average for the industrial world (6.3 years). In the twentieth century expectation of life at birth has followed similar trends in England and Wales, Northern Ireland and the

D. A. Coleman

Irish Republic. Northern Ireland and the Republic have shared almost
identical female mortality since the 1960s. Both converged with English
mortality rates in the postwar period and for the last two decades have
maintained the same trend in improvement but with lower life expectation
in both parts of Ireland (Figure 13). This is consistent with what might be
expected from the different standards of living in these areas. However,
these remaining mortality differences derive mainly from adult mortality.
Infant mortality (both sexes) in the Irish Republic, Northern Ireland and
England and Wales have converged throughout the postwar period. Since
the early 1980s the infant mortality rate (deaths under age 1 per 1000 live
births) in the Irish Republic has been the lowest of the three (Figure 14).

Data on mortality at different ages are only available for the area of
the Irish Republic from 1926. By that time there was a small female
superiority (0.4 years) in expectation of life at birth but females had lower
expectation of life than males from age 5 to age 20. From the 1930s up to
the Second World War, females enjoyed a greater advantage in survival
over males, but even in 1961 the overall female excess expectation of life
was just under 4 years—about 2 years less than in other developed
countries. A truly modern pattern was only achieved in the life table
centred on 1981 (Figure 15). It is not known for how long the older pattern
obtained in Ireland. The life table for the whole of Ireland based on 1891
showed a nearly 1 year female deficiency in expectation of life at birth,
declining to 0.4 years by 1901 and becoming slightly positive by 1911. By

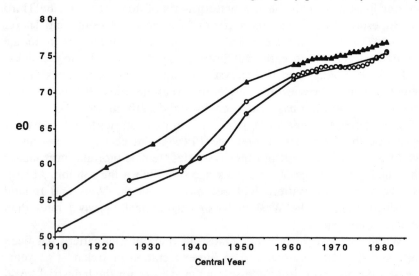

Figure 13. Expectation of life at birth, females 1911–1982, in Irish Republic (◗), Northern
Ireland (○), England and Wales (▲). Sources: Registrar-General Northern Ireland (1989),
OPCS (1990b), CSO (1990a).

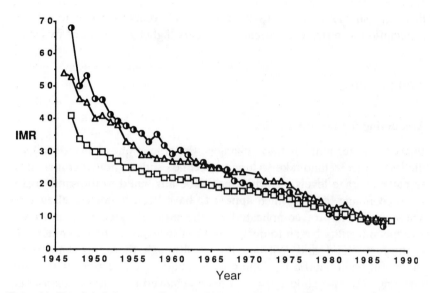

Figure 14. Trends in infant mortality rate, 1945–1987, in Ireland (◑), Northern Ireland (△), England and Wales (□). Sources: OPCS (1990b), CSO (1990a), Registrat-General Northern Ireland (1989).

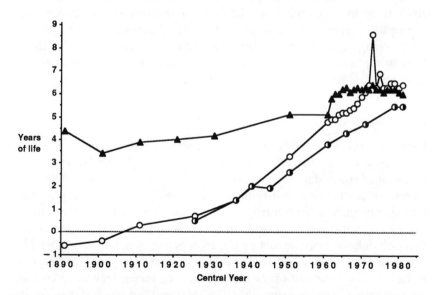

Figure 15. Excess expectation of life at birth for females, 1891–1985, in Irish Republic (◑), Northern Ireland (○), England and Wales (▲). Sources: OPCS (1990b), Registrar-General Northern Ireland (1982, 1989), CSO (1985).

1891 the female excess in England and Wales was already 4 years. The first English life table of 1840 (e_0m = 40.2 years) showed female life expectation at birth to be already 2.0 years higher than that of males.

Conclusions

Accounting for fertility decline

In trying to account for these changes, the crucial questions are: (i) why did fertility in Ireland take so long to decline? and (ii) now that it is falling to more average levels, can this decline be attributed to the same sort of socio-economic factors which appear to have been important elsewhere? These problems are complicated by the lack of agreement as to why European fertility began to decline in the first place in the late nineteenth century (Cleland and Wilson, 1987), although there has been much successful econometric modelling of subsequent fluctuation of the birth rate once the two child norm has been achieved (see de Cooman *et al.*, 1987). In the Irish case, these two processes have been happening at the same time in a 'compressed' demographic transition (Kennedy, 1989). In the analysis of fertility decline, it is customary to begin by partitioning the fertility into those technical 'proximate' components which must, in sum, account for its departure from the 'natural' level, which were mentioned in an earlier section. The changes in marriage discussed above have, other things being equal, tended to increase rather than decrease the birthrate. Clearly the main influence must be the deliberate limitation of fertility through more general use of birth control.

Family planning

Normally, the availability of modern contraceptive methods is held to make only a marginal difference in the fertility of populations already accustomed to older methods of contraception. By the 1930s most European populations had reduced their family size below replacement rate simply with coitus interruptus, the condom and illegal abortion. But supply side improvements, while in part reflecting changed attitudes, may themselves have more impact on the Irish population, which has been less accustomed even to 'traditional' methods of contraception. Contraception in Ireland has come out of the closet following recent legislative changes. A Supreme Court decision in 1973 (McGee) established the legality of contraceptive sale for 'bona fide' purposes (whatever they are), a provision formalised by legislation in 1979. In 1985 further legislation made non-medical contraceptives of all kinds available to anyone over 18 years without prescription. However, contraceptive supply is still hedged with impediments. In February 1991 the Dublin Virgin Megastore store was fined £500 in the Dublin High Court for selling condoms and was told that it had 'got off lightly', and indeed the penalty was later raised to £700.

The rather limited information on family planning practice suggests that Ireland is rapidly converging with the rest of the industrial world: 66 per cent of a sample of 600 married couples in 1975 had used some form of birth control. In the whole sample, 37 per cent had used 'natural' (church approved) methods, 19 per cent had used the pill and 10 per cent other artificial methods. This seemed a surprisingly high proportion, especially as both husbands and wives reported an ideal family size of 5.6 children. Use of contraception was strongly associated with higher social class, higher education and younger age: 30 per cent of wives aged under 25 had already used the pill. Even in 1975, few of those who avoided contraception mentioned specifically religious reasons, although 13 per cent thought the pill 'immoral' (Wilson-Davis, 1982). Results from a smaller sample of 100 married and 100 unmarried mothers of first-born children in a Dublin hospital suggest rapid change in contraceptive practice in ten years: 81 per cent of the married mothers had used some form of contraception, 61 per cent had used the pill, 13 per cent other (mostly artificial) methods, only 7 per cent 'natural' methods; 20 per cent of the married women's pregnancies had been unwanted, 89 per cent of the single women's; 28 per cent of the single women had considered abortion in the UK. It has been estimated that 37 per cent of pregnant single women in Ireland in the early 1980s sought abortion in the UK (Dean, 1984). The poor contraceptive practice among the single women (22 per cent had used the pill, 64 per cent had used no method) was regarded as a damaging legacy of low levels of knowledge of family planning and restricted supply (Greene *et al.*, 1989). It is difficult to put these limited data into the context of other western countries but it looks as though younger married women in Ireland are rapidly approaching modern levels of contraceptive practice.

What, in turn, are the ultimate factors which have changed attitudes towards desired family size and the acceptability, or necessity, of family planning? In the European fertility decline of the late nineteenth century, and subsequent declines after the 1960s baby boom, a number of factors are thought to be important: increased costs of children arising from the need to educate them to meet the needs of a skilled workforce but thereby delaying the time when they could earn money themselves; the effects of near-universal literacy and higher education standards (especially among women) in eroding traditional and religious inhibitions and spreading knowledge of family planning methods; and latterly the general entry of married women themselves into the workforce. All these depend on a modernised, literate, mobile, open society with a modern economy offering rewards to skills and education. It used to be thought that urbanisation and industrialisation were the driving forces, but recent research emphasises more the spread of knowledge and education (Lesthaeghe, 1983; Cleland and Wilson, 1987). For many years, and very fast since the late 1950s, the Irish economy and society have been changing in ways which would be expected to lead to a fertility decline (Kennedy, 1989). Up to the 1950s Ireland was a rural society with 40 per cent of jobs on the land. Since then Irish employment has shifted to urban, manufacturing and service jobs: only 15 per cent worked in agriculture in 1987. Movement away from rural smallholdings undermined one of the main props of long-delayed marriage or celibacy. Elsewhere such economic changes have usually brought small family size. So a classical fall in fertility would be expected. But there do not seem to have been any formal economic analyses of the Irish fertility decline. Analyses using, for example, 'new home economics' models might show whether the decline is in line with that experienced elsewhere or whether, as seems likely, fertility remains higher than the level that would be expected from Irish economic and social development.

Women in the workforce

In econometric modelling of birth rate fluctuations, especially those which marked the end of the baby boom, pride of place usually goes to the entry of married women into the non-agricultural workforce (Ermisch, 1990; De Cooman *et al.*, 1987). This greatly increases the opportunity cost of children. In 1971 only 7.5 per cent of married women in Ireland were in the workforce compared with over 40 per cent in most Western countries. This had increased threefold to 23.1 per cent in 1988, but was still the lowest in the EC except for Spain (see Courtney, 1990). At young ages workforce participation of married women is only slightly below the EC average (51.4 per cent in 1988 compared with 58.2 per cent at ages 15–24). But older married women are progressively less likely to be in work: 45.5 per cent at age 25–34 compared with the EC's 59.1 per cent, 29.7 per cent at age 35–44 against the EC's 58.5 per cent (Eurostat, 1991). This presumably reflects rapid changes in behaviour by successive cohorts of women. The proportion of married women in the workforce in Britain, for example, had risen to 62 per cent by 1982. By 1989, 63 per cent of women aged 16–59 with dependent children were economically active, and 78 per cent of women without dependent children (OPCS, 1990b). But the international correlation of workforce participation rates with fertility is rather low (West Germany has only average rates, those in Italy are below average). It is easier to correlate time trends in fertility with the participation rates in each individual country. Without an econometric analysis of Ireland's fertility decline in relation to its socio-economic variables we cannot know how large is the 'residual', if any, which needs to be accounted for by the effects of religion or of high migration levels.

A Catholic explanation?

The obvious explanation for the persistent high birth rate of the Irish fertility regime is the dominance of the Roman Catholic church in Ireland, the pronatalism of its doctrines being translated into demographic consequences by Irish religiosity. Irish religiosity is clearly higher than almost anywhere else in Europe, and the particular influence of the hierarchy on government policy on, for example, abortion and contraception is easily shown. But there are too many international exceptions to allow that simple hypothesis to pass unchallenged. In his comprehensive analysis of this question, Day (1968) concluded that the only circumstances in which Roman Catholic influence was important, or even detectable, over and above the level expected from socio-economic development, were when Roman Catholicism acquired particular authority through being a focus for the national sentiments of a minority in larger population (see Siegel, 1970). That minority had to be in a politically or otherwise disadvantaged position—Roman Catholic influence was only important if it were reinforced by ethnocentrism and the needs of group survival.

This formulation helps with the apparent Polish and Irish exceptions. In both, the Catholic church has been the only institution surviving as a focus for national identity during the absorption of the society into a wider polity. But neither has been a 'minority' for seventy years, so the survival of this response for religious reasons in Ireland may seem surprising. Whatever the case in the past, public opinion surveys in the 1980s show that a majority of adults in Ireland (especially young people) no longer accept the Catholic church's teaching on contraception and instead approve of its use (cf. Greene et al., 1989). And just at a time when traditional attitudes have apparently been reaffirmed officially in the Republic through the referenda on abortion (1983) and divorce (1986), clear signs have also emerged of rapid declines in fertility and of the rise of the 'second demographic transition', characterised by cohabitation and high levels of illegitimacy, which has also destroyed an old high-fertility regime in Catholic rural Quebec (Henripin et al., 1978). Furthermore, although abortion remains illegal in Ireland, the number of abortions to Irish nationals in the UK alone is, as earlier noted, equivalent to an abortion ratio of 69 per 1000 live births; far from the lowest in Europe.

The emigration factor

Other factors need to be invoked to explain the persistence of high fertility so long after independence and so long after almost all other Catholic countries have adopted a low fertility regime. The Irish case is greatly complicated by the survival of the unique emigration tradition begun in the 1840s. This has permitted high levels of natural increase to co-exist with declining population size for over a century and has dominated the Irish fertility regime since. It has destroyed demographic feedbacks from high natural increase at the population level. Without emigration, population growth and density would have become uncomfortable many decades ago, increasing land values, rents and prices. It would have been difficult to create jobs at the rate of population growth implied by high fertility without the check of emigration. Studies of other high fertility, high emigration countries (e.g. Puerto Rico; see Mosher, 1980) have shown that emigration and fertility decline can be regarded as alternative demographic responses to population growth (Davis, 1963). Long-term high levels of emigration retard the modernisation of fertility.

Emigration may have selective effects on cohorts, leaving behind the more conservative (Walsh, 1972). The fertility of Irish immigrants in the UK is closer to the UK average than it is to that of Ireland. High emigration from Ireland is accompanied by very low levels of immigration of persons without previous connection with Ireland (North or South). There are no large minority groups except the 5 per cent of Protestants whose ancestors have been in Ireland for centuries. Unlike most industrial countries Ireland has experienced no major influx of population from the rest of the EC or from the rest of the world, and therefore has had less exposure to modern attitudes to fertility and religion. Few people go to live in Ireland except those of Irish origin returning home. Those that do tend to be high-status foreigners seeking retirement or second homes, or on short term business sojourns. Neither group will have much effect on the attitudes of local people.

At present rates of change, it looks as though the distinctive Irish fertility regime is finally over, and will join those of Quebec, Spain, Portugal and other Catholic countries as problems of recent history rather than of the contemporary world. But, despite its decline, Irish fertility may not become indistinguishable in pattern from that of the rest of Europe. Other, lesser differences, such as the particularly low fertility of Germany and its neighbours, have persisted for almost two decades. Ideological explanations of fertility change are becoming popular because of the inadequacy of socio-economic models alone to explain the international trend and timing of fertility transitions and regional differences (Cleland

and Wilson, 1987; Lesthaeghe, 1983). These owe much to the analysis of characteristic attitudes which extend over a much wider range than those of institutional religion and which are often discussed in terms of the materialist/postmaterialist or 'fundamentalist/pragmatic' division (Simons, 1986). Ireland returns conservative scores in European attitude surveys, as do other relatively high fertility countries such as England and France, where religiosity is much lower.

While 'Catholic fertility' has disappeared in the rest of the industrial world, other differences concerned with sexual behaviour have not. Although illegitimacy is growing in almost all industrial countries, it is doing so at very different rates and from different starting points. Catholic countries (with Quebec's exception) have markedly lower illegitimacy rates than others. It may be a matter of time before they catch up. We must wait and see whether a further example of the exceptionalism of Catholic societies, and of Ireland in particular, may be in the making. The example of Quebec may provide the most appropriate parallel. In contrast with other cases, fertility was particularly high, Catholics were in a minority position in historical circumstances which had given the church great prestige and influence, they were distinguished by a different culture as well as religion and, until the 1960s, the population was mostly rural. The collapse of the old high fertility regime, and of church influence, were particularly dramatic. Quebec in the early 1980s had almost the lowest fertility of any large western population (TFR = 1.4), much lower than that of its English-speaking neighbouring provinces, and its illegitimacy rates—about 40 per cent of live births—are now higher than those of other Catholic populations. It may be that Irish fertility, and the influence of the church, are facing similar eclipse.

Proceedings of the British Academy, **79**, 79–104

The Significance of Small-scale Landholders in Ireland's Socio-economic Transformation

DAMIAN F. HANNAN* & PATRICK COMMINS†

* Economic and Social Research Institute, Dublin;
Member of the Royal Irish Academy
† Teagasc, Dublin

Introduction

THE STARTING POINT of this paper is the proposition that Ireland's process of modernisation does not conform to the convergent pattern of development expected under the liberal model of industrial society. This posits a growing similarity in both labour force structures and social mobility regimes with expanding industrialisation (Gallie, 1990: 31–33). In Ireland's case, however, rapid industrialisation has not led to increasing social fluidity, as the convergence thesis would suggest, and the modern Irish labour force has also remained unusual in the persistence of a substantial landholding sector. In addition, property holding groups continue to enjoy distinctive economic as well as mobility advantages (see Breen and Whelan, this volume). We attempt to show in this paper not only how and why landholding persisted, but also argue that the survival of landholders is one of the significant factors contributing to the distinctive character of the Irish social mobility regime.

Our first objective, therefore, is to document one important dimension on which the Irish case deviates from the convergent pattern of development expected to occur under the liberal model. The Irish divergence is manifested by the persistence, into modern times, of a vibrant, small-scale landholding sector and, especially, by the manner in which members of that sector have been relatively successful in adapting to the modernisation of the country's economic and social structure. We develop this point in

Read 7 December 1990. © The British Academy 1992.

the first part of the paper by analysing some of the main 'survival strategies' adopted by small-scale landholders in face of agricultural modernisation and industrial development from 1960 to 1980, the crucial decades of Ireland's transition. We see these strategies as including adjustments to commercially-oriented, full-time farming at one end of the spectrum and, at the other end, a retreat from active farming with almost complete dependence on state welfare payments. The main focus of our attention, however, is on a substantial segment of the smallholder class whose members adapted to change by securing non-farm employment and other sources of income while retaining possession of their holdings. In light of this, we draw attention to the dangers of misinterpretation that arise in using conventional occupational categories in studying class transformation in Ireland; a concentration on 'main occupation' will conceal the extent to which extensive landholding persists among people with non-farm employment.

The second aim of the paper is to contrast the Irish smallholding class's adaptation to, or insertion into, the modernising economic and social structure with the fate of the country's lower working class. Working class families have generally failed to acquire their proportionate share of the new opportunities emerging with industrialisation. The new industries were clearly not concentrated in areas where traditional industrial employment declined but were widely scattered geographically. In addition, the rapid transformation of the Irish occupational structure after 1960 was associated with a much enhanced importance of educational and training certification for occupational entry. Families of smallholders capitalised on this change, to a greater extent than working class families, by taking advantage of the extended system of free post-primary education to secure employment for their children. Moreover, the continuing high natural increase in the Irish labour force and the rapid exodus from (full-time) agricultural employment, together with a slow growth in total employment, significantly increased competition for desirable jobs. In these contexts, the relative competitive ability of the Irish working class did not improve and, in important respects, indeed declined.

Our third aim is to show how the survival capacity of the small scale landholding class in the post-1960 period can be related to certain features in the historical development of the Irish family farm system; the 'specific, historically formed circumstances' (Goldthorpe, 1990: 333–336) of the initial stages of recent industrialisation. A quite distinct economic and social structure, elsewhere characterised as a 'peasant system' (Hannan, 1972), emerged among the smaller farmers of the west of Ireland in the late nineteenth and early twentieth centuries. Its cultural autonomy and effective mechanisms of social reproduction ensured the survival of this system until the 1960s. Compared to the Irish working class, small scale landholders were better placed to capitalise upon the opportunities emerging in the post–1960 modernisation of Ireland's economy.

The fourth aim of the paper is to show how the persistence of the Irish small farm sector is linked to the country's political context and culture. In this regard, we review those public policies which have been particularly sympathetic to the smallholding class and argue that these, in turn, have to be understood with reference to prevalent ideological perspectives, to interest group mobilisation, and to the nature of political styles in Ireland.

In a final section we draw together the main strands of the argument. We contend that by describing and offering explanations for the persistence of the small farming sector in Ireland and, by describing that sector's disproportionate presence in the country's more recent socio-economic transformation, we have identified significant factors accounting for Ireland's non-conformity to the liberal model of societal change in the course of industrialisation.

A general theoretical position underlies our analysis. We consider that in relation to the restructuring of the Irish agricultural economy, an account in terms of 'modernisation' is the most useful approach. As we show later, the impact of capitalist macroeconomic forces on Irish agricultural production has been especially pronounced since the 1960s (cf. Commins et al., 1978). However, purely structuralist theories of agrarian change over-emphasise the deterministic effects of economic forces and do not give sufficient weight to several influences that mediate the impact of capitalist development on agricultural communities. Such theories need to be modified to allow for the decision-making capacity—the 'survival strategies'—of individual farm owners (Leeuwis, 1989: 16; van der Ploeg, 1989; Long, 1986: 10). They also need to take into account the role of local cultures, and their associated communal arrangements and institutional forms. And further it is necessary to acknowledge the extent to which structural change in agriculture is substantially mediated by the strong interventionist role of the state.

Surival Strategies of the Smallholder Class

Three main types of adaptation to economic change characterise the original landholding class from the 1960s onwards: full-time commercial farming, which has become increasingly concentrated on the larger farms; off-farm employment, combined with part-time farming or farm rental; and, finally, the adaptation of a category of small-scale landowners, whose principal occupation has remained in farming but whose household income sources have become quite dispersed.

Somewhat over 40 per cent of all landholders in 1987 were estimated to be full-time farmers whose main occupation and income source was farming. A further 30 per cent of all landholders, whose main occupation was recorded as 'farming', received only a minority of their total household income from that source. Over half of this category depended mainly on state income transfers. Finally, approximately 30 per cent of all landowners were estimated to be part-time farmers, whose main occupation was not in farming. (*Agriculture and Food Policy Review*, 1990: 23–25; Callan *et al.*, 1989: 102).

These different outcomes from the significant restructuring that has occurred in Irish agriculture since the 1960s do not accord with what is predicted by theories invoking the 'logic of industrialism'. Land consolidation has been minimal, with small-scale landholders, by and large, holding on to their land. While conventional analyses show both a rapidly declining agricultural workforce and a substantial increase in industrial and service employment (Rottman and O'Connell, 1982; Rottman *et al.*, 1982), they ignore the continuance of landholding among the new classes of industrial and service employees. At the same time, analyses of poverty and inequality in Ireland, also based on 'main occupation' categories, exaggerate the extent of marginalisation and impoverishment among the smallholding class by ignoring the favourable position of the part-time farming group.

To elaborate on the significance of these trends in the Irish occupational structure, we first analyse the limited extent of land consolidation since the 1960s, despite the very rapid decline in farming as an occupation. Secondly, we show the significant growth in part-time farming and related occupations. Thirdly, we contrast the consolidation of commercial production on larger and more productive holdings with the adoption of less labour-intensive farming on smaller holdings. The trends towards part-time farming and dependence on many alternative income sources on the smaller farms mean that actual household income inequalities within the total landholding group are much smaller than previously estimated. Indeed, such inequalities may have narrowed significantly over the past twenty years. In all of these developments, both state and EC policy have had the paradoxical effect of maintaining the landholding structure and impeding land consolidation; outcomes directly opposite to those theoretically expected and to the long established objectives of agricultural modernisation.

Decline in farming, stability in landholding

Over the past quarter of a century there has been a sharp decline in the numbers returning their principal occupation as 'farmer' for census purposes. This has been of the order of 1.5 per cent per annum since the mid-1960s. This decline has been most pronounced among small farmers. The number of farmers with under 30 acres declined by 62 per cent between 1971 and 1986, as compared to a mere 5 per cent among those with holdings over 100 acres. The total decline was of the order of 30 per cent. These trends accorded with theoretical expectations, and with early policy objectives.

Table 1. Percentage change in farmers and landholders.

Farmers 1971–86		Landholders 1975–87	
Size groups (acres)	% change	Size groups (hectares)	% change
<15	−72.7	<10	−5.8
15–20	−56.6		
30–50	−35.4	10–20	−10.3
50–100	−9.6	20–30	+2.5
100–150	−4.2	30–50	−0.1
150–200	−5.9	50–100	+0.1
200+	−8.0	100+	−0.5
Total	−34.3	Total	−4.8

Source: *Census of Population*, 1971, vol. 4, 1986, vol. 2; CSO, *Farm Structures Surveys*, 1975 and 1987 (special tabulations).

By contrast, however, there has been remarkable stability in the number of *landholders*. These declined at an average rate of only 0.5 per cent per annum over the same period. Available data do not correspond with census returns for either time-frame or farm-size groups, but the substantially lower rates of decline among landholders are clearly evident in Table 1. Whereas farmers of under 50 acres declined by one-half during 1971–86, landholders in this group fell by less than 8 per cent in 1975–87. Obviously, a high proportion of those who were landholders in 1986–87 had taken up part-time farming.

Table 2 shows clear gradations of exclusive farming dependence by holding size. Nationally, one-third of all landholders have another occupation besides farming. This proportion, however, is over one-half for those with under 10 hectares, and rises to around two thirds of those on holdings of less than 5 hectares.

Studies of part-time farmers (e.g. Higgins, 1983) show that their

Table 2. Status of farmwork among landholders, 1985: % of landholders for whom farming is sole, major or subsidiary occupation.

Size Group	Farmwork as occupation		
(hectares)	Sole	Major	Subsidiary
<5	34.9	9.2	55.9
5–10	52.5	11.3	36.1
10–20	70.5	10.2	19.3
20–50	80.2	9.7	10.1
50–100	84.2	9.1	6.7
100+	78.6	11.8	9.5
Total	66.1	10.1	23.9

Source: CSO, *Farm Structures Survey*, 1985 (special tabulation).

number increased by 71 per cent between 1961 and 1987. They are heavily concentrated near larger urban centres, and tend to be younger than their peers, and more likely to be married and in the early to middle stages of the family life cycle. Such part-time farmers also hold a wide range of jobs, with only a minority in unskilled manual work. This suggests that they have attained at least moderate levels of education or training (Higgins, 1983: 25). Most intend to continue both in farming and in their non-farm jobs, and anticipate their heirs maintaining this pattern. Thus, most of the original smallholders with commercially non-viable holdings have held on to their land. Approximately half these surviving smallholders have off-farm jobs and adequate household incomes, to which of course farm production or rental income contribute. But the symbolic significance of being a landholder and its status implications probably count for more than its purely economic returns.

Full-time commercial farming has become increasingly concentrated on the larger holdings, while, on the other hand, those smallholders who are too old, unqualified or too distant from off-farm opportunities to avail of them, now constitute one of the most poverty prone groupings in Irish society (Callan *et al.*, 1989: 102).

This quite relentless process of economic and social differentiation that has occurred among landholders is now clearly reflected in the socio-demographic and income characteristics of their households. Table 3 summarises some of the more relevant data for the present discussion.

It is clear from Tables 2 and 3 that between 40 to 60 per cent of smaller landholders and/or their spouses have off-farm jobs. Compared to these, the small-scale landholders who are completely dependent on farming for market income are much older, much less likely to be married, or, if married, much more likely to have no children at home. They have therefore much smaller households, and are generally at the end stage of

Table 3.   Different characteristics of landholder households, 1987. A = Farm operator and/
or spouse with off-farm job. B = Farm operator and/or spouse *without* off-farm job.

		Acres				
		<30	30–50	50–100	100+	All
1. % of all farms	A	38	37	20	17	29
	B	62	63	80	83	71
2. Age of operator	A	46	44	43	44	45
(average)	B	60	57	50	48	54
3. % married	A	74	80	90	89	81
(farm operators)	B	48	56	59	68	57
4. % with pensions	A	30	28	31	27	29
	B	56	38	31	25	38
5. % with Smallholders'	A	14	14	7	7	12
Assistance	B	38	20	9	7	19
6. Non-farm income	A	75	76	53	38	62
as % of earned income	B	0	0	0	0	0

Source: Derived from Power and Roche (1990).

the family cycle. Partly because of their advanced age and incomplete family status, most have substantially disengaged from farm activities. In turn, their households are highly dependent on state welfare payments. Pensions and 'Smallholders Assistance' (the 'farmers' dole') are the main sources of income of a substantial proportion of these households.

Differentiation in farm production

One correlate of this economic and social differentiation in farming has been an increasing distinctiveness in the volume and type of production found on the different kinds of holding. There is increasing concentration of intensive dairying and tillage on the 'full-time', larger farms as against extensive dry cattle and sheep production on the smaller holdings. This is clearly illustrated in Table 4.

In 1960 only 40 per cent of the tillage acreage, and 28 per cent of dairy cows, were on holdings of over 100 acres. By 1987, tillage concentration on holdings over 100 acres had increased to 59 per cent, and dairying to 34 per cent. At the other extreme, tillage had by 1987 almost disappeared from small holdings; and the decline in dairy cow numbers on the small farms, from 22 per cent to 8 per cent, was even more precipitous. So, the highest income yielding enterprises, tillage and dairying, have shown substantial shifts up the farm size scale, while, on the other hand, the more extensive and lower income yielding types of farming, such as dry cattle and sheep, have become much more characteristic of the small farm category.

Table 4. Distribution (%) by size of holding of types of agricultural production, 1960 and 1987.

Size of holding (acres)	Tillage		Dairy cows		Other cattle		Sheep		Arable (crops and pasture) land	
	1960	1987	1960	1987	1960	1987	1960	1987	1960	1987
<30	15.6	6.9	22.0	7.2	18.0	14.8	15.7	12.7	17.4	13.9
30-50	16.6	9.0	20.5	18.6	18.3	18.2	17.7	14.3	18.5	17.2
50-100	27.7	24.7	29.9	39.8	27.7	32.0	25.9	30.0	27.8	31.5
100+	40.0	59.3	27.7	33.8	36.0	35.0	40.7	43.0	36.3	37.4
Total	1,651.9	1,066.6	1,274.7	1,587.4	3,442.5	5,273.2	4,285.0	4,991.5	11,147.2	11,519.3
	(000 acres)		(000s)		(000s)		(000s)		(000s acres)	

Source: *Agricultural Statistics*, 1960, and special tabulations from CSO, *Farm Structures Survey*, 1987.

Although in postwar agricultural policy intensive dairy farming was strongly advocated as the solution to the 'small farm problem', the reality has been that small-scale farmers themselves opted for the less lucrative drystock (cattle) farming. The growth of off-farm employment, and the increasing age and deprived family status of the remaining full-time small-scale farmers have led to a substantial fall in labour supply on small farms. Thus, despite the lower incomes from extensive drystock farming, this pattern of land use accords more readily with reduced labour and also more restricted capital resources on small farms. Drystock farming is also more compatible with part-time farming than dairying. Higgins (1983), for instance, found that 72 per cent of part-time farmers were mainly in cattle and/or sheep production, as against 53 per cent of full-time farmers (see also Lucey and Kaldor, 1969). National Farm Survey (NFS) returns show clear gradations by farm size in the contribution of cattle and sheep to gross farm output. In 1988 this contribution ranged from 66 per cent in the 2–10 hectare category to 36 per cent for the category of over 100 hectares (Power and Roche, 1990: 2.43).

Over time, therefore, most landholders have adapted quite rationally to market opportunities and constraints. They took up off-farm employment where their own farm resources were insufficient, where their job qualifications were adequate and off-farm opportunities were available. Where land resources were sufficient they intensified and increased output and incomes. Close to one fifth of the smallholder class, however, are quite impoverished, being mainly dependent on state welfare payments. In fact, as we detail later, state and EC supports to a large extent bankroll *all* farm-owning categories. Such assistance is provided through a series of production subsidies and market supports. 'Headage' payments for cattle and sheep on the small to medium sized holdings are of particular importance. The cumulative impact of welfare payments, supports and the removal of all land taxes, has been to encourage the vast bulk of the original landholding class to retain their land, albeit in varying degrees of comfort.

The maintenance of such a 'pre-industrial' property holding class right through into the 1990s has not been recognised in most analyses of contemporary Irish society, including Breen *et al.* (1990). Such an outcome can, however, hardly be unexpected, given the historical importance of this class and its favoured political status. Its unusual capacity to survive can be illustrated even more clearly by examining trends in household income sources and levels since the early 1970s.

Inequalities increasing in farm incomes, declining in total household incomes

Analyses of incomes derived from farming between the 1950s and 1980s show a growing economic differentiation, and increasing farm income inequality between the large commercial farmers and those on smaller farms (Commins 1986: 56). However, these conclusions about *farm income* need to be qualified by reference to data available from Household Budget Surveys for *total household* income. These surveys show that for both gross household income and disposable household income, the gap between the largest and smallest 'farmer' category narrowed between 1973 and 1987. In 1973, gross household income on farms of under 30-acres, where the main occupation of the head of household was 'farmer', amounted to 34 per cent of that on farms of over 100 acres. By 1987, the corresponding figure was 44 per cent. Gross household income rose faster on the smaller farms, as did disposable income, despite the fact that income from agricultural production showed a reverse trend. The factor of major influence here was the increasing contribution made on the smaller farms by non-farm earned income and by state transfers. While farm income increases have favoured the larger farms, changes in non-farm earned income, in state transfers and also in direct taxation have had the opposite effect.[1] The proportionate changes in incomes calculated per farm household are shown in Table 5. While farm income growth increased directly with farm size, non-farm earned income, and gross domestic household income, show the opposite growth pattern. Thus, even in the case of those holdings where the 'main occupation' of the household head remains in farming, and where farm incomes have *declined* in relative terms since the early 1970s, the total disposable income of smaller farmers' households has

Table 5. Percentage increase in components of farm household incomes 1973–1987, by size of farm (1973 = 100).

	Acres				
Income component	<30	30–50	50–100	100+	Total
Farm income	310	293	413	439	483
Non-farm earned income	934	1076	798	890	912
Total direct income	541	472	456	485	559
Total state transfers	1032	1091	1288	1535	985
Total gross income	669	548	502	512	605
Total disposable income	642	518	481	479	576
Average weekly disposable income, 1987 (£s)	156.25	165.27	230.18	357.50	224.22
% of workforce in households unemployed, 1987	13.3	8.5	6.8	7.0	6.5

Source: Calculated from *Household Budget Surveys* 1973 and 1987 (CSO, 1977, 1990b).

[1] Further details are given in Central Statistics Office (1980); and Rottman, Hannan, *et al.* (1982).

increased at a relatively faster rate than on the larger farms. As a consequence, total household income inequalities have narrowed.

State transfers

In Household Budget Surveys, 'gross household income' is composed of earned income, other 'direct' but unearned income and state transfers. The main components of state transfers are old age and retirement pensions and unemployment benefit and assistance payments. The household economy of the smaller farms is now predominantly based on non-farm employment and state transfers. Combined, they account for over two-thirds of gross household income on farms under 50 acres. The changes between 1973 and 1987 are shown in Table 6.

Table 6.   Percentage Composition of Gross Household Income, 1973 and 1987, by size of farm.

Year	Income component	Acres			
		<30	30–50	50–100	100+
1973	Farm income	32.8	57.0	69.3	81.6
	Non-farm income	25.1	16.7	14.2	8.4
	Other direct income	15.9	14.0	10.9	7.5
	State transfers	26.1	12.3	5.5	2.5
	Total	100.0	100.0	100.0	100.0
1987	Farm income	15.2	30.5	53.6	70.0
	Non-farm income	34.9	32.8	22.6	14.5
	Other direct income	9.4	12.2	9.7	7.9
	State transfers	40.3	24.5	14.0	7.5
	Total	100.0	100.0	100.0	100.0

Source: Calculated from *Household Budget Surveys*, 1973 and 1987 (CSO, 1977, 1990b).

The proportionate contribution of farming to total gross household income has halved on farms under 50 acres, while barely changing on the farms over 100 acres. Even within the farm income component on smallholdings, an increasing proportion is accounted for by livestock headage payments or other income subsidies. It is estimated that by 1989 almost two-thirds of family farm income on sheep farms, and 40 per cent on dry cattle farms, was represented by such production subsidies (Power and Roche, 1990). Clearly, 'market income' has a very particular meaning in these circumstances!

State transfers as a proportion of total household income display almost the exactly opposite pattern to farm income, accounting for over 40 per cent of total household income on small farms in 1987 and less than 10 per cent on large farms.

Farming households, therefore, vary widely in their income sources. Although most small farms depend on incomes from a number of sources, three sub-groups are discernible:

1 a minority whose farming operations ensure a viable household income;

2 those 'pluriactive' households where farm incomes are mainly supplemented by non-farm earnings from various sources, and by different people within the household;

3 those farm households relying predominantly on state transfers, though with some farm income.

This last sub-group paradoxically may have survived, despite their impoverishment, because they had no realistic alternative.

Household Budget data, it should be noted, refer to 'farmer households' and do *not* include around a third of all landholding households where the 'main occupation' of the head of household is not in farming. Unfortunately, it is not possible from currently available sources to include these latter households in any combined classification. If it were, it would in fact be revealed that the original smallholder class has increased its income at a far faster relative rate than is shown in the gross income disparities in Table 5.

The Adaptations of Smallholders and of the Lower Working Class: Some Comparisons

Having battled so long for their land, the Irish smallholders have been very loath to give it up. Except for a sub-group, they are not nearly as marginalised as most previous analyses have suggested (see Rottman *et al.*, 1982; Commins, 1986; Breen *et al.*, 1990). Only analyses using conventional occupational categories to describe complex class positions could have come to that conclusion. Although only 14 per cent of the workforce are now employed in agriculture, almost a quarter of all households in Ireland still own land. It is instructive to compare the changing situation of smallholders to that of the Irish working class.

From the 1970s to the late 1980s the market income of those smallholders who remained on farms improved to a far greater extent than that of the lower working class. Unemployment among the latter is now at crisis level. At the same time, the educational and social mobility chances of the children of smallholders are far more favourable. Ireland's class structure and class cultures are, therefore, both more complex and more 'traditional' than allowed for by modernisation theory or 'the logic of industrialism'. It is the Irish working class whose situation is now problematic, and who are experiencing economic and cultural alienation.

In the following we first examine the extent to which the rural and the urban working classes gained from Ireland's modern industrialisation process. Secondly, we examine the degree to which children from both class backgrounds gained from educational mobility.

Income and employment changes: 1973–1987

The analyses of household income changes by family farm size and by social class, in Tables 5 and 7 respectively, show relative increases in different sources of household income between 1973 and 1987. The results demonstrate clearly that, even where small-scale landholders have remained in full-time farming, total disposable household income on these farms has not only increased at a much faster rate than on larger farms but also substantially faster than in all working class households.

The main reason for this trend is the extraordinarily rapid growth in unemployment among the lower working class. If one includes school leavers still seeking their first job, by 1987 44 per cent of all adults in the

Table 7.   Percentage increase in components of household income by 'social class' categories, 1973 to 1987 (1973 = 100).

Income component	Social class of head of household					
	Higher and lower professional	Salaried employees and intermediate non-manual	Other non-manual	Skilled manual	Semi- and unskilled manual	Total
Earned income	621	598	561	509	377	563
Total direct income	623	603	573	513	393	566
Total state transfers	1,094	1,068	1,060	1,354	1,100	1,036
Total gross income	635	632	624	583	510	615
Total disposable income	555	562	575	539	496	556
Average weekly disposable income 1987 (£s)	302.96	224.91	197.67	198.08	158.97	200.96
% of workforce in households unemployed in 1987	6.1	12.5	21.1	25.0	37.0	18.0

Source: Calculated from *Household Budget Surveys*, 1973 and 1987 (CSO, 1977, 1990b).

labour force in lower working class households were unemployed. This rate has almost tripled since 1973.·

Actual income levels on farms of under 30 acres are much the same as in lower working class households (Tables 5 and 7). Similarly, state transfers account for around 40 per cent of total disposable income in both cases. In lower working class households state transfers comprise mainly unemployment payments. On smallholdings, in contrast, such transfers are made up mostly of pensions and 'Smallholders Assistance', a specific income supplement not dependent on 'unemployment'.[2] If one adds in that proportion of farm income that is accounted for by state and EC supports, statutory income support for the smaller, poorer farmer is substantially greater, and of a less dependency-creating nature, than that for working class households. This holds true despite the fact that, at first glance, the latter households are in a far more deprived position than small farm households. In many respects, if one is to be unemployed it certainly pays to have some land! In addition, the social and psychological 'diswelfare' effects of unemployment and low incomes are far more serious in working class households (Whelan *et al.*, 1991).

Relative educational mobility and employment chances of smallholders' and working class children

With the exception of a brief period in the 1970s, the expanding Irish economy never provided enough places for all young people leaving full-time education and seeking employment (Sexton *et al.*, 1991). Fertility increased rapidly up to 1980 as did the natural increase in the labour force. At the same time, substantial employment declines occurred in both agriculture and traditional industries (Breen *et al.*, 1990: 60). Thus, even though total employment increased in most periods, it was not sufficient to absorb both the increasing number of new entrants to the labour force and the older unemployed workers displaced from declining sectors. Moreover, although the agricultural workforce had almost halved between 1961 and 1981, the number of farmers' children (of less than 15 years old) declined by only 20 per cent. And of course, their tendency to stay on the farm lessened significantly, from about 30 per cent of the cohort of the early 1960s to around 15 per cent of that of the early 1980s. As a combined result of these trends, the actual volume of outflow from farm backgrounds into the nonfarm labour market declined only minimally from 1961 to

---

[2] At various points throughout this chapter we draw conclusions which are derived from calculations based on official statistics. An additional set of tables documenting these calculations is available from the authors on request.

1981. Given the general over-supply of labour and, as we shall see, the greater educational attainments of those from farming backgrounds, working class school leavers faced severe competition in the Irish labour market over most of the period.

The rather dramatic level of employment and occupational restructuring that occurred from the mid-1960s to the early 1980s is clearly described by Breen *et al.* (1990). There were substantial declines in small scale farming, agricultural labouring, and unskilled manual employment. Most of the new positions demanded, at least, second level educational and training qualifications. With employment and occupational mobility chances becoming increasingly dependent on educational attainment, the relative underachievement of children from working class backgrounds put them at a very serious disadvantage in the labour market (Breen, 1984a; 1991b; Hannan, 1986).

Educational participation rates increased rapidly from the mid-1960s, particularly from the introduction of 'free education' in 1967. In the mid-1960s almost one third of all primary school leavers finished education at that stage, the participation rate for 14 to 19 year olds being only 25 per cent (OECD, 1966: 169, 170). By 1971 the latter rate had almost doubled, while school leaving at primary level had almost ceased. By the end of the 1980s over 70 per cent of the relevant age-cohort were completing second level education, and only 6 per cent were dropping out of second level schools before taking any junior cycle examinations.

Social class and regional inequalities were very pronounced in the 1960s, with disparity ratios of almost five to one between upper middle class and lower working class children in their chances of completing second level education (Rottman *et al.*, 1982: 52). But these ratios had narrowed considerably even by the beginning of the 1970s. By the end of the 1980s, the ratio of upper middle class to lower working class children completing the Leaving Certificate had fallen to two to one (see Table 8).

What is striking about the figures for the 1960s is the similarity in the low participation rates at second level of boys from lower working class and small farm (<30 acres) origins. Around half of both groups did not go further than primary education (Hannan, 1970: 66, 70). Although the one study available for this period of participation rates by size of farm is small and highly regional, later studies for the 1970s and 1980s show equally wide variation in this respect. Within the agricultural sector, therefore, 'class' inequalities were just as marked in life chances as in the non-farm sector.

By the late 1980s, however, less than 15 per cent of children from farm backgrounds came from farms of less than 30 acres, compared to 40 per cent in 1961. Such smallholdings are now predominantly operated on a

Table 8. Educational participation rates by social class, 1960s and 1980s.

Father's class	1960s		1988–9 (National)	
	1961 (National) %left school at Primary Level	1964 (Cavan) % Primary only[a]	%with Leaving Certificate	%to Third Level
Farmers				
<50 acres	—	35	66	21
50–100 acres	—	23	75	34
100+ acres	—	19	83	42
All farmers	25	33	73	31
Non-farm				
Upper and intermediate non-manual	12	10	87	45
Other non-manual	20	21	68	21
Skilled manual	17	21	70	19
Semi-skilled and unskilled manual	46	49	48	11

[a] For the Cavan study valuation of farms was used a variable rather than farm size: an approximate conversion would be: <£30 = <50 acres; £30–£44 = 50–100 acres; £45+ = 100+ acres.

Sources: OECD (1966); Hannan (1970); School Leavers' Survey (1988–9).

part-time basis, and parents are not classified as farmers. Thus, we now have reliable figures only for farms of under 50 acres. Comparing the educational attainments of school leavers from such small farm origins with those from working class origins, as in Table 8, we find that the former have been substantially more successful than the latter. Two-thirds of children from small farm backgrounds complete the Leaving Certificate and over one in five go on to third level. The attainment levels of children from lower working class background are, proportionately, almost a third lower at Leaving Certificate level, and one half lower at third level. By the end of the 1980s the attainments of children from small farm backgrounds had come to resemble those from skilled manual and lower non-manual backgrounds.

Over the whole period, not only have smallholders as a class succeeded in retaining their property and relative income position, but they have also succeeded in capturing a significant proportion of local off-farm employment opportunities. They have been more effective than working class families in utilising the education system to gain access to such off-farm opportunities for their children. Thus, both demographic pressures from the farm sector and the greater educational achievements of farmers' children helped ensure that the upward mobility of working class children was significantly constrained.

We now turn to place the foregoing discussion in the context of the origins and enduring nature of the small scale farm sector in Ireland prior to the adaptations of recent decades.

The Importance of the Traditional 'Peasant' System

There are distinctive features in the historical development of the Irish family farm system that relate directly to the changes that occurred in the post-1960 period. The 'peasant' or small-scale farming system emerged late in Ireland, based on the far-reaching land ownership transfers between 1870 and 1920. These transfers led to the metamorphosis of the impoverished tenant farmers of the post-Famine period almost entirely into peasant proprietors, to the destruction of the rigid and exploitative landlord system, and to the emergence of a new stratification order dominated by 'middle peasants' (Crotty, 1966; Lee, 1973; Hannan, 1979). By the beginning of the 1920s the immense structural changes in the rural and national stratification order, which had occurred over the previous fifty years, had brought about substantial absolute rates of upward mobility for the mass of small-scale and middle-sized farmers, as well as significant improvements in their living standards. Such improvements, however, were not maintained owing to apparently declining productivity levels on their newly owned farms (Crotty, 1966: 92–107). What appears to have occurred up to the late 1950s is the stabilisation of a pattern of agricultural production significantly oriented to subsistence, particularly in the small farms of the west and south-west (Hannan, 1979).

The transition from tenancies to widespread property ownership had far-reaching economic effects, as well as outcomes of social, cultural and political significance. It took place in a context of severe economic rationalisation in the rural economy, so that by the mid-1920s dependence on farm employment had increased greatly relative to the 1870s. By 1926 56 per cent of total Irish male employment was in agriculture. The quite diversified rural economies of the 1870s were replaced by an economy dominated by family farming, with most of the active population being either farmers or farmers' 'relatives assisting' (Rottman et al., 1982: 39–74). Furthermore, while the status, security and wellbeing of the peasant proprietors themselves improved substantially over the period in question, the life chances and the local reproduction opportunities for non-inheritors painfully contracted (Hannan and Hardiman, 1978; Hannan,

1979). The reason for this lay in the extremely discriminatory nature of the single heir inheritance system on family farms, combined with the virtual extinction of most local off-farm economic opportunities for non-inheritors. Arensberg and Kimball (1940) provide a classic description of this 'stem family' system at work.

The economic rationalisation of the rural economy, accompanied by large-scale outmigration of the 'surplus' population on farms, did, however, leave intact a relatively comfortable small farmer class. In fact, the social structure of that class appeared so stable and 'traditional' that Arensberg and Kimball (1940) not only invoked functionalist explanations for the high degree of mutually supportive relationships present, but also culturalist explanations of 'immemorial custom'—which custom had, however, a very brief history indeed.

Despite this lack of historical depth, particularly in comparison with that of peasant life in other West European countries, at least in Connacht and west Munster a particular form of peasant economy, culture and social structure prevailed up to the 1960s (Hannan, 1979). Its most notable feature was perhaps its highly effective, but discriminatory, survival and reproduction pattern. Marriage rates among inheritors remained high until the 1940s, and fertility rates among married farmers were extremely high (Walsh, 1968; Hannan, 1972; 1979). Moreover, while inheritance rules discriminated severely in favour of a single heir, there were effective arrangements for the dispersal and social placement of non-inheritors. Such arrangements included emigration—often managed through kinship networks abroad. But particularly notable was the tendency to seek secure, off-farm, employment opportunities for brighter non-inheriting children. Educational attainment and examination success were seen as the path to professional and public service employment. On this point, it is remarkable that the highest second level completion rates, and third level entry rates, for recent youth cohorts occur, precisely, in those counties which historically shared the main features of this peasant society (Clancy, 1988).

Resilient though this system was, it did experience increasing strains, especially as a result of the income difficulties faced by farmers on the smaller holdings. Among the latter, marriage rates declined rapidly from the 1940s onwards. Consequently, in the face of declining economic circumstances, the formation of complete nuclear families, fully dependent on family farm income, became increasingly problematic. Thus, by the 1960s a considerable proportion of smaller farmers were old and unmarried or, if married, had no direct heirs (Scully, 1971). Moreover, their objectively poorer situation was now less protected by a high level of cultural autonomy, or by strong and supportive local kinship and neigh-bour groups (Hannan and Katsiaouni, 1977; Hannan, 1979). However, what is noteworthy about this heirless and poverty stricken category of small farmers is that the general expectation of their holdings coming on the market, and supposedly resulting in the creation of larger and more economically viable farms, was not realised. Heirs appeared from unexpected places, but mostly from wider kinship networks, with the result that little decline occurred in the total number of landholders. As a consequence, farm consolidation proceeded very slowly. Increasingly, small-scale landholders came to depend less on farm production for their sole livelihood.

If, therefore, we consider the full set of differentiated adaptations of the smallholding class as a whole, rather than concentrating on the residual catgory of 'farmers', their economic marginalisation was not as pronounced as might seem. In fact, their generally successful process of adjustment clearly belies the negative prognoses that were made on the basis of the deprived status of small farmers in the 1960s (Scully, 1971).

By 1961, 42 per cent of total male employment in Ireland was still in agriculture, mostly in small-scale family production units, with a median size of 38 acres (Hannan, 1979: 27–66). The system still retained a strong, self-confident sense of its own culturally independent importance, and politically 'deserving' status, within Irish society. This helps explain why, when the Irish economy started to grow rapidly in the 1960s, the small scale landowners were in a much better position than the working class to use the new opportunities that became available.

State Policy, Political Context and Culture

The persistence of the Irish small farm sector cannot be understood without reference to its generally favourable political treatment, in particular in agricultural and industrialisation policies and in income maintenance measures.

Land immobility and small farm policy

We are concerned here with the way in which the rigidities of the Irish land structure and related agrarian policies have helped to sustain the small landholding class. High levels of immobility in ownership and user rights to agricultural land have been characteristic of Ireland since the late nineteenth century. Connell (1968: 116) argued that the land legislation of that time, in converting farmers from tenants to proprietors, made them more ambitious in their yearning to establish the family name on particular pieces of land. It does appear that ownership solidified the strong bonds of attachment to the land. Certainly, the system of peasant proprietorship, introduced against a background of rapacious landlordism, stifled the evolution of any form of long-term leasing of land (Inter-Departmental Committee on Land Structure Reform, 1978: 26). As already noted, despite declines in agricultural employment, land consolidation to allow farm enlargement did not take place to any significant extent.

Instead, the land policies of the new Irish state were highly redistributive in character. The Irish Land Commission (the state agency responsible for land restructuring) became an extensive purchaser and distributor of land, creating new holdings mainly through the sub-division of those large estates that survived from the days of landlordism. While the Commission gradually obtained strong compulsory powers to acquire land which was not achieving adequate production, such powers proved difficult to use in the face of local popular opposition and frequent legal challenges. The Commission's redistribution policy brought only one-third of its farm enlargements up to its own standards of viable size. Irrespective of its stated priorities, the Commission had to have regard to 'the situation on the ground' and, in practice, the only feasible policy was to give a little land to everybody deemed to qualify (*Inter-Departmental Committee on Land Structure Reform*, 1978: 39). Nevertheless, even these marginal improvements enabled a large proportion of smallholders to remain in farming for at least an additional generation, thereby satisfying their deepest aspirations. Landless farm labourers and non-inheriting sons were not, however, extended this advantage. By the time of rural industrialisation in the late 1960s most of them had already left the countryside.

Another factor contributing to the retention of landholdings was that, for most of the period from the 1960s onwards, it was more economically attractive to retain possession of land than to sell it. In times of rapid inflation and rising land values, it made sense to hold on to land. Furthermore, assessment of means, against payment of the Old Age Pension, was likely to result in a lower imputed value to production from the family holding than the actual income that could be obtained from selling the land. Receipt of the Old Age Pension also conferred other benefits such as free public travel. In this context, special pension schemes to induce elderly farmers to retire, and release the use or ownership of their land to other farmers, did not prove attractive to the targeted population. In addition, younger low income, small-scale farmers could obtain Smallholders Assistance. Such income support could not be as easily secured if the land were sold. It should be noted also that there has been little imposition, such as property taxes, on landholders, and none at all over the past fifteen years.

Besides land policy, several related turning points can be discerned in the 1960s in state action in relation to small farms. An Inter-Departmental Committee on the Problems of Small Western Farms (1962) declared boldly that, for the most part, holdings under 15 acres were fundamentally non-viable. The Committee advocated certain measures to support small-farm development, such as production incentive bonus schemes, intensive advice, and a pension scheme enticing elderly owners to relinquish their land for use by active farmers. The 1965 Land Act did in fact provide for an early rertirement pension but few farmers found it attractive.

The Committee, however, also recommended that the weight of future efforts by the state in small-farm areas should be directed towards providing non-farm employment through industrialisation, afforestation, tourism development and 'other ancillary activities'. The Second Programme for Economic Expansion accepted that programmes of agricultural development in small farm areas were not, of themselves, capable of meeting the problems of these areas. It recognised the need for 'an integrated approach' to rural development. In other words, the policy goal of stabilising the population on *farms* gradually ceded way to the objective of stabilising the *rural* population. By 1969 the Government's Third Programme for Economic and Social Development had consolidated the shift in ideas and strategies. It was stated (1969: 44–45) that:

> In the long run the only real solution to the problems of farms which cannot be made to provide a reasonable livelihood lies not in agriculture alone but in the comprehensive development of rural areas through the expansion of industry.

Rural industrialisation policy

Policy debates about industrialisation in the late 1960s and early 1970s revolved very much around the centralisation or dispersal issue. The Buchanan Report (1968), mindful of the need to maximise new employment in total, favoured a strategy of moderate concentration, focused on the promotion of regional centres. Recognising the obvious risks to its political support in favouring such a proposal, the government instead opted for a wide dispersal of industrial development 'in order to minimise internal migration and population dislocation'. Accordingly, the Industrial Development Authority (IDA) embarked upon a strategy of setting manufacturing job targets for groups of towns (*Regional Industrial Plans*, 1973–77). Mainly as a result of these policy changes, male industrial manufacturing employment grew by 107 per cent between 1961 and 1981 outside Dublin and Leinster—where such job increases were only of the order of 20 per cent. Indeed, in Dublin city itself such employment actually fell, as the traditional industrial base declined rapidly. Overall, the IDA's policy of rural industrialisation had substantial success in generating local employment opportunities, which enabled many smallholders to supplement their meagre farm incomes and thus remain on the land.

The EC experience

Policy measures consequent on Ireland's membership of the EC have also made a contribution to the persistence of small-scale landholding. While it is a fact that the price and market policies of the Common Agricultural Policy (CAP) have skewed the financial benefits of EC membership in favour of the larger producer, Ireland has been quite successful in directing non-price policies to the advantage of its smallholders. Over recent years considerable lobbying has led to a substantial extension of measures in support of farming in 'disadvantaged areas'. Livestock farming which, as we have seen, is the mainstay of small farms, is now heavily subsidised by the EC.

Political context

State policy 'favouritism' towards the small-farm sector derives from the institutional and cultural context of Irish politics and from the small-farm, and generally petty bourgeois base, of the dominant political party. Moreover, the civil and public service has traditionally attracted people from medium- to small-farming backgrounds. Thus, the legitimacy of the political bias towards small farming has rarely been challenged from within the state system.

However, the historical dominance of the rural petty bourgeoisie in Irish economic and political life, and their uniquely advantaged position in the state's taxation and transfer systems (Rottman, *et al.*, 1982; Breen, *et al.*, 1990), are only partly based on their favoured status in the nationalist ideology. They are also very practically grounded in the capacity of small farmers for political organisation. The public articulation and promulgation of their interests is based on skilful ideological use of the mass media and effective mobilisation to protect and advance their shared interests. Several characteristics of farmers as a class make such mobilisation possible. First, there is the political transparency of their class interests in product prices and in a whole range of other state and EC supports, which have increasingly become politically negotiated. Second, farmers live in long established, and generally class homogeneous, communities which have strong local descent group characteristics and limited geographical mobility. Third, farmers' organisations also represent much wider landholding and property interests, and use a rhetoric whose resonance extends far beyond their own membership. In all these respects, the contrast with the working class, and its relatively limited capacity for mobilisation, is obvious.

Even with the emergence of neo-corporatist arrangements for the negotiation of state policies, farmers have retained privileged access to the bargaining table. And although the issues articulated in agricultural policy discussions may reflect primarily the concerns of the larger farmers, the fact remains that the interests of small farmers still receive greater attention than those of the working class.

Political culture and ideology

In considering the survival of the small farm sector, the analysis of Irish political culture is highly relevant. As a predominantly agrarian society, and one in which land issues were associated with a long struggle for national political independence, the new Ireland inherited powerful strains of rural fundamentalist ideology. The writers of the Literary Revival of the late nineteenth century popularised a vision of rustic dignity and virtue while often spurning 'this filthy modern tide' (Brown 1981: 83). The founders of the modern co-operative movement were also inspired by a vision of a rural civilisation. Irish rural fundamentalism, like that found in other largely agrarian societies, was expressed through a set of values and beliefs which stressed: (i) the advantages of family-owned, family-operated farms and of a numerous class of landholders; (ii) the healthy nature of farming as an occupation, and open country farming communities as ideal settlement models; and (iii) agriculture as the basis of national prosperity. Support for the family farm ideal, as well as for having as many people as possible working on the land, was even inserted in the Irish Constitution of 1937.

This Irish version of rural fundamentalism was also congruent with Catholic social thought, which advocated the wide diffusion of private property ownership together with the desirability of owner-operated farms (Commins, 1986: 52). Significantly also, leading churchmen espoused the cause of small farming and rural development (Lucey, 1955: Bohan, 1979) while there is little equivalent episcopal concern on behalf of the lower working class.[3] In the postwar decades it became increasingly difficult to

---

[3] Despite the increasing deterioration in the conditions of the lower working class in Dublin over the past two decades, it is almost inconceivable that an equivalent Episcopal response would arise to that of the recent Western Bishops' Conference on the problem of the small farm Communities of the West of Ireland.

reconcile the rhetoric of rural fundamentalism with the economic realities of small-scale farming, but state action programmes still actively pursued various strategies to maintain viable rural communities.

Ireland affords an example of a polity in which the political concerns and style of the rural periphery came to invade and dominate the urban centre for more than a generation (Garvin, 1974: 324). Rural ideological perspectives, Garvin argues, have persisted in an urban context because patterns of mobility are such that a large proportion of those influential in urban society are likely to have a rural cultural background. The core of the Dáil in the 1980s, just as in the 1960s, was provided by farming and small-business groups, with strong rural and small-community affiliations (Garvin, 1982: 28; Chubb, 1970). Governments led by Fianna Fáil, the dominant political party, systematically spread their cabinet appointments around as many counties as possible, usually giving the western periphery a disproportionately generous share (Garvin, 1974).

In a rural society, where survival is linked closely to state transfers and subsidies, 'the political style will be extremely familial, personalistic and clientelistic' (Carty, 1981: 9). Moreover, patron–client structures are a typical outcome in societies where peasant values and social institutions exist. In the Irish political culture, there have been mutually reinforcing tendencies between peasant survival and patronage politics. Fianna Fail has owed much of its electoral success to support from the small-farm counties. Although it gradually accommodated itself to an emerging urban bourgeoisie, it continued to favour its original political base. While public administration has grown more complex and centralised, political styles remain dominated by intercessionary politics, with members of the Dail 'going around persecuting civil servants' in return for the favour of support at election time (Chubb, 1970). The personalism of clientelistic politics is inextricably bound up with the primary relationships of an agrarian-based rural society.

In this political context, and given the particular culture and forms of Irish political organisation, it is therefore, hardly surprising that the Irish smallholder class should have received such favoured attention.

Conclusions

We have outlined the survival of a numerous land-holding class in Ireland right into the 1980s. Between the 1960s and the 1980s, although the number of those whose main occupation was farming declined at a rate of 1.5 to 2 per cent per annum, landholders declined at less than 0.5 per cent per annum. Even when landowning people shifted occupation from farming, they mostly held on to their land. By the end of the 1980s at least a third of all those with 'farm' holdings with some agricultural activity, and a somewhat higher proportion of all landholders, were mainly dependent on off-farm employment. Until at least this time, little land sale or consolidation had occurred. Off-farm employment, therefore, has been one of the most successful 'survival strategies' adopted by the original smallholding class.

The communities of this class have disproportionately benefited from industrial expansion policy, and its members have adapted with relative success to the educational demands of the labour market. In an economic and demographic context in which labour supply has consistently outstripped demand, the Irish smallholding class has consistently won the competition with the working class for industrial jobs, as well as for upward educational and social mobility for its children.

The late survival of a substantial small-scale landholding sector in Ireland created not only a large reservoir of displaced labour but one that possessed specific cultural and institutional advantages. At least up to the mid-1980s, the 'cultural adaptiveness' of families and individuals from the older peasant, or small farmer, communities has in fact been much more in evidence than the cultural and social–psychological demoralisation of these communities perceived by some anthropologists (e.g. Brody, 1973). There appear to be at least three underlying reasons for this. One is the well-oiled reproduction and dispersion strategies of the stem family system, developed in the most straitened economic circumstances, which have provided small-farm communities with a 'significant beginning advantage' (Hannan, 1979). The 'stem family' system, it should be noted, has no counterpart among the urban working class. Secondly, such farm communities are still largely based on local descent groups, with much stronger ties of mutual support and shared identity than are generally found even within homogeneous working class communities—which, in any case, even in the 1960s when they were more stable and secure than now, held only a minority of all working class families. Thirdly, within the smallholder class, mobility aspirations are higher and more varied, and perceived social and geographic barriers to their attainment less constraining, than among the working class. Thus, over a number of generations, farm families have developed much more widely dispersed kinship and status connections (Hannan and Katsiaouni, 1977; Hannan, 1979).

Such advantages have been reinforced by favourable state intervention. Crucial policy decisions were taken in the late 1960s which recognised the futility of attempting to maintain employment in small-scale farming. Regional and industrial location policy shifted away from the creation of new growth centres, and from supporting declining centres, towards the goal of a widely dispersed industrialisation. The expected marginalisation and likely impoverishment of small farmers were matters of much greater political concern in the late 1960s and early 1970s than that of declining employment opportunities for the urban working class. The importance of the allegiance of small farmers to Fianna Fáil was hardly incidental. Indeed, Irish political culture has, in general, been disproportionately influenced by this class.

Finally, though, these positive conclusions about the survival capacity of the smallholder class need to be balanced by two more negative findings, which may offer pointers to the future. First, those smallholders who are unable to supplement farming income by off-farm employment now constitute one of the main recruitment bases for poverty in Ireland. Secondly, preliminary evidence on land inheritance and sale trends at the end of the 1980s suggests that either the older 'heirless' owner, or his or her heir, is now less likely than before to hold on to the patrimony. But, whatever about the future, there is no denying the numerical, cultural and political significance of the 'peasant residue' in modern Ireland. Previous accounts have provided a predominantly negative evaluation of this phenomenon (Brown, 1981; Garvin, 1974, Lee, 1989). Our argument counters this view, and draws attention to the manner in which the persistence of this landholding class constitutes a crucial respect in which the Irish case deviates from the pattern of social development that would be envisaged under the liberal model.

Proceedings of the British Academy, **79**, 105–128

Industrialisation, Class Formation and Social Mobility in Ireland

CHRISTOPHER T. WHELAN,*
RICHARD BREEN† & BRENDAN J. WHELAN*
* *Economic & Social Research Institute, Dublin*
† *The Queen's University of Belfast*

Industrialisation and Social Mobility

FEW SOCIETIES have changed so rapidly and so radically as has the Republic of Ireland since 1960. Success in the form of state initiatives to promote industrialisation brought a more general promise that the fruits of independence would finally be realised. The associated expectations and excitement were captured in the catch phrase of the 1960s 'the rising tide that would raise all boats'. Such a sanguine view of the relationship between economic growth and social mobility was, until recently, shared by the bulk of sociologists.

In fact, as Goldthorpe (1985: 554) concludes, the evidence on which such confident conclusions regarding the relationship between economic growth, industrialisation and social mobility are based is 'confused and uncertain'. In the literature of the late 1950s and 1960s the discussion of mobility in industrial societies was linked with the question of whether American society was distinctive in the amount of social mobility it displayed. The conclusion reached by Lipset and Bendix (1959) and Blau and Duncan (1967) was that economically advanced societies had *in common* a level of mobility which is, by any reckoning, high. To explain the strikingly similar 'total vertical mobility rates', Lipset and Bendix sought factors universal throughout industrial societies. Among the processes inherent in all modern social structures which, they argue, have a direct effect on the rate of social mobility, two in particular are of importance: (i) changes in the number of available vacancies, and (ii)

Read 7 December 1990. © The British Academy 1992.

changes in the legal restrictions pertaining to potential opportunities. Industrial societies are those with expanding economies which need increasing numbers of workers in higher-level professional, administrative and managerial positions; and further, in the course of industrialisation the family firm gives way to the bureaucratic enterprise with its formal methods of selection, where education becomes a more significant deter-minant of occupational position than occupational inheritance (see also Heath, 1981: 38–39). Emphasis on shifts in occupational structure directs attention to overall, or absolute, mobility rates. On the other hand, highlighting the trend towards universalism, that is, towards the application of standards of judgement or decision-making which derive from considerations of rationality and efficiency and which are detached from the particular values or interests of different membership groups, leads to a focus on relative rates.

The evidence from the CASMIN project (see Erikson and Goldthorpe, 1992) which overcame many of the problems associated with previous work on comparative mobility, is that relative mobility rates show only limited cross-sectional variability. Consequently, increases in absolute mobility associated with economic development must be primarily an outcome of structural effects. However, as Goldthorpe (1985: 558–559) stresses, such effects are exerted in different ways. One basic distinction is between 'shift' and 'compositional' effects. Shift effects refer to consequences of change in the 'shape' of the structure within which mobility is being observed. Compositional effects arise from the fact that different classes have different inherent propensities for immobility. Three main conclusions emerge from the CASMIN analysis.

1 Absolute rates are a great deal more variable than relative ones.
2 While shift effects are often generated by economic development, at comparable levels of economic development the importance of shift effects can vary enormously.
3 There is no evidence that shift effects on mobility will steadily increase with economic development or that their importance is closely correlated with prevailing rates of economic growth.

It is important in attempting to understand class structural change, Goldthorpe stresses, to stop treating structural factors as merely a nuisance:

> . . . insufficient weight has been given to the large variations in the speed, rhythm and phasing of such change. (Goldthorpe, 1985: 560)

This conclusion holds even though it is by no means clear how amenable such structural factors are to accounts which are couched in theoretical rather than historical terms.

The Irish Case

In an earlier work we have stressed that while the core processes that formed the change to Ireland's class structure are typical, their sequencing was not (Breen et al., 1990). While the decline of the agricultural sector is crucial in promoting structural mobility, the actual pattern of decline and its association with other structural changes is quite variable (Goldthorpe, 1985: 561). Late and rapid industrialisation meant that the masive decline in opportunities for agricultural employment could not be compensated for by alternative opportunities in Ireland. Emigration filled the gap. The class structure today reflects the selective process of emigration to Britain as much as it does growth in new opportunities (Hughes and Walsh, 1976; Hannan, 1970).

The main dynamic of class change until the 1960s was the mass exodus from the land. Between 1926 and 1961 the percentage of gainfully occupied males in agriculture fell from 58 per cent to 43 per cent. This was counterbalanced by growth among the non-manual middle class and the non-agricultural working class (Breen et al., 1990: 54–56). Those changes, however, occurred within the context of a decline in the total of gainfully occupied males from 950,000 in 1926 to 820,000 in 1961. The broad stability of the class structure over this period was largely attributable to emigration.

Such stability contrasts with rapid changes after 1960. Between 1961 and 1985 males in agriculture as a percentage of all gainfully occupied males fell from 49 to 20 per cent. By 1985, employed professionals formed some 17 per cent of the work-force, more than tripling their representation since 1951; skilled manual employees also grew markedly over that period from 10 to 20 per cent of the work-force. The number of 'lower' middle-class workers also increased but less dramatically from 14 to 22 per cent. Semi-skilled and unskilled manual workers made up nearly one-quarter of the work-force in 1951 and 12 per cent in 1985.

The swiftness of its class transformation sets Ireland apart from the experience of most other countries. An orderly consolidation in which decline in opportunities in traditional sectors is compensated for by the gradual expansion of alternative opportunities is the antithesis of the Irish experience over recent decades. While some aspects of the post-1950 changes, such as the contraction of the agricultural labour force and the expansion of the white-collar sector, were continuous processes, most changes were not. In the 1950s the spectre of emigration overshadowed all trends by reducing the size of the male labour force by one-seventh. The real growth in skilled manual and junior white-collar work only commenced in the 1960s and continued unabated through the 1970s. Small farmers, agricultural labourers, and unskilled manual workers had a combined decline of 259,000 over the full thirty year period, with the heaviest losses concentrated in the early part of that period. The upper white-collar and skilled manual worker categories ultimately expanded by 120,000 but their pre-1961 increase was virtually nil. So there were no opportunities to compensate for the massive losses in traditional forms of work.

Social Mobility in Ireland

Census data allow us to reconstruct the context within which the structural sources of mobility in Ireland evolved. However, there are limits to the conclusions which can be drawn from such data. An examination of the actual pattern of intergenerational mobility requires that we draw on survey data. Up to this point, analysis of social mobility in Ireland has been based on data sources which do not take us beyond the early 1970s (Breen and Whelan, 1985; Erikson and Goldthorpe, 1987a, 1987b, 1992; Hout, 1989; Hout and Jackson, 1986; Whelan and Whelan, 1984). There are obvious limitations imposed by reliance on such data in order to assess the impact of industrialisation on social mobility in Ireland.

1 The changes in class structure which occurred throughout the 1970s and 1980s were just as substantial as those occurring in the 1950s and 1960s. Thus, between 1971 and 1985 the proportion of males at work in agriculture fell from one-third to one-fifth while the number at work in non-manual occupations rose from three out of ten to four out of ten.

2 Employment creation in the 1970s had particularly distinctive features. By far the largest area of employment growth was in services: employment here grew by 136,000 between 1971 and 1981. However, the bulk of this (85,000 jobs) was in the public sector (Sexton, 1982: 36).

3 In the period of the 1960s and early 1970s the role of manpower policy was seen to be in training the labour force and generally facilitating the efficient matching of the supply of, and demand for, labour. In the mid-1970s, employment subsidies were introduced, as were training and temporary employment schemes, to combat unemployment. In the 1980s manpower policy had, for all intent and purposes, become employment policy.

4 By the early 1970s it was not yet possible to observe the impact of the introduction of free education in 1967. In 1970, 70 per cent of all 15 year olds were remaining in school. By 1985 this had risen to over 94 per cent.

5 Finally, while in 1971 6 per cent of males were unemployed, by 1985 this had risen to close to 20 per cent.

Thus, while on the surface the relationship between economic growth and occupational change looks rather similar for the 1960s and 1970s, somewhat different causal influences were at work. In the 1960s there was a smfll net change in employment, the decline in agriculture being offset by growth, particularly in the manufacturing and public sector. However, in the 1970s, growth in manufacturing and building slackened and the government responded through measures intended to give extra impetus to economic growth and, in the late 1970s, through the use of the public sector as a vehicle for the creation of jobs.

In this paper we will draw on data from the ESRI 1987 Survey of Income and Life-Style to provide a more up-to-date analysis of Irish social mobility patterns. The analysis that follows will relate exclusively to males. The data available in the ESRI survey is particularly suitable for analysis of the implications of different choices concerning the appropriate unit of analysis in mobility studies, and it is our intention to look at this question in considerable detail in our future work. However, the traditionally low levels of participation in the labour force by married women in Ireland reinforces our view that focusing on the mobility experience of men is unlikely to be misleading so far as the study of *class* mobility is concerned. Our analysis is based on a nationally representative sample of 2,394 men aged between 20 and 65.

Classes and Classification Concepts

Our approach to the analysis of social mobility in Ireland draws on Goldthorpe's (1987) model of the mobility process. Under this model, patterns of mobility are shaped by three factors operating alongside structural influences. These are the relative desirability of different class destinations; the resources available to individuals within each origin class which help them gain access to more desirable destination classes; and barriers to movement between classes. Typically, we think of resources as 'economic, cultural and social resources' (Erikson and Goldthorpe, 1987a: 64) while barriers to mobility would include the necessity to own the means of production, educational and other qualifications needed for entry into the occupations that comprise a class grouping, and so forth.

The Goldthorpe framework for class analysis is operationalised through a threefold procedure. First, respondents are placed in occupational groups according to the content of their jobs; second, they are given an employment status that reflects their social relationships at work. In both cases the categories and definitions used are those adopted in Britain by the Registrar General for the analysis of official statistics. Finally, a social class position is obtained for each individual by cross-classifying the relevant occupational title and employment status (Marshall, 1990: 55). In our case we started with occupations coded according to the Irish Census Classification, and with an employment status variable comparable to the British one. Since we lacked the resources to conduct a full scale recoding of occupations according to the British procedures, we mapped the Irish occupational codes on to the British 1970 OPCS scheme. Where we felt that an occupation coded according to the Irish Census classification could not be unambiguously allocated a code in the OPCS classification and that this could affect the respondents' ultimate allocation to a class category, coding was carried out on the basis of the original information in the questionnaire. Thus, in the same way as Ganzeboom and Ultee (1988), we have attempted to 'mimic' the Goldthorpe class schema.

Goldthorpe's procedures bring together within each class position occupations whose incumbents share similar market and work situations. Hence, class categories are made up of occupations whose members are typically comparable in terms of their sources and levels of income, their degree of economic security, their chances of economic advancement and their degree of autonomy in performing work tasks and roles. It is inadequate to think of the schema as deriving solely from the Weberian market based tradition. The classification is based on an understanding of the importance of the development of class relations within large scale capitalist organisations and the nature of control in such organisations (Goldthorpe, 1982: 167–168, Marshall, 1990, Kurz and Müller, 1987: 421–422).

The range of classes distinguished in the CASMIN analysis is set out in Table 1. The most detailed classification distinguishes eleven classes. Frequent use is also made of the seven class schema which is also reproduced in Table 1. In the analysis which is reported in this paper and that by Breen and Whelan in this volume a couple of additional distinctions are made at various points: the first involves separating out the semi-skilled manual group from the unskilled while the second involves breaking down farmers into three categories on the basis of farm size.

Changes in the Class Structure 1973–87

Origins and destinations

In Table 2 we provide a comparison of the origin and destination distributions of classes in Ireland in 1973 and 1987. For origins, the decline in agriculture is the most striking trend. The percentage in the petty bourgeoisie also declines, as does the figure for agricultural workers. All

Table 1.   The class schema.

	Full version		Seven-class
I	Higher-grade professionals, administrators and officials; managers in large industrial establishments; large proprietors	I+II	Service class; professionals, administrators and managers; higher-grade technicians; supervisors of non-manual workers
II	Lower-grade professionals, administrators and officials; higher-grade technicians; managers in small industrial establishments; supervisors of non-manual employees		
IIIa	Routine non-manual employees, higher grade (administration and commerce)	III	Routine non-manual workers; routine non-manual employees in administration and commerce; sales personnel; other rank-and-file service workers
IIIb	Routine non-manual employees, lower grade (sales and services)		
IVa	Small proprietors, artisans, etc., with employees	IV a+b	Petty bourgeoisie: small proprietors and artisans, etc., with and without employees
IVb	Small proprietors, artisans, etc., without employees		
IVc	Farmers and smallholders; other self-employed workers in primary production (i) owning 100 acres or more (ii) owning 50–99 acres (iii) owning less than 50 acres	IVc	Farmers: farmers and small-holders and other self-employed workers in in primary production
V	Lower-grade technicians, supervisors of manual workers	V+ VI	Skilled workers: lower-grade technicians; supervisors of manual workers; skilled manual workers
VI	Skilled manual workers		
VIIa	(i) Semi-skilled manual workers (not in agriculture, etc.) (ii) Unskilled manual workers (not in agriculture, etc.)	VIIa	Non-skilled workers: semi- and unskilled manual workers (not in agriculture, etc.)
VIIb	Agricultural and other workers in primary production	VIIb	Agricultural labourers: agricultural and other workers in primary production

other categories display increases in their relative sizes, with a particularly substantial increase occurring for technicians and skilled manual workers. Comparison with the results reported by Goldthorpe (1987: 331) indicates that there is a clear tendency for the Irish profile to come closer to that of other European countries, particularly Swede, and to a lesser extent

Table 2. Distributions (%) of class origins and destinations for 1973 and 1987.

		Origins		Destinations	
		1973	1987	1973	1987
(I+II)	Professional, administrative and managerial (service class)	6	8	14	17
(III)	Routine non-manual	5	7	9	10
(IVa+b)	Petty bourgeoisie: small employers and self-employed	10	6	8	7
(IVc)	Farmers	39	27	22	10
(V+VI)	Lower technical, manual supervisory and skilled manual	14	20	20	28
(VIIa)	Non-skilled manual	20	27	21	24
(VIIb)	Agricultural workers	7	5	7	3

France. In fact, the degree of dissimilarity between the Irish distributions at the two different points in time is as great as that between Ireland in 1987 and Sweden and France.

Focusing on destinations, we find that the two classes which exhibit a decline over the period are farmers (from 22 to 10 per cent) and farm labourers (7 to 3 per cent). Substantial growth is evident among the professional, administrative and managerial class and also the skilled manual and technical class and the non-skilled manual class. Little change is evident elsewhere. Comparing the Irish data with the other countries, the Irish distribution in 1987 comes very close to that for France, and to a lesser extent, Sweden.

Taking origins and destination together, the evidence available from the CASMIN project shows that England, with extremely low percentages in agriculture for both distributions, lies at one end of the continuum, while the eastern European countries are at the other extreme. Ireland lies in the middle with France and Sweden but has relatively low percentages in the professional, administrative and managerial group. The evidence from the 1987 Survey points to the convergence of class marginal distributions in Ireland towards a pattern quite common in industrial societies in the early 1970s. Consequently, whatever differences we observe between the Irish mobility pattern in 1987 and that of such societies will be less open to explanations in structural terms than would have been the case in 1973.

Absolute mobility rates

The degree of mobility that is observed in any society depends on the number, size and character of the class categories distinguished. A comparison of results for 1973 and 1987 leads to the conclusion (which holds across different versions of the class schema) that there has been a significant increase in the level of absolute social mobility in Ireland. In the case of the seven-class schema the rise is from 58 per cent to 63 per cent; or in other words the percentage remaining immobile in their class of origin declined from 42 per cent to 37 per cent. Of other western European countries in the 1970s, only Sweden displays a decisively higher level.

Class composition

Discussion of absolute levels of mobility leads fairly directly to consideration of issues of social closure and class formation. In dealing with such issues, what matters is not so much the degree of inequality in class mobility chances but the outcome of those chances in terms of class composition (Goldthorpe, 1987: 46). In Table 3 we set out some selected cross-national comparisons.[1] An examination, first, of the results for the professional, managerial and administrative group, or service class, shows that in Ireland, as in other countries, the most striking feature is not the extent of social closure but the degree of heterogeneity of the origins from which recruits are drawn. Ireland is distinctive among western European nations in having a relatively high inflow to the service class of men from agricultural classes and a below average contribution from the industrial working class. This pattern can be compared with England, where a particularly high proportion of recruits come from the industrial working class, and France which is distinctive because of the degree of self-recruitment and recruitment from the self-employed. Relatively little change has taken place since 1973 with a slight increase in the inflow from the industrial working class occurring and a corresponding decline in the inflow from the agricultural classes.

   When we turn to the industrial working class, an obvious point of comparison is England where this class forms a self-recruiting block in which three-quarters of its members may be reckoned as at least second generation. In Ireland in 1987 almost two-thirds were second-generation, although almost one-quarter came from agricultural classes. In fact, only

[1] All figures other than for Ireland 1987 are taken from Goldthorpe (1987) with the exception of those relating to Ireland in 1973, which are derived directly from the CASMIN data.

Table 3. Comparative inflow rates: percentage in selected classes from different class origins.

% of the professional, administrative and managerial class (I + II) originating in				% of the industrial class (V/VI + VIIa) originating in			
Industrial working class (V/VI + VIIa)		Agricultural classes (IVc + VIIb)		Industrial working class (V/VI + VIIa)		Agricultural classes (IVc + VIIb)	
England	45	Poland	34	England	74	Hungary	46
FRG	41	Hungary	25	FRG	65	Poland	46
Sweden	40	Ireland 1973	23	Ireland 1987	63	Sweden	32
Poland	35	Ireland 1987	18	Ireland 1973	57	France	29
Hungary	32	Sweden	17	Sweden	51	Ireland 1973	27
Ireland 1987	32	France	10	France	47	Ireland 1987	24
Ireland 1973	28	FRG	8	Poland	42	FRG	16
France	28	England	4	Hungary	39	England	7

in England is self-recruitment substantially higher. Eighty per cent of recruitment to the industrial working class in Ireland is drawn from small farmers, agricultural workers and the industrial working class together. Between 1973 and 1987 a significant increase in self-recruitment occurred, matched by a corresponding drop in recruitment from the petty bourgeoisie. Within the industrial working class the percentage of skilled manual workers coming from farm backgrounds almost doubled— increasing from 10 per cent to 18 per cent, while inflow from farm origins to the non-skilled manual group fell from 24 per cent to 16 per cent. This change is particularly significant because the skilled manual group increased by close to 50 per cent during this period.

Further, (though not shown in Table 3) the petty bourgeoisie in Ireland have particularly high inflows from farming, with one-third of their members originating in this group. In this respect, Ireland comes closest to Sweden and can be distinguished from England, which has a particularly large inflow from the industrial working class, and France, where there are very high levels of self-recruitment. In Ireland between 1973 and 1987 there was a dramatic decline in the level of self-recruitment to the petty bourgeoisie and a corresponding increase in recruitment from the industrial working class. In 1973 32 per cent of men found in petty bourgeois positions had been self-recruited, compared with 15 per cent in 1987; while the corresponding percentages for inflow from the industrial working class are 20 and 37 per cent. The composition of the routine non-manual class in Ireland comes closest to France, mainly because of similar figures for recruitment from farming but, as in England, there is a high inflow from the industrial working class. Between 1973 and 1987 the share of recruitment from the former class declined while that from the latter increased. Finally, in Ireland, as in France, recruitment into farming from non-farming backgrounds is extremely rare.

To summarise, by 1987 in Ireland

1   the service class was a heterogeneous group;
2   the petty bourgeoisie displayed a significant decline in the level of self-recruitment and had also become a relatively heterogeneous class;
3   the industrial working class displayed high levels of self-recruitment even when the substantial inflow from agricultural classes was taken into account.

Class mobility chances: outflow patterns

In moving from an inflow to an outflow perspective, we become concerned with class mobility chances or with the probability of men of given class origins being found in particular class destinations. In Table 4 we present selected outflow rates for Ireland for 1973 and 1987 and again provide cross-national comparisons, using the CASMIN seven-class schema. A remarkable degree of similarity is shown in the two Irish surveys in the outflows from the professional, managerial and administrative classes; and also in mobility from the industrial working classes. At both points in time just over half of those from service class origins were found in this class and just over one-fifth in the industrial working class. These figures are quite typical of those for other western European countries in the early 1970s. When we direct our attention to men from industrial working class origins, we find that one in nine are located in the service class and seven out of ten have remained intergenerationally stable. The Irish figures for immobility here are comparatively high, with only the FRG, of the western European countries, reaching this level, and with Sweden coming eight percentage points lower. It is, however, the extremely low levels of long range intergenerational upward mobility which give the Irish pattern a quite distinctive character. All of the other countries have outflows from the industrial working class to the service class which are at least five percentage points higher and the corresponding figures for the FRG and Sweden are double those for Ireland. It is true, however, that since the industrial working class increased in Ireland from 40 per cent to 50 per cent of the total between 1973 and 1987, the overall percentage experiencing such mobility has increased.

The picture of stability for the service class and industrial working class contrasts with the substantial changes in the mobility chances of those from

Table 4. Comparative outflow rates: percentage of those of selected class origins found in different classes.

% of those of professional, administrative and managerial origins (I + II) found in				% of those of industrial working class origins (V/VI+VIIa) found in			
Professional, administrative and managerial class (I + II)		Industrial working class (V/VI + VIIa)		Professional, administrative and managerial class (I + II)		Industrial working class (V/VI + VIIa)	
Poland	67	Hungary	34	FRG	22	Hungary	73
FRG	61	FRG	26	Sweden	22	Poland	71
France	60	Poland	25	Poland	21	FRG	69
England	59	Sweden	25	England	18	Ireland 1987	69
Sweden	56	England	22	France	17	Ireland 1973	68
Ireland 1987	56	Ireland 1987	22	Hungary	16	England	66
Ireland 1973	55	Ireland 1973	21	Ireland 1987	11	France	63
Hungary	52	France	21	Ireland 1973	11	Sweden	61

petty bourgeois and farming origins. A major improvement took place in the chances of mobility to the service class for the sons of small employers and more particularly for those of the self-employed. The percentage succeeding in making this transition rose from 30 per cent to 36 per cent for the former group, and from 13 per cent to 36 per cent for the latter. The percentage remaining immobile in these classes dropped sharply and the flows to the non-skilled manual classes were halved; in the case of the self-employed, from one in four to one in eight. The outflow of sons of small employers is now broadly similar to that for France in the early 1970s but with a much lower percentage reaching destinations in the industrial working class. Those from self-employed origins, on the other hand, enjoy distinctively high rates of upward mobility.

In the case of farmers, the most obvious shift is the decline in immobility, where the relevant figure drops from one half to just over one-third. The percentage becoming agricultural labourers is almost halved. This change is accompanied by a significant increase in the flows to the service class but more particularly to the skilled manual group where the figure rises from 4 per cent to 14 per cent. Apart from sharing with France a relatively high level of immobility, those from farming origins also have a particularly low outflow to the non-skilled manual class.

Previous studies of social mobility in Ireland have not been in a position to distinguish between farmers by farm size. In what follows we compare the mobility chances of the sons of farmers with (i) less than 50 acres; (ii) 50–99 acres; (iii) 100 or more acres. The first point to be made is that the percentage remaining in farming shows little variation by farm size. The outflow variations to other categories are as we might expect; almost one-fifth of those from large farm origins gain access to the professional, administrative and managerial class compared with one in thirteen of those from small farm backgrounds. Correspondingly, almost four out of ten of the latter group are currently in the industrial working class compared to one in four of the former. It is noticeable that with men from each of the farm origin categories, the numbers in the skilled manual and non-skilled manual classes are very similar. This contrasts with the situation of those from non-skilled manual origins who are only half as likely to be in the skilled manual class as in the non-skilled.

With the exception of the sharp reduction in immobility among the petty bourgeoisie and farming classes, there is relatively little evidence that changes between 1973 and 1987 involve movement towards some norm for industrial society. The Irish outflow pattern displays the following distinctive, and obviously not unrelated features:

1   opportunities for long-range mobility from the industrial working class into the service class are extremely limited;
2   the advantages enjoyed by property owning groups in the competition to gain access to the service class and avoid entering the non-skilled manual class are unusually strong.

The paper by Breen and Whelan in this volume pursues the issues, first, of whether such advantages should be thought of as accruing to propertied classes in general or whether particular classes such as farmers are particularly favoured; and, secondly, of whether the relative advantages enjoyed by propertied groups are related to changes in the underlying pattern of advantages between 1973 and 1987 or simply involve the exercise of constant advantages in a changing structural situation.

One important point which we wish to note here relates to the relative size of the petty bourgeoisie and farming classes. While the change in outflow rates is greatest among the petty bourgeoisie, it is the changes in the mobility chances of those from farming origins which have the most serious implications for those from working class origins because of the size of the outflow from farming. The paper by Hannan and Commins in this volume elaborates on the manner in which, in a situation of particularly high fertility rates in the farming class and limited employment growth, the success of sons of farmers effectively led to the 'crowding out' of those from working class origins.

Class Mobility and Unemployment

The foregoing analysis takes no account of unemployment and consequently, despite the scale of the class inequalities documented, it fails to bring out the full extent of the disadvantages suffered by the working class.

We have noted earlier that the impact of economic growth on occupational change operated through rather different mechanisms in each decade. By the 1980s a continuation of previous economic policies was no longer feasible. Negative growth rates between 1981 and 1985 were reflected, not in obvious changes in the class structure but in a seemingly inexorable climb in the unemployment rate, coupled with a process of 'trading down' for middle-class school leavers (Breen, 1984a).

Despite the creation of many thousands of jobs since 1958, unemployment levels in Ireland remain high by international standards. Unemployment in Ireland has been characterised by a high overall rate and a high level of long-term unemployment. As economic conditions have worsened and the debt crisis has effectively precluded the public sector from its previous role as the major source of job creation, not only has the Irish unemployment rate worsened but so has the proportion of long-term unemployed. Currently, over one in six workers is unemployed and nearly half of all registered unemployed males have been out of work for a year or more.

The degree to which unemployment has been concentrated in the working classes is striking. Unemployment among non-agricultural unskilled workers has hardly fallen below 30 per cent since 1961, while that for the upper middle class has only once exceeded three per cent. The persistence of high levels of unemployment within the former category points to the absence not only of social but also of geographical mobility. Such people could neither advance in the occupational structure nor, apparently, could they migrate in search of greater opportunities. The position of the unskilled group was exacerbated by the logic of Irish industrial development policy through imbalances or disjunctures between the forms of employment created and the kinds of jobs which have been lost. In broad terms, the jobs which have been lost have been in traditional, indigenous industries, which failed to survive once protectionism was dismantled, and have been of relatively low skill levels, predominantly located in urban areas, notably Dublin. The jobs which have been created have often required greater levels of skills and have been more widely dispersed throughout the country (Breen *et al.*, 1990: 143–147; cf. also O'Malley, this volume).

In Table 5 we introduce unemployment as a destination and compare Irish and English outflow rates. The three-class schema employed includes all routine non-manual workers and the technicians' group in the 'intermediate' category. Not surprisingly, the probability of unemployment varies by class origin for both countries but there is a particularly high probability of one in four for those of manual origins in Ireland. Commenting on the English data, Goldthorpe and Payne (1986: 17–18) conclude that mobility chances for manual workers have polarised between 1972 and 1983 with more experiencing upward mobility, but more too being downwardly mobile into unemployment. The return of mass unemployment 'has had the general effect of "raising the stakes"'. In Ireland no such improvement in the prospects of upward mobility has occurred for those from manual backgrounds but undoubtedly their risk of unemployment has grown rapidly with one in four being located in this category. In England, men from manual origins are twice as likely to appear in the service class as to be unemployed but in Ireland this probability is reversed. It is for the 'intermediate' class that such a polarisation has occurred, while at the top there has been relatively little change.

Our expectation would be that the effect of class origins on the risk of unemployment would operate throughout its impact on current class position. In order to pursue this issue further, in Figure 1 we look at the relationship between labour force status and class, making use of the eleven-class schema for non-farming classes. The indicator of labour force

Table 5. Outflow rates, including to unemployment.

		Respondent's class			
Father's class		Professional, administrative and managerial (I + II)	Other non-manual and farmers (III + IVa, b, c + V)	Manual and agricultural workers (VI + VIIa + b)	Unemployed
Professional, administrative and managerial (I + II)	Ireland 1987	56.3	28.5	11.8	3.4
	England 1983	63.1	23.2	9.3	4.4
Other non-manual and farmers (III + IVa, b, c + V)	Ireland 1987	16.5	44.2	27.8	11.4
	England 1983	32.7	36.2	22.8	8.2
Manual and agricultural workers (VI + VIIa, b)	Ireland 1987	10.3	23.1	41.4	25.1
	England 1983	20.5	29.5	39.5	10.5

Source for English figures: Goldthorpe and Payne (1986).

Christopher T. Whelan et al.

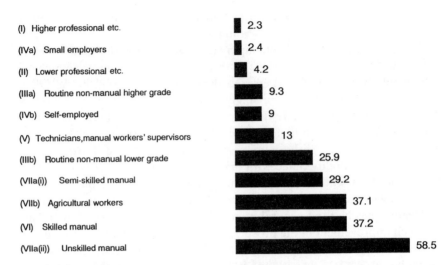

Figure 1. Labour force status by class: percentage unemployed or permanently unable to work through illness or disability (men 20–64).

status taken on this occasion is the percentage unemployed or permanently unable to work because of illness or disability. In opting for this measure we are taking into account the fact that the extent to which an illness will cause a person to be 'unemployable' will vary under different labour market conditions, and the burden of increased risks are borne disproportionately by vulnerable groups (Bartley, 1987: 97). Less than three per cent in the higher professional, administrative and managerial group are 'out of work' compared to close to six out of ten of the unskilled manual group. The lowest risk among the working class is one in four, with the exception of the technicians' group where it falls to one in seven. The highest risk in the 'intermediate' classes overall is one in eleven. Within the working class it is notable that skilled manual workers actually have a somewhat higher risk than semi-skilled workers. This is likely to be due to the difference in their sectoral distribution.

It is, of course, perfectly possible that any relationship which exists between the risk of being out of work and class origin can be accounted for entirely by the association between class of origin and present class and between the latter and labour force status, leaving no independent or 'carry-over' effect for class origins. In this situation a log-linear model which embodies the hypothesis that the odds of a man being out of work rather than in employment or retired are dependent upon his current class position but not on his class of origin (though allowing for the association between origin and destination) should provide an adequate fit. In log-linear terms, this model is

$$\log F_{ijk} = \lambda + \lambda^{US} + \lambda^{FS}$$

where F_{ijk} is the expected value in cell ijk of a three-way table of class of origin (F) with I categories, class of destination (S) with J categories and employment (U) with K categories. Such a model does indeed provide an adequate fit to the 1983 English data analysed by Goldthorpe and Payne (1983). However, from Table 6 it is clear that such a model does not come close to fitting the Irish data. Adding the association between class origin and employment status, reduces the G^2 value by 40.9 for a loss of two degrees of freedom. Thus the final model is

$$\log F_{ijk} = \lambda + \lambda^{US} + \lambda^{FS} + {}^{UF}$$

Table 6. Fit of log linear models of the association between employment status, class and class origins.

Model			G^2	df
FS	US		49.8	8
FS	US	UF	8.9	6

The strength of the independent or carry-over effect of class origin is illustrated in Figure 2. The three-class schema utilised here, unlike the previous one, allocates the industrial working class, agricultural workers and lower grade non-manual workers to the 'working class', and the higher grade non-manual together with the farming and petty bourgeois groups to the 'intermediate' class. At each level of current class position, class origin has a substantial impact. Thus for those in the service class the percentage out of work varies from 0.3 per cent to 5.8 per cent depending on class background. For the intermediate class the range of variation is from 3.2 per cent to 10.4 per cent; the corresponding figures for the working class other than the unskilled manual are 11.2 per cent and 32.9 per cent; and, finally, while none of the members of the unskilled working class come from service class backgrounds, the probability of being out of work rises from one-third for those from intermediate class backgrounds to two-thirds for those from working class origins. It is beyond the scope of this paper to investigate the processes through which class origin has such an impact. The most plausible interpretation is that in a country where a situation of a long-term excess of labour supply exists, class origin may serve not only as a good predictor of current class position but also distinguish within classes between those with stable and unstable work histories.

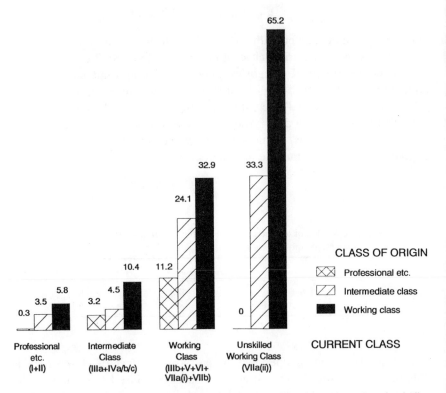

Figure 2. Percentage out of work by class origins, controlling for current class (excluding those currently in farming).

The Nature of the Unskilled Manual Class

The results reported in Figure 2 direct our attention to the distinctive nature of the unskilled manual class which forms 10 per cent of the destination class distribution. In the first place, while close to one in four of the semi-skilled manual group is intergenerationally mobile out of the working class, this is true of only one in seven of the unskilled manual group. An inflow perspective, perhaps, brings out the distinctive nature of the class more clearly. While just over 85 per cent of the members of the semi-skilled manual group are drawn from working class or small farm origins, this holds true for 94 per cent of the unskilled manual group.

Contrary to conventional expectations, the unskilled manual group are not concentrated in urban areas, as we can see from Figure 3. In fact, as the counterpart of the concentration of professional, administrative and managerial respondents in Dublin, the unskilled manual class are

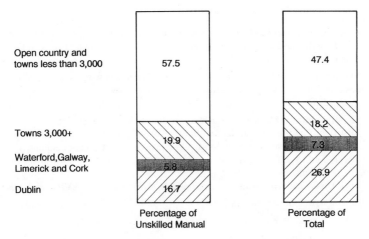

Figure 3. Location of the unskilled manual class.

underrepresented here. On the other hand, they are overrepresented outside the main urban areas. Over half are located in open country or in towns of less than 3,000, and more than three-quarters are located outside the major urban areas. This finding is confirmed by analysis of the small area data from the 1986 Census which shows that employing the Census definition of unskilled, 67 per cent are found outside the major urban areas. The corresponding figure from our data set is 73 per cent. One difference that does arise, though, is that while one-third of unskilled manual workers in rural areas are aged over fifty, this is true of only one-sixth of those in the major urban areas.[2]

Marginalisation and Poverty

In this final section we provide evidence for the consequences of marginalisation. The indicator of poverty we employ combines information on income and life-style and is derived from a conceptual framework in which poverty is understood as *exclusion* arising from lack of resources (Callan *et al.*, forthcoming). In Table 7 we set out a list of deprivation items. We have defined as poor those residing in households who suffer an *enforced* lack of any one of these items and whose incomes, adjusted for household composition, fall below 70 per cent of average household income. In Figure 4 we break down poverty by class. With the exception of farmers,

[2] For an earlier discussion of the implications for the Irish mobility regime of the existence of a rural proletariat see Erikson and Goldthorpe (1987b: 155).

Table 7.   Primary life-style deprivation items.

1.   Household manager has had to go without heating during the last year through lack of money, i.e. has had to go without a fire on a cold day, or go to bed early to keep warm or light a fire late because of lack of gas/fuel.

2.   Household manager has had a day in the last two weeks when she/he did not have a substantial meal at all—from getting up to going to bed.

3.   Household:
   (i) is currently in arrears on rent, mortgage, ESB or gas
   or (ii) has had to go into debt within the past 12 months to meet ordinary living expenses such as rent, food, Christmas or back to school expenses.
   or (iii) had to sell or pawn anything worth £50 or more to meet ordinary living expenses
   or (iv) has received assistance from a private charity—such as SVP—in the last year.

4.   Lacking new, not secondhand, clothes.

5.   Lacking a meal with meat, chicken or fish every second day.

6.   Lacking two pairs of strong shoes.

7.   Lacking a warm waterproof overcoat.

8.   Lacking a roast meat joint or its equivalent once a week.

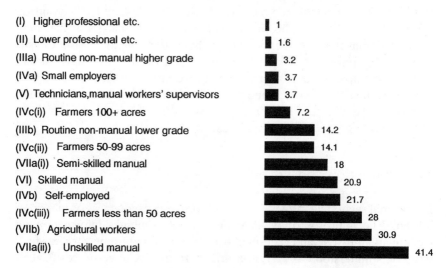

Figure 4.   Poverty by class: the risk of being in a household which is in poverty (%).

the risk of residing in a household which is in poverty for men between 20–64 remains rather low outside the working class. The risk reaches just over one in six for the semi-skilled manual and then rises to one in five for the skilled manual class; this finding is consistent with our earlier results relating to the distribution of unemployment. For farmers with less than

50 acres and agricultural workers, the figure rises to almost one in three. Finally, for the unskilled manual class the risk of poverty is just over four out of ten.

Not surprisingly, in view of the evidence we have presented in relation to the risk of being out of work, class origin also has a significant independent impact on poverty. Employing the same three-class schema that was employed in that analysis, we find that close to one out of two unskilled manual workers with working class origins are living in households which fall below the poverty line; for no other group does the figure rise above one in four.

Conclusions

Politicians in Ireland shared with many social scientists a sanguine view of the relationship between economic growth and industrialisation. In fact, the kind of changes in occupational structure which are associated with social mobility can vary enormously at comparable levels of economic development. The speed, rhythm and phasing of structural change is crucial. In Ireland, late and rapid industrialisation meant that the decline in opportunities for agricultural employment could not be compensated for by alternative opportunities in Ireland. Emigration filled the gap.

The nature of the shift and composition effects taking place in Ireland between 1973 and 1987 were such as to produce a convergence of the marginal distributions of the Irish class mobility table onto a pattern not untypical of modern industrial societies. By 1987 the overall level of mobility in Ireland came close to the norm for western European societies.

In terms of class composition, the Irish service class had, in common with those in other countries, inflows from a heterogeneous set of sources but was notable for the relatively high inflow from farming. The petty bourgeoisie in Ireland became a great deal more heterogeneous between 1973 and 1987, with a significant decline in self-recruitment and a substantially increased inflow from the industrial working class. In the industrial working class, however, despite a significant inflow from the agricultural classes, two-thirds of its occupants had been intergenerationally immobile.

With regard to mobility chances, we observed a remarkable stability in class mobility chances at the extremes of the Irish class hierarchy. In contrast, a major improvement took place in the upward mobility prospects of those born into the petty bourgeois and farming groups. The upwards flow from self-employed origins is distinctively high when placed in a comparative context. The most striking finding, however, is the extent of the barriers to upward mobility into the service class from origins in the industrial working class. These barriers are of a scale sufficient to mark out Ireland as an exceptional case.

The degree of disadvantage suffered by the working class is even greater than would be suggested by conventional mobility analysis because it conceals the dramatic increase in the risk of unemployment for this group. In England in 1983 those from manual backgrounds were only half as likely to be unemployed as to be upwardly mobile into the service class. In Ireland in 1987 men from manual backgrounds were over twice as likely to be unemployed as to be mobile into the service class.

A more detailed breakdown showed that the risk of being 'out of work' was particularly high among the unskilled group of whom more than 60 per cent fell into this category. Furthermore, in Ireland, unlike England, class origin has a substantial independent or carry-over effect on employment status, with two-thirds of those from working class backgrounds who are currently in the unskilled manual group being out of work. The unskilled manual group is one which experiences particularly severe obstacles to upward mobility and, in turn, is an extremely homogeneous group, with well over 90 per cent of its members being drawn from the working class or small farm backgrounds.

The changes in the class composition of the Irish work-force emerged from industrial development that was more rapid, occurred later and was more state-inspired than in most western societies. So intense were the changes that it is easy to overlook their incompleteness. A substantial share of the work-force was in residual classes stranded in the course of industrial development, especially farmers on marginal holdings and labourers without skills. Their position was exacerbated by the logic of Irish industrial development.

The dispersal of industrial location to rural areas in the 1960s and 1970s had long roots in Fianna Fáil policy and more generally in the ideology of rural fundamentalism. However, during the recent past, its purpose has been not simply to provide an alternative to agricultural employment for those who could no longer acquire it but also to yield a second occupation for those farmers whose acreage is too small to ensure their viability.[3] It has been argued that the costs of the policy of locating industry in 'new' areas was carried by the urban working class—particularly the lower working class—whose jobs in indigenous firms were fast disappearing. As Hannan and Commins point out above, the latter difficulties did not become obvious to politicians or those affected by them until the 1970s while the marginalisation of small farmers was apparent by the mid-1960s.

---

[3] See Hannan and Commins (this volume) for a more detailed discussion of these issues.

While the urban working class clearly did suffer from this policy, our analysis shows that the non-skilled manual class are not wholly concentrated in urban areas but are, in fact, widely geographically dispersed. While industrial policy may have favoured those outside the urban areas, it appears that those from unskilled manual backgrounds lost out in the competition for the new rural positions to the petty bourgeoisie and farmers. Of particular quantitative importance here was the strong outflow of men of farming backgrounds to the skilled manual class. One feature which distinguishes the urban and rural unskilled manual groups is their age profile. Because much new industry requires a more skilled workforce, younger rather than older workers are favoured because of their higher educational levels. A 1979 IDA survey showed that 55 per cent of jobs created in new grant-aided industries were held by people less than 25 years of age (IDA, 1980). The influence of this is reflected in the fact that while in the major urban areas one-sixth of the unskilled manual class are over 50 this figure rises to one in three for those outside such areas. Thus, an explanation of the relationship between industrial development and the poor position of the unskilled working class must deal not only with the geographical disjuncture between areas where jobs were being lost and those where jobs were being created, but also with differences between the old jobs and the new. In other words, the disjuncture between the age and skills profile of those whose jobs in indigenous industries were disappearing and the skill requirements of the new industries.

Although opportunities in unskilled or 'nearly' skilled work are continually diminishing, there is at the same time little provision for either intra- or intergenerational mobility out of the marginalised working class. The absence of large scale adult training and re-training means that unskilled adults cannot acquire skills, while the Irish educational system does not serve as a vehicle by which children of lower working class families are taught skills. There remains a large proportion of each cohort of school leavers—about 12 per cent—who come into the labour market each year wholly lacking in formal qualifications. The available evidence on the composition of emigrants suggests that, unlike in the 1950s, few opportunities now exist for those without skills and qualifications to work outside Ireland. So emigration reflects an extension of mobility differentials: those with educational qualifications but unable to find work in Ireland can search elsewhere. Those without such qualifications and who cannot find work remain unemployed in Ireland (NESC, 1991). So a marginalised class is being reproduced through the educational and training systems, while being sustained by social welfare provisions. The creation of employment for members of this class was an option which was

Proceedings of the British Academy, **79**, 129–151

Explaining the Irish Pattern of Social Fluidity: The Role of the Political

RICHARD BREEN* & CHRISTOPHER T. WHELAN†

* *The Queen's University of Belfast*
† *Economic and Social Research Institute, Dublin*

Introduction

THE EMPIRICAL FOCUS of this paper is the pattern of intergenerational social mobility in the Republic of Ireland as revealed through data collected in 1987, and the degree to which this has changed in comparison with results obtained from an earlier mobility survey undertaken in 1973. The conceptual starting point of the paper, however, is a concern to examine the broader question of the relationship between politics and social mobility using, as evidence, the Irish data.

It is clear that political decisions in areas concerned with economic policy and development can influence social mobility. In Ireland, for example, since the 1950s the state has been active in shaping the structure of job opportunities (Breen *et al.*, 1990). In some cases—as in, say, the subsidising of small farmers—the impact of policy on mobility patterns may be readily identifiable, but in other areas, such as public sector job creation or expenditure on training, an assessment will raise complex questions related to the probable outcomes that would have arisen in the absence of such interventions (Breen, 1991a). Overall, then, we are in broad agreement with the view expressed by Goldthorpe (1990: 417) that, while the effects of such structural change on mobility levels and patterns are substantial, it seems unlikely that a useful sociological theory of occupational change or class structural change can be advanced. As a consequence

Read 8 December 1990. © The British Academy 1992.

. . . class analysis must take a given structural context as its starting point
and concentrate on the elucidation of the processes occurring within that
context, mobility included. (Goldthorpe, 1990: 412).

In assessing the impact of politics on social mobility we therefore focus
attention not on overall or 'absolute', rates of social mobility but, rather,
on relative rates (or 'social fluidity'). The primary determinants of absolute
rates are structural changes in a nation's occupational distribution over
time. In mobility tables such shifts are reflected, albeit in a complex way
and confounded with other effects, in the differences between the origin
(fathers') and destination (sons') marginal distributions. Social fluidity, on
the other hand, captures the degree of openness in intergenerational
mobility net of structural effects as they are embodied in the marginal
distributions of the mobility table. In other words, by concentrating on
social fluidity we can then assess the degree to which relative mobility
chances and the level of inequality of mobility opportunities are a
reflection of the ideology of a country's political regime and the policies
pursued by governments, possibly over long periods of time. As is by now
well known, the appropriate measure of such relative chances is the odds
ratio. The odds in question are the odds of being in one destination class
rather than another, conditional on the sizes of those destination classes
and a given class origin. An odds ratio is thus the ratio of two such odds,
each of which is taken relative to a different class origin.[1]

The best known argument concerning politics and social fluidity is that
of Featherman, Jones and Hauser (1975), the so-called FJH hypothesis.
This states that 'rates of social fluidity are basically the same in industrial
societies with a market economy (and) a nuclear family system' (Erikson,
1990: 3). The FJH hypothesis posits a similarity independent of politics.
Studies such as those of Treiman (1970) reach a similar conclusion. These
results are in contrast with the work of a number of earlier authors (such
as Glass, 1954) who believed that politics and specific policy programmes
could increase social mobility (Erikson, 1990).

Research undertaken in the late 1970s and 1980s has been equivocal
on the relationship between politics and social fluidity. While many studies
have shown that the FJH hypothesis does not hold when subjected to strict
test (see Erikson, Goldthorpe and Portacarero, 1982; Breen and Whelan,

---

[1] For example, a typical odds-ratio would measure the chances of a man born in the skilled
manual class remaining in that class rather than moving to the agricultural labourer class,
relative to the chances of a man born into the agricultural labourer class moving into the
skilled manual class rather than remaining in the agricultural labourer class. Thus social
fluidity is seen in terms of competition among men of different origins for particular
destinations.

1985, among others), and that there are interesting and important cross-national deviations from a common pattern of social fluidity, there is little evidence regarding the causes of these deviations. In one study which specifically addressed this issue, Grusky and Hauser (1984) found that measures of inequality and social democracy did not explain such deviations.[2] In their work on the CASMIN data-set, Erikson and Goldthorpe (1987b: 162) have reformulated the FJH thesis to allow for the possibility of the political helping to shape social fluidity:

> . . . a basic similarity will be found in patterns of social fluidity . . . across all nations with market economies and nuclear family systems where no sustained attempts have been made to use the power of the modern state apparatus in order to modify the processes, or the outcomes of the processes, through which class inequalities are intergenerationally reproduced.

The phrase 'sustained attempts' directs attention, in particular, to the impact of periods of socialist transformation in eastern European societies and long-term social-democratic ascendancy in Sweden. Erikson and Goldthorpe's perspective, however, is clearly compatible with the notion of a continuum of levels of purposive action, implemented by the State through political decisions which affect

1   inequality of condition and, in particular, inequality of income;
2   the intergenerational transmission of wealth and the magnitude of the advantages associated with property;
3   equality of educational opportunity.

Our approach to the question of the link between politics and social mobility draws directly on these sorts of consideration. Ideally our empirical approach would be as follows. Given data on a set of countries (or the same country at different times), we begin by modelling social fluidity in terms of a number of independent variables which we believe account for social fluidity in all industrialised nations. The cross-national variation in such fluidity would then be attributable to two things: first, variation in the strength of effect of these independent variables; and, secondly, cross-national differences in the distribution of these variables. These variables would, following our earlier discussion, measure such

---

[2] However, there are reasons to view this result with caution. Grusky and Hauser analysed mobility in 16 countries in the form of a set of 16 three category classifications—white collar, blue collar and agriculture. Such a crude classification obscures potential differences in class —as opposed to sectoral—mobility. Furthermore, their explanatory variables—such as social democracy and inequality—are, at the same time, crude approximations to what they sought to measure while probably being too general in themselves (even if they had been measured without error) to capture important political dimensions of difference between the countries in the study.

things as educational qualifications and the ownership of property and wealth—factors which are, actually or potentially, open to modification by government action. Conditional on the correctness of our hypotheses about the specific factors determining social fluidity, this approach would shift the explanatory focus of cross-national analyses away from social fluidity *per se* towards variations in the distribution and relative strength of effect of the determinants of mobility and the causes of these.

Needless to say, in this paper we are constrained from implementing such an ambitious approach by the unavailability of the necessary data. Our data comprise mobility tables for Ireland in 1973 and 1987. Together with the 1987 mobility data we also have a good deal of other information concerning the respondents to the survey and their origins. We therefore begin by fitting a model, which accounts for mobility in Ireland in 1987 in terms of a number of independent variables, to the mobility table deriving from the 7-class version of the class schema set out in the paper by Whelan, Breen and Whelan above. We then proceed to extend the analysis to the 14-class schema. Mobility in Ireland in 1973 (for which we do not have appropriate measured independent variables) is then compared with that in 1987 employing the 7-class schema. The purpose of this comparison is to assess whether such changes as we observe can be explained in terms of the changes we know to have taken place over the period in the independent variables we identify as important in accounting for social fluidity in 1987.

Theoretical Models of Social Fluidity

In this paper we take as our basic theoretical model that outlined by Goldthorpe (1980: 99). Under this model the pattern of social fluidity is considered to be shaped by three factors. These are the relative desirability of different class destinations; the resources available to individuals within each origin class which help them gain access to more desirable destination classes; and barriers to movement between classes. Typically we think of resources as 'economic, cultural and social resources' (Erikson and Goldthorpe 1987a: 64), while barriers to mobility would include the necessity to own the means of production, educational and other qualifications needed for entry to the occupations that comprise a class grouping and so forth.

The approach to modelling social fluidity outlined in the previous paragraph has been operationalised previously by Erikson and Goldthorpe (1987a, b). Since our approach differs from theirs in some important respects, we first describe their model before going on to outline our own.

In their 'core model of social fluidity' (henceforth CoSF), Erikson and Goldthorpe employ four types of effects to explain the observed pattern of relative mobility rates: 'hierarchy effects' with three levels distinguished; 'inheritance effects' distinguishing between an overall effect, an effect for those classes containing employers or self-employed, and an effect for farmers; a 'sector effect' capturing movement into and out of agriculture; and 'affinity effects' which are intended to 'capture additional effects on mobility which derive from particular linkages or discontinuities between classes' (Erikson and Goldthorpe, 1987a: 67). The first such affinity term relates to the movement between the service class and that of agricultural workers and is intended to allow for factors which make exchanges between such classes particularly improbable. The second affinity term covers instances where a higher propensity for immobility is attributed than would otherwise be the case.

All these effects are modelled as dummy variables. Thus there is no immediate relationship, in the CoSF model, between social fluidity and factors which might be considered to influence social fluidity. In our model, by contrast, we seek, so far as possible, to explain social fluidity in terms of measured independent variables. We are able to do this for our 1987 data, though not for our 1973 data. In our 1987 data we have measures relating to destination and origin classes. We identify the former with the desirability of class destinations and the barriers to mobility into such destinations, and we identify the latter with resources for mobility.

Turning first to destination classes, here we have four possible measures. These are

Y1: gross mean household income in each destination class;
Y2: mean score in each destination class on a 20-item consumption scale;
Y3: mean percentage of men in each destination class permanently unable to work due to illness or unemployed at the survey date;
Y4: mean percentage of men in each destination having more than primary education.

Y1, Y2, and Y3 plausibly represent different aspects of the desirability of destinations, while Y4 is a measure of the barriers to class entry due to educational requirements.

Turning to our origin class measures, we use two measures:

X1: mean percentage of fathers in each origin class having only primary education;
X2: mean score in each origin class on a scale measuring the respondent's perceptions of his family's relative financial deprivation when he was growing up.

Both X1 and X2 can be viewed as measures of resources for mobility.

As yet we have said nothing about ownership of the means of production: this is clearly both a resource for mobility among men of farming, petty bourgeois and proprietorial origins, as well as a barrier to entry among those from the remaining class origins. We operationalise these by using two further measures:

P1: the proportion of fathers in each origin class who are self-employed;
P2: the proportion of men in each destination class who are self-employed.

A very specific resource for mobility is demonstrated by the tendency for class inheritance. For all classes, an origin in a given class is a resource which improves one's chances of remaining in that class relative to the chances of men born in other classes entering that class. The reasons for this are diverse but they include such things as direct inheritance of the means of production, family tradition and access to social networks. To capture this we fit a single parameter to the cells on the main diagonal of the mobility table.

Within the model we include two further parameters which capture the special position of the agricultural sector. The first of these is a single parameter for farm inheritance over and above the general level of inheritance. The second captures the barrier to mobility into the agricultural sector. Note that this is a unidimensional barrier: it does not apply to movement out of agriculture. Indeed, we believe that to model a two-way barrier (into and out of agriculture) with the same parameter is likely to prove very misleading.

Finally, although we sought to capture the effects of ownership of the means of production as both a resource and a barrier, we find that we require one additional parameter to capture the propensity of men of petty bourgeois and farm origins to move into the higher professional, administrative and managerial and large proprietor class.

We have, then, five variables which score our table's destinations and a further three scoring the origins. We could enter these into the model as terms formed by multiplying each origin score by each destination score, to give terms such as Y1X1, Y1X2, Y2X1, and so on. This would yield 15 terms, each using a single degree of freedom, and, indeed, we have fitted such a model. Such a model would tell us, for example, how each of the possible combinations of different desirability/barriers and resources measures influences social fluidity. The model we discuss here, however, is rather more parsimonious. What we want is a model in which some overall measure of desirability/barriers and some generalised resource measure are used to shape the pattern of social fluidity. To arrive at such measures we simply took the first principal component of the origin scores, X1 and X2, as a measure of generalised resources (labelled X), and the first principal component of the destination scores Y1, Y2, Y3 and Y4, to yield a measure of desirability and barriers (labelled Y). We excluded from the principal components analysis the more specific measures of resources and barriers associated with ownership of the means of production. These measures—P1 and P2—were multiplied together to form the variable P12 which captures the level of ownership of the means of production in each origin/destination combination.

Our final model thus includes, apart from the origin and destination main effects, the following variables:

Agriculture: AGB: the term reflecting the barrier to movement into agricultural destinations from non-agricultural origins.

Hierarchy: XY: which captures the effect of generalised resources, desirability and barriers, conceptualised in a hierarchical fashion. Note that this term models the effects of desirability and barriers as varying according to the resources for mobility enjoyed by the different origin classes, and similarly, the effect of resources varies according to the level of desirability/barriers of each destination class.

Property: P12: a measure of ownership of the means of production in each origin/destination combination;

SLP: the term for movement between petty bourgeois or farm origins and the higher professional, administrative and managerial class. Together the P12 and SLP terms capture the pattern of movement within the classes which own the means of production;

Inheritance: INH1: the term for overall class inheritance; and INH3: the term for farm inheritance, measured as additional to the level of overall class inheritance.

We can write this model as

$$\log F_{ij} = \lambda + \lambda^F + \lambda^S + \lambda^{SLP} + \lambda^{INH1} + \lambda^{INH3} + \lambda^{AGB} \\ + \alpha(XY) + \beta(P12) \tag{1}$$

where F_{ij} is the expected value in the ijth cell of the table, alpha is the parameter of association between X and Y and beta that between P1 and P2.

Results

We fitted this model to the 7×7 1987 Irish mobility table and also to a 14×14 mobility table. The definition of the classes in each of these is set out in Table 1 of the preceding paper by Whelan, Breen and Whelan.

Table 1.　Results of applying model (1) to the Irish mobility data for 1987 classified according to the 7-class version of the class schema.

A. Goodness of fit

	G^2	df	rG^2
Independence model	1112.9	36	—
Model (1)	40.19	30	96.0

B. Principal component scores

		Rows	Columns
(I+II)	Professional, administrative and managerial (service class)	1.73	1.71
(III)	Routine non-manual	0.42	0.43
(IVa+b)	Petty bourgeoisie	0.39	0.73
(IVc)	Farmers	−0.24	−0.47
(V/VI)	Technicians, supervisors of manual workers and skilled manual	0.10	−0.17
(VIIa)	Non-skilled manual	−0.37	−1.05
(VIIb)	Agricultural workers	−0.75	−1.10

C. Parameter estimates

estimate	s.e.	parameter
0.2586	0.0633	INH1(2)
1.344	0.3361	INH3(2)
−1.796	0.2335	AGB(2)
0.7602	0.1327	SLP(2)
1.259	0.1719	β
0.6058	0.0494	α

Table 1 contains the results of applying model (1) to the 7×7 1987 Irish mobility table. Panel A shows the goodness of fit relative to the independence model. Our model reduces the G^2 for this latter model by 96 per cent. By conventional criteria the model (1) provides a good fit to the data (the 5 per cent critical value for G^2 with 30 df being 45.5).

In panel B we show the two principal component scores for origins (resources) and destinations (desirability/barriers). The higher the principal component score the greater the resources for mobility (in the case of the row scores) or the greater the desirability of specific classes and the barriers associated with access to them (in the case of the column scores).

Panel C shows the parameter estimates for the six terms that shape odds ratios under the model.

We also fitted the model to the disaggregated 14-class table for 1987. The only adjustment we made was to add one extra parameter which captured mobility between the three farming classes (IVc(i), IVc(ii) and IVc(iii)). We refer to this as model (1a). For the 14×14 table, Table 2 shows that the independence model yields a G^2 of 1543.0 with 169 df,

Table 2. Results of applying model (1a) to the Irish mobility data for 1987 classified according to the 14-class version of the class schema.

A. Goodness of fit

	deviance	df	rG^2
Independence model	1543.0	169	—
Model (1a)	247.79	162	84.0

B. Principal component scores

		Rows	Columns
(I)	Higher-grade professionals, administrators and office managers in large industrial establishments	2.20	2.01
(II)	Lower-grade professionals, administrators and official higher-grade technicians; managers in small industrial establishments: supervisors of non-manual employees	1.48	1.53
(IIIa)	Routine non-manual employees in administration and commerce	1.22	1.15
(IIIb)	Sales personnel; other rank-and-file service workers	−0.06	−0.04
(IVa)	Small proprietors, artisans, etc., with employees	0.73	0.97
(IVb)	Small proprietors, artisans, etc., without employees	0.07	0.54
(V)	Lower-grade technicians; supervisors of manual workers	0.31	0.61
(VI)	Skilled manual workers	0.04	−0.49
(VIIai)	Semi-skilled manual workers (not in agriculture)	−0.06	−0.40
(VIIaii)	Unskilled manual workers not in agriculture	−0.57	−1.88
(VIIb)	Agricultural and other workers in primary production	−0.74	−1.10
(IVci)	Farmers; < 50 acres	−0.55	−0.99
(IVcii)	Farmers; 50–99 acres	0.07	−0.43
(IVciii)	Farmers; 100+ acres	0.09	0.41

C. Parameter estimates

estimate	s.e.	parameter
0.3451	0.0640	INH1 (2)
2.204	0.3553	INH3 (2)
0.9578	0.3692	INH4 (2)
−1.736	0.2332	AGB (2)
0.7013	0.1314	SLP (2)
1.220	0.1670	β
0.6212	0.0411	α

while our model has a G^2 of 247.79 with 162 df. Although this falls marginally short of reaching the usual criterion for fitting the data (the critical value of G^2 for 162 df is approximately 198), the model nevertheless provides a remarkably good fit to the data, reducing the G^2 by 84 per cent of its value under the independence model, while using up only seven degrees of freedom.[3] Such a high level of fit to such a disaggregated table is very unusual and is evidence, we believe, of the validity and explanatory power of our model.

Table 2 also shows the principal component scores and the parameter estimates for model (1a). If we compare the parameter estimates for this model with those displayed in Table 1 their stability, over the two tables, is very striking. The overall inheritance parameter, the parameter for the agricultural entry barrier (which is negative as we should expect), the parameter for movement between property owning classes, and the β and α parameters, are remarkably similar when estimated using either the 7×7 or 14×14 table. In all cases the parameter estimates have the sign and magnitude that we should expect.

The principal component scores in Table 2 show the value of moving to the highly disaggregated 14-class categorisation. The dichotomisation of class III into routine non-manual and rank and file service workers shows that the latter class is much more poorly placed than the former in terms of resources (where it ranks about equal with semi-skilled manual workers) and in terms of desirability/barriers. The distinction between semi-skilled and unskilled workers is important in terms of their resources and desirability, although it is in the latter case that the difference is most extreme with the unskilled class having the lowest score by a wide margin. Furthermore, when we distinguish between these categories it becomes apparent there is relatively little difference between the semi-skilled and skilled manual classes, but there is a considerable difference between them, on the one hand, and the unskilled workers and agricultural workers, on the other. These latter classes display the lowest level of resources.

Generalising the Model

The model we have presented was developed as an attempt to operationalise the basic theoretical approach which sees social fluidity as determined by resources, desirability and barriers to mobility. However, it is possible also to use the model to provide a simple account of the factors shaping social fluidity. The model suggests that social fluidity is shaped by three basic things: first, the barrier that exists to entry into the agricultural sector; second, a hierarchical, or vertical dimension, captured by the ordering of rows and columns (and corresponding to hierarchical measures

---

[3] A model which fitted this data at the 5 per cent level would reduce the independence G^2 by 88 per cent or more.

of resources, desirability and barriers); and thirdly, the pattern of mobility flows related to the ownership of the means of production. We refer to this as the Agriculture, Hierarchy and Property (AHP) model. We believe that such a model can yield a parsimonious and theoretically meaningful account of the observed pattern of social fluidity in modern industrial societies (Breen and Whelan, 1991).

How could we test this assertion? Given that data were available for other countries we could test models such as those reported on in Tables 1 and 2. Furthermore, one important advantage of such a model would be that, by fitting separate independent variables (rather than principal component scores) we could provide an account of the various dimensions of social fluidity. However, the lack of appropriate independent variables for other countries (and, more particularly, for the Irish 1973 data) precludes any such ambitious undertakings. Instead, we ask whether a model that includes only agriculture, hierarchy and property effects can give an adequate account of Irish social fluidity in both 1973 and 1987. To do this we develop a model that includes the barrier to movement into the agricultural sector from outside, a hierarchical effect, and a set of parameters that seek to model social fluidity among the owners of the means of production. In other words, we can proxy the AHP model. For our hierarchical effect we turn to Goodman's Row and Column Effects Model II (RC2) (see Goodman, 1979; Breen, 1984a; Breen and Whelan, 1985). This model provides a scoring of rows and columns so as to maximise the association between the row and column variables conditional upon other effects in the model. We also fit a single parameter, INH1, to the main diagonal of the table to reflect class inheritance. For our property effects we use a dummy variable, INH2, for inheritance among the petty bourgeoisie, and a variable for inheritance among farmers, INH3, together with a single parameter, P, applied to cells representing movement between any pair of the property owning classes (i.e., cells I+II, IVa+b; I+II, IVc; IVa+b, I+II; IVa+b, IVc; IVc, I+II; IVc, IVa+b in the 7×7 table). Finally we add the parameter AGB for the barrier to movement into agriculture.

We write this model as:

$$\log F_{ij} = \lambda + \lambda^F + {}^S + \lambda^P + \lambda^{AGB} + \sum_{i=1}^{3} \lambda^{INHi} + \gamma\, u_i v_j \qquad (2)$$

where γ is the parameter measuring association between the estimated row and column scores, u_i and v_j.

It is important to be clear on the role, within the model, of our very general specification of the hierarchical effect in terms of the RC2 model.

Clearly, since this model scales the rows and columns so as to maximise the association between them then, if the AHP model fails to fit the data, it is most unlikely that a model which used known scores for rows and columns in the construction of the hierarchical effect (as in model (1)) would provide an adequate account of mobility. Conversely, if the AHP model fits the data it leaves open the possibility that exogenous measured variables may also give rise to row and column rankings which, when combined as one or more hierarchical terms, would form part of a model that would also fit the data.[4]

In fitting this model we began by asking how well it compares with the more detailed model when applied to the 1987 Irish data. Detailed results of fitting the AHP model to the 7×7 and 14×14 tables are available from the authors. In summary, however, for the 7×7 table the AHP model returns a G^2 of 31.57 with 20 df thus fitting the data using conventional criteria. This compares with a G^2 of 95.48 with 28 df for Erikson and Goldthorpe's (1987a, b) core model of social fluidity (CoSF).

Our model also provides sensible parameter estimates. It yields a rank ordering of rows and columns very similar to that shown in panel B of Table 1. The other parameter estimates show a positive overall inheritance effect, with significantly higher inheritance among the petty bourgeoisie and among farmers. There is a substantial barrier to movement into agriculture and a substantial tendency for movement among origin and destination classes which own the means of production.

For the 14×14 table, the AHP model returns a G^2 of 228.95 with 137 df. Again the parameter estimates are very similar to those of Table 2.

Ireland 1973 and 1987

Our next step was to fit the AHP model, to the 1973 Irish data, with results as shown in Table 3. Initially, we discovered that the pattern of class inheritance was somewhat different than in 1987. First, the level of class inheritance among skilled manual workers was such as to require the addition of another parameter, INH5, to account for this. Secondly, as panel C of Table 3 shows, when this parameter was included, together with INH2 and INH3, the overall inheritance parameter, INH1, became insignificant. Thus, all class inheritance in the 1973 Irish data is confined to the petty bourgeois, farm and skilled manual classes.

---

[4] Our belief that this would be so derives not least from the fact that, if we had measured variables scoring rows and columns we could enter 11 such pairwise effects (e.g., X1Y1; X1Y2; and so on, as described earlier) without exceeding the degrees of freedom used by the RC2 specification.

Table 3. Results of applying the AHP model to the Irish mobility data for 1973 classified according to the 7-class version of the class schema.

A. Goodness of fit

	G^2	df	rG^2
Independence model	1181.2	36	—
CoSF model	66.9	28	94.3
AHP model (2a)	32.4	19	97.2

B. Estimated row and column scores

		Rows	Columns
(I+II)	Professional, administrative and managerial (service class)	2.0593	1.6612
(III)	Routine non-manual	0.5918	0.6210
(IVa+b)	Petty bourgeoisie	−0.1863	−0.1595
(IVc)	Farmers	−0.7675	0.1655
(V/VI)	Technicians, supervisors of manual workers and skilled manual	0.1670	0.0389
(VIIa)	Non-skilled manual	−0.8326	−0.4245
(VIIb)	Agricultural workers	−1.0316	−1.9027

C. Parameter estimates

estimate	s.e.	parameter
−0.1717	0.1116	INH1(2)
2.087	0.2578	INH2(2)
2.582	0.2542	INH3(2)
1.133	0.1927	INH5(2)
−1.935	0.2049	AGB(2)
0.9965	0.1352	P(2)
0.6205	0.05473	γ

The model adjusted to include this extra parameter—which we call model (2a)—marginally fails to fit the data (though it does fit if we drop the non-significant parameter INH1). It is nevertheless a substantial improvement on the CoSF model.

If we use the CoSF model to compare the changes in the Irish mobility regime between 1973 and 1987 we are faced with a problem. A model which constrains all the social fluidity parameters to be constant across the two data sets provides as adequate a fit to the data as does a model which allows all these parameters to take different values in each table.[5] But the latter fails, by a long way, to fit the data. Aggregating the G^2s from the CoSF model applied to the 1973 and 1987 tables gives a G^2 of 162.3 with 56 df. Clearly, if the nature of Irish social fluidity has changed between

---

[5] The difference between the two models has G^2 of 5.6 with 8 df.

the dates of the two inquiries any such changes lie outside the scope of what is captured by the CoSF model.

In order to determine what these changes might have been we use the AHP model to carry out a formal analysis of the change in the Irish mobility regime between 1973 and 1987 following the logic set out by Breen (1985). As we noted earlier, we use the RC2 formulation to proxy hierarchical measures of resources, desirability and barriers. The γ coefficient and scoring of the origins and destinations under the RC2 specification are estimated so as to maximise the (conditional) association between the two. Since γ, u_i and v_j are not separately identified, a change of parameterisation of say, u_i and v_j will affect γ. Had we exogenous measures, the model would yield parameter estimates based on the maximisation of the conditional association between origins and destinations given the scorings of these two. In the latter case we could speak of the effect, on social fluidity, of specific measures of resources, desirability and barriers. In the former case we cannot. Rather, we must interpret our results by posing two questions. First we ask: given the estimated hierarchical orderings of origins and destinations, what do the results imply about social or political processes? We then ask: are these implications plausible?

The results of this analysis are given in Table 4. We begin by fitting a common (homogenous) model, that is, model (2a) to the two Irish mobility tables, with the addition of only one parameter to allow for the different sample sizes of the two inquiries. We label this the Common Mobility Model (line 1 of Table 4). The reason for fitting such a model is that, conditional on model (2a) being true of both tables, we can relax successive homogeneity constraints to determine the relative contribution of different factors to an account of the changes in Irish mobility. The common model clearly falls a long way short of fitting the data. At the other extreme, if we fit model (2a) to each table separately (a completely heterogeneous model), this returns a total G^2 value of 63.98 with 38 df. This is model (3a) which allows all mobility effects to differ between 1973 and 1987 and is shown in line 3 of Table 4. What we want to explain in our comparative analysis, however, is the difference in the G^2 values of these two models —the common model of line 1 and the completely heterogeneous model of line 3. This difference has a value of 249.72 and is associated with 29 df, as shown in panel B of Table 4. We term it the total mobility difference G^2.

Our next step is to allow the origin and destination effects—but not the interaction effects which shape odds ratios—to vary between the two tables. This model is labelled 2b, and has G^2 of 97.48 with 55 df, as shown on line 2 of Table 4. The difference between this model and the common

Table 4. Accounting for changes in social mobility in Ireland 1973–87 in terms of the AHP model: results for the 7-class version of the class schema.

A. Goodness of fit of models	G^2	df
1. Common mobility model (2a) (homogeneous, allowing for differences only in sample size)	313.7	67
2. Heterogeneous absolute mobility, common social fluidity (2b)	97.48	55
3. Heterogeneous absolute mobility and social fluidity with agriculture, hierarchy, property and inheritance parameters being allowed to vary (3a)	63.98	38
4. Heterogeneous absolute mobility and social fluidity with the parameters for INH1 and INH5 being allowed to vary while all other fluidity parameters are held constant (3b)	86.52	53

B. Decomposition of deviance		
Total mobility difference (2a–3a)	249.72	29
Absolute mobility difference (2a–2b)	216.22	12
Social fluidity difference (2b–3a)	33.50	17

C. Row and column scores (model 3b)

Rows	Columns
2.027	1.832
0.590	0.825
0.069	−0.157
−0.762	−0.193
−0.029	−0.023
−0.662	−0.760
−1.233	−1.523

D. Parameter estimates
Common

estimate	s.e.	parameter
1.795	0.1834	INH2(2)
2.551	0.1958	INH3(2)
1.001	0.0881	P(2)
−1.749	0.1535	AGB(2)
0.4995	0.0298	γ

Heterogeneous

1973		1987		
estimate	s.e.	estimate	s.e.	parameter
−0.0387	0.0894	0.1784	0.0808	INH1(2)
0.9237	0.1770	0.2007	0.1499	INH5(2)

mobility model gives a G^2 of 216.22 using 12 df (shown on the second line of panel B in Table 4). Since the model shown on line 2 of panel A retains homogenous odds ratios, this additional G^2 value is attributable to structural mobility—defined to mean the effect of a change in only the marginal distributions of the table. This model is not far short of reproducing the data, and accounts for 87 per cent of the mobility difference G^2. In other words, a model which says that all the difference between the 1973 and 1987 mobility tables is caused by changes in the origin and destination effects, and is in no way due to a change in social fluidity, very nearly fits.

That it does not suggests that there has been some change in social fluidity. Indeed, the third line of panel B of Table 4 shows that this is associated with a G^2 of 33.50 which represents 13 per cent of the total mobility difference G^2 value. The question then is, how, and where, has this come about? In our model there are four sets of effects which influence social fluidity. These are the estimated row and column scores and their associated parameter, γ; the four inheritance effects; the agricultural barrier; and the term for mobility within the property owning classes. We find that, of these, a model which allows only two of the four inheritance effects to vary between the two tables fits almost as well as a model which allows all four sets of effects to vary. This model (3b) (shown on line 4 of Table 4) returns a G^2 of 86.52 with 53 df. In Panel D of Table 4 we show the estimates of those parameters which shape social fluidity.

The first set of parameter estimates relate to those which are constant over time, namely, the row and column association parameters (the scorings are also constant and are shown in panel C), the agricultural barrier parameter, the parameter, P, reflecting internal mobility among the classes which own means of production, and the inheritance parameters for the petty bourgeoisie and for farmers. Below that we give the 1973 and 1987 values of the parameters which change over time.

The only source of change between the two surveys is in the inheritance of class position. The distinctively high levels of class inheritance among the skilled manual class disappear between 1973 and 1987, but the overall level of class inheritance increases somewhat. These parameter changes reflect, to some extent, changes in the likelihood of movement out of the class of origin, though they are, of course, partial effects which are not independent of the other effects in the model. In the 1973 data, 42 per cent of cases are found in the diagonal cells, compared with 37 per cent in 1987. A more useful measure, which takes account of the change in origin and destination distributions, is the number of cases on the diagonal expressed as a percentage of the maximum possible number. This is shown in Figure 1.[6] This yields a value of 51 per cent in 1973, 46 per cent in 1987.

---

[6] Let n_{ij} be the number in the ij th cell, n_{i+} the total in the ith row and n_{+j} the total in the jth column. The measure reported in the text is then

$$100n_{ii}/\min(n_{i+}; n_{+i})$$

summed over all i.

CLASS CATEGORY

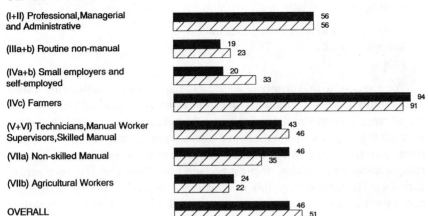

(I+II) Professional,Managerial and Administrative	56 / 56
(IIIa+b) Routine non-manual	19 / 23
(IVa+b) Small employers and self-employed	20 / 33
(IVc) Farmers	94 / 91
(V+VI) Technicians,Manual Worker Supervisors,Skilled Manual	43 / 46
(VIIa) Non-skilled Manual	46 / 35
(VIIb) Agricultural Workers	24 / 22
OVERALL	46 / 51

Figure 1. Number of cases on main diagonal as percentage of the maximum possible, Ireland, 1973 (▨) and 1987 (■). 7-category classification.

These figures suggest that the overall level of class inheritance has been most influenced by structural changes and that, controlling for these, the fall in the likelihood of class inheritance is a less important feature than the change in its distribution. Figure 1 shows that immobility has fallen to any appreciable extent only among the petty bourgeoisie, and indeed has risen among the semi-skilled and unskilled manual classes. There has been virtually no change elsewhere. It is important to note, furthermore, that two of the inheritance parameters shown in Table 4—relating to the petty bourgeoisie and farmers—do not change significantly between the two inquiries. This indicates that, relative to levels of class inheritance in other classes, these two classes have maintained their level of class inheritance.

Conclusions

Theoretical and methodological

In this paper we have sought to operationalise the resources/desirability/barriers model of social mobility using, as far as possible, measured independent variables. We discussed how such variables might be introduced into mobility table analyses and we successfully applied the model to the 1987 Irish mobility data, using both a seven and a fourteen class classification.

This led us to formulate a more general mobility model which has three basic components. These are

1 a barrier to mobility into agriculture;
2 hierarchical effects;
3 property effects.

We suggested that a model based on these three components would give a good account of mobility in modern industrialised societies.

There is a long standing dichotomy between 'class-based' approaches to studying social stratification and those approaches, which, following Blau and Duncan (1967), assume a continuum of positions in society ranked in terms of status or prestige (see also Kelley, 1990). We concur with Goldthorpe's conclusion that, when individuals are thought of as distributed across sets of positions that are defined relationally, important types of mobility are detected which cannot be adequately characterised in terms of movement along a vertical dimension. Despite this, there is no reason why a class perspective is incompatible with an emphasis on the importance of hierarchy as one crucial dimension of the mobility space. Erikson and Goldthorpe (1987a, 1987b) characterise hierarchical effects in terms of a couple of discrete steps. Indeed for Ireland, where one of their hierarchical effects proves to be insignificant, this reduces to one step. Hout's (1989: 153) analysis employing a prestige measure leads him to conclude that Erikson and Goldthorpe understate the importance of hierarchy in Ireland. It is possible to view continuous and discontinuous models of mobility simply as alternative descriptions of the same reality. We believe, however, that the AHP approach demonstrates that it is possible to incorporate, in one model, both continuous hierarchical and discontinuous non-hierarchical effects both of which are conceptualised in terms of class rather than of, say, status. Furthermore, if we are to move towards incorporating, into mobility analyses, independent measured variables as characteristics of classes, it is difficult to see how we can avoid hierarchical rankings.

A crucial illustration of the superiority of the AHP model over the Erikson and Goldthorpe CoSF model is that whereas the former provides a means of describing the distinctive Irish social mobility regime in terms of general theoretical dimensions, the CoSF model does not. Rather, Erikson and Goldthorpe (1987b: 154–55, 160) find it necessary to explain the departures of the Irish data from the expectations generated by their core model in terms of idiosyncrasies.

A final feature of our modelling is that it is very parsimonious. Model (1a), for example, when applied to the 14×14 category table, accounts for virtually all of the G^2 under the independence model with only seven degrees of freedom. All the models we use either fit the data or could be made to do so with the addition or subtraction of one or two parameters.

We believe that, in cross-national or inter-temporal comparisons it is important to develop models which fit, or very nearly fit, the data, using conventional criteria. The reason for this is that, given such models, comparison will be rendered relatively straightforward by seeing how far, and which, parameters of the model can subsequently be constrained to be cross-nationally equal (Breen, 1987: 76–77).

The alternative is to employ a model which does not fit the data and examine the residuals to determine how the mobility regime differs between countries or inquiries. The difficulties with this are twofold. First, the residual from such a model will include both systematic effects that were omitted from the model and sampling and other error. The model itself cannot disentangle these. Second, as our discussion of the CoSF model applied to the Irish data for 1973 and 1987 illustrated, if the dimensions of difference between two or more mobility tables lie outside the fitted model, then the model is of no utility in telling us how—and, more importantly, why—the tables differ.

Changes in Irish social mobility 1973 to 1987

Changes in the Irish mobility regime between 1973 and 1987 were quite modest. Eighty seven per cent of the change in mobility was attributable to change in the pattern of absolute mobility. There was, as a result, a high level of constancy in social fluidity. The lack of significant change in the row and column scores is consistent with a stable situation relating to inequality in resources and attractiveness/barriers and in the association between them. Changes in the pattern of social fluidity, as indicated by our results, were confined to class inheritance: the overall inheritance parameters for classes other than farmers and the petty bourgeoisie tended to become more equal, though there was no evidence that the relative advantage enjoyed by these latter two classes in passing on the ownership of the means of production was in any way diminished.

If we are to look for explanations of why the period 1973–87 should show so little change we must begin by recognising that the full working through of any policy-induced changes, in terms of their impact on origins and destinations, might well take another twenty years. Yet there is a variety of policy effects which can plausibly be hypothesised. A detailed examination of the relationship between changes in income, inequality and taxation will form a central objective of our future work. It is, though, perhaps worthwhile pointing here to a couple of specific conclusions and one of a more general methodological kind.

Our failure to observe any change in the γ coefficient in our models between 1973 and 1987 provides strong evidence for the validity of our earlier conclusions (based on rather more limited evidence) that the transformation of the Irish educational system has had very little impact on the level of social fluidity in the society (Whelan and Whelan, 1984; Breen *et al.*, 1990).

Some policies it seems, though, have had an impact. In particular the retention of advantage by the petty bourgeoisie and farmers is consistent with our understanding of the impact of policy in the area of taxation and redistribution.[7] Over the period in question there was a relatively marked decline in the revenue shares from tax on property, inheritance tax and Corporation income tax. Property tax declined through a series of electoral promises that led ultimately to the removal in 1978 of all taxes on domestic dwellings. The career of capital taxation was even more dramatic. Until 1973 estate duties were the only form of capital taxation in Ireland. After 1973 a series of reforms were attempted as part of the agreement that led to the formation of the Fine Gael/Labour Coalition Government of 1973–77. Capital Acquisition Tax (1974) and an ill-fated Wealth Tax (1975) were introduced to replace the old estate duties, and a Capital Gains Tax was directed at profits from speculative activities. The central aim of these changes was to introduce greater equity into the tax system.

In practice, these reforms were so structured that they failed to secure this objective. Such was the opposition to the proposal for a Wealth Tax that the package finally implemented was ineffectual. Other forms of capital taxation were neutralised by generous exemptions, provisions for indexation with inflation and tapering relief. The total contribution of capital taxation to government revenue fell precipitously, even before Fianna Fáil removed the Wealth Tax in 1978. The old estate duties had been more than three times as effective as a revenue source than the taxes that replaced them were in 1985. Ireland's distinctive tax profile is very much a product of state policy. Tax revenue from capital or corporate income was limited in the pursuit of economic expansion and more recently justified as a basis for job creation (Breen *et al.*, 1990: ch. 4).

Rottman and Reidy's (1988) analysis of the impact of taxation and transfers between 1973 and 1980 showed that farmers enjoyed a unique relationship with the cash transfer system. Regardless of their income levels, all farm categories received substantially more in cash transfers than

---

[7] See Hannan and Commins (this volume) for a more detailed discussion of the advantages enjoyed by farmers.

their households paid in taxation. Once direct transfers and taxes were taken into account, non-agricultural proprietors were, on average, worse off in 1980 if they belonged to the 'large proprietor' category and better off, quite significantly so, if they were 'small proprietors'. In contrast, all categories of employees, except unskilled manual workers, were worse off. The tax advantages conferred by property ownership is most starkly illustrated by the fact that in 1980 large proprietors and unskilled manual workers shared a common effective tax rate of 16 per cent. Cash transfers were allocated among classes on a progressive basis but taxes were only weakly progressive. In practice, this had two main effects. First, for employees state actions left income differences based on the market largely unaltered. Second, state policies generally acted to improve the relative financial situation of families earning their income mainly through family property.

The most general conclusion which we wish to draw from our analysis follows from the fact that the distinctiveness of the Irish social mobility regime can be described in terms of general dimensions derived from an explicit theory of the mobility process. As a consequence of this, it should be possible in principle to provide a genuinely macro-sociological explanation of the Irish case. However, as we move away from 'single number' approaches to describing mobility regimes, it becomes clear that comparative analysis which relies on crude overall measures of inequality, education or political systems has little to offer. Thus, any comprehensive assessment of the impact of politics in Ireland would need to take into account that in areas such as education the state's role is often indirect, with the state acting as financier and paymaster but with private institutions making key decisions on how the money will be used. The Irish experience, where progressivity in personal income tax and in cash transfers produced little impact on the pattern of inequalities because of other features of the structure of taxation, demonstrates the need to go beyond the issue of expenditure and consider control, financing and distribution of benefits. Expenditure can then be viewed as part of a set of state interventions capable of altering life chances. Here, it would appear that we can draw useful lessons from the literature relating to political influences on the welfare state which points to the limitations of simple measures of policy outcomes and the complexities involved in assessing the impact of political partisanship and the structure of party systems (Shalev, 1983; Myles, 1984).

Acknowledgements. We would like to thank John Goldthorpe and William Roche for comments on an earlier draft.

Appendix: Some Mobility Models Explained

1. Quasi-perfect mobility (QPM)

The independence or perfect mobility (PM) model says that all odds ratios are equal to one: in other words, in the competition for any destination class, being born into any particular origin class is no more advantageous than is being born into any other. The QPM model modifies this slightly to say that being born into a given class confers an advantage in competition for entry into that class but not in the competition for entry into any other class.

2. Levels models

A levels model allocates all cells in a mobility table into k mutually exhaustive and disjoint sets (i.e., each cell is allocated to one and only one level) by means of a set of dummy variables. The result is that odds ratios formed from cells drawn from the same level will be equal to one, while odds ratios formed from cells drawn from one or more levels will not. The model thus posits equality of competition for pairs of origins and destinations at the same level and inequality of competition for pairs of origins and destinations drawn from different levels.

3. Models which score rows and columns

In the uniform association (UA) model the odds ratios can be written in terms of scores applied to the rows and columns of a table. Let $x(i)$ be the score for the ith origin class, $y(j)$ the score for the jth destination class. Then any odds ratio depends upon the distance apart, in terms of their x and y scores, of the cells involved, weighted by a parameter (call it β) which measures the strength of the association between x and y. In the RC2 model not only is β estimated but so are the $x(i)$ and $y(j)$ so as to maximise the association between the scored origins and destinations. In such models origin classes which have high scores have the highest relative chance of entering highly scored destinations. Equally, low scoring origins have a higher relative chance of entering low scoring destinations. Thus the scores derived from models like RC2 lend themselves to interpretation in terms of an origin hierarchy of relative advantage in access to destinations which themselves are scored in terms of relative exclusivity in drawing their inflow disproportionately from more advantaged origins.

4. Erikson and Goldthorpe's Core Model of Social Fluidity (CoSF)

This is a variant of the levels model in which cells of the table are allocated to mutually exhaustive but not necessarily disjoint levels. Erikson and Goldthorpe develop the CoSF model as a set of overlapping levels models. Unlike the original levels models, each of Erikson and Goldthorpe's levels is meant to reflect the operation of a specific set of influences on social fluidity. So, three of their levels attempt to capture hierarchical mobility processes, others seek to model inheritance effects, and so forth. Each levels model is fitted using a single dummy variable. Odds ratios under this model depend upon the set of levels into which the cells in question fall.

Proceedings of the British Academy, **79**, 153–172

Change in Intragenerational Mobility in the Republic of Ireland

BRENDAN HALPIN

Nuffield College, Oxford

Introduction

THE PRECEDING PAPERS have examined the effect of industrialisation on intergenerational social mobility in the Republic of Ireland. This paper continues the theme by considering one of the processes that goes to make up intergenerational mobility, namely, intragenerational mobility—the mobility of individuals during their lifetimes. The focus throughout much of this book is on the question of how other aspects of a society change when it undergoes industrialisation. It is often found that underlying patterns of social mobility or, in other words, of social fluidity, are very resistant to change, as has been partially borne out by the preceding paper. The question must then be asked: 'By what mechanisms does change at the level of the occupational structure bring about, or fail to bring about, change at the level of social mobility?' In an attempt to begin to answer this question, I examine intragenerational mobility as one of the components of intergenerational mobility, and continuous worklife mobility as the process by which the life-time trajectory of intragenerational mobility is actually constructed.

   In looking for change in these different aspects of social mobility in mid-twentieth century Ireland, I find no evidence of new patterns of association between classes of origin and destination in inter- or intra-generational mobility, but I do find evidence of change in patterns of continuous work-life mobility. That is, after controlling for changes in class distributions, I find that people are ending up in the same sorts of places as before, but also that—to an extent—they are taking different routes to achieve this.

Read 8 December 1990. © The British Academy 1992.

Under conditions of industrialisation a number of pressures towards change might be expected to affect processes of social mobility. Among these would be greater universalism in social selection, a greater role of education, more bureaucratically directed careers, and so on. But the actual way in which the structural pressure for change will translate into new patterns of social mobility is not deterministic. The conditions change and, as a result, what happens to individuals changes; but people will react to changed conditions with changed strategies. Typically, those with advantage under the old regime will manage to a greater or lesser degree to retain this advantage.

To gain a fuller understanding of this process, it is necessary to treat it at several distinct levels. At the most structural level, the intergenerational relationship between class origins and destinations must be examined. This relationship must be elaborated through an understanding of its component processes; that is, of the link between origin and initial placement in the labour market (and how this is based on inheritance, education, social networks and so on), and in turn of the link between initial placement and 'mature' class position. Then finally the continuous processes which bring about the patterned outcomes of the transition from origin to entry (or 'first') class and from entry to mature class must be dealt with. In this paper I am exclusively concerned with intragenerational mobility, and attempt to examine the nature and significance of change in both mobility between class at entry to the labour market and mature class (taken to be class at age 35 for practical purposes, and generally referred to hereafter as destination or last class) and continuous mobility between classes throughout the work life (also up to age 35). The focus is on how patterns of association between classes change, once shifts in the overall distributions of class positions are taken into account. Allowing for these shifts, does change occur in the relative ease or difficulty of movement between classes?

As I have mentioned, the underlying patterns of intergenerational social mobility are understood to be relatively resistant to change. Cross-sectional research tends to bear this out, even across countries with substantially different absolute mobility rates (see, for instance, Erikson and Goldthorpe, 1992). Similarly, Breen and Whelan (this volume), show that the change which has taken place in the underlying mobility regime in Ireland between 1973 and 1987, while real, is relatively small. But although the patterns of net association of parent's class with child's class tend to be quite similar across many societies, the processes which bring about these patterns can differ substantially. That is, the same origin–destination pattern can be created by a variety of origin-to-first-class and first-class-to-destination-class patterns, since the two components may vary to compensate for each other. Thus, the first–last (i.e. entry-class to mature-class) mobility process can be viewed as being constrained by the origin–destination process. But a given first–last pattern can be constituted by different patterns or sequences of work-life mobility. The first–last pattern is built up out of the accumulated steps of ongoing work-life mobility, while also constraining the pattern of these steps, though not absolutely.

These are the sorts of issues this paper seeks to explore. Structural change is expected to bring about change in the processes of social mobility, over and above its direct effect of simply shunting people about; but it is not clear how much change there will be, or what the relationship is between pressures for change in different aspects of mobility. Thus the questions must be asked (i) if change can be seen, and (ii) if yes, of what nature and extent, in both ongoing work-life mobility, and first–last class mobility. Does the structural change of industrialisation cause change in processes of work-life mobility? If so, does the accumulated experience of new patterns of work-life mobility result in new intragenerational mobility outcomes?[1]

Data Sources

The following analysis is based on data from the Irish Mobility Study of 1973–4. This is the only source of comprehensive work-life data for the Republic of Ireland, and, while lacking information on more recent periods, it covers the bulk of the mid-twentieth century. I look at the complete careers, up to age 35, of men in a series of cohorts, and examine how their experience of the work-life career has changed. For modelling purposes, I group the cohorts into three ten-year groups.

The original survey interviewed males aged between 18 and 65, and collected each respondent's complete work-life history. This gives much more information than I use in the present context, as I discard all information for workers under age 35 at the time of interview, and all information on events after age 35 for those workers older than this at interview. While this entails a substantial loss of information, it allows me to compare the experience of successive birth cohorts. The choice of age 35 in this regard is the result of a trade-off. I feel that there is little point

---

[1] The discussion in this paper focuses exclusively on intragenerational mobility, but it is worth stating at this stage that the modelling techniques used in the body of this paper have also been applied to intergenerational mobility data, and show that there is no evidence of change in the underlying pattern over the relevant period.

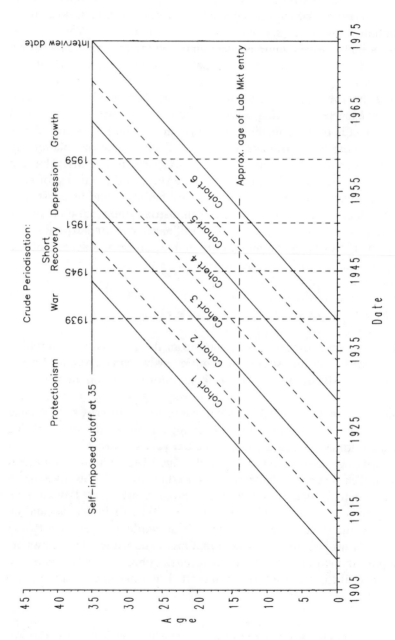

Figure 1. The cohorts in historical context.

in extending the length of career at the expense of number of cohorts, as most mobility will take place before age 35, and further that the addition of extra cohorts at the expense of shorter careers will tend to lose useful information.

The period I can examine is constrained by the available data, which effectively cover from about 1925–30 to 1973. This period can be crudely dichotomised into a period of protectionism and stagnation before the Whittaker Report[2] and one of foreign investment and growth after, but there is rather more detail to the picture in reality. The periodisation I favour, at least for exploratory purposes, begins with (i) the phase of indigenous industrialisation under protection, which was largely a feature of the 1930s, and had reached a plateau well before (ii) the period of austerity and increased isolation of the Second World War. This was followed by (iii) a short period of recovery in the late 1940s, which in turn gave way to (iv) the partially artificially induced depression of the 1950s, before we reach (v) the relatively vigorous growth and innovation of the 1960s.

Figure 1 serves to show how the historical experience of successive birth cohorts differs. It can be seen that the members of cohort 1 entered the labour market well before the Second World War, and spent the later part of their careers, to age 35, during the 'Emergency'. Cohort 2 has a similar experience, but works through the short post-war recovery as well. Cohorts 3 and 4 enter the labour market, by and large, during the war, and experience both the short recovery and the depression of the 1950s. Cohort 5 enters during the post-war recovery, and then works through both the depression and the boom of the 1960s. Finally, cohort 6 has perhaps the experience with the greatest internal contrast, arriving on the scene at the start of the depression but then enjoying the long subsequent period of growth. If the cohorts are paired, as in some cases becomes necessary to avoid an undue sparsity in the data, some of these distinctions of experience are blurred. Cohorts 1 and 2 have a substantial part of their careers under their belts before the war, but also experience the war. Cohorts 3 and 4 for the most part enter the labour market during wartime, have become established by the short post-war recovery, but spend some time in the slump of the 1950s as well. The final pair, cohorts 5 and 6, combine what appear to be two quite different experiences: cohort 5 enters the labour market during the post-war recovery while cohort 6 enters more or less at the beginning of the slump; but, together, they experience the full duration of the slump and of the 1960s growth period.

[2] The internal Department of Finance report, *Economic Development* by T. K. Whittaker, is seen as marking a turning point in the attitude of government to development and, notionally, as the beginning of modern Irish industrialisation.

   The analyses that follow are based on the seven-category version of the Goldthorpe class schema as described in Table 1 of the paper by Whelan, Breen and Whelan, above. The choice of this version of the schema represents a compromise between comprehensiveness and simplicity; it blurs a few interesting distinctions but the data would not allow us to model reliably with a much more disaggregated version.

Looking for Patterns in the Data

Table 1 shows first-to-last class mobility aggregated over the six cohorts. Even with the relatively condensed seven-category class schema, there are a number of zero cells, most notably those representing exit from classes IVab and IVcd, the urban petty bourgeoisie and the farmers. Classes I and II, (generally referred to hereafter as the service class), have markedly high proportions of apparent life-time stability, with only 11 per cent of those who enter the labour market in this class not also being there at age 35. But this is a relatively small class. In contrast, the proprietorial classes (IVab and IVcd), while also retentive, have a much smaller proportion entering as first class (because of the need to wait for inheritance, or to acquire the skills, contacts or capital necessary to set up on one's own etc.), and thus a much smaller population from which to generate outflows to other classes. The industrial working classes (V, VI and VIIa) also hold on to a large proportion of those who enter there, but not to the same extent as the service class or the petty bourgeoisie, while the routine non-manual class (III) seems to be a staging post for mobility. Little more than a third of those entering the labour market in this class are also in it at age 35. Class III sends a lot of its members to the non-agricultural classes, and

Table 1. Class at entry to the labour market by class at 35.

| Entry Class | \multicolumn{8}{c}{Class at 35} |
	I–II	III	IVab	IVcd	V–VI	VIIa	VIIb	Total
I–II	63	3	1	1	1	0	70	
III	37	51	14	5	14	25	1	147
IVab	1	0	5	1	1	1	0	9
IVcd	0	1	0	18	0	0	0	19
V–VI	10	6	29	6	101	35	5	192
VIIa	15	22	26	10	65	145	11	294
VIIb	8	16	24	186	40	139	223	635
Total	134	99	99	227	222	346	240	1366

Table 2. All class spells by class of spell and outcome.[a]

				Destination				
Class of spell	I–II	III	IVab	IVcd	V–VI	VIIa	VIIb	Total
I–II	126	20	13	2	5	8	0	174
III	66	68	21	8	33	82	15	293
IVab	7	1	77	4	20	33	12	154
IVcd	1	1	0	213	1	15	8	239
V–VI	33	22	66	10	160	173	29	493
VIIa	20	98	60	38	230	254	175	874
VIIb	8	24	30	267	62	366	92	849
Total	261	234	267	542	511	931	331	3076

[a] Censored spells are on the diagonal.

recruits mainly from the industrial and agricultural labouring classes (VIIa and VIIb).

However, this picture is exclusively in terms of a two-point life-time trajectory, and says nothing about what happens in between. Table 2 lists all class episodes, or 'spells', experienced by respondents during their careers to age 35,[3] and gives us a different perspective. Possibly the strongest feature of the comparison is the 'absorbing' nature of farming: though very few persons enter it as a first class, those who enter it at any stage are highly unlikely ever to leave it. Conversely, it can be seen that the urban petty bourgeoisie is not so retentive, showing quite substantial flows to and from the working classes (V, VI, VIIa and VIIb), and from the routine non-manual class. The service class still appears quite retentive, though with 28 per cent of spells in the service class ending in transition to other classes, not as retentive as the first–last table suggests. The working classes, too, show increased mobility, though interestingly the increase is mostly in short-range moves.

There are, as noted, two problems with the first–last table. As well as being blind to the possibility of multi-stage careers, it is very sensitive to the distribution of entry class—that is, it is distorted by the fact that certain classes are disproportionately unlikely to be entered as first classes, with the result that their patterns of retentiveness and association with other classes are not well reflected in the table. Conversely, there are also problems with the table of episodes. It fails to distinguish between long and short spells, giving twenty years in a class the same weight as a month, and it loses sight of the sequential nature of mobility, the importance of

[3] Censored spells (i.e. those still going at age 35 and thereby having no observed destination) are presented on the diagonal.

the trajectory of the whole career. However, since their failings are to some extent complementary, to consider the two tables together adds to our understanding.

To see evidence of historical change, we now look at changes in class distributions across cohorts. Table 3 below summarises the last-class distribution over the six cohorts. There is very little unbroken trending. We see uneven growth in the three white-collar classes, and in the higher manual classes (V and VI), also to some degree in the urban petty bourgeoisie, while there is decline in agricultural labour.[4] Table 4 shows how class of entry changes across cohort. Very small numbers of jobs begin

Table 3. Class at 35 by cohort.

	Class at 35							
Cohort born	I–II	III	IVab	IVcd	V–VI	VIIa	VIIb	Total
before Sept 1913	9	9	8	31	34	55	66	213
Oct 1913–Sept 1918	22	15	13	48	30	57	51	236
Oct 1918–Sept 1923	14	15	20	36	30	70	39	224
Oct 1923–Sept 1928	26	22	16	37	41	60	41	243
Oct 1928–Sept 1933	23	18	23	47	35	58	20	224
Oct 1933–Sept 1938	40	20	19	28	52	45	23	227
Total	134	99	99	227	222	346	240	1366

Table 4. Entry class by cohort.

	Entry class							
Cohort born	I–II	III	IVab	IVcd	V–VI	VIIa	VIIb	Total
before Sept 1913	5	10	0	5	30	42	121	213
Oct 1913–Sept 1918	16	23	2	4	26	35	130	236
Oct 1918–Sept 1923	6	16	2	1	32	49	118	224
Oct 1923–Sept 1928	14	26	1	2	32	59	109	243
Oct 1928–Sept 1933	13	33	1	5	29	64	79	224
Oct 1933–Sept 1938	16	39	3	2	43	45	79	227
Total	70	147	9	19	192	294	635	1366

[4] Interestingly, there is no real evidence in these figures of a decline in farming. This is partly due to the facts that most of the decline in agricultural employment was among agricultural labourers, and that some farmers subsidise their farming by a second job, or are subsidised by the state; but it might also reflect a lowering of the age of inheritance—perhaps a greater proportion of those who are going to inherit have done so by age 35 in the later cohorts than in the earlier, and this masks a decline in the number of people who ever become farmers.

in Class I and II, though there is some evidence of an upwards trend. Entry to the labour market through Classes III, and to a lesser extent, V–VI and VIIa increases across the cohorts, though not monotonically.

Two simple measures of mobility during the work life are recorded in Tables 5 and 6: the distribution of episodes across cohorts by the class in which they occurred, and the average number of episodes experienced, shown in relation to class at 35 and cohort. While the absolute numbers of spells show some trends—increases in the service class, the routine non-manual class and the skilled working class, declines in agricultural labour—they do not diverge greatly from the trends in class size. On the other hand, the average number of spells experienced by members of each class at 35 shows few trends, with the exception of an increase for the service class.

From Tables 3 to 6, we can thus see trends in class distributions—notably the growth in the white collar classes and the supervisory and skilled working classes—and also the general pattern of mobility between classes. We can also see how this mobility differs, depending on whether we view

Table 5.   Class spells by class of spell and cohort.

	Class of spell							
Cohort born	I–II	III	IVab	IVcd	V–VI	VIIa	VIIb	Total
before Sept 1913	9	21	16	32	65	131	161	435
Oct 1913–Sept 1918	25	44	31	52	66	143	182	543
Oct 1918–Sept 1923	19	37	27	38	83	142	145	490
Oct 1923–Sept 1928	34	59	26	38	93	170	148	568
Oct 1928–Sept 1933	40	65	28	49	77	159	112	530
Oct 1933–Sept 1938	48	67	26	30	109	131	101	512
Total	175	293	154	239	493	875	849	3078

Table 6.   Average number of spells ever experienced by class at 35 and cohort.

	Class at 35							
Cohort born	I–II	III	IVab	IVcd	V–VI	VIIa	VIIb	Total
before Sept 1913	1.6	1.9	2.8	2.8	2.0	2.4	1.5	2.1
Oct 1913–Sept 1918	1.6	2.5	3.8	2.4	2.5	2.9	1.8	2.4
Oct 1918–Sept 1923	2.8	2.6	2.6	2.6	1.8	2.6	1.6	2.2
Oct 1923–Sept 1928	2.2	2.0	3.1	2.8	2.6	2.5	1.6	2.4
Oct 1928–Sept 1933	2.3	2.4	2.8	2.8	2.7	2.2	1.9	2.4
Oct 1933–Sept 1938	2.1	2.2	2.7	2.4	2.5	2.6	1.5	2.3
Total	2.0	2.3	2.9	2.6	2.4	2.5	1.6	2.3

it from the perspective of the first–last trajectory, or from that of the cumulated moves made during work life. But it is difficult to deal with more complex relationships than these, other than in an intuitive rather than an analytical way. We cannot tell, for instance, if the pattern of association between classes changes across time, nor properly understand how the pattern of class spells relates to life-time trajectories, nor how that relationship changes across time. For this, formal modelling has to be resorted to, which is introduced in the next section.

Modelling Trends in Life-Time Mobility in Ireland

The analytical exercise that follows is essentially simple in nature. In brief, I have created two tables from the data: (i) the 'first–last table', representing the relationship between class of entry and mature class position, for each of three pairs of the initial six birth cohorts; and (ii) the 'cumulated spells table', classifying, again by cohort, every class spell experienced by each respondent by the class in which it took place and the outcome of the spell—that is, the class to which the respondent moved at the end of that spell, or remained in until the cut-off point at age 35.[5] I then apply a series of loglinear models to these tables in order, first, to identify patterns of association between classes independently of the absolute distributions; and then to identify change in these patterns of association, if any can be found.

With both tables the same technique is used to search for historical change: the sample is divided into cohorts, discarding any cohorts whose youngest member had not achieved the age of 35 at interview, and discarding any information about individuals' histories after age 35. This gives comparable information on cohort members' complete careers up to age 35 and, at the expense of throwing away data, avoids problems of cohorts having different ranges of experience.

Because of sparsity in the data, models are presented using a three cohort scheme, rather than the six cohorts represented in Figure 1. This

---

[5] The analysis of tables of counts of class spells or of transitions between classes has been used in several contexts over the past few years. It has notably been advocated for the study of social mobilty by Featherman and Selbee (1988). However, my approach differs from theirs, and I would argue that it is an improvement in terms of interpretability. The critical difference is that I tabulate all *spells*, which includes spells not finished at the time of observation, whereas they tabulate only *transitions*, thereby excluding such censored spells, together with the awkward inclusion in cells on the main diagonal of the spells of those respondents who were still in their first episode at the time of observation and therefore had had no transition. This makes their table difficult to interpret, and the inclusion of all spells, censored or otherwise, avoids this problem.

reduces the historical resolution but means that any trends found are relatively long term and robust. The cohorts are (i) those born before September 1918, (ii) those born thereafter and before September 1928, and (iii) those born after that and before September 1938. A three-cohort set-up is easy to handle, and the larger numbers in the cells of the table mean that the modelling is more efficient, but there are problems: three cohorts allow only two consecutive contrasts, and the cohorts contain persons up to ten years apart in age, and thus cover a wide range of historical experience. It will therefore be hard to pick up detailed historical change, but any changes which emerge will be of a more enduring kind.

Given that the two sets of data are organised in tables of similar structure, the same set of models can be applied to them to search for trends. In order to test for change in the patterns of association between classes, I use the following approach. First, I fit a model which takes account of the changing distributions of class origins and destinations[6] across cohorts, and assumes that the pattern of association between classes does not change across cohorts. This can be referred to as the 'no-trend' model. Then I fit a similar model with the addition of terms which allow the associations between each possible pair of classes to change in a constant fashion across cohorts. This can be called the 'constant-trend' model. In this model, individual elements of the association, the flow from class x to class y, can be declining or increasing, but the change will be proportionately constant across each adjacent pair of cohorts.

In loglinear modelling terms, the no-trend model includes all the two-way interactions in the tables,[7] which is to say it assumes that all the information or pattern in the data is contained in the distributions of origins and destinations, how these change across cohorts, and how origins and destinations relate to each other, irrespective of differences across cohorts. The 'fit' of the model is a measure of how well a table generated under these assumptions replicates the observed values.[8]

The no-trend model can be written as

$$\text{Log } F_{ijk} = \lambda + \lambda^O + \lambda^D + \lambda^C + \lambda^{OD} + \lambda^{OC} + \lambda^{OC} + \lambda^{DC}$$

[6] The terms origin and destination are used here for simplicity, and mean respectively the class in which a spell takes place and the new class, a move to which ends the spell. Alternatives such as 'class of spell' and 'transition class' are too clumsy.

[7] In terms of the GLIM program which I use, the model is, Origin*Destination + Origin*Cohort + Destination*Cohort.

[8] The fit is expressed as the relationship between the deviance (a measure of the difference between the observed and predicted values) and the degrees of freedom, which are inversely related to the complexity of the model. It is necessary to take both into account because it is generally possible—but not always useful—to reduce the deviance by adding extra elements to the model.

The constant trend model then is

$$\text{Log } F_{ijk} = \lambda + \lambda^O + \lambda^D + \lambda^C + \lambda^{OD} + \lambda^{DC} + \beta^{OD}T$$
$$T = 1, 2, 3$$

where F_{ijk} is the expected frequency in the ijk-th cell. As can be seen, the constant-trend model is closely related to the no-trend model, differing only in the addition of a term taking account of change across cohorts in the relationship between origin and destination. For each origin–destination pair, it estimates the parameter, β^{OD}, where β^{OD}.T measures the changing association across cohorts, and T is a continuous variable having the same values as the cohort variable (i.e. T = 1 for cohort 1, etc.).[9] That is, it adds to the no-trend model the assumption that the association between each origin–destination pair will deviate from the base pattern of association by an amount which increases by a fixed proportion from cohort to cohort, in fact one that is linear in the logs (cf. Payne, Payne and Heath, 1991).

Table 7 reports the model search process for both the first-last table and the cumulated spells table. With both tables, we find a big reduction in G^2 with the introduction of the constant-trend variable. However, when the change in degrees of freedom is taken into account, the reduction is significant only for the cumulated spells table.[10] Thus, it can be said that there is evidence for change in the patterns of association between classes in terms of the movements of men during the work life, but not in the patterns of association between first class and last class.

The constant-trend model fits the cumulated spells table well, but it may be overly restrictive. Specifically, the assumption that the trending

Table 7. Model fit statistics.

	Cumulated spells table		First–last table	
	G^2	df	G^2	df
No trend	125.85	72	69.77	72
Constant trend	40.35	36	25.56	36
−Improvement	85.51	36	44.21	36
Significance of improvement	p<0.0001		p=0.164	

[9] In GLIM terms, the constant trend model adds Origin*Destination*T to the no-trend model, where T has the same values as Cohort but has not been declared a factor (i.e. a categorical variable).

[10] The probability figure given for the improvement achieved by the constant trend model represents the probability of the reduction in G^2 occurring by chance (the lower the probability, the more likely the improvement is real).

change in association between classes can be modelled by a proportionately constant increase can be challenged. The pace of the trend might change over time or the trend might be subject to occasional temporary reverses. If this is the case, the assumption of the model that change is proportionately constant will not reflect reality accurately. To deal with this, a third model can be fitted, which, instead of taking a linear set of values for the trend variable (i.e., T = 1, 2, 3, etc.), uses an iterative procedure to estimate the best values. This is akin to saying that while the constant-trend model places the cohorts at equally spaced intervals on an underlying continuum of change, the 'estimated-trend' model searches, rather, for the best places to position each cohort. The estimated-trend model is a version of Goodman's log-multiplicative model (Goodman, 1984: 203–222), and is more complicated than that of constant trend. However, it is conceptually close to the latter, in that it searches for the set of values for the T variable which make for the best fit. In other words, the constant-trend model can be viewed as a special case of the estimated-trend model, where the trend variable is constrained to 1, 2, 3, etc.

One problem that arises is how to choose between the constant-trend and the estimated-trend models. Although they are not actually hierarchically related, the solution that will have to be taken up[11] is to treat them as if they were so related, and to take the difference in G^2 as distributed as χ^2 with k-2 degrees of freedom, where k is the number of levels of the trend variable.

The estimated-trend model was fitted to both tables, and while in the case of the cumulated spells table, it did improve significantly over the no-trend model it did not do so over the constant-trend model. This suggests that, at least on the basis of cohorts, trends are constant in proportional terms. However, this may be due to the small number of contrasts available, so models were also estimated using the initial six cohorts. These did show an improvement in fit achieved by the estimated-trend model for the cumulated spells table. Results are not presented here because the data were relatively sparse and the modelling therefore less reliable, but the indication is that on closer examination the trend in the cumulative spells table may not be a straight line. Most notably, a significant reversal of trend is shown up in the final cohort, which could be speculatively attributed to the fact that the early part of this cohort's work history falls in the depression of the 1950s.

---

[11] Personal communication from Sir David Cox.

Table 8. Trends in work-life mobility identified by comparing fitted no-trend values with observed values.[a]

Class of spell	Destination						
	I–II	III	IVab	IVcd	V–VI	VIIa	VIIb
I–II	−[b]	+	+		+	+	
III		−		+			+
IVab			+				−
IVcd							
V–VI				+			+
VIIa	+				−	+	−
VIIb							

[a] Censored spells are treated as transitions to the same class.
[b] − implies a decreasing tend, + an increasing trend, and a blank means no clear trend.

Looking at the Change in the Cumulated Spells Table

Given that the modelling tells us that the pattern of association between class positions during worklife is changing, it is then of interest to determine exactly what sorts of changes are actually happening. An obvious approach seems to be to look at the parameters of the constant-trend model; but these are not completely determinate, as they are structured as the interaction between two dummy variables and vary substantially if the null categories are changed. However, given that the constant-trend model fits better than the no-trend model, we can compare the fitted or predicted values under the no-trend model with the actual values. The trends we can see there in the residuals (the differences between the observed and fitted values), to the extent that any are apparent, are precisely what is picked up by the trend model.

The simplest strategy is to choose those origin–destination pairs whose residuals have a consistent pattern: that is, pick out those pairs for which the difference between the observed and the fitted values either rises or falls consistently over the three cohorts, and to exclude those whose residuals have a V-shaped (or inverted V-shaped) course.[12] The pattern of trends thus established is presented in Table 8.

[12] This is simple in the 3-cohort case, but becomes more complicated if a cohort variable with more values is used. Even in this case, though, we could discount cases where intermediate figures are very close to either the first or the last, though outside their range and therefore do not present a monotonic progression; and we could take account of the size of trends, and ignore particularly small movements. In fact, neither adjustment makes a large difference to the picture reported in the text.

Sixteen of the forty nine class pairs in the table show a systematic pattern in the residuals under the no-trend model.[13] A reading of 'increase' means that the difference between the observed and the fitted values gets greater over the three cohorts—the model over-predicts the earlier, and under-predicts the later values. That is, an increase presumes

$$R_1 < R_2 < R_3, \text{ where } R = \text{Observed} - \text{Fitted}$$

Thus, an increase means that flows from the origin to the destination class are growing across cohorts, allowing for changes in the sizes of these classes. An alternative way of saying this is that the 'propensity for mobility' from the origin to the destination class has increased.

Looking for patterns in residuals is often useful, but the fit of models based on such examination is statistically suspect—the data suggest the model which is then tested against the same data. However, in this case, since it is first found that the relationship exists, and only then are the residuals that go (in part) to make it up examined, I can claim to be innocent of data-dredging. What it is legitimate to do here is to fit a model based purely on the residuals, just to see how much of the improvement of the constant trend model relative to the no-trend model is represented by the sixteen specific trends noted. To do this I created a categorical variable set equal to 1 for any row-column combination which does not show a trend, to 2 for any combination trending upwards and to 3 for any combination trending downwards. I then fitted the no-trend model with the addition of this new factor, interacting with the cohort variable. This improves the fit substantially, and if the new model is compared with the constant-trend model, the latter is not found to be clearly better—showing that a significant amount of the explanatory power of the constant-trend model resides in the sixteen trends identified.

Interpreting the Trends

When we look at Table 8 we see some interesting patterns. Notable is the fall in the retentiveness[14] of the white collar classes (that is, the service

---

[13] Of these, twelve are robust to the extent of also appearing in the model in which censored spells are treated separately, rather than as transitions to the same class as here. Treating them as transitions to the same class involves regarding a class's retentiveness as closely related to its attractive power, which is why it is favoured here.

[14] The retentiveness of a class, or its ability to hold on to its members, shows up in this data only as censoring. A censored spell is one which was still going on at the cut-off point of age 35, and thus one which does not have a destination, since no transition is recorded. To deal with counts of spells we lose information on their length, and can only distinguish retentiveness as the absence of a transition. In the modelling these are treated as transitions to the same class, and are presented on the diagonal.

classes, I and II, and the routine non-manual class, III). The service class, especially, used to consist of extremely secure positions, but this is less the case in the later cohorts. Associated with this lower—though still relatively high—retentiveness of the service class are increased propensities for mobility from the service class to all other classes except the two agricultural classes; while in contrast there are increased propensities for mobility from the routine non-manual class to the agricultural classes. The only change in the picture from the point of view of recruitment is the increased inflow to the service class from the semi- and unskilled working class.

In the case of the petty bourgeoisie we see greater retentivness, and increased inflows from the service class. There is also a significant drop in the propensity for mobility to agricultural labour.

The two agricultural classes show no patterns in items of exits, but share in new patterns of recruitment, with increased flows from the routine non-manual class, and the skilled and supervisory working class, and declines in flows from the non-skilled working class.

Finally, when we look at the working classes, we see an increased propensity for mobility from the non-skilled class to the service class (and, if we slightly loosen our definition of trend,[15] also to the routine non-manual class). Flows from the skilled class to both the agricultural classes increase, while those from the less skilled decline. There is also an increase in flow from the non-skilled to the skilled working class.

Can the Trends be Interpreted Historically?

Is it justifiable to treat the three cohorts as proxies for distinct phases of history? The first of the three cohorts can be characterised as pre-war/war, the second as war/post-war/1950s, and the third as 1950s-slump/1960s-recovery. Because these are very broad cohorts, our ability to relate change in behaviour to specific historical events is compromised. But their historical experiences are still sufficiently distinct for us to expect significant differences in mobility between them. The first cohort will have worked through what was a generally austere and isolationist period, the second through more varied times of both growth and recession, and the third has had an experience the others have not, of relatively sustained growth, though also enduring initially a very significant period of depression and emigration. (It would be extremely interesting to have data on

[15] By allowing the middle value to be outside the range of that of the first and last cohorts, but within ten per cent of one of them.

one more cohort, to test the hunch that where men enter the labour market in a time of growth, rather more distinct changes in patterns of mobility will result).

Apart from this periodisation, certain underlying trends have been more or less steadily at work, and in respect of these the cohorts can be regarded as being positioned on a continuum. The main trend is the decline in employment in agriculture, which Census figures show to be steady throughout most of the century and to accelerate after 1946. The second trend, but one that is not as steady or as long-term as the agricultural decline, is the growth in white-collar classes and in the skilled and supervisory working class. Thus, it is generally valid to treat differences between the cohorts partly as reflecting different (broad) periods in Irish social history, and partly as consecutive stages on various continua of development.

In sum, we can regard the younger cohort(s) as in general experiencing more economic growth, more exposure to foreign influences (cultural as well as economic), a higher level of industrialisation with concomitant growth in manufacturing and white-collar occupations and a decline in agricultural occupations, somewhat greater urbanisation, and a higher level of education (although the data miss the effect of the 1967 expansion in free education, there is some evidence of growth before). What we can then say on the basis of the present analysis is that, concurrent with these trends and changes, we have evidence of changes in the patterns of association between classes during the work life.

What Does it Mean?

The cumulated spells table shows many changes but it picks up a few centrally important processes. Two in particular are worth considering more closely. First is the growth in white collar occupations and the penetration of their influence throughout much of the society. Second is the broadening range of experience of those entering the agricultural classes.

Perhaps the most striking set of effects here is the broadening of the associations of the white-collar classes, with their drop in retentiveness and increased outflows to a range of other classes. Indeed, between them they show increased mobility propensities to *all* other classes. This suggests that the nature of the service class and of the routine non-manual class is changing. Examination of the raw data shows that while the service class used to be very small, very exclusive and very secure, as it grows it becomes increasingly less selective, and less retentive. This may be because the 'old' service class and the 'new' service class comprise very different distributions of occupations—formerly, mainly the professions, small in number and well established; latterly, many more bureaucratic positions where contingency or the career structure exposes more people to the probability of changing class. In the earlier periods, members of the service class would largely have been doctors, lawyers, teachers and so on; they would have enjoyed great security, and had little desire or opportunity to change occupations. But the growth of the class was mainly due to growth in other types of occupation, notably in management and administration in industry, commerce and government. While still relatively secure, these occupations expose their incumbents to a slightly greater hazard or opportunity of changing to an occupation in a different class, especially, we can speculate, on a temporary basis. Thus, for instance, a junior manager (Class II) may switch to a supervisory post on the factory floor (Class V) in the expectation that the experience might fit him for a more senior managerial position (Class I).

The patterns of entry into the two agricultural classes also show interesting trends. Both classes show the same increase in inflows from routine non-manual work and from skilled working class positions, and decreased inflows from the non-skilled working class. Given that the overwhelming majority of men entering farming are farmers' sons, and that many agricultural labourers are also farmers' sons waiting to inherit (increasingly so in later cohorts, with the mechanisation of farming), we can interpret this changed inflow pattern as evidence of new kinds of activity on the part of farmers' sons before they come into their inheritance. It is interesting that the pattern leans towards greater involvement in both the routine non-manual class and the skilled rather than the non-skilled working class. This suggests that farm children, who tend to have slightly more than average education, may have a certain advantage in acquiring positions which require some form of certification. And the fact that farmers' sons spend time in the routine non-manual class suggests that they are being exposed to the probability of much wider mobility, given the nature of routine non-manual work as a kind of class crossroads.

Such an educational advantage on the part of farmers' sons could be seen as evidence of the process identified by Breen *et al.* (1990), of a move from a society based on property to one based on educational qualifications, but in which the classes with property-based advantages in the past manage to retain their advantage under the new conditions by adopting new strategies. We also see evidence of the other proprietorial class, the petty bourgeoisie, improving its situation, with greater retentiveness and a closer relationship with the service class. Counter-evidence for this advantage-retention thesis exists insofar as the non-skilled working class also enjoy increased flows to and from the service class, although, if it were possible to make the distinction, I would not expect this favourable access to apply to the particularly low-skilled urban working class, whom Breen *et al.* identify as being especially disadvantaged in modern Ireland.

To put the foregoing into perspective, it must be repeated that these trends in question are visible only in the cumulated spells table, and not in the overall first–last transition, nor yet in the intergenerational pattern of mobility. Furthermore, they are based on a blunt, three-cohort comparison. But the trends are nonetheless real, and show changes in the way social mobility works that are significant, and that may underlie subsequent change in more general aspects of social mobility. They also show evidence of people adapting to new situations by new strategies and of change at the level of the year-to-year processes of social mobility, even if, as yet, no change in the intragenerational, nor yet intergenerational, outcomes is apparent.

Conclusion

In the short run, while many things change in the course of industrialisation—the actual distribution of class positions, the economy, education and its role in formal recruitment, etc.—the relative desirability and the relative advantages of various class positions do not alter quickly, barring fundamental social upheaval. Thus, long term aims, and the less intentional consequences of established practices, will tend to bring about the same sorts of mobility outcomes as before. When general conditions change the immediate opportunities and short term pressures for mobility will also change—for instance, a farmer's son may take a clerical job in an office while he waits to inherit, whereas before he would not have had the right qualifications and the job would not have existed locally. Nevertheless, we may still expect that, in time, the older power of property will draw him back to the established intergenerational route.

At the same time, in this ephemeral change may lie the promise of more fundamental alteration. To continue with the same example, as farmers' sons get used to the idea of working off the land, even temporarily, the attractions of, and familiarity with, urban life are likely to weaken the power of property. Poorer farms will tend to be abandoned because they cannot compete, whereas, previously, the moral value placed on the land and on the rural lifestyle would have outweighed its relative poverty. That is, when new conditions obtain, the initial push for change will be at the level of immediate opportunities and pressures, but people will attempt to adapt to the conditions in the light of their longer-term expectations and strategies. Thus, we can have a new pattern of work-life mobility that results in the same first–last outcome, or new patterns of origin-first and first-last mobility that result in the same intergenerational mobility regime. However, there is the possibility that short-term change can begin to change the general topology of class mobility by establishing new routes, if initially only on a short-term basis; it can bring certain classes nearer together and push others farther apart, with the result that, in the long run, the context within which first–last and intergenerational mobility operates is itself reshaped.

I would suggest that such processes are what the present analysis reveals. A different sort of research is needed to examine the mechanics of these processes—to investigate the strategies employed by families to retain advantage when its basis changes and to understand the conditions under which change of this order will bring about change of a more long-term kind. But with the techniques used here it has been shown that while structural change can leave the patterns of intergenerational and first-last mobility apparently unaltered, it is nevertheless possible for patterns of mobility during the work-life to change independently. The analysis shows us that some people took new routes through their work lives as the Republic of Ireland industrialised. But in the period up to 1973, these tended to be different routes to the same sort of place; or, if to different places, were few enough in number not to make a perceptible difference to the final intragenerational outcomes.

Acknowledgements. This paper has benefited greatly from the comments and suggestions of a number of people, notably those of Richard Breen, Sir David Cox, John Goldthorpe, Crispin Jenkinson, Pat McGovern, Clive Payne, Bill Roche and Chris Whelan.

Proceedings of the British Academy, **79**, 173–203

Income Distribution and Redistribution: Ireland in Comparative Perspective

TIM CALLAN & BRIAN NOLAN

Economic and Social Research Institute, Dublin

Introduction

TWO VIEWS of the distribution and redistribution of income in Ireland may be discerned. The first sees Ireland as a particularly unequal society, with state policy doing little to counteract inequalities arising from market and property incomes; a view reflected in the recent synthesis of Breen *et al.* (1990).[1] The second sees the Irish labour market as suffering from an excessively redistributionist policy which imposes high taxes on work and provides high replacement incomes to those not at work. In this paper we seek to shed some light on these contrasting views.

Our focus is broader in some respects, and narrower in others, than that adopted by proponents of these two different views. It is broader, in that it puts the Irish income distribution and the redistributive process firmly into an international comparative perspective; and that it pays particular attention to the debate on the effects of economic development on income distribution. As in most studies of income distribution, our focus is on the way in which incomes from the market are redistributed through direct and indirect taxes, cash transfers and non-cash benefits. Proponents of each of the views outlined above have also argued, in different ways, that state intervention affects the distribution of market incomes themselves; these wider effects of state intervention are outside the scope of the present paper.

Read 8 December 1990. © The British Academy 1992.

[1] Breen *et al.* argue that 'the benefits of Ireland's economic development have been very unevenly distributed' (1990: x) and that 'Despite the enormously bloated role of the state as an economic intermediary, it has been monumentally unsuccessful either in ensuring sustained economic growth or in moderating inegalitarian tendencies in the class system' (1990: 209).

We begin by briefly reviewing the debate on the relationship between economic development and inequality, noting in particular some of the more recent evidence. We then turn to the empirical evidence on the distribution and redistribution of income. Research in this area has been hampered by the lack of truly comparable cross-country data. A recent paper by O'Higgins, Schmaus and Stephenson (1989) has, however, provided a set of baseline measures of inequality based on the most comparable data now available: the micro-datasets assembled by the Luxembourg Income Study (LIS). We use data from the ESRI Survey of Income Distribution, Poverty and State Services to construct comparable measures of the distribution of cash incomes for Ireland. Since all but one of the countries considered by O'Higgins *et al.* is at a higher level of economic development than Ireland, we supplement this material with available statistics on other countries at similar or somewhat lower levels of real income. We also use the available LIS-based statistics on redistribution of cash incomes, together with some more detailed material for Ireland and the UK. As far as non-cash benefits are concerned, we concentrate primarily on the Irish and UK situations, for which comparable analyses based on household expenditure surveys are available. The implications of the differences in net income distributions for relative poverty are then explored. Finally, we draw together the main findings.

Economic Development and Income Distribution

Does the process of economic development itself have a major impact on the distribution of income? Or are international differences in income distribution to be explained mainly by factors other than the level of development? These questions have been the subject of considerable controversy. Here we review briefly the main lines of the literature on the relationship between development and income distribution, before assessing the current Irish income distribution in the light of differing theories.

The starting point for any review of this topic must be what has become known as the Kuznets hypothesis (Kuznets, 1955): that inequality increases as countries move from the lowest levels of development, but decreases in the later stages of development. The rationale for this 'inverted-U curve' is that at the lowest levels of development limited economic opportunities lead to low levels of inequality. As the process of development gets under way, economic opportunities are unevenly distributed (for example, between a subsistence and a market sector, and perhaps between regions within countries), leading to an increase in inequality. Later in the development process economic opportunities become more widely spread (for example, as the subsistence sector shrinks and is absorbed in to the market economy). This was the kernel of Kuznets' argument.

The Kuznets hypothesis has been subjected to extensive empirical investigation. Most studies have been based on cross-section comparisons of countries at different levels of development, and have been treated as broadly confirming the main thrust of the hypothesis. Some recent studies have, however, called these results into question. Here we summarise these early and later studies, before drawing out the implications for a study of the Irish income distribution.

Simple cross-sectional comparisons, such as that by Paukert (1973), were found to confirm the Kuznets hypothesis: on average, the Gini coefficient was about 0.42 for the least developed countries, rising to an average of 0.50 for a substantial group of developing countries, and falling to 0.40 or below for the most developed countries in Paukert's sample. Cross-sectional regression analyses which took into account some other influences on inequality (e.g., Ahluwalia, 1974, which focused in particular on the income share of the bottom 40 per cent of the population) were also found to support the hypothesis of an inverted-U relationship between development and inequality. Ahluwalia noted, however, that this should not be regarded as an 'iron law' of development.[2]

These empirical findings supporting the Kuznets hypothesis have recently been questioned on two main grounds. First, it has been argued that the inverted-U shape relationship estimated in cross-sectional regressions may be the product of an inappropriate functional form. Anand and Kanbur (1986) explored the relationship between inequality and development using a variety of functional forms, each of which would allow either a U-shaped or inverted-U shaped relationship, depending on the estimated parameters. For a subset of Ahluwalia's data for which the income concept and recipient unit were held constant, they found that the best fit is provided by a U-shaped relationship:[3] inequality first falls and then rises with income.

The second challenge to the established view has come from the work of Fields and Jakobsen (1990). They use a data-set which includes repeated measurements of inequality for some countries, and their method of analysis allows for 'fixed effects' corresponding to each country; that is, there is a common relationship between inequality and development, but

---

[2] Adelman (1975) also noted that growth with an equitable distribution was possible and had occurred.

[3] More formally, non-nested tests reject alternative specifications but cannot reject that giving rise to a U-shaped relationship.

it may be shifted up or down by a constant for each country. They find that the inverted-U shape does not hold if the data is analysed in this way:[4] the relationship may be either U-shaped or monotonically decreasing with per capita income, depending on the measures of income used. When Fields and Jakobsen revert to the standard approach, treating the 'panel' data as a cross-section, it yields the familiar inverted U-shape. Fields and Jakobsen explain these cross-sectional findings as reflecting the fact that Latin American countries have high levels of inequality, but levels of income intermediate between those of Asia and the OECD. Their explanation for the change in shape is, however, less convincing:

> A look at the underlying data shows the reason for the change in shape. For five of [six selected countries] . . . inequality fell and then rose. By contrast, in Brazil, we see the more familiar inverted-U shape. We would expect that a family of parallel curves fit to these six countries would also be U-shaped

But there are many other countries in the sample which show rising inequality as they move from low levels of development, some of which also show the inverted-U shape: the data do not provide as clear-cut an answer as the above quotation might suggest.

One thing which does emerge clearly from studies of the Kuznets hypothesis is the diversity of country experience. Countries at similar levels of development may have very different levels of inequality; countries which have similar levels of inequality may have very different levels of income; and countries starting from similar levels of development and with similar growth rates may experience increases or declines in measured inequality. Thus, the relationships estimated can only reflect a dominant experience and not a necessary one. (cf. Adelman and Morris, 1973; Ahluwalia, 1974).

While most of the empirical studies of the Kuznets hypothesis have included countries at high levels of development,[5] their focus has typically been on what countries at low or middle levels of income, by world standards, can expect as the income distribution consequences of economic growth. Rather less attention has been paid to what may be expected at somewhat higher levels of development. How applicable is the basic Kuznets thesis to countries such as Ireland? Broadly speaking, small farming could be identified with the low-income sector in the Kuznets-type model. Given the proportion of population engaged in that sector in recent decades, Ireland might be expected to have experienced declines in

---

[4] This result holds for either of the main functional forms (quadratic in levels of per capita income, or quadratic in logs of per capita income) examined by Anand and Kanbur.

[5] Some have also re-estimated their results, excluding more developed countries.

inequality from the flow of population from small farming. Alternatively, one could view the broader farming sector as having relatively more unequal incomes, so shrinkage in this sector, even in a way which left a constant differential between farm and non-farm sectors, would also contribute to inequality reduction. In short, the secular decline in agriculture may be associated with declining inequality within the sector and/or between it and the non-farm sector. The empirical studies, with the exceptions noted above, suggest an inverted-U curve: Ireland's income per capita places it well above the turning point on such a relationship. Thus, countries somewhat below Ireland's level of development would be expected to have more inequality, while more advanced economies would be expected to have less inequality. If welfare state intervention is positively related to levels of per capita income, this would also suggest a similar pattern. Level of development is not, however, the only influence on the extent of welfare state intervention, which may therefore be regarded as an index for some independent influences. If Ireland's welfare state is more extensive than would be expected for its level of development,[6] one would expect this to be reflected in income distribution statistics.

Income Distribution

Methodological considerations

Cross-country comparisons of income distribution are bedevilled by problems of comparability. Is the income recipient unit the individual or the household? Is household income adjusted for differences in the size of household, and if so, how? Is income measured before or after deduction of income taxes? Over what period is income measured? Published national studies rarely tally on all of these counts, making international comparisons extremely difficult. It was largely in order to circumvent such difficulties that a group of researchers began the collation of an international data-base, harmonised to the greatest extent possible in terms of variable definitions and coverage, known as the Luxembourg Income Study. In recent years, a number of analyses using these data have appeared, including a baseline study of income distribution by O'Higgins, Schmaus and Stephenson (1989).

O'Higgins et al. identify four major methodological issues for income

---

[6] See the interchange between Geary (1973), O'Hagan and O'Higgins (1973) and Walsh (1974); and the paper by O'Connell and Rottman in this volume.

distribution studies. The first is the choice of income concept—gross as against net cash income, or as against 'direct' or 'market' income.[7] Each of the income concepts tells us about different aspects of the income distribution: comparison of market incomes with gross incomes tells us about the impact of cash transfers, while comparison of gross with net incomes tells us about the impact of the tax system. Thus, each of these concepts will be examined.

The second methodological choice is whether the income of families of different sizes is to be compared directly, without adjustment, or is to be adjusted for size by some 'equivalence scale' intended to take differences in needs into account.[8] Many national studies simply publish information on the distribution of family income without adjustment for size, but the distribution of income per equivalent adult[9] is often thought to provide a better measure of the distribution of economic welfare. Both methods were applied in the LIS-based study and will be applied here. The equivalence scale used by O'Higgins *et al.* was 1 for the first household member, 0.5 for all others, and 6 for households of 10 or more.

Most studies assume complete income sharing within families. But a choice still arises between using the family or the individual as the unit of analysis. O'Higgins *et al.* refer to this as the choice of 'weighting of income units'. Does each family count as one unit, or as N units, when there are N persons in the family?[10] Each formulation has its merits. We may be interested in the distribution of equivalent income across families; but we may also be interested in how many people are affected by the differences in equivalent income, in which case an individual unit of analysis is preferable.

In general, income distribution analysis measures the distribution of a particular income concept over units ranked by that same income concept. But O'Higgins *et al.* note that it is possible to break this link. In particular, they note that it may be of interest to ask questions such as what percentage of total family income goes to the poorest 20 per cent of individuals ranked by total family income. This can be answered by

[7] Broader income concepts might also take into account non-cash benefits or indirect taxes; but for the moment we concentrate on cash income concepts.

[8] For example, a two-adult household can benefit from economies of scale in terms of housing, heating, and cooking, while a child's needs would typically be less than those of an adult. This could be represented by an equivalence scale such as 1 for the first adult, 0.6 for other adults, and 0.4 for children.

[9] Henceforth referred to as equivalent income—what the Institute for Fiscal Studies calls 'equivalised' income. It is arrived at by simply dividing total income by the number of 'adult equivalents' in the household.

[10] In other words, the issue is to whether to attribute a weight of one for each family, or attribute a weight of one to each person.

analysing the distribution of per capita income over individuals ranked by total family income (without adjustment for size differences).

While in principle various combinations of choices regarding equivalence scale (including the possibility of no adjustment for size), unit of analysis, and rank ordering are possible, several of these can be ruled out as inconsistent. O'Higgins et al. concentrate on three combinations: the distribution of unadjusted family income over families ranked by unadjusted family income, the distribution of equivalent income over persons ranked by equivalent income, and the distribution of per capita income over persons ranked by family income.

Data

Details of the LIS data-set may be found in Smeeding and Schmaus (1990). Here we outline briefly some of the features most relevant to the present analysis. The surveys on which the data-set is based typically aimed at covering the population of private households, with the institutional population and the homeless being excluded. Further exclusions were made in Germany, where households headed by a foreigner were excluded; and in Israel, where rural inhabitants (living in settlements of fewer than 2,000 people) were excluded. Definitions of income sharing unit also varied. Some surveys had sufficient flexibility to be able to produce information both for households (defined by common living arrangements) and for families (persons related by blood, marriage or adoption).[11] For Germany and Israel, information could only be analysed on a household basis but only 2.4 per cent of German and 2.2 per cent of Israeli households have multiple families. Sweden and Norway have data on families defined in a slightly narrower fashion: adult children are treated as independent units. The compromise chosen by O'Higgins et al. is to undertake comparisons on a broad family unit basis where possible, since this also ties in with the household definition for Germany and Israel in almost all cases. The narrower Swedish and Norwegian units pose a problem: it should be borne in mind that their income distributions would most likely be more equal in comparisons based on broad family units.

The Irish data for this comparison of income distributions are drawn from the Survey of Income Distribution, Poverty and Usage of State Services, undertaken by the ESRI in 1987. The coverage of the survey was very similar to that of the surveys providing the LIS data-base: private households were included, but institutions and homeless people were excluded. Less than one per cent of Irish households contained more than

---

[11] One-person families are sometimes referred to as 'unrelated individuals'.

Table 1. GDP per capita in selected countries adjusted to a common purchasing power standard.

Country	Year	Index of GDP per capita[a]
Ireland	1985	46.4
Israel	1979	52.8
UK	1979	69.8
Sweden	1979	76.9
FRG	1981	84.6
Norway	1979	92.3
USA	1979	100.0
Canada	1981	100.4

[a] Percentage of US GDP per capita in 1979.
Source: Summers and Heston (1988).

one family, in the sense of persons unrelated by blood or marriage, so that Irish households can be considered as closer than their German or Israeli counterparts to the core concept of family unit in the comparisons which follow. A detailed description of the survey is given in Callan *et al.* (1989). However, it is important to note that in the present paper we use an annual income measure for the first time, in line with the practice in the LIS data-set. This was constructed by using information on participation in the labour market and receipt of social security payments over the 12 months prior to the survey.[12] It is also important to note that our annual income distributions are not directly comparable with those from earlier studies for Ireland, which are based on current income.

Empirical results

Our discussion of the Kuznets hypothesis cautioned against comparing Irish income distribution with that of other countries without taking into account differences in the level of development. Table 1, therefore, presents data on GDP per capita, adjusted to a common purchasing power standard and expressed as a percentage of US GDP per capita in 1979. It

---

[12] For a significant number of cases, however, information was only available on a current basis. For such cases annual income is treated as the annual equivalent of current income. As a result, the estimated annual income distributions reported here may tend to be slightly more unequal than the true annual income distribution. Methods of improving the estimates are under investigation. Recorded income taxes and social insurance contributions were used when available: this constituted the majority of cases. But where such information was not recorded, procedures were developed to allocate the difference between recorded net and gross pay to income taxes and social insurance contributions.

Table 2. Composition of gross and net income: average value of income source/tax as percentage of average gross income.

Income from	Canada 1981	US 1979	UK 1979	FRG 1981	Sweden 1979	Norway 1979	Israel 1979	Ireland 1987
Wages and salaries	75.7	75.8	72.0	63.1	64.5	69.9	66.1	61.9
Self-employment	5.4	6.7	4.5	16.7	3.7	11.1	16.8	15.2
Property	7.2	5.8	2.7	1.1	2.7	2.7	4.4	2.8
Factor Income	*88.3*	*88.3*	*79.3*	*80.9*	*70.8*	*83.7*	*87.3*	*79.9*
Occupational pension	1.8	2.6	2.5	2.3	0	1.2	3.4	2.9
Market Income	*90.1*	*90.8*	*81.7*	*83.3*	*70.8*	*84.9*	*90.6*	*82.8*
Child benefits	0.9	0.0	2.2	1.4	1.3	1.2	2.7	1.8
Means-tested benefits	1.4	1.3	2.1	0.6	4.4	0.3	0.4	5.7
Other cash benefits	6.7	6.8	12.9	14.5	23.6	12.7	5.3	9.5
Total cash benefits	*9.1*	*8.0*	*17.2*	*16.5*	*29.2*	*14.1*	*8.3*	*17.0*
Private transfers	0.0	0.6	1.0	0.2	0	0.8	1.0	0.1
Other cash income	0.8	0.6	0.1	0.0	0	0.1	0.0	0.0
Gross income	*100*	*100*	*100*	*100*	*100*	*100*	*100*	*100*
Income tax	15.2	16.5	13.6	14.8	28.5	19.1	23.4	15.6
Employee payroll tax	0	4.5	3.3	7.7	1.2	6.2	5.3	3.7
Net Cash Income	*84.8*	*79.0*	*83.1*	*77.5*	*70.2*	*74.7*	*71.3*	*80.7*

Sources: Ireland: ESRI Survey of Income Distribution, Poverty and Usage of State Services, 1987. other countries: O'Higgins *et al.* (1989: Table 1).

is clear that a substantial gap exists between Ireland and Israel and the more advanced countries included.

Before comparing the distributions of income, we compare in Table 2 the average composition of gross and net income in Ireland with that in the countries covered by O'Higgins *et al.*

O'Higgins *et al.* emphasise the importance of the basic distinction between gross income arising from market activities (earnings from employment and self-employment, property income and occupational pensions) and that arising from other sources, predominantly state transfers. Their data show that market income accounts for more than 90 per cent of gross income in the US, Canada and Israel, leaving only a small role for transfers. In Sweden, on the other hand, transfers account for almost 30 per cent of gross income, with market income at just over 70 per cent. The UK, Germany and Norway form an intermediate group, with transfers accounting for between 15 and 20 per cent of gross income. Ireland also falls into this intermediate category, with transfers constituting 17 per cent of average gross income.

However, composition of market income and of state transfers in Ireland shows some interesting differences from the dominant patterns elsewhere. Ireland has the lowest share of wages and salaries in gross income, but one of the highest shares of self-employment income: farm income is obviously of particular importance in the Irish case.

Perhaps even more striking is that means-tested benefits are of much greater importance in Ireland than elsewhere, at 5.7 per cent of gross income, as against levels of no higher than about 2 per cent in almost all other countries. The only exception is Sweden, but the high figure for means-tested benefits there reflects the overall importance of transfers. O'Higgins *et al.* note that the *relative* role of means-tested benefits in total state transfers in Sweden is similar to that in the UK, the US and Canada. Means-tested transfers in Ireland, on the other hand, account for over one-third of total cash benefits, as against about one-eighth in Sweden, the UK, the US, and Canada. Cyclical factors may play a role here. The Irish data were collected in 1987, after several years of low or negative growth: rising unemployment, and particularly long-term unemployment, would have led to a rise in means-tested transfers over that period. Data for the other countries were collected in 1979 or 1981, at the peak of the business cycle or early in the downturn: means-tested transfers would certainly have played a much greater role in the UK by 1987. Even allowing for this time difference, however, it seems likely that the figures also reflect more fundamental differences in the structures of social security systems and income composition.

The balance between income taxes and social security contributions differs considerably across countries. In discussing the role of taxation, therefore, we concentrate on the size of the total direct tax take. This total tax take in Ireland (income tax plus employee PRSI contributions) is, at 19.3 per cent, in the middle of the spectrum. Only Canada and the UK have a lower direct tax take. Here again, though, we must note that differences in the dates of the surveys may be important: the widespread international trend towards reductions in income taxes in the 1980s could be expected to alter at least some of the rankings.

One measure of the 'leverage' which government policy has on the distribution of income is given by the sum of direct taxes and cash benefits as a proportion of gross income. O'Higgins *et al.* found the highest 'impact potential' on this measure in Sweden, at about 60 per cent, the lowest in the US at about 30 per cent, while other countries returned figures of between 35 and 40 per cent. Ireland also falls in this intermediate range, at 36.3 per cent. Thus, both the Irish 'welfare effort' in terms of cash transfers and its tax take are similar to those in countries at much higher levels of development, such as the UK and Germany.[13]

---

[13] The time difference between the Irish data and that of other countries may play some role in the precise rankings, but it is clear that Ireland's welfare effort places it in the intermediate group. The paper by O'Connell and Rottman in this volume finds that the Irish welfare effort is exceptionally high, and investigates why this is so.

Table 3. Distribution (%) of gross and net income over families.

	Quintile	Canada	US	UK	FRG	Sweden	Norway	Israel	Ireland
Gross income	Lowest	4.6	3.8	4.9	4.4	6.6	4.9	4.5	4.5
	Second	11.0	9.8	10.9	10.2	12.3	11.4	10.5	9.2
	Third	17.7	16.6	18.2	15.9	17.2	18.4	16.5	15.6
	Fourth	25.3	25.3	25.3	22.6	25.0	25.5	24.9	24.2
	Top	41.4	44.5	40.8	46.9	38.9	39.8	43.6	46.6
	Gini coefficient	37.4	41.2	36.5	42.9	32.9	35.6	39.5	42.4
Net income	Lowest	5.3	4.5	5.8	5.0	8.0	6.3	6.0	5.5
	Second	11.8	11.2	11.5	11.5	13.2	12.8	12.1	10.8
	Third	18.1	17.7	18.2	15.9	17.4	18.9	17.9	16.4
	Fourth	24.6	25.6	25.0	21.8	24.5	25.3	24.5	24.0
	Top	39.7	41.0	39.5	45.8	36.9	36.7	39.5	43.4
	Gini coefficient	34.8	37.0	34.3	40.9	29.2	31.1	33.8	38.1

Sources: As for Table 1.

Turning now to income distributions, we show in Table 3 distributions over families. The Gini coefficients suggest that Ireland is the second most unequal country, after Germany. This is not because of a particularly low share going to the bottom quintile: the Irish figures for the shares of both gross and net income going to the bottom quintile are not very different from those of several of the other countries. The source of the inequality lies instead in low shares for the second and third quintiles, together with an exceptionally high share for the top quintile.

But does this apparently high inequality simply reflect differences between household sizes in Ireland and elsewhere? Suppose two countries have precisely the same distribution of incomes over individuals but, in one country, all individuals live in two-person households, while, in the other, some live in one- two- or three-person households. Measures of inequality on a household basis will then show the latter country as more unequal. It is of considerable interest, therefore, to move, as in Table 4, to an individual level of analysis, using income per equivalent adult for each person.

The Irish distributions still rank among the most unequal. The share of net equivalent income going to the bottom quintile of persons in Ireland is the second lowest, although close to that observed in Israel, Germany and Canada. The share of this income going to the top quintile of persons is, however, greater than in all countries except Germany. The Gini coefficient also suggests that Ireland ranks as the second most unequal country. Part of this may have to do with macroeconomic conditions: one might expect the increase in Irish unemployment over the 1980s to have

Table 4. Distribution (%) of equivalent gross and net income over individuals.

	Quintile	Canada	US	UK	FRG	Sweden	Norway	Israel	Ireland
Equivalent	Lowest	6.7	5.1	7.9	7.2	9.4	8.1	6.1	6.2
gross	Second	12.6	11.4	13.0	12.1	14.6	13.6	10.3	10.7
income	Third	17.5	17.1	17.9	16.0	18.5	17.9	15.9	15.6
	Fourth	24.0	24.2	23.7	21.3	23.3	23.4	23.7	23.0
	Top	39.2	42.1	37.5	43.4	34.3	37.0	44.0	44.8
	Gini coefficient	32.7	37.1	29.7	36.3	24.9	28.9	38.2	38.3
Equivalent	Lowest	7.6	6.1	9.0	7.5	10.6	9.9	7.5	7.4
net	Second	13.3	12.8	13.5	12.7	16.1	14.8	11.7	12.1
income	Third	17.9	18.1	18.0	16.1	19.1	18.4	16.8	16.5
	Fourth	23.8	24.4	23.4	20.7	23.1	22.9	23.7	22.7
	Top	37.4	38.6	36.1	43.0	31.1	34.1	40.3	41.7
	Gini coefficient	29.9	32.6	27.3	35.5	20.5	24.3	33.3	34.1

Sources: As for Table 1.

increased income inequality, so that in a comparison with other countries based on 1980 data Ireland might appear less unequal.[14] Some limitations of our estimates of 12 month income should also be noted: annualised current income is used for a significant proportion of cases. This might tend to overstate inequality, though the difference between annualised current and 12 month income may be small for most of the individuals involved.

In the context of a concern with the relationship between income distribution and levels of development, however, perhaps the most striking feature of Table 4 is that the distribution of equivalent income over persons in Ireland and Israel is very similar.[15] The distributions of unadjusted income were quite different, but in Table 4 the quintile shares of gross income do not differ by more than one percentage point, leading to almost identical Gini coefficients, and the quintile shares of net income are also very close, leading to Gini coefficients which diverge by just one percentage point.

O'Higgins *et al.* suggest that the Kuznets hypothesis may help to

[14] But to some extent Irish macroeconomic performance diverged from world trends during the 1980s: the recovery, particularly as regards employment, was more sluggish at least until 1987. Thus, results of a comparison based on 1987 data for all countries might be intermediate between the present ones and those based on a 1980 comparison. An alternative concept of standardisation would be to average over the 'business cycle' influences at national level. Time lags in the transmission of cyclical influences across countries may make this concept different from calendar time standardisation.

[15] The exclusion of rural inhabitants from the Israeli survey has already been noted; if they were included, one might expect to find the Israeli distribution slightly more unequal than Ireland's rather than, as in the Table, slightly less unequal.

explain the relatively high inequality in Israel. In terms of income composition, the proximate causes for high inequality in that country are the greater role and more unequal distribution of self-employment income, and the lack of a strong role for cash transfers. This is offset, however, by the strong role for income taxes, which account for almost 30 per cent of gross income. The relative importance of cash transfers and income taxes are reversed in Ireland, but self-employment income plays a similar role and the outcomes in terms of equivalent income per person are also similar.

The similarities between Ireland and Israel, and the differences between them and more advanced countries, suggest that a broader comparison, using more countries at or below the Irish level of development, would be of interest. Unfortunately, the availability of data for such countries is quite restricted, and the comparability of income distribution

Table 5. Income distribution and level of development.

Country and year	Real GDP per head[a]	Gini coefficient[b]	Quintile shares (where available)				
			1	2	3	4	5
Brazil 1983	3075	0.57	2.4	5.7	10.7	18.6	62.6
Taiwan 1985	3581	0.27					
Malaysia 1987[b]	3636	0.48	4.6	9.3	13.9	21.2	51.2
Singapore 1972/3	3680	0.40					
Hong Kong 1971	3731	0.43					
Mexico 1977	3768	0.50					
Chile 1971	3845	0.46					
Singapore 1978/9	4820	0.37					
Hong Kong 1976	5216	0.43					
Ireland 1987[c]	**5389**	**0.38**	**5.5**	**10.8**	**16.4**	**24.0**	**43.4**
Trinidad and Tobago 1975/6	5775	0.47					
Israel 1979	6124	0.34	6.0	12.1	17.9	24.5	39.5
Spain 1980/1	6134	n.a.	6.9	12.5	17.3	23.2	40.0
Singapore 1982/3	6836	0.42	5.1	9.9	14.6	21.4	48.9
Hong Kong 1981	7751	0.45	5.4	10.8	15.2	21.6	47.0
UK 1979	8094	0.34	5.8	11.5	18.2	25.0	39.5
Sweden 1981	8916	0.29	8.0	13.2	17.4	24.5	36.9
FRG 1981	9820	0.41	5.0	11.5	15.9	21.8	45.8
Norway 1979	10708	0.31	6.3	12.8	18.9	25.3	36.7
USA 1979	11602	0.37	4.5	11.2	17.7	25.6	41.0
Canada 1981	11650	0.35	5.3	11.8	18.1	24.6	39.7

[a] From Summers and Heston (1988).
[b] Distribution of unadjusted household income over households, except for Malaysia (per capita income over households); real GDP per capita refers to 1985.
[c] The latest available Summers and Heston estimate of real GDP for 1985 has been updated by national accounts measure of growth in GDP to 1987.
Sources: Fields and Jakobsen (1990), Summers and Heston (1988), World Bank (1990).

figures cannot be assured to anything like the degree possible with the LIS data. We have drawn on a number of sources, however, to compile Table 5, which presents data on real GDP per capita (adjusted to a common purchasing power standard) and on income distribution measures.

The table strikingly illustrates the diversity of country experience referred to earlier. For example, Taiwan's Gini coefficient of 0.27 can be compared with figures of 0.50 or above for its near neighbours in the income league. The earlier detailed comparisons can also be seen as cautioning against over-interpretation of small differences between the distributions in this table: we have seen that the difference between the Irish and Israeli distributions vanishes if the income concept is changed to reflect the distribution of equivalent income over persons. The literature on the Kuznets hypothesis would suggest that over the income range of the countries in Table 5, inequality would decline with increases in GDP per capita. While there is considerable individual variation, it is true that, on average, inequality is greater for countries at or below the Irish level of development than for those above it. The average Gini coefficient for countries below the Irish level is 0.43, or 0.46 excluding Taiwan; for those above, it is 0.37, or 0.35 for those at or above the UK level of GDP per head. On this basis, it would be difficult to argue that the Irish distribution is particularly unequal for its level of development: if anything, it appears slightly more equal than one might expect.

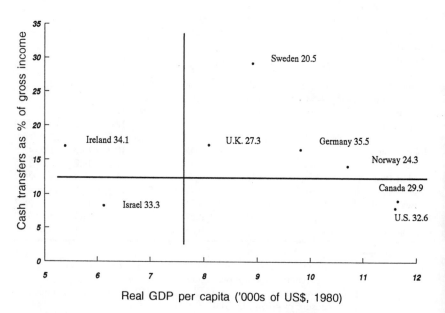

Figure 1. Income inequality (Gini), income level and rate of cash transfers.

We noted earlier that the extent of welfare state intervention could be seen as an influence on income distribution which is somewhat independent of level of development. It is possible to illustrate this point for Ireland and the countries in the LIS data-set. Figure 1 uses cash transfers as the single most important index of welfare state intervention and real GDP per capita as the index of development. The position of different countries is plotted in this space, and the Gini coefficient for the distribution of net equivalent incomes per person is indicated.

If income inequality declined continuously with GDP per capita and with increases in cash transfers, we might expect smooth 'iso-inequality' contours. Alternatively, these effects might be somewhat discontinuous, in which case a division of the type illustrated into regions of high/low income and high/low rates of cash transfers could be more helpful. In this latter case low income inequality would be expected in the top right hand quadrant, high income inequality in the bottom left-hand quadrant, and moderate income inequality in the other two quadrants. The pattern shown conforms to these expectations in some respects, but Israel and Germany are exceptions, for different reasons.[16]

Income Redistribution

Redistribution through cash benefits and income taxes

Thus far, analysis of each income concept (net or gross income) has been on the basis of persons or families ranked by that income concept. This is appropriate in making comparisons of the level of inequality at particular stages in the redistribution process. But in order to examine that process itself, an analysis on the basis of a single ranking is also of interest. We need to ask, for example: what is the share of factor income, gross income and net income for the bottom or top 20 per cent of persons ranked by

---

[16] The particularly high (and progressive) direct tax take in Israel can be seen as reducing its inequality more than its rather low rate of cash transfers would suggest: the other country with a particularly high tax take is Sweden, where the combination of high transfers and high taxes leads to the lowest inequality, despite other countries having higher levels of GDP per head. But the most puzzling anomaly is the case of Germany which has a Gini coefficient well above that of other countries with similar levels of development and cash transfers. The analysis of the redistribution process which follows will show that this arises from an exceptionally skewed distribution of factor incomes, rather than from an ineffective redistribution by transfers and taxes; but the underlying causes of this phenomenon lie outside the scope of the present paper.

Table 6. Distribution and redistribution of income: income shares (%) of quintiles of persons ranked by family gross income.

	Quintile	Canada	US	UK	FRG	Sweden	Norway	Israel	Ireland
Factor income	Lowest	5.4	4.2	4.0	2.3	6.5	4.4	4.9	2.2
	Second	14.9	12.8	15.0	13.8	18.5	17.0	11.6	8.7
	Third	19.2	19.2	19.9	17.1	18.8	19.6	16.0	16.6
	Fourth	24.5	25.1	24.9	22.0	23.0	24.2	24.3	25.2
	Top	36.0	38.8	36.3	44.7	33.2	34.9	43.2	47.7
Gross income	Lowest	9.5	7.5	10.9	10.7	13.7	12.0	9.3	9.2
	Second	15.6	14.3	15.6	14.7	20.5	17.8	12.5	11.6
	Third	18.7	18.8	18.7	16.2	18.6	18.4	15.8	16.5
	Fourth	23.0	23.6	22.0	20.1	20.1	21.6	22.7	22.9
	Top	33.2	35.9	31.9	38.2	27.1	30.3	39.8	40.2
Net income	Lowest	10.8	9.0	12.4	13.1	16.4	14.7	12.0	11.2
	Second	16.4	15.9	15.9	15.3	21.2	18.6	14.1	13.1
	Third	18.8	19.5	18.6	16.0	18.3	18.6	16.8	16.9
	Fourth	22.6	23.6	22.4	19.3	19.9	21.0	22.1	22.3
	Top	31.4	32.0	30.6	36.2	24.2	27.2	35.0	36.8

gross income?[17] This is the perspective adopted by O'Higgins *et al.*; so in order to compare Ireland's redistributive process with that of the other countries, the same perspective is adopted here, with results as reported in Table 6.[18]

Since the data have been ranked by gross income in all cases, the distributions over other income concepts are 'hybrids': the main interest is in changes in the shares of different income concepts going to the income quintiles ranked by gross income. The change which cash transfers brings about to the share of the bottom quintile is of particular interest.[19] Here we find increases of 7 or 8 percentage points in the UK, Sweden, Norway and Germany; Ireland also falls in this group, with an increase of 7 percentage points. In the US, Canada and Israel, by contrast, the share of the bottom quintile rises by just 3 to 4 percentage points. The proportionate

[17] The ranking by gross income also differs from those presented earlier: the present analysis deals with the share of aggregate family income going to successive quintiles of persons ranked by total family income.

[18] Other perspectives on the redistribution process would also be of interest. For example, Gini coefficients for re-ranked distributions of market and gross income would help to show the role of cash transfers in different countries; this information is not available from O'Higgins *et al.*, though it could in principle be obtained from direct analysis of the LIS datasets. Comparisons of this type are presented for Ireland and the UK later in this paper, though not based on LIS data.

[19] An initial distribution of market incomes would be preferable for this analysis; but it is clear that the dominant role in changes between factor and gross incomes is played by cash transfers rather than occupational pensions.

increase in the share of the bottom quintile is greatest by far in Germany and Ireland, where the distribution of factor incomes appears most unequal; the lowest proportionate increases are again in Israel, the US and Canada. Cash benefits in Ireland also have a relatively high impact on the share of the second quintile: the increase of almost 3 percentage points in their share is greater in absolute and proportionate terms than elsewhere. The shift from factor to cash incomes also sees a higher percentage point drop in the share of the top decile in Ireland than in the other countries.

The changes caused by direct taxes are more modest in all countries. In Ireland, the share of the bottom quintile rises by a further two percentage points, as against 2.4 to 2.7 percentage points in Germany, Sweden, Norway and Israel, but 1.5 percentage points or less in Canada, the US and the UK. The proportionate rise in Ireland is, however, about as high as in any other country.

Overall, then, it appears that cash transfers and direct taxes have at least as large an impact in Ireland as elsewhere. The fact that net incomes are distributed somewhat more unequally in Ireland than elsewhere reflects a high level of inequality in factor incomes—the dominant component of market incomes in all countries.[20]

Redistribution through non-cash benefits and indirect taxes

In addition to income tax and social insurance contributions and social welfare cash transfers, the well-being of households at different points in the income distribution is affected by indirect taxes and services provided in free or subsidised form by the state. An evaluation of the impact of such taxes and non-cash benefits is therefore necessary if the full redistributive effects of state policy are to be seen. Unfortunately, attempting such an evaluation poses major methodological problems, and comparative data across countries in this area are rather scarce. Here our limited objective is briefly to describe the way in which indirect taxes and non-cash benefits in Ireland are structured, to set out what is known about their redistributive effects, and to add what can be said to provide a comparative perspective.

In doing so, we draw on the exercises carried out by the CSO on the basis of the 1973 and 1980 Household Budget Surveys (CSO, 1980; 1983), and studies based on these exercises by Nolan (1981), O'Connell (1982a), Murphy (1984) and Rottman and Reidy (1988). (A more up-to-date analysis by the CSO, based on the 1987 Household Budget Survey, is to be published shortly but no results are currently available.) These exercises

---

[20] Only Germany shows a similar level of inequality in factor incomes, as noted earlier.

follow the conventional methodology adopted in studies of fiscal incidence by the UK CSO and other agencies. The limitations of this approach and the care with which results are to be interpreted are discussed at length both in the Irish studies mentioned, and in, for example, Meerman (1978), Bird (1980), O'Higgins (1980) and O'Higgins and Ruggles (1981). Not all taxes and expenditures are included in the analysis, the cost rather than the benefits of services provided by the State are allocated, and, perhaps most crucially, both taxes and benefits themselves influence the distribution of market income. The observed distributions of gross and net incomes reflect that influence. Further, the distribution of factor incomes used in the analysis is constructed by simply adding and subtracting income transfers. This constructed distribution does not, therefore, represent what the distribution of factor incomes would be in the absence of taxes and benefits. The exercises thus aim to show flows of taxes and benefits to and from particular groups of households in a given year, rather than their impact on the distribution in any more fundamental sense.

It is also important to note that using this data-base means that income now largely refers to that received in the last week, rather than the (estimated) annual income employed in our analysis of distribution and redistribution in cash terms. (For the self-employed, though, income over the previous twelve months is generally used in the HBS as the basis for current income.) We deal first with indirect taxes, then with non-cash benefits, and finally with the combined effects of both and the overall redistributive impact of taxes and benefits together.

Indirect taxes

Taxes on goods and services are a particularly important source of government revenue in Ireland. Currently they account for about half of all tax revenue for budgetary purposes, or about 42 per cent of all revenue including contributions to the Social Insurance Fund. This is well above the average for the OECD countries, which is 30 per cent of total revenue (including social insurance), or the UK share which is 31 per cent (OECD, 1990: Table 25). Taxes on goods and services account for about 17 per cent of GDP in the Irish case, well above the OECD average and the UK figure, both of which are 12 per cent (OECD, 1990: Table 24). About half the receipts from such taxes in Ireland are raised through Value Added Tax, and most of the remainder is from excise duties, particularly on alcohol, tobacco, motor vehicles and oil. An important feature of the Irish VAT system in a redistributional context is that food and children's clothing are zero rated.

The analysis of distribution carried out by the CSO using the 1980 Household

Budget Survey allocated VAT, fiscal duties, motor tax and local water charges among households in the sample. Each household's VAT and fiscal duty was estimated by applying the appropriate tax rates to the reported expenditure on different items. This, the conventionally adopted approach, involves the assumption that the incidence of indirect taxes falls entirely on the consumer.

The CSO study showed that, when households were classified by income range, indirect tax paid was generally a higher proportion of income at low than at high incomes.[21] Such a comparison takes no account of the fact that households of different composition are not evenly spread throughout the distribution. The published data also showed, though, that indirect tax as a proportion of income was low at higher incomes for households of each main composition type, classified by market income (CSO, 1983: Tables 4A and 4M). Murphy, presenting a detailed analysis of the CSO results, used equivalent market and disposable income and calculated two frequently used progressivity indices, the Kakwani and Suits measures, for indirect taxes as a whole and for the main constituents. These indicated that total indirect taxes and each main element were regressive (1984: Tables 23 and 24).

This conforms to the pattern generally found elsewhere. The data available allow few direct comparisons, however, so it is difficult to assess the degree of regressivity in comparative terms. Suits indices for sales and excise taxes in the US (for 1966 and 1970) were similar to the results reported for Ireland in 1973 by Nolan (1981). The variation in indirect taxes as a proportion of income over the UK income distribution, as shown in the UK CSO's redistributive studies and in O'Higgins and Ruggles (1981), also reveals the same general pattern as in the Irish data.

More generally, the overall redistributive impact of direct and indirect taxes taken together appears to be quite limited in Ireland, which is also the case for a number of other developed countries. Saunders and Klau (1985), in their review of studies of the redistributive effects of taxes and benefits in OECD countries, concluded that for almost all countries covered the tax system had relatively minor effects on the income distribution. This was a result of progressive income tax being largely neutralised by the impact of regressive social security contributions and indirect taxes.[22] For Ireland, this is very much the pattern revealed by Murphy's results (1984: Table 24): compared to either cash or non-cash

---

[21] See CSO (1983: Table J, p. xxi, Table 1, pp. 2–3, Table 10, pp. 46–47). This was the case whether market, gross or disposable income was employed.

[22] Sweden was identified as an exception to this general pattern, where a markedly progressive income tax means that taxes do affect the distribution.

benefits, taxes as a whole had little impact on the distribution.[23] While the incidence assumptions underlying such exercises may be open to question, it is worth noting Saunders and Klau's conclusion that the broad pattern of the results internationally was not unduly sensitive to changes in these assumptions.

Non-cash benefits

The structure and delivery of publicly-provided services in the health, education, housing and transport areas, and their redistributive effects, have been analysed in detail in Rottman and Reidy (1988), again based on the CSO's exercises using the 1973 and 1980 Household Budget Surveys. Only the briefest outline of these structures can be given here. Entitlement to publicly provided health services is determined on the basis of income, with about 38 per cent of the population eligible for the entire range of services free of charge, about 47 per cent entitled mainly to hospital services, and the top 15 per cent entitled to hospital accommodation but liable for consultants' fees.[24] Given this differential pattern of entitlements over the income distribution, and the fact that services will be heavily utilised by groups concentrated in particular parts of the distribution (notably the elderly), the potential for a substantial redistributive impact is clear. In education, all children are entitled to free primary and secondary education, but those not availing of it still benefit through state spending on fee-paying schools. State spending on third-level education also heavily subsidises those receiving it, fees paid being well below the cost of provision. As Rottman and Reidy put it, the redistributive impact of educational spending is primarily a function of class-specific 'take-up' rates of education beyond the legal minimum age, and the cost per student to the state at each level. Expenditure on health and education account for most of public social expenditure, excluding cash transfers, but the much smaller amounts going on subsidies to local authority housing and public transport are also included in the redistributional analyses.

The CSO exercises allocate the 'benefit' of state social spending on the basis of reported or estimated utilisation patterns and the cost of providing the service in question. Thus, households containing a pupil in primary school will be attributed benefit amounting to the cost per student to the

---

[23] It is worth noting, though, that whereas for 1973 social security contributions were seen to be regressive (as in Nolan and O'Connell's results), in 1980 Murphy shows that they were mildly progressive.

[24] Since 1987, the second and third categories are also liable for charges of £10 per night spent in hospital, and for attendance at outpatient clinics. A full description of the system of entitlements etc., as it applied in 1980, is given in Rottman and Reidy (1988: ch. 3).

state of providing that level of education. This follows the conventional methodology adopted by, for example, the UK CSO; no attempt is made to measure the value to the recipient of the service received. While some studies, mostly in the US (see, for example, Smeeding, 1982), have explored various approaches to evaluating utility in this context, as yet these have not been widely applied. The more common method simply seeks to allocate the value of the resources used in providing the service.

The CSO's results for 1980 show public expenditure on health being relatively evenly spread over the (disposable) income distribution in absolute terms. In proportion to their incomes, then, lower income groups gain considerably more. Education 'benefit', on the other hand, rises as household income rises, but as a proportion of income is highest for those in the middle of the distribution rather than at either tail.[25] Clearly, though, the amounts attributed to particular households are crucially dependent on their composition, and looking at households ranked by equivalent rather than unadjusted incomes is of particular interest. Table 7 shows the distribution of health, education, 'other', and total allocated non-cash benefits by equivalent disposable income quintile, derived for 1980 by Rottman and Reidy (1988).

Health expenditure goes disproportionately towards lower income households: 50 per cent of spending goes to the bottom 40 per cent of households ranked by equivalent income. This reflects both the extra entitlements of those towards the bottom and the over-representation of the elderly in the middle and bottom rather than towards the top of the distribution. Education spending in aggregate also goes more to the bottom and middle of the distribution than the top—the top 20 per cent of households receive only 12 per cent of expenditure. However, this aggregate is made up of quite disparate patterns for different levels of education. Primary and secondary education spending go disproportionately to bottom and middle income groups, while third level, and especially university, spending go more to upper income groups (cf. Rottman and Reidy, 1988: Table 4.6). With the much smaller sums allocated for housing, transport and other subsidies also going more towards lower than higher income groups, the total of allocated spending is seen to benefit low-income groups quite substantially relative to their share of disposable income. The bottom 20 per cent of households received 24 per cent of these benefits, whereas the top 20 per cent received only 13 per cent.

---

[25] See CSO (1983), Tables 10 and 11—these conclusions apply whether direct, gross or disposable income is used to classify households.

Table 7. Distribution (%) of non-cash benefits by household equivalent income quintile, Ireland 1980.

Quintile	Health	Education	Other[a]	Total non-cash benefits
Lowest	25.4	21.6	24.9	23.8
Second	24.6	23.1	21.9	23.5
Third	19.8	23.7	18.8	21.3
Fourth	17.3	19.2	18.0	18.2
Top	12.9	12.1	16.5	13.2
All	100.0	100.0	100.0	100.0

[a] Housing, transportation and other subsidies.
Source: Rottman and Reidy (1988: Tables 3.7 and 4.6 and Appendix Table 7.2).

The impact of cash transfers, taxes and non-cash benefits on the income distribution

Given the profile of indirect taxes and non-cash benefits, what impact does this have on the level of inequality in the income distribution? The customary approach to assessing this impact is simply to take each household's disposable income, subtract the indirect taxes and add the non-cash benefits attributed to that household, and thus derive what is usually termed 'final' income. This clearly represents a construct quite different in nature to disposable income itself. Whereas disposable income measures the resources available to the household for consumption, non-cash benefits do not represent generalised purchasing power. None the less, final income does provide a benchmark—a starting-point for the assessment of the overall extent of state intervention and its impact on the distribution of income.

Focusing first on unadjusted rather than equivalent income, Table 8 shows the distribution of market, gross, disposable and final income in 1980. Comparing disposable and final income, the overall impact of indirect taxes and non-cash benefits is to produce a more equal distribution —the Lorenz curves do not intersect, the top quintile has a smaller share of final than disposable income and the bottom two quintiles have larger shares. This is reflected in the Gini coefficient, which is 3 per cent lower for final than for disposable income. However, this difference is relatively small when set against the impact of cash transfers and direct tax taken together—seen by comparing market and disposable income distributions. A simple measure of the redistributive effect of taxes and transfers is provided by the percentage reduction in the Gini coefficient, which is termed the Musgrave-Thin index. The overall impact of taxes and benefits

Table 8. Market, gross, disposable and final household income distribution, Ireland 1980 (% of total income).

Quintile	Market	Gross	Disposable	Final
Lowest	0.5	4.6	5.2	5.8
Second	8.5	10.6	11.6	11.9
Third	17.1	16.8	17.2	17.2
Fourth	25.7	24.2	24.0	24.0
Top	48.1	43.8	42.0	41.2
All	100.0	100.0	100.0	100.0
Top decile	29.7	27.0	25.7	25.1
Gini coefficient	0.468	0.385	0.360	0.348

Source: Murphy (1984: Table 5).

Table 9. Redistributive impact of taxes and transfers, Ireland and UK 1980.

Percentage reduction in Gini coefficient, redistribution from	Ireland	UK
Market → gross income	17.7	21.8
Gross → disposable income	6.5	7.8
Disposable → final income	3.3	2.7
Market → final income	25.6	29.6

Source: Calculated from Murphy (1984: Table 5) and *Economic Trends*, January, 1982.

in 1980 was to reduce the Gini from 0.468 to 0.348, a fall of 26 per cent. But about 70 per cent of this reduction was attributable to the effect of cash transfers, 20 per cent to direct taxes, and only 10 per cent to indirect taxes and non-cash benefits combined.[26]

This conforms to the general pattern found in similar studies in other developed countries, in particular the UK. A direct comparison can be made with the results of the corresponding exercise carried out by the UK CSO, also for 1980, as shown in Table 9.[27] A slightly higher overall 'redistributive effect' is seen in the UK, as measured by the fall in the Gini coefficient of 30 per cent from market to final income, compared with the Irish figure of 26 per cent. Once again, in the UK case 74 per cent of this reduction was attributable to cash transfers, 20 per cent to direct taxes, and only 6 per cent to indirect taxes and non-cash transfers combined. Saunders and Klau (1985), having reviewed available studies for OECD

---

[26] The Theil inequality measure, also calculated by Murphy, shows a very similar pattern to the Gini coefficient.

[27] Rottman and Reidy (1988: ch. 7) present a similar analysis, with slightly different levels for Gini coefficients, based on discrete rather than decile data. Here we use the latter, presented by Murphy (1984), to maintain consistency with those for equivalent income below.

countries, concluded that public expenditure programmes, particularly cash transfers, have been almost totally responsible for the changes in income distribution which governments have brought about. Ireland appears to fit comfortably within this general pattern.

These results refer to the income distribution among households, without adjustment for differences in household size and composition. It is also of interest to look at the overall impact of taxes and benefits on the equivalent income distribution. Table 10 shows the distribution of market and final equivalent income in Ireland in 1980.[28] Final income is once again a good deal more equally distributed than market income, the differences being concentrated in the larger share of the lowest quintile and the smaller share of the top decile. Compared with unadjusted income, the redistributive impact of taxes and benefits is considerably greater when assessed on an equivalent income basis. The Gini coefficient is reduced from 0.46 to 0.27, giving a Musgrave-Thin index of 41 per cent, compared with 26 per cent for unadjusted incomes. This comes about because there is little difference between unadjusted and equivalent market income distributions, but equivalent final income is a good deal more equally distributed than unadjusted final income.

While fewer studies are available for other countries on an equivalent income basis, a comparison can be made with the UK. The UK CSO carried out an exercise with 1985 data, comparing the redistributive effects of taxes and benefits using equivalent as opposed to unadjusted income.[29] This showed an overall reduction in the Gini coefficient of about 47 per

Table 10. Direct and final equivalent income distributions (%), Ireland 1973 and 1980.

Quintile	1973		1980	
	Direct	Final	Direct	Final
Lowest	1.7	7.7	0.7	8.8
Second	10.5	13.5	9.3	14.3
Third	16.9	17.2	17.0	17.5
Fourth	24.5	22.1	25.3	22.3
Top	46.5	39.5	47.6	37.0
All	100.0	100.0	100.0	100.0
Top decile	29.4	25.0	29.8	22.7
Gini coefficient	0.434	0.306	0.459	0.272

Source: Murphy (1984: Tables 9 and 17).

[28] The equivalence scales employed by Murphy, from whom these results are taken, differ from those used earlier in this paper—see Murphy (1984: 72).
[29] See *Economic Trends*, July 1987.

cent (from market to final income) for equivalent income, compared with 33 per cent for unadjusted income. The overall redistributive impact is again slightly higher than in Ireland. However, it should be noted that both the inequality in market income and the overall redistributive impact in the UK appear to have risen between 1980 and 1985. Thus comparison based on equivalent income for the same year would probably reveal even less difference between the two countries in overall redistributive impact.[30]

Rottman and Reidy (1988), in addition to looking at redistribution in terms of the income distribution in the 1973 and 1980 Household Budget Surveys, also examined the redistributive impact of taxes and transfers on households in terms of a social class categorisation. While the pattern revealed is a complex one, large proprietors and, even more so, large and medium scale farmers were seen to be more favourably treated in terms of overall redistributive impact than the professional and managerial classes. Small and marginal farmers were also more favourably treated than unskilled workers. While these class differentials affect the degree of vertical redistribution taking place across income groups, their significance from an income distribution perspective may be greatest in terms of horizontal equity—'equal treatment of equals'. The relationship between class-based analysis and the income distribution perspective clearly deserves greater attention than it has received in the literature. But a major problem with the class-based analysis is that it does not allow us to say whether the pattern for Ireland is more or less extreme than elsewhere. Cross-country comparisons face great difficulty in arriving at a class categorisation which is consistently articulated and applied. This is perhaps the principal reason why most studies aiming at a cross-country perspective on redistribution, like the present one, rely on income rather than class categories.

Trends over time in redistributive effects

Finally, what can be said about trends over time in the redistributive effects of taxes and benefits in Ireland? Currently, relevant analyses are only available for 1973 and 1980. Rottman and Reidy (1988) analysed trends over this period in depth, and on the basis of the distribution of unadjusted income showed a significant increase in overall redistributive impact. This

---

[30] The equivalence scales used in the Irish and British studies differ, and the coverage of the UK exercise is slightly broader, complicating the comparison. The UK exercise found the results to be insensitive to the precise scales adopted however. The UK CSO has now changed to equivalent income as the basis for its redistributive exercises (see *Economic Trends*, May 1990).

they attributed primarily to increases in levels of direct taxes and cash transfers. While inequality in market incomes rose, this was counteracted by an expanded redistributive effort, so that inequality in final income was actually lower in 1980 than 1973. The distributions of market and final equivalent income for 1973, presented by Murphy and shown in Table 10 along with the 1980 figures, reveal a similar picture. While the Gini coefficient for equivalent market income was lower in 1973 than 1980, the reduction brought about by taxes and benefits was only 29 per cent in 1973 compared with 41 per cent in 1980, leaving the Gini for final income higher in the earlier year. When the corresponding CSO exercise based on the 1987 HBS becomes available it will be possible to update these findings through the 1980s. Given the very substantial increases in levels of unemployment, public expenditure and taxation, it may be speculated that both the inequality in market incomes and the overall redistributive impact of taxes and benefits will show a continuing rise in Ireland, as they have in the UK.

The main features of the redistribution of income through taxes and benefits in Ireland may now be summarised. Taken together, taxes and benefits have a major impact on the distribution, leading to greater equality. As in other OECD countries, most of this is attributable to cash transfers—the tax system has relatively little effect, regressive indirect taxes offsetting progressive income tax, while non-cash transfers are mildly progressive. The overall 'redistributive effect', as reflected in the decline in the Gini coefficient brought about by taxes and benefits, was slightly less than in the UK in 1980. Given the differences between the two countries in level of development, the overall impact of taxes and benefits in Ireland may thus be regarded as relatively substantial. The 'redistributive effect' increased over the 1970s in Ireland, as direct tax and cash transfers in particular became more important, and this is likely to have continued through the 1980s.

Relative Poverty

Relative poverty in EC countries

In placing the distribution and redistribution of income in Ireland in a comparative perspective, it is also of interest to look very briefly at the extent of poverty and the effectiveness of social security transfers in alleviating it. To do so, we focus on poverty measured using relative poverty lines, and compare results for Ireland with those for other EC countries. The conceptual and methodological issues raised by such an

Table 11. Percentage of persons below half average equivalent income, EC countries, 1980 and 1985.[a]

Country	1980	1985
Belgium	[7.6]	7.2
Denmark	[13.0]	[14.7]
France	17.7	[17.5]
FRG	6.7	[8.5]
Greece	24.2	[24.0]
Ireland	**19.2**	**22.9**
Italy	9.4	11.7
Luxembourg	[7.9]	7.9
Netherlands	7.0	7.4
Portugal	27.8	[28.0]
Spain	20.5	[20.0]
UK	9.2	12.0

Note: [a] Figures in square brackets have been estimated—see source, Annex 1; dates refer to nearest available year.
Sources: O'Higgins and Jenkins (1989: Table 1), except for Ireland, for which see Callan *et al.* (1989: Table 5.4).

exercise are discussed in Callan *et al.* (1989) and Nolan and Callan (1990) and will not be addressed here.

The first set of comparisons which can be made with data available across EC countries is based on results presented in O'Higgins and Jenkins (1989). Poverty lines are derived as 50 per cent of average equivalent household income in the country in question, using a common set of equivalence scales. Table 11 shows the percentage of persons in each country in households falling below these 50 per cent relative poverty lines for 1980 and 1985 or the nearest available year. The Irish figures are based on the ESRI's survey carried out in 1987 and the 1980 Household Budget Survey.[31] Without placing too much emphasis on the precise figures shown, the position of Ireland compared with the other countries may be noted. There is a higher proportion of the population below the 50 per cent relative poverty line in Ireland than in any of the other EC countries, except Portugal and Greece, in each of the years. Spain has a similar percentage below the line; France shows a lower, and other countries a considerably lower figure.

A similar comparison on a somewhat different basis may also be made. EUROSTAT has produced figures showing the percentage falling below 50 per cent relative poverty lines in each EC country, based on household

---

[31] The Irish figure for 1980 presented here differs from that in O'Higgins and Jenkins (1989), being derived from direct analysis of the HBS micro-data rather than by interpolation. The 1987 figure is also slightly revised.

Table 12. Percentage of persons below 50 per cent of average equivalent expenditure, EC countries, 1980 and 1985.

Country	1980	1985
Belgium	7.1	5.9
Denmark	7.9	8.0
France	19.1	15.7
FRG	10.5	9.9
Greece	21.5	18.4
Ireland	**18.4**	**19.5**[a]
Italy	14.1	15.5
Netherlands	9.6	11.4
Portugal	32.4	32.7
Spain	20.9	18.9
UK	14.6	18.2

[a] Relates to 1987.
Source: Eurostat Rapid Reports, *Population and Social Conditions*, 1990, 7.

equivalent expenditure rather than income. These figures are based on the Household Budget Surveys carried out in the various countries, again for 1980 and 1985 (or nearest available year). Table 12 shows the percentage of persons falling below this line in each country. The Irish figures (which are for 1987) are not very different from those on an income basis, and are now about the same as those for Spain and Greece, and much lower than for Portugal. Italy, Portugal and the UK have higher percentages below the expenditure-based lines than in Table 11, but the relative position of Ireland is not much affected.[32]

Clearly, the extent of relative poverty in the various EC countries is related to the level of development attained, with the less developed countries—Ireland, Spain, Greece and Portugal—having higher poverty figures, even on a purely relative basis. However, the relationship—like that between income inequality and level of development discussed earlier —is not a simple or rigid one, and no attempt will be made here to tease out the complex influences at work.

Relative poverty in Ireland and Britain

It may be of interest in the present context to examine in more detail the comparison between Ireland and the UK. To make a precise comparison with the official British Department of Social Security data on 'Households Below Average Income', we have applied the methodology used in this

---

[32] The comparison between the income and expenditure-based results is complicated by the fact that for some countries—including Ireland for 1987—different data sources were used.

Table 13.   Percentage of persons below relative income cut-offs, Great Britain and Ireland, 1987

Cut-off	% of persons below cut-off	
% of mean equivalent income[a]	Great Britain	Ireland
50	14.3	17.4
60	25.5	28.5
70	36.2	39.6
80	45.9	48.9
90	54.8	57.1
100	63.4	63.8

[a] Income is before housing costs.
Sources: DSS (1990), Table C 1; Nolan and Callan (forthcoming: Table 3).

new series—including the equivalence scales—to data from the ESRI 1987 sample. This involves calculating average equivalent income, deriving income cut-offs as 50 per cent, 60 per cent, 70 per cent and up to 100 per cent of that average, and looking at the percentage of persons falling below each. (The results for the 50 per cent cut-off differ from those given in Table 11 because, although the general approach is the same, there are differences in its detailed application.)[33]

The DSS produce figures for Great Britain—Northern Ireland is not included—based on the Family Expenditure Survey, recently updated to 1987, and Table 13 compares these to the corresponding Irish results for the same year. The table shows that, consistently at all cut-offs up to average income, a higher proportion of persons fall below the relative thresholds in Ireland. It is worth noting, though, that the differences between the two countries are much less striking than in the comparison presented in Nolan and Callan (forthcoming), which employed British data for 1985. This is because there was a dramatic increase in the percentage of British persons falling below most of the thresholds between 1985 and 1987—the percentage below the 50 per cent line rising from 9.2 per cent to 14.3 per cent.

Differences in the composition of those at low incomes in the two countries are also of interest. An analysis of the risk and incidence of poverty in the two countries reveals a number of important differences. The risk of being below the 50 per cent or 60 per cent line is significantly higher for the elderly in Britain, whereas the non-elderly generally face a

---

[33] In particular, the equivalence scales employed in the two exercises differ, and the DSS average equivalent income across persons, whereas O'Higgins and Jenkins compute the average across households.

higher risk in Ireland. As a result of both their higher risk and higher weight in the population, families with children constitute a much higher proportion of those below the cut-offs in Ireland than in Britain. About 69 per cent of those below half average income in Ireland are families consisting of a couple with dependent children, compared with 45 per cent in Britain.

Conclusions

Is the Irish income distribution particularly unequal? And is state redistributive policy particularly ineffective in Ireland? Here we summarise the main findings as regards these basic questions underlying our investigations.

The Irish income distribution does appear unequal when compared with countries at higher levels of development. However, comparison with countries at similar or lower levels of development suggests that the Irish income distribution is *not* particularly unequal. Relative poverty rates—on either an income or an expenditure basis—were likewise found to be greater in Ireland than in the more developed EC countries, though not dissimilar from those in Spain and Greece, and below those of Portugal.

The Irish welfare effort is rather higher than might be expected on the basis of level of income per head. As elsewhere, most of the redistributive effect is attributable to cash transfers, with direct taxes playing a less important redistributive role; the progressive effect of non-cash benefits is in large part offset by regressive indirect taxes. Detailed comparisons with the UK, and more limited comparisons with other countries, suggest that this intervention is no less effective than in other countries. Thus, the greater degree of inequality in Irish incomes after government intervention can be traced back to greater inequality in market incomes.

What factors account for the differences between these findings and the view of the redistributive process put forward by Breen *et al.* (1990)? First, many of their arguments concerning the ineffectiveness of state intervention refer to class rather than income categories. One clear message from this paper is that the relationship between class categories and income deciles is a complex one, deserving of greater attention than it has received up to now. Second, Breen *et al.* have in mind a broader assessment of the state's role, including not only policies usually encompassed by redistribution studies, but also the provision of economic subsidies to industry and agriculture and the state's role as employer, which influence the distribution of what is termed 'market' income. There is, however, a third factor which the present analysis suggests should not be underestimated. It is that conclusions regarding the distribution and redistribution of income in Ireland can be heavily influenced by the international perspective in which they are located. Conclusions based on comparisons with the UK, or with other countries at higher levels of development than Ireland, may need to be substantially modified when a wider perspective, including countries at similar or lower levels of development, is adopted.

Acknowledgements. We would like to thank participants at the Nuffield conference, in particular the discussants, Michael O'Higgins and Mairéad Reidy, and the editors of this volume, for helpful comments and suggestions.

Proceedings of the British Academy, **79**, 205–239

The Irish Welfare State in Comparative Perspective

PHILIP J. O'CONNELL* & DAVID B. ROTTMAN†

* *Economic and Social Research Institute, Dublin*
† *National Center for State Courts, Williamsburg, USA*

Introduction

MOST INTERPRETATIONS of the transformation that Irish society has experienced since 1960 treat industrialisation as the central underlying dynamic. Typically, these interpretations also pay homage to the crucial role played by state industrial policies. This chapter explores an alternative interpretation of that transformation. Over the past three decades social citizenship rights have steadily expanded. In our view, this expansion of social rights constitutes a fundamental dynamic shaping contemporary Irish society, but neither the trend nor its significance has been sufficiently recognised. We argue that the expansion of social rights amounts to a silent revolution, one that vies for importance with industrialisation as a driving force in shaping Irish society.

Social citizenship refers to the bundle of social rights—to welfare, equality and security—to which citizens are entitled, unconditionally, by virtue of their membership of the national community. In Ireland, the range of exigencies from which people are protected has expanded dramatically over the past three decades. So has the proportion of the population enjoying such protection on an insurance rather than an assistance basis. The state increasingly takes responsibility not only for providing income replacement for the aged, the sick and the unemployed, but also for employment and for equality of opportunity. The progressive enhancement of social rights is a basic trend running through the changes that Ireland has experienced since 1960.

To argue that social citizenship has expanded in Ireland in recent

Read 8 December 1990. © The British Academy 1992.

decades is not, however, to assert that its quality has vastly improved. Inequalities were neither eliminated nor even greatly abated. While all citizens may have come to have virtually equal entitlements to a comprehensive range of social rights, services, and benefits, the interaction of those rights with market-generated inequalities generally results in the reproduction of inequality. What has evolved is a pay-related welfare state in which minimal levels of universal entitlement to income and services are supplemented by market-based resources. Thus, we argue that the expansion of the welfare state, and of social citizenship, was accomplished in such a manner as to leave privilege essentially undisturbed.

The impact of industrialisation in Ireland is not, in our view, as comprehensive or well-defined as that of the expansion of social rights. Industrial production and employment certainly expanded after 1960, but the change can hardly be deemed an industrial revolution. Moreover, although state industrial policies were undoubtedly important in shaping that growth, those policies represented but one moment in a more general process in which there was a marked expansion of state intervention in all important spheres of social and economic life. We do not believe that the expansion of social citizenship was an inevitable consequence of the development of industrial society in Ireland. Expansion occurred despite the strong opposition of the main economic planners. Rather, the real import of industrialisation may be that enhanced industrial productivity generated the increased surplus that is a necessary, but by no means sufficient, prerequistite for welfare state expansion.

This paper sets out our interpretation of how and why the Irish welfare state expanded and with what societal consequences. We look first at the degree to which the major existing theories of welfare state expansion apply to the Irish case, concluding that a state-centred approach is the most appropriate. Second, we define the welfare state as a political mode of allocation and distribution of resources, and, therefore, of life chances, independent of market forces.[1] Third, we detail the main features of the Irish welfare state as it evolved, concentrating on the period since 1960. Finally, we return to the central problem of explaining how and why the Irish welfare state expanded in so distinctive a manner and with consequences that proved to be so favourable to privilege.

---

[1] We follow Giddens (1973: 130–131) in understanding life chances to refer to 'the chances an individual has for sharing in the socially created economic or cultural "goods" that typically exist in any given society'.

Applicability of General Theories of the Welfare State to Ireland

Three general approaches to the study of the welfare state can be identified that recognise important national differences in welfare policies: the 'logic of industrialism', the 'social democratic' and the 'state-centred' approaches. These identify important factors in the development of welfare states, but no single approach appears to provide a satisfactory account of the Irish case. The logic of industrialism theory argues that the welfare state is a functionally necessary accompaniment to industrialisation. Economic development, giving rise to demographic change and social structural upheaval, generates both new needs and new resources for the expansion of the welfare function (Kerr *et al.* 1960; Wilensky, 1975). A similar functionalism is also evident in certain Marxist formulations, in which social policies are held to aid capital accumulation and serve needs for legitimacy (O'Connor, 1973). Functionalist theories generally fail to specify the mechanisms translating systemic needs into policy outcomes and encounter difficulties in accounting for welfare state variation among countries at similar levels of development. This is particularly evident when the welfare state is operationalised in terms of levels of spending on state transfers and benefits (Castles, 1982). Ireland is a case in point. The level of spending on welfare state functions, conventionally measured, is underpredicted by level of development.

The social democratic approach, in contrast, emphasises the strength of working-class interests and the capacity of unions and political parties representing those interests to press for welfare policy reforms (Shalev, 1983b; Stephens, 1979). A substantial body of empirical evidence, finding that nations with strong and centralised union movements and stable and enduring social democratic governments have high levels of welfare spending, supports the social democratic theory (Cameron, 1978, 1984; Castles, 1982; Furniss and Tilton, 1977; Korpi, 1980, 1983, 1989). Support for this thesis is qualified, however, in the light of assertions that the effect of social democracy is contingent on macroeconomic conditions and political system characteristics, and that social democracy is not the only route to the expansion of the welfare state (Shalev, 1983a; Skocpol and Amenta, 1986). In the Irish case, although union membership is somewhat above the European average, the labour movement is deeply fragmented. Moreover, the Labour Party has never enjoyed much electoral support and has generally been excluded from power, except as a minor partner in coalitions dominated by the right-wing Fine Gael party. Despite working-class weakness, however the share of welfare expenditures in Gross Domestic Product (GDP) has been higher in Ireland than in

Austria, Finland, Norway, and the United Kingdom—countries where the working-class is substantially more organised and mobilised.

Both the logic of industrialism and social democratic approaches view the state as determined by, or responsive to, societal forces and interests. The state-centred approach, in contrast, regards the state as an organisation with interests of its own to pursue. State-centred theories explain national differences in the timing and content of welfare policies in terms of historical variations in state structures. Crucial structural variables are the adminstrative capacities of states to introduce, finance and implement policies; prior state actions and policies that shape future policy innovations; and the degree to which states can act independently of powerful organised interests (Skocpol, 1981; 1985). The major criticism of this approach is that it overestimates the autonomy of the state and underestimates class biases within the state (Carnoy, 1984; Quadagno, 1987).

Advocates of a state-centred approach argue, howeer, that autonomy is a variable, 'not a fixed structural feature of any governmental system. It can come and go'. Autonomy is variable because 'the very *structural potentials* for autonomous actions change over time, as the organisations of coercion and adminstration undergo transformations, both internally and in their relations to societal groups and to representative parts of government' (Skocpol, 1985: 14). A state-centred view does not necessarily entail turning the society-centred view of the state on its head, as it were, by making the state into the dominant force in history.[2] Poggi (1990: 98) argues for a 'state centred view of the state itself', in which the state is a distinctive social force pursuing its own interests. But, he argues, that view needs to be juxtaposed with one recognising the importance of forms of social power other than the political that shape the structure and action of the state.

Our interpretation of the expansion of the welfare state in Ireland and of the consequences of that expansion relies on a state-centred approach. The Irish state has been an important agent of change since 1960, assuming a prominent role in the determination of the life chances of its citizens. But we do not argue that the welfare state has developed in isolation from its social context. On the contrary, our interpretation recognises the economic and political constraints on state interventions, as shaped by the particular pattern of democratisation, industrialisation, and class formation. Such an interpretation, moreover, can explain the quality of social citizenship in the welfare state, rather than simply the amount of money being spent.

---

[2] Although some interpretations will, of course, try to do just this: 'vulgar' statism as an antithesis to 'vulgar' Marxism.

What is the Welfare State?

The essence of the welfare state is that it confers social citizenship: a package or regime of programmes and policies that guarantee socially acceptable living standards independent of pure market forces (Marshall, 1950; Myles, 1988, Esping-Andersen, 1990). This conceptualisation of the welfare state returns to the inherent tension between politics and markets, between economy and society, that Polyani identifies in *The Great Transformation* (1944). The market cannot be separated from society. Market logic requires that land, capital and labour be treated as commodities, governed exclusively by the laws of exchange. But the reduction of individuals to mere commodities, subject to the laws of supply and demand, and thus to a market logic that threatens to exploit workers to such an extent that they become unable to reproduce themselves, undermines the social basis of the market itself. Polanyi argues that it falls to the state to counteract the deleterious consequences of an otherwise unfettered market in capitalist societies. Welfare state institutions and policies are thus essential characteristics of advanced capitalist societies, although states may differ greatly in how they organise welfare.

The welfare state, understood in terms of political intervention to protect individuals from disadvantages suffered in the marketplace, encompasses a far wider range of policy intervention than what is conventionally designated as 'social policy': that is, income maintenance, transfer payments, and services in health, housing, and education (Castles, 1988; Esping-Andersen, 1990).

Castles (1988: ix) provides an informal listing that indicates the multiplicity of policy actions protecting the individual in the welfare state:

> It can take the form of tariff protection, designed to cushion the impact of competitive market forces on wage levels or it can assume the character of industrial restructuring measures aimed at ensuring that individuals do not find themselves dependent on low-wage employment. It can focus on creating the conditions for full employment or it can provide compensation for those who cannot obtain jobs. It can seek to control wage levels or it can use state action to redistribute income through the tax-transfer system.

Esping-Andersen (1990: 2) also argues for a broad conceptualisation of the welfare state in terms of the quality of social rights: '. . . issues of employment, wages and macro-economic steering are considered integral components in the welfare-state complex', as is the impact of state policies on general social structure. Korpi (1980), moreover, identifies a series of stages of public intervention in the distribution of resources. Initial public interventions take the form of legislation affecting minimum wages and the bargaining power of unions. Policies affecting employment and labour force participation then shape the distribution of market incomes. Subsequent interventions, including taxes, transfers and public services shape the distribution of disposable incomes or 'buying' power. The welfare state is thus the political mediation of life-chances: the policies by which the state intervenes in, and interacts with, markets to protect the individual. How social rights are defined, how they are pursued, and with what resulting quality of social citizenship varies considerably among countries; but a broad definition, based on the notion of social citizenship, offers the most meaningful and analytically useful way of approaching the welfare state.

The welfare state as social citizenship rights can be captured empirically by focusing on three sets of state policies, programmes and activities designed to alter market outcomes:

1 state actions that affect the range of positions within the class structure available for market participation;
2 policies that have an impact on the processes by which persons are recruited into positions within the class structure;
3 state interventions that mitigate market-based income inequalities by levying taxes and distributing benefits.

The first set of welfare state policies is directed at the number and structure of positions in the labour market. The state is a significant employer in most of the advanced capitalist societies and underwrites a significant proportion of positions in the private sector, including those of proprietors and the self-employed. Employment in the public sector itself is the most obvious manifestation of this set of policies. 'In most major Western nations, the period since 1951 has seen a doubling in public employment as a proportion of the workforce' (Rose, 1985: 10). Public employment accounted for between a quarter and a third of the workforce in the early 1980s in Britain, France, Germany and Italy; the percentage in the United States, though considerably lower, was still substantial at 18.3 per cent (Rose, 1985: 11). Welfare state employment covers a broader set of positions located in both the private and public sectors. Denmark and the United States indicate the range of variation for the advanced societies. It is estimated that the welfare state (*c.* 1985) accounts for 28 per cent of employment in Denmark and 17 per cent in the United States. However, virtually all of that employment in Denmark (90 per cent) is in the public sector, in contrast to less than half (45 per cent) in the USA (Esping-Andersen, 1990: 158). Countries also differ in subsidies to proprietors and the self-employed that make such positions economically viable. Industrial policy more generally may have profound implications for the set of positions available to labour market participants, if, for example, it subsidises capital intensive, rather than labour-intensive, investment.

The second set of policies concern state interventions to structure the flow of individuals into the positions available for market participation. These policies are therefore concerned with the state role in fostering, or otherwise, equality of opportunity. Education policy plays a particularly large role in determining the degree of openness in the processes of recruitment of individuals to fill class positions. These policies also include efforts to counter discrimination by gender or race. The converse of these are policies that inhibit female labour force participation or, more specifically, labour force participation by married women.

The third, and most conventional, set of welfare-state policies refers to the redistribution of income that occurs through taxation and benefits. Benefits in principle include all social expenditures on income maintenance, health, education, housing and transportation. These may take the direct form of transfer payments or publicly provided services, or the more indirect forms of subsidies to users and 'tax expenditures', such as tax relief for mortgage interest payments or for personal pension contributions (both of the latter amounting to public subsidies to private saving). Participants in social insurance programmes transfer income from points at which income is being received to other points when income is absent owing to contingencies such as retirement, illness, or temporary unemployment. Participants and non-participants benefit from transfers from other age-cohorts funded from general tax revenue. Social security and similar programmes, however, capture only a part of what is being exchanged. Tax expenditures to persons accumulating private pensions can approach or exceed the value of what the state provides directly as cash income to the retired (Munnell, 1982; Hughes, 1991) and mortgage interest relief subsidises the purchase of a family home that will be owned outright by the point of retirement from the labour market.

A comprehensive understanding of the welfare state alerts us to the problems inherent in adopting more restrictive definitions. The share of national resources being devoted to social spending is an inadequate index of welfare effort because it is restricted to one way in which welfare objectives may be met (Heald, 1983). Similarly, income redistribution through state benefits and taxes does not represent the essence of a welfare state. Redistribution depends on two features of government taxation and expenditure: the average tax/benefit and the progressivity with which it is levied/distributed. If we look at the degree to which cash transfers are redistributive, for example, the United States may appear as a more efficacious welfare state than, say, Sweden, because the proportion of transfers going to the poor is higher (Myles, 1988: 268). This is due primarily to the residual nature of the American welfare state: spending is targeted as income replacement in the poor-law tradition and is consequently highly 'progressive', with the average rate of benefit declining as income increases. This progressivity is sufficient to offset the low levels of benefits in the United States relative to average labour market earnings.[3]

Of course, the more broadly we define the welfare state, the more likely it is to exert a significant impact on the market determination of life chances. Comparative or historical analysis, however, requires such breadth because most welfare state objectives can be pursued by, separately or jointly, intervening in the operation of the labour market, restructuring processes of recruitment to positions, or modifying the distribution of market incomes.

The Welfare State in Ireland, 1960–91

It is our contention that the Irish welfare state over the last three decades substantially (i) altered the range of positions within the class structure, (ii) shaped the rules by which individuals are recruited into those positions, and (iii) extended the range of collective entitlements or social rights in such a manner as to restrict the degree of inequality generated in the labour market, without, however, undermining the position of privileged groups. This section identifies what we regard as the main tendencies and trends within each sphere of the welfare state.

Class transformation and welfare state expansion

Over the last three decades in Ireland agricultural employment continued in its long-term decline, there was some increase in industrial employment, and massive growth in employment in services. Two overarching trends affecting the labour force accompanied these sectoral changes: an up-grading of the quality of positions in the labour market and a marked expansion in public sector employment. Moreover, from the mid-1970s onwards, the ranks of the unemployed rose steadily. The main underlying logic to the transformation these changes represent, however, is not the

---

[3] Generally, the redistributive impact of cash transfers depends, first, on the distribution of market earnings and on the proportion of the population without market incomes; second, on the degree to which transfers are targeted selectively to low- and zero-market income groups, rather than as universalistic entitlements to transfer income; and, third, on the level of benefits offered under various transfer programmes.

replacement of positions lost in agriculture, nor even the upgrading of skills within manufacturing. Instead, the predominant shift is away from positions governed by pure market forces and toward those dependent on state intervention. State industrial policies may have been instrumental in setting the class transformation in motion; state policies in other arenas proved equally, if not more, influential in reshaping the class structure.

The change in the class structure is most clearly shown in the changing composition of the male work force, as described in Table 1 for the years 1951–89.[4]

Late industrialisation in a peripheral economy does not transform the class structure in the manner previously experienced by the core group of advanced capitalist societies (Breen *et al.* 1990; O'Malley, this volume). In the Irish case, growth in manufacturing employment was modest and peaked during the second decade of export-led industrialisation. Manufacturing output in the Republic of Ireland rose almost fivefold between 1959 and 1988; manufacturing employment in 1988, however, was but one quarter higher than in 1959 (Kennedy, 1989: 36).

While industrialisation generated only modest gains in the numbers employed in manufacturing, the timing and location of Irish industrialisation did put its stamp on the class and occupational structures. What types of positions were created and reproduced over the three decades of industrial development? Skilled manual workers grew from 93,000 in 1961, representing 12 per cent of the work force, to 163,000 in 1981, just over one-fifth of the work force. Over the 1980s, however, both the numbers and the share of the male work force in skilled manual employment declined. Positions in semi-skilled and unskilled manual work also declined sharply over those years, and by 1989 accounted for only 8.9 per cent of the work force. Therefore, employment in industry did not compensate for the persistent decline in agriculture. For industrial workers with minimal or low skills, moreover, the trends represent job losses, not upgrading to new positions in modern manufacturing.

The rise after 1961 in the proportion of the work force occupying skilled manual positions is overshadowed by the more sustained growth in positions available for upper middle class employees and for non-agricultural proprietors (including here both employers and the self-

---

[4] Excluding the unemployed focuses attention on positions available for market participation. However, the size of the total number at work varies significantly due to emigration (outward migration in the 1950s and 1980s; return migration in the 1970s) and the high rates of unemployment since the late 1970s. This means that the numbers in a class can remain constant over time while its share of the work force rises or falls. Table 1 therefore includes both the numbers in each category, by year, and the percentage of the work force each class represents.

Table 1. Males at Work by Class Categories, 1951–1989.

	Number					%				
	1951	1961	1971	1981	1989	1951	1961	1971	1981	1989
EMPLOYERS AND SELF-EMPLOYED										
Agriculture										
(i) employers	27,844	14,001		13,540	10,500	3.1	1.8		1.7	1.7
(ii) self-employed and relatives assisting	314,768	265,524	212,982[a]	140,841	120,400	35.1	34.2	27.5[a]	17.5	16.4
Non-agricultural										
(i) employers	19,689	12,582		35,679	37,200	2.2	1.6		4.4	5.1
(ii) self-employed and relatives assisting	52,522	47,897	64,624[a]	42,408	62,400	5.9	6.2	8.3[a]	5.3	8.5
EMPLOYEES[b]										
(i) upper middle class	47,780	58,959	84,512	128,499	133,400	5.3	7.6	10.9	16.0	18.1
(ii) lower middle class	123,011	121,134	139,991	163,012	153,400	13.8	15.6	18.0	20.3	20.8
(iii) skilled manual	90,400	92,632	128,056	163,021	131,400	10.1	12.0	16.5	20.3	17.9
(iv) semi/unskilled manual										
(a) agricultural	94,957	64,753	40,245	25,780	22,000	10.6	8.4	5.2	3.2	3.0
(b) non-agricultural	124,789	96,731	105,384	89,962	65,000	13.9	12.5	13.6	11.2	8.9
TOTAL AT WORK[b]	896,624	774,540	776,507	808,670	737,700	100.0	100.0	100.0	100.0	100.0
TOTAL UNEMPLOYED[c]	36,115	46,989	55,157	91,279	157,300	3.7	5.7	6.6	10.1	17.6

[a] Employers and self-employed were not distinguished in the 1971 Census.
[b] Total numbers at work includes a small number of individuals who could not be allocated to a class, and excludes theological students, 'professional students', and 'articled clerks'; in 1981 it also excludes persons in hospital.
[c] Percentage figures = unemployed as % of gainfully occupied.
Sources: 1951, 1961, 1971 and 1981 *Census of Population of Ireland*; unpublished 1989 Labour Force Survey tabulations provided by the Central Statistics Office.

Table 2. Percentage changes in class membership, 1961–89.

	1961–71	1971–81	1981–89
Upper middle class employees	+43.3	+52.0	+3.8
Non-agricultural proprietors and self-employed	+6.9	+20.8	+27.6
Skilled manual workers	+38.2	+27.3	−19.5

employed). Table 2 expresses the percentage change in the numbers in these classes over each decade. By that index, opportunities for labour market participation were expanding most rapidly for upper middle class employees during the 1960s and 1970s, and for proprietors during the 1980s. The most resilient growth trend is in the class most likely to benefit in terms of enhanced employment prospects from state expansion: upper middle class professionals, administrators and managers.

The direct effect of state intervention in labour markets was the increase in employment in the state itself. Employment in the state sector grew from 118,000 in 1961 to 235,000 in 1981 (Kennedy and McHugh, 1984). If state-sponsored bodies are included, by 1981 the public sector employed one-third of the non-agricultural labour force (Humphreys, 1983: 88). Until the mid-1980s, the rate of expansion in the public sector continued to outstrip growth in the total labour force. The trend of public sector growth over the 1960s and 1970s, and decline in the latter half of the 1980s, is summarised in Table 3. In the 1960s, growth in the central civil service (male and female employees) approached that experienced for skilled manual work; by the 1970s, opportunities in the public sector (and especially in the central civil service) were expanding at a far higher rate than in industry. This is consistent with the experience of most European democracies. Generally, public sector growth was greater in the more prosperous, social democratic countries. Ireland and Italy, however, are exceptions, with substantial growth in public employment in the absence of either prosperity or social democratic dominance (Rose, 1985: 7).

The expansion of opportunities for middle class employment was not, of course, confined to the public sector. Some of the growth in the upper middle class reflects the employment of senior managers, engineers and accountants in the industrial sector. Employment in the private services sector also benefited from purchases of services by manufacturing firms and their employees. But the expansion of the state was so rapid as to have generated the bulk of the growth. Industrial production and its trickle down effects certainly contributed to financing the rise in public spending and, thus, employment (although the effects were muted by the virtual immunity from taxation enjoyed by foreign capital). Yet public

Table 3. Percentage growth in the public sector, 1961–90.

	1961–71	1971–81	1981–90
Central civil service	34.6	57.8	−18.1
Total public sector	23.7	42.1	−8.2

Sources: Ross (1986: 289, 303) for 1961 to 1981; IPA (1990: 395) for 1981–90.

employment, and particularly the expanding welfare state, proved the more substantial and durable factor in class transformation. Even in the 1980s, public employment in health and education was essentially stable, despite an overall decline of 8.2 per cent in the total public sector and of virtually the same magnitude, 8.8 per cent, in the total number at work (IPA, 1990: 395).

The transformation of Ireland's class structure appears distinctive in the degree to which it fostered an expansion in the number of non-agricultural proprietors and an enlargement of their share of the work force. Industrialisation is typically associated with a general shift from self-employment into wage-employment. In Ireland, non-agricultural self-employment did decline consistently from 1926 to 1961, but thereafter began to expand with increasing vigour in successive decades (see Tables 1 and 2 above). This coincided since the mid-1970s with a general trend in EC countries—especially Belgium, Italy, and the United Kingdom—toward growth in self-employment (Steinmetz and Wright, 1989). Ireland may therefore be seen as a precursor of a structural reversal in the fortunes of the petty bourgeoisie, although such an interpretation is open to debate (cf. Linder and Houghton, 1990; Steinmetz and Wright, 1990). However, the state can undoubtedly play a key role in reducing the risks of starting a business. Taxation policies may favour the self-employed, labour market and industrial programmes may underwrite the start up costs of a small business for those unemployed, and the self-employed can in various ways be incorporated into state subsidised social insurance schemes. More recently, and of likely import in Ireland, attempts to reduce the size of the state sector, and thereby state expenditure, have resulted in the transfer of tasks (and professional workers who perform them) to the private sector. Early retirement and redundancy packages facilitate the duplication in the private sector of positions once formally within the state sector but no less dependent on state support for their viability.

State employment policies also offer incentives to entrepreneurship, a quality some believe to be inadequately emphasised in Irish culture (Kenny, 1984; Lee, 1989). That concern seems misplaced, in view of the fact that one in twenty members of the male non-agricultural work force is an employer and a further one in twelve is self-employed—a strikingly high percentage by European standards. It is particularly so, given the degree to which industrial policy has sought, successfully, to create employment by offering incentives to foreign capital and, since the mid-1960s, without excessive regard for native industry's share of the home market. Native entrepreneurs seem nonetheless to have been encouraged by the substantial package of tax incentives, adaptation grants, advisory bodies, subsidised labour, and sectoral specific schemes established by the state.

It appears, therefore, that industrial workers were not the sole beneficiaries of state policies in recent decades. Foreign capital is tempted to invest in Ireland by the offer of subsidies that are extraordinarily generous by the standards of other industrial democracies (OECD, 1978). Native entrepreneurs, employees with secure and well remunerated positions in the state bureaucracy and professionals in medicine and other fields who provide social services subsidised by the state are also filling positions in the class structure that depend on the state, and, more specifically, on the welfare state.

Finally, one should note a further twist to the new class structure that is attributable to state policy. Regional policy led to a decentralisation of industry. As a result, the working class beneficiaries of jobs in industry are not labouring, for the most part, in industrial cities. Late industrialisation in Ireland intruded more upon the rural than the urban landscape, as the bulk of manufacturing plants—and industrial employment—were located outside of the major urban areas. Office blocks and sprawling commuter suburbs, not factories or warehouses, give Dublin its current 'character' and account for its ever growing population. In fact, Irish industrialisation was perhaps of primary benefit to small farmers, who were able to use the new positions to forge successful adaptive strategies that allowed them to survive on the land with a respectable standard of living (Hannan and Commins, this volume).

In sum, the increasing salience of the state mediation of life chances is evident in

1   state policies that fostered public employment;
2   welfare state expansion that created jobs not only for public employees, but also for self-employed professionals and private sector employees;
3   state economic, social and taxation policies which underwrite property-based market capacities that would not be otherwise viable;
4   rationalisation strategies implemented in pursuit of fiscal rectitude which, in recent years, shifted positions from the state sector into self-employment; and
5   regional policies which redistributed industrial jobs from urban to rural areas.

Together, these state interventions were as influential as industrial policy in determining one of the most fundamental of life chances: the possibility for secure market participation. We turn next to how the state affected the distribution of access to those positions in the period 1960-90.

Recruitment and state policies

Within the span of twenty years, roughly 1950 to 1970, the Irish class structure shifted from one based primarily on property ownership to one based on educational credentials and wage-employment. Access to the most valued credentials governed, by and large, who would be recruited into the positions created for skilled manual work and for white collar professional, administrative and managerial employment.

The transitional process is one of formal equality of opportunity interacting with considerable inequality of conditions. In the mid-1960s a series of reforms left the basic structure of the educational system largely unaffected but nonetheless vastly expanded its scope (see Tussing, 1978; Hannan *et al.*, 1983). The chief reform was free education at the post-primary level, introduced in 1967. Institutional change through the introduction of non-denominational comprehensive schools and the establishment of a Higher Education Authority can also be traced back to that period. But the main impact was in educational participation. Among 16 year olds, the participation rate was 36.8 per cent in 1963–64; by 1984–85 it had reached 80.3 per cent. The change over those years among 19 year olds was from 8.8 per cent to 23.6 per cent (Breen *et al.*, 1990: 127).

The effect of this expansion of social citizenship was shaped by the interaction between the method of state financing for education and social class differentials in the take-up of the new educational opportunities. State support for education per pupil at second level is essentially a constant amount across private and public, fee paying and 'free' schools, with the bulk of teachers' salaries being paid by the state. Costs have been assumed by the state for parents with children in the 'free' sector. Where parents enrol their children in fee-paying schools, the state subsidy forms the foundation on which the fees they pay will support enhancements. Also, the schools in the 'free' second level (approximately 440 out of 500 secondary schools in 1986) differ in their resources according to what additional resources parents and schools make available (Breen, 1984a; Breen *et al.*, 1990: 114). Tuition and fees paid by the pupils' parents and endowments, if any have been established, supplement what the exchequer provides. Until 1986, fee paying schools also received a slightly reduced capitation grant. State financing of education was, therefore, a key instrument for expanding social citizenship. The state underwrote the full cost of second level schooling, allowing for a dualism in which the market could supplement the bedrock minimum that the state undertook to provide. Scholarships and grants to individual students also facilitated and encouraged continued educational participation beyond the mandatory age of 15 (raised from 14 in 1972).

The vastly expanded opportunities to obtain educational qualifications offered by the state subsidy were overwhelmingly taken up by children from middle class families. True, rates of participation increased for all class categories, resulting in differentials between classes that were roughly the same in the 1980s as they had been in the 1960s (Breen *et al.*, 1990). Participation by working class children in second and third level education, however, remains so low as to effectively inhibit their mobility outside of their parents' class. The emphasis on formal qualifications extended to competition for apprenticeships, one of the traditional ladders of working class mobility from low skilled backgrounds into skilled employment. Thus, in the keenly competitive Irish labour market of the 1980s, middle class children were able to 'trade down' their non-vocational credentials for access to secure and well paid jobs (Breen, 1984a).

In fact, the disadvantages associated with early school leaving appear to expand rather than to abate over time. Making the shift from unemployment into a job depends on two related factors. 'The first of these is educational qualifications, the second is the individual's labour force record, where the duration of current unemployment is important in reducing the chances of getting a job' (Breen, 1991b: 81). This leads to a vicious cycle, in which the initial gap in labour market success associated with credentials expands: 'because they have no qualifications and a poor employment record early leavers are unable to get a stable job—which further worsens their employment record . . .' (Breen, 1991b: 80).

Class barriers proved resistant, by and large, to state initiatives that sought to equalise access to education and, as part of economic development policy, upgrade the skills of the Irish work force (the two facets of state policy and the links to contemporary OECD thinking are discussed in Breen *et al.*, 1990: 124–126). Family resources rooted in the old, proprietorial class structure facilitated acquisition of the credentials and qualifications that governed access to the new class positions in services, industry, and the welfare state. A formal expansion of a major right of social citizenship, that to education, did not generate a real change in the degree of openness in Irish society.

Gender barriers proved to be equally resistant. Ireland's economic development policy might be expected to have facilitated the entry of more women into the labour force, creating more openness as expressed in higher female labour force participation and a shift away of women workers from traditional female occupations (Pyle, 1990: 3). But the female share of the Irish work force rose only from 25.9 per cent to 28.4

per cent in the first two decades of active state development policy, and Ireland's female labour force participation rate in 1981 was the lowest in the OECD, well below the weighted average of 37.0 per cent (Pyle, 1990: 26).[5] This modest overall increase masks two trends: a slight decline in the participation rate by single women and a substantial increase—a doubling over the 1970s—in participation by married women (Blackwell, 1989; Mahon, 1991). Gender inequalities interact with those located in the educational system and, more generally, in the class structure: there is a strong correlation between labour force participation and the level of education attained (Review Group, 1991: 8). State policies, often reinforced or compelled by EC regulations and rulings, removed most formal barriers to female labour force participation. Regional policy, industrial policy, taxation policy and social welfare policy combined, however, to shape and limit the extent of women's involvement in the labour market.[6]

For our purposes, the recruitment and promotion of women within the state sector itself is of particular relevance. After all, formal barriers to recruitment, retention, and promotion were abolished in the 1960s and 1970s. The presence of women in the various grades constituting the central civil service is shown in Table 4. In describing women's place within the civil service, this is one of the rare situations where the data do speak for themselves. Untangling the factors that create this outcome is more complex, requiring reference to, first, the selection process through which candidates are recruited into the main promotional grades and, second, the rates of promotion upward from those grades. Recruitment into the main promotion grades works to the disadvantage of female candidates. In part, this can be traced to the winnowing effects of face-to-face interviews, since female applicants score as well or better than males on written tests and other universalistic criteria. The impact is cumulative: 'A low recruitment of women to these posts now will in time mean the continuity of vertical segregation: their absence from the top level posts' (Mahon, 1991: 24). The restricted access by women to the main promotional grades is then exacerbated by a selection process that discourages women from applying and imposes standards of 'suitability' that are not gender neutral (Mahon, 1991: ch. 5).

From the 1960s onwards, there was a substantial increase in the intervention of the state into the processes by which positions in the class

---

[5] Toward the end of the decade the rate had risen to 31.9 per cent, but was still the lowest in the EC (Mahon, 1991: 2).

[6] Pyle (1990) appears to underestimate the powerful disincentives in the tax code to married women's labour force participation.

Table 4. Representation of women in civil service grades, 1987.

Grade	% Female
Secretary	0
Assistant Secretary	1
Principal Officer	5
Assistant Principal Officer	23
Administrative Officer	26
Higher Executive Officer	34
Executive Officer	44
Staff Officer	67
Clerical Officer	68
Clerical Assistant	83
Overall	38

Source: Mahon (1991: 21)

structure are filled. Social citizenship was extended in ways that nominally opened access to the more advantaged positions in the class structure regardless of class or gender. But formal equality of opportunity interacted with inequality of conditions with the result that the actual change effected was slight in contrast to the massive changes in legislation and state funding. In education, and we shall argue in other areas of policy in the pay-related welfare state, intervention spread thin, in the form of minimal social rights, rather than deep, in the form of programmes targeted to those most in need, was not sufficient to overturn privilege.

Redistribution through benefits and taxation

Three general trends are evident in traditional welfare state policies to alleviate market-based inequalities: the erection of an assistance-based safety net of support at higher levels of benefit; the growth of the proportion of the workforce incorporated into social insurance; and the development of a pay-related form of service delivery, particularly in health care and education, in which a basic universal subsidy serves as the foundation on which those with advantaged positions in the class structure can purchase a better quality of service.

The strongest expression of social citizenship took the form of a patchwork of income maintenance programmes created as the state granted official recognition and redress for an increasingly wide range of specific contingencies. Today, virtually all of the standard welfare contingencies are covered by state programmes (although some only on a means tested basis) and most of the labour force is protected by full social insurance. This is a marked change from the 1950s, when provision was

Table 5.   Social Insurance Coverage, 1953–90.

	Number insured	% of labour force with full coverage
1953	724,000	51.7
1961	713,000	56.8
1971	808,000	65.5
1981	1,129,000	74.2
1990	1,471,019	75.3

Sources: Maguire (1987: 468, Table 7) for 1953–81; Department of Social Welfare (1991: 9, Table A8) for 1991.

made for only a narrow range of contingencies and only a small proportion of the workforce was insured against those contingencies on a non-means tested basis.

Universalism, however, is largely limited to the health and educational systems. In income maintenance programmes there are significant disparities between differing categories of beneficiaries. Several groups are excluded from social insurance: married women not at work in the labour market being the most numerous category. Finally, the tax system operates in ways that often cut across the effects from the social welfare system. The heavy reliance on indirect taxation ensures that even those living off social welfare payments return a significant proportion of their incomes to the exchequer (Rottman and Hannan, 1981; Breen *et al.*, 1990).

(i)   The framework of entitlements

Social insurance extended only to manual and other low paid employees until the late 1970s. The trend toward universalism is evident in Table 5, which traces the change in the number of insured persons and the percentage of the labour force covered for all contingencies. The circumference of the social insurance umbrella expanded dramatically in the 1970s and 1980s. In 1974 social insurance was extended to all white collar employees under the new Pay Related Social Insurance (PSRI) scheme. The number of persons with social insurance entitlements grew by 40 per cent over the decade. By 1990, virtually all employees apart from 'permanent and pensionable' public servants were covered for the full range of benefits. Persons on training schemes were included, as were those who were unable to work but entitled to be credited with contributions (25 per cent of all insured persons). In terms of breadth of coverage, the universalistic component of the welfare state had truly 'grown to its limits' with the inclusion of the self-employed.

The changing balance between means-tested assistance and universalistic

Table 6. Trends in the incidence of insurance and assistance.

	Insurance		Assistance		Total
	Number	%	Number	%	number
1947	56,926	19.3	237,748	80.7	294,674
1966	170,090	50.0	170,044	50.0	340,134
1971	211,273	52.6	190,415	47.4	401,688
1982	350,230	56.8	266,054	43.2	616,284
1990	382,843	52.2	350,454	47.8	733,297

Sources: Commission on Social Welfare (1986: 60) for 1947–82; Department of Social Welfare (1991: 5) for 1990.

social insurance cash benefits is further revealed in Table 6 which shows trends in recipients. First, an expanded state role is evident: the number of recipients of weekly social welfare payments rose two-and-a-half times from 1947 to 1990. Most of that growth occurred in the 1970s. Second, by the 1960s, a rough balance had been reached in which about half of all recipients received insurance-based payments and one-half means-tested assistance. The two systems are linked for several key contingencies, notably unemployment, where insurance entitlements have a fixed duration after which payments are made as means-tested assistance. The growth in the proportion of the long-term unemployed in total unemployment may account for the shift back between 1982 and 1990 toward assistance payments. The provision made for recipients of both insurance and assistance became more generous over recent decades. To varying degrees, the level of payment offered in the various programmes rose more rapidly than inflation from the 1960s to the 1980s (McCashin, 1982; Department of Social Welfare, 1991), closing the gap between those dependent on social welfare for their income and those with market incomes.

When we assert that social citizenship has expanded since 1960, the reference is most immediately to the increase in the contingencies against which state provision is made. Income maintenance programmes are created to cater for long-term illness, unemployment, marital desertion, retirement, and other eventualities. Typically, as the range of contingencies expands, so does the proportion of the population that can seek shelter under the umbrella of the welfare state. This expansion is not, however, an inexorable march towards convergence in actual life circumstances among the population or towards reduction in the extent to which privilege is transmitted from one generation to the next.

The Irish experience of welfare state expansion in fact stands in stark contrast to the Scandinavian pattern. In Scandinavian welfare state expansion, changes occurred along two main dimensions: first, universalistic entitlements created solidarity among classes and between other social categories; second, a commitment to the levelling of inequalities was given expression in all spheres of social policy (Myles, 1989: 62). In the Irish case, commitment to reducing inequality has been slight, showing strength only in the mid-1960s (Maguire, 1986). There was greater stress, concentrated in the 1970s and 1980s, on achieving social solidarity through an expanded social insurance system. This coincided with experimentation with neo-corporatist arrangements (Hardiman, 1988). However, unless tied to a commitment to reduce inequality, the extension of social insurance to the middle classes or the universal provision of services can exacerbate rather than reduce inequalities.

That is what we believe occurred in Ireland. The expansion of old age pensions provides a good illustration of how the pay-related welfare state reproduces market inequalities. Provision for old age originated with a general means-tested pension established by the British Administration.[7] Subsequently, in 1960, an insurance based pension system was established offering a flat rate pension at age 70 for manual workers and low paid service workers. Insurance coverage was extended in 1974 to all employees and the normal pension age gradually reduced to age 66 (by 1977). The self-employed were incorporated into the insurance system in 1988. A parallel retirement pension is available from age 65 but requires the recipient to leave the labour force, an action that is not a prerequisite for receiving the old age pension (Maguire, 1986; Hughes, 1991). The pension system that has emerged reflects both the expansion of social citizenship and the way in which social and market rights interact in Ireland. There are three tiers. Entitlement to non-contributory old-age pensions, which provide for those with intermittent or marginal labour market participation, is subject to a means test. Contributory state pensions form a second tier and can be universally attained in the private sector and by the self-employed, and are open to most state sector employees. Where state contributory pensions are combined with occupational and private pensions, a third tier is formed.

All three tiers benefited from the rise in the real value of state pensions —by just over 50 per cent in both the 1960s and 1970s (Maguire, 1986: 285), and by a more modest 11.6 per cent in the 1980s (Department of Social Welfare, 1991: 15–16). That rise in benefit levels is the main gain achieved by the semi-skilled and unskilled working class. For most working-class employees, passing a means test would not pose an insurmountable obstacle to receiving a state pension. The higher level of benefit

---

[7] The Old-Age Pension Act, 1908, went into effect in 1909, and responsibility for the system was assumed by the Irish government after independence.

that they receive is only possible, however, because of the broad inclusive-
ness sought and achieved by social insurance policy. That is to the benefit
of the middle class and the basis for the third tier of the system. Middle-
class employees can combine a social insurance pension with occupation
pension entitlements, private pensions and savings, all subsidised through
tax expenditures, in order to attain financial comfort in old age. Those
covered by private occupational pensions are likely to be in white collar
rather than manual employment, males rather than females, in large rather
than small firms—in other words, to occupy secure, well-paid employment. All public sector employees in Ireland enjoy the security of an
occupational pensions scheme, as compared to an estimated 32.3 per cent
(in 1985) of private sector employees (Hughes, 1991). Occupational
pensions are earnings related; state pensions are set at a flat rate. The
result is that privately financed, but state subsidised, occupational pensions
yield incomes that, as indexed by the replacement ratio, tend to be above
international targets, while the income afforded by state pensions falls
below that target (Hughes, 1991: 79–80). Retired middle-class employees
consequently enjoy a considerably enhanced income compared to retirees
in other classes (Whelan and Whelan, 1988).

The significance of the interaction between private provision and
welfare state programmes is considerable. Occupational and private
pensions represent an accumulation of money that increasingly matters.
Pension assets amounted to 6 per cent of GNP in 1975, 10 per cent in 1980
and 38 per cent in 1989 (Hughes, 1991: 14). The tax expenditure underlying those assets is nearly as large as direct state expenditure in the form
of pension payments. In 1989, tax relief on the income of approved pension
schemes amounted to 172 million pounds (Hughes, 1991: 68). A universal
entitlement to a state-guaranteed minimal pension is, therefore, supplemented by private savings and insurance based schemes that are subsidised
by state tax expenditure for higher income groups, thus reinforcing market
based inequalities. This echoes the pattern found in education, whereby a
universal entitlement forms a foundation on which parents can build by
adding their own money to the state subsidy to obtain a higher quality of
education. Similarly, free hospital care, until changes in 1991, underwrote
part of the costs of a stay in a private hospital ward, with the patient and/
or insurer paying the difference between the subsidy and the actual cost
(Rottman and Reidy, 1988; Nolan, 1991). This amounts to a 'pay-related'
welfare state, premised on a mixing of private and public components to
attain a final level of benefit.

Although the degree to which the Irish middle class in fact benefited
from the expansion of social citizenship is demonstrable, its inclusion was
a result of state policies, not demands expressed and realised through party

politics. Middle and high income white collar workers had the opportunity to contribute to social insurance on a voluntary basis before 1974; the self-employed similarly could contribute prior to their mandatory incorporation in 1988. But few in either group volunteered to participate. There were some 6,000 voluntary contributors in 1974 prior to the abolition of the earnings limit for non-manual workers and fewer than 900 voluntary contributors in 1984 when the self-employed represented the only major non-insured segment of the labour force (Commission on Social Welfare, 1986: 498).

(ii) Financing the welfare state

Citizenship entails both obligations and rights.[8] The obligations of citizens in a welfare state are most immediately expressed in the manner through which public social expenditure is financed. Two aspects of the financial obligations of welfare state citizenship receive attention here: the structure of taxation as it affects the impact of social expenditure and the question of who funds social insurance.

The progressivity or regressivity of tax collection alternatively enhances or blunts the impact of state income replacement programmes and social service provision. The stratification outcomes of any given social policy will depend on the taxes used to finance public spending and debt. Currently, about one half of the income dispensed by the Irish welfare state is drawn from general tax revenue or borrowing (Department of Social Welfare, 1991). If spending on health, education and housing is taken into consideration, the overwhelming proportion of the welfare state is funded through taxes.

There are some important consistencies in Irish taxation policy that bear on the amount of redistribution from social expenditure, and some notable changes in direction as well. Tax policy in Ireland has been shaped by subservience to the goal of economic development, a narrow base for taxation of income, historical and political associations that make government reluctant to levy tax on land, and the effects of inflation. These features of the tax burden are important, but neglected, factors for understanding the quality of social citizenship achieved in Ireland.[9]

The changing profile of Irish taxes can be traced in Table 7. One consistency is a general preference for taxing goods and services rather

---

[8] Citizenship in the modern state is 'a set of mutual claims and reciprocal involvements binding together the state and the individuals' (Poggi, 1990: 33).
[9] Murphy (1984) summarises the results from conventional redistribution analyses using Irish data. Callan and Nolan (this volume) place Irish redistribution patterns in comparative perspective.

Table 7. The structure of taxation, 1955–1985.

	% of total tax revenue			
	1955	1965	1975	1985[a]
Personal income	16.4	16.7	25.2	31.3
Corporate income	7.4	9.1	4.8	3.2
Employer social security	2.4	3.3	8.2	9.4
Employee social security	2.2	3.2	5.6	5.2
Property	19.2	15.1	9.7	4.0
Goods and services	52.4	52.6	46.5	44.4
Total	100	100	100	100[a]
total tax as % of GDP	22.5	26.0	31.5	38.9

[a] Since 1980 an 'employment and training levy' and a 'health contribution' of 1 per cent have applied to all earnings (up to an upper income limit for the 'health' levy) and, between 1983 and 1986, a special levy of 1 per cent was imposed to raise revenue for unspecified uses. All three were collected in conjunction with PRSI. Employees pay the current levies unless they hold 'Medical Cards', in which case the employer pays the tax. The resulting revenue is classified in the OECD accounts as being derived from 'payroll taxes' and represented 2.3 per cent of total tax receipts in 1985.
Source: OECD (1989b: Tables 3, 47, 112 and 115).

than income, for, as a Fianna Fáil Minister for Finance put it in the late 1960s, 'it discourages excessive spending but not earning or saving' (quoted in Sandford and Morrisey, 1985: 50). Corporate income is not a substantial source of tax revenue. Economic development policies offered 'negligible' corporate tax rates (Telesis, 1982) and high depreciation allowances as part of what became the most generous tax-expenditure package for investors in the OECD.[10] Therefore, although foreign capital generated a level of corporate income hitherto unavailable for taxation, tax from that source declined in importance after an initial boost in the early 1960s.

Sheer growth in taxation is the most dramatic change. Total tax revenue in 1955 amounted to 22.5 per cent of Ireland's GDP, commensurate with the state's limited ambitions during the early decades of independence. By 1985, tax revenue had grown to the equivalent of 38.4 per cent of GDP, with much of the increase having occurred in the 1970s. Even so, this only partly funded the more active state of recent decades —total public expenditure in 1985 representing just under two-thirds (65.8 per cent) of GDP. The rising tax burden was accompanied by a shift away from property tax and towards taxes on income. Tax on property declined significantly as a revenue source in recent years, particularly after a

[10] The generosity of the subsidies presented difficulties for those undertaking comparative evaluation: 'Ireland's extremely large subsidies require a different scale' (McKee, Visser and Saunders, 1986).

commitment made in the course of the 1977 general election was honoured. An attempt by the Coalition government ousted by that election to introduce a wealth tax was also terminated, but even in its heyday generated little revenue but much controversy (Sandford and Morrisey, 1985).

The compensating increases came from taxes on personal income and from social insurance contributions. In the inflationary 1970s, the failure to act sufficed to significantly raise revenue from income tax because inflation steadily—and rapidly—eroded the real value of tax bands and tax exemptions. The result was more revenue but less progressivity (Rottman and Hannan, 1981). Social insurance contributions also soared, particularly with the expansion of PRSI in 1974. Overall, social insurance represented 4.6 per cent of tax revenue in 1955 and 14.6 per cent in 1985 and the share borne by employers increased four-fold and that by employees doubled.

Taxation in Ireland constrained what was achieved through welfare state policies. Targeting consumer spending as the primary source of tax revenue and exempting property and corporate incomes meant that the costs of welfare state expansion were borne by working class and middle class households alike. Progressivity in personal income tax and the substantial (relative to the average wage) levels of benefits make the overall effect of state interventions redistributive. This needs to be assessed, however, in the light of the sizable proportion of the Irish population without a market income and the income tax rate accruing to employees with modest incomes. Further, the favourable tax position afforded to farmers and to proprietors generally served to underwrite the viability of their positions within the class structure.

Beyond the general impact of the tax structure, the shares paid by employers, by employees and by the state define the nature and impact of social insurance. The share funded by each of the three contributors varies among countries and, in Ireland, varied over the decades. Tripartite funding was characteristic of continental European welfare states from their inception. However, in Britain greater deference was made to the interests of private insurers (Ashford, 1986: 163), an influence that was yet more pronounced in Ireland, where a powerful producer group, the medical profession, allied with the Catholic hierarchy, successfully lobbied for exclusion from key British reforms in the 1911–13 period (Barrington, 1987: 39–66). The welfare state framework that Ireland inherited in 1922, therefore, relied more on actuarial principles than on social solidarity in justifying social insurance and defining to whom it applied. Professionals and institutional providers of services in areas such as medicine and education were able to shape public policy—a further aspect of the more general pattern in which middle class actors enjoy greater capacity to determine outcomes in the welfare arena in their own favour.

In Europe a shift toward a broader conception of social insurance is evident from the late 1940s. There has been a movement away from a social insurance system heavily reliant on state subsidy to one that is heavily funded by employers' contributions. In Ireland, however, employer social insurance contributions have essentially kept the corporate sector's share of total tax revenue at its 1955 level, and the actual rates of tax involved are low relative to those found in countries such as France or Germany.

The increased yield from social security taxes did not fund the expanded rights to income replacement. Before the incorporation of white collar employees into PRSI, the Social Insurance Fund was truly tripartite in funding: 30 per cent from employers, 28 per cent from employees, and 40 per cent from the state (see Table 8). With most employees included, the burden shifted in the direction of employer PRSI contributions with the state's share initially falling, then rising again in the early 1980s and in 1990 falling to 5.9 per cent of the Fund, as a result of strenuous efforts to reduce the budget deficit. The share financed from employee contributions was 26.2 per cent in 1990, little changed from twenty-five years before.[11] The insurance based segment of the welfare state, expanding substantially in importance since the 1960s, was therefore funded primarily by employers' contributions and by a considerable state subsidy. That subsidy could not be sustained when the late 1980s brought massive demands for expenditure on assistance based programmes, including from those whose entitlement to short-term income support had expired. Fiscal rectitude reappeared as a prime political virtue toward the end of the decade, making the reduction of the public debt a priority. The state's contribution to the Social Insurance Fund was a place where cuts could be effected. Yet, the commitment to maintaining the real value of social welfare payments and the level of social services remains. So does the principle of tripartite social insurance funding although its integrity seems somewhat tattered. In *Social Security* a 'white paper' issued in 1949, tripartite funding was justified on the basis that employees, employers, and the state all benefit: employees are insured against contingencies, employers gain in worker productivity, and the state enjoys an enhanced 'standard of efficiency, contentedness and security of the workers' that makes it 'equitable that the Exchequer, that is to say, the community as a whole, should also continue to bear its

---

[11] There was less change over the period in the state's share of the total social welfare budget: 69.6 per cent in 1965; 57.8 per cent in 1975; 60.2 per cent in 1985; and 52.9 per cent in 1990 (the latter year is atypical, the 1989 share was 57.2 per cent).

Table 8. Percentage shares of Social Insurance Fund finance.

Year	Employers	Employees	State	Self-employed	Other	Total
1965	29.5	28.0	39.9	–	2.6	100
1975	47.3	29.3	22.8	–	0.5	100
1985	47.9	23.2	28.8	–	0.2	100
1990	63.8	26.2	5.9	3.7	0.4	100

Sources: Department of Social Welfare (1967: Table 43D; 1976: Table 48E; 1987: Table 78; 1991: Table G6).

share of the burden of social insurance and so keep the contribution of the individual worker down to a reasonable level' (quoted in the Commission on Social Welfare, 1986: 272).[12] However, it is questionable whether the current levels of social citizenship can be sustained through 'reasonable levels' of employee and employer contributions in the absence of a more substantial state subsidy.

Having described the transition from a minimalist to a more comprehensive but pay-related welfare state, we turn next to the questions of how and why that transition occurred in the Irish case.

Explaining the Development and Consequences of the Irish Welfare State

In general, the rise and expansion of welfare states in Western Europe can be understood as responses to the two fundamental transformations of the modern era: the development of industrial capitalism and the growth of national states and mass democracies (Flora, 1985). The particular pattern of these two transformations appears to be of substantial importance for the interaction of state and economy and for the development of the welfare state. Ireland combines a dependent, peripheral and relatively less-developed economic structure with the liberal democratic political institutions of an advanced capitalist society. The distinctiveness of Irish welfare state development derives from this unusual combination of economic and political characteristics.

That distinctiveness requires that we give priority to the structure and policies of the state itself. That necessity derives from Ireland's peripheral location in the international economy. Malloy (1985: 28) notes a general tendency in peripheral countries: 'the need to consciously adapt to

[12] The document paved the way for the Social Welfare (Insurance) Act, 1952, which extended coverage to agricultural and domestic service workers and integrated the assorted contingency specific schemes.

processes generated in the centre in a sense forced the peripheral countries to develop an activistic mode of statecraft prior to some centre countries'. But our state-centred interpretation is contingent on three other variables that constrain the autonomy of the state: political system characteristics; class structure and mobilisation; and the capacities of other interest groups.

Most western European societies emerged from the Great Depression and the Second World War with commitments to both extend social rights and abolish unemployment. Ireland was an exception. Sustained expansion of social citizenship had to await the 1960s. We need therefore to explain both the absence of welfare state expansion before the 1960s and its rapid advance thereafter.

Why did Ireland lag so far behind its European neighbours in developing its welfare state? The legacy at independence was mixed in respect of social citizenship. Ireland in 1922 had an underdeveloped economy, full adult male suffrage, which was immediately extended to the adult female population, and a minimalist state. The inheritance included a somewhat attentuated version of British welfare institutions, including the poor relief system, an embryonic social insurance system providing unemployment and sickness compensation for certain categories of workers, some health and housing services, and subsidised education. Spending on social services accounted for about 36 per cent of total central government spending during the 1920s (Maguire, 1986: 245). 'Welfare effort', as measured by the percentage of GNP devoted to social expenditure, was thus comparatively high in the 1930s, although this must be interpreted in the light of a low level of national income (Goodin and Dryzek, 1987: 57). The Free State thus inherited a substantial set of obligations—a precocious set of social rights that had expanded during the final decades of British rule—relative to the development of the economy and to the tax-base. The value of the entitlements this afforded to Irish citizens could be cut—as in the 10 per cent reduction in Old Age Pensions in 1924—but the obligations were sacrosanct, to the chagrin of civil servants and politicians (Fanning, 1978; Lee, 1989). Rights, once extended, appear to be difficult to rescind in a liberal democracy.

Arguably, the most important part of the post-colonial legacy can be seen in the policy stance of the state itself. The Department of Finance, which, following the Treasury model inherited from the British adminstrative system played a dominant role in state policy formation for much of Ireland's post independence history, was opposed in principle to increases in state expenditure and taxes, and in particular to increased commitments to social welfare. The Department, especially during the protracted secretaryship of J. J. MacElligott, consistently argued from a classically liberal position against the expansion of social programmes on the grounds that the state should not interfere with markets and that its responsibilities should be limited to the relief of destitution. Thus, for instance, in opposing a government proposal for universal payments of family allowances in 1942, MacElligott criticised the proposal because it would increase the degree of bureaucratic control over the domestic affairs of families, and argued, more generally, that

> social schemes in this country up to the present have tended to develop on lines of too great reliance upon the state as a source of help and assistance towards a situation where below a given wage level the incentive to work will be totally destroyed (quoted in Lee, 1989: 281).

Given its dominant position in the civil service, the Department of Finance represented a powerful champion of the liberal cause. It was joined in this by the Central Bank (see Bew *et al.*, 1989). There is little evidence to suggest that MacElligott had changed his mind by the time he resigned in 1953, and the Department suspicion of 'social schemes' was evidently still alive when T. K. Whitaker, its secretary in 1958, argued in *Econmic Development* for cuts in social spending.

The political system generated few welfare innovations in the first decades of independence. The conservative Cumann na nGaedheal government, fixated on promoting agricultural exports, preferred to keep both welfare spending and taxes down, and relied on emigration to alleviate high levels of unemployment in the late 1920s (Breen *et al.* 1990; Maguire, 1986). The Fianna Fáil party, which replaced Cumann na nGaedheal after winning the general election in 1932, appealed to the less well-off sections of society—small farmers and business people, and urban and rural manual workers—who had fared poorly under the previous government. Fianna Fáil promised to increase the state commitment to social welfare, and to fight unemployment and promote industrial development through protectionism. Unemployment benefits and old age pensions were increased and new income-maintenance schemes were introduced; unemployment assistance came in 1933 and widows' and orphans' pensions in 1935. The major initiative of the first Fianna Fáil government was, however, an ambitious housing programme. An average of 12,000 new houses were built with state aid between 1932 and 1942, compared to 2,000 per year between 1923 and 1931 (Lee, 1989: 193). Need was urgent, given the overcrowded and inadequate condition of much of the nation's housing stock, and it was a particularly effective social policy since it was targeted directly at the most derprived sections of the community. There were additional advantages. The housing programme functioned as a Depression era public works scheme; housing, along with other welfare reforms and a commitment to increase employment, encouraged working-class support; and new house construction enhanced Fianna Fáil's relationship with another important group—property speculators and builders. Thereafter, renewed activity in housing occurred between 1949–53 (Kennedy, 1971), and in the 1950s eligibility for public hospital services was extended to about 85 per cent of the nation, and unemployment insurance coverage was extended to male agricultural workers (Maguire, 1986). Nonetheless, these reforms still lagged far behind the rate of innovation in other European countries. Development of social rights in Ireland had to await the 1960s, and the elimination of unemployment proved quite beyond the capacity of the state.

Ireland's reluctance to emulate other European countries is also partly explicable by its economic predicament and by the petit-bourgeois cast of its class structure (Rottman and O'Connell, 1982). Total social expenditure actually fell from 16 per cent of GNP in 1951 to 14 per cent in 1959. How could this be during a decade of economic stagnation and declining employment? Part of the answer must lie in the decision by 400,000 citizens to emigrate; the departure of approximately 13.5 per cent of the population relieved both the fiscal and potential political pressure on the state. There was, moreover, a coincidence of policy preferences between the state and powerful interests. The early post-war attempts at reform were discouraged by opposition from the Roman Catholic Church to an expansion of state involvement in welfare. In the 'Mother and Child Scheme' incident in 1951 the church blocked a major extension of public health care to provide free ante- and post-natal care to mothers and free medical care to all children without a means test. It is perhaps ironic that the church and the 'premier' department in the state should be joined in their opposition to increased state commitment to social welfare. The ideological roots of the church's opposition, were, in fact, quite antipathetic to the liberalism of the Department of Finance. Catholic social thought of the period was heavily influenced by the corporatist rejection of both unfettered markets and state bureaucratic regulation. The specific objection by the church to the Mother and Child scheme, entered on behalf of the medical profession, was that it allocated to the state responsibilities rightfully the preserve of intermediate institutions to which the family could have direct access.[13]

[13] As in the 1911–13 period, the material interests of the medical profession and the principles of the Catholic hierarchy happily coincided: 'The true clash had, in any case, always been between the wishes of a reforming minster (and his department) and the self-interested conservatism of the Irish Medical Association. When the latter proved able to persuade the bishops that the survival of private practitioners in the field of public health was crucial to the safeguarding of Catholic morality a specious cloak of principle was very effectively thrown over what had, from the start, been essentially a fight over cash and the privileges cash can buy' (Hoppen, 1989: 244).

The quality of social citizenship expanded markedly from the early 1960s to the mid-1970s as services were improved and the coverage of income maintenance payments were extended and upgraded. Why did the welfare state expand so decisively and rapidly during the 1960s and 1970s after such inauspicious beginnings in the earlier post-war period? Our explanation is a state-centred conjunctural one that examines both the state itself and the major organised interests in Irish society during the crucial decade of the 1960s.

First, state intervention in the economy expanded dramatically in the wake of the early planning documents of the 1960s. The strategy adopted by the state to resolve the economic and social crisis of the 1950s—export-led industrialisation relying on foreign capital—necessitated the development of a welfare state for business, replete with capital grants and other incentives and generous tax breaks. This has been well documented elsewhere (Breen *et al.*, 1990; Lee, 1989). But the expansion of the state role did not necessarily entail an expansion of social citizenship: in fact, quite the contrary. From the onset of increased state economic intervention, Whitaker envisaged a reduction in social expenditures and the diversion of funds to investment in economic development. Such a 'free-market' approach would have been quite consistent with state strategies in other late-industrialising nations, in which restricted citizenship rights allowed non-democratic governments to keep down consumption in order to free funds for investment in expansion (cf. Chirot, 1986: 128). That social rights expanded and welfare budgets grew despite Finance reluctance and in the midst of a state-sponsored industrialisation drive, suggests the importance of political and economic constraints on state policy formation, and should serve as a caution against overestimating the autonomy or monolithic nature of the state.

However, part of the impetus for the expansion of social citizenship may also be found within the state itself, where bureaucratic politics appear to have been undergoing some changes. After the initial spurt of state intervention in the late 1950s, the dominance of the Department of Finance waned. There is substantial evidence to suggest that the Departments of Finance and Industry and Commerce were in conflict during the late 1950s and 1960s over fundamental policy issues, with Finance defending restrictive deflationary policies and Industry and Commerce advocating expansionary policies, and that Finance was defeated on crucial issues (Bew and Patterson, 1982; Girvin, 1989). It was also during the 1960s that the main social spending departments, headed by new energetic and ambitious ministers in the departments of Education, Local Government, Health and Social Welfare, were successful in overcoming Finance's traditional resistance to increases in spending (Kennedy,

1971: 244–245).[14] Moreover, part of the expansion and construction of social citizenship represented the specific interests of the state as an organisation. Perhaps the most obvious example of such a state-centred logic is the crucial decision to extend PRSI coverage first to all employees (1974) and ultimately to the self-employed (1988), which promoted the social solidarity needed to accomplish the extension of social citizenship, and helped to legitimate the extraction of taxes to finance the welfare state. It was a decision that followed from the logic of state policies, not in response to political pressures or in pursuit of political advantage.

Second, though welfare issues assumed greater importance on the political stage, there is no simple correspondence between political parties and welfare issues. Fianna Fáil, for instance, controlled government both during contractions in welfare spending (1951–54, 1957–61, and from 1987) and during the period of its most rapid expansion (1963–73). Likewise, Fine Gael, the other major contender, has also had a chequered history on welfare policy, and while the Labour Party has been more consistent in its support for social welfare, its electoral support has been weak. Nevertheless, electoral politics has been important in the expansion of the welfare state.

Fianna Fáil is a populist and corporatist party that attempts to mobilise support across class lines. It articulates an ideology that emphasises social harmony and economic growth (Mair, 1987). During the early 1960s its leader, Sean Lemass, argued that social progress would follow from, but was contingent upon, economic development (Bew *et al.*, 1989). Fine Gael, was also a catch-all party, but it had traditionally found its greatest support among large farmers and other substantial propertied interests, and had accordingly favoured conservative social and economic policies. Fine Gael policy underwent a major change in the mid-1960s with the party's discovery of a social democratic concern with social justice and, after the publication of its *Just Society* programme in 1965, it began to advocate increased state commitment to social welfare. This coincided with electoral gains by the Labour Party, which also advocated welfare policy reform. Both Fine Gael and Labour made social policy a major issue of the 1965 election. From 1965 onwards, Fianna Fáil responded to increased electoral competition over social issues by emphasising its own commitment to social spending and the reform of social welfare programmes. The 1965 budget was pronounced a 'social services budget' by the Minister of

[14] The power struggle between the Departments of Finance and Industry and Commerce is well researched in Girvin (1989), Fanning (1978), and Bew and Patterson (1982). Little evidence is available, unfortunately, through which to characterise the relationships among other departments.

Finance (Maguire 1986: 334), indicating, incidentally, the extent to which the imperatives of political strategy had overcome the market oriented fiscal orthodoxy of the officials of his own department.

Party politics thus underwent major changes and welfare issues became more salient to party competition. It became likely that electoral success would go to the party or coalition of parties promising the most to the greatest number of beneficiaries—thus reinforcing the tendency toward universal provision of services. This intensification of concern over welfare issues coincided with relatively strong economic growth, which thus provided the necessary revenue buoyancy to finance the competition. Later, when growth slowed, revenue would be replaced by borrowing.

Third, several aspects of the social structural changes wrought by state-sponsored economic development were of particular importance for the subsequent shape of the Irish welfare state. The increase in waged and salaried employment entailed growing needs for social-insurance-type provision for security. The particular timing and nature of economic development also led to an upgrading in the quality of labour-market positions in both the public and private sectors. The class structure was thus transformed into one dominated by middle class professionals and proprietors. Deference to their interests was a prerequisite for any expansion of the welfare state. By contrast, working class families fared poorly.

The expansion of the wage-dependent work force increased the strength of trade unions. Wage pressure intensified over the 1960s as Irish workers attempted to raise their living standards closer to those in other European countries, and in the 1970s returned migrants brought enhanced expectations of the state. The strategy of export-led industrialisation with foreign capital necessitated, however, harmonious industrial relations and wage competitiveness. One of the responses of the state to the intensification of distributive conflict in the 1960s was the establishment of a number of tripartite neo-corporatist institutions to encourage cooperation between trade unions, employer organisations and government in matters relating to economic development. By the 1970s the state had become centrally involved, underwriting incomes restraint with welfare spending and tax reforms (Hardiman, 1988; O'Brien, 1981; O'Connell, 1982). This politicisation of incomes policies and the displacement of distributional conflict from the private sector to the state intensified over the decade. In the late 1970s, centralised bargaining had been extended, through the 'National Understanding', to include a wide range of state activities, including employment creation, industrial relations, social welfare, health, education and housing services, as well as wages and taxation. The expansion of the welfare state must therefore be understood in relation to these attempts to maintain international competitiveness and foster labour-market conditions favourable to economic growth.

Moreover, class mobilisation in the period encouraged welfare state expansion through party politics and sectoral bargaining alike. The standard interpretation, represented, for example, in Bew and Patterson (1982) and Bew et al., (1989: ch. 3) focuses on just one aspect of class mobilisation: that of the working class. But political mobilisation in Ireland took the form of parties attempting to mobilise individual voters by appealing to their class interests rather than classes mobilising through parties. The transformation of the class structure is crucial here. During the 1960s, the middle class was consolidating its position and putting its imprint on party politics. Irish industrialisation meant the numeric decline, fragmentation, and geographical dispersion of the working class and, simultaneously, the growth and consolidation (particularly in Dublin) of the middle class. In our interpretation, middle class political mobilisation and the expression of middle class preferences and interests proved the dominant force.

Fourth, the Roman Catholic Church, which had successfully opposed increased state involvement in welfare in the 1940s and 1950s, also underwent change during the 1960s. The corporatism of Catholic social thought actually embraced two different components. One was represented by the vocationalist tradition which gained popularity in Ireland in the 1940s. The other, more familiar in Latin America, Spain and Portugal, favoured a strong interventionist state which pursued the common good of all its subjects (Stepan, 1978). The latter tradition is clearly far more amenable to welfare state expansion, and appears to be reflected in the substantially greater concern with social justice adopted by the Catholic Church in Ireland in recent years.

Conclusion

Our interpretation of the expansion of social citizenship counters the excessive importance that has sometimes been placed on state industrial policy and economic planning in understanding the transformation of Irish society. Stressing the growth of social citizenship also identifies some aspects of the welfare state in Ireland that have gone largely unremarked and certainly under-researched. The creation of a pay-related welfare state, in our view, reflects the undoubtedly wide range of social rights to which Irish citizens are now entitled, but also the degree to which those rights reinforce, rather than mitigate, market inequalities. Minimal levels of security and service are guaranteed to all resident citizens. However, the welfare state is 'pay-related' in that it permits those with advantages generated in the market to supplement their citizenship rights with their own resources. Purchasers of private health and education continue to enjoy virtually the same level of state subsidy as the users of public services, but they enjoy a more expensive and, presumably, better product. Thus, for example, the consequences of such a system for providing education is evident in the remarkably low rate of social mobility in Ireland (Breen and Whelan, this volume). In income maintenance programmes, the dual system means that those with higher incomes are entitled to higher rates of compensation, and minimal state pensions can be supplemented with private pensions, thus replicating market inequalities in old-age. This dual nature of social citizenship reflects middle class interests in security and in quality of services. But the inclusion of the middle class was essential both to legitimate the large welfare role of the state and to justify the high rates of taxation faced by higher income employees.

Focusing on the principles underlying social rights and welfare institutions, and on the social forces articulating those principles, allows us to explore a conjunctural explanation for why social citizenship expanded during the 1960s and 1970s. This conjunctural explanation suggests that in those decades shifts occurring both within the state and within Irish society relaxed some of the opposition to welfare state expansion, and simultaneously strengthened social forces favouring the growth of social citizenship.

What, then, can be learned from the Irish case about the process of welfare state development in general? First, the theory of industrialism does not fare well in Ireland. While the coincidence of industrial development with the expansion of social citizenship appears at first sight to provide compelling evidence in favour of the logic of industrialism, closer inspection reveals that the expansion of social rights—as they are experienced by people and as they affect life chances—is nominal rather than real. The restricted nature of this expansion is revealed both by the pay-related structure of the welfare state which replicates, rather than mitigates, market advantages, and by the persistence of inequality of opportunity—the failure, therefore, of advancing industrialism and expanding social citizenship to create a more open, achievement-oriented society. Moreover, from the standpoint of the logic of industrialism, the role of state is determined by socioeconomic forces (Kerr *et al.*, 1960) and political development is a function of economic development (Lipset, 1960; Huntington, 1968). The state in Ireland, however, must be seen as an independent rather than a dependent variable; this inverts the causality that the theory of industrialism asserts.

Secondly though, the social democratic approach does not contribute much more than that of the logic of industrialism. The welfare state expanded in Ireland in spite of the weakness of left-wing political parties, and neither the timing of that expansion nor the nature of the new citizenship rights can be explained by reference to working class strength. Welfare state expansion occurred in Ireland during a process of late industrialisation that consolidated the position of the middle class, not the working class.

We have argued, instead, for a state-centred approach. States in less developed peripheral societies tend to be activistic in pursuit of what they define as national priorities. Liberal democratic states are expected to be responsive to the demands of their citizens. Ireland is one of the few nations combining both of these state-expansionary tendencies, and the role of the state is therefore particularly important. State-centred approaches cannot, however, be applied mechanically. In the Irish case, such an application leads to the expectation that social citizenship would have been restrained during the period of economic development. This was, after all, the explicit policy position of the Department of Finance, the core of the Irish state in the first decades of independence. That social citizenship nonetheless expanded indicates that the state is far from monolithic and that it must formulate policies in concert with other powerful social actors. In our interpretation, then, political factors are subsumed within the state centred approach. The emergent welfare state was shaped to attract the support of the middle classes; it was not targeted at the working class, as it had been in other European countries from the late nineteenth century onwards. The influence of politics on an emergent welfare state therefore depends on the nature of the class structure and the material interests associated with those market processes to which the state is responsive.

Acknowledgements. Comments, criticism, and advice that we received on earlier drafts were used to the best of our ability. We acknowledge the contribution made at various stages along the way by Peter Bearman, Craig Calhoun, Roger Hanson, and Ciaran McCullagh, as well as the response to the first draft by the participants in the Nuffield Conference and to the second draft by the participants in an ESRI Department of Sociology and Social Policy Seminar.

Proceedings of the British Academy, **79**, 241–263

Catholicism and Industrial Society in Ireland

TONY FAHEY

St Patrick's College, Maynooth

> I fear, wherever riches have increased, the essence of religion has decreased in the same proportion . . . Religion must necessarily produce both industry and frugality, and these cannot but produce riches. But as riches increase, so will pride, anger, and love of the world in all its branches . . . So, although the form of religion remains, the spirit is swiftly vanishing away (John Wesley, as quoted in Weber, 1958: 175).

Introduction

MAX WEBER, more than most, credited religion (especially ascetic Protestantism) with a part in creating the 'tremendous cosmos of the modern economic order'. But echoing the prescient thoughts of Wesley, he also gave classic expression to the view that the economic order which Protestantism helped create had by his day lost the spirit of religion and had become based instead on the technical and economic conditions of machine production. The culture of the machine and the spirit of religion, in his view, were simply incompatible, and the triumph of the former had made the latter irrelevant to economic organisation in the modern industrial world. Weber's linkage of industrialisation with secularisation became a commonplace in subsequent social theory. Technical rationality, large-scale urbanisation, the decline of community, institutional differentiation and other social changes associated with industrialisation have been widely viewed as inimical to religion and as responsible in particular for a long-term decline in the place of institutional Christianity in the western world (for characteristic statements of this position see Acquaviva, 1979 and Wilson, 1982).

Read 8 December 1990. © The British Academy 1992.

However, this view of the fate of Christianity during industrialisation does not tell the whole story. Ireland, and particularly Catholicism in Ireland, seems to have had a somewhat different experience, and the purpose of this paper is to assess how real and wide that difference was. But Ireland was not the only exception. The broader picture of the western world offers many contradictions of the view that industrialisation was generally antithetical to religion. If we are able to grasp properly the peculiarities of the encounter between Catholicism and industrialisation in Ireland, we first need to get a better sense of what the broader picture was.

General Patterns

In Max Weber's lifetime, many parts of the western world were experiencing a religious boom of sorts. This took the form especially of a surge of growth in the main Christian churches in much of western Europe and North America. Protestant churches were invigorated by waves of revivalism and evangelisation, especially in the early decades of the nineteenth century, and the Catholic church achieved new levels of organisational strength and popular adherence. In Britain, all the churches thrived in the second half of the nineteenth century: 'membership, attendance and related series indicate that in the major churches organisational expansion continued to the eve of the First World War' (Gilbert, 1980: 76). In Weber's own Germany, the Catholic church flourished in an unprecedented way up to the end of the Weimar republic, not only in the traditionally Catholic south but also in places such as the Rhine valley and the Ruhr district where industrialisation was most intense (Sperber, 1984). In the United States, the emerging giant of the industrial age, Christianity 'came to the mid-twentieth century on a rising tide' such that in 1961 the 'proportion of the population who were members of the Christian churches was higher than in any other year in the nation's history' (Latourette, 1962: 135). The success of the Catholic church in the United States was especially striking. From a base of 6.25 million members in 1880 (just over 8 per cent of the population), the Catholic church grew to nearly 44 million members in 1963 (roughly 23 per cent of the population), with its main support base in the working and middle classes in the highly industrialised north-east states (Dolan, 1987: 139; Hennessey, 1981: 175). Church attendance remained high—about 70 per cent of Catholic adults in the U.S. attended church regularly in the mid-1950s, according to Gallup surveys at the time (Hennessey, 1981: 287). And church organisation continued to expand until the mid-1960s: between 1954 and 1965, the number of religious sisters in the American Catholic church rose from 158,000 to 181,000, the number of brothers rose from 8,700 to 12,500 and the number of priests rose from 47,000 to 60,000 (Hennessey, 1981: 287). Generally within the industrialising west—that is, in addition to Africa and Asia where western colonialism presented the Christian churches with new opportunities for missionary expansion—the first century of industrialisation in many ways enhanced rather than retarded the position of institutional Christianity.

The paradox is that the vitality of western institutional religion in this period, though real, does not contradict the idea of secularisation as a feature of the industrial age. In the Victorian era, secularisation and ecclesiastical vitality went hand in hand, a paradox summed up in the heading used for the 1850–1914 period in Bihlmeyer's *Church History*: 'Church grows stronger; Increasing secularisation of state, society and culture' (Bihlmeyer and Tuchle, 1966, vol. 3). Church growth took place within a framework of institutional differentiation such that larger, better organised churches were but one dimension of the increasing size, scale and organisational complexity of the social system as a whole. It was thus possible for churches to expand and popular religious practice to become more regular and disciplined even while religion lost influence in major areas of cultural and intellectual life (especially science) and in the major institutions of state (Dobbelaere, 1987: 117–118).

In addition, church expansion was uneven. In some regions, rural as well as urban, Christianity weakened steadily. France in the nineteenth century, for example, became a patchwork of intensely Catholic and intensely secular regions; with no easily discernible logic in the resulting patterns of affiliation. An area such as the Limousin region, which was poor, rural and mountainous, was as firmly on the anti-clerical, secular side as the the left-leaning working classes in the big cities. In Spain and Portugal, the important contrast in religious terms was not between urban and rural but between the devout north and the anti-clerical south (McLeod, 1981: 54). Other social cleavages were also reflected in the unevenness of church growth. Women became more devout than men, though in some areas the gender gap was much wider than in others. Class divisions between workers and the bourgeoisie were sometimes reflected in differential attitudes to religion, though the nature of the differences varied from place to place. Working class religiosity was strong in many areas, so that the idea that the working class tended to reject organised religion as a bourgeois device is as often wrong as it is right (McLeod, 1981).

As well as being socially and regionally uneven, religious growth was limited by time. As the twentieth century progressed, church expansion, Catholic as well as Protestant, gradually slowed down, halted and turned into decline—though even this temporal pattern had many variations and some apparent exceptions (examples of which can today be found in eastern Europe). Gilbert (1980) identifies the First World War as the turning point in Britain, the 1930s or the 1940s might be thought of as more decisive in other western European countries, while in the United States the crisis (for the Catholic church at least) did not arrive until the 1960s. Most indicators today, especially those related to church membership and attendance, suggest that 'de-christianisation' is now far advanced in many countries, particularly in western Europe.

However, though ecclesiastical contraction is now common in most of western Europe and North America, so was the growth of the Christian churches which preceded it. This suggests that in these regions industrialisation was accompanied by a curving trajectory within institutional religion, beginning with a phase of rapid (albeit uneven) ecclesiastical expansion from around the mid-nineteenth century onwards, followed by a levelling-off period which in most cases occurred sometime between 1900 and 1960, and followed in turn by a decline of varying steepness up to today. The present-day sociology of religion has given little attention to the first phase of this evolution—the spurt of church growth which took place within the first century of industrialisation—as it has concentrated on developments since the 1940s. De-christianisation provided the impetus for the revival of sociological interest in religion in the 1950s and placed questions about how far industrial society had killed off religion at the centre of interest (Beckford, 1990; Dobbelaere, 1987). Some sociologists disagree that western society in recent decades can be assumed to be more secular simply because the traditional churches are contracting. Religious sentiment may survive in 'civil religion', as Bellah (1967) has argued, or as privatised 'invisible religion', as Luckman (1970) has claimed, or indeed Christianity may not be dying so much as migrating to a separate, narrower realm of modern life (on this argument see Dobbelaere, 1987: 117–118). However, a certain kind of secularisation has undoubtedly occurred, in that the indicators of churchly religious adherence which became so strong in so many western countries since the early nineteenth century have now almost everywhere shown a decline.

No satisfactory theoretical explanation has yet been provided either for the general shape of the religious growth curve since early industrialisation or for the many local variations in that curve which can be observed across the regions and social groups of western Europe and north America. Theoretical interest has concentrated on the ways in which industrialisation has been inimical to organised religion, though even this interest has tended to focus on the centres of industrial expansion and has not examined how negative effects have spilled over into rural hinterlands and peripheral regions. Countervailing positive influences which fostered religous expansion in both core and peripheral regions have attracted less attention, though it is clear that these positive influences were as much a part of industrialisation as the negative ones. This is shown nowhere more clearly than in the appeal of religion to the migrating populations in nineteenth and early twentieth century industrialisation—among European ethnic groups migrating to North America and among rural-to-urban migrants within Europe itself. For many such groups, churchly religion acquired a significance and vitality in their new urban-industrial settings that it had in some cases lacked in their traditional homelands. Churchly religion in these circumstances was important not only as a psychological bridge between the old and the new, a stable reference point in the midst of change, but also as a practical institution which provided social contacts and a system of supportive services in unsettled urban communities. Churches, especially the Catholic church, were rich in organisational and ritual resources. These gave to churches a range of strengths in responding to local communal needs which secular systems often lacked and which gave the churches the capacity to complement, and sometimes compete with, secular systems as objects of loyalty and identification. The Catholic church especially deployed this capacity both in the evangelisation of new urban populations and in the revival of its position in older rural hinterlands (for overviews, see Dolan, 1987; McLeod, 1981; for sample case studies, see Sperber, 1984; McLeod, 1989).

Churches in the industrialising world thus were not simply struggling survivors of pre-industrial peasant piety, though their pre-industrial roots and traditions were important. Rather they were creative, adaptive institutions playing an active role in shaping the new order. Weber may have been right in saying that the economic order of the nineteenth century was no longer open to religious influence in any fundamental way. But the same was hardly true of the political order in the age of Bismarck's *Kulturkampf*, of the Dreyfus affair in France, of the conflict over the papal states in Italy, of the politics of church versus chapel in Victorian Britain, of Protestant triumphalism in the United States. Nor was it true of social organisation when religion provided a reference point for communal solidarity and ethnic identity during the migratory upheavals and cultural dislocations of the industrial era. In many ways, therefore, the question to be asked is not just whether in the West in recent decades industrialisation has killed religion—or even institutional Christianity—but also how the development of industrial society interacted with the remarkable growth in organised religion which preceded the recent decline and which provides the benchmark against which that decline is measured.

The Irish Exception?

It is against this background that religion in Ireland is of interest.[1] No doubt at one level, Ireland attracts attention simply because it has stayed so Catholic for so long. Irish Catholics today practise their religion with exceptional regularity and in exceptional numbers and, on some issues at least, pay more attention to the teachings of their church than in any other western country. In everything from sport to education to the mass media, Irish society accords a prominence to the church and to religion that makes the image of the post-Christian society an exaggeration if not entirely irrelevant. However, Catholicism in Ireland is equally interesting because of its typicality. Although there are differences in timing and degree, it too shows signs of the standard expansion–contraction sequence which has been a feature of so much of institutional religion in the west in the last hundred and fifty years or so. For Catholicism in Ireland, the expansionary phase ran from about the middle of the nineteenth century to the middle of the twentieth. That expansion has certainly halted in the last two decades or so and, despite the continuing importance of the church in Irish society, there are significant signs of incipient decline. Only time will tell how far or how fast that decline will proceed, and so we shall have to wait and see if the full sequence will be run through.

But much of the sequence—the expansion and levelling-off stages— has already happened. That gives us a country-level case-study of the dynamics of ecclesiastical expansion and of its relationship to the development of industrial society. Ireland itself (or at least the Catholic part of it) could hardly be called industrial in the narrow sense for much of the period in question. Economic output and employment were dominated by family farming, the bulk of the population lived in the countryside and small towns, and such heavy industrialisation as occurred was concentrated in the mainly Protestant north-east (particularly Belfast). On the other hand, Ireland since the industrial revolution was closely integrated into the international capitalist economy. It was a major supplier of emigrant labour to the burgeoning industrial centres of Britain and North America; emigrants' remittances regularly have amounted to a significant level of its

[1] This paper focuses on Catholicism in the Republic of Ireland. As a result, the religious situation in Northern Ireland, both on the Catholic and Protestant sides, is referred to only in a marginal way, even though it is closely intertwined with that of the Republic, both historically and at the present time, and is equally relevant as a case-study of religion in industrialising societies. However, the differences between the two regions, both in their religious life and in their experience of industrialisation, are great enough to justify concentrating on one at a time, as far as that it is possible, and this is the course taken in the present paper.

national income; its domestic economy was until recently geared very much to the production of agricultural commodities for the British market; and its consumption patterns have long relied on the importation of finished industrial goods. Internally, the concentration of industrial development in the north-east of the island became a major influence on social structure and political developments. Because of the pervasiveness and importance of these external and internal links, industrialisation thus had direct and immediate ramifications for Catholic rural Ireland as well as for places like Belfast, Coventry and Pittsburg, though rural Ireland experienced these ramifications as a peripheral rather than a core region of the industrial system.

And of course Christianity in Ireland, especially Catholicism, was also part of an international system. Indeed, the Catholic church as a whole in the nineteenth century came the closest of any church at any time, Christian or otherwise, to being a world church. From a vigorous European base (and in addition to its large but in some ways organisationally weak presence in Latin America) it built up a powerful position in North America and Oceania in the nineteenth century, made substantial inroads into Africa and expanded its bridgeheads in China, India, Japan and other Asian countries. The Irish church was a notable force in this international expansion of Catholicism. It retained a strong sense of its membership of an international ecclesiastical community not just because of its allegiance to Rome but also because of the 'spiritual empire' which its floods of emigrant priests, religious and laity had fashioned around the world. Irish Catholicism thus encountered industrialism not as a small isolated religious tradition facing up to an overwhelming revolution in international economic and social structures, but as a branch of a powerful, international ecclesiastical system which it proudly proclaimed to be the universal church.

The interaction of religion and industrialisation in Ireland, therefore, was not a discrete national experience constructed in isolation from developments elsewhere. Nor is it a recent experience dating only from the spurt towards internal industrialisation in the Ireland of the 1960s. Rather it was a local variant of patterns that were widely echoed elsewhere and that were in constant evolution since the industrial revolution. Sperber (1984: 292–294) suggests that Ireland in the nineteenth century provides the outstanding example of a model of Catholic revival which was quite widespread throughout central and northern Europe at that time. The north-west region of Germany, studied by Sperber, was characterised prior to 1850 by a debilitated, disorganised Catholic church, lax religious practice among an impoverished, rapidly growing rural population, strained relations with a hostile Prussian state and a Catholic bourgeoisie

heavily influenced by enlightenment secularism. Following a rural subsistence crisis in the 1850s, the region was marked by rapid industrialisation
and urbanisation, fed in population terms by high levels of rural to urban
migration, along with a Catholic revival in rural and urban areas brought
about by a reassertion of clerical leadership, a transformation of popular
piety in both cities and countryside towards new, disciplined religious
practices and an accommodation between the church and the Prussian
state. In this case, then, Catholic revival began with a disorganised church
struggling to administer to an over-burdened rural subsistence society and
generated out of that a revitalised, more streamlined church successfully
finding its place in a rapidly changing, newly integrated rural-urban social
system. The generality of such a revival model in Europe and North
America may be open to question. The reason for its success in some areas
and its failures in others, along with the widespread crisis which has
affected it in recent decades, may also be hard to specify. But echoes in
the Irish situation are fairly obvious and invite us to consider Irish religious
history since the nineteenth century not as an exceptional case on the
fringes of Europe but as a reflection of tendencies that were closely tied
to broader patterns of social and religious change in the contemporary west
as a whole. We shall look in turn here at the Catholic revival in Ireland
since the early nineteenth century and at its levelling-off since the 1960s,
before returning in the final section of the paper to the question of the
exceptionalism or otherwise of the Irish experience in the context of
general patterns in the industrialising West over this period.

The Catholic Revival in Ireland

The revival and expansion of Catholicism and the Catholic church was a
major feature of nineteenth century Irish history, affecting politics, culture
and social structure. The revival was such that by 1880, 'the Catholic
church was beginning to take on some of the characteristics of an
establishment' (Corish, 1985: 226), even though it was not then and never
became an established church in the legal sense.

As in other regions which experienced a Catholic resurgence, Catholic
revival in Ireland was founded upon the restructuring and revitalisation of
clerical organisation. The Catholic church in most dioceses in Ireland in
1800 was in a disorganised, weakened state following the anti-Catholic
penal laws of the eighteenth century. Priests were scarce, church buildings
poor or non-existent, clerical discipline was lax and diocesan structures
were in disarray, with the result that the day-to-day pastoral functions of
the church were performed poorly or not at all. By 1900, parish and

diocesan structures had been thoroughly restored and the Irish church as a whole had been brought under firmer allegiance to papal authority. The number of priests had increased from 1,850 in 1800 to almost 3,500 in 1900, despite rapid population decline over the latter half of that period. A surge of church building also in the latter half of the nineteenth century had equipped every Catholic parish with at least basic centres of worship. All parish clergy by then were equipped with a narrow but effective training for pastoral work and were subject to thorough episcopal control. The church was not a significant owner of land or commercial property but rather derived its finances largely from popular subscription, thus strengthening the ties between church and people. The clergy were drawn mainly from the middle classes in the small towns and countryside and identified closely with the concerns of their largely rural populations, but even in the largest towns and cities church presence was strong. By the early twentieth century, the supply of priests had begun to exceed the domestic needs of the Irish church and thenceforth was sufficient to man a steadily expanding missionary effort, directed first at the Irish diaspora in Britain, the United States and Australia and subsequently at the 'pagan' mission-fields of the British colonies and elsewhere.

In many ways, the reorganised Catholic church in nineteenth century Ireland implemented the reforms worked out at the Council of Trent in the 1560s and in that sense was a neo-Tridentine institution. However, in its approach to women, the nineteenth century church, in Ireland as elsewhere, introduced a number of innovations which departed in some ways from Tridentine ideas and which proved fundamental to the vitality and popular impact of the church. The most obvious of these was the evolution of female relgous congregations, an institutional device for harnessing the energies of women to the pastoral work of the church which was one of the major institutional innovations within Catholicism in the nineteenth century. Since the thirteenth century, church teaching had insisted on total and permanent cloister as the only acceptable basis for the religious life of nuns. This approach was reiterated at Trent and again on a number of occasions up to the mid-eighteenth century. The injunction to cloister was frequently flouted by women religious, sometimes out of disregard for the spirit of the religious life and sometimes out of the impulse to live it more fully and actively. But it effectively shackled the female religious orders, confined their members to lives of seclusion and silence and prevented women from performing any extensive pastoral role in the church.

Some successful breaches in the church's resistance to active female religious had been made as early as the seventeenth century. But it was not until the nineteenth century that the active female religious congregation became an accepted element of church organisation and indeed it was only in the early 1900s that its canonical position was regularised. The concept of the active female religious congregation was introduced into Ireland in the form of the Presentation Sisters, founded in Cork (in the face of considerable clerical resistance) in the 1780s and 1790s. Two other major Irish foundations, the Sisters of Mercy and the Irish Sisters of Charity, along with a number of lesser foundations, helped secure the institutional basis for the active female religious life in the 1830s and 1840s. From about the mid-nineteenth century, in Ireland as in other countries, the movement took off in spectacular fashion. The number of sisters in Ireland grew from around 1,500 in 1851 to just under 9,000 in 1911. The growth continued until it peaked at around 16,000 in the mid-1960s and was such that for most of the preceding sixty years nuns had outnumbered male clergy and religious of all kinds by more than two to one. The main contribution of this new force to the church lay in the network of schools and other social services which the female congregations built up over this period. By the 1920s, convent schools catered for some 17 per cent of children in the primary school system and all Catholic women primary teachers were trained in teacher training colleges run by nuns. Up to the 1960s, secondary schooling for Catholic girls was provided almost exclusively by convent schools. In the medical field, the largest hospitals in the country were run by nuns and much of the nursing profession was formed in nursing schools attached to these hospitals. Nuns were active also in orphanages, reformatories and other social services. Although nuns continued to endure a humble and subordinate status within the male-run church, it was largely as a result of their efforts that, in addition to the ministry and pastoral work of the clergy in the parish system, the church was enabled to enter people's lives through the education, health and social services which the female religious congregations provided on such an extensive scale (Fahey, 1987; Clear, 1987).

The increase in female religious in the Catholic church was paralleled by a certain 'feminisation' of the church's support base in the population at large. In Ireland as elsewhere, religion among lay people in the nineteenth century often came to be seen as primarily women's business. In some areas, the gender gap in religious adherence became very wide: women became or remained devout while men drifted away from religion or became actively hostile (McLeod, 1981). In other countries, of which Ireland was one example, the gap was much narrower since religious adherence was high among men as well as women. But even here there still remained a sense in which women were more important than men as carriers of the faith, especially within the family where they were ascribed the main responsibility for preserving a religious ethos in the home and for passing on the faith to children (see Inglis, 1987: 187–214, where the theme of the Catholic mother as the key figure in the church's lay support is developed). The particular links between women and religion in the nineteenth and twentieth centuries is still a largely unresearched area, but changing definitions of femininity and of the nature and significance of women's roles clearly enhanced both the appeal of churchly religion to women and of women to churches in this period. Consequently, changes in the position of women in economic life, in the family and in the wider community emerge as an important mediating factor in the relationship between religious and social change during industrialisation.

The pastoral work of the clergy, along with the educational and social service work of the religious congregations, thus provided a powerful machinery for church growth and consolidation. It also placed a strong, clerically-dominated church at the centre of the religious life of Irish Catholics. For most Irish Catholics the church and religion were synonymous, thus giving a strong institutional expression and focus for popular religious faith. In some ways, Irish Catholicism may have been more church-oriented than elsewhere. It produced less in way of lay Catholic action (in the form of Catholic political, business or trade union organisations, for example) than the Catholic church in many European countries. But, in general, the features of Irish ecclesiastical expansion just described were not unusual by the standards of the Catholic church in much of the rest of the western world and reflected a general trend towards making the church internally stronger and more present in the daily religious lives of believers.

Yet another important feature of the success of the institutional church in Ireland was the degree to which it became embedded into the system of social services developed under the nineteenth century British state. Despite the tension between the colonial state and the Catholic tradition in Ireland in the nineteenth century, the basic outlines of a tacit concordat between the two had been worked out by the end of the century. That concordat was based, on the one hand, as Whyte (1980) puts it, on a certain aloofness between church and state. For the most part, the church kept its distance from state affairs and the state likewise steered clear of such potentially contentious issues as episcopal appointments and state payments for clergy. On the other hand, there was a small but vital range of areas where church and state closely intermingled.

By far the most important of these was education. The distinctiveness of the Irish school system from a religious viewpoint was not so much the denominational character of schools supported by the state (other countries where state support was provided to denominational schools are mentioned by Whyte, 1980). Rather, denominational control of Irish schools lay to an exceptional degree in the hands of the clergy and religious orders rather than of lay representative bodies, so that it was the institutional church—clergy, brothers and nuns—rather than the Catholic laity which stamped the schools with their denominational character. At the foundation of the national primary school system in 1831, local management of schools devolved onto the clergy and religious orders by default rather than by design, in that nobody else came forward to do the job, reflecting the weakness of local civic leadership at the time. But having gained that position, the church clung to it. Although responsibility for the curriculum and for the payment of teachers was centralised under state control, the managerial role of clergy and religious orders at local level gave the church powerful leverage at all levels of the system. The effectivness of this leverage was shown, for example, in the 1880s when the state in effect handed control of primary teacher training to denominational teacher training colleges, largely because of the long-standing refusal of Catholic school managers to hire teachers trained in 'godless' state colleges. In the same period, the state began to extend modest financial support to second-level schools, most of which were owned and run by religious orders. Subsequently the secondary school system emerged as a publicly funded but privately owned network of church-run schools. The end result was an education system which at primary and secondary levels gave unparalleled ownership, access and local control to the church, while the burden of the financial and central administrative responsibility was carried by the state.

The pattern in education was repeated to a more limited extent in a number of other social services, including hospital services, the care of orphaned and homeless children, the 'rescue of fallen women' and a limited range of services for the poor and for unemployed women (Clear, 1987; Inglis, 1987). In each case, the church was the only institution capable of sustaining a level of provision which approached that evolving under state direction. The response by the state at some points was hostile or competitive. But for the most part partnership of some sort was the preferred option, with the result that key areas of the social services became a joint venture between 'voluntary' church effort and official funding and administration.

The most obvious expression of Catholic vitality in nineteenth and twentieth century Ireland was the high level of popular religious practice. This practice went beyond church membership and minimum church attendance to include plentiful and varied forms of day-to-day religious ritual. Some years ago, the historian Emmet Larkin used the term 'devotional revolution' to refer to the sudden emergence of this pattern among Irish Catholics around the mid-nineteenth century. Since then there has been some debate as to whether we should speak of an evolution over a longer time rather than of a sudden revolution (Connolly, 1985: 42–60 reviews this debate). But the consensus is that whatever about timing and pace, the new devotionalism represented an unprecedented expansion and strengthening of orthodox Catholic practice in daily life. Miller (1975) has argued with some basis in quantitative evidence that attendance at Sunday Mass in rural Ireland in the 1830s was low, reflecting the shortage of priests and churches and the weakness of clerical influence on popular practice. It is also clear that many ritual customs of the pre-Famine era, such as wakes and patterns, owed more to pre-Christian tradition than to post-Tridentine orthodoxy. These were a particular target of reformist clerical concern. By the end of the century, universal weekly Mass attendance had become the norm for Catholics throughout the country and in all social classes, even in the cities. Indigenous ritual had been rooted out and had been replaced on clerical prompting with a panoply of Italian and French-style devotions—benedictions, novenas, the rosary, first Friday Masses, forty hours adoration, and so on. By then, mass attendance and regular devotional practice came to be seen as the outward and necessary signs of being a Catholic and became a routine part of Irish Catholic life on a very wide scale.

The popular spiritual significance of Catholic religious practice was intensified by a pervasive sense of the reality of sin and of the potency of the miraculous in daily life. Sin was for many identified less with internal lapses of the spirit than with external breaches of social respectability, that is, with anything that hinted, however remotely, of debauchery. Drink was considered one of the great sources of sin. Attitudes towards drink were ambivalent, however, and its immovable place in large segments of Irish popular culture made the church reluctant to attempt an all-out offensive against it. The attitude to sex was less uncertain: sexual immorality often seemed to be the central form of sin and resistance to the temptations of sex became a central preoccupation of Catholic morality. Sexual repression seemed to intensify in Irish Catholic culture as the nineteenth century progressed, though in this, as in other areas, Irish Catholicism was an extreme example of patterns common throughout the Victorian world rather than an utterly deviant case. Popular faith in the miraculous powers of certain saints, relics and sites of pilgrimage sometimes bordered on the unorthodox and prompted watchful attention on the part of church authorities. However, it was a central focus of religious commitment among ordinary Catholics and the church provided abundant approved locations and methods for its expression.

Apart from the personal consolations and satisfactions it offered to believers, Catholic ritual and religious doctrine also acted as a symbol of the distinctively Catholic view of the world and so served as a way of marking and maintaining boundaries between Catholicism and the world around it. To further this boundary maintenance, the international Catholic church regularly threw itself into symbolic confrontation with key strands of modernity. In the age of progress it harked back to medieval Thomistic models for its image of the good society; in the age of democracy it promulgated the doctrine of papal infallibility and of the authority of the magisterium; in the age of technical rationality it cultivated a popular devotionalism which was suffused with a sense of the supernatural as a living force in the practicalities of daily life; in the age of the melting-pot it fostered a sense of Catholic distinctiveness even among those urban-industrial communities subject to the standardising influences of modern production systems. These assertions of a distinctively Catholic view of the world served not to undermine popular support but to give an unmistakable, clearly identified profile to which Catholics could offer their allegiance.

The assertion of a distinctive Catholic identity found an especially receptive audience in Ireland. The communal bonding effect of shared religious practice among Irish Catholics had been reinforced since the Reformation by a shared alienation from Protestantism. In the wake of the collapse of the Gaelic tradition, Catholicism provided a substitute badge of identity in an Anglo-centric world and, as the era of modern nationalism dawned in the nineteenth century, Catholic history provided Irish nationalist myth-makers with a fertile source of material for national self-definition and consciousness raising. Thus, as nationalist sentiment gathered force in nineteenth century Ireland, Catholic alienation from Protestantism merged with the Irish nationalist alienation from British rule and the modern nationalist identification of Irishness with Catholicism took firm hold. Politically this was expressed in an alliance between the church and the constitutional nationalist political movement. That alliance provided much of the Church's political strength in the struggle over education, just as it helped to give nationalist movements, particularly as represented by the Home Rule party in the 1870s and 1880s, a broad base of popular support.

In the longer term, the identification of Catholicism with nationalism helped secure the Church's position in the new state created after independence in 1921. Most of the Protestant population was sectioned off into the northern six counties and in the remaining twenty-six, Protestants dwindled from about 10 per cent of the total population prior to independence to 5 per cent by the 1950s. With Catholics forming almost 95 per cent of the population in the independent state, the religious community, the nation and the state became as one. Reflecting its unchallenged place in an homogeneous, solidly Catholic culture, the church allowed an air of smugness and triumphalism to creep into the conduct of its affairs and the few fragments of a Catholic liberal intelligentsia which existed complained of the stifling and oppressive cultural atmosphere. The church was allowed to consolidate its position in education and social services, and the Catholic ethos was acknowledged overtly in legislation and in the public utterances of politicians. But formal arrangements with the state were avoided, and as Whyte (1980) says, the tradition of aloofness between ch·irch and state in most political areas, combined with a ready acceptance of church interest in certain key areas, remained characteristic of church–state relations in the decades after independence.

The Levelling-off Period

The upheavals in the Catholic church brought by the Second Vatican Council were fully reflected in Ireland and were part of the overall disturbance in economic and social life which gave the 1960s the appearance of a watershed in recent Irish history. The economic policies of the inward-looking nationalism of the preceding decades had failed and this failure rubbed off to some extent on the old allegiance to Catholicism. The question of the 1960s for Catholicism in Ireland was how it would adapt to the new wave of economic prosperity, social freedom and openness to outside influences then sweeping the country. The experience of other countries at the time suggested that the old religious adherence would not live easily with the new prosperity and would succumb rather quickly to what was thought of as the corrosive effects of secular liberalism. From the vantage point of the early 1990s, we can see that change has not been so dramatic: the strength and pre-eminence of Catholicism in Irish culture has been reduced in many ways but has not been radically undermined. However, in judging the significance of recent developments in Irish religious life, the comparison with countries which have experienced rapid religious decline in the post-war period may not be the most appropriate one. Rather the preceding period of levelling-off in church expansion and the onset of incipient decline may provide more relevant parallels. Ireland may be thought of as relatively late in reaching the plateau stage in the sequence of expansion and contraction rather than as an entirely deviant case (though the fact that the American Catholic church likewise did not reach its plateau until the 1960s should remind us that Irish lateness in this regard was neither entirely unique nor entirely linked to economic

Table 1.   Catholic clerical and religious personnel working in Ireland, North and South, 1970 and 1986 (excluding Irish church personnel working overseas).

	1970	1986	% Change 1970–86
Diocesan clergy	3,813	3,697	–3
Clerical orders (male)	4,019	2,789	–31
Sisters	15,145	12,332	–25
Brothers	2,195	1,230	–44
Total	25,172	19,113	–24

Source: Weafer (1988: 502).

marginality). At any rate, we will review in this section some of the main indicators of recent trends in Catholicism in Ireland.

First of all let us look at the church in organisational terms. In the late 1960s, the Catholic church in Ireland (North and South) had at its disposal a full-time staff of well over 30,000 priests and religious, of whom over 25,000 lived and worked in Ireland. This was the Irish church's highest number of personnel in its history and, relative to the population it served, made it the most heavily staffed in the western world. Since then, it is scarcely surprising that there has been a fall-off in numbers from this high peak. The numbers of diocesan clergy have fallen the least, declining only by 3 per cent between 1970 and 1986 (see Table 1) and projections from current rates of entry to the priesthood and from losses through death and departure suggest that this rather stable pattern is likely to hold for the near future (Weafer, 1988).

The stability in the numbers of diocesan clergy provides a relatively strong basis for the future of the parish system at least in the short-to-medium-term and renders the issue of lay participation in parish ministry somewhat less pressing than in other Catholic countries. Among the other personnel, however, decline is quite sharp. Male clerical orders, congregations of sisters and congregations of brothers have dropped between 25 and 44 per cent in numbers over the period 1970 to 1986. Intake of new members has fallen even more sharply so that those organisations now have a rapidly ageing membership. These developments bring the future of many of these orders and congregations seriously into question, and for some of them, amalgamations, rationalisations and the closing of houses have already become facts of life.

The contraction of the religious orders and congregations is important not only because of what it suggests about changed public attitudes to the religious life but also because it contributes to a marked loosening of the church's traditional partnership with the state in important areas of the social services. The most notable of these is secondary education, which until recently was dominated by religious order schools supported out of state funds. Attempts in the 1960s to build up a community-based comprehensive school system as a counter-weight to the religious order schools were resisted by the church, failed to generate popular enthusiasm and had little success. But now, church influence in the post-primary school system is declining by default rather than as a result of public policy. Because of shortage of personnel, the religious presence in the secondary system is waning rapidly and religious personnel in those schools have been concentrated into administrative positions. On the other hand, however, there is little public demand for a secularisation of the school system and considerable sympathy for attempts to preserve a religious ethos in schools in spite of the weakening of the direct religious presence. In primary schools, the clergy continue to play an important and widely accepted role in management boards and the majority of primary teachers accept an obligation to teach orthodox Catholicism as part of their work. Thus in the field of education, as in other areas, Catholicism now faces a period of re-organisation and of noticeable reduction in its position but it is by no means confronted with radical eclipse.

Impressions about the high level of religious belief and practice in Ireland were given their first systematic test in 1973–74 by means of a large-scale sample survey conducted by Maire Nic Ghiolla Phádraig of the Irish Bishops' Research and Development Commission (Nic Ghiolla Phádraig 1976, 1987). The results of the survey more than confirmed the view that religous adherence was, in fact, very strong. Almost 91 per cent of Catholics reported that they attended Mass at least once weekly and participation in other forms of devotion was correspondingly high. The results also showed that Catholics seemed to be more given to devotion and practice than to belief and conviction. Levels of belief in items of Catholic doctrine, and even knowledge of doctrine, seemed to be lower than the high levels of practice would imply, thus giving an indication that convention and social conformity rather than strong personal conviction might underly some of the devotionalism of Irish Catholics.

Subsequent studies of a type similar to the 1973–74 baseline enquiry enable us to make some assessment of recent trends (see Table 2). The main impression for this intervening time-span is that, while change has occurred, it has been limited. The proportion attending Mass at least once a week has dropped from 91 per cent in 1974 to 82 per cent in 1988–89, and monthly confession has dropped quite sharply (from 47 per cent in 1974 to 18 per cent in 1988–89). The trend in orthodox doctrine is also downwards, though not much: the proportion who believe in God is down from 96 per cent in 1974 to 93 per cent in 1984, while the proportion who

Table 2.   Selected indicators (%) of religious practice and belief among Irish Catholics, 1974–1984.[a]

	1974	1984	1988–89
Attend Mass at least once per week	91	87	82
Attend Mass more than once per week	23	30	21
Receive Communion weekly	28	38	43
Attend Confession monthly	47	26	18
Pray daily	80	85	71
Fully accept belief in God	96	93	n.a.
Fully accept that the Catholic Church is the one true Church	83	73	n.a.
(N)	(2,499)	(1,006)	(943)

[a] The data for 1984 are based on measures which replicated those used for the 1974 data, while the 1988–89 data are based on somewhat different measures. Thus while the 1988–89 data are reasonably comparable with the 1984 and 1974 data, that comparability is not complete.
Sources: 1974 and 1984 data, Weafer (1986b); 1988–89 data, Mac Gréil (1991).

believe that the Catholic church is the one true church is down by a bit more. On the other hand, some important indicators of practice are stable or have actually risen: about the same proportion, 21–23 per cent attended Mass more than once weekly in 1988–89 as in 1974 (this indicator having risen to 30 per cent in 1984), while the proportion who receive communion weekly has risen from 28 per cent to 43 per cent.

Some other patterns from survey data in the 1980s gave additional support to the notion that secularisation is taking place in Ireland at a considerably slower pace than had been expected. The 1973–74 study had shown a markedly lower level of belief and practice among young adults, 21–25 year olds especially, than in the rest of the population. However, by 1984, church affiliation among 21–25 year olds had risen and generally the rate of decline in other 'high-risk' groups (males, urban-dwellers, the highly educated) was relatively slight. Weafer (1986b: 517) concluded on the basis of these findings that 'the state of religion among Catholics in the Irish Republic is in a relatively stable conditon, with high levels of belief and practice persisting into the mid-1980s'.

Other indications of church influence seem to show the same pattern of change alongside continuity, with continuity often seeming to be the stronger. Artificial contraception, long banned under Irish law and opposed by the Catholic church, was legalised without too much protest in 1979. However, recent referenda on the Constitution have re-affirmed the constitutional ban on divorce and installed a ban on the legalisation of abortion, leaving Ireland in a quite exceptional position in developed countries on these issues. The visit of Pope John Paul II to Ireland in 1979 evoked an enthusiastic response, with one million people (almost one-third of the population) attending his open air Mass in Dublin alone. In 1988, the newly formed Progressive Democrats, a political party with a secular-liberal slant, proposed a new national Constitution which omitted reference to God and quickly retracted the proposal once its unpopularity among its own members became clear. (It was said that the proposal was adopted at a party conference on a Sunday morning when many of the delegates were at Mass). Straws in the wind such as these often surprise commentators. They indicate a stubborn durability in conservative Catholic allegiance in Ireland which seems out of step with Ireland's other image as a rapidly changing, increasingly liberal, secular society of a typically modern, western type. On the other hand, none of the trends mentioned above contradicts the notion that Catholicism in Ireland has reached a plateau and may be about to begin a descent. They suggest rather that the pace of that descent is slower and more uneven than has often been expected.

Conclusion

The historical record shows that institutional Christianity continued to act as an important part of the social fabric in western societies during industrialisation, at least, in most cases, until well into the twentieth century. Indeed in many places, in both metropolitan and peripheral regions, its significance grew as the early disruptive effects of capitalist industrialisation became more pronounced. In general terms, therefore, the strengthening influence of the Catholic church in Ireland in this period is not as far out of step with developments elsewhere as we often tend to think. However, this very general point does not make it any easier to specify the precise links between the dynamics of industrialisation and religious change, either in Ireland or in other countries. It may be tempting to interpret those connections in functional terms, looking at the role of religion as a mechanism of social integration during a time of rapid social change. However, while religion undoubtedly had certain integrative effects, it did not have the field to itself in this regard: nationalism, secular liberalism and socialism also offered themselves as potent ideological systems. These sometimes worked alongside and sometimes dislodged religion as means of group integration. Thus while the need for cultural identity and social integration offered religion a social function, it does not explain why religion, rather than any of the competing ideologies, sometimes fulfilled that function and sometimes did not. Nor does it explain the difficult question of the social level at which the integrative effects of religion operated. In the United States, among Catholics at least, religious identity and cohesiveness were most evident at the level of the ethnic neighbourhood (McLeod, 1986b), while a more general, non-confessional patriotism bound religious-ethnic groups into American society as a whole. In Germany, Catholic organisations—workers' associations, trade unions and political parties—played a similar role at sub-national level (McLeod, 1986b), but here too nationalism succeeded in transcending confessional affiliation to provide an ideological underpinning to German society as a whole. Elsewhere, religion could be integrative at one level and disruptive at another. In Ireland, religious and national communities tended to become co-terminous, leading to the breakaway from the United Kingdom of the largely Catholic independent state in the south and the formation of the 'two nations'—Catholic-nationalist and Protestant-unionist—in the north. Cases such as Poland suggest that the importance of religion in defining national identity is not unique to the south of Ireland, while the Balkan states show how even today competing religious allegiances can, as in Northern Ireland, tend to sunder fragile political entities. Further complications arise when we consider that patterns of religious adherence have changed even since industrialisation: in most cases, churches grew, levelled off and went into decline, though the pace and timing of that evolution have varied greatly from country to country and even between regions, social classes, gender groups and ethnic groups within individual countries.

The variety of religious patterns during industrialisation thus defy easy summation, though for Catholicism at least there are a number of regularly recurring features. The most obvious of these—all of them well-represented in the Irish case—can be listed as follows.

1   Strong ecclesiastical organisation, founded on a plentiful supply of well-organised, effectively equipped and efficiently deployed clergy and religious.
2   A particular appeal to, and association with, the world of women, as reflected both in the floods of women who joined female religious congregations from about the mid-nineteenth to the mid-twentieth centuries and in the widespread tendency to identify religion as women's business, particularly within the confines of the home and in connection with the socialisation of children.
3   Strategic flexibility in shaping the local-level presence of the church to suit local circumstances: in American cities, the parish was linked to ethnic neighbourhoods, in rural Ireland it was identified with a strong sense of local place, while in many continental countries, the Catholic organisation was the key focus of local Catholic attachment.

4 The top–down cultivation of a rich ceremonial devotionalism, coupled with a sexually repressive morality and a tolerant approach to the popular demand for a quasi-magical or miraculous element in the veneration of saints, shrines, relics and pilgrimage sites.

5 The building up of extensive Catholic services in education, health-care and social welfare as an adjunct to pastoral ministration. Sometimes (as in Ireland since the days of British rule, or as in other European nations for varying periods of their recent histories) these were provided to some degree or other in formal cooperation with the state, while sometimes (as in the United States) they were provided as independent systems running parallel to or even in competition with state services. Religious congregations, particularly of women, provided much of the personnel and financial resources which enabled the church to provide these services on such a large scale.

6 A pragmatic approach to church–state relationships, with an emphasis on finding a workable *modus vivendi* in dealing with the political authority rather than on ideological confrontation.

It is hard to move from this list of features to anything like a formal model of the relationship between religion and industrialisation which would successfully account for the peculiarities of Catholic history in western countries since the early nineteenth century. All we can say is that the ways in which those features worked together in different countries help us to account in an *ad hoc* way for one of the paradoxes of Catholic development during industrialisation: Catholicism was the most successful of the larger Christian denominations in riding out the upheavals that accompanied industrialisation, even though it was widely perceived—by Catholics as much as by non-Catholics—as the least at home with the culture of the industrial world. The church's symbolic defiance of many of the main strands of modernity gave it sympathetic appeal for many population groups who shared a sense of alienation, while its pragmatism and organisational strengths helped those same groups cope with the social forces pushing them towards the margins.

The Irish case is in many ways typical of this combination of resistance and accommodation in the Catholic church's relationship with the industrialising world up to the mid-twentieth century. In Ireland, despite the vigour and pace of the Catholic church's advance, there was undoubtedly something closed and defensive about its ethos. That defensiveness was generated in part by the Irish church's position as the only substantial Catholic church in the British Empire, a world which had long been dominated by Protestantism, which was rapidly becoming secular and was revolutionising its economic and social structures at a bewildering pace. As a result of the collapse of the Gaelic tradition, the Irish church lacked the cultural defense of a separate language to ward off the influences of that environment and consequently bristled with antipathy to the many of the cultural currents flowing from it. The training it gave to its clergy was narrow and anti-intellectual, and was as much concerned with shunning new ideas as stimulating the capacity to deal with them. Its powerful role in education was accompanied by little in the way of new educational thought; it was generally strong on instruction but weak on creativity. Its social base lay in the countryside and the middle-sized farming classes. In common with the nationalist tradition with which it identified, it was committed ideologically to a rural fundamentalism which was suspicious and fearful of the industrial city and it glorified the family farm and the little village as the pillars of social and economic life. It was a church, in other words, which often gave the appearance of being in, but not of, the larger industrialising world in which it was embedded.[2]

At the same time, the church's unease with much of the greater world around it was an important source of affinity with the marginality felt by Irish Catholics, first of all within the British empire and later, after independence, within the broader industrialising world. That sense of affinity was an important pre-disposing factor for the close and vigorous alliance between the Catholic church and Irish nationalism which grew with the nineteenth century. But the translation of this predisposition into achieved fact also required the church's organisational capacity to cope with both the threats and opportunities the wider world offered. The church may have disliked modernity but it did not dismiss or disregard its instruments. The church's internal structural reforms—greater centralisation of control in the papacy, tighter vertical integration through the episcopacy, better trained, more numerous and more rationally deployed clergy, the proliferation of new, functionally specialised religious congregations—were themselves representative of the increasing organisational rationality of nineteenth-century social systems and suggests an organisation coping with rather than fleeing from change. In Ireland, the broader

---

[2] Many general arguments have been advaced to the effect that the Catholic ethos was in one way or another hostile to the performance culture of modern capitalism, or in some way hindered the cultural developments common to modernisation in other western countries (see, e.g., Inglis, 1987; Lee, 1989). In addition, some attempts have been made to find structural links between Catholicism and poor economic performance in Ireland in the last hundred years. Kennedy (1978), for example, argued that church building in the nineteenth century hampered economic development by diverting a significant share of domestic capital away from productive uses. Concerning the more recent past, it has been argued that the church's influence in key institutional areas such as education has hampered the state's capacity to direct social development and so has hindered economic progress by impeding state action rather than by direct effects on the economy (Breen *et al.*, 1990).

society in which the revitalised church carved its place was visibly modernising, even if its economic structures remained fairly stagnant, and there were many ways in which the church both benefitted from and promoted that modernisation. Outside of normal parish ministry, the church's most important agent was the teacher in the primary school and its grasp of mass schooling in Ireland placed at its disposal one of the principal instruments of modern social engineering. Through the work of the religious congregations, the Irish church not only gained a foothold in the rapidly emerging system of social services, it also did much to mould the profession of lay teacher, as well as other modern 'caring' professions such as that of nurse and social worker. Its pastoral, educational and social services were focused very much on the family and it promoted a familial piety which reflected the increasing nuclearisation of the family and the growing importance of women as the moral centres of family life. No doubt the appeal to tradition was an important basis for the church's authority. But the church of the nineteenth century was a new species of organisation, fertilised in part by tradition but endowed also with much of the newly evolved social and cultural equipment of the modern world growing up alongside it.

The tension between resistance and accommodation was thus a source of creativity and strength for the Catholic church in the first century of industrialisation. Resistance came from the sense of the main strands of modernity as a threat to Catholic traditions, accommodation from the pragmatic awareness that modernity could not be avoided. A 'fortress mentality' was endemic in the church even where it was locally or nationally strong, since it always perceived the menace of external cultural forces. But the fortress was a base from which the church did business with the world, often with impressive effect. It mattered a great deal for the position and impact of the church whether its 'fortress' was built on a national population, as happened in Ireland, or whether it was based on sub-national regions or ethnic groups, as happened in many other cases. But in all these situations, the adaptive devices at its disposal had many general similarities. The Irish case demonstrates in an especially striking way how effective these devices could be. But there were many other success stories for the church and together these suggest how central to the history of industrialised societies organised religion continued to be until well into the present century at least.

Proceedings of the British Academy, **79**, 265–290

Social and Religious Transformations in Ireland: A Case of Secularisation?

MICHAEL P. HORNSBY-SMITH

University of Surrey

Introduction

IN HIS WELL-KNOWN ESSAY on the alleged demise of the supernatural, Berger claimed that it was 'reasonable to assume that a high degree of secularisation is a cultural concomitant of modern industrial societies' (1971: 30). In an earlier study he defined secularisation as 'the process by which sectors of society and culture are removed from the domination of religious institutions and symbols' (1973: 113).

This paper aims to address this secularisation thesis and its supposed relationship to the processes of industrialisation and modernisation by considering the major social and religious transformations which can be discerned in the Irish Republic over the past three or four decades. First, it will outline the changing social and religious context within which religious world views strive for plausibility (Berger, 1973). Of particular importance are the social concomitants of the economic transformations which have taken place since the 1950s and the religious transformations, especially in Roman Catholicism since the Second Vatican Council (1962–65).

Secondly, the extent to which one can find in recent decades evidence not only of secularisation but also of counter-tendencies will be explored. For this purpose I will review data on the religious transformations in Ireland in terms of Dobbelaere's three dimensions of secularisation (1981) and levels of analysis (1985). It will be suggested that the evidence indicates that there is no necessary link between industrialisation and secularisation. Thirdly, the implications of our findings for secularisation theory and the interpretation of the religious transformations in Irish Catholicism will be considered.

Read 8 December 1990. © The British Academy 1992.

Among social scientists generally, the secularisation thesis in an age of industrialisation, modernisation, rationalisation, bureaucratisation and urbanisation is 'the conventional wisdom' (Hammond, 1985: 1). Even so, the proliferation of 'new religious movements', the evident strength of an aggressive conservative Christianity and the 'religious right', the resurgence of fundamentalist Islamic movements, and the power of the basic Christian community movement legitimated by Third World liberation theology, should all give empirically-oriented sociologists grounds for reappraisal (Hadden and Shupe, 1985). The stance taken here is one of empirical agnosticism. It is necessary to take seriously Dobbelaere's requirement that 'we should be ready to falsify our theories on the basis of new empirical material' (1989: 28). Post-war Ireland provides an important test-case for the secularisation thesis.

In a recent literature review (1992), the author has suggested that Martin's early critique of the concept of secularisation (1965) remains important, although he has since modified his position (1969; 1978). In the first place, the existence or not of a process of secularisation is largely a definitional matter involving 'the very notions of religion and the sacred' (Ireland, 1988: 1). In its simplest formulation, Wilson defined it as 'the process whereby religious thinking, practice and institutions . . .' (1966: xiv) or 'by which religious institutions, actions, and consciousness, lose their social significance' (1982: 149). Given an exclusive, substantive definition of church-oriented religion, evidence of institutional decline appears to be a clear indication of secularisation. In his earlier work Wilson seems largely to have taken this view and he commences with a comprehensive review of statistical trends of religious indicators. On the other hand, when an inclusive, functionalist definition of religion is employed, secularisation seems to be ruled out. Luckmann's 'invisible' religion (1970) seems to fall into this category. Related problems arise where different interpretations are placed upon the same religious indicator —for example, church attendance—in different social and cultural settings —for example, the United States and Poland; and also where the cultural meanings and significance of the same religious phenomena—for example, traditional devotions or styles of spirituality—change over time.

Secondly, the concept of secularisation refers to a *process* so that historical data of some kind are necessary for any empirical testing of the secularisation thesis. In a recent analysis of religious trends in post-war America, Greeley (1989) has taken this quite literally and confined himself to an investigation of survey findings only where the same question wording has been employed at two points in time. But given the 'oscillating' nature of religious phenomena (Wilson, 1979: 11), the choice of the earlier point is inevitably contested and arbitrary (Martin, 1965). In my own studies of English Catholicism I have argued that there never was a 'golden age' of consistently high levels of religious belief, practice and commitment (Hornsby-Smith, 1987: 26-31), and suggested that there are close similarities between the interview responses of grassroots Catholics in the London of Booth's survey at the turn of the century (McLeod, 1974; 1981; 1986a; 1990) and the 'customary' religion of 'ordinary' Catholics in the 1970s and 1980s (Hornsby-Smith, 1989; 1991). In the case of Ireland an 'alternative popular culture' existed in pre-famine days and religious practice was much lower at the beginning of the nineteenth century than later (Kirby, 1984; Connolly, 1982).

There are, then, good reasons to be wary of an uncritical assumption of inevitable secularisation resulting from processes of social and economic change such as industrialisation and urbanisation. In order to explore the social implications of the religious changes which have taken place in recent decades, it is necessary to recognise the complexity of those changes and to identify appropriate criteria for monitoring them.

Dobbelaere (1981: 11–12; 1985) is one of several researchers who has sought to clarify this complexity. In particular he has distinguished three dimensions of the problem of secularisation:

1 *laicisation* at the macro or societal level—the process of structural differentiation whereby 'institutions are developed that perform different functions and are structurally different';
2 *religious involvement* at the micro or individual level, which 'refers to individual behaviour and measures the degree of normative integration in religious bodies'; and
3 *religious change* at the organisational level which 'expresses change occurring in the posture of religious organisation . . . in matters of beliefs, morals, and rituals, and implies also a study of the decline and emergence of religious groups'.

Dobbelaere postulates 'an underlying modernisation process—i.e. differentiation, rationalisation, societalisation, industrialisation, urbanisation, bureaucratisation, mobility, etc.—on the disengagement of modern man from religious bodies' (1981: 136–7). On the other hand, he allows for contrary processes of 'delaicisation' and 'desecularisation', and argues that 'secularisation is not a mechanical process, and it allows for religious groups to react' (1989: 37). Dobbelaere's framework is helpful and will be used in this paper to summarise religious changes in Ireland over the past three or four decades. Before considering the evidence in the case of Ireland, however, it is first necessary to review in outline the changing social and religious context.

The Changing Context

Social and economic change

Of relevance for the analysis of religious transformations are the changes which have taken place in economic structures and loci of control, demographic changes, processes of urbanisation, and the indications of major shifts in values resulting from the opening up of Irish society to external forces and influences. As we shall see, in this process the role of the Catholic church has been transformed.

In the first place, the Republic of Ireland in large measure reflects its former status as a colony of Britain (Nic Ghiolla Phádraig, 1988; Hechter, 1975). Thus, Mair (this volume) argues that one consequence of the British occupation was that the forces of clericalism and conservative nationalism became legitimised after independence. Catholicism and nationalism had become the two main pillars on which Irish political culture rested. A further reflection of its long historical domination by Britain is the fact that Ireland has exported some eight million people, or twice the present population of the whole island, over the past two centuries, as its agricultural economy, structure of landholdings and system of inheritance failed to absorb a large increase in population (Hornsby-Smith and Dale, 1988; Kennedy, 1973b; Drudy, 1985; Lyons, 1974; Breen *et al.*, 1990).

Hannan and Commins (this volume) argue that the rural fundamentalist ideology which was inherited by the new Irish state was congruent with Catholic social thought and was espoused by church leaders. It was also legitimated by the romantic claim that Ireland 'did not place as high a value on economic development as other countries did' (Kennedy, this volume). The steady bleeding away of the young, however, reflected the failure of an economy based on private enterprise and protective barriers and the absence of a 'constructive social vision' on the part of the church. It was not until the late 1950s that there was a shift to an explicit drive for economic growth by means of an 'aggressive capitalism' largely aligned with the 'project of the bourgeoisie' (Peillon, 1982). Although the immediate consequence of the drive for industrialisation in the 1960s was that the international migration flow was reversed in the 1970s, in the more unsettled economic conditions of the 1980s, both emigration and unemployment rates increased significantly (Breen *et al.*, 1990: 144–145, 147).

With the dash for growth, agriculture declined in importance and a major process of urbanisation was generated by the migration of workers from the land and peripheral regions to the towns. The population of Dublin increased by one-sixth between 1971 and 1978, faster than any other western European capital (Lee, 1989: 605). The result is that around one-third of the population now lives in the greater Dublin area. But as the economy faltered in the 1980s, the frustration of expectations of higher living standards led to higher levels of anomic disturbance: crime, marital breakdown and drug abuse increased, especially in working-class areas (Nic Ghiolla Phádraig, 1988: 208).

The new economic strategies of the 1960s resulted in a significant shift of employment from agriculture to manufacturing and services. There was also a steady increase in the female labour force participation rate. This was especially striking for married women, the increase being from one in twenty in 1961 to one in five in 1987 (Breen et al., 1990: 101, 117). Associated with this is evidence that contraceptive practices in Ireland are converging with those of other industrialised nations and that a majority of the population no longer accepts the teaching of the Catholic Church on contraception (Coleman, this volume).

Mention must also be made of the undoubted impact of the mass media in opening up the Irish consciousness to the social and cultural changes which were taking place elsewhere and especially in Britain. The proclivity to censorship in Roman Catholic Ireland collapsed in the face of the range of developments in mass communications in recent years, especially television, pirate radio, video recorders and satellite broadcasting (Farrell, 1984: 115). A greater openness to external influences also resulted from membership of the EC and was reflected in the impact of equality legislation and the judgements of the European Court (Nic Ghiolla Phádraig, 1988: 213).

Religious changes

Around 95 per cent of the population of the Irish Republic declare themselves to be Catholics (Fogarty et al., 1984: 125; Mac Gréil, 1991: 2–3). 'It is the only predominantly Roman Catholic country in the English-speaking world' (Nic Ghiolla Phádraig, 1988: 205) and 'with the loss of the Irish language [the Catholic church] became the single most important mark of [Irish] separate identity' (Kirby, 1984: 62). For Catholics, the Second Vatican Council (1962–65) was a watershed between the 'late Tridentine Victorian' Catholicism 'combining Roman ultramontanist legalism with British Victorian prudery' (Nic Ghiolla Phádraig, 1988: 206–7; cf. also McRedmond, 1980; Kirby 1984) of the pre-Vatican church and the new post-Vatican model (Hornsby-Smith, 1987, 1989). Any understanding of religious change must take due account of the renewal processes taking place since, and as a consequence of, the Council

(Abbott, 1966; Butler, 1981). The historian of church–state relations in Ireland has observed that 'it would be natural to expect that in so intensely Catholic a country as Ireland these effects should have been particuarly strong', and he refers especially to the growth of the ecumenical movement, the growing freedom of discussion in the church, and the development of Catholic social teaching since Pope John XXIII's 1961 encyclical *Mater et Magistra* (Whyte, 1980: 345–5).

Up to the end of the 1960s the sociological reality of the church corresponded closely to the institutional model identified by Dulles (1976). The emphasis here is on the church as a structured community led by office holders with clearly defined rights and powers. Dulles suggests that by itself this model tends to be doctrinaire and to result in rigidity and conformity. In a stable, unchanging world the church manifested such characteristics of a 'mechanistic' organisation as a distinct hierarchical structure of control, authority and communication; tendencies for interaction between superiors and subordinates to be vertical, and for normal behaviour in the institution to be governed by instructions and decisions issued by superiors; and an insistence on loyalty to the institution and obedience to superiors as a condition of membership (Burns and Stalker, 1966; Fulton, 1991). The hierarchical authority structures were seen as mediating grace and truth to the laity and there was a marked tendency for the institution to be concerned with its own maintenance and survival.

The pre-Vatican church stressed the virtues of loyalty, the certainty of answers, strict discipline and unquestioning obedience (Greeley, 1972). In this model the priest was viewed as a 'man apart' and the 'sacred' ministry of the priest was asserted over the priesthood of all believers (Moore, 1975). In the pre-Vatican theology, with its fidelity to tradition (*Pro Mundi Vita*, 1973), God was seen as remote, unchanging and perfect (Neal, 1970). There was a close relationship between an emphasis on a transcendent God, a hierarchically structured church, an authoritarian clergy and social distance between the clergy and the laity (Sharratt, 1977). At the parish level there was an emphasis on the objectivity of the sacramental system and a discouragement of full lay involvement in liturgical worship. The sermon provided an opportunity to legitimate traditional practices and reinforce traditional status and power differentials. Control of information was monopolised by the priests who discouraged ecumenical ventures and independent lay initiatives. The 'sacredness' of the separate Catholic community was preserved by insistence on marital endogamy and religious socialisation in separate Catholic schools. Separation from contamination by the world was emphasised and, though there was the exercise of charity to save souls, social and political involvement as a requirement of the gospel was rejected (Leslie, 1980).

However, it was becoming increasingly clear that this model of the church was inadequate in the post-war, post-colonial world of the nuclear threat, democratic imperative, new contraceptive technology and mass communications. The strategy of suppression or intransigence (Berger, 1973: 156), which had been ruthlessly followed for over half a century since the condemnation of modernism, was beginning to break down. The Vatican Council's emphasis on collegiality and participation by all the 'People of God' can be seen as indicating a shift within a changing world to an 'organic' management structure with far more emphasis on lateral consultation than vertical command (Burns and Stalker, 1966). The church was to be transformed from a pyramid of organisation and power into a community of service and mission on the move (Moore, 1975: 34–5). Alternative 'community', and also 'sacrament', 'herald' and 'servant', models of the church were to be given increasing emphasis (Dulles, 1976).

What was involved was nothing less than the adoption of a strategy for transformation and revitalisation, which has been the subject of intermittent conflict between competing exponents in the more pluralistic post-Vatican Church. The Church had a completely 'new agenda' with less emphasis on the defence of the faith and more on the interpretation of religious symbols (Greeley, 1975). There was a movement away from the legalistic following of institutional rules and regulations to a concern with how Christians were to live fully human and liberated lives. This was legitimated by significant shifts of theological emphasis from 'tyrannous transcendentalism' to 'radical immanentism' (Daly, 1981: 220–2) and by the promotion of pluralist participation. Whereas the pre-Vatican church had been top-heavy with 'duty-language', the Second Vatican Council stressed reciprocal rights and duties, dialogue and consultation (Coleman, 1978). A major feature of the post-Vatican period has been its doctrinal relativism (McSweeney, 1980) and, for the individual Catholic, the loss of the fear of hell—that is 'the traditional Hell of Roman Catholics, a place where you would burn for all eternity if you were unlucky enough to die in a state of mortal sin' (Lodge, 1980: 113).

Irish Catholicism was seriously unprepared for the Vatican Council. The liturgical reforms and new ecumenical openness were dutifully encouraged according to the letter, though not perhaps the spirit of the Council (McRedmond, 1980: 42; Nic Ghiolla Phádraig, 1988: 209). All the same, the European Value Systems Study Group (Fogarty et al., 1984: 104) noted that there was clear evidence that the Council had influenced Irish Catholics in three ways:

> it revealed to many Catholics the possibility of a private world of conscience and behaviour; it stressed that the Church was not merely the pope and

bishops but the entire people of God whose common convictions carry an inner truth of their own; and it transformed religious thinking from being introverted and pessimistic to be outward-looking and optimistic.

While the Second Vatican Council undoubtedly initiated transformations globally in the Roman Catholic church, its impact varied from society to society, depending largely on the proportion of Catholics in the population. Martin, in his encyclopaedic study of patterns of secularisation (1978), has suggested a fundamental contrast between an organicist Catholicism and a pluralist Protestantism. This leads him to distinguish situations of monopoly, duopoly and various forms of pluralism.

The Republic of Ireland clearly presents a case of Catholic monopoly and has been regarded as 'an unself-consciously Catholic state' (Nic Ghiolla Phádraig, 1988: 206). Martin argues that in the post-Tridentine period Catholicism was a kind of 'reaction formation . . . as a sociological consequence of an organic system trying like a limpet to defend itself by clinging with more and more intense desperation to the rock . . . of Peter' (1978: 37). It manifested, in other words, an ultramontane deference to Roman centralism. However, by way of modification, he notes that in the case of Ireland, as of other nations such as Poland, 'an indissoluble union of church and nation arises where the church has been the sole available vehicle of nationality against foreign domination'. Such countries continue to be characterised by high practice and belief (1978: 107).

A second modification follows from Martin's analysis of centre–periphery relations. Where there is no viable alternative language as a source of identity and where 'the centre is perceived as different, . . . then religious nationalism is the likely outcome' (1978: 148). But the case of Ireland is unusually complex:

> Ireland is peripheral to England but England is peripheral to Europe and to Rome. The Roman centre at its moment of weakness before the barbarians, was strengthened on its distant Irish periphery, from which the faith returned to Scotland and England . . . So Ireland like Poland is the hard circumference of the Roman centre of the circle. Since Ireland is indeed peripheral to England and England defines its marginality in relation to Europe through Protestantism, Ireland is strengthened in her Catholicism and in her relation to England's historic enemies, Catholic Spain and France . . . In Southern Ireland where Catholicism and the State are one, the historical enmity no longer obtains. The Protestant cause is defeated without any doubt . . . Five per cents are rarely dangerous . . . (1978: 150)

Finally, in a recent appraisal of global Catholicism, Martin has warned that 'the seeming power of religion when linked to feelings of repressed national identity, as in Eire . . ., is not to be interpreted as proof of the eternal and inevitable role of faith in the psyche and in the community' (1978: 28).

Secularising and Counter-secularising Tendencies

This review of the historical context of religion in Ireland and of the social, economic, political and religious changes which have taken place in recent decades, is the setting in which we can ask how far secularisation is a concomitant of the modernisation process. In this section we will review the evidence for religious transformations in Ireland in recent decades in terms of Dobbelaere's three dimensions of secularisation.

In a famous broadcast for St. Patrick's Day in 1943, De Valera expressed the dominant and 'stifling Catholic nationalist orthodoxy' (Kirby, 1984: 18) in his 'unworldly vision' (Murphy, 1975: 84) of the good society:

> That Ireland which we have dreamed of would be the home of a people who valued material wealth only as a basis of right living, of a people who were satisfied with frugal comfort and devoted their leisure to things of the spirit —a land whose countryside would be bright with cosy homesteads, whose fields and villages would be joyous with the sounds of industry, with the romping of sturdy children, the contests of athletic youths and the laughter of comely maidens; whose firesides would be forums for the wisdom of serene old age. It would, in a word, be the home of a people living the life that God desires that man should live. (Moynihan, ed., 1980: 466).

Critics have suggested that this dream was unrealistic, 'bore no relationship' to people's material and spiritual lives (Kirby, 1984: 18) and was a totally unsuitable basis for the construction of national economic policy (Lee, 1989: 334). It does, at all events, illustrate a strong Catholic suspicion of industrial capitalism and its attendant materialism and consumerism. But there seems little doubt that continuing economic stagnation and the huge loss of young people by emigration in the post-war years led eventually to the search for new economic policies of growth which were not premised on an unrealisable nostalgic vision of a benevolent rural society. In 1964 Garret Fitzgerald, writing in the Jesuit journal *Studies* on 'seeking a national purpose', suggested that

> in some respects the thinking of the Catholic Church in Ireland has lagged far behind Catholic thought elsewhere. This has been particularly notable in relation to such matters as social welfare. One cannot resist the conclusion that in the 1930s and 1940s the Irish Church took a wrong turning in its thinking on these matters. (quoted in Whyte, 1980: 334)

Table 1. Secularising and counter-secularising tendencies in the Republic of Ireland.

TENDENCY	Societal	LEVEL Organisational	Individual
	Laicisation	DIMENSION Religous Change	Involvement
SECULARISATION	Accommodation strategy Process of differentiation — education — health — law	Indicators of decline — fall in and aging of personnel — fall in vocations	Indicators of decline — erosion of traditional beliefs — erosion of traditional practices
RELIGIOUS REVITALISATION	Special purpose groups — abortion amendment — divorce referendum Moral monopoly — 'conscience of nation'	Emergent 'People of God' — *Trocaire* — justice concerns Moral monopoly	Emergent laity — participation — social awareness — small groups

Six years previously T. K. Whitaker had in fact heralded the search for new strategies of state economic planning in his report, *Economic Development*. Is it right, however, to regard these new economic goals and their consequences as implying a process of secularisation? Table 1, which is based on Dobbelaere's analysis, summarises the evidence and suggests that the answer is not as clear-cut as some have supposed.

Church–state relations: secularising tendencies

Focusing first on Dobbelaere's societal level, evidence of processes of structural differentiation in recent decades, and particularly developments in education, health and law, has been taken to indicate 'a gradual secularisation' (Breen *et al.*, 1990: 108–11). The 'moral monopoly' of the church (Inglis, 1987) in these three areas has loosened since the 1960s with the emergence of 'a form of pro-religious anti-clericalism' on the part of middle-class laity (Fulton, 1991: 194).

In Ireland the control of schools and of cultural tranmission by the Roman Catholic church dates from the colonial period in the middle of the nineteenth century. Fulton sees schooling in Ireland as an instance of 'political religion' (1991: 171–97). A schools system emerged which was paid for by the state but was effectively under clerical control. In this way the religious socialisation of young Catholics was ensured, differentiation from Protestants and an ethnic sense of identity reinforced, the threat of secularising influences countered, hierarchical clerical control over the laity maintained and the power of the church to define morality extended. In exchange the church provided legitimation for the state. This clerical control of schools has been jealously guarded as 'the single most important institutional means of reinforcing Catholic precepts' (Peillon, 1982: 92). For much of its history the education system was firmly rooted in dogmatic 'truth peddling'. However, the rapid expansion in the provision of second level education and the decline in the numbers of those in religious orders resulted in a significant laicisation process and the decline in the proportion of teachers in religious orders at the second level from over one half in 1961 to 16 per cent in 1983 (Breen et al., 1990: 109). Concessions from a traditional intransigence regarding the Catholic control of education were also made in the 1970s. The new flexibility of the hierarchy first showed itself in the lifting of the ban on Catholic students attending Trinity College and later over the issues of community schools and multi-denominational schools. Whyte has observed that 'to anyone who knows the previous history of Irish education, the astonishing thing is that [the Catholic bishops] conceded so much' (1980: 395).

A similar process of laicisation occurred in the health services. 'As hospital services mushroomed, the dominance of religious orders in hospital administration and staffing dwindled' (Breen et al., 1990: 109). Early post-war proposals for state welfare failed in large part owing to the strong opposition of the Catholic church on two main grounds: (i) a deep suspicion of state power over the individual and consequently its advocacy of the principle of subsidiarity, that is, that the state should not undertake what smaller bodies can properly do; and (ii) its concern that improper health advice, not according to Catholic moral teaching, for example on contraception, might be given. A similar concern with the growth of state power on the part of the English Catholic hierarchy had led initially to their opposition to the construction of the welfare state in post-war Britain (Coman, 1977).

The strong overt and covert opposition of the Catholic bishops to Dr. Noel Browne's 'Mother and Child Scheme' was dramatically exposed when the Minister resigned at the request of his party leader in 1951 and in an unprecedented move released the relevant correspondence to the press (Whyte 1980: 196–272, 419–38). Whyte's judgement (pp. 260–1) that Browne 'courted a showdown' and 'wished to bring about a collision between the Irish State and a powerful vested interest . . . [and so] crack the mould of Irish society' in order to bring about radical social change, has the ring of plausibility. The 1951 crisis does seem to have been an important milestone even if 'the growth of State power was a genuine problem in Ireland, especially in view of the centralising tendencies and the impatience with interest groups that were so noticeable in Irish administration'.

In reviewing the role of the Catholic church in Ireland in the post-war years, Peillon has argued that it abandoned its former vision of a society constructed on corporatist principles, which provided an alternative to both capitalism and communism, and has, in recent years regarded the increasing dominance of Irish society by large national and multinational enterprises with growing concern. However, the church

> will adapt to the society which is today in the making, but will make no creative contribution to its elaboration. In the past it looked with aversion on the advance of urbanisation and industrialisation in Ireland and found itself incapable of holding it back. Today it no longer proclaims commitment to a particular type of society and to this degree it has ceased to be a social force. The Irish Catholic Church professes a social doctrine but no longer entertains a coherent social project. (Peillon, 1982: 99)

The third example of laicisation is the increasing independence of the law and judiciary in the determination of social policy, even in areas where previously the hegemony of the Catholic church was unchallenged. Some changes were clearly designed with a view to appeasing the fears of Northern Ireland Protestants. One instance of this was the removal from De Valera's 1937 Constitution, following a referendum in 1972, of the reference to 'the special position' of the Catholic church (Whyte, 1980: 388–9; Murphy, 1975: 90). A second was the changes in the law relating to the sale and distribution of contraceptives (Whyte, 1980: 403–16; Breen *et al.*, 1990: 109–10). Following the McGee case in 1973, in which the Supreme Court held that a 1935 law which forbade the importation of contraceptives was unconstitutional and violated basic human rights, the law was finally amended in 1979. One of the most unexpected aspects of the debate, however, was the statement by the bishops in 1973 that 'there are many things which the Catholic Church holds to be morally wrong and no one has ever suggested, least of all the Church herself, that they should be prohibited by the State' (*Irish Independent*, 26 November 1973; quoted in Whyte, 1980: 407). A third instance, which also reflects the increasingly independent role of the courts and the failure of the church to maintain a previously intransigent position, relates to the matter of legal adoption. A revision of the law in 1974 for the first time allowed a couple of mixed religion to adopt a child.

Whyte has characterised the secularising tendencies we have reviewed as 'adjustment by consent' (1980: 380) and there are signs that the response of the Catholic church in Ireland to the massive economic and social changes since the 1950s has increasingly been one of accommodation (Berger, 1973: 156). Thus it no longer espouses a commitment to a rural society based on small scale agriculture. On the other hand, it has not replaced an earlier vision grounded in pre-war papal encyclicals (chiefly Leo XIII's *Rerum Novarum* of 1891 and Pius XI's *Quadragesimo Anno* of 1931) with 'a coherent social project'. While this reflects the 'great flexibility and political realism' of the church in the pursuit of its essential survival goals (Peillon, 1982: 89), it also demonstrates that the church has become increasingly divorced from participation in major areas of social and economic policy determination.

The election in 1990 of Mary Robinson, a well-known campaigner for individual and minority rights and for a pluralistic, modern Ireland, as President of the Republic, has been interpreted as a tacit sign of the emergence of a 'new' Ireland (O'Sullivan, 1991) and of the inability of the religious authorities in the Roman Catholic church seriously to retard such developments. In this sense the result can be seen as an indication of latent secularising tendencies.

Church–state relations: religious revitalisation

The evidence we have reviewed above does not give the whole story of the religious transformations which have taken place. It is also necessary to evaluate the evidence for religious revitalisation and counter-secularising tendencies.

In a recent study of religious change in the United States, Wuthnow has drawn attention to the growth of special purpose groups and their increasing public role. These groups clearly constitute 'one of the ways in which the faith is continually revitalised' (1988: 121). It might be argued that such lay-initiated and lay-run organisations have also been enormously successful in the Irish Republic in mobilising Catholics in defence of traditional positions regarding abortion and divorce in the two referenda in the 1980s. Any secularisation thesis has to face the fact that the aggressive Pro-Life Amendment Campaign (PLAC) on the very first occasion 'that they [had] openly initiated and directed such a campaign' (Inglis, 1987: 86), successfully persuaded the Irish electorate to constitutionalise the issue and insert an anti-abortion clause into the constitution. Article 40, paragraph 3, section 3, now reads:

> The State acknowledges the right to life of the unborn and, with due regard to the equal right of life of the mother, guarantees in its laws to respect, and, as far as practicable, by its laws, defend and vindicate that right.

One view of the referendum was that it was a rite of renewal directed at the maintenance of traditional cultural supremacy and an attempt to pre-empt the democratic consideration of alternative rights and liberties (O'Carroll, 1991). Other commentators regarded the referendum as a 'vulgar farce' since about 4,000 Irish women were going to Britain for abortions each year and abortion was already illegal in Ireland. Rather 'the exercise was symbolically significant . . . It was a cleansing ritual, of a type central to the traditional value system . . . [which] had now broken up, but substantial fragments still survived' (Lee, 1989: 653–4). Inglis saw this as the first time that the full power of Catholic laity to split any major power bloc or alliance in Irish society with its demand for loyalty to traditional Catholic morality had been demonstrated (1987: 86).

The second successful mobilisation of Catholic laity was demonstrated in the victory of the anti-divorce lobby in the referendum of 1986 on amending the constitution to allow divorce in certain circumstances, despite evidence of increasing marital breakdown. The emergence of the lay-run 'special purpose' groups is a new phenomenon and must reasonably be considered as evidence of powerful counter-secularising forces in Irish society. Thus, in an analysis of recent movements for social change in the Republic of Ireland, and in particular the mobilisation of the Catholic 'ideological bloc', Hannigan concludes that 'secularisation . . . has not proceeded in Ireland in an evolutionary, linear fashion'. Rather, given the dualistic nature of the bloc—conservative in private morality and liberal on social justice issues—'it appears more useful to conceputalise secularisation in Gramscian terms as a process of ideological contestation in each of the main societal sectors' (1989: 83).

Lee suggests that the abortion referendum was a device for diverting attention back to traditional concepts of personal morality and away from areas of social morality and the operation of capitalistic enterprises (1989: 654–5). However, the Catholic hierarchy had begun to develop a critique of social policy in the 1970s as unemployment levels and attendant social problems rose as a result of major social and economic reconstruction and increasing exposure to global economic forces. This concern culminated in the publication of the joint pastoral letter *The Work of Justice* in 1977. While it seems to have made little public impact, Whyte observes (1980: 396–7) an interesting shift of methodology. Whereas previously the bishops had slavishly attempted to apply the papal social encyclicals to the Irish situation, now they 'started looking at Ireland as it actually was, and applied their consciences to the evils they saw'. Hannigan speculates about the consequences of 'social justice' elements in the Catholic bloc allying with reformist political elements in a way which 'could significantly affect, and perhaps realign, the power relations between the main contending social classes in their dispute for hegemony in Ireland' (1989: 82).

In his masterly review of the evidence of church–state relations in Ireland, Whyte concluded that there were only sixteen measures out of about 1,800 statutes enacted by the Irish parliament between 1923 and 1970 where there was clear evidence that one or more bishops had been consulted or made representations (1980: 363–4). This led him to reject any suggestion that Ireland was a theocratic state. He also rejected an alternative view that the Catholic hierarchy was simply one interest group among many and, following the suggestion of Liam Ryan (1979), concluded that 'the best model to use for the hierarchy's current role is to see it as seeking to be *the conscience of society*' (1980: 416). In this role the hierarchy is seen less as the close collaborator of the state and more as 'a left-of-centre' social critic on behalf of the poor, deprived and those oppressed and vulnerable as a result of social and economic change. In my view, it is misleading to see such a transformation of social role as evidence of secularisation. Rather it is appropriate to regard the change as evidence of a slow process of revitalisation in Roman Catholicism which commenced a century ago with the first modern social encyclical but which in recent years dates from the reforms of the Second Vatican Council.

Organisational decline: secularising trends

While some secularisation theorists are chiefly concerned with the influence of religion at the societal level, attention is also given to the organisational and individual levels. At the organisational level, Kirby (1984: 38) has pointed to evidence of a significant fall in the numbers of church personnel to serve Ireland's growing population:

> The numbers of priests, sisters and brothers have shown a steady decline since 1970. In that year the total number was 33,092 while in 1983 it was down to 28,607. In every year since 1974, when these statistics first began to be compiled at a national level, the numbers of deaths or departures from the ranks have far exceeded the number of entrants. Another important factor is the age structure of Church personnel. Whereas in 1970 40% were under the age of 40 and 41% were over the age of 50, by 1981 only 25% were under 40 and 55% over 50. Smaller numbers of young priests, sisters and brothers have to support ever larger numbers of older ones. This is going to be a major drain on the financial resources and freedom of action of many religious orders in years to come. (1984: 38)

The former director of the Irish bishops' Council for Research and Development reported that 'in 1989, the total strength of the Irish Catholic church clerical and religious personnel was 24,546' (Weafer, 1990), a fall of more than one quarter in the past twenty years. The number of new entrants was only two-fifths of the number in 1970. Other commentators have bemoaned the failure of the Catholic church in Ireland to exploit the potential of the Vatican Council's reforms and have suggested that it has remained wedded to 'outmoded parish structures' and 'more concerned with maintaining the institutions functioning rather than with fostering new forms of mission through which this generation of Irish people could be excited by a vision of what it is to be a Christian' (Kirby, 1984: 32). Tendencies such as these appear, then, to indicate processes of institutional decline and hence of secularisation.

Institutional reform: counter-secularising tendencies

It is, however, necessary to balance the consideration of institutional decline with an assessment of the huge scale of the Catholic church's physical and bureaucratic organisation. In his comprehensive review of the situation in 1982, Inglis (1987: 33–62) has indicated that for an estimated Catholic population (in the whole island) of 3.7 million there were 1,322 parishes, 2,639 churches, 591 Catholic charitable institutions (including hospitals, homes for the deaf and blind, and reformatories and 3,844 primary and 900 secondary schools. He argues that it is the sheer scale of these resources which enables the Catholic church 'to control the moral discourse and practice of the Irish people' and maintain a 'moral monopoly'.

Of course, the sheer size of the institution does not bear directly on the processes of religious decline or revitalisation. It is mentioned simply in order to guard against too hasty a judgement of decline. In spite of the fact that some commentators have felt it necessary to ask *Is Irish Catholicism Dying?* (Kirby, 1984), there are indications of processes of religious revitalisation following from the reforms of the Second Vatican Council. There is evidence of a stirring among the laity to realise their newly discovered status as 'the People of God', to resist 'top-down' traditional styles of religious authority, to 'reclaim their story' and insist on their right to participate in the determination of priorities (O'Kelly, 1986). Seeds of a transformed Catholicism are also to be found in the success and international recognition of the work of *Trocaire*, the main Irish development agency, in the charismatic movement and in various forms of basic Christian communities. A growing number of groups are working in inner-city areas or with deprived groups and attempting to raise awareness of some of the social injustices associated with uncontrolled forms of western capitalism (Kirby, 1984). In my judgement, it would be perverse to regard such new stirrings of a revitalised religious faith as evidence of secularisation.

Finally, Peillon (1982: 90) has observed that the dual nature of the church's structure, that is, a diocesan clergy which serves the everyday needs of parishioners and members of religious orders who have the autonomy to respond more rapidly to changing needs (teaching, nursing, charitable works, etc.), contributes to institutional resilience. This flexibility is also manifested in a 'plurality of languages' which enables clergy speaking from a variety of standpoints to maintain some contact with marginal groups and even the 'enemies of the moment'. By means of a variety of strategies—organisational flexibility, the plurality of its languages, adaptable methods of clerical recruitment, control over the schools, and so on—the church continues with a high measure of success to reproduce itself.

Individual involvment: declining traditional practice

Between the 1971 and 1981 censuses in the Irish Republic there was a fivefold increase in the number of people who declared that they had 'no religion' from 0.3% to 1.2% in an increased population. Such figures 'seem to support the assertion of some people that Ireland is witnessing the gradual but persistent movement towards a secularist society' (Weafer, 1986b: 507). As we shall see, however, the evidence in terms of individual involvement is by no means all in the direction of secularisation.

There is no shortage of survey data about the changing religious beliefs and practices of Irish people over the past two decades. Chief sources are the national survey of 1974, a subsequent survey in 1984 designed specifically to monitor changes over the ten-year period (Breslin and Weafer, 1985), and more recently another national survey of religious practice and attitudes (Mac Gréil, 1991). There have also been two national surveys conducted by the European Values Systems Study Group in 1981 (Fogarty et al., 1984) and 1990 (Whelan, forthcoming).

Weafer (1986a,b) has reported the main findings: a small decline in orthodox beliefs and weekly Mass attendance and a big decline in the use of monthly private confession. Orthodox belief was found to increase with age, to decrease with educational qualifications, and to be higher among women and lowest in urban areas. Similarly higher sacramental participation was found among women, those living in rural areas and those in higher social classes. In a comparison of the findings from surveys of the religious beliefs and practices of Irish university students in 1975–76 and 1987–78, MacAirt also reported lower levels of 'basic' beliefs, much lower levels of Mass attendance more than weekly, and concluded that 'the spiritual climate in Ireland is changing rapidly' (1990: 183).

Of particular interest for the purposes of both trend and cohort analysis are the two surveys of the European Value Systems Study Group. The findings from the 1990 study will be reported in due course. On the basis of the 1981 study it was reported that:

> there is the shift across generations from stronger to weaker acceptance of orthodox beliefs and religious practice and of the authority of the Church . . . The shift has been sharpest in attitudes to the Church and the authoritativeness of its teaching: and in this area the age and generation shift has been reinforced by a similar, though modest, trend towards a more critical attitude to the Church and its authority among those with higher levels of education and occupational qualification (Fogarty *et al.*, 1984: 12).

This survey also reported that the unemployed stood out as a particularly alienated group and that women in employment were, if anything, running ahead of trends away from orthodoxy. As we noted earlier, there were large increases in the size of both these groups in the 1980s.

Where longitudinal data are not available, tests of the secularisation thesis have been claimed by comparing more modern and more traditional groups or sectors of the population. For example, Nic Ghiolla Phádraig, using data from a national survey in 1973–74, showed that men were less religious than women, younger cohorts less religious than older cohorts (apart from the 18–20 age group), urban residents less religious than rural residents, farmers more religious than those in the non-farming sector, those with emigration experiences less religious than those who had not been exposed to such influences, and those with a higher consumption of foreign media less religious than those with lower exposures. She concluded that 'indicators of modernisation are negatively related to measures of religiosity and so provide some support for the secularisation theory' (1986: 153).

In a review of the survey evidence, Ryan has suggested that 'a picture emerges of a people largely believing in God and in the Church, but in possession of a belief which increasingly has little impact, not just on the wider world of business and politics, but also in many areas of private morality' (1983: 6). A new type is beginning to appear among middle-class Catholics, similar to Greeley's 'communal Catholic' (1976), wanting a less authoritarian and more participative style of leadership and demanding that the leadership speak out more authoritatively on social morality but less on moral matters which affect his or her private life.

Individual involvement: resilience and reform

In the surveys we have briefly reviewed not all the indicators support a secularisation thesis. For example, there were small but quite consistent declines in the proportions rejecting basic church doctrines between 1974

Table 2. Religious and moral values in the Republic of Ireland: average scale scores 1981–1990 (N = 2,217).

	Scale				
	Traditional religious beliefs	Religiosity	Confidence in the church	Permissiveness	Civic morality
1981	5.36	3.60	1.65	2.09	8.11
1990	5.30	3.63	1.45	2.49	8.43
p (1981–90)	NS	NS	<.01	<.001	<.001
European average, 1990	3.18	2.57	1.21	3.81	8.37
Items in scale	7	6	3	8	14
Max. score	7	6	3	10	10

Source: Hornsby-Smith and Whelan (forthcoming), where full details of the scales, based on work at the University of Tilburg, are given. The items forming the three religious dimensions are all dichotomous and the scores are the average number of items agreed with. The items in the two morality scales are scored on a scale from 1 ('never justified') to 10 ('always justified') and the scale scores are the average scores on the items included.

and 1984, an increase in the proportions attending Mass more than weekly (from 23 to 30 per cent), and a big increase in the proportions receiving Holy Communion weekly (from 28 per cent in 1974 to 43 per cent in 1988–89). More people said they prayed daily and more said their families prayed together at home. In sum, 'the state of religion among Catholics in the Irish Republic is in a relatively stable condition' (Breslin and Weafer, 1985; cf. Weafer, 1986b) Mác Greil, 1991).

The two European Values surveys have also demonstrated the substantial stability of religious and moral values in the 1980s. The findings show that whatever secularising trends there might have been in the Irish Republic in recent years, they have gone 'nowhere near so far in Ireland as in Britain or in Europe generally' (Fogarty et al., 1984: 12; Harding et al., 1986). The results summarised in Table 2 show that overall there has been no change in the level of traditional Christian beliefs or in religiosity, a modest decline in confidence in the church, a significant increase in permissiveness and a strengthening of civic morality. A comparison of Ireland with Western European countries as a whole shows that the scores of Irish respondents on the religious dimensions are well above the European average and that they also display lower levels of permissiveness and a slightly more absolutist view on civil morality.

There are no significant social class variations in the measures of traditional religious beliefs and religiosity but the unskilled manual workers express higher levels of confidence in the church and lower levels of permissiveness than all other social classes. Interestingly, educational level has no significant impact on traditional religious beliefs though religiosity is significantly lower for those with third level education, but only for those under 40. Confidence in the church falls and permissiveness increases with increasing educational qualifications. In the case of women, both traditional religious beliefs and religiosity decline and permissiveness increases as they move from home duties to part-time and full-time employment, as might have been predicted (Luckmann, 1970), but the highest levels of alienation are expressed by the unemployed. Levels of confidence in the church are not significantly related to employment status.

The largest variations are associated with age and are a great deal more substantial than period effects. In general terms, in both 1981 and 1990, the older the respondent the higher the levels of traditional religious beliefs, religiosity and confidence in the church and the lower the level of permissiveness. Cohort analysis shows that during the 1980s, traditional religious beliefs and religiosity showed no overall tendency to decline. These results are not consistent with the secularisation thesis at the individual level.

When individual items of religious belief are looked at, comparison with the European averages shows how exceptional the Irish are. They are twice as likely to believe in heaven, hell and the devil, and susbtantially more likely to believe in God, life after death, and sin. There was no change in the 1980s in the proportion believing in God, very slight increases in belief in life after death, a soul, and heaven, and slight decreases in belief in hell, the devil and sin. The overall picture is of no significant change in the past decade, but of a move towards a more optimistic interpretation of religion. Finally, the Irish are also much more likely than people in Europe as a whole to pray and to obtain comfort and strength from religion. Cohort analysis shows that the proportions of middle-aged respondents (in their thirties and forties in 1990) who draw comfort and strength from prayer has increased significantly over the past decade. Again, this result does not support the secularisation thesis.

Other survey data point to a growing 'awareness of the social responsibility deriving from one's religion' and increasing proportions involved in parish activities such as reading the lesson, helping to organise parish social events, and serving on parochial committees (Weafer, 1986a). Among Irish university students there was also a slight increase in the proportions conforming to the weekly Mass attendance obligation between the mid-1970s and the late-1980s (MacAirt, 1990).

We have previously noted Martin's (1978) qualifications about the extent to which secularisation occurs where there is a close linkage between religion and national identity. Likewise, Nic Ghiolla Phádraig has noted that 'the colonial inheritance of an underprivileged Church, which had often mediated on behalf of an underprivileged people, has headed off anticlericalism at source and provided loyal, if not always uncritical support' (1986: 142–3). This was illustrated in the report of the conference of the 1987 Synod of Bishops on the role of the laity in the church and in the world (O'Kelly, 1986). As in the United States (cf. Wuthnow, 1988), 'there has been some increase in polarisation among Irish Catholics, with some moving away from legalism to spirituality, on the one hand, and secularism on the other'. Thus, while some have taken the 'option for the poor' and identified with the needs of marginalised groups and worked alongside the left on welfare and human rights issues, others have allied themselves with those resisting amendment in the traditional Catholic positions on abortion, divorce and traditional sexual morality (Nic Ghiolla Phádraig, 1988: 210–1; Hannigan, 1989).

A balanced interpretation of recent religious changes in Ireland would therefore recognise that not all religious indicators have been in decline but that there is evidence of a considerable transformation in what was until recently an extremely rigid and authoritarian church, with emergent groups struggling to articulate new interpretations of their Catholic faith. As in England (cf. Hornsby-Smith, 1991):

> a rigid adherence to the rules and regulations of the Church has been giving way to a more individually principled ethics. Irish Catholics are now more willing to make up their own minds about what is right and wrong rather than to follow the dictates of the Church (Inglis, 1987: 217).

The conclusion is, therefore, that rather than a process of secularisation following inevitably from the processes of industrialisation promoted since the late 1950s, religious changes in the Irish Republic have been complex and multiform. Certainly there have been major changes in the way in which the largely implicit assumptions of an inevitable alliance between the Roman Catholic church (or rather its clerical leadership) and the state have been expressed in recent decades. But this has also gone along with transformations in Roman Catholicism encouraged by the Second Vatican Council and resulting in a patchwork of renewal processes which have revitalised some aspects of Irish Catholicism. Catholics seem clearly to have emerged from a state of dependence and legal conformity to face the more challenging demands of lay participation in the church and responsibility for the civic society and the wider world.

Discussion

In this paper we have summarised recent social and religious changes in the Irish Republic in order to test the proposition that modernisation processes have led inevitably to secularisation. Although we have not been concerned here with the situation in Northern Ireland, it is evident that, with its high levels of religious affiliation and practice after more than a century's experience of industrialisation, any assumption of a direct causal link between industrialisation and secularisation in that province is preposterous. In the case of the Irish Republic, using a model of three levels and dimensions of secularisation derived from Dobbelaere, it has been shown that at each of the societal, institutional and individual levels it is possible to discern both secularising tendencies, on the one hand, and counter-secularising tendencies or evidence of religious revitalisation, on the other. In other words, the reality is a great deal more complex than evolutionary theories of religious decline would suggest.

The first century of industrialisation in Europe, as Fahey (this volume) reminds us, coincided with an expansionary phase for institutional religion. In the case of Irish Catholicism, this ran from the post-famine period to the middle of the twentieth century when there was a period of levelling off in church expansion. Fahey suggests that while in some respects Catholicism may have entered a period of incipient decline, the evidence for this is uneven and, in any event, the pace is slower than elsewhere in Europe. This leads him to speculate that Ireland is not so much a deviant case as at an earlier stage in an (inevitable) process of secularisation. Given the evidence reviewed in this present chapter, this conclusion seems both premature and overly pessimistic. The evolutionary expectations of the secularisation thesis seems to be a theoretical cul-de-sac and a diversion from the search for explanations of the multifarious ways in which religious phenomena emerge, are transformed, or disappear during periods of rapid, economic, social or political change.

The role of the Roman Catholic church in Irish politics has been the focus of much debate. There seems little doubt that the power and influence it has wielded and the substantial absence of serious anti-clericalism, can be attributed to the role of the clergy in resisting the British Protestant state and articulating the distinctiveness of an Irish Catholic identity during the colonial period. This resulted in a privileged status for the church after independence, and while the Republic might not have been a theocratic state, neither was the church simply another interest group. It used its 'moral monopoly' to keep key issues, such as educational policy, off the state's agenda for many decades.

Recently, however, it has become evident that there has been an 'adjustment by consent' (Whyte, 1980: 380) in the relations between the clerical leadership of the church and the state. The election of Mary Robinson as President may be interpreted as indicative of this trend. On the other hand, the 1990 European Values study showed that very large majorities of the Irish people believed that the church should speak out on a wide range of political, social and moral issues, though only a minority favoured its intervention in government policy.

A process of structural differentiation has been discerned, especially in education, health and law. There is also evidence of a significant decline in the number of priests and personnel in religious orders and some decline in adherence to traditional beliefs and practices. On the other hand, there have been powerful counter-secularising tendencies, manifested for example in the emergence of powerful lay-led 'special purpose groups' to strengthen the traditional opposition to abortion and divorce. In the maintenance of its 'moral monopoly', the church has shifted its strategy from one of coercion to one of being the 'conscience of the nation'. With the economic and social transformations of the past three decades the Republic has experienced increasing problems of unemployment, urban deprivation and alienation. This has called forth notable responses from the church or its agencies and there is growing evidence of a more participative and socially aware laity seeking ways of realising a Christian dimension in their everyday lives.

It is tempting to regard some of the religious changes which have been noted as indicative of a 'protestantisation' of Catholicism. Thus, the evident tendency for increasing proportions of Irish Catholics to make up their own minds on contraception points to the greater prominence of private judgement and moral decision-making. Nevertheless, such a view is unsatisfactory, not least because of the continued salience of the Catholic identity, sharply distinguished from Protestantism. Such emphatic self-definition must be respected as socially meaningful to the actors themselves. Secondly, the evidence from both historical (e.g. Hynes, 1989) and ethnographic (e.g. Taylor, 1989; 1990a; 1990b) studies shows that the ordinary lay Catholic has always made up his or her own mind on some matters. Religious beliefs and practices have always been 'in flux' (Hynes, 1989) even if religious power has been unevenly distributed. A process of 'protestantisation' misleadingly implies that Catholics have simply assimilated to a clearly identifiable static model of Protestantism. It seems altogether more satisfactory to regard the religious transformations which have undoubtedly taken place as evidence for a process of normative convergence (Goldthorpe and Lockwood, 1963) in a modernising society.

Some final methodological reflections may not be out of place. For some sociologists, secularisation is a self-evident consequence of the process of modernisation, industrialisation, rationalisation, bureau-cratisation and urbanisation. Others see in the emergence of new religious phenomena an obvious refutation of ideological assertions of inevitable evolutionary change. The attempt to provide an appropriate framework for the empirical testing of the thesis (Dobbelaere, 1981, 1989) is therefore very welcome. This framework has been employed in this chapter but, even so, the relative weights to be attributed to secularising and counter-secularising trends at each level of analysis will remain a matter of judgement.

Thus, in the analysis of the power of the Catholic church in Ireland, there is a considerable gap between the claim, on the one hand, that it possesses a 'moral monopoly', and on the other hand, the argument (on the basis of an estimate that the hierarchy made direct representations to the government on only a tiny fraction of the legislative measures since independence) that there is no automatic deference to the hierarchy by the government. It is difficult to avoid the conclusion that the sociologist must proceed systematically to examine at each level whose interests count in the determination of specific policy issues, who controls the economic, social and political agenda, and who can mobilise bias to include or exclude issues (Lukes, 1974). In other words it is necessary to examine empirical instances of the 'dialectic of control' (Giddens, 1986: 16), involving a variety of actors, including the church hierarchy and emergent lay groups and politicians, in order to arrive iteratively at a better understanding of the power of the Catholic church in Ireland today and in what ways and to what extent it is changing.

In our review of the transformations which have taken place in Catholicism in Ireland in recent decades, we have in the main drawn on two types of data. First, we have referred to historical analyses, especially of the interrelationship between the Roman Catholic church and the Irish state since independence. Secondly, we have reviewed data from a large number of structured surveys carried out over the past two decades. Recently, however, pleas have been made for an empirically-based anthropology that 'does justice to the range of human experience, and will develop some systematic methods of asking how different moral principles become acceptable and different versions of reality plausible' (Douglas, 1982: 18). Such an approach can contribute to understanding 'the mutual conditioning of power and meaning' and the 'antagonistic inter-dependencies' which exist in rival religious regimes, the dynamics of which depend on shifting balances of power (Bax, 1987).

In the case of Ireland, Taylor has recently contributed some note-worthy anthropological studies of popular Catholicism in Donegal. These include an account of the radical shift in the religious discourse of the parish mission with its accommodation to a changing world, for example, in its neglect of hell, while continuing to stress 'the necessary sacramental structure of the Church' (1989: 13). In a second study of a charismatic 'healing Mass' Taylor stresses that beneath the superficial impression of great ritual unity, those attending felt and thought very differently about it (1990a: 101) and that it provided 'significantly different religious experiences' for the participants. Taylor, like other anthropologists of religion who stress 'essentially loyal heterodoxies' (Brandes, 1990: 188), shows how devotional innovations may nevertheless be 'incorporated into pre-existing frameworks' and contribute to 'the solidification of clerical domination in a firmly established diocesan regime' (1990a: 106). This was apparent in the dramatic shift away from the expressive emotional and noisy form of charismatic prayer in the early days of the Irish Catholic charismatic movement to an emphasis on non-participatory contemplative worship, personal spirituality and a stress on the 'deeper' meanings of silence (Szuchewycz, 1989). Thirdly, in a study of the stories of the healing powers of drunken priests, Taylor notes how they can be read as a commentary 'on the longer historical process of the growth of institutional Church power through priestly domination' and 'the dynamic nature of the relationship between local and official religion' (1990b: 181–3).

In these various studies there are two significant conclusions. Firstly, historically there has been, and still is, a wide variety of ways of 'being a Catholic' in Ireland, and there is no strong evidence that ordinary Catholics have ever found 'different orders of belief irreconcilable or even particularly discordant' (Hynes, 1989: 53). Secondly, neither individuals nor communities are entirely passive in their stance towards their Catholicism. There is no simple top-down imposition of orthodoxy. Ordinary Catholics always have made up their own minds on some issues (for example, boycotting in the nineteenth century, contraception today). In spite of the religious status of the priest, authority is enhanced where it resonates well with everyday experiences and situations (Hynes, 1989: 56–7). In the present state of 'flux' there are opportunities for emergent groups to contest the existing distribution of power and authority.

In sum, in spite of considerable social turmoil and the religious transformations over the past three decades, it is clear that modernisation processes in Ireland have not been accompanied unambiguously by secularisation. The case illustrates the dangers of a simplistic and deterministic view of the relationship between modernisation and secularisation. More generally, it demonstrates that religion in particular and culture in general have a resilience which is at least partially independent of industrialisation processes. The study of industrialisation is, therefore, incomplete without some consideration of the religious variable.

Proceedings of the British Academy, **79**, 291–327

The Liberal Theory of Industrialism and the Development of Industrial Relations in Ireland

WILLIAM K. ROCHE

University College Dublin

The Liberal Theory of Industrialism and Industrial Relations

THE CENTRAL CONCERNS of liberal theory with respect to industrial relations can be divided into one set of propositions concerning the effects on unions and employers of the *'take-off'* into industrialisation and three further sets of propositions concerning the effects, following take-off, of long-term development towards an increasingly industrialised society. The major arguments regarding take-off and secular change can be stated as follows.

1 Worker and union militancy and radicalism peak early in the course of industrialisation and represent a protest against social dislocation occasioned by the rigours of industrial organisation and urban life. The faster the pace of industrialisation, the more severe the disjuncture with traditional patterns of life and the greater the degree of militancy with which workers respond (Kerr *et al.*, 1973: 218–9; Lipset, 1969: ch. 6). Industrial technology and its supposed 'imperatives' are attributed major, indeed almost exclusive, importance in influencing trends in behaviour and organisation. Other concomitants of industrialisation, such as the development of markets, growing regional and international economic interdependence, and the effects of business cycles, have virtually no place in liberal theory. The impact of take-off is, however, believed to be compounded by the social and political circumstances in which it is achieved. Of particular importance in this respect is the *sequencing* of 'national, political and industrial "revolutions" in a country relative to the

Read 8 December 1990. © The British Academy 1992.

rise of the labour movement' (Dunlop, 1958: 313 and ch. 8; cf. Kahn-Freund, 1972: 39–40; Commons, 1932: 683; Sturmthal, 1951; Kendall, 1975; Lorwin, 1954). Relatedly, it is noted that the social divisions of rural society may 'carry over' into industrial society through pre-capitalist traditions of militancy which continue to influence newly recruited industrial workers and their unions.[1]

The three remaining sets of propositions of the liberal theory are addressed to long-run change in industrial relations.

2 Sustained employer resistance to union recognition and collective bargaining results in union demands becoming utopian and eventually revolutionary. The prospect of a spiral of politicisation, in which employer resistance and union militancy reinforce each other, leads in most national cases to a revision of employer strategy. A class compromise of a kind is achieved which allows a 'containment spiral' to take effect. The waning of employer resistance reduces significantly the *intensity* of industrial conflict. What Kerr calls the 'glacial impact' of institutionalised compromise gradually transforms industrial relations. Gradually the exercise of industrial authority comes to be shared between managers and managed. A 'constitutional approach' to the governance of work replaces confrontation. Following an early decline in the intensity of industrial conflict comes a long-run decline in the *level* of industrial conflict (Ross and Hartman, 1960). The progressive development of a 'constitutional approach' to the governance of the workplace—the elaboration of a 'web of rules', or the emergence of 'industrial citizenship', as the process is sometimes described —is the guarantor of long-run social integration and economic stability (Kerr, 1955; Slichter, Healy and Livernash, 1960; Flanders, 1970). Pluralist industrial relations strategy involves a rejection of 'monism' or 'unitarism'. Efforts at total control of employees' attitudes to employment are viewed as superfluous and damaging (Kerr, 1955: 16–7; Fox, 1966).

3 Geographical and social mobility increase in response to economic development, the spread of educational opportunity and the gradual growth of occupations requiring higher levels of skill (Kerr *et al.*, 1973: chs. 1 and 8). Class structures decompose and give way to social structures in which people's identities in the labour market are formed no longer on the basis of class allegiance but on the basis of occupation or 'status position'. Occupational identities and interests cannot be accommodated in large 'inclusive', multi-occupational unions. In consequence, general and industrial unions experience long-run decline at the expense of more

---

[1] For a somewhat different version of this approach see Gallie's discussion and critique of the 'Mann-Giddens' thesis (Gallie, 1983: ch. 11).

'exclusive' types of trade unions, such as craft and occupational unions (Kerr *et al.*, 1973: 274). Trade unions lose the capacity to act in concert in pursuit of the common interests of all workers.

4   Changes in social stratification and the institutionalisation of industrial conflict result in the scaling-down of trade union objectives. The very idea of labour organisations as 'component parts of class movements urging programmes of total reform' ceases to have meaning (Kerr *et al.*, 1973: 274). Politics and industrial relations become distinct spheres of activity, responding, as it were, to their own cycles. Cleavages in industry and politics arise around different issues. Political parties originating on the left open-out to embrace issues not traditionally polarised in terms of a left-right split and, as a result, the interests of unions and 'progressive (socialist, labour) parties' diverge (Dahrendorf, 1959: 267–318). The state continues to be powerful and active, but operates as an honest broker, overseeing the 'rules of the game', and protecting civil liberties in a society dominated by interest organisations.[2]

These propositions have had a major impact on sociological thought regarding the development of relations between employers and employees in western industrial nations. For adherents of the liberal canon, they are no less applicable to Third-World, Asian and east European nations (Kerr *et al.*, 1973). It will be argued in this paper that the development of Irish industrial relations confounds liberal theory in a number of major respects. The shortcomings of the liberal position will be examined by reviewing the Irish experience against each of the four sets of propositions in turn. In addition to testing the liberal propositions in the Irish case, the paper is concerned to advance alternative, and more empirically grounded, explanations of the forces that have shaped industrial relations in Ireland.

Working-class Militancy in Sociological Context: 1900–1922

In the period from about 1907 to 1920 unionisation first became a mass economic and social force in Ireland. Prior to the early twentieth century, only skilled craftsmen working in the towns and cities of the eastern,

---

[2] Clearly the liberal representation of the maturation of labour movements over the course of industrialisation carries strong undertones of the 'end of labour history'. Regulated or institutionalised industrial relations is presented as the really momentous social invention of industrialism. 'Constitutional' decision-making in industry, involving professional managers and workers organised independently in unions, halts the political and social momentum of industrial conflict. The study no less than the practice of industrial relations becomes properly concerned with the complex 'web of rules' through which the pragmatic day-to-day compromises between managers and workers receive expression (Dunlop, 1958).

southern, and western seaboards had attained significant levels of sustained union organisation. The majority of these craftsmen were members of Irish branches of several of the formidable British 'new model' unions (Clarkson, 1926; Keogh, 1982: ch. 2). It was a British trade union activist, James Larkin, who set off the avalanche of unionisation which began in 1907. The Irish Transport Union (later, the Irish Transport and General Workers' Union) was founded by Larkin in 1909, following a dispute with his own union, the British National Union of Dock Labourers. The ITGWU was to be at the centre of the remarkable transformation of Irish industrial relations in the years to 1920. The sequence of events during this period need only be considered here in outline.

The membership of unions affiliated to the Irish Trade Union Congress rose from about 30,000 in 1894 to 250,000 in 1920. The Irish Transport alone reached a membership level of over 100,000 by 1920 (Greaves, 1982). In very rough terms total trade union membership in that year represented about 25 per cent of wage earners. From the incomplete statistical data available on strike trends, it is clear that a major strike wave occurred during the period, with particularly high levels of strike participation registered during the years 1917 to 1920 (Fitzpatrick, 1980). From the many descriptive studies of strikes during the period, it is clear that industrial conflict was of unique intensity compared to subsequent strike waves (O'Connor, 1988: Greaves, 1982; Lysaght, 1982).

The period as a whole can be divided into two sub-periods, each characterised by a distinct cycle of unionisation and militancy. In the first period, covering the years from 1907 to the great Dublin lock-out of 1913–14, the self-styled syndicalist ITGWU concentrated on gaining membership and recognition in the towns and cities of the 'maritime economy' that had been the bulwarks of craft unionism. The urban membership drive of the nascent general union was centred on relatively mature working-class occupational communities of dockers, transport workers, millers and engineering workers. This drive for membership and also recognition met with concerted employer resistance, and resulted in a series of major lock-outs, culminating in the great Dublin lock-out of 1913–14, which all but destroyed the ITGWU. In the years 1914 to 1917 the union was virtually dormant. The years to 1920 witnessed the second cycle of unionisation and militancy, this time focused on rural areas, and in particular on agricultural labourers. The rank-and-file militancy of this second cycle showed signs of social radicalism. Land seizures and factory occupations became common. These initiatives were encouraged by the widespread collapse of civil order during the Anglo-Irish War. From 1919, attempts by employers to cut wages also spurred workers into militant action. The rhetoric and sometimes the tactics of trade union militancy were influenced by the

Bolshevik revolution (Mitchell, 1974: 141–2; Lysaght, 1982; Fitzpatrick, 1977 ch. 7).[3]

As outlined above, liberal theory attributes major importance to the traumas associated with the take-off into industrialisation in explaining the tendency for 'worker protest to peak early in the course of industrialisation and decline in intensity thereafter' (Kerr et al., 1973: ch. 6). However, the intense strike wave and worker militancy in Ireland between 1907 and 1920 cannot meaningfully be regarded as a response to economic and social dislocations resulting from industrialisation. In many of the towns and rural areas in which working-class militancy was particularly intense, take-off into industrialisation in any real sense had yet to be attained—or reattained. In other areas with a more developed industrial base, militancy arose in a context of industrial stagnation or decline.

Table 1. Percentage of total workforce in agricultural employment in Ireland and other European countries, 1891–1971.

	Ireland	Great Britain	France	Italy	Sweden
1891	44.2[a]	10.4	40.3	59.4 (1901)	53.9
1901	44.6[a]	7.7	41.8	59.4	49.8
1911	43.0[a]	8.1	42.7 (1906)	55.5	45.6
1926	51.3	6.0 (1931)	38.3	47.3 (1931)	35.4 (1930)
1951	39.6	5.0	27.2 (1954)	40.0	20.3
1961	35.2	3.6	20.3 (1962)	28.2	13.8
1971	25.4	2.5	12.2 (1975)	16.3	8.1

[a] Irish data for 1891–1911 relate to all Ireland.
Sources: Data for European countries derived from Flora et al. (1983). Data for Ireland for 1891 derived from Coyne, ed. (1902: 65) and for 1901 and 1911 from the Census of Population for Ireland 1911, *General Report*, occupational tables.

The standard indicators of levels of industrialisation presented for Ireland and other European countries in Tables 1 and 2 indicate that in the 1890s and early 1900s overall levels of industrial employment and non-agricultural employment in Ireland were on a par with continental European countries, though well behind Great Britain, the world's 'first industrial nation'. The regional penetration of industrialisation in early twentieth century Ireland was nonetheless very uneven. The heaviest concentration of industrial employment was found in the North East, centred on Belfast. Generally, levels of industrial employment were lower in the late nineteenth and early twentieth centuries than they had been in

[3] The most detailed accounts of union militancy during the period can be found in O'Connor (1988) and Lysaght (1982).

Table 2. Percentage of total workforce in industrial employment in Ireland and other European countries, 1891–1971.[a]

	Ireland	Great Britain	France	Italy	Sweden
1891	27.2	44.5	28.1	23.7	14.4
1901	32.6	45.6	30.0	23.7	19.7
1911	33.8	44.6	29.5	26.8	24.7
1926	14.5	46.1	33.0	29.4	30.9
1951	24.4	49.2	35.7	30.4	40.6
1961	25.5	47.4	38.5	39.4	45.1
1971	31.5	42.2	34.7	42.2	40.3

[a] Time points as in Table 1.
Sources: As in Table 1.

the early nineteenth century (Booth, 1902; Cullen, 1972). The available evidence suggests that the pace of output growth in Ireland over the period since the middle of the nineteenth century was slower than in any other European country (Kennedy *et al.*, 1988: ch. 1). Thus, in many parts of Ireland the nineteenth century and early 1900s witnessed 'deindustrialisation'. The 1890s saw the beginnings of an economic revival on this shrinking industrial base (Cullen, 1972). The circumstances of the Great War rendered uneven the fortunes of different sectors of Irish industry between 1914 and 1920. Sectors that could take advantage of war contracts prospered, as did parts of the food industry, but sectors that had relied heavily on imported raw materials or on export-markets were adversely affected (Riordan, 1920).

The relevant point here is that, even in the absence of reliable indicators of aggregate industrial output, liberalism's social dislocation theory is clearly redundant in explaining the intense worker militancy of early twentieth century Ireland. No severe disjuncture in living or working conditions was experienced by Irish industrial or agricultural workers such as might explain the extreme intensity of the industrial and class conflict of the period. An alternative explanation for the 'peaking of worker protest' and the course of union militancy in Ireland between 1907 and 1920 can be found in the interaction of three sets of factors: first, the two cycles of economic activity in industrial and agricultural Ireland; second, the progress of the Anglo-Irish War and the associated near-collapse of civil order in rural areas; and third, the response of employers and farmers to attempts by the unskilled to unionise.

The early success of Larkin and his Irish Transport Union in organising urban workers occurred against the background of industrial revival (Cullen, 1972). While the numbers employed in manufacturing generally continued to fall between 1891 and 1911, employment rose in occupations in transport and communications which represented the early focus of unionisation. The rate of growth in occupations in the Census classification of 'general labourers' was only about one third of that achieved over the period 1841–81 (Booth, 1902; Census of Population, 1891; 1909; 1911). This might suggest that a combination of economic revival and slow-down in the growth of the labour supply at the base of the occupational structure contributed to the first cycle of unionisation and militancy in urban areas.

The second cycle of unionisation and militancy from about 1917 to 1920 occurred against an economic background of war-time food shortages, spiralling inflation and sharply falling real wage levels. In such conditions workers developed an intense conviction that employers and shop keepers were profiteering by creating artificial shortages and by hoarding goods (Fitzpatrick, 1977; O'Connor, 1988). Workers in urban-based industries faced highly uneven economic conditions, but the net employment situation in the towns appears to have been poor throughout the War. The position of agricultural labourers was more conducive to unionisation and militancy. Rural workers faced similar problems of inflation and relative deprivation to those faced by workers in the towns. However, soaring agricultural prices during the Great War led to a boom in farming. Rural labour markets were thus generally tighter than those in the towns, especially following the imposition of compulsory tillage, backed by legal minimum wages, between 1917 and 1919. The growth of agricultural trade unionism was dramatic. By the end of 1919 agricultural labourers had become the single biggest membership category of the Irish Transport, accounting for just under 30 per cent of the total union membership (Greaves, 1982: 259). More generally, the Irish Transport enjoyed spectacular membership growth and quickly became by far the largest trade union in Ireland, although its progress was very uneven geographically (Kenny, 1985; Fitzpatrick, 1977: 247).

'Modern' or revisionist explanations of the spectacular, but geographically uneven, rise in the unionisation of agricultural labourers usually stress the importance of the rise in tillage acreage. Because tillage is more labour intensive than pastoral farming, an increase in tillage acreage is understood to have increased the demand for labour. This in turn is taken to have enhanced the bargaining power and confidence of agricultural workers and increased their propensity to unionise and press claims on farmers. (Fitzpatrick, 1977: ch. 7; Kenny, 1985: ch. 3). The revisionist position among historians and historical geographers tends, at the same time, to down-play the role of resurgent nationalism in legitimising the strongly republican ITGWU and enhancing its attractions to wage earners (see esp. O'Connor, 1988). The participation of the union's acting general secretary, James Connolly, in the 1916 Rising and his subsequent execution, gave the union a symbolically powerful place in the pantheon of Irish revolutionary martyrdom. During the Anglo-Irish War union officials were actively engaged in the independence movement. The union participated in a series of major political strikes and in the campaign against conscription (Mitchell, 1974). The potency of nationalism among rank-and-file trade unionists was apparent in a wave of breakaway activity by the Irish branches of British trade unions during and after the Anglo-Irish War.

The results obtained by modelling the county-level branch penetration of the ITGWU in 1920 throw interesting light on the mediate and proximate factors contributing to the dramatic growth of the union in the second cycle of unionisation and militancy during the First World War and Anglo-Irish War. Data on the incidence of branches by county are available for 1920. (Unfortunately, no data are available on the membership of branches, so the incidence of branches represents but a rough indicator of relative union strength in different counties.) Also available by county are data on tillage acreage in 1918, on changes in tillage acreage from pre-war levels in 1911, on approximate numbers of agricultural labourers employed on large commercial farms, on inter-county variations in contemporary nationalist political organisation, and on the incidence of rural militancy and conflict prior to the advent of unionisation ('outrages' during the Land War of 1879–82).

The results of regressions of 1920 ITGWU branch numbers by county on these and other control variables are reported in Table 3. Comparable data are not available for the six counties subsequently to be partitioned into Northern Ireland. In the Ulster counties with significant protestant and unionist populations, however, the ITGWU made little headway. This was due, no doubt, almost entirely to the union's nationalist pedigree.

The most dramatic result to emerge from the regression analysis is that branch incidence is very strongly associated with variations between counties in the size of the agricultural labouring class employed on large commercial farms. This variable is highly significant statistically ($p > 99$ per cent) and accounts for the greater part of the inter-county variance in branch incidence, as revealed in model 3.1. Variations in the size of the labouring populations working on large farms proves to be a much better predictor of ITGWU branch incidence than either the sizes of county populations or agricultural populations. The permanent agricultural workers on the large commercial farms of the east, the midlands and the Golden Vale constituted an agricultural proletariat. The scale of the farms on which they worked was such that they were less tied to farm owners by

Table 3. Influences on ITGWU branch penetration in 1920 (BRANCH), standardised OLS coefficients.[a]

	Model			
	3.1	3.2	3.3	3.4
Independent variables[(a)]				
AGPROL	0.90**	0.95**	0.86**	0.88**
TILLAGE		−0.32		
TILLRATE		−0.24		
SINN FEIN			0.06	
OUTRAGES			0.22*	
ACTIVISM				0.26**
TOWN BRANCHES				0.12
R^2	0.81	0.85	0.88	0.87
F	124.30**	41.38**	66.12**	63.84**
DW	1.56†	1.99†	2.70‡	2.59‡
F.Ch.				15.18**

Statistical significance at the 1% and 5% levels is indicated by ** and *; † indicates the absence of first-order serial correlation at the 1% level; ‡ indicates an inconclusive Durbin Watson test. (The DW value of 2.59 in equation 3.4 is just at the boundary for an inconclusive test: $4 - 2.59 = 1.41$; the upper limit of the inconclusive zone, with $N = 26$ and three variables, is also 1.41.)

[a] All results relate to the 26 counties of what was to become the Irish Free State. BRANCH = numbers of ITGWU branches by county in 1920; AGPROL = numbers of permanent agricultural labourers employed on holdings of 100 or more acres (1912); TILLAGE = tillage acreage by county in 1918; TILLRATE = the percentage rate of change in tillage acreage between 1911 and 1918, by county; SINN FEIN = members of Sinn Fein per thousand of the population by county in 1919. (The variable has been scored on a scale with a minimum value of 1 [0–100 members] and maximum value of 7 [600–1,000 members]); OUTRAGES = agrarian outrages per 10,000 of the population by county during 1880–82. (The variable has been scored on a scale with a minimum value of 1 [up to 10 outrages] and a maximum value of 5 [40 or more outrages]); ACTIVISM = an index combining unweighted scores on the scales of SINN FEIN and OUTRAGES; TOWN BRANCHES = number of branches based in urban areas in 1917, by county. Information on sources is available from the author.

bonds of paternalism and deference than farm workers on smaller farms. Whereas many of those working on smaller farms in the west and north west might still have harboured hopes of benefitting from land redistribution under the Land Acts of 1881–1909, labourers employed on large commercial farms were probably more resigned to remaining wage workers permanently. In areas where labourers still harboured hopes of becoming farmers, the ITGWU faced competition from local Land and Labour Associations. These organisations combined trade union functions with a programme of lobbying for the establishment of small holdings through land redistribution. Where the class basis of agriculture was more propitious for simple trade unionism, many of these associations were absorbed by the ITGWU (see Greaves, 1982; Fitzpatrick, 1977: ch. 7).

A further interesting result to emerge is that the impact of proximate economic factors, like the level of tillage acreage in counties, or differences in the scale of the shift into tillage farming, appears a good deal more indirect or remote than suggested in the historical literature. Model 3.2 includes tillage acreage in 1918 and the rate of increase in tillage acreage over 1911 levels. The rationale for including the former variable is straightforward: the scale of tillage farming represents a rough indicator of county-level differences in the gross demand for agricultural labour. Including the rate of change in tillage acreage as a variable tests the hypothesis that the propensity of agricultural workers to unionise may have been affected by *changes in the demand for labour*, in addition to the current level of demand. Both aspects of the new pattern of agriculture from 1917 have been linked with the explosion of ITGWU branch activity in rural Ireland (see Kenny, 1982: ch. 3). In model 3.2 the coefficients on both variables are incorrectly signed and statistically insignificant. Logging tillage acreage to allow for the possibility of a non-linear relationship with the number of branches produced no better results. Tests for interaction effects, making the impact of tillage acreage and changes in tillage acreage depend on variations in the size of the agricultural proletariat, also produced negative results.[4]

Further interesting results emerge when levels of Sinn Fein membership and Land War outrages are entered in model 3.3. The coefficient on the outrages variable is significant and positively signed. This suggests that traditions of rural militancy influenced the early growth of trade unionism. The coefficient for the variable measuring levels of Sinn Fein membership by county is also positively signed but insignificant. The correlation between county-level Sinn Fein membership and Land War outrages is strong ($r = 0.7$). Given such a high level of inter-correlation between independent variables, and the small number of cases available to estimate the model, simultaneously entering the two variables results in multicollinearity. The options available are to derive principal components

---

[4] The only specification of a tillage acreage variable that produced statistically notable results was where tillage acreage was expressed as a ratio of numbers working in agriculture (including farmers and 'relatives assisting'). Such a variable might be regarded as a very rough indicator of county-level differences in the balance of demand and supply of agricultural labour. When this variable was entered it produced a statistically significant coefficient. The coefficient was negatively signed, however, contrary to theoretical expectation, and would suggest that where the balance of demand over supply favoured workers, there was a lower propensity to organise. The result is thus probably a statistical accident and can be ignored.

scores for these variables, or to combine the variables into an index to measure variations in underlying levels of social and political activism—past and current—in different counties. The former strategy is, however, also compromised by the small N, so in model 3.4 an 'index of activism' is entered. The coefficient is correctly signed and significant; an F test confirms that the addition of the index significantly improves the explanatory power of the model.

The results overall can be interpreted as suggesting that traditions of social and political activism at county level positively influenced the spread of unionisation to rural areas between 1917 and 1920. The dominant factor appears to have been a tradition of rural militancy prior to the advent of unionisation. The stronger were pre-existing traditions of rural activism, the greater appears to have been the predisposition of workers to organise in unions. Contemporary Sinn Fein strength seems to have exerted a similar influence. The greater the strength Sinn Fein had attained at county level, the more prone workers were to organise collectively, or possibly, as well, the more receptive they tended to be to the blandishments of the 'republican' Irish Transport. The union's activities, of course, inevitably conflicted with Sinn Fein's ideology of class harmony. Model 3.4 introduces as a variable the number of urban branches of the union in existence in 1917. This was included to control for any positive effect that pre-existing ITGWU branch activity in county towns up to 1917 might have had on the general growth of branches (see Kenny, 1982: ch. 3). The results provide no evidence of any such effect.

Given the shortcomings of the available data, the results of the modelling exercise must obviously be regarded as tentative. Nonetheless, by integrating them with the historical record, a number of conclusions can be drawn regarding the roots of unionisation and working-class militancy in Ireland in the early decades of the century. The pace, character or process of industrialisation is not directly relevant to an understanding of the scale and intensity of worker militancy during the period 1907–20. The most militant sections of the urban working class were those working and living in relatively mature communities in the main cities and towns of the maritime economy. The most highly organised and militant agricultural workers were labourers on larger commercial farms who had probably become reconciled to their status as an agricultural proletariat. The growth of trade unionism in town and country thus reflected the mediate influence of dispositions formed by stable social arrangements, rather than putative processes of social dislocation or 'anomie'. The demands of Irish workers during this period give no hint of any atavistic rejection of industrial or commercial economic relations. What is striking, rather, is the precocious nature of much of the militancy of the period, considering that the great majority of the workers involved had little tradition of trade unionism (cp, for example, O'Connor, 1988 and Cronin, 1979: ch. 5).

On the other hand, liberal theory's emphasis on the role of employer resistance in spurring working-class militancy is broadly consistent with the record in Ireland. After the first intense set-piece confrontations with new unionism in the towns, employers appeared to accept, however grudgingly, that union recognition and collective bargaining could not be fought off indefinitely. Employer resistance to the rudiments of collective bargaining was also intense in rural Ireland from 1918 to 1920. This probably contributed to the volatility, violence and intermittent radicalism of rank-and-file militancy in the countryside. Here the onset of the post-war slump in agricultural prices from late 1920 defused rural class struggle by undermining working-class power and confidence. So a spiral of politicisation failed to take hold in Irish industrial relations, in part because working-class insurgency in the face of intense employer militancy was not sustained for sufficiently long to have critically transformed the socio-political values of workers.

In sum, then, cyclical recovery in the urban economy, followed by the abnormal economic and social conditions of wartime in urban and rural economies alike, gave rise to economic conditions conducive to unionisation and militancy. The proximate economic influences on the surge of unionisation between 1917 and 1920 appear to have been those that affected more or less all agricultural labourers: in particular, the prosperity of employers, a general tightening of labour markets, inflation and stagnant or falling real wages. Legal provision for guaranteed minimum wages was also important in that it provided the ITGWU with a prop in its dealings with farmers and cast the union in the role of custodian of public policy (Greaves, 1982: ch. 10). Variations between counties in unionisation appear from the data available not to have been affected in any direct or simple way either by the scale of tillage farming or the growth in tillage acreage.

In addition, the subsidiary liberal idea of 'sequence' effects is useful in a number of respects in appreciating the distinctiveness of Irish industrial relations. The geographical pattern of unionisation appears to have been influenced by nineteenth century traditions of rural agitation and by contemporary nationalist political mobilisation. More generally, the sequencing of industrialisation and unionisation in Ireland was unusual owing to the influence of British institutions and ideas. At independence, trade unionism in Ireland was organised along similar lines to British trade unionism, in spite of the dramatic difference between the two countries in levels of industrial and economic development. Strong craft and occupational unions coexisted with industrial and general unions in a fragmented trade union system. The occurrence of the national revolution was to fragment Irish trade unionism further by causing a wave of breakaway activity in the Irish branches of virtually all of these types of British unions.

The simultanaiety of national revolution and mass unionisation contributed both to the emergence and containment of social radicalism in the period 1918–20, and at the same time to the marginalisation of the Labour Party in the formative period of Irish politics. The land seizures and factory occupations were spurred by the political upheaval of the Anglo-Irish War and Civil War and the virtual collapse of civil order over much of the country. Radicalism was also contained by the balance of class forces in the national revolution. The revolutionary political elite sought to contain class conflict during the struggle for independence, initially to promote united insurgency, and later to placate farming and business interests and maintain the status quo (Strauss, 1951: 265; Laffan, 1985: 205). In this they were aided by the successors of Larkin and Connolly and the leaders of the Irish Labour Party and Trades Union Congress. In general, labour leaders during period 1917–20 drew back from rank-and-file militancy, using their energies instead to build and consolidate trade union organisation.

In deference to the strength of the nationalist movement, and constrained by the weakness of party organisation at constituency level, the Labour Party failed to contest the first election held under universal adult suffrage in 1918. This election ultimately led to the establishment of the independent Irish State. The civil war, which began shortly after the truce in 1922 and continued into 1923, set the mould of party politics in Ireland. By mobilising support around the national question, the parties drew electoral support from across the class structure.

The critical formative influences on Irish industrial relations are thus to be found in the interaction of mediate influences that imply social dispositions formed in a context of stability rather than dislocation, influences arising from cyclical and wartime economic conditions, and the kind of sequence effects viewed by liberal theory as little more than subsidiary influences on the impact of industrialisation.

Trends in 'Exclusive' and 'Inclusive' Trade Unionism

Liberal theory predicts a secular rise in the membership shares of craft and occupational unions at the expense of general and industrial unions. This trend gradually attenuates unions' inclination or capacity to act in concert to achieve common objectives. In short, liberal theory argues from trends in organisation to trends in union strategy, predicting a secure future for trade unions, but the end of *trade union movements*.

The level of trade union 'density' attained by Irish unions increased from less than 20 per cent in the 1920s to a peak of over 60 per cent in 1980 (Roche and Larragy, 1989: 22). Short- and medium-term fluctuations around this rising secular trend can be attributed to business cycle and institutional influences on unionisation (Roche and Larragy, 1990). The membership of Irish unions also became occupationally and industrially more diverse over this period. Of particular sociological interest, however, are trends in the distribution of this growing level of union membership across unions along the continuum from 'inclusive' to 'exclusive' unionism. General unions are the most inclusive of all unions in aspiring to organise the 'entire working class' or workforce, whereas pure craft and professional unions are the most exclusive in restricting membership to trained members of the craft or profession. Often craft and professional unions impose barriers to entry in order to restrict labour supply. They also try to 'police' the work of members to preserve the 'integrity' of the craft or profession against encroachment by other occupations. Between these extremes of union character fall unions of more or less inclusive membership and ambition. Industrial unions and unions organising workers engaged in broadly similar or 'allied occupations'—possibly in different industries—are closest to general unions. Unions of single occupations are closest to pure craft and professional unions, differing perhaps only in their inability to exercise closure over entry to the occupation, or to control the boundaries of the jobs done by their members.

Table 4 presents the distribution of union membership across unions grouped into these three broad types at ten-year intervals since 1930. Data for 1985 are also presented, as this is the most recent year for which

Table 4. Percentage distribution of union membership by organisational type.[a]

	General unions	(Quasi-) industrial and allied occupational unions	(Ex-) craft and occupational unions
1930	38.4	30.8	30.8
1940	46.0	27.1	26.9
1950	54.8	20.9	24.2
1960	56.8	19.5	23.7
1970	52.3	19.6	27.7
1980	49.5	20.7	29.8
1985	45.2	22.5	32.3

[a] The membership of a small number of unions of indeterminable status has been omitted. Rows may not sum to one-hundred due to rounding.

Source: Dues Data Series on Ireland, available from the author.

Table 5. Percentage distribution of union membership by organisational type (excluding general unions).[a]

		(Quasi-)industrial	Allied-occupations	Occupational	(Ex-)craft
Blue-collar unions	1930	36.0 (6)	9.1 (7)	1.3 (2)	53.2 (50)
	1940	28.2 (7)	14.3 (7)	0.9 (4)	56.6 (50)
	1950	25.2 (5)	13.6 (7)	0.0	61.2 (44)
	1960	22.4 (4)	16.4 (8)	0.0	61.2 (42)
	1970	14.9 (4)	20.9 (8)	2.4 (2)	61.8 (26)
	1980	9.3 (3)	17.9 (7)	2.6 (1)	70.2 (22)
	1985	7.8 (3)	19.2 (7)	2.9 (1)	70.0 (16)
White-collar unions	1930	31.8 (6)	22.9 (8)	45.2 (16)	
	1940	40.8 (5)	19.4 (11)	39.8 (25)	
	1950	33.9 (5)	20.8 (10)	45.2 (34)	
	1960	30.5 (5)	21.0 (11)	48.4 (40)	
	1970	22.0 (7)	24.3 (13)	53.7 (43)	
	1980	13.6 (5)	34.1 (12)	52.1 (38)	
	1985	12.2 (5)	34.9 (13)	52.9 (33)	

[a] Percentages express the shares held by different types of unions of total blue-collar and white-collar union memberships for the years shown (the membership of general unions being excluded from these totals). Rows may not sum to one-hundred due to rounding. Membership of a small number of unions of indeterminable status has been excluded. Figures in parentheses show numbers of unions in each category.
Source: As for Table 4.

reliable data can be obtained.[5] The terms 'quasi-industrial' unions and 'ex-craft' unions are used in the tables to indicate that not all industrial unions aspire to complete organisation of their industrial domain, and that many craft unions, though originating in organisations restricted solely to apprenticed tradesmen, have 'opened' and admitted semi-skilled workers over time. This point is elaborated later. The table indicates that the share of total union membership organised by general unions remains by far the largest of any union type. General unions, quasi-industrial unions, and unions organising allied occupations combined, still in 1985 organised 68 per cent of all Irish trade union members—more than double the combined share of craft and occupational unions.

If the level of membership accounted for by inclusive unions is inconsistent with liberal theory, the *trend* in membership shares might still be interpreted as providing it with some support. The period covered by

[5] In interpreting relative shares for that year it has to be borne in mind that 1985 was the trough of a deep labour market recession. This would have affected the membership share of the more 'exposed' general unions more than other union types, and would, thus, have led to a short-run cyclical drag on the relative performance of open unions.

the data appears to break down into two distinct sub-periods. During the first, from the 1930s to about 1960, the trend favours general unions. The share of the intermediate union types declines sharply, as does that of craft and occupational unions. From then on, however, the share of intermediate types fluctuates around a fairly level trend; the share of general unions declines and that of occupational and craft unions (in fact, of occupational unions alone) rises. On closer inspection, however, the support provided by these data is far from compelling.

First of all, the unions classified by type in Table 4 have themselves undergone significant change. General unions have in practice become progressively more general or inclusive over time. Their ambition to organise workers of all industries and occupations is closer to their actual achievement in recent years than in the past. The 45 per cent of trade union membership accounted for by general unions in 1985 is much more heterogeneous in occupational and industrial terms than the 57 per cent organised in 1960. It follows that the inclusive unions have been capable of accommodating an increasingly diverse membership, whereas the prediction of Kerr and his associates was that occupational identities would become increasingly unmanageable in unions of this type. A similar trend holds at the other end of the organisational spectrum, at least for craft unions. A major trend among craft unions for many years has been to engage in mergers, where necessary, with contiguous craft unions. As a result, many craft unions are now in reality conglomerate organisations of craftsmen and unskilled workers in related job territories. Thus, the rising share held by craft and occupational unions since the 1960s masks the growth of occupational diversity within at least some unions of this type. A final problem concerns the allocation of unions to the typology. Any typology of union type or character inevitably gives rise to difficult cases, and in the typology of Tables 4 and 5 the difficult cases arise in the occupational unions category. Several unions defined as occupational unions in the breakdowns of Tables 4 and 5 might arguably be better defined as industrial unions. The Irish Bank Officials' Association is a case in point. The IBOA organises the great majority of officials in Irish banks, from entry grade up to, and including, management levels. Thus, it might be regarded as an industrial union of all bankers. However, the IBOA does not attempt to organise manual and craft workers in the industry, and has long adopted an exclusive strategy which has involved remaining outside the ICTU and avoiding alliances with blue-collar unions. So it seems more valid to define the union as an exclusive occupational union. At the same time, the vertical integration of different levels of the same occupation in IBOA, and in other similar unions, means that unions in the occupational category range from small civil service grade associations, representing only workers at the same level in the public service, to much wider ranging occupational unions taking in all grades from the bottom to the top of a particular profession. In other words, the changing distribution of membership shares across inclusive and exclusive unions masks growing internal occupational and industrial diversty across nearly the whole range of union types—a trend inconsistent with liberal theory's predictions.

A second reason for caution in interpreting organisational trends as favouring these predictions is that there seems nothing inexorable about the overall trend towards occupational unions since the 1960s. Of particular relevance in this respect has been the upsurge of merger activity involving occupational unions in recent years. A notable example is the declared intention of three separate unions of teachers and a union of lecturers to consider merger into one industrial union for education; an interim federal organisation of teaching unions has already been formed. Again, a significant number of civil service grade unions and staff associations are merging into increasingly conglomerate unions in the public sector. These currently comprise such a significant share of the 'closed' unions category that the outcome of their merger activities may decisively affect the future overall trend. Finally, the merger in 1990 of the Irish Transport and General Workers' Union and the Federated Workers' Union of Ireland into the self-styled 'super union', SIPTU, has resulted in new recruitment and organisation campaigns which could lead to a revival in the membership share of general unions.

One last reason for scepticism regarding the long-run sociological significance of the overall organisational trend since the 1960s emerges if we consider white-collar and blue-collar unions separately (omitting general unions from the analysis). This is done in Table 5. The table indicates that within the blue-collar group the most salient trend is the decline of quasi-industrial unionism. This has not occurred through organisational disintegration, resulting from the conflicting pressures exerted by a diverse membership, but typically because the unions affected suffered from the long-run decay of their industrial domains. An example is the Irish Shoe and Leather Workers' Union, which transferred to the ITGWU when the Irish leather industry collapsed in the wake of increased international competition. More important is the trend among white-collar unions, where occupational unionism appears to have reached a plateau and the major development is the sharp growth of conglomerate unions of allied occupations. Given that the white-collar workforce is destined for future relative growth, and that recent merger activity appears to reinforce the trend apparent in the table, the prototypical union form may well be the large conglomerate and not Kerr's narrow craft, occupational and professional union. It is also significant in this respect that so diverse have some major white-collar unions of this type become, for example, The Manufacturing, Science and Finance Union, that they are increasingly described as general unions or 'white-collar general unions'.

Several further features of the trend in union organisation in Ireland bear comment in regard to the question of fragmentation. The first is the long-run decline which has occurred in the number of unions relative to the number of union members. In 1930 in the region of 100 unions and associations organised about 104,000 workers. In 1985 83 unions and associations organised 500,000 workers. Also relevant is the level of organisational concentration. The share of membership held by the top five unions in 1980 was 56 per cent—the same level of concentration as in 1930, though a drop from the high point of 63 per cent reached in the 1960s. In terms of the predictions of liberal theory, organisational concentration might be expected to have undergone secular decline as an outcome of growth in occupational and grade-based unionism. The 'monopoly' of the Irish Congress of Trade Unions as the peak federation of Irish unions is likewise relevant in considering trends in organisational cohesion. ICTU-affiliated unions have organised in the region of 90 per cent of trade union members since the federation was re-established in 1959, following a 1945 split which led to the establishment of two rival federations. Attempts by white-collar unions to establish a separate white-collar federation have had little effect on ICTU's monopoly: the vehicle of white-collar exclusivism, the Irish Conference of Professional and Service Associations, has remained ineffectual.

One secular trend that has gone contrary to any tendency towards fragmentation is the declining share of union membership organised by unions with headquarters in the United Kingdom—'British unions' in the parlance of the Irish trade union world. The British–Irish divide has long been a source of deep conflict in collective bargaining and policy-making within the ICTU. Most British unions are philosophically opposed to centralised, national wage bargaining and particularly to tripartite agreements involving government. The preference of most British unions for 'free collective bargaining' contrasts with the more pragmatic approach of Irish unions. The share of British union membership in total membership, and commensurately the influence of British unions on the policies of the Irish labour movement, have declined steadily over time. In 1930 about 30 per cent of Irish trade union members were represented in British unions, compared with 14 per cent in the mid-1980s. The declining membership share of British unions can be accounted for in part by the prolonged influence of nationalism. Nationalist sentiment appears to have both encouraged secession by the Irish branches of British unions and retarded their membership growth (Roche, forthcoming).

What, then, may be emphasised is the degree to which the Irish case deviates from the liberal pluralist prediction of an increasingly sectionalist trade unionism, fragmented by occupational interests, and progressively less capable of conceiving of itself as a 'movement' transcending the immediate priorities of its many component groups. Though already fragmented by the circumstances of their early development, Irish unions have had sufficient capacity for concerted action to enter centralised wage agreements in nineteen of the twenty-nine 'wage rounds' which have occurred since 1946. Four such agreements have formally involved government in tripartite deals. The objectives of the ICTU in centralised tripartite bargaining have included 'wage solidarism', tax reform, employment creation and the preservation and extension of social policy. The degree to which these objectives have been attained is a subject of continuing trade union and academic debate. And it cannot be denied that the fragility of cohesion in the trade union movement and the limited authority of the ICTU have been evident in such centralised bargaining (Roche, 1987a; Hardiman, 1988). Yet the evolution of trade union organisation in the course of industrialisation has not rendered it impossible, or progressively more difficult, for unions in Ireland to act in a concerted manner, or to pursue policies which are in significant respects class-oriented. The ideal of trade unions as components of a social movement has not altogether disappeared; it remains a compelling ideal, albeit one that meets with variable support from different types of trade unions and different trade union leaders. Though the alliances of unions involved in centralised bargaining have always been contingent and thus insecure, they have nonetheless pursued social democratic objectives that challenge market outcomes in the common interest of working people. Acting concertedly to influence macro-economic and social policy, unions in Ireland have retained a pivotal influence over the granting or withholding of consent by employees to government policy. Some sixty years after the Irish state first began actively to promote industrialisation, unions still debate the mission of their organisations. Though no longer engaging in militant class insurgency, they are still capable of creating alliances which transcend narrow occupational interests. The future of such alliances is open and not predetermined by an inexorable 'logic of industrialism'.

That no clear trends towards 'exclusive' trade unionism or progressive fragmentation can be identified in the Irish case points to a number of weaknesses in liberal theory's grasp of the effects on union organisation and strategy of industrialisation and economic development. The departure of craft unions from exclusive organisational strategies and the growing prominence of unions of allied occupations can be attributed in part to the effects on union policies of technological and industrial change. Changing technology in many instances blurred established lines of demarcation between crafts and other occupations, making it more difficult for exclusive unions to control job boundaries and thus to restrict these jobs to their members. If the work traditionally done by union members can be allocated to semi-skilled workers, or to the members of other craft or occupational unions, a union may be forced to respond by trying to organise the potential substitute workers. This can then result in the merger of craft unions into a craft conglomerate; in the admission of semi-skilled workers; or in the addition of allied non-craft occupations to a core craft membership.

Another force linked with economic development but going counter to fragmentation is the state's policy of encouraging trade union 'rationalisation'. The impetus behind this policy is the belief that union multiplicity encourages inter-union conflict and compromises economic growth. A series of legislative initiatives by successive Irish governments have addressed this issue. It has been made progressively more difficult for groups of workers to establish new unions. As well as encouraging newly unionising occupational groups to opt for representation in existing unions, this policy has also made it harder for disaffected groups to secede from unions in order to set up more exclusive organisations. State policy favouring large inclusive unions also gave unions like the Irish Transport an advantage in organising the new workforces of incoming multi-national companies. The process of change within unions themselves is further inimical to fragmentation and exclusivism. Much of liberal writing on change in trade unions has focused on how processes of 'union maturation' transform unions from militant organisations to 'sleepy bureaucracies' (Lester, 1958). Other effects of 'maturation' should also be recognised. As unions become more concerned to represent members 'professionally', introducing to this end an increasing range of services and 'selective incentives', the size-threshold for financial viability probably rises. Craft and occupational unions tend to be small unions, and such unions are particularly vulnerable to financial pressure arising from membership setbacks, inflation and relative improvements in the services and benefits offered by larger unions. Unlike larger organisations, they may be unable to scale-down administrative overheads to weather financial difficulties. Financial vulnerability to merger with predatory inclusive organisations has long been a weakness of exclusive unions, and such vulnerability has probably increased with the general 'professionalisation' of union activities.

The overall conclusion must therefore be that the prediction of an inexorable drift towards exclusive unionism lacks validity in the Irish case. Irish trade unions remain capable of operating in concert as a 'movement'.

The impact of industrial and technological development on trade union structure and strategy has been more complex than grasped by liberal theory. The future, with respect both to trade union structure and strategy, is open rather than predetermined.

The Development of Pluralist Industrial Relations Practices

The *conduct* of industrial relations in Ireland has evolved more or less along 'liberal pluralist' lines, but the *outcome* of liberal pluralist practices has not been as predicted. Little development in industrial relations institutions or practices occurred in the new Irish State until after the Second World War. During the period of intense industrial and social conflict from 1907 to 1920 Irish employers were already retreating from dogmatic opposition to the unionisation of the unskilled, and were pragmatically accommodating to collective bargaining (O'Connor, 1988). Through its membership of the International Labour Organisation, independent Ireland was bound by resolutions concerning the right to freedom of association and the promotion of collective bargaining. The Irish constitution of 1937 granted citizens the right to 'form' associations and unions.

The establishment of the Labour Court in 1946 was a watershed in Irish industrial relations. The Court was established to provide a facility for conciliation or adjudication in industrial disputes. It was philosophically disposed towards encouraging the spread of collective bargaining, and intervened early in disputes over union recognition in a number of industries. While the Labour Court was beginning to foster a pluralist model of 'good industrial relations' in the private sector, collective bargaining was also gaining acceptance in the public services. As a result of developments from the late 1940s, civil service unions and associations gained recognition as representative organisations in conciliation and arbitration schemes.[6] As unionisation increased, a system of collective bargaining emerged which was dominated by multi-employer and multi-union bargaining units. Wage bargaining came to be heavily influenced by a series of recurring economy-wide 'wage rounds'. In establishing an economy-wide 'orbit of coercive comparison' for wage rises, the industrial bargaining structure virtually 'took wages out of competition' across the entire economy.

Certain elements of pluralist industrial relations were thus in place

---

[6] They were not, however, to enjoy the same strike immunities as private sector workers until the 1980s.

Table 6. The growth of professional personnel management.

A. Estimated national totals of personnel managers in firms with different levels of employment (1964 and 1973)

	Employing less than 100	Employing 100–499	Employing over 500	All Firms
1964	21[a]	16[a]	53	90
1973	93[a]	135[a]	155	383

B. Estimated number of firms with a designated personnel office, 1981–82, in different sectors

Manufacturing/industrial (including construction)	550
Financial	70
Other services/distribution etc.	150
Total	770

[a] Estimates are likely to be imprecise due to survey sampling errors. Very small firms (less than 20 employees in 1964 and less than 25 employees in 1975) were excluded from the surveys.
Sources: Data for 1964 and 1973 are derived from results reported in Gorman *et al.* (1975: 36–9). Data for 1981–2 are derived from Institute of Public Administration (1982).

early in state's history, while other elements evolved slowly but progressively. From the 1960s state development agencies successfully followed a policy of encouraging foreign companies to adapt to local practices. Many incoming international firms concluded 'pre-production' agreements with unions covering recognition and procedural arrangements for the conduct of industrial relations.[7] The 'constitutional' approach to the governance of the workplace entered a new phase during the 1960s and 1970s with the professionalisation of personnel and industrial relations management. Up to then, apart from in large enterprises, industrial relations activity was mostly conducted at industry level. It was at that level that wage bargaining was concentrated and there was little more to industrial relations. From the 1960s, workplace bargaining and associated policies and procedures began to be elaborated, and enterprise-level industrial relations assumed growing importance.

Table 6 indicates the increase in the number of professional personnel managers and departments. In a survey of 141 manufacturing companies in 1984 Murray (1984: 21) found that 74 per cent of companies had a personnel function. Compared with the situation in the mid-1960s, when only 4 per cent of companies had a personnel executive reporting to the company's chief executive, in 1984 the head of personnel was directly accountable to the top manager in 84 per cent of companies with a

---

[7] A review of industrial relations in multi-nationals in the early 1980s, concluded that they were not 'materially different from home-based companies' (Kelly and Brannick, 1985).

personnel function; and 24 per cent of personnel directors had a seat on company boards. Further, almost 90 per cent of companies claimed to have a written personnel policy. So-called 'comprehensive agreements', covering pay, conditions and procedures, became more common and fixed-term agreements became standard (McCarthy et al., 1975). Management education in personnel and industrial relations also expanded in universities, third-level colleges and professional institutes like the Irish Management Institute and the Institute of Personnel Management. The canons of 'good industrial relations' taught in higher education and professional bodies were stridently pluralist in character.

Studies conducted during the 1970s and 1980s indicated that techniques of 'rational' personnel and industrial administration—such as selection, training, employee appraisal, disputes and grievance procedures—were by then extensively used (Gunnigle and Shivanath, 1988; Keating, 1987; Murray, 1984; Wallace, 1981; Gorman et al., 1975). During the 1960s, in contrast, they were seldom used even in large companies (Tomlin, 1966: ch. 15). Productivity bargaining, some of it certainly spurious, also became common during the 1960s and 1970s (McCarthy, 1982; O'Brien, 1981). The growth of professionalisation and rationalisation was encouraged by the main employers' industrial relations body, the Federated Union of Employers (later the Federation of Irish Employers). The Federation followed a policy of broadly supporting collective bargaining in companies where some degree of unionisation had occurred. During the 1960s and 1970s, FUE increased its level of penetration of Irish business and developed an extensive set of services for member firms (Commission of Inquiry on Industrial Relations, 1981: ch. 4; O'Brien, 1987).

The evidence that a process of extensive and intensive professionalisation and rationalisation in the management of Irish industrial relations gathered pace during the 1960s and 1970s is thus compelling. The changes which occurred at the level of the firm endorsed the basic principles of liberal pluralism. Collective bargaining remained the cornerstone of professional industrial relations and personnel management. The new techniques and practices were implemented with a view to rationalising collective bargaining, and often to extending its scope. By the end of the 1970s pluralism's 'constitutional approach to the governance of work' reigned almost supreme in Irish industrial relations.

The question that then arises is what effect these changes had on industrial relations and on the policies of trade unions. There is no simple answer to this question. But what can be suggested is that a number of trends and developments indicate that the consequences of professionalisation, in all its forms, have been a good deal more complex than is presumed in the liberal pluralist model. The liberal pluralist claim that the *intensity*

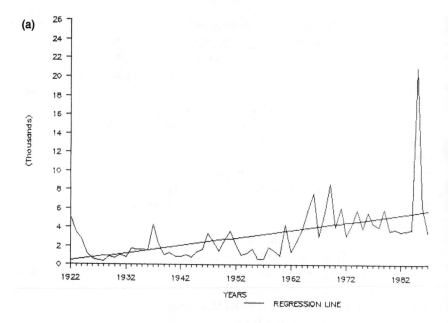

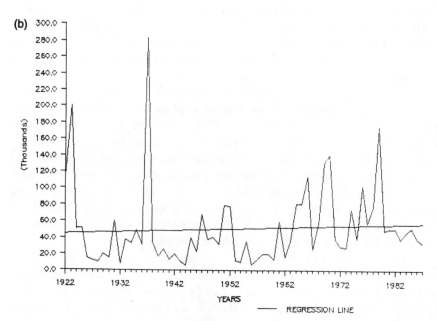

Figure 1. (a) Workers involved in industrial disputes and (b) working days lost, annually per hundred thousand civilian employees at work.

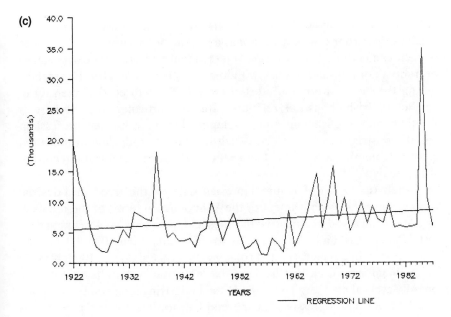

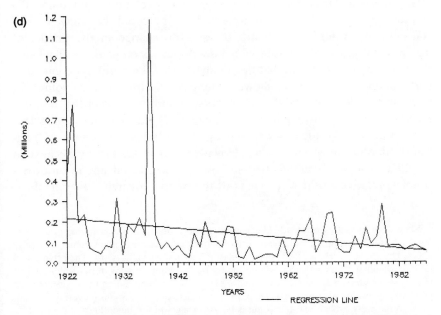

Figure 1. (c) Workers involved in strikes and (d) working days lost, annually per hundred thousand trade union members.

of industrial conflict peaks early in the course of industrialisation and declines thereafter can be accepted as a reasonable portrayal of the course of such conflict in Ireland. Employers' gradual and pragmatic acceptance of trade unionism, and unions' withdrawal from militant class insurgency, during the period from 1907 to the early 1920s defused the intensity of conflict in Irish industrial relations. But of particular interest here is whether the establishment and development of pluralist and profession-alised industrial relations practices led to a long-run decline in industrial conflict. One obviously critical indicator of any such trend is the record of strike activity.

Panels (a) to (d) of Figure 1 present data on the trend in industrial conflict since the establishment of the Irish State, in terms of the numbers of workers involved in industrial disputes and the numbers of working days lost. Panels (a) and (b) show levels of conflict per 100,000 civilian employees, while panels (c) and (d) show the same data per 100,000 trade union members. Clearly, the level of industrial action fluctuates in a broadly cyclical manner. To bring out the underlying long-run trends, each panel fits an autoregressive linear trend-line to data for the period as a whole. This provides a way of identifying any long-run decline in the propensity of employees or union members to engage in industrial action across the troughs and peaks of the business cycle.[8] As pluralist practices relate in particular to the conduct of industrial relations with unionised workers, trends in the union-weighted series could be viewed as a conceptually preferable indicator of long-run change in the impact of management practice and institutional developments on worker behaviour.[9] Panels (a) and (c) indicate that the numbers of workers and trade unionists participating in strikes have shown no long-run decline, and the volume of working days lost per 100,000 employees, as shown in panel (b), has also failed to decline. Only in panel (d), which relates the trend in working days lost to number of trade union members, do we find any indication of long-run decline in industrial conflict. However, this arises largely because in the 1920s and 1930s unions had so few members to engage in industrial conflict, relative to the later years of the period covered. Overall, then,

---

[8] While such measures of trend, like any others, are open to criticism, they are useful nonetheless in bringing out underlying secular patterns. All autoregression trends are clearly affected by 'outliers'. These affect, in particular, trends in working days lost. Their 'typicality' raises conceptual problems which will not be considered here. What is of particular interest in the present context is the lack of evidence of a declining trend during the period of most pronounced development of workplace pluralist practices and institutions (covering the mid-1940s to the early 1980s); and this result is not seriously affected by outliers.

[9] For a rejection of the view that union-weighted series are the relevant indicators of trends in industrial conflict, see Hibbs (1976: 1034–7).

Figure 1 would suggest that there has been no secular decline in the propensity of employees or trade union members to engage in industrial conflict.

What also clearly emerges is that levels of industrial conflict failed to respond to any significant degree to the professionalisation of industrial relations at workplace level. The rise in strike participation and working days lost during the 1960s and 1970s occurred in spite of the rising incidence of procedures for conflict avoidance and the growing resort to the conciliation and investigation services of the Labour Court. In addition, a diverse repertoire of other sanctions apart from strikes became evident in industrial relations during this period—for example, go-slows, overtime bans, bans on flexible working, refusal to work co-operatively and so on. It is difficult to identify trends in their occurrence with certainty but in many large organisations, like ESB, such sanctions both became more common and were deployed with greater sophistication. Murray's 1984 survey of manufacturing found that the incidence of non-strike forms of industrial action was triple the incidence of strikes (Murray, 1984: 8); and an exploratory study, based on the reportage of such tactics in a specialist industrial relations news periodical during the 1980s, also concluded that there appeared to have been an increase in the level of sophistication with which non-strike sanctions were deployed (Moore, 1988).

The growing formalisation of wage bargaining structures also had economic effects that were unanticipated in liberal theory. Research on wage rounds during the 1960s suggested that the system of wage fixing had become almost entirely unresponsive to market signals and conditions. Prevailing micro-economic and macro-economic conditions seemed to have little effect on wage determination in comparison with the 'micro-political' dynamic enjoined by inter-union relations and the determined use of collective organisation (McCarthy et al., 1975). Wage pressure on direct labour costs began to rise from the 1960s, and so too, it appears, did pressure for concessions on a range of fringe benefits and conditions of employment. The scope of collective bargaining began to widen to encompass allowances of various kinds (Hardiman, 1988: 155–8). To the traditional union policy of claiming wage-round increases and the maintenance of relativities were added an opportunistic seizing of bargaining opportunities wherever they arose and an entrepreneurial flair for creating such opportunities where none had existed before. Orbits of coercive comparison also began to widen as blue-collar groups for the first time pursued parity of pay and conditions with white-collar workers (Roche, 1981). In this context, disillusionment set in among employers with some of the most 'progressive' techniques of the period, and with productivity bargaining in particular.

Some of the consequences of pluralist industrial relations practices have been as expected and intended. Pluralist systems of industrial authority have afforded employees greater job protection, reduced their vulnerability to arbitrary or capricious management decisions, and provided them with a means of voicing grievances. Professionalisation along pluralist lines has also given companies greater predictability in respect of wage costs, and greater stability in the intensity with which work is performed. By routinising and even ritualising industrial conflict through procedures, the parties to industrial relations have defused its intensity and volatility. Pluralist practices have also made it possible to build up a body of precedents regarding equity in wage determination. However, other consequences of pluralist professionalisation seem at variance with the expectations of liberal theory. Worker grievances and industrial conflict have proved to be 'durable'. Attempts to democratise and constrain the exercise of managerial authority have expanded the bargaining agenda of unions and have probably encouraged worker 'entrepreneurship'. The development of wage-bargaining structures has resulted in the suppression of market signals. In short, while some, though not all, of the anticipated effects of pluralism have been achieved, other effects, scarcely considered by liberal theory, have probably had no less an impact on industrial relations. And these unintended consequences, as well as the unrealised effects of pluralism, point to weaknesses in liberal theory. In this theory, the various forms of joint regulation are viewed primarily as providing a series of channels for 'draining away' conflict and worker dissent. This view neglects entirely the complex ways in which institutions can interact with day-to-day industrial relations to heighten awareness of bargaining opportunity and, as it were, 'create their own supply' of grievances and demands. The idea that professional management and its institutional supports can contain or reduce worker militancy or 'pushfulness' ignores a number of problems. The establishment of procedures for conflict avoidance appears often to result in a tactical use of such procedures during the course of disputes. Far from commanding normative commitment, the various stages and levels associated with procedure agreements are often viewed in an instrumental way. Procedure is frequently exploited tactically as a resource for furthering a dispute; and procedural rules can be ignored by either side as the occasion demands (see Murray *et al.*, 1984; Wallace and O'Shea, 1987). The adoption by managers of a more professional and strategic approach to containing industrial action may evoke a similar response on the part of unions and their members. This can result in a widening of the repertoire of methods of industrial action. The more sophisticated employees become in responding to management professionalism, the more they may resort to methods that are acknowledged by managers to be very difficult to counter: for example, a tacit refusal to work flexibly, or a withdrawal of goodwill. By establishing committees, tribunals, representatives and channels for processing claims, pluralist forms of industrial relations can foster worker opportunism and 'entrepreneurship'. By encouraging orderly and stable union organisation at the level of the enterprise and the workplace, professional managers may strengthen their 'adversaries' and their capacity to pursue claims effectively. In elaborating a web of rules in the workplace, pluralist forms of industrial relations may institutionalise job boundaries and demarcations. Career-ladders and rights of access to jobs and promotional opportunities are usually highly regulated by collective agreements, as are wage relativities between different grades. In these ways pluralist practices further compound the bureaucratic organisation of work.

If pluralist practices can in this way *build up codified work rules* which intensify bureaucracy, they may also *erode social norms* which facilitate organisational integration and the control of work by managers. It is now widely recognised that productivity bargaining serves often to heighten bargaining awareness and to encourage an instrumental attitude to work. By focusing attention on the wage-effort bargain, productivity bargaining may encourage employees, in effect, to 'ration' work effort and sell it at the margin. In the same way, where a strong predisposition develops among employees to trade work-effort marginally, aspects of effort which may in the past have been offered 'free'—conceded, that is, as 'non-contractual elements of contract'—for example, enthusiasm, co-operation, flexibility, a willingness to adjust to change etc., are subsumed to the logic of exchange (Roche, 1987b). The result may be a further need for rules and standards to *substitute for* the social norms eroded through the routine conduct of collective bargaining.

The evolution of Irish industrial relations since about 1960 illustrates many of the lacunae and unintended effects of pluralism. When faced with an increasingly confident and strongly organised workforce, companies resorted to a model of 'good industrial relations' which built upon the foundations of long-established traditions and practices. This model seems not to have reduced worker pressure on wages, contained industrial conflict or increased the leeway available to companies to organise work and direct work effort without provoking strong and well-organised employee resistance. What emerges in the Irish case, therefore, is hardly an instance of industrial relations conflict becoming little more than a 'frictional' force in an otherwise smooth progression towards advanced industrial society. During the 1960s and 1970s, on the contrary, industrial relations conflict and union wage pressure appeared to government and employers to be intractable to existing industrial relations practices and prescriptions. The wage-price spiral came to be seen by the same parties as a chronic threat to competitiveness, and the trend in industrial conflict as a serious discouragement to foreign investment—the cornerstone of the State's strategy of industrialisation and economic development. In spite of the growing sophistication of industrial relations, the model of 'good industrial relations' enshrining pluralist practices was brought increasingly into question and a growing sense of industrial relations 'crisis' arose.

The major exponents of the 'crisis' argument were employers and governments, but trade unions too sometimes questioned the viability of current practices (McCarthy, 1973). The immediate result of growing disillusionment in the 1970s was a progressive politicisation of wage bargaining—a trend at variance with one of the central predictions of liberal theory. On the side of employers, one of the longer-term consequences has been a new popularity of versions of 'monistic' or 'unitarist' industrial relations in which the role of trade unions is restricted. This is one of the most salient developments in Irish industrial relations during the late 1980s and 1990s. In common with their counterparts in other countries, Irish employers have shown growing interest in 'human resource management' techniques, and other departures from established pluralist practice can also be identified. Thus, in many sectors of Irish business, employers have sought to promote 'flexibility' by dismantling standardised conditions of employment and job security; and flexibility has also been pursued by hiving-off of parts of production, maintenance or amenities to sub-contractors, by making greater use of part-time workers, and by increased resort to 'untypical' forms of employment contract. Moreover, in some companies and sectors, the challenge to pluralism has been less sophisticated, involving growing resistance to union recognition, or the reassertion of traditional doctrines of managerial prerogative (Roche, 1991; McGovern, 1988).

In sum, the creation of a system of industrial citizenship based on the 'joint regulation' of working conditions has proved not to be a panacea for the economic and social conflicts released by industrialisation and economic development. In the 1990s the very survival of major features of pluralist industrial relations at company and workplace levels is coming into question. 'Unitarism' in various guises is back on the employers' agenda. The Federation of Irish Employers appears no longer to be disposed to encourage new companies to concede union recognition rather than explore other industrial relations strategies. Unions have also complained that the IDA has tacitly retreated from its traditional policy of encouraging incoming multinationals to adapt to local industrial relations practices (McGovern, 1988: 89–90). Unions are obviously very aware of recent revisions in the ideological and strategic positions of employers and the state. Thus far, they have not regarded the reappearance of unitarism as the most serious threat with which they are faced. But there is growing concern and debate within the union movement about the likely future impact on unionisation of the waning support for industrial relations on the pluralist model.

The Politics of Industrial Relations in Ireland

Liberal theory predicted the progressive depoliticisation of industrial relations. At face value, party politics in Ireland seems consistent with the liberal prediction. The political ideologies of the major parties with respect to industrial relations have not been distinctive, and thus the governments they have formed have not followed markedly different industrial relations strategies. Both Fianna Fáil and Fine Gael have sought—and, to a greater or lesser degree, managed to sustain—working-class support for their policies. The main parties' 'catch-all' approach to political mobilisation has meant that conflicts arising from the sphere of industrial relations have not been politicised in a visibly class-partisan way. In contrast with the United Kingdom, industrial relations has never figured as a key issue in Irish elections. The policy of the Labour Party on industrial relations issues has traditionally been distinct from those of the two major parties in placing emphasis on the extension of industrial and economic democracy. But Labour policy on these issues has had little direct effect on Irish industrial relations owing to the electoral weakness of the Labour Party and, consequently, the Party's minority status in inter-party and coalition governments since 1945.

While the similarity of approach of the major parties is the most salient feature of party politics in industrial relations, important differences of emphasis and 'political style' can nonetheless be identified. Fianna Fáil governments have favoured active involvement in industrial relations and collective bargaining rather less equivocally than inter-party governments or Fine Gael–Labour coalitions. The political ideology of Fianna Fáil, which views the party as a 'national' party or party of 'national consensus', places few ideological constraints on intervention in industrial relations, if this is seen to be warranted by circumstances. Indeed, the promotion of 'social partnership' between the state and the peak federations of unions and employers has come to be regarded as the direct expression in economic policy of the Party's emphasis on fostering 'national consensus'.

Fine Gael ideology is permeated by political and economic liberalism of a character which reflects the party's original support-base among larger farmers, the propertied middle class and the professions. From the 1950s the Party moved towards a more social-democratic politics, which found its clearest expression under Garret Fitzgerald's leadership, and this facilitated the adoption of a more *dirigiste* approach to economic policy-making. The liberalism still inherent in Fine Gael's political ideology, even under Fitzgerald, resulted in a higher level of equivocation on union involvement in public policy-making than was characteristic of Fianna Fáil. Nonetheless, Fine Gael's liberalism stopped short of distaste for active state involvement in pay bargaining, and well short of that expressed in the 'free market' policies of the Thatcher Conservative Governments in the United Kingdom. In any case, the Party's stance was tempered in government during the 1970s and early 1980s through its being in coalition with Labour.

The absence of clear class-based party politics in Irish industrial relations cannot, however, be understood in terms of forces unleashed by industrialisation. The character of Irish party politics must be traced to the circumstances in which the Irish party system emerged. In this sense, much of the politics of industrial relations in Ireland has to be understood in terms of the 'pre-history' of modern industrial relations, considered earlier in the paper. Nor should the broadly similar positions of the main political parties on industrial relations be viewed as unchangeable. In the mid-1980s a new party, the Progressive Democrats, emerged on the liberal-right of Irish politics. In spite of its origins as a breakaway from Fianna Fáil, the PD Party espoused a neo-liberal ideology which declared itself hostile to restrictive and monopolistic institutions and practices. The Party polled impressively in the 1987 election. For a time, the PDs seemed set to coalesce in future elections, and possibly governments, with Fine Gael— itself experiencing realignment following the retirement of Fitzgerald. This raised the prospect of a more ideologically divided party-politics of industrial relations. It was a prospect that did not go unnoticed by trade union leaders when they entered talks on a national wage agreement with a Fianna Fáil government after the 1987 election. The fortunes of the PDs declined sharply in the general election of 1989, and the organisation opted to participate in coalition with Fianna Fáil. However, the realignment in party politics threatened by the appearance of the PDs indicates that political circumstances are still capable of recasting the politics of industrial relations in Ireland in a more class-partisan mould.

If considerable electoral and ideological scope has long existed for the adoption by government of an active, interventionist approach to industrial relations, up to the 1960s only the exceptional circumstances of war-time were seen to warrant a departure from a non-interventionist approach. For much of the state's history, a preference prevailed for keeping politics out of industrial relations (Roche, 1987a). However, in the 1960s, in response to growing trade union organisation and power, a rising level of industrial conflict and forceful trade union wage pressure, Irish governments began to adopt a more interventionist stance. In the following decade, pay determination became increasingly politicised, as unfettered collective bargaining fell from favour and governments sought to promote concertation with union and employer federations.

The limited success of national bargaining during the 1970s has been examined in a number of studies of the period (O'Brien, 1981; Roche, 1987a; Hardiman, 1988 and this volume). In attempting to explain the weakness of centralised wage bargaining in Ireland, Hardiman concludes (1988: 151) that the involvement of unions in concertation during the 1970s tended to 'take a pluralist, pressure-group form rather than one characteristic of (neo-corporatist) political exchange'. While the limited success of concertation during the 1970s cannot be denied, what bears emphasis in the present context is the degree to which pluralist interest representation was modified at the political level during the decade, as successive governments sought to avoid the damaging effects attributed to 'free', or politically unfettered, collective bargaining. The politicisation of industrial relations between 1970 and 1981, though heavily compromised by practices and structures built up for long before, represented a significant departure from the politics of industrial relations as projected by liberal theories of industrialism.

In liberal theory, industrial relations are supposed to become 'insulated from the political process'. In neo-corporatist concertation, this obviously is not the case; indeed, the objectives of the 'social partners', and of unions in particular, come to be shaped in important respects by the opportunities opened up by access to public policy. Specifically, wage pressure in the labour market is traded off, in the main, against economic and social policy measures which benefit employees in general, irrespective of their occupational situation or status. In consequence, politicised wage bargaining tends to stand opposed to pressures towards sectionalism in the trade union movement (cf. Goldthorpe, 1984: 326; Regini, 1984: 124–5).

Nor has the experiment in tripartism of the 1970s and early 1980s proved to be an aberration—in the face of international economic upheaval—from a secular trend towards depoliticisation. Between 1987 and 1990, unions, employer associations and government again entered a central, tripartite agreement, the Programme for National Recovery (PNR), after five years of decentralised bargaining. Considerable controversy remains regarding the achievements of the PNR—as distinct from the benign effects on the Irish economy of the international economic recovery with which the agreement coincided in the late 1980s. The parties to the PNR were critical of its limited achievements; the unions, in particular, felt that little progress had been made in tackling unemployment. Yet in a manner unprecedented in the history of tripartism in Ireland, all parties to the agreement pointed to areas or issues with respect to which they considered themselves 'winners'. The success attributed to the PNR was a major factor in the background to the negotiation of the Programme for Economic and Social Progress (PESP) in early 1991. A second cycle of politicised wage bargaining has thus lasted over four years and is scheduled to last at least for six. This raises the question of the factors responsible for the emergence of a more stable tripartism, and the related question of whether secular trends in Irish industrial relations may lead to the *institutionalisation* of political exchange as a more or less permanent feature (see further Hardiman, this volume).

The economic and political conjuncture in which the PNR was negotiated and implemented was very different to that obtaining during the informal and formal experiments in tripartism of the 1970s and early 1980s. In 1987 the Irish economy was almost universally seen to have reached its nadir. The public finances had run virtually out of control; the level of unemployment was unprecedented in the state's history; emigration had risen sharply, and union membership had declined dramatically over the preceding seven years. In such a context, market forces began to impinge decisively on free-for-all bargaining, progressively widening pay differentials hitherto fixed by institutional forces. More generally, as discussed earlier, the pluralist model of industrial relations was coming under threat from employers. In addition, the realignment of Irish politics attending the emergence of the PDs held out the prospect of growing support for neo-liberal policies and politics. Faced by these circumstances, Irish trade unions thought it advisable to take stock and opt for politics— as much as anything else to find shelter from the storm. In the event a slow economic recovery set in during the life of the PNR and the party political base for neo-liberal policies seemed to disappear in the General Election of 1989.

Against the background of such extreme contingencies, 'political exchange' proved to be more stable than before and unions and employer associations more inclined, or better able, to 'deliver' the consent of their respective constituencies. The terms of the PESP provide for slightly higher pay rises than those of the PNR, but allow more scope for local bargaining in the private sector and relax restrictions on 'special' relativity claims in the public services. The viability of PESP commitments by the government on pay and social policies was seen to depend at the time of negotiation on optimistic assumptions regarding economic growth. By mid-1991 these assumptions were confounded by the worsening international economic situation. The Minister for Finance responded in the Autumn of 1991 by calling for the renegotiation of the PESP. A torrent of protest came from the unions, especially those in the public services. The future of PESP and of the rehabilitated version of politicised wage bargaining hangs in the balance.

It may be that the economic and political contingencies of the late 1980s were of critical importance in underpinning tripartite wage bargaining. They may also appear, with hindsight, to have been highly unusual. Specifically, the PNR may come to be viewed as an agreement negotiated, as it were, 'out of the last ditch'—providing an Irish parallel to the successful and, never again to be repeated, British incomes policy of the late 1940s and early 1950s.

What, however, also bears consideration in the context of the theory of liberal pluralism, is the possibility—one cannot, it has to be said, speak of the probability—of an alternative scenario. The pronouncements during and after the PESP negotiations of a number of senior trade union officials regarding future strategies give rise to the possibility that Congress may attempt to institutionalise 'political exchange' in the context of a ten-year programme of trade union policies. These policies include collective goods and services of a distinctly class-related character—employment, social policies, union rights etc (see ICTU, 1990). Such an approach could indicate the operation of a 'learning curve' on the part of union leaders concerning the constraints and opportunities of centralised, tripartite bargaining. It might also point to deepening pessimism regarding the likely future achievements and consequences of free-for-all bargaining, given the changes in employer strategies now in train. In short, influential sections of the Irish trade union movement have perhaps made a strategic decision to 'opt for politics' in a potentially more far-reaching way than in the recent past. Such a strategy will, of course, have to be contingent on the results of tripartism. The alternative unions now face is to revert to decentralised bargaining in a changing system of industrial relations, and attempt to engage in 'pressure-group' politics to counter any trends not tractable to collective bargaining alone.

Sixty years on from the beginnings of industrialisation in the independent Irish State, the choice between politicised industrial relations and the 'autonomous' industrial relations envisaged by liberal theory remains open to trade unions, employers and the State. It is a choice of major significance for the political economy of Irish society. It has not been precluded—nor will its outcome be determined—by social forces associated with industrialisation or economic development. The electoral viability of an interventionist stance on industrial relations arises from the catch-all nature of Irish party politics. In the Irish case, politicised industrial relations and catch-all party politics *coexist*, albeit in an unstable amalgam

and in a manner which limits the effectiveness of tripartite concertation (Hardiman, 1988). Politics and national governance currently
turn in important respects on the government's success in managing
tripartism. The future is open. Political realignment to the liberal
right could undermine tripartism, as, in the short term, could economic
circumstances. At the same time, underlying trends in industrial relations
could lead to the institutionalisation and stabilisation of political exchange.

Conclusion

This paper has presented a review of the development of Irish industrial
relations in the context of the liberal theory of industrialism. It has been
found necessary to question the overall validity in the Irish case of the
successive claims made by the theory. The peaking of worker militancy in
the period 1907–20 was shown to have no meaningful link with the pace
or character of industrialisation. Its roots were to be found, rather, in the
contagion of British ideas and institutions, cyclical economic developments
and the abnormal economic, political and social conditions of the First
World War and Anglo-Irish War. While attempts to promote or engage in
concerted action by Irish unions have always been compromised by union
multiplicity and organisational fragmentation, no clearly defined trend
towards 'exclusive unionism' can be identified. Some of the forces unleashed by industrialism were shown to *constrain* union fragmentation
and to encourage more 'inclusive' forms of organisation, increasing the
capacity for concerted action by trade unions. The evolution of practices
and management techniques consistent with a pluralist understanding of
'good industrial relations' failed to bring about a secular decline in strike
activity. Thus far, at least, industrial conflict has proved to be 'durable'.
The growing conviction of Irish governments that collective bargaining
needed to be harnessed more directly to business performance and macroeconomic management led to the growing politicisation of industrial
relations during the 1960s and 1970s. In the recession of the 1980s
employers also showed renewed interest in essentially unitary models of
industrial relations, and these are now subject to significant experimentation. The new vogue in unitarism and the reassertion of managerial
prerogative at company level have been paralleled by the re-emergence
since 1987 of politicised industrial relations at national level. Both trends
run directly counter to the predictions of liberal theory. Options as
between different sets of social and political arrangements for the
conduct of industrial relations are still available to unions, employers

and governments. These options, furthermore, have strikingly different economic and social consequences. Ultimately, this is the most telling evidence against the supposed logic of industrialism on which the liberal theory relies.

Proceedings of the British Academy, **79**, 329–358

The State and Economic Interests:
Ireland in Comparative Perspective

NIAMH HARDIMAN
Somerville College, Oxford

Introduction

IRELAND'S ECONOMIC AND POLITICAL DEVELOPMENT has often been
assumed to be very different from that of other western societies. However, corporatist or 'concertative' pay agreements have been a recurring
theme in Irish economic management. In this way, Ireland's experiences
resemble those of many other industrialised countries, and especially the
smaller European countries with which Ireland may perhaps most appropriately be compared. Some commentators have argued that all small
countries experience a special incentive to adjust in a co-ordinated way to
international economic pressures, in view of their vulnerability to trade
fluctuations (cf. Katzenstein, 1983, 1985). Ireland's growing economic
openness since the 1960s provided the context for the emergence of
centralised pay agreements (Hardiman, 1988: ch. 2). This paper will use
comparative studies to draw out the conditions of success or failure of
corporatist pay agreements, the better to account for the particular
features of the Irish experience.

The heyday of corporatism has often been seen as the 1970s.[1] During
the 1980s, the dominant tendency appeared to be for comprehensive,
centralised bargaining systems to founder, or to be reconstituted at lower
levels or 'sectors' of the economy (Schmitter, 1991), a development
sometimes termed 'meso-corporatism' (Cawson, 1985). The return to
centralised agreements in Ireland in 1987 might be thought of as a move
against the general trend. However, an analysis which is less focused on
Northern Europe and Scandinavia reveals that Ireland was far from

Read 8 December 1990. © The British Academy 1992.
[1] An extensive academic debate was initiated primarily by Schmitter's article, originally
published in 1972 (see Schmitter, 1979), entitled 'Still the Century of Corporatism?'.

unique in seeking a centralised solution to economic difficulties during the 1980s.

Corporatism in Advanced Industrial Societies

Corporatism became a widely used strategy for macroeconomic regulation, with greater or lesser degrees of success, during the years between the end of the Second World War and the oil-price crises of the mid-1970s. These were the years of the 'long boom'. Although the experiences of different countries varied, these years can be said to have been characterised by steady growth, virtually full employment, and an increase in trade union strength. Corporatist networks linking the conduct of collective bargaining to government policy-making provided a means of reconciling the potentially conflicting policy priorities of full employment, growth, and control of inflation. Most western countries became involved in corporatist experiments in these years (Schmitter and Lehmbruch eds., 1979; Lehmbruch and Schmitter eds., 1982; Goldthorpe, 1984).

The form taken by centralised agreements, and the extent of participation of government in employer–labour bargaining, varied considerably. In the Nordic countries, employer–labour collective bargaining succeeded for many years in combining steady growth with egalitarian redistributive policies, with no direct government role, but with considerable public policy support for full employment and 'active labour market' policies (Korpi, 1978; Esping-Andersen, 1985; Arter, 1987). In Austria, egalitarian objectives featured less prominently, and pay agreements were negotiated within highly institutionalised tripartite consensus-building processes. But this process also facilitated the maintenance of high levels of employment with low levels of inflation (Lehmbruch, 1979; Scharpf, 1981; Marin, 1983). In the Netherlands and, in a somewhat different form, in West Germany, collective bargaining initially facilitated post-war economic reconstruction under heavy political influence. In both countries, the mechanisms for representing employer and labour interests at various levels of economic and political decision-making were extensive. Pay bargaining thus contributed to controlling inflation in a context of strong growth, whether the government involvement was direct or indirect (Flanagan *et al.*, 1983; Gourevitch *et al.*, 1984; Markovits, 1986; Scholten ed., 1987; Scharpf, 1991). While few countries failed to attempt some form of co-ordination of pay policy with government objectives, it is generally acknowledged that the strongest, most successful exemplars of corporatist wage agreements were the centralised agreements negotiated in Austria and in the Scandinavian countries.

From the mid-1970s, 'stagflation' put unprecedented stresses on Keynesian techniques of demand management. Additional public expenditure deferred the emergence of mass unemployment but, in many countries, unemployment began to creep up in the 1970s and increased more rapidly in the early 1980s (Johannesson and Schmid, 1980; Scharpf, 1984, 1991; Therborn, 1986; Schmidt, 1988).

The 1980s saw the emergence of a new set of economic problems in the advanced countries. Economic growth no longer ensured employment expansion. Control of inflation assumed a different significance in slacker labour markets. Further problems emerged from the increasing interdependence of the international economy. The old Keynesian remedies no longer seemed relevant. Many governments entered the 1980s with sizeable fiscal deficits, which they could sustain in the short term to support employment levels, but which had to be tackled eventually. The changed economic circumstances brought about a shift in the terms on which organised economic interests were involved in political processes. For some, the British experience was a paradigm of the new direction, with trade unions excluded from political influence, unemployment allowed to rise as a discipline on labour markets, and the introduction of legislation to further reduce unions' organisational strength (see, e.g., Longstreth, 1988; Crouch, 1990).

However, the diversity of political responses apparent in this period was greater than at any time since the war (Goldthorpe, 1984, 1987; Lash and Urry, 1987: ch. 8). The unions' bargaining position was, on the whole, weaker (cf. Baglioni and Crouch eds., 1990) but there was no common tendency towards an undermining of union organisation, and no convergence towards Britain's experience in the rest of the advanced capitalist countries (Goldthorpe, 1987; Hardiman, 1990). Still, the solutions adopted to economic problems often entailed a shift away from the 1970s model of neo-corporatism; and where 'social partnership' agreements were negotiated, the terms on which they were concluded had to take account of new circumstances.

The co-ordination of pay bargaining with macroeconomic policy remained central to the 'policy repertoire' in Austria (Gerlich et al., 1988), in Norway (Lafferty, 1990), and in Finland (Arter, 1987). In these countries, open unemployment was avoided through a variety of policy responses to which the established corporatist networks were central. The 'Swedish Model' was under more obvious stress, as the unity of the main blue-collar federation (LO, Landsorganisationen i Sverige) was threatened from within, primarily by the metalworkers' union—a move supported by their employer counterparts, who attempted to shift to industry-level bargaining. The LO's leadership role in collective bargaining was also increasingly challenged as the rapidly expanding and diverse white-collar unions, with their own separate organisational structures, sought to develop independent strategies (Lash, 1985; Ahlen, 1989). But, at least until 1991, the economic problems of the Swedish economy were managed within the existing system.[2]

A number of other countries experimented with the introduction of centralised agreements for the first time during the 1980s: these were Australia, Spain, Portugal, and Greece. Australia already had a national-level system of wage bargaining, which had facilitated the rapid diffusion of wage gains during the 1970s. Thus, employers as well as unions supported the National Accord, which was first negotiated between the unions and the Labour Party in 1983 and renewed at intervals thereafter (OECD, 1988, 1990).[3] The Accord was one element of a government strategy to liberalise Australian monetary and trade policies, the consequences of which were likely to involve some hardship among employees. But the unions were committed to a centralised strategy which could help to prevent unemployment from worsening, their views being explicitly inspired by the examples of the Scandinavian countries (Archer, 1991).

The newly-democratised countries of Southern Europe, Spain, Greece, and Portugal, with their relatively underdeveloped economies, faced special problems of adjustment to the conditions of EC membership. In Spain and Portugal the legacy of protectionist state intervention from the pre-democratic era was also still strong. Agreements between government, employer organisations and trade union movements were attempted in each case to facilitate the necessary adjustments to more liberal and competitive conditions (Perez-Diaz, 1986; Roca, 1987; Pinto, 1990; Featherstone, 1990). Trade union membership levels were low, and in Spain in particular union weakness was compounded by internal political divisions (Estivill and Hoz, 1990; Gillespie, 1990). But more seriously for the prospects of corporatist pay agreements in Spain and in Greece, popular expectations of what governments of the left should achieve were high. The pay agreements were restrictive, and the fiscal commitments of governments were limited. In Greece, allegations of political corruption within the Socialist Party further soured relations between unions and

---

[2] During 1990, in an attempt to control strikes and secure its budgetary position, the Social Democratic government had threatened to introduce a range of legislative controls on union actions. It survived without doing so. But in the autumn of 1991, the Social Democrats finally lost office, and with it the political hegemony they had held for so long, even while in opposition.

[3] In New Zealand, the Labour governments elected in 1984 and 1987 also pursued liberalization policies, but with no negotiated agreement with the unions (Whitwell, 1990; Walsh, 1991).

government; in Spain, popular discontent resulted in sizeable popular and industrial protests. By the early 1990s, only Portugal had a functioning corporatist pay agreement, facilitated by fiscal relaxation in the late 1980s (OECD, 1991a).

The terms of the agreements in each of these countries differed in a number of ways from the stable neo-corporatist practices established elsewhere in an earlier and economically more buoyant period—and this, as will be seen, was true of the Irish experience of the late 1980s as well. Medium-term economic stabilisation was the first consideration, but pursuit of long-term growth also involved adjustment to a more open and competitive international economic environment. The economic problems to be addressed thus included control of high levels of unemployment, reduction of public spending, and liberalisation of market conditions both in domestic and international activities. For government and employers, corporatist agreements could provide some assurance that union strength would not worsen an already grave economic situation. For organised labour, corporatism could no longer provide a means of pursuing full employment policies. Its participation in such agreements could help prevent economic performance from worsening, but the assurances that economic outcomes would improve were weaker than previously, and governments could make relatively few fiscal concessions to underpin union co-operation. Moreover, by the late 1980s, new disciplines on economic policy were felt in the EC countries, and in those countries such as Sweden and Norway which had decided to link their currencies with the EC's Exchange Rate Mechanism. Commentators argued that these developments accorded greater significance to domestic pay policy. Scharpf, for example, suggested that 'the structurally weak countries with greatest pressure for unsustainable pay rises will become even weaker because they will not be able to use the exchange rate to pass on costs'.[4]

Conditions Facilitating Corporatist Agreements

This brief profile of corporatist experiences leads us to consider the conditions which facilitate the negotiation and successful implementation of such agreements (cf. Korpi and Shalev, 1980; Schmidt, 1982; Schmitter, 1981; Cameron, 1984; Western, 1991). The formal, organisational conditions will be outlined first, followed by the strategic considerations relevant to each side in the negotiating process.

[4] Quoted in 'An orderly model that enforces restraint', *Financial Times*, 3 May, 1991.

Corporatist agreements might be described as 'class-compromise' agreements, because organised labour undertakes, in its negotiations with employers, to restrain industrial militancy and to hold back on maximising its short-term wage gains; the objective is to improve medium-term economic performance in ways that would benefit both workers and employers (Przeworski, 1985). The result can be thought of as a 'positive-sum' outcome from which both sides benefit. Control of inflation can be thought of as a 'public good' desired by employers and unions alike. Employers might also be expected to value industrial peace, and the predictability of wage increases. Trade unions attach priority to real pay increases, but also to control of unemployment. Their central organizations may be thought of as having 'class-wide' interests, because labour-market conditions are crucial to the collective well-being of all employees (Korpi, 1978, 1983; Cameron, 1984; Offe, 1985).

Where employer and trade union organisations cover a relatively large proportion of their respective potential memberships, the authority of their federations would be expected to be great. 'Encompassing organisations', that is, organisations that span the whole, or the greater part, of their total potential constituency (Olson, 1982), are best placed to take a broad overview of economic performance, of how their activities affect it, and of strategies to improve it.

High levels of industrial concentration facilitate employer organisation (Ingham, 1974; Cameron, 1978). Where employers are relatively homogeneous, they are likely to experience less difficulty in organising effectively and building up high levels of membership of employer associations. The kind of trade union organisation which is most conducive to corporatist agreements in turn requires high union density, a unified trade union movement, and a high degree of authoritative centralisation on the part of the union federation (Schmitter, 1981; Schmidt, 1982). An industrial basis of organisation may be more favourable than a combination of craft and general unions, because industrial unions facilitate the absorption of rank and file tensions within the organisation, thus reducing open conflict. They also make it easier to centralise bargaining at the national level. The nature of the legal framework of industrial relations can also be important in stabilising agreements, as strong juridification of industrial relations can contribute to strengthening the authority of the central union federation (Crouch, 1985).

The character of the manufacturing sector of the economy may have a significant bearing on the unions' willingness to participate in wage agreements. If that sector which is most exposed to international trading conditions is relatively large, and also highly unionised, these unions are likely to exert a strong, perhaps dominant, influence within the trade union federation. The need to protect competitiveness is therefore more likely to be recognised within the labour movement, and the exposed sector will take the lead in pay bargaining (Crouch, 1991, 1992). The Swedish unions' strategy on pay from the 1950s on, which resulted in one of the paradigm cases of 'concertative' agreements, was based on the explicit recognition of two sectors in the Swedish economy: an exposed, competitive, manufacturing sector, and a sheltered sector of non-tradeable goods and domestic services (Edgren *et al.*, 1973; Gourevitch *et al.*, 1984). An additional feature which helped the 'Swedish model' to become well established in the 1950s and 1960s was the relative weakness of white-collar trade unions and the dominance of the trade union federation organising private sector industrial employees (the LO) over other federations. This greatly facilitated acceptance of the primacy of the needs of the exposed sector (Gourevitch *et al.*, 1984).

Close relations between the trade union movement and the governing party or parties will further improve the prospects that comprehensive pay agreements will be successful. The political character of the party or parties in power may be important in either of two ways. First, a Social Democratic or Labour government in power can help to secure agreements by boosting the confidence of the trade union movement that the government of the day is seriously committed to objectives which the movement shares. Secondly, where (as in most cases) a leftist party does not occupy a 'hegemonic' position, what may be more important is the ideological distance between parties in the political spectrum, especially with regard to the management of the economy. Where the government is formed by a coalition of parties, co-operation between them may require 'consensus-oriented' pay agreements (Scharpf, 1991). Such a narrow range of disagreement among the main parties has been a feature of Austrian politics, and also, though to a lesser degree, of politics in West Germany and the Netherlands. In contrast, where it is likely that the orientation of economic policy will be reversed with a change of government, stable and successful concertation of economic interests is less likely (as, for example, in Britain).

For each participant, though, wage-regulation agreements must provide a credible means of advancing at least some of the interests that are most important to its members. If such agreements succeed in improving medium-term economic performance, all sides acquire a vested interest in their continuance. During the 1960s and 1970s, these agreements held out the prospect of generating growth without producing damaging inflation. The countries in which corporatist structures were well established tended to be characterised by low inflationary wage pressures, the continued preservation of low unemployment, high levels of employment, and low strike rates (see, e.g., Korpi and Shalev, 1980; Schmidt, 1982, 1988; Cameron, 1984). The 'politics of the virtuous circle' was evidently functioning successfully (Castles, 1978; Lange, 1984). This 'positive-sum' game provided enough incentives for all sides to remain committed to corporatist agreements. But economic contingencies affect the probability that a positive-sum outcome will be possible. Similarly, even where formal conditions appear to be favourable to such agreements, the relationships between unions and employers, unions and government, and employers and government, are contingent and subject to strategic calculations.

During the 1980s, it became increasingly apparent that the relationship between the level of wage bargaining and economic performance was not linear, as earlier analysts had argued, but rather follows a 'U-curve'. Steady growth and low levels of unemployment were not only evident in the centralised systems: they were also to be found in countries with weak and highly decentralised labour market organisations and fragmented collective bargaining arrangements, generally governed by parties of the right or centre-right (Garrett and Lange, 1985; Calmfors and Driffill, 1988; Paloheimo, 1991). The most prominent exemplar of this 'free-market' approach to growth and employment creation during the 1980s was the USA (Esping-Andersen, 1990: ch. 9).

One explanation of these alternative paths to successful economic performance can be found in Olson's (1982) analysis of the effects of organised labour on growth prospects. He suggests that where unions have relatively little power to disrupt market processes, employer responses to market signals can be swift, and changes in demand and in competitive conditions can easily be accommodated. If union density increases but unions are fragmented, each can pursue its own short-term advantage while disregarding the consequences for the rest of the economy; an individual union need not concern itself if its members' pay increase is passed on elsewhere as a price increase. The cumulative effect of a multitude of such decisions will, however, be highly disadvantageous at the aggregate level. But if union density is high, and unions have an effective means of co-ordinating their activities, the union leadership can take an overview of the consequences of union activities at the macroeconomic level. An 'encompassing' union organisation can devise a strategy to avoid the disruptive consequences of unions' disaggregated pursuit of their interests. Thus, according to this analysis, good economic performance would be expected both in countries in which unions were weak and ineffective and in countries in which they were strong and 'encompassing'.

On the opposite side of the 'U-curve' from countries following the free-market model during the 1980s were those with a co-ordinated approach to economic management. But there were in fact two clusters of countries featuring high levels of labour market co-ordination, of very different sorts. Austria, Sweden, and Norway were all characterised by strong and centralised trade union organisations, and large Social Democratic parties in parliament (though not always in government). Their experiences correspond most clearly to Olson's analysis of the role of 'encompassing' union organisations. A second cluster, however, comprised Japan and Switzerland, (and Germany, though its higher levels of unemployment during the 1980s remove it somewhat from the 'pole' of successful economic performance). These cases reveal a very different means of providing co-ordination in industrial relations institutions, labour market policies, and pay determination processes. Organised labour is not a strong actor at the centralised or national level, but is integrated into policy-making and wage formation at lower levels in a variety of ways (Therborn, 1986; Soskice, 1990, 1991).

None of this is to suggest that either the decentralised or the centralised models were without their own difficulties. The US model encountered increasing problems in employment generation and fiscal stability during the 1980s, and a variety of unsolved 'public goods' problems in social provision, through its pursuit of market-based solutions. On the other hand, most of the centralised systems encountered limits to the effectiveness of planning under the changed economic conditions. The prospect of EC economic integration impelled several countries which were not members of the EC, including Sweden, Norway, and Austria, to reorient their own economic policies to cope with the new situation. Greater mobility of labour and capital, 'harmonisation' of tax systems, and fixed exchange rates made it far more difficult for domestic economic strategies to function independently of trends in other countries. By 1990, Sweden and Norway had aligned their currencies with the European Monetary System, and Sweden and Austria had applied for EC membership. Whether or not centralised systems would continue to be the dominant strategies in these countries remained an open question, but the preferences of the Swedish employers had shifted decisively towards decentralised and market-based solutions.[5] Furthermore, in many western countries, electoral considerations were weakening the relationships which parties of the left had previously cultivated with organised labour (Peterson, 1987; Hall, 1990).[6]

[5] See 'Business plans five-year campaign to end Swedish economic model', *Financial Times*, 8 November, 1990.
[6] The Spanish Prime Minister, Felipe Gonzalez, was reported to have commented with relief on the unions' breach with the party, as parties of the left all over Europe needed to 'recover their autonomy'. Interview, *Financial Times*, 17 December, 1990.

Nevertheless, the curvilinear relationship between bargaining systems and economic performance crystallises the problem faced by countries with 'intermediate' arrangements, whose economic performance has been generally poor: it is not clear in which direction change would most improve their performance. Ireland can be taken as 'intermediate' in this sense. It has relatively decentralised labour market institutions with 'some tendencies' to centralisation (Paloheimo, 1991: 120; cf. Roche, this volume). It has a political system in which the major parties do not divide on the conventional left–right spectrum, and the main parties have not typically evinced pro- or anti-labour strategies (see Mair, this volume).

The next section deals with the emergence of interest in centralised, corporatist pay agreements in Ireland during the 1970s, and investigates the reasons why, by 1981, all sides had come to believe that their usefulness had been exhausted. The subsequent section analyses the Programme for National Recovery (PNR) of 1987 and the Programme for Economic and Social Progress (PESP) of 1991. It discusses whether anything fundamental had changed in the attitudes and commitments of each side, and evaluates the prospects for agreements of this kind becoming central and stable elements of national policy.

The Politicisation of Collective Bargaining in the 1970s

The move toward centralised pay agreements in Ireland, as elsewhere, arose from the problems of economic growth. A strike wave in the late 1960s developed for reasons similar to those which obtained in several other European countries: economic growth and tighter labour markets facilitated a shift of power to the workplace level of organisation (Crouch and Pizzorno eds., 1978, vol. 1). In the Irish case, craft workers' pay rates exercised a 'leadership' role which intensified wage pressures and heightened industrial militancy (McCarthy, 1973; McCarthy *et al.*, 1975).

The National Wage Agreements (NWAs) of 1970 to 1978 were not negotiated primarily to facilitate the macroeconomic management of inflation, unemployment and growth. The objectives were to negotiate increases in employee incomes in a more orderly way than hitherto, to provide a mechanism for dispute settlement, and to keep government out of direct involvement in pay determination. The trade union negotiators were mandated to take as their central objective the protection of living standards through pay compensation, particularly during the years of high inflation in the mid-1970s, following the oil price crisis.[7] The centrally-agreed norm also permitted increases above the norm to be sought, on certain conditions, through local bargaining: the NWAs were 'two-tier' agreements from the outset (O'Brien, 1981; Hardiman, 1988).

Governments became more interested in the terms of the agreements in the course of the 1970s. They wished to exercise a direct influence on the terms of the public service pay bill. But in addition, the centralised pay agreements came to assume considerable importance for their own macro-economic objectives, first during the oil-price crisis and then during the international recovery of the later part of the decade. The first cautious attempts to influence pay norms through tax concessions were made by the Fine Gael–Labour coalition, in 1975 and 1977. But a much more overt proposal linking budgetary concessions with pay outcomes was made by the Fianna Fáil government in 1978. The National Understandings of 1979 and 1980 represented the culmination of this expanded bargaining agenda. Both involved some tax concessions to employees and a range of government spending commitments on employment, health, education and other matters, in addition to the public and private sector pay agreements (see Roche, 1982).

However, by 1981 all sides took the view that the agreements had not worked to their advantage. Wage drift had grown to proportions which the private sector employers held were no longer sustainable (cf. Fogarty et al., 1981). Moreover, by the late 1970s the growing incidence of industrial conflict had further reduced the attractiveness of the agreements (Hardiman, 1988: ch. 4). Considerable political pressure had been brought to bear on the private sector employers to agree to the terms of the second National Understanding in 1980, but after it expired, they withdrew altogether from any further negotiations.

A significant source of discontent for employers and employees alike was the growing 'tax wedge' between real and disposable income. The tax base of the economy had remained narrow, because industrial policy required company taxation to be relatively light, and agricultural interests and the self-employed constituted powerful traditional lobbies against attempts to extend the reach of the tax system. Despite reform at the margin, the tax system came to rely ever more heavily on employees during the 1970s, as rapid nominal pay increases drew more and more into the tax net (Hardiman, 1988: ch. 4; Breen et al., 1990: ch. 4). The tax burden

---

[7] Ruaidhri Roberts (ICTU) cited a typical comment on ICTU's bargaining policy in the mid-1970s, reflecting the lack of economic sophistication among many union activists: 'Let's go for a really big wage increase this time, one so big that inflation just can't catch up with it' (in interview in 1983).

had itself become an object of employee dissatisfaction, occasioning massive street protests in 1979. Employers in turn increasingly held tax rates reponsible for stimulating excessive pay demands. Although grievances arising from the tax structure risked undermining continued support for the centralised pay agreements, problems in public finance by the end of the 1970s made significant reductions very difficult.[8]

By the early 1980s, government found itself facing heavy public spending commitments, and a sizeable fiscal deficit, much of it financed by increased foreign borrowing (Hardiman, 1988: ch. 4). The increased borrowing and spending undertaken by the Coalition government in the mid-1970s had largely been brought under control by 1977 (OECD, 1982: 38). The public spending commitments undertaken by Fianna Fáil proved far more difficult to curb, and the fiscal deficits thus generated were to dog successive governments during the 1980s.

What, then, went wrong? The pay agreements had appeared to develop into a classic form of 'concertation' whereby the outcomes of pay determination were negotiated to complement macroeconomic objectives. Yet these agreements did not become successful 'class compromises'. Four factors may be identified to account for this. First, employers' interests were diverse and difficult to co-ordinate effectively. Secondly, the trade union leadership faced organisational difficulties in any attempt to advance collective, 'class-wide' interests. Thirdly, the cleavage structure of the party system made it difficult for governments, under conditions of fiscal expansion, to establish firm policy priorities. Fourthly, the structure of the economy itself cast doubt on the credibility of a strategy of employment growth through wage regulation agreements.

Employer diversity

The employers' main concerns were to secure wage costs consistent with the requirements of competitiveness, and to minimise the incidence of industrial conflict. But the changing nature of the Irish economy limited their ability to take a common line.

The principal feature which differentiated the Irish economy from other small economies with a longer experience of stable wage regulation agreements was the rapid development during the 1970s of a foreign-owned sector of manufacturing. This was concentrated in the most modernised, developed, and export-oriented industries (NESC, 1982,

---

[8] The tax wedge continued to worsen: between 1979 and 1983, real after-tax wages of the average employee fell by 15 per cent, while real labour costs to firms rose by 12 per cent (OECD, 1989a: 46).

1983; O'Malley, 1989 and this volume). Increasingly, Irish manufacturing industry was becoming differentiated between an older, often labour-intensive sector, largely indigenously-owned, and a newer, more capital-intensive and predominantly foreign-owned sector. The traditional industries suffered most heavily with the onset of recession, and wage costs were clearly of considerable significance to them. But the companies in the foreign-owned sector generally tended to be capital- rather than labour-intensive, so pay costs represented a lower proportion of their total costs. The export-oriented, mainly foreign-owned sector also tended to be far more profitable than the domestic productive sector (O'Hearn, 1989: Table 11, 592). This increased the incentives to employees in these firms to seek ways to improve their relative pay position through additional workplace bargaining.[9] Many firms, especially in the foreign-owned sector, were willing to make additional payments to skilled labour in excess of the basic terms of the pay agreements. This counteracted the compression of differentials which the basic provisions of the pay agreements alone would have effected (cf. Fogarty *et al.*, 1981: 16).

Foreign-owned companies were also likely to have a weaker interest in, or long-term commitment to, employer solidarity than Irish-owned companies. In a survey undertaken for the IDA in 1984,[10] foreign-owned firms were found to be almost as likely as Irish-owned to be members of an employers' association, but almost all of them conducted their bargaining as individual companies rather than as part of a group (only one-third of Irish-owned companies did so); they were also significantly more likely to use their membership of the employers' association for information only. In these cases, the most the FUE (Federated Union of Employers; Federation of Irish Employers, or FIE, from 1989) could do was to encourage these firms to make additional payments in ways that would not involve too transparent a breach of the terms of the centralised agreements.[11]

Such differences among employers therefore made it difficult for them

[9] It would not be correct, though, to assume that the 'modern', largely foreign-owned sector, always pays the highest wages. Other factors such as the structure of the workforce are also relevant. For example, electronics, health care products, textiles, and clothing have a high proportion of female assembly-type workers, and wages are at or below the average for industry. The drink, chemicals, and pharmaceuticals industries have relatively high average wages: they are highly capital-intensive and have a higher proportion of technical and other skilled workers (cf. O'Hearn, 1989: 592–3).

[10] *Survey of Employee/Industrial Relations in Irish Private Sector Manufacturing Industry,* conducted for the Industrial Development Authority, Autumn 1984.

[11] Dan McAuley, former FUE Director General, stated in interview in 1983 that American companies would 'run a mile' if they thought the FUE was trying to influence their in-house industrial relations.

to devise a common strategy on pay policy (cf. also Hardiman, 1988: ch. 6). Furthermore, many FUE member companies were ill-prepared for two-tier bargaining. Collective bargaining prior to the 1970s had involved more multi-employer or industry-level bargaining, especially in the industries producing for the domestic sector. The centralised agreements increased the volume of claims advanced at firm- or plant-level, and many employers found it difficult in the circumstances to resist them. The private sector employers lacked the co-ordination to establish the pay agreements on terms more favourable to their own interests.

Problems of trade union co-ordination

A number of the characteristics of the Irish Congress of Trade Unions (ICTU) diminished its scope for authoritative policy-making. The pecularities of the early development of the trade union movement gave it contours which would, under any circumstances, render it difficult to devise a common, collective strategy (cf. Roche, this volume). Pre-independence Ireland already had a trade union structure on the British model before it had very much of an industrial base at all (McCarthy, 1977). The Irish trade union movement included craft unions, general unions, public sector unions, and quasi-industrial unions. The unions' organisational fragmentation was reduced somewhat during the 1970s and 1980s[12] But the legacy of British patterns of decentralised organisation and collective bargaining, combined with a permissive legislative system in industrial relations, meant that the capacity of ICTU to articulate 'class-wide' interests and to devise collective strategies was always limited.

Furthermore, trade unions which had their head-offices in Britain continued to organise Irish members in post-independence Ireland. The division between British-based and Irish-based unions overlapped, to some extent, with a division in unions' ideological orientation to collective bargaining and relations with government. Though there were exceptions, the Irish-based unions tended to favour a pragmatic approach to negotiations with government, while the British-based unions tended to be deeply attached to a workplace focus of collective bargaining, and were particularly opposed to any form of incomes policy (see, e.g., McCarthy, 1977: 578–9; Roche, this volume). The latter group of unions, along with some Irish-based, mainly craft unions, constituted a recurrent problem for the union leadership, because they opposed all moves towards centralised bargaining. They were motivated by ideological disdain for pay

---

[12] There were 95 trade unions in 1970, 75 in 1985, and 69 in 1989. See Roche this volume.

negotiations with the state, or by economic self-interest (since they organised among the more highly-paid employees), or by both considerations.

During the 1970s, changes in the employee workforce introduced new divisions of interest into the union movement. First, the growth of new industries, as outlined above, differentiated the interests of employees in manufacturing. Crouch (1991, 1992) has suggested that unions in the exposed, competitive sector of the economy are crucial for the development of union commitment to corporatist pay agreements. But employees in this sector in Ireland could scarcely be expected to play such a role. Employees in the exporting sector were not organised in a single union or bloc of unions, comparable, say, to the metal-workers' unions in some other European countries. Employees in manufacturing in both the foreign-owned and domestic-owned sectors tended to be organised by the same unions.

Secondly, during the 1970s employment increased steadily in services and especially in the public sector (Conniffe and Kennedy, 1984: 261). This contributed to the steady increase in white-collar trade union membership (Roche and Larragy, 1989). More than seventy unions were affiliated by ICTU by the mid-1980s, and by then about half of all trade unions had a membership confined wholly or mainly to the public sector (Cox and Hughes, 1989). These unions steadily gained in influence within ICTU but, more significantly for pay policy, public sector employees were also organised by a wide range of other unions—craft unions, and the big general unions—which were not primarily public sector unions. It was estimated that, by the mid-1980s, at least half of the country's trade union members were public sector employees, and that only about fifteen unions had no public sector members (Cox and Hughes, 1989). This helped to prevent conflicts of interest between different categories of employee from being expressed as clashes between discrete organisations; but at the same time it made it difficult for unions to establish clear priorities between the diverse interests of their memberships. In attempting to generate any strongly centralised strategy, the senior officers of ICTU had no independent base of support. The Executive Council comprised trade union leaders who were subject to a variety of particularistic pressures emanating from their own membership, and focused on pay and pay-related benefits. Thus, with no real opportunity for constructing an overarching, collective definition of economic interests, ICTU had little option during the 1970s but to press for the widest scope for two-tier bargaining.[13] The 'vectors' of divergent interests were therefore crucial in shaping the priorities adopted (see Hardiman, 1988: ch. 5).

---

[13] Ruaidhri Roberts, in interview in 1983.

Political commitment to pay agreements

The Irish political system, lacking the articulation of class or distributive issues in party organisation, facilitates the formulation of concertative strategies in some of the ways suggested earlier. The largest party, Fianna Fáil, has consistently drawn significant cross-class support; and the alternative of a Fine Gael–Labour coalition, which formed governments in the mid-1970s and between 1982 and 1987, also had a cross-class support profile, though rather different in kind (Chubb, 1982; Mair, 1987 and this volume). The commitment first by the Coalition government and later by Fianna Fáil to support a form of social partnership with wage negotiation at its core fulfils one of the conditions specified above for effective concertation.

However, the nature of that commitment deserves further scrutiny. As Mair in his paper below shows, awareness of distributive conflicts is widespread in Irish society but the party system tends to blur its articulation. Coalition governments of Fine Gael and Labour have been characterised by cross-cutting priorities of economic liberalism and social welfare. However, the contradictions within Fianna Fáil have been of greater significance for the fortune of wage regulation agreements. Its cross-class electoral support and its ideology of national interest and national unity have disposed it more strongly than the Coalition governments to seek support from, and co-operation with, all sections of Irish society (Chubb, 1982: ch. 6; Bew *et al.*, 1989; Lee, 1989). And although trade unions' political affiliation, where they have any, is to the Labour Party, trade union leaders recognise that Labour's influence, when in government, is not great. Links between sections of the trade union movement and the Fianna Fáil party are strong, and influential union leaders have attached greater significance to their relations with Fianna Fáil than to those with any other party (Hardiman, 1988: ch. 7; Bew *et al.*, 1989: ch. 4).

Fianna Fáil's own vaunted freedom from ideological commitments disposes it to adopt a relatively short time-scale in its approach to mediating distributive conflict. This feature is not unique to Fianna Fáil (nor indeed to Irish democratic politics). But the content of such short-term calculations is further moulded by an electoral system which encourages localism and particularism at the expense of a sense of national priorities (Carty, 1981).

The role of the pay agreements in mediating adjustment to the shocks of inflation and unemployment, particularly in 1975 and 1976, was generally deemed positive. Indeed, the incoming Fianna Fáil government of 1977 was prepared to approve the centralised agreements more overtly than its predecessors. But this political support for continued centralised bargaining itself added a new element to employer and trade union expectations. The trade union movement came to see the growing involvement of government in the process, particularly that of the Fianna Fáil government, as providing an additional forum for pursuing gains on issues under the direct control of government. The degree to which fiscal concessions were seriously conditional upon the level of pay increase in the agreement had never been clear, though trade union negotiators understood that an element of give-and-take was required in the (confidential) negotiations. But by the end of the decade, the unions were aware of the *political* importance which government attached to securing agreements, and knew that once pay terms were not too far above the limits indicated, government was very unlikely to rescind its offers. A senior trade union leader, centrally involved in the negotiations of the period, commented in retrospect that for a while during the National Understandings, ICTU exercised 'a lot of clout—more than it should have been able to'; and that where this happens in bargaining situations, 'what is implied is ineptitude on the part of the other side'.[14]

Fianna Fáil has at various times evinced a pragmatic commitment to containing and absorbing conflicts, and to finding ways of accommodating discontent without alienating important constituencies of support. But this characteristic of its electoral strategy contributed to what came to be seen as the excessively high political and economic cost of achieving the last two centralised agreements of the 1970s.

The structure of the economy

The scope for government to exercise significant control over economic performance was limited, most obviously so in the areas of inflation and unemployment (Hardiman, 1988: chs. 2, 4). Government's capacity to control inflation was restricted by the openness of the economy and its close trade links with Britain, and by the parity which was maintained between the Irish pound and sterling until 1979. These factors meant that Irish inflation levels were heavily dependent on those obtaining in Britain.

From the trade union side, one of the essential elements of concertative wage agreements, the assurance that wage restraint would improve longer-term employment prospects, was particularly uncertain in the Irish case. Industrial growth was heavily based on attracting foreign investment. This

---

[14] Ruaidhri Roberts, in interview in 1983. Another senior trade union leader commented that negotiating public service pay increases in 1980–81 was like 'pushing at an open door, with a smiling Taoiseach sitting behind an open coffer asking, how much do you want?'.

strategy of 'dependent' development meant that there was no guarantee that the economic benefits of wage restraint would translate into domestic investment (O'Hearn, 1989; O'Malley, 1989). Trade union scepticism regarding the commitment of foreign industry to the Irish economy deepened during the 1970s as evidence accumulated of the extensive repatriation of profits to the overseas parent companies.[15]

It also seemed evident to the unions that tax incentives were more important than pay levels in attracting direct inward investment. Industrial policy was based on providing attractive corporate tax rates, grants, and a variety of allowances and tax expenditures to attract direct foreign investment and to boost an export orientation. This resulted in relatively heavy employee taxes which implicitly disfavoured employment-intensive investment. The relative prices of capital and labour were distorted, to labour's disadvantage, throughout the 1970s (OECD, 1979: 37). There was, therefore, a degree of tension between pay policy and employment creation policy which governments found it difficult to manage convincingly. Governments could argue that in the absence of pay agreements, job creation prospects would be worsened. But it appeared to the unions that the connections between pay restraint and employment expansion were very tenuous. Public sector job creation could alleviate unemployment to some degree, but it became increasingly clear in the late 1970s that this entailed excessive fiscal costs.

In sum, although many of the conditions impelling the 'social partners' towards concertative agreements were present in Ireland during the 1970s, there were also powerful reasons why the agreements did not develop as successful elements of a macroeconomic 'virtuous circle'. In this light, the shift away from centralised collective bargaining between 1981 and 1987 was relatively unsurprising. Fiscal crisis left no scope for government interest in concertation agreements (Roche, 1989). High and rising unemployment limited trade union militancy. The employers' associations provided strong support for a more vigorous approach to company-level bargaining. In Ireland, as elsewhere in western Europe (Streeck, 1990), this did not necessarily mean overt hostility to trade unions or a radical revision of collective bargaining arrangements. Some issues, such as the introduction of new technology, increased responsibility, and task flexibility, required greater employee involvement in work processes and could only be negotiated effectively at company level. During these years,

---

[15] 'The size of profit repatriation by foreign-owned companies significantly affects the current external balance'; in 1977 it amounted to 2.5 per cent of GNP; this had risen to 10.5 per cent by 1988. (OECD, 1989a: 41).

however, ICTU found itself fragmented in its organisation and in its pay negotiation functions, and unable to influence the apparently inexorable rise in unemployment. From this chastening experience, and from a determination to avoid the fate of political irrelevance which had overtaken the British trade union movement, a new approach to trade union strategy was developed. But it needed the return to government of Fianna Fáil in 1987 to give it effect.

The Centralised Agreements of the 1980s

Both the Programme for National Recovery (PNR) and the Programme for Economic and Social Progress (PESP), like the earlier National Understandings, may be seen as 'concertative' agreements. The most obvious difference from the earlier agreements, though, was the economic climate in which they were negotiated. The enormous fiscal problems of the 1980s, and rising unemployment and emigration, left little room for manoeuvre. This time the trade unions' bargaining strength was weaker, and employers and government alike were working within much tighter constraints.

Both the PNR and PESP involved three-year phased pay agreements —a longer term than any that had been negotiated during the 1970s. The PNR, negotiated in October 1987, consisted of two parallel pay agreements, one for the public and another for the private sector, which averaged out at approximately 2.5 per cent per annum. The private sector agreement (though not the public sector one) ruled out any additional cost-increasing claims, to avoid the re-emergence of two-tier bargaining.[16] On the government side, spending commitments were restricted to employee tax relief. Public spending was cut sharply in the following budget, in line with government commitments and with the support of all parties to the PNR, in order to reduce the ratio of public debt to GNP and to make progress towards further reducing the fiscal deficit. Only in this way, it was argued, could economic recovery begin and employment prospects improve.

When the PNR was due to expire, it was initially unclear to the employers or to government that a second agreement on similar terms would be obtainable, in view of the economic improvement already under way. In the event, an agreement was reached in January 1991 for a pay agreement averaging approximately 4.8 per cent per annum over three years.[17] The union side pressed for some element of local bargaining in

[16] For details, see e.g. *Irish Times*, 10 October, 1987.
[17] For details, see e.g. *Irish Times*, 16 January, 1991.

this agreement; employers conceded limited rights. This agreement, like the PNR, was developed as the central element of a broader government economic plan. The PESP involved tax concessions and further government commitments to spending on social welfare, education, and health.

Several aspects of the PNR and PESP mark them off from the agreements of the 1970s. First, a firmer consensus on the problems of the economy appeared to have been reached during the mid-1980s, which might be seen as improving the stability of any ensuing neo-corporatist arrangements (cf. Armingeon, 1986). Secondly, although it is too soon at the time of writing to draw any firm conclusions about the PESP, the PNR received a positive evaluation across a relatively broad spectrum of opinion. How much, then, one may ask, has really changed since the 1970s, and how stable are these agreements likely to be in the altered economic circumstances of the 1980s and early 1990s?

The economic analysis which underlay the PNR originated with an influential report produced by the tripartite consultative body, the National Economic and Social Council (NESC). Through the involvement of all the major economic interests and of government representatives, that body had functioned during the mid-1980s as never before as a forum for discussing the economic crisis, particularly the crisis in the public finances, and the political options for tackling it. The NESC report, *A Strategy For Recovery* (November, 1986), was explicitly intended as a consensual statement; no minority, dissenting opinion was appended. There was no mention of pay policy in the report, but it identified the central problems of the Irish economy which would need to be addressed. Although it had been commissioned by the Coalition government, it was widely perceived as non-party document.

The advent to power of Fianna Fáil in 1987 was crucial to the possibility of a return to centralised pay bargaining. While still in opposition, Fianna Fáil had proposed building on the NESC consensus; it had incorporated proposals for a tripartite agreement in its election manifesto, and had given priority to the negotiation of the PNR upon taking office. Fine Gael had made it clear while in government (with the Labour Party) between 1982 and 1987 that it did not intend to diminish the distance it had imposed between the trade union movement and government.[18]

The performance of the economy during the three years of the PNR was considerably better than that of the preceding few years. The strategy

---

[18] In his memoirs, ex-Taoiseach Garrett Fitzgerald commented that 'Meetings with ICTU were formal, often tense, and on the whole unproductive throughout our term' (Fitzgerald, 1991: 454).

of the PNR was summarised by an influential economic commentator as one of 'deflationary expansion' (McAleese, 1990). The current Budget deficit was brought sharply down, and Exchequer borrowing was reduced.[19] Tax expenditures were a central part of the PNR strategy, and government spent approximately three times the amount originally committed in budgetary tax relief, targeted primarily at the PAYE sector.[20] The debt-to-GNP ratio had been reduced from 130 per cent in 1987 to about 123 per cent by the end of 1989, with prospects of further reduction.[21] Of the industrial countries which started the decade with sizeable fiscal deficits, Ireland was one of the worst placed; yet by 1990 it ranked second only to Denmark in the size of the transformation which had been accomplished (McAleese, 1990). Both interest rates and inflation had been held below the EC average during the second half of the decade, an unusual experience for Ireland. Despite the severe retrenchment in public spending, growth increased each year between 1987 and 1990. Improved levels of confidence in economic performance permitted producers and exporters to take advantage of an upturn in international economic conditions.

Of greater immediate significance for the trade union movement, real disposable incomes actually increased somewhat between 1987 and 1990, through a combination of negotiated pay increases and tax concessions, following the years of real pay decline earlier in the decade.[22] Estimates of the figures involved have varied, depending on the assumptions made, but the tripartite PNR Central Review Committee estimated that, whereas average earnings had fallen by between 8 and 10 per cent between 1980 and 1987, they had increased by between 4 and 9 per cent between 1988 and 1990.[23] And although unemployment remained very high, at around

[19] The current Budget deficit fell from 8.3 per cent of GNP in 1986, and 6.5 per cent in 1987, to 1.7 per cent in 1988 and 1.3 per cent in 1989. Exchequer borrowing declined from 12.8 per cent in 1986, and 9.9 per cent in 1987, to 3.3 per cent in 1988 and 2.3 per cent in 1989 (McAleese, 1990: Table 2).
[20] Between 1988 and 1990, the standard rate of income tax was reduced from 35 per cent to 30 per cent, and the top rate from 58 per cent to 56 per cent, allowances were increased, and the (hitherto very narrow) bands for the standard and 48 per cent rates were broadened.
[21] PNR Central Review Committee, *Progress Report*, February, 1990: 20.
[22] This contrasted with the terms of the centralised agreement negotiated by the Finnish centre-right government in November 1991, which involved a two-year pay freeze as part of a package of measures to deal with economic crisis.
[23] The *Quarterly Report* of the Monitoring Unit of the Department of Labour, July–September 1989, similarly estimated that during 1988 and 1989, increases in real take-home pay for those on average earnings and average male earnings ranged from 3 per cent to 7 per cent.

18 per cent, it was estimated that employment had increased by some 30,000 between April, 1987 and April, 1989.[24]

The low inflation and low interest rates of the late 1980s not only increased the real value of the pay agreement to employees, but did so in a way that did not impose costs on the private sector employers. Over the course of the PNR, in contrast with the 1970s, the share of profits in national income increased and that of employees' wages and salaries decreased.[25] The private sector employers had been slow to become involved in centralised processes again, particularly in view of the 'irrationality' of the terms on which the second National Understanding had been concluded.[26] They only became involved when it was clear that a headline-setting public sector agreement was imminent. They insisted that second-tier bargaining should be prohibited for the duration of the agreement. Once the union negotiators had accepted this, the employers were persuaded that there were real advantages to be gained from the PNR.

Their willingness to support the PNR is further explained by the fact that the outcomes of decentralised collective bargaining between 1980 and 1987 had not been altogether to their satisfaction. The incidence of additional cost-increasing claims had been reduced, and industrial militancy was depressed by unemployment and recession. But nominal wage increases were less flexible than they wished: competitiveness was protected by exchange rate movements more than by pay developments.[27] In contrast, competitiveness improved markedly between 1987 and 1990, as hourly earnings in common currency declined in 1988 and 1989 and unit wage costs fell even more dramatically.[28] Unlike in the 1970s, those

---

[24] PNR Central Review Committee *Progress Report*, February 1990. The rate of employment gain was expected to be 13,000 in 1990. Notified redundancies in 1989 were 13,400, but this was the lowest since 1979 and over 40 per cent lower than in 1988. The Department of Labour *Annual Report*, 1989, reported that the average rate of unemployment for 1989 was 17.9 per cent, compared with an average of 18.4 per cent in 1988. Net outward emigration was 27,000 in 1986/87, 32,000 in 1987/88, 46,000 in 1988/89, but was forecast, on the basis of ESRI data, to decline by about 20,000 between April 1989 and April 1991 (*Annual Report*, 1989: 18).

[25] Paul Tansey, 'The negotiations will really be a struggle for economic power', *Sunday Tribune*, 11 November 1990.

[26] This and other comments in this paragraph are drawn from an interview with John Dunne (FIE).

[27] Gross hourly earnings in Ireland rose by three-quarters between 1980 and 1985, and by less than half in competitor countries; productivity gains and a recovery in sterling in relation to the punt reduced the loss of competitiveness expressed in terms of common-currency unit wage costs (see Hardiman, 1988: 219–21).

[28] Hourly earnings in common currency, (1980 = 100), stood at 116 in 1986 and 115 in 1987, but 111 in 1988 and 107 in 1989. Unit wage costs stood at 85 in 1986, 77 in 1987, 68 in 1988, 63 in 1989 (McAleese, 1990: Table 2).

in stronger market positions did not engage extensively in additional bargaining 'above the odds', visible in the forms of wage drift. Some pay increases above the terms established by the PNR were indeed negotiated, especially in industries such as pharmaceuticals, chemicals, and electronics.[29] But the national pay terms evidently exercised a dominant influence on pay movements, and senior officers of the FIE reported that when account was taken of increased output and extra overtime, the extent of wage drift was actually very small.[30] The relatively low levels of wage drift were attributed to managers' experiences during the earlier years of the 1980s when they 'learned how to manage again'.[31] Strike levels fell over this period to their lowest in many years.

However, the successes of the PNR owed a great deal to the improvement in the international economy in the late 1980s.[32] Many of the underlying problems which had created difficulties for the agreements of the 1970s were still in evidence. The stability and durability of pay agreements were not yet assured. In what follows, the aim is not to attempt to predict the eventual outcome of the PESP in any detail, but rather to consider the various factors which might tend either to strengthen or to weaken the prospects of corporatist pay agreements in Ireland.

Tensions within the trade union movement

During the 1980s, influential trade union leaders increasingly saw a return to the national stage as their only hope of escaping organisational decline. In the context of falling membership and increasing unemployment, one union leader had commented that: 'The trade union movement can hardly now be called a movement; it is more a loose federation of organisations

---

[29] The surveys of pay developments by the Central Statistics Office and the Department of Labour Monitoring Unit make this clear. While actual real take-home pay was estimated to have increased by between 3 and 7 per cent during 1988 and 1989, it would have increased by between 1 and 5 per cent for those receiving only the standard increases.

[30] Interviews with John Dunne and Gerry Dempsey (FIE). Jim O'Brien, a director of FIE, estimated that the first phase of the pay agreement was applied as written in 85 per cent of agreements and to 74 per cent of employees. 'Only 3 per cent of the 1000 agreements analysed by FUE differed from the PNR for no apparent reason—and these involved only 1.5 per cent of employees in the sample of 433,516 employees covered by the analysis. All in all this was an unparalleled degree of commitment to what was, in essence, a modest three year pay agreement' (O'Brien, 1989: 146).

[31] Interview with John Dunne (FIE).

[32] For a sceptical view of the role of the PNR in economic recovery up to 1990, and a distinctly negative prognosis for the PESP, see, for example, Durkan (1991); also Sean Barrett, 'A Case of National Misunderstanding', *Business and Finance*, 24 January, 1991.

each dismally engaged in pursuing sectional interests'.[33] The trade union movement had therefore to take part in any stabilisation and recovery strategy, 'if it was not to be seen as part of the problem rather than as part of its solution'.[34] The leadership of ICTU also took the view that unemployment was primarily a political issue, one which would not be remedied without political intervention (ICTU, 1984)—an unlikely prospect in the mid-1980s. The need to develop a credible policy on this issue became pressing as unemployment worsened.[35] The clear implication of these reflections was that a more calculated political presence and policies with a longer time-scale would be the only way to remain viable as a collective voice.[36]

Many union leaders increasingly looked to other west European countries for their models, a tendency strengthened by ICTU's increased involvement with the European Trade Union Confederation (ETUC), arising particularly from debates over the EC's Social Charter. An ICTU policy document (1990) stated that:

> The overall aim of the long-term strategy should be the development of a modern efficient social market economy in Ireland similar to Germany—a market economy, with regulations on competition, company law and consumer rights with regulations that bite, low levels of unemployment and a high level of social protection. In devising the strategy we should also learn from the achievements of small open economies such as Austria, Denmark and Finland which have more developed economies, higher living standards and lower unemployment than Ireland. These they achieved through National Programmes agreed centrally but implemented with a high level of worker participation and involvement at the level of the individual company.

However, the trade union movement continued to be characterised by the diversity of interests discussed earlier. Some rationalisation of trade unions occurred during the 1980s, the most significant merger being that between the two largest general unions in 1990.[37] The resulting union,

---

[33] Phil Flynn (general secretary, LGPSU), at the ICTU Annual Delegate Conference, July 1985.
[34] Interview with Peter Cassells (ICTU).
[35] ICTU leaders may also have seen other pragmatic reasons for developing their policies on this matter: 'The poverty lobby and the Catholic Church have become a real thorn in the government's side. They could do horrendous damage to the unions if they can make ICTU look like a pressure-group for the employed only. The PNR keeps up our profile on the issues of poverty and unemployment'. Interview with Bill Attley (SIPTU).
[36] See, for example, ICTU (1989); also 'A Programme for Economic and Social Development', in ICTU (1990). On changed views on trade union legislation and privatisation, see ICTU *Executive Council Report*, 1990, p. 70.
[37] These were the Irish Transport and General Workers' Union (ITGWU) and the Federated Workers' Union of Ireland (FWUI), both of which had been founded by Jim Larkin.

SIPTU, comprised over 40 per cent of all union members affiliated to ICTU. But ICTU remained constrained by the limited authority it could exercise over its constituent unions, and by the diversity of interests represented within individual unions. Debates within the trade union movement in the course of the PNR, and preceding the negotiation of the PESP, revealed the fragility of the consensus achieved under the PNR. Trade union members tended to evaluate it primarily in terms of how well it performed in securing protection for living standards and reductions in tax levels, and greater equity in social and health services. The fall in inflation levels gave a fillip to the defenders of the agreement and mollified many of those who had been critical of what it had delivered. But the international upturn of the later 1980s could not have been foreseen; senior trade union leaders had initially been very cautious in their estimation of the durability of the pay settlement.[38]

At ICTU delegate conferences from 1987 on, approximately 60 per cent of delegates have supported the centralised agreements, and up to 40 per cent have opposed them, out of a combination of principled opposition and calculated attempts to put pressure on government. This is much the same pattern as was evident during the 1970s (Hardiman, 1988: ch. 5). Trade union leaders accepted that this was likely to continue to be the case, and concentrated on securing as much of the majority vote as possible.[39]

The core of organised challenge to ICTU's strategy continued to reside in the minority of trade unions, largely composed of British-based unions and some Irish-based craft unions, which still opposed any departure from 'free collective bargaining' as a matter of principle.[40] The unions opposed to the PNR came close to embarrassing the ICTU strategy severely, by forcing a Special Delegate Conference to be held in February 1990 to debate ICTU withdrawal from the PNR. The resolution discussed at the conference had taken the leadership of ICTU by surprise, and all its leadership resources were mobilised to secure its defeat. It was defeated, but by a close margin.[41] The level of dissatisfaction with government policy expressed by many other union representatives revealed the highly conditional nature of support for the PNR.

[38] 'Most of us were surprised at the speed with which things improved. We had thought it would take a minimum of three years to make a dent in the economic situation. We had wanted to take pay off the agenda for as long as that took'. Interview with Peter Cassells (ICTU).

[39] Interviews with Peter Cassells (ICTU), and Bill Attley (SIPTU).

[40] A leading figure in this group maintained that ICTU's role should be confined to *lobbying* on matters such as social policy, tax reforms, etc. Interview with Brian Anderson, MSF.

[41] See e.g. *Irish Times*, 6–9 February, 1990; *Business and Finance*, 15 February, 1990.

Divisions within the trade union movement, and indeed within individual unions, persisted during the 1980s, making it difficult for union leaders to establish clear priorities between the potentially conflicting interests of public sector employees and private sector employees, between those in the domestic and foreign-owned sectors, or between white-collar and blue-collar employees.

Public sector 'special' pay increases, recommended by the Arbitrator under the Conciliation and Arbitration Schemes (see Cox and Hughes, 1989), added significantly to total public expenditure during the 1980s. The PNR in 1987 and the PESP in 1991 both postponed the phasing-in of various 'special' increases, and limited the right to advance further claims. But in a situation where the public finances deteriorated, and these claims were further delayed, public service grievances could become acute. Public sector employees possess considerable disruptive power. During 1991, strikes in electricity supply, the postal services, and in public transport underlined once again the difficulties of trade union leaders in committing their members to pay agreements.[42]

The political factor

Fianna Fáil returned to (minority) government in 1987 with a consensus-based recovery plan. But the difficulties inherent in a cross-class approach to accommodating distributive conflict became more apparent in the years that followed.

The election of 1987 saw a shift of urban working-class support towards Fianna Fáil, in protest at the harshness of the measures proposed by the coalition (see Laver *et al.*, 1987). For Fianna Fáil, maintaining good relations with the trade union movement was a familiar element of its economic approach.[43] But although it had campaigned actively against the 'uncaring' Coalition and the hardships involved in public expenditure cuts, its own public spending cuts, especially in health, were greatly resented (Marsh and Sinnott, 1990). The election called in mid-1989, to try to gain an overall majority while the government's prospects still seemed good, revealed the depth of popular dissatisfaction (the same dissatisfaction voiced at ICTU's Special Delegate Conference in February 1990). Its

---

[42] See, for example, 'Programme in question after electricians' strike', *Irish Times*, 27 April, 1991. The power workers' strike accounted for 48 per cent of all days lost in strikes between January and September 1991.

[43] The leadership of ICTU also welcomed the opportunity to play a centre-stage role again: 'Before our first meeting with the Fianna Fáil government, we were like schoolboys, down in Raglan Road (ICTU head offices), all in good suits, delighted to be talking directly to the government again'. Interview with Bill Attley (SIPTU).

policies lost Fianna Fáil some measure of working-class support to both Labour and the Workers' Party. The 1989 election appeared to signal an emergent left-right division in the Irish political spectrum (see Gallagher *et al.*, 1990; Mair, this volume). Not only did Fianna Fáil once again fall short of an overall majority, but its claim to be the 'natural party of government' appeared to be at an end when it formed a coalition government with the Progressive Democrats (cf. Bew *et al.*, 1989).

However, if the party's electoral strategy was receiving a battering, its preference for consensus-based economic policies had not diminished. There were some signs in 1990–91 that, once again, the political primacy of securing an agreement could take priority over what might be considered economically desirable. The rate of reduction of the public borrowing requirement slowed, and public spending was given more rein. During the run-up to the negotiation of the PESP, the government made some advance concessions on public spending to secure the support of influential public sector unions (for example, to the teachers' unions). In the course of the pay talks, the private sector employers were understood to be under strong pressure from the Labour Minister, Bertie Ahern, and from the Taoiseach himself, to make further concessions in order to secure an agreement.[44]

It is as yet too soon to evaluate the outcome of the PESP. Nevertheless, the constraints on governments in the early 1990s have prevented the same recourse to the use of fiscal policy as in the late 1970s. During 1991, budgetary overruns impelled the Fianna Fáil-led government to propose not only to postpone the public sector 'special' increases due in the future, but to take the unusual step of limiting the amount eventually paid, on a tapered scale most favourable to the low-paid. Union protest was widely expected at what was interpreted as a breach of the agreement on the part of the government.[45] Early in 1992, a compromise seemed likely to be found whereby the scheduled increases would be deferred, but would be paid in full before the end of 1994; economic growth and a more buoyant economy were expected to ease budgetary problems by then. The union leadership sought a solution which would prevent the breakdown of the agreement; government made some gains in the timing of its budgetary problems, if not in their ultimate volume. The scope for an agreed

---

[44] See 'How a deal was struck', *Business and Finance*, 24 January 1991. The Minister for Labour was recognised as taking a strongly sympathetic view towards the trade union position on other matters, particularly employment: see 'Employers "owe it" to help generate jobs, says Ahern', *Sunday Tribune*, 19 November 1989.

[45] See, for example, 'Unions to meet on plans to fight pay negotiations', *Sunday Tribune*, 15 September 1991.

recognition of what the economy could sustain was greater in the early 1990s than it had been in the late 1970s.

The structure of the economy

The mechanisms through which pay restraint would translate into employment creation were as problematic in the 1980s and 1990s as they had been during the 1970s. A persistent problem in the Irish economy was that improvements in employment levels followed much more slowly than improvements in other economic indicators. The experience of 'jobless growth' was not confined to Ireland, but Ireland had little prospect of experiencing the strong and sustained levels of growth which would be needed to make an appreciable difference to employment levels. The tax system continued to constitute a serious obstacle to employment-creation, while the system of grant-aiding industry increasingly came under criticism; there was still little evidence of a coherent national strategy for job creation.[46] The widely publicised financial scandals during 1991 may also have made the need for pay restraint even less convincing to many employees. Cynicism about the meaning of the national interest, and the distribution of the sacrifices required to achieve it, was widespread. The 'social partners' had reached a consensual analysis of the problems of the national economy in 1986. But the difficulties of devising a credible and sustainable strategy on pay policy to address these problems, and one which would command sufficient support among the employee workforce, still seemed considerable by the early 1990s.

Conclusion

It was noted earlier that during the 1980s economic performance in terms of the main indicators of growth, inflation, and unemployment, appeared to show a U-shaped distribution in relation to the organisational centralisation of the major economic interests and the centralisation of collective bargaining. In its industrial relations system, Ireland is generally taken by commentators to be a 'decentralist country with some centralist tendencies'. Such cases may find they attract many of the disadvantages and few of the advantages of the two main alternative economic management options, the decentralised, liberal approach, and the centralised, corporatist approach.

---

[46] These points were made unambiguously in the report of the Industrial Policy Review Group, appointed by the government, entitled *A Time For Change: Industrial Policy for the 1990s*. See *Irish Times*, 11 January 1992.

In Ireland, governments have at various times tried to centralise the system of industrial relations. But the evidence would suggest that this solution is not firmly based. Certainly, the agreements of the 1970s did not work successfully as a mechanism for improving national economic performance. The PNR of 1987 was generally judged to have been successful—but so were the first few NWAs in the early 1970s. What remains uncertain is whether corporatist pay agreements may become more securely established in the future. No definite evaluation can yet be offered of the PESP and of the prospects of a successor to it. Nevertheless, many characteristics of Irish politics and society, and Irish economic structure, continue to make it difficult to predict with confidence the future of corporatist pay agreements.

As discussed earlier, the trade union movement finds it hard to establish priorities among the competing interests of its membership. The exporting sector has not been at all as firmly rooted into the domestic economy in Ireland as in those countries which have been the paradigm cases of corporatist pay policies. Employees in this sector do not constitute a distinct organisational bloc. The economic disciplines of centralised agreements are unlikely to come from conditions in the exposed manufacturing sector in Ireland.

Economic management strategy has not, to date, become sufficiently politicized in Ireland to generate support for an alternative, more thorough-going decentralised approach. But the difficulties of implementing stabilisation policies with trade union support became increasingly severe for a government seeking to maintain a centrist position. It is possible that a growing 'Europeanisation' of the Irish party system will in the future alter the terms of the debate on economic policy, and will propose a different set of costs and benefits related to corporatist pay agreements. But this remains no more than a possibility at present.

The experience of other countries suggests that where corporatist pay agreements are seen to produce successful economic outcomes, this reinforces and stabilises them. Sustained positive feed-back of this sort has yet to be seen in the Irish case. Special problems arise due to the distinctive structural features of the Irish economy and the nature of its industrialisation strategy. Nevertheless, on the evidence of the pragmatic adjustments to the changed domestic and international economic circumstances which has been evident in trade union thinking and in the leadership of the political parties since the mid-1980s, corporatist pay agreements could yet become more firmly established as part of the national 'policy repertoire' during the 1990s.

Proceedings of the British Academy, **79**, 359–381

Are Irish Parties Peculiar?

MICHAEL LAVER

University College Galway

Introduction

PEOPLE WHO WRITE about Irish politics sometimes describe Ireland as a rather peculiar sort of place, as something quite out of the European mainstream. This argument typically takes two forms.

The first has to do with Irish parties, and is based upon the assumption that the key features of Irish party politics have developed in response to social forces that are quite distinct from those to be found in the rest of western Europe. Symptoms of this are: the continued success of the two main parties, Fianna Fáil (the Soldiers of Destiny) and Fine Gael (the Tribe of the Gael), whose distinctive origins derive from the Civil War; the fact that these parties are difficult to classify according to any general western European schema of political party types; and the fact that policy differences between the main parties are small and ambiguous, so that party electoral appeals appear to play more upon traditional and enduring family loyalties than upon any sort of rational policy calculus.

The second type of argument about the peculiarity of Irish party politics is related to the first, and has to do with voting behaviour. Irish voters, it is claimed, simply do not behave like their European counterparts. Symptoms of this are: the fact that Irish voting patterns appear to be only weakly structured by social class; the fact that, despite the size of the Irish working class, Ireland has by far and away western Europe's weakest left.

In this paper I review these arguments, devoting by far the more attention to the alleged peculiarity of Irish parties. This argument is usually made rather informally in terms of party policies. The bulk of the paper presents some more systematic evidence on the role of policy in comparisons between the party systems of Ireland and the rest of western Europe. Before turning to this matter, however, I review very briefly the argument

Read 9 December 1990. © The British Academy 1992.

about the distinctiveness of Irish voting behaviour, an argument that has been much more extensively treated elsewhere.

The Social Bases of Party Choice

One of the first studies to compare patterns in Irish voting behaviour with patterns to be found elsewhere was produced by Whyte, author of the Irish chapter in Rose's edited volume *Electoral Behaviour: a Comparative Handbook* (1974). Using public opinion poll data from 1969, Whyte set everyone talking, in a phrase that spawned a thousand undergraduate essay titles, about 'politics without social bases'. This pithy epithet derived from the conclusion that there appeared to be very little difference in the social backgrounds of voters supporting different Irish parties. Writing several years later, Carty re-emphasised this line of argument in his book *Party and Parish Pump: Electoral Politics in Ireland*, with the claim that 'social characteristics do not structure voting behaviour in Ireland' (Carty, 1981: 24). The argument that Irish voters are peculiar was thus based upon the observation that, everywhere else in western Europe, there appeared to be much more difference in the social backgrounds of voters supporting different political parties.

In the past twenty years, however, the tools of comparative political research have been applied with increasing enthusiasm to the Irish case and the 'politics without social bases' thesis has been heavily revised. There have been two thrusts to this revision.

The first is that the social bases of partisanship in Ireland have been imperfectly estimated—this shortcoming is a product of the absence (now unique in western Europe) of an Irish academic election study. The resulting lack of crucial data has forced political scientists to rely upon public opinion polls, and thus upon the 'social grade' classifications used by market researchers. When more appropriate 'sociological' definitions of social class are employed in survey work, a social patterning of Irish voting behaviour, otherwise masked by the social grade classifications, becomes more apparent (Laver, 1987; Laver, Marsh, and Sinnott, 1987b).

The second argument for revising the 'politics without social bases' thesis is that Irish voting behaviour may have become more structured by social class since 1969, even if class is measured using imperfect social grade indicators. This argument sets on one side the small, and declining, level of support for the Irish Labour Party, and looks at the social bases of support for the other parties, particularly Fianna Fáil. The argument is based on the evidence summarised in Table 1, which analyses voting intention at Irish elections by social grade, in selected elections since 1969.

Table 1. Percentage of different social grades supporting Irish parties 1969–89.

Party[a]	Year	Social grade					
		Professional and managerial (AB)	Other non-manual (C1)	Skilled manual (C2)	Unskilled manual (DE)	Farmers with over 50 acres (F50+)	Farmers with under 50 acres (F50−)
Fianna	1969	37	48	40	43	38	53
Fáil	1981	34	48	46	45	35	49
	1987	26	32	45	41	30	48
	1989	32	42	39	41	43	
Fine	1969	37	26	21	14	46	26
Gael	1981	46	31	29	24	53	26
	1987	34	24	23	15	45	35
	1989	35	30	21	14	39	
Labour	1969	10	15	27	28	2	5
	1981	9	10	10	16	4	2
	1987	1	6	4	7	1	2
	1989	6	9	14	15	5	
Prog.	1987	18	18	9	9	10	2
Dems.	1989	10	6	6	7	4	
Workers'	1981	1	0	2	4	1	0
Party	1987	1	2	3	4	0	1
	1989	3	2	5	10	2	

[a] Support for 'other' parties and 'don't knows' excluded.
Sources: 1969–87, Laver, Marsh and Sinnott (1987: 102); 1989, Marsh and Sinnott (1990: 125).

(The 1969 data are precisely those on which Whyte based his conclusions. Unfortunately the 1989 data were reported, for farmers, in even cruder categories).

The first thing that is clear from Table 1 is that, even in 1969, voting behaviour in Ireland was to some extent structured by social grade. The cross-class support for Fianna Fáil is of course quite striking and is the feature of these figures that is usually cited as evidence for the 'politics without social bases' thesis. However, support for both Fine Gael and Labour was more strongly structured by social grade. Large farmers were *much* more likely to vote for Fine Gael than were unskilled workers; unskilled workers were *much* more likely to vote for Labour than were large farmers.

Changing patterns of party support are also evident from Table 1. By 1987, the cross-class basis of Fianna Fáil support appeared to be declining

—manual workers were significantly more likely than nonmanual workers to support Fianna Fáil. In addition the Progressive Democrats (PDs), a new party which first contested an election in 1987, clearly appealed more to nonmanual than to manual workers. These figures led analysts of the 1987 election to the conclusion that 'the class basis of Irish politics is more evident now than at any time in the previous twenty years' (Laver, Marsh and Sinnott, 1987b: 112).

In 1989, however, this trend was reversed. Fianna Fáil gained ground among large farmers and nonmanual workers, and lost support most significantly among manual workers. The PD vote fell sharply across all social grades, but especially among nonmanual workers. The net result was the apparent re-emergence of Fianna Fáil as a catch-all party, causing political scientists to re-evaluate the argument that the trend in Ireland is towards class-based voting behaviour: 'although 1989 involved significant class-related shifts in voting behaviour . . . it did not produce a strong class-based alignment. This was because such movements as occurred mainly served to redress the class pattern that emerged from the 1987 election' (Marsh and Sinnott, 1990: 125).

Perhaps the most striking comparison in Table 1, however, is between 1969 and 1989. For the two main parties, the social patterning of the vote is almost identical for the two years, and well within the realms of sampling error. By 1989, the PDs were not making a very big impact on the overall picture and the most striking difference that we can see has to do with the splitting of the left wing vote. This was united behind Labour in 1969, and divided between Labour and the Workers' Party in 1989.

The general trend in western Europe is for class-based voting to decline but certainly not to disappear (Gallagher, Laver and Mair, 1991). When class voting in Ireland was apparently increasing, there appeared to be a convergence with western Europe. The reversal of this trend leaves Ireland at the low end of the European class voting continuum. Voting behaviour is nothing like as strongly structured by social class as it is in Scandinavia, for example, but the pattern to be found in Ireland is not completely out of the European mainstream. As in 1969, the degree of social patterning in popular support for Fine Gael, Labour and the Workers' Party means that we do have useful information about how people are likely to vote if we know their social grade. And the crude social grade measures that continue to be used in Ireland, given the continued lack of an academic election study, undoubtedly mask a more subtle pattern of party choice.

Comparing Irish Parties with their European Counterparts

The argument that it is Irish parties, rather than Irish voters, that are peculiar can be found in various guises. Its pervasiveness is illustrated quite clearly by the fact that both of the current standard treatments of the Irish party system (Gallagher, 1985; Mair, 1987) feel it necessary to confront in their opening pages the widespread perception that Ireland is a deviant case. Both authors cite Whyte's famous comment that Irish party politics are *sui generis* (Whyte 1974: 648), and both note Garvin's now-familiar argument that patterns of party politics in Ireland fit the models of political science much better if they are compared with other post-colonial states, rather than with the developed polities of western Europe (Garvin, 1981). Gallagher (1985: 140–141) provides a striking review of the weird, wonderful and inconsistent ways in which various non-Irish authors have attempted to categorise Irish parties in comparative European terms. While Mair, and also Sinnott (1984), argue strongly that Ireland is not a deviant case, they do not do so on the basis that Irish parties are in any sense like their European counterparts. Rather they argue that standard political science theories, and notably that of Lipset and Rokkan (1967), can in general terms be used to account for the development of the Irish party system.

In the remainder of this paper I explore the argument that the Irish parties are much less peculiar than any of these authors have thus far been prepared to admit. I do this by comparing the role played by each party in the Irish party system with the roles played by equivalent parties in other western European party systems. Obviously, in order to do this, I need to develop a method of describing parties and party systems that allows such comparisons to be made. This method depends upon describing party systems in terms of the weights and policy positions of the parties concerned, and is elaborated in the following section.

Policy constellations

One way of describing a party system is to think of it as a collection of different parties, each with particular electoral and legislative weights, and each with a particular policy position. If we assume that policy positions can be represented in a 'space' defined by a set of policy dimensions, we can describe a party system as a constellation of parties in this space. The use of such 'policy spaces' is by now a very conventional way of describing the policy positions of political actors, typically associated with the seminal Hotelling-Downs model of party competition (Hotelling, 1929; Downs, 1957; and cf. Laver and Hunt, 1992). On this account, many important features of electoral competition, legislative behaviour, government formation and policy bargaining can be analysed in terms of the structure of policy positions and bargaining weights of the actors in such a space.

If we can describe key features of politics in two countries in terms of the same basic policy dimensions, then we can compare aspects of the structure of party competition in these countries. For example, we can compare two countries in which there is a party with a particularly 'central' location in the policy constellation—such as the Christian Democrats in Italy and Luxembourg—and note that such a party will be very difficult to exclude from government coalitions, no matter how well or badly it does at elections. In what follows, therefore, I compare the Irish policy constellation with other European policy constellations, locating each in a space defined by the same two policy dimensions, both highly salient in a wide range of European countries.

There are two basic reasons for doing this. The first, to which I will return at the end of the paper, has to do with the electorate. If we assume that the constellations of party policy positions in these spaces are the parties' equilibrium responses to the strategic problem of maximising votes at election time, then comparing policy constellations and party weights allows us to compare electorates. The second has to do with government formation. If we assume that senior politicians must pay attention to the constellation of party policy positions when they engage in government formation negotiations, then different party constellations define different government formation games, and hence imply different political outcomes. The existence of similar party policy constellations implies important underlying similarities in the government formation game in two countries. I make no bones about an assumption that underlies this entire discussion, which is that the government formation game is the single most important feature of party competition in any parliamentary democracy.

Estimating party policy positions

In order to make such comparisons, it is necessary to estimate the position, on a range of policy dimensions, of political parties in each western European country. The estimates reported in this paper are derived from a large scale 'expert survey' of party policy positions, conducted in 1989. The survey was conducted by the author as part of a larger project to build an integrated comparative data-set on the policy bases of party competition in all parliamentary democracies. In addition to information on party policy positions, various other data on the role of policy in party competition were assembled. These include trade-offs between office- and policy-oriented motivations among politicians; the location within parties of decision making on matters of policy and government formation; the role of policy disputes in cabinet politics; the relative salience of different cabinet portfolios, and so on. The study is described, and the data are reproduced extensively, by Laver and Hunt (1992). The main current application of the data is in the empirical elaboration of a new model of the role of cabinet portfolios in the government formation game, described by Laver and Shepsle (1990a, 1990b, 1991). A rudimentary application of this approach to the government formation game in Ireland in 1989 is reported by Laver and Arkins (1990). A more extensive application of the data to government formation in the Irish case, among others, can be found in Laver and Hunt (1992), and a full empirical exploration of the implications of the new model for the case of Ireland is part of ongoing work.

Essentially, a long quesionnaire on the policy positions of political parties in particular countries was sent to the universe of political scientists specialising in the country in question, identified using various directories. Each expert was asked to make a judgement about the position of each party on each of the policy dimensions defined *a priori* and listed in Table 2. Each was then asked to rate the political salience of each dimension for each party. Respondents were also given the opportunity to 'write in' their own, country-specific, policy dimensions, and many took the opportunity to do this. The data used here are mean expert judgements on party positions on each policy dimension in each country, based on a total of 356 expert responses.[1]

The relative importance of each policy dimension for each country was estimated by calculating a mean saliency score. More salient dimensions in a given country received scores of more than 1, while relatively less salient dimensions received scores of less than 1.[2] These estimates are reported in Table 3. They show that two particular dimensions, a 'taxes

---

[1] Several alternative techniques are available for estimating party positions, including the content analysis of party manifestoes (Budge, Robertson and Hearl, eds., 1987) and the dimensional analysis of mass and elite survey data (Inglehart and Klingemann, 1976; Sani and Sartori, 1983). These data sources are in some senses 'harder' than a Delphic poll of country specialists, but none provides a comprehensive comparative description of a range of different party systems in terms of a common set of ideological dimensions.

[2] These scores were derived as follows. The mean expert judgement of the salience of a given dimension in a given country for a given party was first calculated. The weighted mean salience of the dimension, for all parties taken together in the country in question, was then calculated—each party-specific saliency score was weighted by the proportion of the legislative seats that the party controlled. A global mean weighted saliency score for all dimensions in the country in question was then calculated—the weighted mean salience of each dimension was then expressed as a proportion of the global mean score. (See Laver and Hunt, 1992, for a more detailed description.)

Table 2.   Policy scales estimated in expert survey.

1.   TAXES VERSUS PUBLIC SERVICES
     Promote raising taxes to increase public services (1)
     Promote cutting public services to cut taxes (20)

2.   FOREIGN POLICY
     Promote development of friendly relations with Soviet Union (1)
     Oppose development of friendly relations with Soviet Union (20)

3.   PUBLIC OWNERSHIP
     Promote maximum public ownership of business and industry (1)
     Oppose all public ownership of business and industry (20)

4.   SOCIAL POLICY
     Promote permissive policies on matters such as abortion and homosexual law (1)
     Oppose permissive policies on matters such as abortion and homosexual law (20)

5.   THE RELIGIOUS DIMENSION
     Strongly anti-clerical (1)
     Strongly pro-clerical (20)

6.   URBAN VERSUS RURAL INTERESTS
     Promote interests of urban and industrial voters above others (1)
     Promote interests of rural and agricultural voters above others (20)

7.   CENTRALISATION OF DECISION MAKING
     Promote decentralisation of all decision making (1)
     Oppose any decentralisation of decision making (20)

8.   ENVIRONMENTAL POLICY
     Support protection of environment, even at the cost of economic growth (1)
     Support economic growth, even at the cost of damage to environment (20)

9.   OTHER SCALE 1
     Respondent asked to interpret endpoints.

10. OTHER SCALE 2
     Respondent asked to interpret endpoints.

versus spending' dimension and a 'social policy' dimension, had the highest salience in the group of countries taken as a whole, as well as higher than average salience in almost every country studied.[3] Having used estimates of dimension salience of to identify key dimensions, expert judgements of party policy positions on these dimensions were then used to generate the policy spaces that formed the basis of comparisons between different party constellations.

In the Irish case, Table 3 shows that a 'user supplied' Northern Ireland policy dimension was rated as being highly salient. In this important sense,

---

[3] The religious dimension and the urban-rural dimension, in contrast, tended to be the least salient in most countries.

Table 3. Weighted means saliency scores, by dimension, by country.

	Taxes vs spending	Social policy	Foreign policy	Public ownership	Environment	Centralisation	Urban vs. rural	Religious dimension	Most salient local dimension
Australia	1.27	1.10	0.86	1.10	1.09	0.99	1.00	0.58	
Austria	1.17	1.06	0.90	1.08	1.14	0.73	1.04	0.88	
Belgium	1.26	1.18	1.02	0.98	0.78	1.13	0.82	0.82	1.37 (Nuclear)
Britain	1.35	1.08	1.10	1.25	0.98	1.01	0.81	0.43	
Canada	1.20	1.13	1.04	1.18	0.98	1.06	0.83	0.58	1.60 (US relations)
Denmark	1.31	1.03	1.28	1.06	1.01	0.85	0.92	0.56	
Finland	1.11	1.03	0.94	1.01	0.97	0.95	1.14	0.85	
France	1.18	1.18	0.94	1.15	0.76	1.06	0.80	0.93	0.85 (Europe)
Germany	1.10	1.15	1.05	0.95	1.16	0.89	0.94	0.76	
Greece	1.16	0.61	1.56	1.18	0.79	1.17	0.69	0.83	
Iceland	1.08	1.16	1.17	1.13	1.25	0.90	1.18	0.14	
Ireland	1.42	1.21	0.80	1.18	0.75	0.55	1.05	1.04	1.46 (N. Ireland)
Italy	0.91	1.15	1.08	1.02	0.95	0.97	0.77	1.17	
Japan	1.28	0.90	1.17	0.76	0.76	1.02	1.08	1.04	
Luxembourg	1.22	1.33	1.18	0.82	1.26	0.48	0.89	0.81	
Malta	0.98	1.09	1.09	1.01	1.15	0.82	0.71	1.14	
Netherlands	1.28	1.32	1.09	0.95	1.29	0.64	0.65	0.77	1.17 (Nuclear)
Norway	1.13	1.20	0.99	1.09	0.98	0.91	0.93	0.78	
New Zealand	1.33	1.14	0.99	1.06	0.98	0.95	1.11	0.44	1.21 (Nuclear)
Portugal	1.04	1.17	0.95	1.28	0.94	1.13	0.82	0.66	
Spain	1.21	1.17	1.11	1.03	0.85	1.26	0.67	0.68	
Sweden	1.24	1.09	0.96	1.16	1.08	0.98	0.82	0.66	
US	1.37	1.44	1.19	0.56	1.21	0.93	0.72	0.59	
Mean	1.20	1.20	1.13	1.06	1.04	1.00	0.93	0.89	0.75

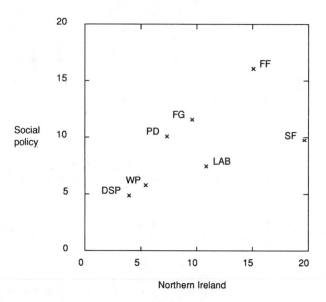

Figure 1. Relationship between social policy and Northern Ireland policy in Ireland. DSP, Democratic Socialist Party; FF, Fianna Fáil; FG, Fine Gael; Lab, Labour Party; SF, Sinn Fein; WP, Workers' Party.

the Irish party system is clearly unique. However, party positions on the Northern Ireland policy dimension are closely related to positions on the social and moral policy dimension, with parties that advocate a hard line with the British on Northern Ireland rated as conservative on social policy and parties that advocate a softer line being rated as more liberal on social policy. This can be seen in Figure 1, which plots Irish party positions on the social policy dimension against positions on the Northern Ireland dimension. Only the Labour Party and Sinn Fein deviate from this very strong pattern, each being more liberal on social policy than might be expected from their positions on Northern Ireland policy. For all other parties, the two policy areas are highly correlated, so that the Irish party constellation that we identify using the 'common' two dimensional analysis based on social policy would be little changed if we were to substitute Northern Ireland policy. The underlying structure of the relationship between the parties would be substantially the same.

Party positions on the 'taxes versus spending' and the 'social policy' dimensions were thus used to structure a common two dimensional view on each system. Party positions in these two dimensional policy spaces can be drawn neatly on a sheet of paper, but this should not for one moment be taken to imply that the policy spaces we are considering are inherently two dimensional, or that any or all of them are best represented by this particular pair of dimensions. Indeed, estimating the 'real' dimensionality of policy spaces, once this is assumed to be less than infinite, involves deep and unresolved issues in political science (aired briefly by Laver and Hunt, 1992). I ignore such issues completely in this paper, in which I am certainly not claiming to present *the* picture of party politics in any particular country; what follows is *a* picture of each country, contributing to a series of pictures, each painted from a common point of view.

There is a major problem concerning the cross national comparability of such policy spaces, one that cannot be avoided. This arises because ostensibly the same policy dimension may in practice have a different meaning in different countries. For example, a relatively mainstream 'liberal' policy on social issues in the Netherlands might include support for free abortion on demand, decriminalisation of drug use and support for voluntary euthanasia. In Ireland, even those who think of themselves as very liberal indeed would never dream of publicly endorsing such policies. There is thus a big 'shift' in the social policy scale, comparing the Netherlands and Ireland.

For this reason, some would argue strongly that there is no basis whatsoever for comparing party positions on any particular policy dimension in two different countries, and that what I do below is to commit a serious methodological sin. It must be emphasised, however, that I make no assumption at all that absolute scale positions can be compared from one system to another—that a 10 on social policy in Ireland means anything like the same thing as a 10 in the Netherlands, for example. Rather, what I am looking for are patterns created by *relative, not absolute*, positions of parties in broadly comparable and salient policy spaces. I am looking for policy constellations, and specifically for types of European policy constellation that might approximate to the party constellation found in Ireland.

Comparing policy constellations

The policy dimensions used here to compare different European party constellations are two important facets of what has traditionally been regarded as a 'socio-economic', 'left–right' dimension. The first reflects economic strategy, the extent to which, if a choice must be made, tax cuts are preferred to public services. The second reflects the extent to which it is felt that the state should intervene in matters of personal morality. The degree to which these two dimensions are independent of each other in practice as well as in theory can be seen from the picture that they generate of the party constellation in the Netherlands, presented in Figure 2. The Dutch party constellation has been selected because it includes sufficient

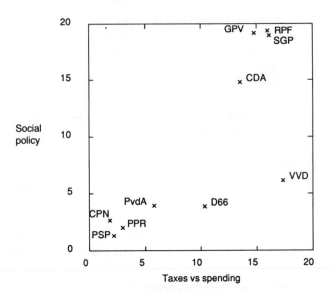

Figure 2. Two-dimensional view of the Dutch party constellation. CDA, Christian Democratic Appeal; CPN, Communist Party; D66, Democrats '66; GPV, Reformed Political Union; PPR, Radical Political Party; PSP, Pacifist Socialist Party; PvdA, Labour Party; RPF, Reformed Political Federation; SGP, Political Reformed Party; VVD, People's Party for Freedom and Democracy.

ideological variety to provide a useful set of reference points, which we can use to calibrate pictures of other party systems.

It is worth taking time to consider the party constellation in the Netherlands, viewed through this particular prism. The three main Dutch parties are the PvdA, a social democratic party, the VVD, a neoclassical liberal party, and the CDA, a biconfessional Christian democratic party. These parties, taken together, comprise an unmistakably triangular policy constellation. The PvdA provides a social democratic pole, anchoring the constellation at the centre-left of both policy dimensions; the CDA provides a Christian democratic pole, anchoring the constellation at the centre right of both dimensions. The VVD, on the other hand, is 'right-wing' on economic strategy and 'left-wing' on social issues, a typical libertarian profile. This provides a liberal pole for the constellation. The position of the minor Dutch parties can be described in relation to these three. The Communists (CPN), Left Radicals (PPR) and Pacifist Socialists (PSP) are all to the left of the PvdA on both dimensions. The three fundamentalist protestant parties (GPV, RPF and SGP) are all to the right of the CDA on both dimensions. The moderate D'66 is liberal on social issues and middle of the road on the economy. Despite the large number

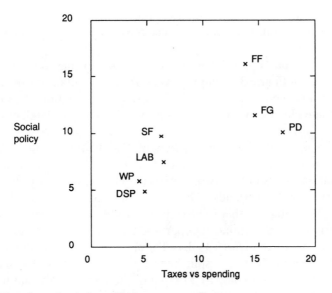

Figure 3. Two-dimensional view of Irish party constellation.

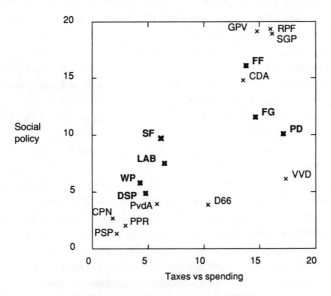

Figure 4. Superimposing the Irish on the Dutch party constellation.

of parties in the Netherlands, only four have been serious players in the government formation game during the postwar era. These are the PvdA, D'66, VVD and CDA. Thus, the main activity in Dutch politics takes place in the region of the policy space bounded by the positions of these parties.

No party inhabits the top left hand corner of the space, a position which would imply supporting left wing economics and a conservative social policy.

The Irish party constellation is described, using the same policy dimensions, in Figure 3. Stripping away irrelevant detail, it can be seen to be similar in several ways to the Dutch party constellation. This comparison is made clearer by superimposing the Irish party constellation on the Dutch, as in Figure 4.

Figure 4 shows that the position of Fianna Fáil in the Irish party constellation is rather similar to that of the CDA in the Dutch party constellation. Ireland has two parties in the role filled by the Liberals (VVD) in the Netherlands. These are Fine Gael and the Progressive Democrats, though neither is as distinctive in its position as the VVD. The Irish party constellation has two parties, Labour and the Workers' Party, filling the role of the Dutch PvdA. The fact that both the liberal and the social democratic poles are split in Ireland does increase the bargaining power of Fianna Fáil, compared to that of the Dutch CDA, but that is not our immediate concern. What we see from Figure 4 is that, taking Fianna Fáil as fulfilling the role of a Christian democratic party, taking Labour and the Workers Party as filling the role of social democratic parties, and taking Fine Gael and the PDs as in some restricted sense fulfilling the role of liberal parties, the Irish party constellation does not look that peculiar when compared to at least one representative European comparator.

Laver and Hunt (1992) discuss the juxtaposition of parties on the 'taxes versus spending' and 'social policy' dimensions for each of the twenty four countries included in their expert survey. They identify four different types of party constellation.

The first, of which the party constellation in the Netherlands is a very good example, is the 'Benelux' constellation. In the other Benelux countries, Belgium and Luxembourg, the basic structure of the party system is the same as that of the Netherlands. Each party constellation has a social democratic pole, a liberal pole and a Christian democratic pole. (In the Belgian case these poles comprise party 'families', each with Flemish and Walloon language wings.) In each case, the liberal pole is distinguished from the Christian democratic pole, despite roughly similar positions on economic policy, because the liberals promote a far less conservative social policy than the Christian democrats. This comparison can be extended easily to Germany, where the unvarnished social democratic (SPD)—liberal (FDP)—Christian democratic (CDU/CSU) triangle can be seen most clearly. Stretching a point, the Austrian party constellation can also be thought of as an example of the Benelux pattern, though there is less separation between the parties than in the other Benelux constellations. As we have seen, the Irish case an be compared to the Benelux constellation if Fianna Fáil is treated as a Christian democratic party and if the rather less distinctive positions of the 'liberal' parties in Ireland are overlooked.

The second pattern suggested by Laver and Hunt is the 'Mediterranean' constellation. Once more, this constellation is grounded in a quite distinctive social democratic pole. The difference with the Benelux constellation concerns the opposition to social democracy. In countries with a Mediterranean constellation (Italy being an exception) this opposition is focused around a populist conservative party with a strong nationalist appeal, neither anticlerical nor particularly liberal on social affairs. This group includes the Gaullists (RPR) in France, New Democracy in Greece, the Nationalist Party in Malta, the Social Democrats (despite their name) in Portugal, and the Coalición Popular in Spain. These countries lack significant liberal parties, so that the underlying structure of party competition is bipolar rather than tripolar.

A good example of the Mediterranean constellation can be found in France, and Figure 5 shows the Irish party constellation superimposed upon the French. The comparisons, once more, are striking. The relative locations of the socialist parties are similar in both systems, though the French parties are at a somewhat greater distance from their rivals on the

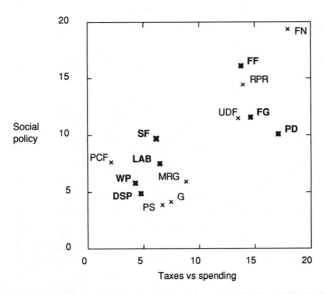

Figure 5. The Irish party constellation superimposed upon the French. FN, National Front; G, Greens; MRG, Left Radicals; PS, Socialist Party; PCF, Communist Party; RPR, Rally for the Republic (Gaulists); UDF, Union for French Democracy.

right. Fianna Fáil fulfils the same role in the Irish party constellation as the Gaullists (RPR) do in the French; Fine Gael fulfils the same role as the French conservatives (UDF). Taking Fianna Fáil as a Gaullist party, the Irish party constellation looks quite plausibly Mediterranean.

The final important set of party constellations can be found in Scandinavia, where commentators have traditionally emphasised the theme of 'two-bloc' politics. In the Scandinavian constellation, a largish secular conservative party tends to coexist with a small, protestant, Christian democratic party. Both of these confront a strong social democratic pole. The Scandinavian constellation differs from the strongly bipolar southern European constellations, however, in that a significant middle-of-the-road liberal or agrarian party tends to bridge the gap between the conservative pole and the social democratic pole. Norway, Sweden, Denmark and Finland all conform to this description. Two other possible candidates for inclusion are Iceland and Canada. In neither of these cases is there even a weak Christian democratic party but, in both cases, middle-of-the-road liberal parties bridge the gap between secular conservative and social democratic poles. A good example of the Scandinavian constellation can be found in Sweden, and the Irish constellation is superimposed upon the Swedish in Figure 6.

Once more we note the striking juxtaposition between the role filled

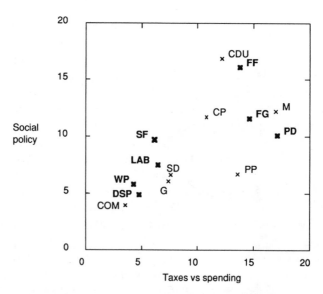

Figure 6. The Irish party constellation superimposed upon the Swedish. CDU, Christian Democratic Union; COM, Communist Party; CP, Centre Party; G, Greens; M, Moderate Unity Party (conservatives); PP, People's Party; SD, Social Democrats.

by Fianna Fáil and that of the Christian Democrats, and between the roles of Fine Gael and the secular conservatives. Once more, the social democratic poles fulfil similar roles in anchoring the left of each party constellation. But the Irish party constellation is unlike the Scandinavian in a number of important respects. In the first place, there is no centrist party in Ireland that bridges the gap between the social democratic and conservative poles, filling the role of the Centre Party (CP) in Sweden. (The positioning of such a party can have an important impact upon government formation games.) In the second place, while Fianna Fáil is close to the Christian democrats, the latter tend to be weak in Scandinavia. And, finally, a matter that we can ignore no longer—the social democrats are very strong in Scandinavia, while they are very weak in Ireland.

Which European party constellation does the Irish constellation most resemble? Overall, though this is very much a matter of taste, the Irish party constellation most closely resembles the Mediterranean. While the Irish constellation is moderately tripolar in shape, its liberal pole is not distinct enough from its 'christian democratic' pole for us plausibly to describe the Irish parties as conforming to the pattern of the Benelux constellation. And the strength of 'christian democratic' Fianna Fáil, coupled with the weakness of the left, leaves Ireland looking distinctly unScandinavian. The Irish constellation does, however, have some striking similarities with several Mediterranean constellations. Notably, in addition to the pervasive role of the main social democratic party, both the Irish and the Mediterranean constellation are defined by the position of a popular, and populist, non-anticlerical conservative nationalist party. There is typically, though not always, a weaker secular conservative party—most evident in France, absent altogether in Malta and Greece—fulfilling a broadly similar role to that of Fine Gael. The left is typically divided in the Mediterranean constellations, as it is in Ireland.

The one important caveat that must be entered in relation to this conclusion concerns previous Fine Gael–Labour coalition cabinets. These data were collected in 1989, two years after the last Fine Gael–Labour coalition had fallen apart over its inability to agree over cuts in public spending. We cannot tell from the data at hand whether Fine Gael and Labour had moved apart by 1989, having once been closer together, or whether Fine Gael–Labour coalitions were, rather, a response to what was then taken to be one of Fianna Fáil's 'core values', its refusal to share government power with any other party. In the latter event, it might have been the case that Fine Gael and Labour were as far apart in 1982 as they were in 1989, but still went into coalition together simply because this was the only hope that either had of ever getting into government. Fianna Fáil renounced this particular core value when it went into coalition with the

Progressive Democrats in 1989. Given this, and considering only party policy, it is now difficult to see future Fine Gael–Labour coalitions being formed without a major realignment of Irish party policy positions. Indeed, an analysis of the Irish government formation game in these terms, using these data, suggests that Fianna Fáil should remain well poised to form stable minority governments after those elections in which it fails to gain a parliamentary majority (Laver and Hunt, 1992).

Keeping this caveat in mind, we can conclude that there seems nothing particularly peculiar about the ideological configuration of the Irish parties. They seem to fit very well with one of the major European party constellations—the Mediterranean model that is characterised by the confrontation between a divided left, on one hand, and a powerful pole of populist nationalism, on the other—a constellation that is typically found among the Catholic countries of Southern Europe.

Party Positions and the Popular Vote

If it is accepted that Irish parties in themselves are not particularly weird or wonderful, then the most important distinctive feature of the Irish party system must undoubtedly be remarkable electoral weakness of the left in general and of the social democratic left in particular, a phenomenon documented extensively by Mair in the following paper. While the left is often divided in 'Mediterranean' party systems, as it is in Ireland, it is nowhere as weak. This weakness benefits not so much Fianna Fáil, the populist nationalist party (such parties tend to be large in each of the Mediterranean party constellations) but Fine Gael, the second-string conservative party, which is untypically large for a Mediterranean constellation.

One way of looking at this in more systematic terms is to relate levels of party support in the electorate to the two dimensional configurations of party policy positions reported in Figures 2 to 6. For obvious reasons, it is very difficult, though not impossible, to locate the electorate directly in these policy spaces. What would be required would be a large scale cross-national programme of mass attitude surveys, designed to estimate the distribution of electoral preferences in each country on the policy dimensions being used to represent party competition. In the absence of this, we can attempt to make inferences about electoral policy preferences from the relationship between the policy positions of parties and their levels of electoral support, assuming that electors are at least to some extent influenced by the relative policy positions of the parties when they decide how to cast their votes.

There has been relatively little systematic work on such inferences, which raise some intriguing methodological problems. First, there is the issue of whether to take electoral tastes as exogenous to party competition, or whether to assume that the tastes of voters can be moulded by the activities of parties. Implicit in almost all analyses of the relationship between policy and party competition is the assumption that electoral tastes are exogenous variables; this is the assumption that I too will make, but it is as well to be aware that it is being made. Assuming electoral tastes to be exogenous, and assuming that electors rank parties, all other things being equal, according to how close party policy positions are to their own ideal policy position, the second question concerns how voters decide which party to support. In a simple two party system it is logical for all parties to support the party that is closest to them in policy space. In all other party systems with a first-past-the-post electoral law, such as that to be found in Britain, a voter may choose to support a second choice party in the interests of keeping out a lower choice party if it seems likely that a first choice party will be defeated. In multiparty systems with proportional electoral laws, rational voters should take account of likely subsequent patterns of coalition formation when deciding how to cast their votes. The modelling of such behaviour is complex, and has only just begun. Results for a three party system with one policy dimension are reported by Austen-Smith and Banks (1988). In what follows, I assume 'naive' decision-making by voters who support the party closest to their ideal point, regardless of their expectations of subsequent coalition bargaining.

Assuming exogenous electoral tastes and naive voting, the interaction of election results and party policy positions can be used to generate information about the policy preferences of the electorate. If voters vote for the party whose policy position is closest to their own tastes, then the policy space can be divided into areas, such that each area is closer to a given party than to any other party. Think of this area as a party's 'policy domain'. Every voter whose ideal point lies within this area will, by assumption, vote for the party in question. Looking at things the other way around, the vote share for a given party is an estimate of the proportion of the electorate whose ideal points lie within the area of the policy space that is the party's policy domain.

We now simply confront the technical issue of drawing the policy domains. This involves drawing, for each party, the section of the policy space that is closer to that party than to any other party. Making the standard microeconomic assumption that the preferences of voters can be modelled in terms of the Euclidean distances between points in policy space, we are very fortunate that an existing packaged computer routine,

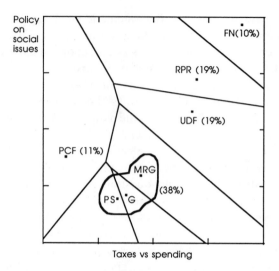

Figure 7. Party regions and party voting in France (votes June 1988).

originally developed by hydrologists, will do just this job for us. The resulting diagrams are technically known as Voronoi tesselations, or Thiessen diagrams.[4]

Figures 7 to 10 show the results of such an analysis. In each case the two dimensional policy space is divided into policy domains. Each domain has a party in its centre, and all points in the domain are closer to this party than to any other party. In addition, Figures 7 to 10 give the share of the popular vote won by each party at the election closest to the time when the data were collected, in early 1989. These diagrams thus allow us to use party constellations to tell us something about the electorate, if we assume that party voters are to be found in the appropriate policy domain. Figure 7 shows the situation in France, our reference Mediterranean constellation.

The pattern in France is repeated in most other European countries. We can draw a line from top left to bottom right of the standard two-dimensional policy space and thereby divide parties of the left from those of the right, taking both social and economic policy into consideration. About 50 per cent of French voters can be found on either side of this line. A broadly similar pattern can be found in the Netherlands (Figure 8) and Sweden (Figure 9).

[4] These diagrams were generated on a Macintosh SE, using the Voronoi Plot routine in the Systat 5.0 statistical package. Other graphics were also generated using Systat 5.0. A tentative exploration of using non-Euclidean metrics to model preferences can be found in Laver and Hunt (1982).

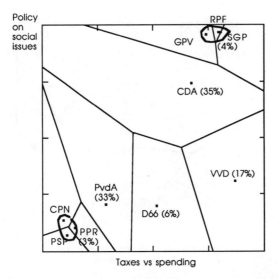

Figure 8. Party regions and party voting in the Netherlands (votes May 1986).

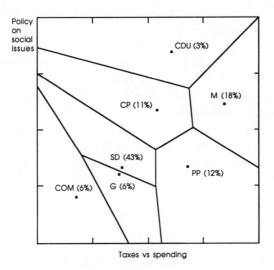

Figure 9. Party regions and party voting in Sweden (votes September 1988).

In the Netherlands, the left is rather weaker, in Sweden it is rather stronger, but the orders of magnitude are the same. In each case, a range of policy positions is offered to voters at election time, in each case there is a broadly even distribution of support between the two sides of the space. (Note that regions in the top left of the space, reflecting positions that are left wing on economic policy and right wing on social policy, tend

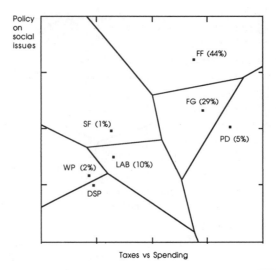

Policy on social issues

Taxes vs Spending

Figure 10. Party regions and party voting in Ireland (votes June 1989).

to be much less densely populated, though irredentist nationalist parties can sometimes be found in them.)

The situation in Ireland stands in stark contrast to this. About 80 per cent of the electorate is to be found in the upper right hand area of the space, despite the fact that a range of policy positions is offered in the bottom left hand region. No other western European country even approximates this distribution.

These diagrams thus give us a systematic picture of the essential peculiarity of Irish politics, seen in comparative western European terms. A number of parties offer policy positions on the left, but few voters support them.

Conclusions

In one sense, the main conclusion to be drawn from all of this is something of an anticlimax, since the data presented in this paper cannot help us to understand the causes of the weakness of the Irish left, clearly the most distinctive feature of the Irish party system. What the data presented have shown quite clearly, however, is that it is the electoral weakness of the Irish left that is *the* distinctive feature of Irish party politics.

Irish parties are *not* peculiar—they are common or garden European varieties, rather than the weird and wonderful mutants that some would have us believe. We do not have to travel far in Europe to find plenty of parties like Fianna Fáil, or even like Fine Gael. The Irish Labour party fulfils a role in the Irish party constellation just like social democratic parties in almost every other European country, while the Workers' Party fills a role much like Communist or new left parties elsewhere. If we had to make a choice, and there is no reason why we should make a choice of course, the Irish party constellation looks decidedly Mediterranean.

What we have seen, in short, is that Irish voters are offered similar alternatives at election time to those offered to their European counterparts. Taken *en masse*, however, Irish voters make different choices between these alternatives. Understanding why this is the case, and estimating whether the pattern is changing, is the key to understanding whether Irish politics really should be seen as a deviant case in the western European context. Exploring these issues is the subject of Mair's discussion in the paper that follows.

Proceedings of the British Academy, **79**, 383–410

Explaining the Absence of Class Politics in Ireland

PETER MAIR

University of Leiden

Introduction: What Needs to be Explained?

IN RECENT YEARS there has been quite a gradual if nevertheless pronounced shift in conventional political science treatments of the Irish case, a shift which has seen an emphasis on the peculiarities of Irish political life being slowly replaced by a new emphasis on essential comparability. In part, this shift has resulted from the internationalisation of Irish political science, and from the incorporation of data and interpretations of the Irish case within cross-national research projects—particularly those projects which, focusing on the European context, go beyond an exclusive emphasis on the major countries or 'pattern states' (Daalder, 1987) in order to include data on the smaller democracies. Whether the topic in question has concerned the role of the cabinet, the policy-making process, the welfare state, the party system, or whatever, elements which once seemed distinctive to Ireland are now seen to fit within more broadly applicable models. In part also, this shift has resulted from a growing perception that Irish political life itself is changing, and that political processes which once seemed *sui generis* are now adapting to more conventional patterns. The keywords here are 'Europeanisation', 'modernisation', and 'secularisation', within interpretations which see Irish peculiarities as the hangover from an increasingly distant and irrelevant past.

The most evident signs of Irish political peculiarities were those highlighted by studies of mass politics and political ideologies. Here, the combination of two very distinctive features—an unusual, preference-based electoral system, on the one hand, and a partisan cleavage which

Read 9 December 1990. © The British Academy 1992.

derived from an intra-nationalist conflict, on the other—were seen to have created a party system and a set of electoral orientations which were quite unlike those of the neighbouring democracies. The most classic statement of the case came from the late John Whyte, whose early survey of the relationship between social structure and political behaviour led him to conclude that, from a comparative perspective, Irish politics was deviant and even unique, its singularities stemming from its own idiosyncratic history. 'It is, then, perhaps a comfort to comparative political analysis that Irish party politics should be *sui generis*', he concluded, for 'the context from which they spring is *sui generis* also' (Whyte, 1974: 648). This refrain echoed more or less persistently throughout the literature on Irish politics in the 1970s and early 1980s, whether that literature was penned by Irish students themselves or by comparatively-minded outside observers. 'Over and over again', noted Carty (1981) in his Preface to a study of electoral politics in Ireland, 'the literature of comparative politics noted simply "except Ireland"'.

More recently, however, as observed, a bias towards a more conventional perspective has emerged. In the first place, while Whyte (1974) had emphasised the peculiarities involved in the sheer lack of correspondence between conventional social structural distinctions, on the one hand, and electoral support for Fianna Fáil, on the other, subsequent analyses found that the elaboration of more nuanced models did help to detect a degree of association between class and voting (see, for example, Laver *et al.*, 1987b; Mair, 1979: 457–9). Second, while many earlier analyses had assumed the persistence, and hence also the persistent non-comparability, of a *sui generis* nationalist political divide in Ireland (e.g. Chubb, 1970; Garvin, 1974; Cohan, 1982), subsequent studies found that the ideologies of the parties actually went beyond a simple nationalist opposition, and reflected policy stances which were quite in line with parties in many of the other European democracies (see, for example, Mair, 1987: 138–206; Laver, this volume). Finally, notwithstanding any ideological or sociological peculiarities, it was also rapidly becoming clear that the strategic behaviour of the parties was far from being unusual, and derived from much the same 'rational' calculus as that which informed (the many) comparable parties in comparable bargaining situations (Laver and Higgins, 1986). In short, despite the early impressions, and perhaps also a little disappointingly, Irish political life was proving to be just as normal and mundane as that in a large number of other countries (Mair, 1990; O'Leary, 1987, 1990).

Yet for all its new-found normalcy, there remains one key aspect in which Irish politics does continue to stand out as a deviant case among the European democracies, and that is in *the striking electoral debility of class-based, left-wing parties.* For even now, despite 'modernisation', 'secularisation', and 'Europeanisation', and even despite the relatively recent emergence of the Workers' Party as an expanding electoral force on the Irish left, the aggregate voting support for 'class left' parties remains distinctively and substantially below that in *any* other country in Western Europe.

This particular Irish peculiarity is more than evident in the voting patterns shown in Table 1, which record the mean levels of electoral support for class left parties (that is, communist, social democrat, and left socialist parties) in the various countries of western Europe in each of the postwar decades.[1] Few, if any, other comparative indicators of political life would mark the Irish case out so distinctively. In the first place, the average support for the class left in Ireland (which is largely the average support for the Labour Party and the Workers' Party) never really rises above just one-third of the average of that won in *all* of the other countries. The Irish figure is 25.5 per cent of that in the other countries in the 1950s, 34.7 per cent in the 1960s, 33.6 per cent in the 1970s, and 32.6 per cent in the 1980s. Second, there is no other *single* country in western Europe which even approaches the weak position of the Irish left: the closest to the Irish position—that is, the second lowest country in terms of a rank-ordering —is Switzerland, where support for the class left averaged almost 29 per cent in the 1950s, 1960s, and 1970s, and almost 26 per cent in the 1980s. At all times, therefore, even this low-ranking country recorded a level of support which has been double that in Ireland.

The purpose of this paper is to tease out a possible explanation for this persistent peculiarity of Irish politics. Two points should be made at the outset, however. First, the heuristic, but nonetheless plausible, assumption under which I am working is that the weakness of the class left in Ireland is something which needs to be explained.[2] Given that electoral support for class left parties in almost all other established western democracies, and especially in western Europe,[3] is substantially above that in Ireland,

---

[1] More generally, the data in Table 1 also serve to emphasise that, contrary to much conventional wisdom, there has been no sustained and substantial erosion of electoral support for the West European class left parties over the postwar years (see also Bartolini and Mair, 1990: 68–124). To be sure, average support for these parties in the 1980s was lower than in the 1950s, 1960s, or 1970s, but an overall decline of just 3 per cent since the 1950s is much more indicative of continuity rather than collapse. In addition, it is also worth emphasising that in five countries, *including Ireland*, the average vote for class left parties in the 1980s was higher than that in the 1950s (the other four countries are Denmark, West Germany, Italy, and Sweden).

[2] On this, see also Gallagher (1982: 8–28), and especially Hazelkorn (1989).

[3] Indeed, among all western democracies, one only really finds a parallel to the Irish case in the United States, where the class left is effectively non-existent.

Table 1.   Mean electoral support for class left parties[a] in postwar western Europe.

Country	1950s	1960s	1970s	1980s
Austria	47.6	46.7	51.2	46.1
Belgium	39.3	34.7	29.5	29.4
Denmark	44.7	47.8	44.9	47.2
Finland	48.0	48.5	42.7	39.3
France	49.8	40.0	43.1	47.4
FRG	31.4	39.4	44.2	39.4
Iceland	35.9	31.3	38.5	32.4
Ireland	**10.9**	**14.8**	**14.1**	**12.8**
Italy	40.7	47.9	46.9	46.3
Luxembourg	48.7	49.0	43.6	37.4
Netherlands	35.7	32.0	39.3	35.8
Norway	51.8	51.2	46.7	45.1
Sweden	49.8	52.6	48.8	50.1
Switzerland	28.7	28.6	29.0	25.6
United Kingdom	46.3	46.1	39.1	29.2
Mean	40.6	40.7	40.1	37.6
Mean (excluding Ireland)	42.7	42.6	42.0	39.3

[a] Socialist, Communist and New Left parties; only parties winning at least 1 per cent of the vote are included.
Source: Gallagher *et al.* (1991).

and given that these other European democracies provide a context in which studies of Irish political culture and behaviour can best be situated (see also Laver, this volume), this assumption seems to me to be an eminently reasonable one. To be sure, it might be argued that this Irish peculiarity exists only nominally, and that in reality Ireland does have a substantial working class party, which just happens to be called Fianna Fáil. Whatever one might think of Fianna Fáil's occasional claims to be a working class party,[4] however, the key point here is that Ireland, unlike any of its European neighbours, does not now maintain, nor has it ever maintained, a *major* party which has *expressly* mobilised as a working-class party of the left and which, as such, has consciously sought to associate itself with the international political movement of the working class.

Second, in seeking to explain the weakness of the Irish left, I am working very much within Sartori's (1968/1990) understanding of the factors which facilitate and promote the development of class politics, in which a major stress is laid on the relevance of organisational intervention

---

[4] Note, for example, de Valera's remark in 1951 that 'although we [i.e. Fianna Fáil] stand for all sections of the people, nevertheless the sections for which we have a special regard . . . are the small farmers on the one hand, and the workers on the other' (quoted in Mair, 1987: 51).

—that is, political intervention, as opposed to simply social structure. More generally, Sartori seeks to distinguish sociological explanations of political behaviour from more strictly political explanations of that behaviour, specifying the different levels of analysis which are involved in discussions of class conditions, class awareness, and, in politics, class action. I will come back to this argument at a later point; suffice it for now to underline that in this paper I will first seek to explore more sociologically-based explanations of the weakness of the Irish left before going on to emphasise a more politically-focused analysis. Hence I will first look at the question of class conditions and class awareness, then briefly examine evidence of class voting, and finally address questions relating to political culture and political style. As a word of warning, it should also be added that, largely for the sake of argument, the conclusions of this paper will tend to over-emphasise the importance of the political as against the social, while a more extensive analysis would inevitably have to take fuller account of both dimensions, as well as of their interaction.

The 'Class Conditions' Explanation

One of the most basic and time-honoured explanations for the weakness of the class left in Ireland concerns class conditions. More precisely, the debility of the class left is seen to derive from the combination of a poorly bounded class structure, and/or the relative weight of the non-labour intensive agricultural sector, and/or the essentially rural culture. Although such explanations have thankfully tended to prove less common in recent years (for a delightfully caustic assault on this perspective, see O'Leary, 1990), and although they have also tended to be primarily concerned with the failure of the left in the early years of the state (e.g. Orridge, 1976), some of the less sensitive comparative assessments still continue to include class conditions, and social conditions more generally, as key factors explaining the weakness of the class left in Ireland. An article by Inglehart is a case in point. Accounting for the dominance of 'conservative' material values, he notes, almost in passing, that 'everybody knows that Ireland is a largely rural nation' (Inglehart, 1987: 1294).

In fact, and this has finally begun to be widely accepted in the comparative literature, class conditions in Ireland are now much less distinctive than was once the case. To be sure, agricultural or other primary sector employment (15.1 per cent of the labour force in 1989)[5] is still more than two-and-a-half times that of the average in the remaining

[5] This and all other figures cited in this paragraph come from OECD (1991b).

fourteen countries listed in Table 1 (5.8 per cent in 1989). But the range among these other countries is also quite wide, and the Irish figure, while relatively high, is only little more than half as big again as that for Finland (8.9 per cent), Iceland (10.2 per cent), and Italy (9.3 per cent), where the class left vote is clearly very substantial. Moreover the Irish figure is also substantially less than the figure for Greece (25.3 per cent), and only slightly larger than that for Spain (13.0 per cent), yet in each of these latter two cases socialist parties constitute the largest single and most successful political force. In addition, in terms of one other indicator normally associated with support for class left parties, that is, the proportion of the labour force employed in industry, Ireland is quite unexceptional, with a figure of 28.4 per cent as against an average of 31 per cent in the remaining fourteen countries. Ireland here ranks higher than Denmark (27.4 per cent), the Netherlands (26.5 per cent) or Norway (25.3 per cent). Finally, there is also one other striking statistic which bears underlining as regards the supposedly 'rural' Irish economy, which is that the overall proportion of unemployed persons in the labour force (15.4 per cent in 1989), and male unemployment in particular (17.5 per cent in 1989), actually *exceeds* the proportion employed in agriculture.

Nor does rurality in the stricter sense of the term appear to offer any more reasonable basis from which to begin an explanation of the weakness of the Irish left. To be sure, urban environments do seem more favourable to left politics than are rural environments: thus, for example, at 16.4 per cent, the combined average vote for the Labour Party and Workers' Party in Dublin in the 1980s was markedly higher than that in the rest of Ireland. But this still begs the question, since even this city vote remains substantially less than the *nation-wide* vote enjoyed by the relatively low-polling Swiss left, and thus underlines the overall problem faced by the Irish left—even in its own 'strongholds'. Hence, while rurality may well be one of the major obstacles standing in the way of a *nationalisation* of left voting, it nevertheless hardly constitutes a satisfactory explanation of the debility of the Irish left in general, and of the urban left in particular.

Finally, and most evidently, the reality is that Irish society is indeed characterised by very high levels of working-class 'self-recruitment', or class reproduction (see Whelan, Breen and Whelan, this volume), which, when coupled with the more general lack of social mobility, underlines the reality of class conditions, and, in particular, make it highly likely that a distinctive working-class culture can be sustained. The evidence adduced by Breen *et al.* (1990) concerning the class structure as a whole is also compelling in this regard. Over and above their documenting of the undeniable realities of a sharply-bounded class structure in contemporary Ireland, they also clearly demonstrate how the low level of social mobility, on the one hand, and limited state-induced redistribution, on the other, have combined 'to mould *economic* class categories . . . into identifiable, cohesive *social* classes' (1990: 60). Indeed, even if we were to disregard the data on class awareness (see below), this 'structural' evidence alone would incline one to doubt the notion that it is an absence of favourable class conditions which now stymies the Irish left. Rather, the problem would appear to lie beyond this, and to concern instead the translation of *social* classes into class *politics*.

The 'Class Awareness' Explanation

But class conditions are one thing; class awareness is clearly something else, and it is obvious that class conditions cannot generate class politics unless there is at least some prior translation of these conditions into a sense of class awareness. Is this perhaps the problem in Ireland? Is the problem that while a class structure exists in reality, it is not perceived to exist by those whom it constrains, and particularly by those, in the working class, who might provide the basis for a class left politics?

There are two points which are relevant here, the first of which concerns comparative levels of subjective class identification. The data that are cited here come from the European Parliament Election Study of 1989, an EC-wide survey in which comparable questions were asked at more or less the same time in all EC member states, thus allowing the relative position of Ireland to be assessed with some degree of precision. The results are striking and, in some senses, surprising. In the first place, some slight support can be found for the suggestion that class distinctions have less relevance in the Irish context than is the case in other European countries, in that almost 9 per cent of Irish respondents either refused or were unable to assign themselves to a social class, a proportion exceeded only in Luxembourg (13.8 per cent) and Belgium (10.4 per cent). But this is of minor importance, for what emerges even more clearly is the remarkably high percentage of Irish respondents who assign themselves to the working class. Indeed, at 41.9 per cent, this figure is second only to that for Britain (45.9 per cent), and well in excess of those for countries such as Denmark (21.9 per cent), Germany (21 per cent), Italy (22.9 per cent) and particularly Spain (12.1 per cent). In sum, these figures not only suggest that class categories mean something to the vast majority of Irish voters, but also that Ireland is characterised by a relatively high level of working-class self awareness.

To be sure, data such as these may be regarded as of dubious value, since 'class' itself, together with its qualifying adjectives of 'working', 'middle', and so on, may mean different things to different people, and may also carry a normative baggage which clouds the cross-national comparability of those surveys which seek to probe class identification. In particular, certain cultures may encourage many 'objectively' working-class respondents to identify subjectively with the middle class, and vice versa. In the case of Ireland, however, as can be seen from Table 2, such confusion as does exist seems almost wholly a function of the misplaced identities of *non*-working class respondents. Thus while Ireland records one of the highest percentages of working class identification among non-working class respondents (27.8 per cent of those in non-working class occupations regard themselves as working class, as against an average of just 13.4 per cent in the other EC countries—the Irish figure is second only to the British figure of 34.3 per cent), it is even more striking to note that it also records the highest proportion of those in working-class occupations who, 'correctly', regard themselves as working class (69.6 per cent as against an average of 47.5 per cent in the other EC countries). Thus, while non-working class respondents in Ireland may be more inclined to regard themselves as working class than is the case in most other EC countries, this is less relevant to our present purposes than the fact that working-class respondents are more likely to regard themselves as working class than in any of the other countries. As far as the working class is concerned, therefore, there seems remarkably little confusion about class identity, a factor which makes the debility of a class left political alternative all the more striking. Indeed, the country which comes

Table 2. Subjective class identification in EC countries. 1989: percentage of respondents claiming to be working class from among different occupational categories (excluding respondents with no classifiable occupation).

Country	% Among skilled and unskilled Workers	% Among other occupational categories
Belgium	58.7	13.5
Britain	60.2	34.3
Denmark	42.9	7.7
France	51.0	13.5
FRG	40.5	10.6
Greece	47.4	23.6
Ireland	**69.6**	**27.8**
Italy	43.9	12.0
Luxembourg	51.1	1.8
Netherlands	58.4	8.6
Portugal	49.2	18.0
Spain	19.0	6.5

Source: European Parliament Election Study, 1989.

closest to the Irish pattern in this regard, that is, the country in which a strikingly high proportion of those in both working-class and non-working class occupations regard themselves as working class, is Britain, where class has long been regarded as the main basis of political choice.

The third piece of evidence which can be cited here concerns levels of trade union density; that is, the proportion of the labour force which is organised within trade unions, and which, in this context, is being stretched in order to be read as an indirect indicator of the extent of popular awareness of collective interests in general and of class interests in particular. It must be emphasised that the figures which can be cited are relatively crude aggregates, which do not distinguish between white-collar and blue-collar unionisation, and which are therefore not specific to working class identity as such. Despite such qualifications, however, the reality is that at least up to the mid-1980s, according to figures on ten west European nations reported by Visser (1987: 21), and to Irish data reported by Breen et al. (1990: 163, citing Roche and Larragy, 1987, and see also Roche, this volume), Ireland is characterised by one of the *highest* levels of trade union density in western Europe. Indeed, with a figure of some 55 per cent of the labour force unionised, Ireland ranks in fifth position within the eleven countries covered, lagging behind Denmark (82 per cent), Sweden (80 per cent), Norway (63 per cent), and Austria (58 per cent), each of which has, of course, a strong socialist tradition; and exceeding the levels in the United Kingdom (46 per cent), Italy (36 per cent), Germany (34 per cent), Switzerland (29 per cent), the Netherlands (24 per cent) and France (15 per cent). Despite the crudeness of the indicator, we can therefore conclude that large sections of the Irish working class are aware of their identity as a class *and* of the need for collective action as a class—at least as far as the labour market is concerned.

The discussion so far can therefore be summarised as follows. First, a class structure exists in reality; second, Irish citizens are aware of this class structure; third, within that class structure, a relatively high percentage of citizens identify with the working class, including a particularly pronounced percentage of those in working-class occupations; and fourth, as indicated by levels of unionisation, a relatively high proportion of the labour force (and hence of the working class) appears to perceive—and to act upon—a collective interest which can be expressed in class (or, at least, in occupational) terms.

In other words, reasonably pronounced class conditions exist, and it is likely that a relatively high degree of class awareness also exists. Both factors would therefore suggest that, *ceteris paribus*, Ireland should possess a relatively strong class left political alignment. But, as we have seen, this is clearly not the case. However, before going on to widen the search for explanations of this increasingly perplexing peculiarity, it is necessary to take a tangential look at the precise character of the left electoral support that does exist in Ireland.

A Note on Class Voting

Since the publication of Whyte's seminal essay (1974) on the relationship between social structure and voting, appropriately entitled 'Politics Without Social Bases', a sporadic debate has ensued within Irish political science concerning the real extent to which class, and other social variables, can be related to voting preferences in Irish elections. In general, it seems that they cannot. Gallagher's (1976) extensive ecological analysis of voting patterns over time, for example, largely confirmed Whyte's findings on the lack of social rootedness of the Irish parties. And while my own re-analysis of the data used by Whyte did note a substantial social effect in relation to the particular division between Fine Gael and Labour supporters, even this social effect was obliterated once the cross-class support for Fianna Fáil was added to the equation (Mair, 1979: 457–9). More recently, Laver *et al.* (1987b), partly employing a more sophisticated categorisation of classes and occupations, have noted that a limited social effect does exist, and that Irish politics may be regarded as having 'some' social basis. In general, however, the broad conclusion of this debate, at least so far, has been that any relationship which does exist between social divisions, on the one hand, and party preference, on the other, is, at most, quite marginal.

The new European Parliament Election Study data which were cited above, and which, being based on actual as opposed to intended vote, provide a reasonably reliable source of information, also tend to confirm this pattern, and also emphasise Irish exceptionalism within western Europe. But it is important to note that they do so with one major caveat: for while the Irish left enjoys relatively little overall support within its 'natural' working class constituency, it enjoys a strikingly *high* share of the working class vote *relative to* its share of the non-working class vote. In other words, while its share of the overall working class vote is relatively low, its support is nevertheless pronouncedly biased towards the working class. The relevant figures are reported in Table 3, which shows voting support for the left among both working class and non-working class voters, as defined both in terms of occupations (objective class) and in terms of class identification (subjective class).

As these simple data indicate, the lack of a distinct social base of support for the Irish left is evident in its ranking in one of the lowest positions among the twelve EC countries in terms of its share of the working class vote. In terms of subjective class, Labour and the Workers' Party actually polled just 20.5 per cent of this vote, as against an average for the left of 34.2 per cent in the remaining eleven countries, and with only the Portuguese left lagging behind the Irish left in this regard. The same pattern is apparent with the objective class indicator. The Irish left polls just 21.7 per cent of the skilled and non-skilled working class vote, as against an average of 32.6 per cent in the other countries. And here again it is only Portugal which lags behind Ireland.

What is also striking about the Irish case, of course, is the low level of left support within the *non*-working class,[6] with Ireland ranking in the lowest position among all twelve countries as far as both class indicators are concerned. And it is this which necessitates the caveat: for in terms of the *ratio of the share of the working class vote to the share of the non-working class vote*, the Irish left ranks towards the top of the list of those included in Table 3. In fact, the ratio in the Irish case is a remarkably high 3.10 as far as the objective class indicator is concerned, ranking highest of all twelve countries; and is 2.23 as far as the subjective class indicator is concerned, being exceeded only by Belgium, Britain and Denmark. Thus, while the Irish left is far from being composed of *parties of the working class*, in that Labour and the Workers' Party win only a small minority of working class support, however defined, it is, nevertheless, in large part composed of *working class parties*, since it relies more heavily on the working class vote than almost all the comparable lefts in the twelve other countries considered. If nothing else, these data confirm that it is not so much the *character* of the left vote in Ireland which is peculiar, but rather, and more simply, its *size*.

In short, the peculiarity of the class left in Ireland is not that it is fundamentally different from that elsewhere in Western Europe; it is just that it is smaller. And since an adequate explanation of this smallness cannot (easily) be derived from the peculiarities of class conditions or class awareness, that is, from a more *sociological* perspective, then it seems appropriate to address the question from a more *political* perspective, in which two distinct categories of explanation are relevant: first, an explanation based on the institutional and behavioural characteristics of Irish politics; and second, an explanation based on political culture and political strategy.

---

[6] A factor which, as Kieran Kennedy and Chris Whelan have emphasised to me, may well be due to the pronounced and very intense attachment to property in the Irish case. This particular cultural phenomenon has long roots in Irish society and, while neglected in this present discussion, does merit substantial analysis.

Peter Mair

Table 3. Class support for left parties in EC countries, 1989.

Country[a]	Subjective Class[b]			Objective Class[c]		
	% Support in working class (1)	% Support in other classes (2)	Ratio (1)/(2)	% Support in working class (3)	% Support in other classes (4)	Ratio (3)/(4)
Belgium	37.9	13.9	2.73	28.7	14.6	1.97
Britain	28.5	12.3	2.32	24.1	15.2	1.58
Denmark	33.0	14.7	2.24	23.8	16.6	1.43
France	22.0	15.0	1.47	26.0	16.6	1.57
FRG	35.3	29.7	1.19	36.3	29.3	1.24
Greece	48.6	37.0	1.31	50.0	45.2	1.11
Ireland	**20.5**	**9.2**	**2.23**	**21.7**	**7.0**	**3.10**
Italy	40.3	27.3	1.48	43.0	29.0	1.48
Luxembourg	41.2	21.0	1.96	44.4	20.9	2.12
Netherlands	32.6	19.0	1.72	27.0	22.0	1.23
Portugal	15.0	14.3	1.05	14.4	15.0	0.96
Spain	42.2	28.4	1.49	40.5	21.1	1.92

[a] All class left parties included, with, in addition to the main social democratic parties, the Danish Socialist People's Party, the French Communist Party, the Greek Left Coalition, the Irish Workers' Party, the Italian Communist Party, Social Democratic Party (PSDI), and Proletarian Democracy, the Luxembourg Communist Party and the Spanish United Left. It should be noted that the levels of support shown do not always correspond closely with the aggregate figures reported in Table 1. There are two reasons for this: first, the earlier figures concerned decade averages, whereas these are from survey data from 1989; second, the preferences of a number of respondents who were not classifiable in terms of either objective or subjective class have been excluded from these calculations.
[b] All respondents defining themselves as belonging to the working class or as belonging to other (specified) classes.
[c] All respondents in skilled and unskilled working class occupational categories, or in other (specified) occupational categories.
Source: As for Table 2.

The 'Institutional and Behavioural' Explanation

Clientelism

One of the first, and most obvious explanations for the apparent inability of class conditions and class awareness to translate into class action, at least politically, lays particular stress on the perceived lack of political relevance of collective, class interests. (I emphasise the political here simply in order to accommodate the fact that, as indicated by the level of trade-union density, collective industrial and labour market interests are clearly perceived as being of relevance). And the most obvious explanation for this perceived lack of relevance is explained, in turn, by the priority accorded to individual interests and individual action, which, it can be claimed, is reflected in the pervasiveness of *clientelistic networks* in Irish politics.

There is little need to rehearse the various arguments which seek to demonstrate the importance of clientelism in Irish politics; nor is it necessary to refer to the vast array of evidence which reveals how politically relevant grievances are often processed in a particularistic or personalistic fashion, constituting an exchange between the individual voter, on the one hand, and the individual (and, in this case, essentially non-partisan) politician, on the other. Unlike in other political systems, therefore, where organised mass parties mobilise collective identities among voters, Irish politics is characterised by a pattern of individualistic mobilisation which is inimical to the pursuit of collective interests. Clientelism therefore acts to disaggregate potential collective interests, including, most obviously, class interests. This point has been highlighted by a number of observers of Irish politics, and little needs to be added to their conclusions. For Higgins (1982: 133), for example, clientelism 'disorganises the poor in that it serves as an impediment to their aggregating their demands or mobility in horizontal associations for the prosecution of such demands'. In a similar vein, Hazelkorn (1986: 338) writes that clientelism 'ensures that incipient (class) conflict can be redirected through acceptable channels which emphasise the role of individuals and not groups or classes'. More importantly, she adds that 'insofar as this is the dominant mode of political organisation, class or mass mobilisation is that much more difficult to achieve. . . . [C]lientelism has helped to keep the working class outside the sphere of active politics . . . [and] retards the political development and consciousness of the economically dominated classes'. Hence, if we can assume that clientelistic practices tend to operate much more extensively within the political sphere, as opposed to the industrial sphere, we can advance at least one attractive and distinctive explanation as to why class action at the level of the trade unions fails to translate into class action at the level of politics and voting behaviour. Indeed, the Labour Party currently affiliates more trade union *members* than it wins popular *votes*.

But, however attractive, clientelism in itself does not seem to offer a really plausible or adequate explanation of this particular Irish peculiarity. And the main reason for this inadequacy, as I have argued elsewhere (Mair, 1987), is that the pervasiveness and exclusiveness of clientelistic links and particularistic ties has tended to be overestimated, as has the degree of individualistic mobilisation; while the importance of party, and hence of more collective mobilisation, has correspondingly tended to be underestimated.

There are several considerations involved here. In the first place, the peculiarity of the Irish electoral system, which, in its preference voting procedures, is one of the factors most often cited as sustaining clientelistic practices, does not derive from its favouring individualistic ties *instead of* party orientations; it derives, rather, from its capacity to promote individualistic ties *as well as* party orientations. Irish voters may well orient towards clientelistic (that is, individualistic) ties; but the evidence of Irish voting studies clearly suggests that they *also* orient towards partisan (that is, collective) commitments, since what is distinctive about the single transferable vote electoral system within multi-member constituencies is its ability to allow both types of orientations to co-exist with one another. Thus, for many (albeit not all) voters, it appears that they *first*, as partisans, choose a party, and *then*, as clientelistic voters, choose an individual within that party as their first-preference selection (Mair, 1987: 66–86). Hence, at least in this case, evidence of the importance of clientelism does not necessarily imply evidence of lack of partisanship, and in this sense the notion of party, and of collective identifications, would appear to be no less strong in Ireland than in a number of other countries.

Second, many of the arguments which have emphasised the importance of clientelism have done so more or less by default, in that they have (mistakenly) assumed an absence of policy differences between the parties (see, for example, Carty, 1981; and, more recently, Lee, 1989: 545–7). Since the parties do not really differ from one another, it is argued, voters are unable to use party *per se* as a guide to voting choice. There is little to sustain this assumption, however. On the contrary, as an analysis of election programmes clearly indicates, the parties do differ substantially, and meaningfully, in terms of their policy preferences, and real policy competition does exist (Mair, 1987: 138–206). Moreover, when Irish parties do enunciate their policy preferences, it is striking to note that they tend to focus more on economic and social policies than is the case in most other west European party systems—an emphasis on the mundane which stands in sharp contrast to the widely held assumption that the Irish parties are interested only in their idiosyncratic divisions on nationalist issues (see Table 4).

Third, and finally, the orientation towards party, and hence the non-exclusiveness of clientelism, can also be seen in that party as such, and particularly the policy performance of parties, matters to voters, as is evidenced by the existence of a clear relationship between the general sense of economic well-being, on the one hand, and the electoral popularity of incumbent parties, on the other (Mair, 1987: 76–7). In short, and as elsewhere in Europe, Irish politics *is* party politics, even if, in contrast with many other countries, it is *also* personalistic politics.

Table 4. Percentage of contents of election programmes devoted to social and economic issues.

Country	% of contents
Austria	49.8
Belgium	40.5
Britain	43.3
Denmark	37.8
France	38.8
Germany	34.9
Ireland	**57.5**
Italy	23.1
Netherlands	46.2
Norway	55.9
Sweden	52.6
Mean	*43.7*

Source: Calculated from the data from the ECPR Manifesto Study.

But there are other, and arguably more important, questions to be asked about the supposed impact of clientelism on the fortunes of class politics. For example, while clientelism may be cited as a factor which acts to disaggregate the working class and therefore impinges directly on the fortunes of the class left, why does it not appear to have had a similarly powerful impact on the collective interests of farmers, which readily, and frequently, translate into political action (a point also emphasised by Hazelkorn, 1986: 357)?[7] Moreover, if clientelism is so important in the political sphere, and if it has been responsible for a political disaggregation of collective interests, why then has this not also spread over to the industrial sphere? Why should collective class interests and collective class action be manifestly relevant at the industrial level, and yet absent at the political level?[8]

[7] Unfortunately there is no room here to explore the development of agrarian politics in Ireland, and the revealing contrasts which it provides with the development of working class politics. One point which should be emphasised, however, relates to an argument which is dealt with later, concerning the bias against the politicisation of social conflict. For, interestingly enough, farmers' parties, in their unabashed avowal of the farmers' interests, seem to have proved much more immune to this bias than have workers' parties, a contrast which may be due to their ability to put themselves forward as reflecting the *national* interest: what is good for the farmers is good also for the country, whereas what is good for the workers is good only for the workers.

[8] Indeed, given the organisational fragmentation of the trade-union movement (see the papers by Roche and by Hardiman in this volume); the disaggregation of welfare clienteles and the importance of means-tested benefits (see the papers by O'Connell and Rottman, and Callan and Nolan in this volume); and the sheer territorial dispersion of the unskilled manual class (see the paper by Whelan *et al.* in this volume), it is surprising that collective action proves to have any real potential at all in the industrial sphere.

The need for an independent working class party

If clientelism is not the (only) answer to the puzzle of the failure of the class left in Ireland, then perhaps an alternative explanation might be that the class left does not constitute a strong, independent electoral force simply because there is no real *need* for such a force. In other words, as far as the potential constituency of the class left is concerned, things are fine as they are, and, in any case, the sort of demands which might be advanced by such an independent movement are already being met by the existing political parties, and particularly by Fianna Fáil.

One way in which to assess the potential of this argument is to consider the sort of outcomes which, in a comparative perspective, might be expected to have followed from the successful mobilisation of a strong party of the left. Were these outcomes actually realised in the Irish case, notwithstanding the absence of such a party, then we might reasonably assume that the need for a strong party of the left had been satisfied through other means. Were these outcomes absent, on the other hand, then an alternative explanation would be required. Three sets of outcomes or demands are relevant here, since in each case comparative analysis suggests that their realisation can be considered as having required a strong class left party: first, participation by a working-class party (or parties) of the left in decision-making; second, the incorporation of the trade unions into the public policy-making process; and third, the creation and maintenance of a strong welfare state.

Let us first address the question of *involvement in decision-making*. The argument here would simply be that unless it can acquire the status of a strong and substantial party, the class left will experience persistent exclusion from government office and from an influence on the policy-making process. In Ireland, however, this is evidently far from being the case. The Labour Party was first established just before World War I, and already by 1918–19 it was being regarded by Sinn Fein as having a legitimate voice in determining the programme of the new Dáil. Up to the late 1920s, in the context of Sinn Fein and Fianna Fáil abstentionism, the party constituted the major 'legitimate' opposition in parliament. In 1932, it provided external support for Fianna Fáil's first (minority) government, being a coalition partner in all but name; and in 1948 it actually entered government as one of the junior partners to Fine Gael. The party was again in government in the late 1950s, and then again in the mid-1970s and for a large part of the 1980s. Given its small size, therefore, its record of sheer length of incumbency compares favourably with that of its counterparts in continental Europe. In the last two decades, for example, the Irish Labour Party has enjoyed a more sustained period in government than has the major party of the left in Italy, the Netherlands, or the United Kingdom.

The second outcome is less directly concerned with formal governmental participation, and relates to *the role of the wider labour movement in the policy-making process*. The argument here is simply that unless a strong class left party exists, and, more arguably, unless it can gain regular access to government, the trade-union voice will be excluded from the more generalised, day-to-day process of public policy formation. To put it another way, the regular political participation of working class parties in government will facilitate the emergence of a more corporatist mode of decision-making (see, for example, Lehmbruch, 1979), and this in turn implies that it is in the trade unions' interests to have a strong class left party in politics. Again, however, the Irish case suggests otherwise. While acknowledging Hardiman's well-taken scepticism about the applicability of a full-blooded neo-corporatist model to the Irish case (Hardiman, 1988; and this volume), it is nevertheless clear that the trade-union movement, however fragmented and inchoate, has rarely been denied a legitimate voice in the policy-making process. Its participatory role was clearly evident in the centralised agreements and 'national understandings' of the 1970s and early 1980s, as well as, if not more markedly so, in Fianna Fáil's Programme for National Recovery in the late 1980s and now in the more recent Programme for Economic and Social Progress. To be sure, this is no fully-fledged 'social partnership', which does perhaps require a sustained governmental role for the left; but, as Hardiman concludes, it is at the same time a process which has given the trade unions 'direct access to government and . . . an unprecedented input to public policy' (1988: 247). And since such access has not only proved possible, but has also been strengthened, under the aegis of 'non-left' (that is, Fianna Fáil) governments, it therefore seems likely that the trade-union movement, at least, does not suffer markedly from the absence of a strong independent political voice on the left.

The third demand which is of relevance here concerns the *creation and maintenance of a strong welfare state*, as well as the acceptance of a concept of social citizenship—a demand which, to judge from the more mechanistic exponents of the 'Do Parties Matter?' school of political science, would appear to require either governments of the left or, at least, a strong voice for the left. In reality, however, the Irish case (together, indeed, with the Dutch and Italian cases) again suggests otherwise, and demonstrates that a commitment to welfare is far from predicated upon a substantial left input into the policy-making process. The most relevant source here is the comprehensive analysis of Maguire (1986), who emphasises how, since the 1960s, Ireland has increased its expenditure on welfare substantially beyond the average increase recorded by other OECD nations:

> In 1960 social expenditure amounted to 11.7 per cent of GDP compared with an average of 13.1 per cent across OECD countries. By 1981 the Irish expenditure share had risen to 28 per cent, compared with an OECD average of 25.6 per cent. The growth of social spending is particularly impressive considering that Ireland is not an especially wealthy country by OECD standards. In 1981, Ireland ranked twentieth in the OECD area in terms of per capita GDP, but eighth in terms of the GDP share of social expenditure (Maguire, 1986: 286–7).

Moreover, much of this expansion was the result of wholly 'non-left' governments, that is, Fianna Fáil governments, rather than of those coalition governments in which Labour played a minor, but not insubstantial, role. Ignoring the very exceptional 1948–51 government, for example, when postwar reconstruction led to an annual growth of social expenditure of some 12.7 per cent, annual growth under coalition governments averaged some 4.5 per cent. Under Fianna Fáil governments, on the other hand, the average annual growth rate of social expenditure reached 5.4 per cent, with the party holding office during all but two of the years from 1963 to 1975, that is, the period in which the welfare state experienced what Maguire refers to as its 'major expansion'. To be sure, Maguire also points out that much of this difference can be explained by differential rates of economic growth, and that the partisan contrasts all but disappear when one controls for changes in the level of GDP. Even then, however, the real point remains: wholly non-left governments have proved at least as willing welfarists as have those in which the left is involved (Maguire 1986: 334–8).

In all three instances, therefore, it appears that Ireland has not suffered unduly from the absence of a strong left party, and in this sense the best explanation as to why the class left remains so weak in electoral terms may perhaps also be the simplest: there is nothing in particular which is offered to voters by the left, and *only* by the left, and hence Irish voters perceive no real need for a strong left party or parties.

Yet it might also be argued that this assessment is actually too simple, and that it subordinates the more important question of the redistribution of resources to the less revealing one of the overall level of welfare expenditure. In this sense, a strong class left party might have been expected to effect not only a growth in general welfare spending, as was the case under Fianna Fáil, but also, and more crucially, a *more equitable redistribution* of national resources. But even in this case, the actual record of the Irish welfare state does not appear so ineffective. In the sophisticated comparative analysis of income distribution reported in this volume by Callan and Nolan, for example, the Irish 'welfare effort', as measured in terms of cash transfers and taxes, is seen not only as comparable to that of other, more developed economies, but also as associated with a distribution of income which is somewhat *more* equal than the level of economic development alone might lead one to expect. In addition, the combined effect of cash transfers and direct taxes is reported as having as large an impact on income redistribution in Ireland as elsewhere, and, moreover, as having improved in effectiveness in the 1970s and, probably, in the 1980s also. In these terms, at least, Ireland not only enjoys a relatively well-financed welfare state but also one which seems reasonably, and increasingly, progressive.

At the same time, though, this is still not the whole story. When one looks at the experiences of the different *social classes*, as opposed to different *income groups* (and thus separates out the experiences of the relatively deprived unskilled working class, on the one hand, and the relatively favoured property-owning small farmers, on the other), the image of egalitarianism, redistribution and progressivity begins to dissipate. As Maguire has further observed, for example, 'the extent to which social programmes have contributed to a more equal sharing out of the fruits of economic progress must be questioned. . . . Such evidence as is available indicates that the redistributive process operates unevenly from a social class perspective, treating the property owning classes in a relatively favourable fashion' (1986: 320). Breen *et al.* draw a similar conclusion, noting that 'the high levels of [social] expenditure and the taxation needed to finance it . . . certainly failed to abate the importance of class in determining life chances' (1990: 97). Their conclusions on the impact of family policy are even more starkly stated: 'the Irish State's policies combine today to perpetuate and even exacerbate class inequalities' (1990: 121). And finally, as Whelan, Breen and Whelan's new data, reported in this volume, clearly indicate, differential levels of various forms of social deprivation are also strongly class-linked.

In short, when looking at occupational categories, and when looking at the class structure, there is little to counter the view that modern Ireland remains a profoundly inegalitarian society. The purpose of this observation is not simply to suggest that the situation might have been different had there been a successful mobilisation of a major class left party. Rather, the point is to emphasise the now very apparent paradox that, despite the existence of favourable class conditions, despite seemingly widespread class awareness, and despite the evidence of large-scale, class-based inequalities and of disadvantaged class interests which might benefit from being served in politics, there has never been a successful mobilisation of a class left party in Irish politics. In other words, the puzzle still remains, and this particular peculiarity, now all the more striking, still needs to be explained.

The Political Culture and Political Strategy Explanation

Before reviewing this final kind of explanation it is necessary to return briefly to Sartori's (1968/1990) theoretical analysis of the factors which both facilitate and promote the development of class politics and class parties. In his closely argued and innovative essay, which seeks to clarify the distinction between the sociology of politics and political sociology, Sartori argues against the pervasive belief that political preferences and behaviour can be seen as the essentially 'automatic' or 'natural' reflection of social divisions—a belief most aptly summarised by Lipset's classic assertion that 'in every modern democracy conflict among different groups is expressed through political parties which basically represent a "democratic translation of the class struggle"' (Lipset, 1960: 220). Were such a translation to be automatic, then it is clear that not only would all modern industrial societies give rise to major working-class parties (which has clearly not been the case in the United States—or modern Ireland) but also that similar social conditions would create similar partisan structures, which, given the long-term presence of radical communist parties in certain western democracies (for example, Finland, France and Italy), and the long-term irrelevance of such parties in others (for example, Britain, Norway and Sweden) is clearly not a sustainable thesis. On the contrary, as Sartori emphasises, the partisan structure of class politics is much more contingent than is implied by any notion of simple 'reflection' or 'translation', and depends on a variety of factors, including the extent of class awareness, class consciousness, and class action, at least as much as on the existence of appropriate class conditions.

The existence of a class structure can therefore be regarded as a *necessary* but a far from *sufficient* condition for the emergence of class politics, which depends also on the degree to which members of different classes, and of the working class in particular, feel themselves to be members of a class, and, most crucially, are willing to act together, *in politics*, on that basis.[9] And this, in turn, depends on the extent to which class identity is seen to be relevant to politics or, as Sartori puts it (1990: 70), on the extent to which members of the class have been 'class persuaded'. Which, rather neatly, brings to the forefront the persuasive role of class organisations and class parties, for the 'most likely and apt

[9] For a later version of much the same argument, see Przeworski (1985).

persuader is the party (or the union) playing on the class appeal resource'. In other words, 'it is not the "objective" class (class conditions) that creates the party, but the party that creates the "subjective" class (class consciousness) . . . [W]henever parties reflect social classes, this signifies *more* about the party end than about the class end of the interaction' (Sartori, 1990: 169).[10]

In the Irish case, then, the most reasonable explanation for the absence of a class alignment in politics, and for the absence of a major class left alternative in the Irish party system, is what at first sight may also appear as the most tautological: unlike in the rest of western Europe, no party, or union, has sought sufficiently hard 'to persuade' such an alignment, and the 'class appeal' in politics has been persistently muted. In concluding, I would therefore like briefly to suggest three related factors which might account for this eschewal of the class motif in political mobilisation, all of which can constitute elements of what might be referred to more generally as a *politics of the national interest*.

The legacy of past cleavages

The first factor is that of the legacy of past conflicts, or past cleavages, in modern Irish history.[11] Two major cleavages dominated the early development and formative years of mass politics in Ireland, involving a nationalist mobilisation, on the one hand, and a Catholic mobilisation, on the other. These cleavages were clearly related, and alike expressed an opposition which might loosely be defined as that between the 'haves' and the 'have-nots', an opposition which acquired a degree of autonomy in most other European states and which, in these other countries, was eventually reflected in the mobilisation of mass working-class parties. In Ireland, however, and unusually so, it is important to realise that the

---

[10] It is interesting to note that although operating from a perspective far removed from that of Sartori, Marxist political strategists have often theorised in a similar way about the class-party linkage. Thus, in *What Next?*, Trotsky writes: 'The proletariat acquires an independent role only at the moment when, from a social class *in itself*, it becomes a social class *for itself*. This cannot take place otherwise than through the medium of a party. The party is that historical organ by means of which the class becomes class conscious.' (quoted in Cannon, 1975: 5).

[11] For reasons of space, I am deliberately avoiding an account of the Irish experience of the more generalised process by which cleavages and party systems were 'frozen' in the wake of mass enfranchisement in western Europe (see Lipset and Rokkan, 1967; Bartolini and Mair, 1990), despite its obvious relevance for the development of the Irish party system and for Labour's failure in particular. Useful discussions of the applicability of the Lipset–Rokkan model to the Irish case can be found in Garvin (1974) and Sinnott (1978, 1984). Cf. also Farrell (1970) and Mair (1987: 43–60).

opposition between 'haves' and 'have-nots' did not really correspond to an internal national divide. Rather, being subsumed within both nationalist and Catholic mobilisation, it was seen to reflect the opposition of the under-privileged Catholic Irish, on the one hand, and the privileged non-Catholic British, on the other. This is, of course, well-known, and has accounted for most of the problems facing the Irish left in its attempts first to cope with, then to absorb, and, most recently, to differentiate itself from, a radical nationalist politics.

An oppositional movement imbued with a nationalist and Catholic identity, which incorporated virtually all of the citizens in what was to become the Irish Republic, left little space in which to mobilise an internal opposition, which might have polarised privileged and under-privileged *within* the Republic itself. Rather, there emerged a new political culture which, in its constant stress on Catholic nationalist uniformity and homogeneity—and through the early development of an institutional structure which had been built on the assumption that partisan politics would fail to develop—proved quite hostile to any notion of politicising internal social divisions. To be sure, such divisions did quickly develop in the new state, and, within the terms of reference of an intra-nationalist opposition, did prove to have substantial social underpinnings and hence to pit the relatively privileged against the relatively deprived. Even then, however, the explicitly social side of this conflict proved short-lived, and was often denied by the actual rhetoric of the mobilisers themselves. This was certainly the case with Fianna Fáil, for example, which, as Bew *et al.* (1989: 78) emphasise, 'sought to mobilise an agrarian constituency of small farmer and labourer aspiration and resentment . . . [while] confin[ing] this constituency within a national project which self-consciously eschewed class polarisation'. In class terms, as in social terms more generally, and despite all polarising political conflicts, the Irish people were to be seen as one. To divide this united people, and especially to promote a politics which would pit class against class, was both anti-national and irrelevant, for there could only be common enemies, and these all lay outside the boundaries of the state. In short, there developed a 'culture of community', an emphasis on the 'uniqueness, unity, and wholeness' of Irish political culture (O'Carroll, 1987: 83–4); and to 'persuade' a necessarily divisive class alignment in such an environment would inevitably prove a most difficult task (cf. also Hazelkorn, 1989).

The role of Fianna Fáil

The second factor which must be highlighted here is the long-term appeal of Fianna Fáil, which has acted to sustain a sense of political homogeneity and uniformity—long beyond the period in which the momentum of both Catholic and nationalist triumphalism might have been expected to fade.[12] Fianna Fáil's ideological posture is based on two mutually reinforcing appeals—the emphasis on territorial unity and traditional nationalist politics, on the one hand, and the emphasis on social harmony and social cohesion, on the other. As early as 1933, for instance, de Valera had insisted that Fianna Fáil was 'a National Party, representing all sections of the community' (*Irish Press*, 20 January, 1933), while on the eve of his retirement as party leader his message was that 'Fianna Fáil is a national movement rather than a political party organisation' (*Irish Times*, 18 May, 1954). More recently, in 1969, Jack Lynch began a review of party policy by declaring his pride in being leader of 'this great democratic organisation, of this broadly based national movement representative as it is of all the people—and I mean all sections of the people—farmers, workers, businessmen and employers. Representing such a broad spectrum of Irish life, Fianna Fáil is in a unique position to produce and put into effect the policies best suited to the needs of the Irish people' (Lynch, 1969: 1). His successor, Charles Haughey, has spoken in similar terms. In 1983, for example, he insisted that 'our hopes, our beliefs, and aspirations are not sectional. They are national. They are not confined or limited by any regional boundaries or attitudes' (Haughey, 1983: 1). And so on.

In general, of course, such Fianna Fáil claims were not without foundation; the party did consistently win support from farmers and from workers, from professionals and employers, from young and old, such that its enduring constituency seemed like a microcosm of Irish society as a whole. Nor was Fianna Fáil averse to employing this cross-class appeal to its advantage, and in this sense the emphasis on social solidarity came easily. Given its constituency, Fianna Fáil could more credibly claim a national political project than could its more sectionally-based opponents. In 1943, for example, when the notion was mooted of replacing a single-party Fianna Fáil government with an inter-party national government, Fianna Fáil leaders argued that 'a government which came from a party representing all sections of the community was much more entitled to be called a national government than would a government composed of the odds and ends of little sectional groups' (*Irish Press*, 16 June, 1943). And it was precisely because Fianna Fáil drew substantial support from all the major social groups that such promotion of social solidarity favoured it electorally. In the first place, and to the extent that the general interest was perceived by the electorate as being of greater importance than any specific sectional interest, then one could anticipate a general drift towards

[12] The following remarks draw heavily on Mair (1987: 177–184).

Fianna Fáil as the most broadly representative 'national' party. More specifically, however, insofar as the promotion of social solidarity militated against the politicisation of social conflict, it also acted against any possible break-up of the party's broad, cross-class coalition. To set one group against another would be to divide the party against itself. To mobilise the town against the country, or worker against employer, would be to undermine the very social solidarity on which the party depended. It was in just such a context that Sean Lemass urged the incorporation of working class interests in party policy in the 1950s and 1960s (Bew and Patterson, 1982): no single social group could be excluded from the remit of the party.

The more widely documented emphasis on territorial nationalism, which has accompanied that on social solidarity, is of course also crucial to an understanding of the Fianna Fáil appeal. As Haughey (1981: 33) once stated in one of his more memorable rhetorical flourishes, 'in the broad sweep of [Fianna Fáil] membership and their faith and devotion to their country, there resides what one might well call "the Spirit of the Nation"'. But it is also important to note that this particular appeal to the nation finds expression in social, as well as in strictly territorial terms. The nation must be united, but it is a unity which derives from social solidarity. Of course, the appeal may also be accompanied by an emphasis on territorial nationalism *per se*, but, in more recent years, it was the social rather than the strictly territorial element which received greater attention. What must be emphasised, however, is that the two appeals do reinforce one another, in that it is precisely a record of militancy in terms of territorial nationalism that lends credibility to appeals to social solidarity and the national interest. The link between the two was perhaps most clearly expressed by Jack Lynch in an interview with the *Irish Times* (28 June, 1975): 'the soul of Fianna Fáil is still anti-Partition', he argued: 'To be in Fianna Fáil you must have a Republican outlook in its broadest conception. One must also have a very strong social sense, the desire to represent the broadest political spectrum of the Irish people'.

Hence, for ideological reasons, as well as for more pragmatic partisan and electoral reasons, Fianna Fáil has persistently sought to stress the need for the nation to be united—socially as well as territorially. In other words, Fianna Fáil has sought to define the political alternatives in such a way as to bias politics against the politicisation of internal social conflict in general, and of class conflict in particular, a strategy which finds many echoes in some of the more extreme populist rhetoric employed in the developing economies of Latin America, where ruling parties have, like Fianna Fáil, stressed the need to achieve economic growth with a minimum of social conflict (Malloy, 1977). Moreover, the impact of such a vision extended far beyond the limits of the Fianna Fáil constituency itself. For it is not only true that 'the definition of the alternatives is the supreme instrument of power' (Schattschneider, 1960: 66) but also that it is the very access to power which enables one to continue to define the alternatives thereafter. Irish political culture, no less than the Irish state itself, still bears a strong Fianna Fáil imprint, an imprint which continues to bias that culture against an acceptance of the political expression of internal social conflict. We may not all be in the same boat, but all our different boats do lie alongside one another, and hence we should all wait, together, for the shared rising tide. It is for this reason also that class politics has been inhibited.

The failed Labour challenge

In seeking to challenge this widespread sense of social solidarity and in attempting to politicise internal class divisions, Labour, as the long-term proponent of social democracy in the Irish state and therefore as the only potential long-term class persuader, has undoubtedly faced an uphill struggle and a far from friendly environment. Nevertheless, even allowing for all the obstacles in its path, one might have expected the party to have achieved some greater success than has actually been the case. While it seems unrealistic to suppose that Labour could have gained the sort of support enjoyed by the Norwegian, Swedish, or even British parties, for example, it seems less implausible to suggest that it might have reached the level of, say, the Belgian or Dutch parties, where religious divisions have done much to curtail the appeal of democratic socialism.

In fact, there is evidence to suggest that Labour has got itself to blame for its own failure—at least in part. For, far from seeking to mount a sustained challenge to the social consensus, much of Labour's strategy has reflected an acquiescence in that consensus. And while there is little scope here to document this assertion adequately, there is also little need to do so, in that there is already ample published material recording the party's failure (see in particular Gallagher, 1982; Horgan, 1986; Bew et al., 1989: 142–206). Two familiar points can however be briefly rehearsed. The first, and most obvious, is that Labour has never really sought to prioritise a strong class appeal or to persuade a class alignment. For much of the party's history, a socialist rhetoric has been most notable by its absence, with the emphasis on a class appeal apparent only as regards the need to voice the demands of trade-unionists. It was only really in the late 1960s, when the party was seen to move to the left, that a more social democratic rhetoric came to the fore. Even then, however, the softness of the party's position was evident. As Gallagher (1982: 69) has noted of the annual conference in 1967 which marked the first major shift to the left, 'almost every delegate made much use of the word "socialism", but it remained an ill-defined term, not backed up by anything tangible, and used almost as a ritual word, as proof of comradeship and as a mark of a distinctive Labour identity'.

The second point which deserves highlighting concerns Labour's strategy, and is perhaps more telling. For, since first standing aside in 1918 in order to allow the new Irish electorate unhampered access to nationalist politics, Labour has virtually always drawn back from attempting to mobilise a genuine *political* alternative to mainstream Irish politics, and has instead opted for the more comfortable strategy of building *governmental* alternatives to Fianna Fáil. This was seen most crucially in 1948, when the hold of Fianna Fáil finally appeared to be weakening, and when, with the mobilisation of both Clann na Talmhan and Clann na Poblachta, it seemed that a genuine, and quite radical, realignment was possible. More recently, the same logic underlay the party's decision to coalesce with Fine Gael in 1973, at a time when it finally seemed in a position to establish an independent identity, and in a period in which it had finally begun to outpoll Fine Gael in Dublin to become the second party in the city. In both cases, the potential for long-term electoral growth was sacrificed in the interests of the short-term advantage of incumbency. More crucially, in both cases Labour entered government as part of a wide-ranging inter-party coalition which, given its overall breadth of representation and given its combined social basis, effectively mirrored the intra-party coalition of Fianna Fáil, and, as such, while providing an alternative government, proved wholly unable to persuade an alternative politics.[13] Even when Fianna Fáil was in opposition, therefore, the logic of its alternatives did not disturb the *status quo*: government was to be in the interests of all sectors of society, no single group or class was to be privileged, and social solidarity was to remain unchallenged.

Thus, any attempt by Labour to mount a sustained challenge to this consensus, any attempt to mobilise a sustained class appeal, would have required it to maintain the independent stance which it had begun to develop in the late 1960s; and this, in turn, would have prevented any coalition with Fine Gael—regardless of the extent to which the latter was then promoting notions of social justice. Conversely, any commitment to coalition, and to the creation of an alternative government in the short-run, necessitated downplaying a potential class appeal, since what was

---

[13] However, this is not to deny that the election programme of the 1973 coalition was striking in its relative commitment to redistribution, and, as such, did have the potential to mark a significant shift in policy emphasis. See Mair (1987: 197–202).

unique to Labour was its class identity and, in coalition, it was precisely the unique which had to take second place.

In sum, Irish party politics grew out of a culture which had emphasised solidarity, cohesion, and homogeneity. This culture was then consciously sustained by Fianna Fáil, which saw itself as a party that represented the interests of the Irish people as a whole, and that decried any attempt to turn sections of this people against others. And, finally, Labour in its own modest and cautious way, acquiesced in this same vision of politics, rarely mobilising, and never sustaining an effective alternative politics. In such a context, no major voice sought to persuade a class alignment. And hence, despite the existence of favourable class conditions, and despite evident class awareness, class itself has never really been seen as relevant to politics. It is the absence of a class persuader which, at least in part, has resulted in the absence of class politics.

Straws in the wind?

Increasing signs of change and fragmentation in the Irish party system since the mid-1980s suggest that the picture presented above may soon cease to reflect the prevailing political realities in Ireland. These signs are, as yet, mere straws in the wind, but they do nevertheless point in a reasonably consistent direction, and, above all, they point to a breakdown in the social consensus. Were this consensus finally to fracture, then the scope for internal opposition would inevitably be increased, and with it the scope for a new politicisation of internal social conflict. In such circumstances, an eventual realignment towards a modern version of 'class' politics would not be impossible.

The signs of change are many and varied but, at least at the political level, they can be easily summarised. In the first place, the emergence of the Workers' Party, with a growing though still minimal level of support, has helped to place class issues on the agenda in a way which is quite unprecedented in modern left politics in Ireland. Second, this new competitor on the left has had the effect of radicalising the Labour Party, in strategic if not pronouncedly ideological terms, and has encouraged Labour to return to a more politically independent stance. Third, and perhaps paradoxically, the legitimacy of such an independent politics on the left has also been strengthened by the emergence on the liberal right of the Progressive Democrats, and by the latter's fairly unashamed avowal of a conservative class politics. Fourth, the capacity of Fianna Fáil to continue to sustain its emphasis on social solidarity, and hence to continue to define the alternatives in a manner which is inimical to the politicisation of social conflict, has of late been undermined, not least as a result of its abandonment of an anti-coalition stance and its consequent transformation into a run-of-the-mill political bargainer. Fifth, and perhaps most importantly, the image of homogeneity and uniformity, the 'culture of community' itself, has been badly shaken as a result of the inter-party, and inter-regional divisions concerning the role of the Catholic church, on the one hand, and the legitimacy of traditional nationalism, on the other. Finally, and perhaps only symbolically, there is now the hope for change which was instilled as a result of the success of Mary Robinson's presidential campaign, and which clearly built on the conjuncture of the new circumstances indicated above.

All of this suggests that opposition and criticism are increasingly legitimate, and that internal differences can now be aired. It suggests, in short, the long overdue waning of the politics of the national interest. Divisions, minority rights, and alternative positions are now more acceptable than ever before, and hence are also more susceptible to politicisation. And within this new world, a world which is characterised by increased social as well as political differentiation, the left, however, it will seek to define itself in future, need no longer appear apologetic. Times are changing, and so too, finally, are Ireland's last remaining political peculiarities.

Acknowledgements. I am grateful to Cess van der Eijk for allowing me access to the data from the European Parliament Election Study which are cited in this paper, and to Mireille Geldorp for her help in analysing these data. I am also appreciative of the useful comments received from other contributors to this volume, and particularly of those from Kieran Kennedy and Chris Whelan.

Proceedings of the British Academy, **79**, 411–431

The Theory of Industrialism and the Irish Case

JOHN H. GOLDTHORPE

Nuffield College, Oxford

Fellow of the British Academy

Introduction

IN THE PRECEDING PAPERS in this collection, authors have attempted to provide empirically well-grounded accounts of various aspects of the development of industrial society in Ireland and, on this basis, have sought to address, where it appeared appropriate to do so, more general questions concerning the nature of industrialism and its social concomitants. This concluding contribution has, however, a rather different emphasis. The substance of the Irish case is here treated only selectively, while theoretical issues become the focus of attention. Specifically, the concern is with the implications of the Irish case for the theory of industrialism that has prevailed—or, at all events, that has had by far the greatest currency—within western social science over the last three decades.

This theory, which will be labelled the 'liberal theory' of industrialism, was elaborated in the 1960s by chiefly American authors (see, esp., Kerr *et al.*, 1960; Kerr, 1969; Parsons, 1960, 1967) in close relation with concurrent analyses, theoretical and historical, of economic growth and yet more ambitious treatments of social and political 'modernisation'. The theory, it is true, never went unchallenged. In fact, it attracted sharp, and mounting, criticism (for a bibliographical review, see Badham, 1984), and by the 1980s was sometimes thought of as being discredited and defunct. This must, however, be reckoned a serious misjudgment. The theory achieved an undoubted centrality within comparative macrosociology and, although in various respects refined and modified in response to both

© The British Academy 1992.

criticism and events (see e.g. Dunlop *et al.*, 1975; Kerr, 1983), still remains
as a major influence—more so in fact today than a decade ago.

Two reasons for this durability may be noted. First, the theory is,
formally at least, a highly attractive one. It starts from the assumption that
industrialism exercises a powerful 'demonstration effect': given the opportunity, non-industrial societies—their elites and masses alike—will opt for
industrialism, primarily on account of the unparalleled material benefits
that it confers. The theory then seeks to show that, once such a commitment to industrialism is made, constraints are gradually but unremittingly
imposed on social structures and processes, and also on political institutions, by an inherent 'logic of industrialism': that is, by the functional
exigencies of the technical and the economic rationality on which industrialism depends. All actual industrial societies will converge in their
development on the 'pure' industrial type (see esp. Kerr *et al.*, 1960: chs.
2, 10). In turn, then, a wide range of quite specific propositions may be
derived about the major trends of change that should be observable in
societies within the industrial world. Few, if any, other sociological
theories have succeeded so well in combining boldness with clarity and
openness to empirical examination.

Secondly, the credibility of the theory has of late been greatly enhanced
by the collapse of the state socialist regimes of eastern Europe. One of the
most challenging arguments to which the theory lead was that regimes that
imposed command economies and sought to maintain a virtual monopoly
of political power could not adequately respond to the demands of
advancing industrialism. The latter required, rather, an essentially liberal
order, of which a market economy and a democratic and pluralist polity
were the defining characteristics. Some exponents of the liberal theory did
indeed expressly predict the demise of state socialism (e.g. Parsons, 1964:
349–50); and, after the event, triumphalist reformulations have not been
slow to emerge (see, notoriously, Fukuyama, 1989).[1]

No apology is therefore required for returning once more to the critical
examination of the liberal theory. And in this respect, as will be seen, the
Irish case offers important strategic advantages, not least in providing an
example of a society within the western world which became industrial
only in the mid-twentieth century. For, whether or not recent events in
eastern Europe do underwrite the liberal theory as unequivocally as is
claimed, it may still be held that it is in regard to developments as yet most

---

[1] One of several ways in which Fukuyama's argument goes beyond that of earlier exponents
of the liberal theory is that he sees no need to accept any degree of 'two-way' convergence
(cp. Kerr, 1983: ch. 1) between liberal and state socialist societies. Liberalism has won 'an
unabashed victory' (1989: 3).

evident in the West that the more serious difficulties faced by the theory arise (cf. Goldthorpe, 1984, 1991). These involve a range of issues which, for the purposes of the review that follows, will be categorised as presuppositional, empirical and ideological.

Presuppositional Issues

The liberal theory of industrialism can be seen as falling in line of descent from both nineteenth-century theories of social evolution and from Marxism. It takes societies—usually national societies—as its units of analysis and seeks to account, in essentially functionalist terms, for the long-term trends of change in structure and process that they display (cf. Nisbet, 1969: ch. 7; Goldthorpe, 1971). For all theories of this general type, crucial questions then arise of how far the units of analysis that are distinguished are to be treated as being independent of each other; and further, to the extent that some degree of *inter*dependence is acknowledged, of the implications that this carries for the explanatory approach that is pursued.[2]

As already noted, the liberal theory does in one respect clearly recognise interdependence, namely, through the demonstration effect: the industrially more developed societies hold up to those that are to follow them 'the image of their own future'. But, beyond this, what would seem to be assumed is that the development of particular societies will be determined primarily by internal or 'endogenous' factors: in effect, by the degree to which aspects of the traditional society and the strategies of dominant elites either facilitate or obstruct the logic of industrialism. The presence of already more advanced nations enters into the analysis, if at all, simply as constituting a more or less benign 'setting'.[3]

This assumption is, however, one to which objections can obviously be raised—and not least when the case of Ireland is considered. To begin with, it is now far more difficult to believe than it was in the 1960s that relations between nations at different levels of industrial development will

---

[2] Such questions were in fact raised in connection with some of the earliest attempts at a functionalist macrosociology: most notably, in the case of Galton's objections to Tylor's analysis of functional associations ('adhesions') in marriage customs, on the grounds that examples drawn from different cultures could not be treated as independent owing to the possibility of diffusion. For further discussion of the 'Galton problem', see Naroll (1970) and Przeworski (1983).

[3] The works earlier cited, both of Kerr and his associates and of Parsons, are indeed remarkable for their almost total lack of reference to international relations, economic or otherwise. Cf. in this respect the apt comments of Nisbet (1969: 233–9).

—in consequence of expanding trade and the principle of comparative advantage—be ones from which 'mutual benefit' may be expected. In this regard, the orthodoxy of neoclassical economics has been powerfully challenged, even if not decisively overthrown, by alternative theories of 'dependency', 'displacement competition', 'late development' etc., which emphasise essentially asymmetric relations between the nations of the 'centre' and those of the 'periphery'. From the complex debate that has ensued, what can perhaps be most safely concluded is that rival theories perform better or worse depending upon the specific historical conditions that obtain; and thus, that in the analysis of particular cases—the Irish included—history must carry at least as great a weight as theory. It is, fortunately, not necessary here to attempt adjudication on the question of whether Irish industrial development has been more aided or impeded by relations with more advanced nations, and especially of course with Britain (for differing views see Crotty, 1986; O'Malley, 1989, and this volume; Girvin, 1989; Lee, 1989: 522–40; O'Hearn, 1989; Mjøset, 1992: ch. 3; Kennedy, this volume). It is sufficient to observe that no one would now wish to suppose that the course and pattern of Irish industrialisation is comprehensible without such relations being taken into account or, that is, simply in terms of the internal dynamics of Irish society itself.[4]

In this connection, a matter of particular relevance is of course that of emigration. As Coleman points out in his contribution to this collection, large-scale emigration has allowed Ireland to establish a remarkable record in demographic history: a hundred years of relatively high natural increase in population without any sustained effect on population size. Emigration has made possible a demographic regime in which 'feedback' on fertility levels from population pressure has been largely eliminated. Emigration has, in other words, substituted for, and thus greatly delayed, the decline in fertility which the logic of industrialism should have engendered: that is, by removing the need for the expansion of employment or, alternatively, for the reduction in living standards that would otherwise have obtained (cf. NESC, 1991).

Furthermore, the effects of emigration on the nature of the industrial society that now exists in Ireland can only be reckoned as far-reaching, even if the counterfactual form in which claims in this regard have usually to be made will always leave some room for argument. Thus, emigration could scarcely avoid having a pervasive influence on family relations—most obviously, perhaps, because of the geographical dispersal of

[4] Debate centres, rather (cf. O'Hearn, 1990) on the *degree* of autonomy that may be attributed to the Irish state and to dominant elites, as against constraints imposed both by internal class and other conflicts and by the international political economy.

kin that it entailed. Further, though, in removing pressure for a reduction in family size or for an increase in employment, emigration helped maintain a traditional sexual division of labour within the family, and can then in turn be reckoned as one factor in the distinctively low labour force participation rates that Irish women continue to display (Pyle, 1990). At the same time, it can also surely be said that the shape of the Irish employment and class structure today 'reflects the selective process of emigration to Britain of young men and women as much as it does the growth of new opportunities' (Breen et al., 1990: 54). And there is likewise good evidence for supposing that emigration effects, although often difficult to determine precisely, have been, and remain, of significance in regard to such other processes as social mobility (see Hout: 1989: ch. 1), political participation (see Mair, this volume; and cf. Hirschmann, 1981: ch. 9) and the formation of national culture and identity (see Lee, 1989: 374 et seq.).

The crucial point to be made here is, then, that in so far as emigration has in fact shaped the development of industrial society in Ireland, the resulting features of this society would appear to fall outside the explanatory scope of the liberal theory. That is to say, they must be seen as reflecting not functional exigencies inherent in industrialism itself, but rather 'functional alternatives' allowed by the—quite contingent—fact that large-scale emigration was a possibility. Irish men and women were able to respond to the demonstration effect of industrialism, and for many it would appear the only feasible response, by seeking its benefits elsewhere—in Britain or the USA. If this possibility had not existed, it is difficult indeed to imagine Irish society tracing the same developmental path as it did or being as it is now.[5]

The implicit presupposition of the liberal theory that societies follow each other on the 'ladder of industrialism' as essentially independent entities, sharing only a common goal, is also involved in, and compounds, certain other basic problems that the theory encounters. Two of these at least are again particularly well illustrated by the Irish case and may here be noted.

The first concerns the nature of the pre-industrial society on which the

---

[5] For a general treatment of the possible implications, for sending nations, of emigration and of its prohibition, see Hirschman (1981: ch. 11). It is of particular interest that Hassner (1989) should note, specifically in response to Fukuyama, the inapplicability of an 'Irish solution' in the event of the former nations of the Communist world failing to achieve capitalist prosperity, despite their citizens' mounting desire for this: 'while all the ideological challenges to the West have failed . . . [it] is as incapable of integrating the hundreds of millions of potential immigrants as it is of creating the conditions, in their home countries, which would make them want to stay there.'

logic of industrialism is seen as exerting its transformative effect. The underlying assumption of the theory is that pre-industrial society is 'traditional' society. The process whereby traditional society yields to the imperatives of economic and technical rationality—or, in other words, becomes 'modernised'—is identified with that through which an industrial society is created. The course of the long-term trends of change for which the theory seeks to account is in effect delimited by a series of simple binary oppositions, which can be understood largely as derivations from the seminal *Gemeinschaft–Gesellschaft* distinction of Tönnies, and which achieve their most elaborate expression in Parsons' 'pattern variables'.

However, the significance of the Irish case in this respect is that it clearly reveals the difficulty that can arise in treating modernisation and industrialisation as if they were but one and the same process. By the criteria that the liberal theory would adopt, the modernisation of Irish society must in fact be seen as running well ahead of its industrial development throughout most of its recent history; and again the part played here by outside influences, especially, though not only, ones emanating from Britain, is of major importance.

For example, under British rule Ireland acquired a modern state apparatus and a modern financial system—which the Free State could take over in 1922 more or less unchanged. Further, the new nation came into being with literacy rates of approaching 100 per cent and also, in Lee's words (1989: 76), 'belonged to a western European pattern of access to higher education.' Again, as Fahey (this volume) brings out, the leading role played by Ireland in the nineteenth-century revitalisation of the Catholic church entailed a remarkable application of one of the major instruments of modernity, that is, organisational rationality—even if in the service of an ideologically anti-modernist movement.[6] And finally, it must be recognised that although until well into the twentieth century Ireland was still an agrarian rather than an industrial nation, this is not to say that Irish agrarian, or rural, society remained set on a traditional pattern. By the time of independence, agriculture was mostly market-oriented; and, as Hannan has shown (1979), while in some areas a form of peasant economy and culture did persist, this could scarcely be equated with traditionalism—despite the imaginative efforts of social anthropologists to suggest otherwise. Thus, for example, the institutional bases of the

[6] The paradox here implied is intensified in that, at the ideological level, the Irish Church was rather distinctively reactionary and unresponsive to new initiatives—as, for example, in Catholic social theory. On the other hand, Fahey's argument is reinforced by an observation made by Lee (1989: 90–1): 'The organisation of the American and Australian Catholic Churches counts among the major administrative achievements of modern history. Those achievements were in disproportionate measure Irish achievements.'

communities in West Clare, described by Arensberg and Kimball (1940) as if their origins were lost in the mists of the past, had in fact been established for no more than two generations.

In a cogent essay, Wrigley (1979) has urged the need for the concepts of modernisation and industrialisation to be clearly distinguished, rather than being set together in polar opposition to that of traditionalism. Furthermore, he goes on to propose that the actual relation between the two processes should be seen as contingent, not necessary: no automatic connection can be shown in either theory of historical experience between, on the one hand, the increased economic efficiency that may be expected from modernisation and, on the other, the economic growth and structural change that are implied by industrialisation. In the context of European history in general, Wrigley suggests, industrial development might be better understood not so much as a seamless continuation of modernisation but rather as a possible solution to a major problem that prior modernisation helped create, namely, that of population pressure—with mass emigration being then the obvious alternative if industrialisation is too long delayed. The Irish case is one that would appear to fit especially well into this line of argument.

The second problem to be noted is that of what might be called 'sequencing'. Various specific trends of change that the liberal theory would envisage may quite typically be observed in societies in the course of their industrial development; but, from case to case, these trends can proceed at differing rates or with a different timing relative to each other. Exponents of the liberal theory have not been unaware of this fact, nor indeed of the long-term consequences that variation in sequencing may have (see, e.g., Dunlop, 1958: ch. 8 and cf. Roche, this volume). But its actual occurrence is something that would again appear to require explanation, and in part at least because of the lack of independence of national cases, in terms that are clearly extraneous to the theory.

Thus, in the Irish case, as in that of any industrialising society, a decline can be traced over time in employment in the agricultural sector and in the size of agricultural classes, along with an increase in size of the industrial working class and also in that of the white-collar salariat or service class. However, as is now well-documented (see, e.g., Breen et al., 1990: ch. 3), surplus labour from the agricultural sector was not in Ireland, as it was, say, in Britain, more or less directly transferred, whether through intra- or intergenerational mobility, into an expanding industrial work force. The surplus could not in fact be absorbed, and for many decades emigration 'filled the gap'—that is in fact, until it proved possible to step up the pace of industrial development in the 1960s. At this point, moreover, rapid growth began in both the industrial working class and the service class *together*, whereas in Britain, as in other early industrialising nations, the growth of the former was close to its peak (and agricultural employment at a near minimum) *before* the main acceleration in the growth of white-collar employment occurred. As Whelan, Breen and Whelan then show in their paper above, this particular sequencing in the process of class structural change is in turn chiefly responsible for certain distinctive features that appear in the pattern of class mobility in present-day Irish society: most notably, a level of service-class recruitment from among the sons of farm families that is unusually high, and especially so relative to that of recruitment from among men of working-class origins.

Another of the preceding papers offers a further and, if anything, yet more striking example of the implications of sequencing: that is, in regard to the growth and present form of the Irish welfare state. O'Connell and Rottman observe that the Irish experience does not accord well with the idea that in western nations welfare state development has occurred essentially as a *response to* the functional requirements of industrialism, with political democratisation serving as little more than a mediating factor (cf. e.g. Wilensky and Lebeaux, 1958; Wilensky, 1975). The legacy of British rule meant that in Ireland democratic institutions, as well as a modern state apparatus, were in place well in advance of the period of rapid industrialisation of the 1960s, as also in fact were a range of welfare provisions deriving from British legislation of the Edwardian period. In the early decades of independence, the particular governmental form that had been inherited—the 'Treasury model'—served to inhibit the further growth of such provision; but, subsequently, industrial development and the extension of the 'social rights of citizenship' went ahead more or less *in tandem*, with the state playing a crucial part, as both 'arena' and 'actor' alike. At the same time, O'Connell and Rottman seek to show that this sequencing also helps explain the distinctive character of Irish welfare programmes and their tendency, even while exerting a major influence on the shape of the class structure, still to leave the extent of class inequalities little altered. Once more, then, the point is well brought out that the functional logic of industrialism that the liberal theory invokes cannot provide an adequate basis for understanding the course of change in particular nations to the extent that the presupposition of essentially independent developmental paths is breached.

Empirical Issues

In this section, the emphasis shifts from features of the Irish case that serve to reveal limitations in principle to the explanatory power of the liberal theory to consideration of Ireland as a strategic case for evaluating the theory within, so to speak, its own frame of reference. In particular, Ireland offers an outstanding opportunity for testing empirically certain claims, central to theory, that concern the effects of industrial development on processes of social stratification and on the nature and extent of social inequality.

According to the liberal theory, the logic of industrialism progressively undermines traditional processes of stratification based on criteria of ascription, and promotes the emergence of new forms based on criteria of achievement. The demands of economic and technical rationality mean that 'social selection' must be determined by what individuals are able to do rather than by who they are, in terms of descent, social background etc. Moreover, with advancing industrialism, human resources become increasingly valuable; talent must be fully exploited wherever in society it is to be found. Thus, educational provision is expanded, and educational institutions are reformed so as to widen access. Changes in economic organisation further encourage the trend towards an 'achievement-oriented' society. Employment becomes increasingly concentrated in large-scale, professionally managed enterprises, while small-scale, family-based concerns, in which ascriptive tendencies are most likely to persist, steadily decline in importance. In sum, what is envisaged is the development of a far less rigid form of stratification than that which previously prevailed. The association between individuals' social origins and their educational attainment will weaken, while that between their educational level and the kind of employment they obtain will strengthen. Thus, an increasingly mobile and 'open' society will be created, in which it will be possible for such intergenerational continuities of social position as may still be observed to be explained—and at the same time legitimated—in essentially 'meritocratic' terms.[7]

In this connection, Irish industrialisation is of significance for two main reasons. First, its critical period is one that is unusually well documented. Largely on account of the fact that a modern state apparatus was already well established, far better information is available for the decisive transformation of Irish society that occurred between, say, the 1950s and the 1970s than for most corresponding periods in either earlier industrialising nations in the West or 'newly industrialised countries' elsewhere. From both official statistics and the results of various other kinds of state-supported investigation, it is possible to trace in some detail the course

---

[7] Further elaboration of this position can be found in, e.g., Blau and Duncan (1967: ch. 12 esp.) and Treiman (1970).

and the concomitants of the changes that led Irish society from being one
in which farmers, farm workers, small proprietors and artisans pre-
dominated to one in which the large majority of the active population are
wage- or salary-earners employed in manufacturing and services.

Secondly, Irish industrialisation over the period in question, through
being promoted and guided by the state, would appear to have been
actually *informed by* ideas integral to the liberal theory—especially as
these were mediated and disseminated by international agencies such as
the OECD, World Bank and IMF (Breen *et al.*, 1990: 128–30). Thus,
educational expansion was undertaken with the explicit aim of meeting the
need that, it was believed, industrialisation imposed to build up the
nation's 'human capital'; and reforms intended to increase access to
secondary and higher education were represented as necessary so that at
one and the same time an economically unacceptable wastage of talent
could be prevented and a greater equality of opportunity established. In
these respects, it is therefore scarcely too fanciful to view the Irish case as
a kind of 'naturally occurring experiment' in which the liberal theory was
applied in the real world.

What, then, one may ask, were the results that this experiment
provided? How far do they lend empirical support to the theory? To begin
with, a substantial increase in participation in the educational system was
clearly achieved, and most notably at the secondary level (cf. Rottman and
O'Connell, this volume). Although the *rate* of increase in enrollments did
not rise much from what it had been since the 1920s, simply through this
rate being sustained the objective of 'secondary education for all' came
close to being realised. Moreover, educational expansion and reform
were associated with some reduction in class differentials in transition
rates through the different levels of the system; or, in other words,
some—slight—weakening did occur in the overall association between
class origins and educational attainment. To this extent, therefore, it
could be said that the expectations of the liberal theory were borne
out.

However, what further emerges from more detailed analysis of the
relevant data (see esp. Hout, 1989: ch. 8; Raftery and Hout, 1990) is that
this reduction in class differentials was the outcome essentially of expansion itself, rather than of any changes in the criteria of educational
selection or of any decline in the influence of class on selection processes.
That is to say, through expansion, the Irish educational system became less
selective and especially in the transition to the secondary level—with some
benefit thus accruing to children from less advantaged class backgrounds;
but, *wherever selection remained*—as, most importantly, *within* the

secondary level and in the transition to higher education—class effects were undiminished.[8]

Further still, there is little evidence to suggest that changes brought about in the distribution of educational attainment have in turn led to changes in rates and patterns of social mobility of a kind that would indicate greater 'openness' and equality of opportunity. Thus, Halpin (this volume) shows that although among men studied in 1973 the propensity for movement between different class positions over the course of working life tended to increase somewhat from older to younger birth cohorts, no corresponding change is to be found in the underlying pattern of association between class as determined by employment on entry into the workforce and class at age 35. Again, both Hout (1989; ch. 3) and Erikson and Goldthorpe (1992; ch. 3), using the same data as Halpin but in order to investigate *inter*generational mobility, report a similar finding. Observed, absolute rates of such mobility clearly changed in response to the transformation of the class structure; but, in intergenerational perspective also, the association between class of origin and of destination considered *net* of all structural effects—or, that is, the pattern of relative mobility rates or of social fluidity—remained little altered over successive cohorts. Finally, Breen and Whelan (this volume), who are able to compare the 1973 intergenerational mobility data with those of a further enquiry of 1987, show that between these two dates the stability of relative mobility rates was largely maintained and that where shifts could be detected, these were by no means ones pointing consistently towards greater openness.[9]

In other words, the idea that changes in processes of social selection, as necessitated by the logic of industrialism, will in themselves create a more fluid society is one that the Irish experience can scarcely sustain. By the 1970s, a class structure recognisably that of an industrial society had emerged and educational expansion and reform had been implemented much on the lines that the liberal theory would anticipate. But although the pattern of actual mobility flows, both over working life and intergenerationally, was thus reshaped and a substantial enlargement of human

---

[8] It should be noted that insufficient time may have elapsed for the effects of more recent educational reforms to show up in the birth cohorts studied by Hout and Raftery. However, as discussed further below, the results they report are very much in line with those emerging from studies in a number of other nations whose educational systems have evolved in quite diverse ways.

[9] To judge by the experience of other nations, it is in fact rather surprising that *any* significant change in relative rates should be detected over a period of no more than a decade and a half, at least on the basis of samples of the size in question. The present author would still incline to the view that Irish 'peculiarities' of some kind or other, most probably associated with mobility propensities into or out of the agricultural sector, are chiefly at work here.

capital no doubt achieved, the supposed effects of such developments in reducing the influence of class on educational attainment and in turn on mobility chances show up but weakly, if at all. Far more striking, it could be thought, is the degree to which class inequalities in these respects have been found to persist, notwithstanding the rapidly changing structural and institutional contexts within which they operated.

However, if the Irish case is here of particular significance, as earlier suggested, this is not to imply that the results it provides are at all atypical. To the contrary, in the light of the foregoing, one could say that its interest lies chiefly in the fact that it lends support, in a detailed yet rather dramatic way, to a conclusion now emerging from research undertaken across a range of other societies: namely, that industrialisation does *not* create a new basis for social stratification of a kind that allows for, and indeed promotes, greater mobility, in the way that the liberal theory would claim. Industrial development may well require educational programmes of the kind envisaged by the theory—and which were accordingly carried through in Ireland. In turn, such programmes may bring about some reduction in class differentials in educational attainment, although it would appear that more often than not they fail to do so (see Shavit and Blossfeld, eds., 1992). But even if some greater educational equality *is* thus achieved, a major empirical difficulty for the theory still remains in that this does not then automatically, or even usually, show up in a greater equality of mobility chances (Erikson and Goldthorpe, 1992: ch. 3 esp.).[10] At this point, the supposed logic of industrialism evidently breaks down; and thus, it may be argued, an inherent weakness in the form of the liberal theory is revealed.

As earlier noted, the theory derives its explanatory potential from the notion of the functional exigencies of an industrial society. But it has then the problem, like all functionalist theories, of showing why the courses of action that are actually pursued by individuals and collectivities—or at least their outcomes—*should be* ones consistent with the exigencies that are specified. Thus, when it is held that an emphasis on achievement rather than ascription in social selection and the creation of a more open society are 'required' by the logic of industrialism, the obvious question arises of

---

[10] A divergent view is to be found in Ganzeboom, Luijkx and Treiman (1989), who believe that they can discern in cross-national and over-time data a 'world wide secular trend towards increased societal openness'. However, it is still unclear how far they would regard their analyses as lending support to the liberal theory, since they also show many nations at a relatively early stage of industrialisation as being more open than more advanced societies; and their results can in any event be questioned, both on grounds of data comparability and of the modelling from which they derive (see Jones, 1991; Erikson and Goldthorpe, 1992: 99–101).

just why this requirement should in fact be met. Why should it not rather be—and as the empirical evidence would indeed suggest—that those individuals and families in superior class positions will use their advantage and power in order to react against what may appear as tendencies dangerous to their position, and quite regardless of the consequences for the functioning of the society at large?

If, for example, educational attainment does become more important to mobility chances, those families in a position to do so can use more of their resources in order to maintain their children's competitive edge in this respect: as Halsey has put it (1977: 184), 'ascriptive forces find ways of expressing themselves as "achievement".' And if, none the less, educational attainments do become somewhat more equally distributed among children of different class origins, then within more advantaged families resources can be applied through *other* channels in order to help their offspring preserve their class prospects—as against the threat of meritocratic selection via education. Thus, to revert to the Irish case, Hout (1989) has emphasised the part that would still appear to be played in mobility processes by patronage, favouritism and other 'particularistic' influences, largely mediated through family relations; while Breen and Whelan (this volume) underline the continuing importance of the possession and transmission of family property.[11]

In short, one could say that what is crucially brought into question by the empirical results reviewed is the *cogency* of the logic of industrialism. Nothing in the liberal theory tells one why it is this logic that should in the end prevail, and especially where, as with social stratification, it is not difficult to envisage an opposing 'logic': that according to which those holding more advantaged and powerful class positions have thereby the capacity, as well as the motivation, to act effectively in order to preserve the *status quo*.[12]

---

[11] More specific analyses are now in fact emerging that call directly into doubt the existence of any long-term trend towards meritocratic selection in industrial societies—at least if 'merit' is taken to be indexed by educational attainment. See for Britain, Heath, Mills and Roberts (1991) and for Sweden, Jonsson (1991).

[12] In other words, just as the old functionalist theory of stratification (Davis and Moore, 1945) did not explain by what means the 'necessary' effects of social inequalities served also to keep these inequalities in being, so the liberal theory gives no account of why 'necessary' processes of social selection making for greater equality of opportunity should in turn guarantee their own persistence. In this connection, it is of further interest to note (as pointed out to me by Christopher Whelan) that the concern of Irish governments with the formation of human capital and the promotion of meritocracy tended in fact to give way after the 1960s to much narrower preoccupations with 'fine-tuning' educational outputs to meet supposed shortages in particular kinds of skilled labour. On the general failure of functionalist explanations in sociology—in contrast with those in biology—to specify appropriate 'causal feedback loops', see Elster (1979) and also Stinchcombe (1968: 58–9, 80–101).

Ideological Issues

To describe the theory here examined as the 'liberal' theory of industrialism is appropriate in that, as earlier noted, a central conclusion to which
it leads is that only a liberal social order, characterised by a market
economy and a democratic and pluralist polity, will in the end prove
functionally compatible with industrialism. Thus, according to the theory
as it was elaborated in the 1960s, the state socialist industrial societies of
the Soviet bloc were fraught with contradictions that threatened their long-
term viability, while other versions of socialism which might be aspired to
were either ones that 'history' had already rejected or merely Utopian.
The inevitable consequence of advancing industrialism, it was held, was
that 'real ideological alternatives' were steadily narrowed down (cf. Kerr
et al., 1960: 283) until in fact only one possibility, that of a liberal order,
remained. With the actual collapse of state socialism in most of eastern
Europe, such arguments have then been reasserted, and in more extreme
forms. Thus, Fukuyama (1989: 4) has proposed that western liberal
democracy should now in fact be seen as marking 'the end of history': with
the universalisation of liberalism, the final form of human government and
'the end point of mankind's ideological evolution' will be reached.

Historicism of this kind is open to major objections in principle, both
intellectual and moral (cf. Popper, 1957; Goldthorpe, 1971). However, in
the present context, attention may better be focused on certain more
specific issues. These arise from arguments, developed after the ending of
the 'long boom' of the post-war years, which have posed a threat to the
liberal theory of industrialism at its very core: that is, in questioning
whether a democratic and pluralist polity, however desirable in itself, *is*
that most conducive to the efficiency and growth of a modern market
economy.

It should be noted, first of all, that the most powerful of these
arguments do not emanate from the left but are advanced, rather, by
authors who would themselves lay claim to a liberal position (see e.g.
Brittan, 1977, 1983; Scitovsky, 1978, 1980; Olson 1982). Their common
concern is that while modern liberal democracies allow, and indeed
encourage, the formation of a wide range of organised interest groups, as
an essential element in pluralist politics, the operation of these interest
groups within the economic system may well have damaging consequences
for its performance. This comes about because trade unions, professional
associations, industrial cartels and the like all seek to strengthen their
members' positions primarily through action that is in some way taken
against market forces— via organisation, regulation, legislation, etc.; and
further, because such bodies tend to concentrate their attention on

'zero-sum' issues, where their own members' interests can only be protected or advanced at the expense of those of other groups. As, therefore, the number of competing organisations grows and pluralist, pressure-group politics intensifies, the tendency is for market mechanisms—and in turn the economic efficiency that they guarantee—to be progressively impaired. Thus, far from democratic pluralism representing the essential political counterpart of a modern industrial economy, its consequences are seen as being, at all events, an important contributory factor in endemic problems of industrial unrest, inflation, unemployment and slow growth.[13]

Such an analysis would therefore suggest that to create the conditions necessary for improved economic performance, change must occur in one or other of two directions. Either relations among major economic interest groups have to become more 'concerted' than the pluralist model would imply, so that distributional conflict is made less damaging to market mechanisms and thus to the economy overall; or, alternatively, *some* economic sectors have to be more fully exposed to market forces in order to compensate for 'rigidities' elsewhere. The main indication of the force of the analysis is then that tendencies in these two directions can in fact be observed in many western nations from the 1970s onwards (Goldthorpe, 1984, 1987). And in this connection, the particular interest of the Irish case lies, to begin with, in the fact that during the recent past attempts have been made to move first in the one and then in the other direction, without, however, any decisive outcome having been so far achieved. The difficulties that may in each case be encountered are thus illuminated, but so at the same time is the extent to which major questions of national political economy remain essentially open and, moreover, ones that offer—indeed demand—crucial ideological choices.

In his contribution above, Roche has described how institutions providing for 'industrial citizenship' and for the 'joint regulation' of employment relations developed in Ireland much on the lines that the liberal theory would propose. But, as he further shows, the consequences that followed proved to be far less consistent with the theory's expectations. Although organised labour abandoned politically-oriented militancy at an early stage, no decline occurred in the level of industrial conflict, no 'withering away' of the strike; and within the institutional framework that was

---

[13] The intervention of these authors thus serves to expose a strong tension within the liberal camp in regard to whether greater weight should be given to freedom of association and collective action or to the 'freedom' of market forces. The divergence between 'political' and 'economic' liberals is well captured in Scitovsky's observation (1980) that the former possess 'an excessive faith in capitalism and in its ability to fly however much its wings are clipped.' A very early statement of essentially the same argument is to be found in Lindblom (1949). Kerr (1955) showed awareness of the argument but sought to play down its importance.

established—the pluralist 'web of rules'—unions were able to increase their capacity to press claims, to expand their negotiating agendas and to create wage-bargaining structures of a kind often inimical to the efficient functioning of labour markets. By the end of the 1960s there was in fact widespread recognition of an industrial relations crisis, manifested in a high level of industrial disputes and in inflationary wage spirals, which undermined Ireland's international competitiveness and the ability to attract foreign investment on which the national economic strategy depended.

It was in response to this situation that the first efforts were made at reconstructing industrial relations on a more orderly basis. These lead through a series of National Wage Agreements (1970–78) to the National Understandings of 1979 and 1980, in which government, along with unions and employers, was directly involved. What was attempted was actually quite modest in comparison with the scope and objectives of similar tripartite arrangements in nations where concertative or 'neo-corporatist' tendencies were more securely established. However, the NUs failed to produce results satisfactory to any of the participants and were abandoned in some disillusionment (Hardiman, 1988). A return to decentralised bargaining followed and indeed a period in which, as Roche further describes, employers took the lead in what could be regarded as attempts to subvert, rather than to go beyond, the institutions of 'pluralistic industrialism': that is, by seeking, where possible, to avoid union recognition and to impose 'monistic' forms of industrial relations (cf. McGovern, 1989), and further by developing 'secondary' labour forces whose members in some degree or other fell outside the protection that industrial citizenship afforded against market forces and managerial absolutism. But although these initiatives were taken in a context of rapidly rising unemployment, with the balance of market power thus clearly in employers' favour, they received little support from government[14] and, in the outcome, unions were not seriously weakened nor labour markets 'dualised' in any radical way. Moreover, as the economic situation deteriorated further, a reversion to a concertative response was signalled by the Programme for National Recovery of the new Fianna Fáil administration that entered office in 1987 and the subsequent Programme for Economic and Social Progress of 1991—the still uncertain prospects for which are considered in Hardiman's paper above.

---

[14] It should, however, be noted that the IDA, having initially played an important role in facilitating 'sweetheart' or single-union arrangements for incoming employers, apparently ceased in the course of the 1970s to advise such employers to accept unionisation (McGovern, 1989).

What is ultimately involved in these shifting, yet inconclusive, approaches to problems of political economy can perhaps best be brought out by going back to the famous metaphor of Lemass for the initial drive for growth of the 1960s: 'the tide that will raise all boats'. This gave graphic expression to a key idea of the liberalism of the post-war era: namely, that economic growth could substitute for attempts at redistribution. Governments that achieved, or at all events that presided over, economic growth would thereby avoid the need to take any serious action on questions of class and other inequalities. However, in the far less congenial economic climate after the ending of the long boom, the inadequacy of this idea is fully revealed. Attempts made to reduce the 'perils of pluralism' for economic performance—whichever direction they take and whatever their degree of success—inevitably raise distributional questions that cannot be disregarded by governments, however much they might wish to do so, and that, still within the context of a liberal polity, create ample scope for ideological division.

Thus, even if a dismantling of pluralist institutions or an increased evasion of their constraints by employers does help produce an increased rate of economic growth, it can scarcely be assumed that this will then simply mean an all-round improvement in living standards, while the pattern and extent of inequality remain unchanged. To the contrary, the probability must be that inequalities will *widen*. The objective is after all to modify the interplay between politics and markets so that certain groups within the labour force are unable to compensate for their lack of strength in the market through either organisational power or regulatory intervention. Furthermore, with such a 'free market' strategy, no linkage can be expected between growth and high levels of employment. Governments will decline responsibility for maintaining employment at any particular level; and the empirical evidence is that dualised labour markets, even while allowing greater flexibility to employers, still show little more tendency to clear than do those operating under pluralistic rigidities. In other words, with any economic 'tide' that is in this way created, the most likely outcome must be that some boats will rise much higher than do others, and that some will indeed be left more or less deliberately stranded.

Concertative strategies have likewise to be seen as implying an attempt to redefine relations between politics and markets. The immediate aim of such strategies is to create arrangements under which conflict among major organised interests within enterprises and labour markets can be so contained as to minimise their economically damaging effects—most typically, through some form or other of wage regulation. However, while such arrangements are often presented in the rhetoric of 'national consensus' or 'social partnership', it is in fact essential to their survival that the conflicts in question should not be merely denied or suppressed. They must, rather, be effectively transferred into the political domain.[15]

Thus, as analysts have recurrently found (see e.g. Lehmbruch and Schmitter, eds, 1982; Goldthorpe, ed., 1984) the continued participation of labour in neo-corporatist institutions depends upon unions being able to achieve politically—and demonstrate to their members—some *quid pro quo* for their abstention from the pluralistic free-for-all. Under 'bad weather corporatism', as attempted in Ireland after 1987, this may be no more than an assurance that labour will not bear an undue share of the costs of recovery programmes (cf. Hardiman, this volume). But in so far as concertative institutions do help to strengthen economic performance, the demands made upon processes of 'political exchange' are likely to mount, at all events from the side of labour. Pressure must be expected for greater priority to be given to the reduction of unemployment (cf. Korpi, 1991) and for fiscal and social policies from which labour can be seen to gain advantage. In Ireland such pressure is indeed already apparent even with the very limited economic improvement of the last few years (cf. Wilkinson, 1991).[16] In other words, concertative strategies in their very nature make it impossible for governments to avoid an involvement in distributional, and especially class distributional, questions. Which boats rise with the economic tide, and how high, cannot be left as the outcome merely of the play of market forces or of pluralistic bargaining, but has in important part to be determined by what Korpi (1983) has described as 'societal bargaining' within the national political arena.

In the context of the foregoing, one further significant feature of the Irish case is then apparent. The dominant position in Irish politics of 'catch-all' parties, the weakness of the class basis of party support and the infrequency with which political agendas are set in class terms would all suggest that Ireland might be regarded as a nation in which 'the end of ideology' was indeed reached *avant la lettre*. In the light of the liberal

---

[15] The one area where a basic consensus would seem necessary is that of economic analysis. As British experience well brings out, it is difficult to develop any concertative strategy if government, employers and unions adhere to quite different theories of the working of the economy. Roche (1989) notes a similar difficulty in the Irish case, but cf. Hardiman (this volume) with reference to the PESP.

[16] Furthermore, as Wilkinson is chiefly concerned to show, the Industrial Relations Act of 1990 seems likely to be a source of future difficulty, since, while conceived as an essential element of a concertative strategy, the advantage to labour is not readily apparent. Thus, the union leadership is exposed to rank-and-file attack for 'trading concessions in return for little benefit' and in turn the strategy as a whole can be represented 'as an attempt not so much to incorporate the unions as social partners in the organization of the economy, but to restrict their ability to protest the neo-liberal economic agenda begun by Fianna Fáil in 1987 and continued since.' (1991: 36).

theory, this seemingly precocious political development should then be of major benefit to the project of industrial advance.[17] However, a directly contrary view is now indicated. It may rather be that the distinctive structure and culture of Irish politics stand as barriers to the resolution of persisting economic problems, precisely because the strategies and policies offering the best chances of success would be divisive in class terms, and could thus be carried through only by parties ready to face such divisiveness and to address the ideological issues that arise.

Thus, as one factor in the failure of the concertative attempts of the 1970s, Hardiman (1988) has identified the reluctance of governing parties, dependent upon cross-class electoral support, to accept the distributive conflicts and associated ideological clashes that would be involved if national pay agreements were to be turned into more stable 'class compromises', through which the achievement of macroeconomic goals might be facilitated. And likewise, as regards the failure of governments to give support to employers' attempts at weakening organised labour, Breen et al. (1990: ch. 8) have argued that, because of the non-ideological character of Irish party politics, any such aggressive 'free market' strategy could not appear electorally attractive (cf. also Roche, 1989). From this standpoint, then, the logical conclusion must be that the 'straws in the wind' noted by Mair (this volume), which suggest in present-day Ireland a waning of the 'politics of national interest', growing socio-political dissensus and the possibility of parties more closely reflecting class interests, ought not to be viewed with dismay. To the contrary, if such straws can indeed be seen, they should be clutched at, since there may be few more hopeful signs so far as the future of Irish political economy is concerned.

Conclusion

The chief aim of this paper has been to exploit the strategic advantages offered by the Irish case for the critical examination of the liberal theory of industrialism. Difficulties arising with the theory have been suggested on several, quite different grounds. First, it has been argued that the implicit presupposition of the theory that societies can be understood as making the transition to industrialism as essentially independent entities must seriously limit its explanatory power. Many features both of the

---

[17] It should, however, be noted that no very obvious explanation for this development is itself derivable from the liberal theory—that is, in terms of the logic of industrialism as this operated in the Irish case.

actual course followed by industrialisation in Ireland and of the society that has by the present time emerged cannot be adequately accounted for in terms of internal processes—that is, of the progressive reshaping of a 'traditional' order by the functional logic of industrialism—but reflect, rather, major external influences, inseparable from Ireland's particular history as a European and a post-colonial nation.[18]

Secondly, it has been shown that in an area where the 'endogenous' processes directly addressed by the liberal theory might be regarded as primary, that of the changing nature of social stratification, expectations deriving from the theory are still not well supported by the empirical evidence. Ireland provides an unusually good test-case for the claim that advancing industrialism is associated with the creation of a more achievement-oriented and open society—which turns out, however, to give largely negative results. Even if, then, it is accepted that a logic of industrialism is here at work, what may still be questioned is its force, and the assumption of the liberal theory that it must prevail when opposed by the actions of individuals and families concerned to maintain the relative power and advantage that they presently possess.

Thirdly, it has been observed that the ideological ambition of the liberal theory—to promote, one might say, the ideology of the end of ideology —though furthered by the collapse of state socialism in eastern Europe, is at the same time threatened in the western world. An awareness has emerged that a pluralist polity may not, at a high level of development, be that functionally most compatible with a market economy. The Irish case well illustrates the unintended and undesirable consequences for economic performance that the institutions of 'pluralistic industrialism' can engender and, in a rather distinctive way, the difficulties of seeking either to transcend or to weaken these institutions in a situation where non-ideological politics are already established.

To end with, then, it would seem appropriate to ask: if such criticism of the liberal theory can be sustained by reference to the Irish case, what in turn follows for Ireland and for those concerned with the future of its industrial society? In response, two things might be said. First, although, as remarked at the outset, the liberal theory is a theory of constraints, it still fails to provide an adequate account of the way in which the development of industrial societies is thus shaped. The emphasis placed on constraints supposed to follow from the functional exigencies of industrialism

---

[18] In this last respect, however, the foregoing analysis would suggest that more emphasis needs to be given to the fact that the Irish situation was one of 'internal' rather than of 'external' colonialism (cf. Hechter, 1975), as a result of which certain 'core' political and social rights were extended to the economic periphery.

would seem exaggerated—to the neglect of others which, in regard to Ireland at least, need to be accorded much greater importance. That is, on the one hand, external constraints deriving from relations with other nations and increasingly, one could expect, with multinational business enterprises and supranational political agencies; and, on the other hand, internal constraints stemming not from the logic of industrialism but from social structures and processes expressing established relations of power and advantage within Irish society that have evident self-maintaining properties. Secondly, though, there is still no reason to accept that constraints of whatever kind operate to such an extent that major political choices are narrowed down in the way that exponents of the liberal theory have wished to claim. The idea that in the more advanced western societies, polity and economy have by now come into such a degree of functional harmony that an 'end state' must be recognised is not one that can withstand empirical examination. Even if the 'universalisation of liberalism' is assumed, significantly different versions of industrial society are still possible, and may be seriously pursued, within the limits thus set. And in Ireland especially, it could be argued that the prospects of creating a more successful industrial society could only be enhanced by changes in political culture and organisation that would encourage the 'real ideological alternatives' that do in fact exist to be more vigorously explored and contested.

Acknowledgements. I am indebted to Christopher Whelan for his helpful comments on an earlier version of this paper, and to Terence Gorman, Niamh Hardiman, Patrick McGovern, Dorren McMahon and Brian Wilkinson for valuable discussion, information and advice.

Bibliography

Abbott, W. M. (ed.) (1966): *The Documents of Vatican II*, London: Geoffrey Chapman.

Acquaviva, S. S. (1979): *The Decline of the Sacred in Industrial Society*, Oxford: Basil Blackwell.

Adelman, I. (1975): 'Development Economies — A Reassessment of Goals', *American Economic Review*, 65: 302–9.

Adelman, I. and Morris C. (1973): *Economic Growth and Social Equity in Development Countries*, Stanford: Stanford University Press.

Agriculture and Food Policy Review (1990): Dublin: Stationery Office.

Ahlen, K. (1989): 'Swedish Collective Bargaining Under Pressure: Inter-Union Rivalry and Incomes Policies', *British Journal of Industrial Relations*, 27: 330–6.

Ahluwalia, M. (1974): 'Income Inequality: Some Dimensions of the Problem' in H. Chenery *et al.* (eds), *Redistribution with Growth*, Oxford: Oxford University Press.

Amoroso, B. (1990): 'Development and Crisis of the Scandinavian Model of Labour Relations in Denmark' in C. Baglioni and C. Crouch (eds).

Anand, S. and Kanbur, R. (1986): 'Inequality and Development: A Critique'. Paper prepared for the Yale University Economic Growth Center.

Archer, R. (1991): 'The Unexpected Emergence of Australian Corporatism' in J. Pekkarinen, M. Pohjola and B. Rowthorn (eds), *Social Corporatism and Economic Performance*. Oxford: Oxford University Press.

Arensberg, C. (1937): *The Irish Countryman*, New York: Macmillan.

Arensberg, C. M. and Kimball, S. T. (1940): *Family and Community in Ireland*, Cambridge, Mass.: Harvard University Press.

Armingeon, K. (1986): 'Formation and Stability of Neo-Corporatist Incomes Policies: A Comparative Analysis', *European Sociological Review*, 2: 138–47.

Arter, D. (1987): *Politics and Policy-Making in Finland*, Brighton: Wheatsheaf.

Ashford, Douglas, (1986): *The Emergence of the Welfare States*, Oxford: Basil Blackwell.

Austen-Smith, D. and Banks, J. (1988): 'Elections, Coalitions and Legislative Outcomes', *American Political Science Review*, 82: 405–422.

Badham, R. (1984): 'The Sociology of Industrial and Post-Industrial Societies'. *Current Sociology*, 32: 1–141.

Badone, E. (ed.) (1990): *Religious Orthodoxy and Popular Faith in European Society*, Princeton: Princeton University Press.

Baglioni, C. and Crouch, C. (eds) (1990): *European Industrial Relations: The Challenge of Flexibility*, London: Sage.

Baker, T. (1988): 'Industrial Output and Wage Costs 1980–87', *Quarterly Economic Commentaries*, Dublin: The Economic and Social Research Institute.

Balassa, B. and Bertrand, T. J. (1970): 'Growth Performance of Eastern European Economies and Comparable Western European Countries', *American Economic Review*, 60: 314–320.

Barrington, R. (1987); *Health, Medicine and Politics in Ireland: 1900–1970*, Dublin: Institute of Public Administration.

Bartley, M. (1987): 'Research on Unemployment and Health in Great Britain' in P. Schwefel, G. Svenson and H. Zoller (eds), *Unemployment Social Vulnerability and Health in Europe*, Berlin: Springer Verlag.

Barry, F. (1988): 'Review Article', *Economic and Social Review*, 20: 59–62.

Bartolini, S. and Mair, P. (1990): *Identity, Competition and Electoral Availability: The Stabilisation of European Electorates, 1885–1985*, Cambridge: Cambridge University Press.

Baumol, W. J. (1990): 'Entrepreneurship: Productive, Unproductive and Destructive', *Journal of Political Economy*, 98: 893–921.

Bax, M. (1987): 'Religious Regimes and State Formation: Towards a Research Perspective', *Anthropological Quarterly*, 60: 1–11.

Beckford, J. A. (1990): 'The Sociology of Religion 1945–1989', *Social Compass*, 37: 45–64.

Bellah, R. N. (1967): 'Civil Religion in America', *Daedulus*, 96: 1–21.

Berger, P. L. (1971): *A Rumour of Angels: Modern Society and the Rediscovery of the Supernatural*, Harmondsworth: Pelican.

Berger, P. L. (1973): *The Social Reality of Religion*, Harmondsworth: Penguin.

Bew, P., Hazelkorn, E., and Patterson, H. (1989): *The Dynamics of Irish Politics*, London: Lawrence and Wishart.

Bew, P. and Patterson, H. (1982): *Sean Lemass and the Making of Modern Ireland: 1945–66*, Dublin: Gill and Macmillan.

Bihlmeyer, K. and Tuchle, H. (1966): *Church History*, Westminster: Newman Press.

Bird, R. M. (1980): 'Income Redistribution Through The Fiscal System: The Limits of Knowledge', *American Economic Review, Papers and Proceedings*, May: 77–81.

Blackwell, J. (1989): *Women in the Labour Force*, Dublin: Equality of Employment Agency.

Blau, P. M. and Duncan, O. D. (1967): *The American Occupational Structure*, New York: Wiley.

Bohan, H. (1979): *Ireland Green*, Dublin: Veritas Publications.

Booth, C. (1902): 'The Economic Distribution of Population in Ireland', in W. P. Coyne (ed.), *Ireland: Industrial and Agricultural*, Dublin: Browne and Nolan.

Bradley, J., Fitzgerald, J. and McCoy, D. (1991): *Medium-Term Review 1991–1996*, Dublin: The Economic and Social Research Institute.

Brandes, S. (1990): 'Reflections on the Study of Religious Orthodoxy and Popular Faith in Europe' in E. Badone (ed.).

Breen, R. (1984a): *Education and the Labour Market: Work and Unemployment Among Recent Cohorts of Irish School Leavers*, Dublin: The Economic and Social Research Institute.

Breen, R. (1984b): 'Fitting Non-Hierarchical and Association Log Linear Models Using GLIM', *Sociological Methods and Research*, 13: 77–107.

Breen, R. (1985): 'A Framework for Comparative Analysis of Social Mobility', *Sociology*, 19: 93–107.

Breen, R. (1987): 'Sources of Cross-National Variation in Mobility Regimes: English, French and Swedish Data Reanalysed', *Sociology*, 21: 75–90.

Breen, R. (1991a): 'Assessing the Effectiveness of Training and Temporary Employment Schemes: Some Results from the Youth Labour Market', *The Economic and Social Review*, 22: 177–198.

Breen, R. (1991b): *Education, Employment and Training in the Youth Labour Market*, Dublin: The Economic and Social Research Institute.

Breen, R., Hannan, D. F., Rottman, D. B. and Whelan, C. T. (1990): *Understanding Contemporary Ireland: State, Class and Development in the Republic of Ireland*, London: Macmillan.

Breen, R. and Whelan, C. T. (1985): 'Vertical Mobility and Class Inheritance in the British Isles', *British Journal of Sociology*, 36: 175–192.

Breen, R. and Whelan, C. T. (1991): 'Cross-National Variation in European Patterns of Social Fluidity: The Effects of Agriculture, Hierarchy and Property'. Unpublished paper.

Breslin, A. and Weafer, J. (1985): *Religious Beliefs, Practice and Moral Attitudes: A Comparison of Two Irish Surveys, 1974–1984*, Report No. 21. Maynooth: Council for Research and Development.

Brittain, S. (1977): *The Economic Contradictions of Democracy*, London: Temple Smith.

Brittan, S. (1983): *The Rise and Limits of Government*, London: Temple Smith.

Brody, H. (1973): *Inishkillane*, London: Penguin.

Brown, T. (1981): *Ireland: A Social and Cultural History 1922–79*, London: Fontana.

Brunnetta, R. and Dell'Aringa, C. (eds) (1991): *Labour Relations and Economic Performance*, Basingstoke: Macmillan.

Buchanan, C. and Partners (1968): *Regional Studies in Ireland*, Dublin: An Foras Forbartha.

Budge, I., Robertson, D. and Heald, D. (eds) (1987): *Ideology, Strategy and Party Change*, Cambridge: Cambridge University Press.

Burns, T. and Stalker, G. M. (1966): *The Management of Innovation*, London: Tavistock.

Butler, C. (1981): *The Theology of Vatican II*, London: Darton, Longman and Todd.

Callan, T., Nolan, B., Whelan, B. J. and Hannan, D. F. with Creighton, S. (1989): *Poverty, Income and Welfare in Ireland*, Dublin: The Economic and Social Research Institute.

Callan, T., Nolan, B. and Whelan, C. T. (forthcoming). *Resources, Deprivation and the Measurement of Poverty*, Oxford: Oxford University Press.

Calmfors, L. and Driffill, J. (1988): 'Bargaining Structure, Corporatism and Macroeconomic Performance', *Economic Policy: A European Forum*, 6: 13–61.

Cameron, D. (1978): 'The Expansion of the Public Economy: A Comparative Analysis', *American Political Science Review*, 72: 1243–1261.

Cameron, D. (1984): 'Social Democracy, Corporatism, Labour Quiescence, and the Representation of Economic Interest in Advanced Capitalist Society' in J. H. Goldthorpe (ed.).

Cannon, J. (1975): *The Revolutionary Party: Its Role in the Struggle for Socialism*, New York: Pathfinder Press.

Carnoy, M. (1984): *The State and Political Theory*, Princeton, N.J.: Princeton University Press.

Carty, R. K. (1981): *Party and Parish Pump: Electoral Politics in Ireland*, Ontario: Wilfrid Laurier Press.

Castles, F. (1978). *The Social Democratic Image of Society*, London: Routledge.

Castles, F. (ed.) (1982). *The Impact of Parties: Politics and Policies in Democratic Capitalist States*, London and Beverley Hills: Sage.

Castles, F. (1988): *The State and Political Theory*, Princeton, N.J.: Princeton University Press.

Cawson, A. (1985): *Organised Interests and the State: Studies in Meso-Corporatism*, London and Beverly Hills: Sage.

Census of Population, *General Reports for Ireland, 1891; 1901; 1911*, London: HMSO.

Census of Ireland (1901), (1902), *Part II General Report*, Dublin: HMSO.

Census of Population (1951): *Volume 3: Occupations*, Dublin: Central Statistics Office.

Census of Population (1961): *Volume 5: Occupations*, Dublin: Central Statistics Office.

Census of Population (1971): *Volume 4: Occupations*, Dublin: Central Statistics Office.

Census of Population (1971): *Volume 5: Occupations and Industries Classified by Ages and Conjugal Conditions*, Dublin: Central Statistics Office.

Census of Population (1981): *Volume 7: Occupations*, Dublin: Central Statistics Office.

Census of Population (1986): *Volume 2: Age and Marital Status*, Dublin: Central Statistics Office.

Chirot, D. (1986): *Social Change in the Modern Era*, Orlando, Fl.: Harcourt Brace Jovanovich.

Chubb, B. (1970/1982): *The Government and Politics of Ireland*, Oxford: Oxford University Press.

Clancy, P. (1988). *Who Goes to College?* Dublin: HEA.

Clancy, P., Drudy, S., Lynch, K. and O'Dowd, L. (eds) (1986): *Ireland: A Sociological Profile*, Dublin: Institute of Public Administration.

Clark, J., Modgil, C. and Modgil, S. (eds) (1990), *John H. Goldthorpe: Consensus and Controversy*, London: Falmer Press.

Clarkson, J. D. (1926): *Labour and Nationalism in Ireland*, New York: AMS Press.

Clarkson, L. A. (1981): 'Irish Population Revisited, 1987–1921' in J. M. Goldstrom and L. A. Clarkson (eds), *Irish Population, Economy and Society*, Oxford: Clarendon.

Clear, C. (1987): *Nuns in Nineteenth Century Ireland*, Dublin: Gill and Macmillan.

Cleland, J. and Wilson, C. (1987): 'Demand Theories of the Fertility Transition: An Iconoclastic View', *Population Studies*, 41: 5–30.

Cliquet, R. L. (1991): *The Second Demographic Transition: Fact or Fiction?* Population Studies No. 23. Strasbourg: Council of Europe.

Coale, A. J., Hill, A. G. and Trussell, T. J. (1975): 'A New Method of Estimating Standard Fertility Measures From Incomplete Data', *Population Index*, 41: 182–210.

Coale, A. J. and Watkins, S. C. (eds) (1986): *The Decline of Fertility in Europe*, Princeton: Princeton University Press.

Cohan, A. S. (1982): 'Ireland: Coalitions Making a Virtue of Necessity' in E. C. Browne and J. Dreijmanis (eds), *Government Coalitions in Western Europe*, London: Longman.

Coleman, J. A. (1978): *The Evolution of Dutch Catholicism, 1958–1974*, Berkeley: University of California Press.

Coman, P. (1977): *Catholics and the Welfare State*, London: Longman.

Commins, P. (1986): 'Rural Social Change' in P. Clancy *et al.* (eds), *Ireland: A Sociological Profile*, Dublin: Institute of Public Administration.

Commins, P., Cox, P. G. and Curry, J. (1978): *Rural Areas: Change and Development*, Dublin: National Economic and Social Council.

Commission on Social Welfare (1986): *Report of the Commission on Social Welfare*, Dublin: Stationery Office.

Committee of Inquiry on Industrial Relations (1981): *Report of the Committee of Inquiry on Industrial Relations*, Dublin: Government Publications.

Commons, J. (1932): 'Labour Movements'. *Encyclopedia of the Social Sciences*, New York: Macmillan.

Compton, P. A. and Coward, J. (1989): *Fertility and Family Planning in Northern Ireland*, Aldershot: Avebury.

Connell, K. H. (1950): *The Population of Ireland 1750–1845*. Oxford: Clarendon Press.

Connell, K. H. (1968): *Irish Peasant Society*, Oxford: Clarendon Press.

Conniffe, D. and Kennedy, K. A. K. (1984): *Employment and Unemployment Policy for Ireland*, Dublin: The Economic and Social Research Institute.

Connolly, S. J. (1982): *Priests and People in Pre-Famine Ireland 1780–1845*, Dublin: Gill and Macmillan.

Connolly, S. J. (1985): *Religion and Society in Nineteenth Century Ireland*, Dundalk: Dundalgan Press.

Corish, P. (1985): *The Irish Catholic Experience*, Dublin: Gill and Macmillan.

Council of Europe (1989): *Recent Demographic Developments in the Member States of the Council of Europe*, Strasbourg: Council of Europe.

Courtney, D. A. (1990): *Women, Parenthood and Labour Force Activity in Ireland during the 1980s*, Paper presented to the Council of Europe Seminar on Present Demographic Trends and Lifestyles. Strasbourg.

Coyne, W. P. (ed.) (1902): *Ireland: Industrial and Agricultural*, Dublin: Brown and Nolan.

Cox, B. and Hughes, J. (1987/1989): 'Industrial Relations in the Public Sector' in T. Murphy (ed.).

Cronin, J. (1979): *Industrial Conflict in Modern Britain*, London: Croom Helm.

Crotty, R. (1966): *Irish Agricultural Production*, Cork: Cork University Press.

Crotty, R. (1986): *Ireland in Crisis: A Study in Capitalist Colonial Underdevelopment*, Dingle: Brandon Book Publishers.

Crouch, C. (1985): 'Conditions for Trade Union Wage Restraint' in L. Lindberg and C. S. Maier (eds), *The Politics of Inflation and Economic Stagnation*, Washington D. C.: The Brookings Institution.

Crouch, C. (1990): 'United Kingdom: Rejection of Compromise' in C. Baglioni and C. Crouch (eds).

Crouch, C. (1991): 'Trade Unions in the Exposed Sector: Their Influence on Neo-Corporatist Behaviour', in R. Brunetta and C. Dell'Aringa (eds).

Crouch, C. (1992): *Industrial Relations and European State Traditions*, Oxford: Oxford University Press.

Crouch, C. and Pizzorno, A. (eds) (1978). *The Resurgence of Class Conflict in Western Europe Since 1968*, Vol. 1: *National Studies*, London: Macmillan.

CSO (1975, 1985, 1987): *Farm Structures Survey* (unpublished).

CSO (1977): *Household Budget Survey*, Dublin: Central Statistics Office.

CSO (1980): *Redistributive Effects of State Taxes and Benefits on Household Incomes in 1973*, Dublin: Stationery Office.

CSO (1983): *Redistributive Effects of State Taxes and Benefits on Household Incomes in 1980*, Dublin: Stationery Office.

CSO (1985): *Irish Statistical Bulletin 1985*, Dublin: Central Statistics Office.

CSO (1989): *Statistical Abstract 1989*, Dublin: Central Statistics Office.

CSO (1990a): *Irish Statistical Bulletin 1990*, Dublin: Central Statistics Office.

CSO (1990b): *Household Budget Survey 1987*, Vol. 2, Dublin: Stationery Office.

Cullen, L. M. (1972): *An Economic History of Ireland Since 1660*, London: Batsford.

Curtin, C. and Wilson, T. M. (eds) (1989): *Ireland From Below: Social Change and Local Communities*, Galway: Galway University Press.

Daalder, H. (1987): 'Countries in Comparative Politics', *European Journal of Political Research*, 15: 3–21.

Dahrendorf, R. (1959): *Class and Class Conflict in Industrial Society*, London: Routledge and Kegan Paul.

Daly, G. (1981). *Transcendence and Immanence: A Study in Catholic Modernism and Integralism*, Oxford: Clarendon Press.

David, P. A. and Sanderson, W. C. (1988): 'Measuring Marital Fertility with CPA', *Population Index*, 54: 691–713.

Davis, K. (1963): 'The Theory of Change and Response in Modern Demographic History', *Population Index*, 21: 345–366.

Davis, K. and Moore, W. E. (1945): 'Some Principles of Stratification'. *American Sociological Review*, 5: 242–249.

Day, L. H. (1968): 'Nationality and Ethnic-centrism: Some Relationships Suggested by an Analysis of Catholic-Protestant Differentials', *Population Studies*, 22: 27–50.

de Cooman, E., Ermisch, J. and Joshi, H. (1987): 'The Next Birth and the Labour Market: A Dynamic Model of Births in England and Wales', *Population Studies*, 41: 237–268.

Dean, G. (1984): *Termination of Pregnancy, England 1983: Women from the Republic of Ireland*, Dublin: Medico-Social Research Unit.

Department of Industry and Commerce (1989): *Strategy for the Irish-Owned Electronics Industry*, Dublin: Stationery Office.

Department of Labour (1989) *Annual Report*, Dublin: Stationery Office..

Department of Social Welfare (1967): *Report of the Department of Social Welfare*, 1963–66, Dublin: Stationery Office.

Department of Social Wefare (1991): *Statistical Information on Social Welfare Services, 1990*, Dublin: Stationery Office.

BIBLIOGRAPHY 439

Dobbelaere, K. (1981): 'Secularisation: A Multi-Dimensional Concept', *Current Sociology*, 29: 3–213.

Dobbelaere, K. (1985): 'Secularisation Theories and Sociological Paradigms: A Reformulation of the Private-Public Dichotomy and the Problem of Societal Integration', *Sociological Analysis*, 46: 377–387.

Dobbelaere, K. (1987): 'Some Trends in European Sociology of Religion: The Secularisation Debate', *Sociological Analysis*, 48: 107–137.

Dobbelaere, K. (1989): 'The Secularisation of Society? Some Methodological Suggestions' in J. K. Hadden and A. Shupe (eds) *Secularisation and Fundamentalism Reconsidered, Religion and the Political Order*, New York: Paragon.

Dolan, J. P. (1987): *The American Catholic Experience: A History from Colonial Times to the Present*, New York: Image.

Douglas, M. (1982): 'The Effects of Modernisation on Religious Change', *Daedalus*, 3: 1–21.

Downs, A. (1957): *An Economic Theory of Democracy*, New York: Harper and Row.

Drudy, P. J. (1985): 'Irish Population Change and Emigration Since Independence' in P. J. Drudy (ed.) *The Irish in America: Emigration, Assimilation and Impact*, Cambridge: Cambridge University Press.

Dulles, A. (1976): *Models of the Church: A Critical Assessment of the Church in All Its Aspects*, Dublin: Gill and Macmillan.

Dunlop, J. T. (1958): *Industrial Relations Systems*, New York: Holt.

Dunlop, J. T., Harbison, F. H., Kerr, C. and Myers, C. A. (1975): *Industrialism and Industrial Man Reconsidered*, Princeton, New Jersey: International Study of Human Resources in National Development.

Durkan, J. (1991): 'Social Consensus and Incomes Policy', paper presented to the Irish Economic Association Conference.

Edgren, G., Faxen, K-O, Odhner, E. (1973): *Wage Formation and the Economy*, London: Allen and Unwin.

Elster, J. (1979): *Ulysses and the Sirens*, Cambridge: Cambridge University Press.

Erikson, R. (1990): 'Politics and Class Mobility. Does Politics Influence Rates of Social Mobility?' in I. Persson (ed.) *Generating Equality in the Welfare State: The Swedish Experience*, Oslo: Norwegian University Press.

Erikson, R. and Goldthorpe, J. H. (1987a): 'Commonality and Variation in Social Fluidity in Industrial Nations, Part I; A Model from Evaluating the "FJH Hypothesis"', *European Sociological Review*, 3: 54–77.

Erikson, R. and Goldthorpe, J. H. (1987b): 'Commonality and Variation in Social Fluidity in Industrial Nations, Part II: The Model of Core Social Fluidity Applied', *European Sociological Review*, 3: 145–166.

Erikson, R. and Goldthorpe, J. H. (1992): *The Constant Flux: A Study of Class Mobility in Industrial Societies*, Oxford: Clarendon Press.

Erikson, R., Goldthorpe, J. H., and Portocarero, L. (1982): 'Social Fluidity in Industrial Nations: England, France and Sweden', *British Journal of Sociology*. 33: 1–34.

Esping-Andersen, G. (1985): *Politics Against Markets*, Princeton, N. J.: Princeton University Press.

Esping-Andersen, G. (1990): *The Three Worlds of Welfare Capitalism*, Princeton, N.J.: Princeton University Press.

Estivill, J. and de la Hoz, J. M. (1990): 'Transition and Crisis: The Complexity of Spanish Industrial Relations' in C. Baglioni and C. Crouch (eds).

Eurostat (1989): *Demographic Statistics 1989*, Luxembourg: EC.

Eurostat (1991): *Demographic Statistics*, Luxembourg: EC.

Eurostat (1991): *A Social Portrait of Europe*, Luxembourg: EC.

Fahey, T. (1987): 'Nuns in the Catholic Church in Ireland in the Nineteenth Century' in M. Cullen (ed.) *Girls Don't Do Honours: Irish Women in Education in the 19th and 20th centuries*, Dublin: The Women's Education Bureau.

Fanning, R. (1978): *Independent Ireland*, Dublin: Helicon.

Fanning, R. (1990): 'The Genesis of Economic Development' in J. F. McCarthy (ed.), *Planning Ireland's Future: The Legacy of T. K. Whitaker*, Dublin: The Glendale Press.

Farrell, B. (1970): 'Labour and the Irish Political Party System: A Suggested Approach to Analysis', *The Economic and Social Review*, 1: 477–502.

Farrell, B. (1984): 'Communications and Community: Problems and Prospects' in B. Farrell (ed.) *Communications and Community in Ireland*, Dublin and Cork: Mercier Press.

Featherman, D. L., Jones, F. L., and Hauser, R. M. (1975): 'Assumptions of Mobility Research in the United States: The Case of Occupational Status', *Social Science Research*, 4: 329–60.

Featherman, D. L. and Selbee, L. K. (1988): 'Class Formation and Class Mobility: A New Approach with Counts from Life History Data' in M. Riley and B. Huber (eds) *Social Structure and Human Lives*, Newbury Park: Sage.

Featherstone, K. (1990): 'The "Party-State" in Greece and the Fall of Papandreou', *West European Politics*, 13: 101–115.

Fields, G. and Jakobsen, G. (1990): 'The Inequality-Development Relationship in Developing Countries', Paper Presented at the 6th World Congress of the Econometric Society, Barcelona.

Fitzgerald, G. (1991): *All In a Life*, Dublin: Gill and Macmillan.

Fitzpatrick, J. D. (1977): *Politics and Irish Life*, Dublin: Gill and Macmillan.

Fitzpatrick, J. D. (1980): 'Strikes in Ireland, 1914–1921', *Saothar*, 6: 26–39.

Flanagan, R. J., Soskice, D. W., and Ulman, L. (1983): *Unionism, Economic Stablisation and Incomes Policies: European Experience*, Washington, D.C.: Brookings Institution.

Flanders, A. (1970): *Management and Unions: The Theory and Reform of Industrial Relations*. London: Faber.

Flora, P. (1985): 'On the History and Current Problems of the Welfare State' in S. N. Eisenstadt and O. Ahimeir (eds). *The Welfare State and its Aftermath*, New Jersey: Barnes and Noble.

Flora, P. (1987): *State, Economy, and Society in Western Europe 1815–1975: A Data Handbook*, Vol. 2, Frankfurt: Campus Verlag.

Flora, P., Krause, F. and Pfenning, W. (1983): *State, Economy and Society in Western Europe, 1815–1975: A Data Handbook*, Vol. 1, London: Campus Macmillan.

Fogarty, M. P., Egan, D., and Ryan, W. J. L. (1981): *Pay Policy for the 1980s*, Dublin: Federated Union of Employers.

Fogarty, M., Ryan, L. and Lee, J. (eds) (1984): *Irish Values and Attitudes: The Irish Report of the European Value Systems Study*, Dublin: Dominican Publications.

Fox, A. (1966): 'Industrial Sociology and Industrial Relations', Royal Commission on Trade Unions and Employer Associations, Research Paper, No. 3, London: HMSO.

Fukuyama, F. (1989): 'The End of History?', *The National Interest*, 16: 3–18.

Fulton, J. (1991): *The Tragedy of Belief: Division, Politics and Religion in Ireland*. Oxford: Clarendon Press.

Furniss, N. and Tilton, T. (1977): *The Case for the Welfare State*, Bloomington: Indiana University Press.

Furtado, C. (1976): *Economic Development of Latin America*, Cambridge: Cambridge University Press.

Gallagher, M. (1976): *Electoral Support for Irish Political Parties, 1927–73*, London: Sage.

Gallagher, M. (1982): *The Irish Labour Party in Transition, 1957–82*, Dublin: Gill and Macmillan.

Gallagher, M. (1985): *Political Parties in the Republic of Ireland*, Dublin: Gill and Macmillan.

Gallagher, M., Laver, M., and Mair, P. (1992): *Representative Government in Western Europe*, New York: McGraw Hill.

Gallagher, M., and Sinnott, R. (eds) (1990): *How Ireland Voted 1989*, Galway: Centre for the Study of Irish Elections.

Gallie, D. (1983): *Social Inequality and Class Radicalism in France and Britain*, Cambridge: Cambridge University Press.

Gallie, D. (1990): 'John Goldthorpe's Critique of Liberal Industrialism' in J. Clark *et al.* (eds.).

Ganzeboom, H. B. G., Luijkx, R. and Treiman, D. J. (1989): 'Intergenerational Class Mobility in Comparative Perspective', *Research in Social Stratification and Mobility*, 8: 3–55.

Ganzeboom, H. B. G. and Ultee, W. C. (1988): 'Comparative Social Mobility in Industrial Nations – An Appraisal with Special Reference to Social Mobility in The Netherlands', Conference on Class Formation and Comparative Social Mobility, Schloss Reisenburg, Germany.

Garrett, G. and Lange, P. (1985): 'The Politics of Growth: Strategic Interaction and Economic Performance in the Advanced Industrial Democracies, 1974– 1980', *Journal of Politics*, 47: 792–827.

Garvin, T. (1974): 'Political Cleavages, Party Politics, and Urbanisation in Ireland: The Case of the Periphery-Dominated Centre', *European Journal of Political Research*, 2: 307–327.

Garvin, T. (1981): *The Evolution of Irish Nationalist Politics*, Dublin: Gill and Macmillan.

Garvin, T. (1982): 'Change and the Political System' in F. Litton (ed.) *Unequal Achievement: The Irish Experience, 1957–1982*, Dublin: Institute of Public Administration.

Geary, R. C. (1973): 'Are Ireland's Social Security Payments Too Small? A Note', *The Economic and Social Review*, 4: 343–348.

Gerlich, P., Grande, E. and Müller, W. (1988): 'Corporatism in Crisis: Stability and Change of Social Partnership in Austria', *Political Studies*, June: 209–23.

Giddens, A. (1973): *The Class Structure of the Advanced Societies*, London: Hutchinson.

Giddens, A. (1986): *The Constitution of Society: Outline of the Theory of Structuration*, Cambridge: Polity Press.

Gilbert, A. D. (1980): *The Making of Post-Christian Britain. A History of the Secularisation of Modern Society*, London: Longman.

Gillespie, R. (1980): 'The Break-up of the "Socialist Family"; Party-Union Relations in Spain, 1982–89', *West European Politics*. 13: 47–62.

Girvin, B. (1989): *Between Two Worlds: Politics and Economy in Independent Ireland*, Dublin: Gill and Macmillan.

Glass, D. V. (ed.) (1954): *Social Mobility in Britain*, London: Routledge and Kegan Paul.

Goldthorpe, J. H. (1971): 'Theories of Industrial Society', *Archives Européennes de Sociologie*, 12, 263–288.

Goldthorpe, J. H. (1982): 'On the Service Class: Its Formation and Future' in A. Giddens and G. McKenzie (eds), *Classes and the Division of Labour*, Cambridge: Cambridge University Press.

Goldthorpe, J. H. (ed.) (1984): *Order and Conflict in Contemporary Capitalism*, Oxford: Clarendon Press.

Goldthorpe, J. H. (1984): 'The End of Convergence: Corporatist and Dualist Tendencies in Modern Western Societies' in J. H. Goldthorpe (ed.).

Goldthorpe, J. H. (1985): 'On Economic Development and Social Mobility', *British Journal of Sociology*, 36: 549–573.

Goldthorpe, J. H. (1980/1987): *Social Mobility and Class Structure in Britain*, Oxford: Clarendon Press.

Goldthorpe, J. H. (1987): 'Problems of Political Economy after the Post-War Period' in C. Maier (ed.), *The Changing Boundaries of the Political*, Cambridge: Cambridge University Press.

Goldthorpe, J. H. (1990): 'A Response' in J. Clark *et al.* (eds).

Goldthorpe, J. H. (1991): 'Employment, Class and Mobility: A Critique of Liberal and Marxist Theories of Long-Term Change' in H. Haferkamp and N. J. Smelser (eds), *Modernity and Social Change*, Berkeley: University of California Press.

Goldthorpe, J. H. and Lockwood, D. (1963): 'Affluence and the British Class Structure', *Sociological Review*, 11: 133–63.

Goldthorpe, J. H. and Payne C. (1986): 'Trends in Intergenerational Class Mobility in England and Wales 1972–1983', *Sociology*, 20: 1–24.

Goodin, R. E. and Dryzek, J. (1987): 'Risk Sharing and Social Justice: The Motivational Foundations of the Post-War Welfare State' in R. Goodin and J. Le Grand, (eds), *Not Only the Poor: The Middle Classes and the Welfare State*, London: Allen and Unwin.

Goodman, L. A. (1979): 'Simple Models for the Analysis of Association in Cross-Classifications Having Ordered Categories', *Journal of the American Statistical Association*, 74, 537–552.

Goodman, L. A. (1984): *The Analysis of Cross-Classified Data having Ordered Categories*, Cambridge, Mass.: Harvard University Press.

Gorman, L., Handy, C., Moynihan, T. and Murphy, T. (1974): *Managers in Ireland*, Dublin: Irish Management Institute.

Gorman, L., Hynes, G., McConnell, J. and Moynihan, T. (1975): *Irish Industry: How It's Managed*, Dublin: Irish Management Institute.

Gourevitch, P., Martin, A., Ross, G., Bernstein, S., Markovits, A. and Allen, C. (eds). (1984): *Unions and Economic Crisis: Britain, West Germany and Sweden*, London: George Allen and Unwin.

Greaves, D. (1982): *The Irish Transport and General Workers' Union: The Formative Years*, Dublin: Gill and Macmillan.

Greeley, A. M. (1972): 'The State of the Priesthood in the United States', *Doctrine and Life*, 22: 351–380.

Greeley, A. M. (1975): *The New Agenda*, Garden City, New York: Image Books.

Greeley, A. M. (1976): *The Communal Catholic: A Personal Manifesto*, New York: Seabury Press.

Greeley, A. M. (1989): *Religious Change in America*, Cambridge, Massachusetts and London: Harvard University Press.

Greene, S. M., Joy, M.-T., Nugent, J. K. and O'Mahony, P. (1989): 'Contraceptive Practice of Irish Married and Single First-time Mothers', *Journal of Biosocial Science*, 21: 379–386.

Grusky, D. M. and Hauser, R. M. (1984): 'Comparative Social Mobility Revisited: Models of Convergence and Divergence in 16 Countries', *American Sociological Review*, 49: 19–38.

Gunnigle, P. and Shivanath, G. (1988): 'Role and Status of Personnel Practitioners —A Positive Picture', *Irish Journal of Business and Administrative Research*, 9: 1–9.

Hadden, J. K. and Shupe, A. (eds) (1985): *Prophetic Religions and Politics*, New York: Paragon House.

Hall, P. A. (1990): 'Pluralism and Pressure Politics', in P. A. Hall, J. Hayward and H. Machin (eds), *Developments in French Politics*, Basingstoke: Macmillan.

Halsey, A. H. (1975): 'Towards Meritocracy? The Case of Britain' in J. Karabel and A. H. Halsey (eds), *Power and Ideology in Education*, New York: Oxford University Press.

Hammond, P. E. (ed.) (1985): *The Sacred in a Secular Age*, Berkeley, Los Angeles, and London: University of California Press.

Hannan, D. F. (1970): *Rural Exodus*, London: Geoffrey Chapman.

Hannan, D. F. (1972): 'Kinship, Neighbourhood and Social Changes in Irish Rural Communities', *The Economic and Social Review*, 3: 163–88.

Hannan, D. F. (1979): *Displacement and Development: Class, Kinship and Social Change in Irish Rural Communities*, Dublin: The Economic and Social Research Institute.

Hannan, D. F. (1986): *Schooling and the Labour Market*, Shannon: CDU, for the Department of Education and the Irish Pilot Projects.

Hannan, D. F., Breen, R., Murray, B., Hardiman, N., Watson, D. and O'Higgins, K. (1983): *Schooling and Sex Roles: Sex Differences in Subject Provision and Student Choice in Irish Post Primary Schools*, Dublin: Economic and Social Research Institute.

Hannan, D. F. and Hardiman, N. (1978): 'Peasant Proprietorship and Changes in Marriage Rates in the Late Nineteenth Century'. Dublin: The Economic and Social Research Institute, Unpublished paper.

Hannan, D. F. and Katsiaouni, L. (1977): *Traditional Families?* Dublin: The Economic and Social Research Institute.

Hanningan, J. A. (1989): 'Containing the Luciferine Spark: The Catholic Church and Recent Movements for Social Change in the Republic of Ireland' in R. O'Toole (ed.).

Hardiman, N. (1988): *Pay, Politics, and Economic Performance in Ireland, 1970–87*, Oxford: Clarendon Press.

Hardiman, N. (1990): 'Capitalism and Corporatism' in J. Clark. *et al.* (eds).

Harding, S., Phillips, D. and Fogarty, M. (1986): *Contrasting Values in Western Europe: Unity, Diversity and Change*, London: Macmillan/EVSSG.

Harris, R. I. D., Jefferson, C. W., Spenser, J. E. (eds) (1990): *The Northern Ireland Economy: A Comparative Study in the Economic Development of a Peripheral Region*, London: Longman.

Hassner, P. (1989): 'Response to Fukuyama', *The National Interest*, 16: 22–24.

Haughey, C. J. (1981): *Presidential Address to the 50th Fianna Fáil Ard Fheis*, Dublin: Fianna Fáil.

Haughey, C. J. (1983): *Presidential Address to the 51st Fianna Fáil Ard Fheis*, Dublin: Fianna Fáil.

Hazelkorn, E. (1986): 'Class, Clientelism and the Political Process in the Republic of Ireland' in P. Clancy *et al.* (eds).

Hazelkorn, E. (1989): 'Why Is There No Socialism in Ireland? Theoretical Problems of Irish Marxism', *Science and Society*, 53: 136–164.

Heald, D. (1983): *Public Expenditure*, London: Martin Robertson.

Heath, A. F. (1981): *Social Mobility*, London: Fontana.

Heath, A. F., Mills, C. and Roberts, J. (1991): 'Towards Meritocracy? Recent Evidence on an Old Problem', SCPR: Nuffield College, Oxford, Joint Unit for the Study of Social Trends, Working Paper 3.

Hechter, M. (1975): *Internal Colonialism: The Celtic Fringe in British National Development, 1536–1966*, London: Routledge and Kegan Paul.

Helleiner, G. K. (1973): 'Manufactured Exports from the Less Developed Countries and Multinational Firms', *Economic Journal*, 83: 21–47.

Hennessey, J. (1981): *American Catholics. A History of the Roman Catholic Community in the United States*, Oxford: Oxford University Press.

Henripin, J. *et al.* (1978): *La Fin de la Revanche du Berceau*. Quebec.

Henry, E. W. (1989): *The Capital Stock of Ireland, 1950–1984*, Dublin: The Economic and Social Research Institute.

Hibbs, D. (1976): 'Industrial Conflict in Advanced Industrial Societies', *American Political Science Review*, 70: 1033–1038.

Higgins, J. (1983): *A Study of Part-Time Farming in the Republic of Ireland*, Dublin: An Foras Taluntais, Economics and Rural Welfare Research Centre.

Higgins, M. D. (1982): 'The Limits of Clientelism: Towards an Assessment of Irish Politics' in C. Clapham (ed.), *Private Patronage and Public Power*, London: Frances Pinter.

Hirschman, A. O. (1981): *Essays in Trespassing*, Cambridge: Cambridge University Press.

Hoppen, K. T. (1989): *Ireland Since 1800: Conflict and Conformity*, London: Longman.

Horgan, J. (1986): *Labour: The Price of Power*, Dublin: Gill and Macmillan.

Hornsby-Smith, M. P. (1987): *Roman Catholics in England: Studies in Social Structure Since the Second World War*, Cambridge: Cambridge University Press.

Hornsby-Smith, M. P. (1989): *The Changing Parish: A Study of Parishes, Priests and Parishioners after Vatican II*, London: Routledge.

Hornsby-Smith, M. P. (1991): *Roman Catholic Beliefs in England: Customary Religion and Transformations of Religious Authority*, Cambridge: Cambridge University Press.

Hornsby-Smith, M. P. (1992): 'Recent Transformations in English Catholicism: Evidence of Secularization?' in S. Bruce (ed.) *Secularization: Recent Trends in Theory and Data*, Oxford: Oxford University Press.

Hornsby-Smith, M. P. and Dale, A. (1988): 'The Assimilation of Irish Immigrants in England', *British Journal of Sociology*, 39: 519–544.

Hornsby-Smith, M. P. and Whelan, C. T. (forthcoming): 'Religion and Morality', in C. T. Whelan, (ed.).

Hotelling, H. (1929): 'Stability in Competition', *Economic Journal*, 39: 41–57.

Hout, M. (1989): *Following in Father's Footsteps: Social Mobility in Ireland*, London, Harvard University Press.

Hout, M. and Jackson, J. (1986): 'Dimensions of Occupational Mobility in the Republic of Ireland', *European Sociological Review*, 2: 114–137.

Hughes, G. (1991): *The Provision of Retirement Incomes by Private and Other Non-Public Institutions: Ireland*, Paris: Organization for Economic Cooperation and Development.

Hughes, J. G. and Walsh, B. M. (1976): 'Migration Flows Between Ireland, the United Kingdom and Rest of the World', *European Demographic Information, Bulletin* 7: 125–149.

Humphreys, P. C. (1983): *Public Service Employment: An Examination of Strategies in Ireland and Other European Countries*, Dublin: Institute of Public Administration.

Huntington, S. P. (1968): *Political Order in Changing Societies*, New Haven, Connecticut: Yale University Press.

Hynes, E. (1989): 'Nineteenth-Century Irish Catholicism, Farmers' Ideology and Natural Religion: Explorations in Cultural Explanation' in R. O'Toole (ed.).

ICTU (1984): *Confronting the Jobs Crisis*, Dublin: ICTU.

ICTU (1989): *Trade Unions and Change: Shaping the Future – Discussion Document*, Dublin: ICTU.

ICTU (1990): *Ireland 1990–2000: A Decade of Development, Reform and Growth*, Dublin: ICTU.

IDA (1980): *Survey of Recruitment Patterns and Age Structure of Workforce in New Industry Grant Aided Companies*, Dublin: IDA.

Ingham, G. K. (1974): *Strikes and Industrial Conflict*, London: Macmillan.

Inglehart, R. (1987): 'Value Change in Industrial Societies', *American Political Science Review*, 81: 1289–1302.

Inglehart, R. and Klingemann, H. D. (1976): 'Party Identification, Ideological

Preference and the Left-Right Dimensions Among Western Mass Publics' in I. Budge, I. Crewe, and D. Farlie (eds), *Party Identification and Beyond: Representations of Voting and Party Competition*, London: Wiley.

Inglis, T. (1987): *Moral Monopoly: The Catholic Church in Modern Irish Society*, Dublin: Gill and Macmillan.

Institute of Public Administration (1982): *Personnel and Industrial Relations Directory*, Dublin: Institute of Public Administration.

Institute of Public Administration (1990): *Administration Yearbook and Diary, 1991*. Dublin: Institute of Public Administration.

Inter-Departmental Committee on Land Structure Reform (1978): *Final Report*, Dublin: Stationery Office.

Inter-Departmental Committee on the Problems of Small Western Farms (1962); *Report*, Dublin: Stationery Office.

Ireland, R. (1988): *The Challenge of Secularization*, Melbourne: Collins Dove.

Johannesson, J. and Schmid, G. (1980): 'The Development of Labour Market Policy in Sweden and in Germany: Competing or Converging Models to Combat Unemployment?', *European Journal of Political Research*, 8: 387–406.

Johnson, D. (1985): *The Interwar Economy in Ireland*, Dublin: The Economic and Social History Society of Ireland.

Jones, F. L. (1991): 'Common Social Fluidity: a Comment on Some Recent Criticisms', Canberra: Australian National University Research School of Social Sciences.

Jonsson, J. O. (1991): 'Towards the Merit-Selective Society?', Stockholm: Swedish Institute for Social Research.

Kahn-Freund, O. (1972): *Labour and the Law*, London: Stevens.

Katzenstein, P. (1983): 'The Small European States in the International Economy: Economic Dependencies and Corporatist Politics' in J. G. Ruggie (ed.) *The Antinomies of Interdependence*, New York: Columbia University Press.

Katzenstein, P. (1985): *Small States in World Markets*, Ithaca, N.Y.: Cornell University Press.

Keating, M. (1987): 'Personnel Management in Ireland', in T. Murphy (ed.).

Kelley, J. (1990): 'The Failure of a Paradigm: Log-Linear Models of Social Mobility' in J. Clark *et al.* (eds).

Kelley, A. and Brannick, T. (1985): 'Industrial Relations Practices in Multi-National Companies in Ireland', *Journal of Irish Business and Administrative Research*, 7: 98–111.

Kendall, W. (1975): *The Labour Movement in Europe*, London: Allen Lane.

Kennedy, F. (1971): *The Growth and Allocation of Public Social Expenditure in Ireland Since 1947*, Ph.D. Thesis, National University of Ireland.

Kennedy, K. A. and McHugh, D. (1984): 'Employment', in J. O'Hagan (ed.), *The Economy of Ireland: Policy and Performance*, Dublin: Irish Management Institute.

Kennedy, K. A., Giblin, T. and McHugh, D. (1988): *The Economic Development of Ireland in the Twentieth Century*, London: Routledge.

Kennedy, L. (1978): 'The Roman Catholic Church and Economic Growth in Nineteenth Century Ireland', *The Economic and Social Review*, 10: 45–60.

Kennedy, L. (1989): *The Modern Industrialisation of Ireland 1940–1988*, Dublin: The Economic and Social History Society of Ireland.

Kennedy, L., Ollerenshaw, P. (eds) (1985): *An Economic History of Ulster 1820–1939*, Manchester: Manchester University Press.

Kennedy, R. E. (1973a): 'Minority Groups and Fertility: The Irish'. *American Sociological Review*, 38: 83–96.

Kennedy, R. E. (1973b): *The Irish: Emigration, Marriage and Fertility*, London: University of California Press.

Kenny, B. (1985): *The Spatial Dimensions of Trade Union Organization in Ireland: A Case Study*, M.A. Thesis, St. Patrick's College, Maynooth.

Kenny, I. (1984): *Government and Enterprise in Ireland*, Dublin: Irish Management Institute.

Keogh, D. (1982): *The Rise of the Irish Working Class*, Belfast: Appletree Press.

Kerr, C. (1955): 'Industrial Relations and the Liberal Pluralist' in *Labour and Management in Industrial Society*, New York: Doubleday, 1964.

Kerr, C. (1969): *Marshall, Marx and Modern Times*, Cambridge: Cambridge Univerisity Press.

Kerr, C. (1983): *The Future of Industrial Societies*, Cambridge, Mass.: Harvard University Press.

Kerr, C., Dunlop, J. T., Harbison, F. and Myers, C. A. (1960/1973): *Industrialiam and Industrial Man: The Problems of Labour and The Management of Economic Growth*, Cambridge, Mass.: Harvard Univeristy Press/ London: Penguin.

Kirby, P. (1984): *Is Irish Catholicism Dying?* Dublin and Cork: Mercier Press.

Korpi, W. (1978): *The Working Class in Welfare Capitalism*, London: Routledge and Kegan Paul.

Korpi, W. (1980): 'Social Policy and Distributional Conflict in the Capitalist Democracies', *Western European Politics*, 3: 296–316.

Korpi, W. (1983): *The Democratic Class Struggle*, London: Routledge and Kegan Paul.

Korpi, W. (1989): 'Power, Politics and State Autonomy in the Development of Social Citizenship: Social Rights during Sickness in Eighteen OECD Countries Since 1930', *American Sociological Review*, 54: 309–328.

Korpi, W. (1991): 'Political and Economic Explanations for Unemployment: a Cross-National and Long-Term Analysis', *British Journal of Political Sciences*, 21: 315–348.

Korpi, W. and Shalev, M. (1980): 'Strikes, Power and Politics in the Western Nations 1900–1976', *Political Power and Social Theory*, 1: 299–332.

Kurz, K. and Müller, W. (1987): 'Class Mobility in the Industrial World', *Annual Review of Sociology*, 13: 417–442.

Kuznets, S. (1955): 'Economic Growth and Income Inequality', *American Economic Review*, 45: 1–28.

Kuznets, S. (1965): *Economic Growth and Structure*, London: Heinemann.

Laffan, M. (1985): '"Labour Must Wait": Ireland's Conservative Revolution' in P. J. Corish (ed.). *Radicals, Rebels and Establishments*, Belfast: Appletree Press.

Lafferty, W. M. (1990): 'The Political Transformation of a Social Democratic State: As the World Moves in, Norway Moves Right', *West European Politics*, 13: 79–100.

Lange, P. (1984): 'Unions, Workers and Wage Regulation: The Rational Bases of Consent' in J. H. Goldthorpe (ed.).

Lash, S. (1985): 'The End of Neo-Corporatism?: The Breakdown of Centralized Bargaining in Sweden', *British Journal of Industrial Relations*, 23: 215–40.

Lash, S. and Urry, J. (1987): *The End of Organized Capitalism*, Cambridge: Polity Press.

Latourette, K. S. (1962): *Christianity in a Revolutionary Age. A History of Christianity in the Nineteenth and Twentieth Centuries*. Vol. V. *The Twentieth Century Outside Europe. The Americas, The Pacific, Asia and Africa: The Emerging World Christian Community*, London: Eyre and Spottiswoode.

Laver, M. (1987): 'Measuring Patterns of Party Support in Ireland', *Economic and Social Review*, 18: 95–100.

Laver, M. and Arkins, A. (1990): 'Coalition and Fianna Fáil' in M. Gallagher and R. Sinnott (eds)., *How Ireland Voted 1989*, Galway: Centre for the Study of Irish Elections.

Laver, M. and Higgins, M. D. (1986): 'Coalition or Fianna Fáil? The Politics of Inter-Party Government in Ireland' in Geoffrey Pridham (ed.), *Coalitional Behaviour in Theory and Practice*, Cambridge: Cambridge University Press.

Laver, M. and Hunt, W. B. (1992): *Policy and Party Competition*, New York: Routledge.

Laver, M., Mair, P. and Sinnott, R. (eds) (1987a): *How Ireland Voted: The Irish General Election 1987*, Dublin: Poolbeg Press.

Laver, M., Marsh, M. and Sinnott, R. (1987b): 'Patterns of Party Support' in M. Laver, P. Mair and R. Sinnott (eds).

Laver, M. and Shepsle, K. A. (1990a): 'Coalitions and Cabinet Government', *American Political Science Review*, 84: 873–890.

Laver, M. and Shepsle, K. A. (1990b): 'Government Coalitions and Intraparty Politics', *British Journal of Political Science*, 20: 489–507.

Laver, M. and Shepsle, K. A. (1991): 'Divided Government: America is not Exceptional', *Governance*, 4: 250–269.

Lee, J. (1973). *The Modernisation of Irish Society*, Gill and Macmillan.

Lee, J. J. (1989): *Ireland 1912–1985: Politics and Society*, Cambridge: Cambridge University Press.

Leeuwis, C. (1989): *Marginalization Misunderstood*, Wageningen: Wageningen Agricultural University.

Lehmbruch, G. (1979): 'Liberal Corporatism and Party Government' in P. Schmitter and G. Lehmbruch (eds), *Trends Towards Corporatist Intermediation*. London: Sage.

Lehmbruch, G. and Schmitter, P. (eds) (1982): *Patterns of Corporatist Policy Making*, Beverly Hills: Sage.

Leslie, J. H. (1980): 'Some Theoretical Issues in a Sociological Analysis of Religious Ideology in a Roman Catholic Parish', *Research Bulletin*, ISWRA, University of Birmingham.

Lester, M. (1958): *As Unions Mature*, Princeton N.J.: Princeton University Press.

Lesthaeghe, R. (1983): 'A Century of Demographic and Cultural Change in Western Europe', *Population and Development Review*, 9: 411–436.

Lindblom, C. E. (1949): *Unions and Capitalism*, New Haven: Yale University Press.

Linder, M. and Houghton, J. (1990): 'Self-Employment and the Petty Bourgeoisie:

Comment on Steinmetz and Wright'. *American Journal of Sociology*, 96: 727–735.

Lipset, S. M. (1960): *Political Man*, New York: Doubleday.

Lipset, S. M. (1969): *Revolution and Counter-Revolution*, London: Heinemann.

Lipset, S. M. and Bendix, R. (1959): *Social Mobility in Industrial Society*, Berkeley: University of California Press.

Lipset, S. M. and Rokkan, S. (1967): 'Cleavage Structures, Party Systems, and Voter Alignments: an Introduction' in S. M. Lipset and S. Rokkan (eds), *Party Systems and Voter Alignments*, New York: The Free Press.

Lodge, D. (1980): *How Far Can You Go?* London: Secker and Warburg.

Long, N. (1986): 'Commoditization: Thesis and Antithesis' in N. Long, J. Van Der Ploeg, C. Curtin and L. Box, *The Commoditization Debate: Labour Process, Strategy and Social Network*, Wageningen: Wageningen Agricultural University.

Longstreth, F. (1988): 'From Corporatism to Dualism: Thatcherism and the Climacteric of British Trade Unions in the 1980s', *Political Studies*, September: 413–32.

Lorwin, V. (1954): *The French Labor Movement*, Boston, Mass.: Harvard University Press.

Lucey, C. (1955): 'Minority Report' in *Commission on Emigration and Other Population Problems 1948–1954 Reports*, Dublin: Stationery Office.

Lucey, D. I. F. and Kaldor, D. R. (1969): *Rural Industrialisation: The Impact of Industrialisation on Two Rural Communities in the West of Ireland*, London: Chapman.

Luckmann, T. (1970): *The Invisible Religion: The Problem of Religion in Modern Society*, London: Collier Macmillan.

Lukes, S. (1974): *Power, A Radical View*, London: Macmillan.

Lynch, J. (1969): *Presidential Address to the Fianna Fáil Ard Fheis*, Dublin: Fianna Fáil.

Lyons, F. S. L. (1973): *Ireland Since the Famine*, London: Fontana.

Lysaght-O'Connor, D. R. (1982): *Class Struggle in the Irish War of Independence and Civil War*, M. A. Thesis, University College, Dublin.

MacAirt, J. (1990): 'Religion Among Irish University Students', *Doctrine and Life*, 40: 172–183.

McAleese, D. (1990): 'Ireland's Economic Recovery', *The Irish Banking Review*, Summer.

McCarthy, C. (1973): *The Decade of Upheaval: Irish Trade Unions in the Nineteen Sixties*, Dublin: Institute of Public Administration.

McCarthy, C. (1977): *Trade Unions in Ireland, 1894–1960*, Dublin: Institute of Public Administration.

McCarthy, C. (1982): 'Productivity Agreements: The Problem of the Spurious'. *Journal of Irish Business and Administrative Research*, 4: 99–107.

McCarthy, W. E. J., O'Brien, J. and Dowd, V. G. (1975): *Wage Inflation and Wage Leadership*, Dublin: The Economic and Social Research Institute.

McCashin, A. (1982): 'Social Policy: 1957–82' in F. Litton (ed.). *Unequal Achievement*, Dublin: Institute of Public Administration.

McGovern, P. G. (1988): *Recent Developments in Antiunionism in Ireland: An Exploratory Study*. M. B. S. dissertation, University College, Dublin.

McGovern, P. G. (1989): 'Union Recognition and Union Avoidance in the 1980s' in T. Murphy (ed.).

Mac Gréil, M. (1991): *Religious Practice and Attitudes in Ireland. Report of a Survey of Religious Attitudes and Practice and Related Issues in the Republic of Ireland 1988–89*, Maynooth: Survey and Research Unit, Department of Social Studies.

McKee, M., Visser, J. and Saunders, P. (1986): 'Marginal Tax Rates on the Use of Labor and Capital in OECD Countries', *OECD Economic Studies*, 7 (August).

McLeod, H. (1974): *Class and Religion in the Late Victorian City*, London: Croom Helm.

McLeod, H. (1981): *Religion and the People of Western Europe: 1789–1970*, Oxford: Oxford University Press.

McLeod, H. (1986a): 'New Perspectives on Victorian Class Religion: The Oral Evidence', *Oral History Journal*, 14: 31–49.

McLeod, H. (1986b): 'Building the "Catholic Ghetto": Catholic Organisations 1870–1914' in W. J. Sheils and D. Wood (eds), *Voluntary Religion*, Oxford: Basil Blackwell.

McLeod, H. (1989): 'Popular Catholicism in Irish New York, c. 1900' in W. J. Sheils and D. Wood (eds), *The Churches, Ireland and the Irish*, Oxford: Basil Blackwell.

McLeod, H. (1990): 'Urbanisation and Religion in 19th Century Britain' in K. Elm and H.-D. Loock (eds), *Seelsorge und Diakonie in Berlin*, Berlin and New York: Walter de Gruyter.

McRedmond, L. (1980): 'The Church in Ireland' in J. Cumming and P. Burns (eds.) *The Church Now: An Inquiry into the Present State of the Catholic Church in Britain and Ireland*, Dublin: Gill and Macmillan.

McSweeney, B. (1980): *Roman Catholicism: The Search for Relevance*, Oxford : Blackwell.

Maddison, A. (1982): *Phases of Capitalist Development*, Oxford: Oxford University Press.

Maddison, A. (1989): *The World Economy in the 20th Century*, Paris: OECD.

Maguire, M. (1986): 'Ireland' in P. Flora (ed.), *Growth to Limits: The Western European Welfare States Since World War II*, Vol. 2, Berlin: Walter de Gruyter.

Maguire, M. (1987): 'Ireland', in P. Flora (ed.), *Growth to Limits: The Western European Welfare States Since World War II*, Vol. 4, Berlin: Walter de Gruyter.

Mahon, E. (1991): 'Motherhood, Work and Equal Opportunity: A Case Study of Irish Civil Servants', *First Report of the Third Joint Committee on Women's Rights*, Dublin: Stationery Office.

Mair, P. (1979): 'The Autonomy of the Political: The Development of the Irish Party System', *Comparative Politics*, 11: 445–465.

Mair, P. (1987): *The Changing Irish Party System: Organisation, Ideology and Electoral Competition*, London: Frances Pinter.

Mair, P. (1990): 'The Irish Party System Into the 1990s' in M. Gallagher and R. Sinnott (eds), *How Ireland Voted 1989*.

Mair, P. (ed.) (1990). *The West European Party System*, Oxford: Oxford University Press.

Malloy, J. M. (1977): 'Authoritarianism and Corporatism in Latin America: The Modal Pattern' in J. M. Malloy (ed.), *Authoritarianism and Corporatism in Latin America*, Pittsburg: University of Pittsburg Press.

Malloy, J. (1985): 'Statecraft and Social Security Policy and Crisis: A Comparison of Latin America and the United States' in C. Mesa-Lago (ed.). *The Crisis of Social Security and Health Care: Latin American Experiences and Lessons*, Pittsburgh: Center for Latin American Studies, University of Edinburgh.

Marin, B. (1983): 'Organizing Interests by Interest Organization: Associational Prerequisites of Corporatism in Austria', *International Political Science Review*, 2: 197–217.

Markovits, A. (1986): *The Politics of the West German Trade Unions*, Cambridge: Cambridge University Press.

Marsh, M. and Sinnott, R. (1990): 'How the Voters Decided' in M. Gallagher and R. Sinnott (eds).

Marshall, G. (1990): 'John Goldthorpe and Class Analysis' in J. Clark *et al.* (eds).

Marshall, T. H. (1950): *Citizenship and Social Class*, Cambridge: Cambridge University Press.

Martin, D. (1965): 'Towards Eliminating the Concept of Secularization' in J. Gould (ed.), *Penguin Survey of the Social Sciences*, Harmondsworth: Penguin.

Martin, D. (1969): *The Religious and the Secular: Studies in Secularization*, London: Routledge and Kegan Paul.

Martin, D. (1978): *A General Theory of Secularization*. Oxford: Blackwell.

Matthews, R. C. O., Feinstein, C. H. and Odling-Smee, J. C. (1982): *British Economic Growth 1856–1973*, Oxford: Clarendon Press.

Meenan, J. F. (1970): *The Irish Economy Since 1922*, Liverpool: Liverpool University Press.

Meerman, J. (1978): 'Do Empirical Studies of Budget Incidence Make Sense?', *Public Finance*, 3: 295–313.

Miller, D. (1975): 'Irish Catholicism and the Great Famine', *Journal of Social History*, 9: 81–98.

Mitchell, A. (1974): *Labour in Irish Politics*, Dublin: Irish University Press.

Mjøset, L. (1992): *The Irish Economy in a Comparative Institutional Perspective*, Dublin: National Economic and Social Council.

Moore, J. (1975): 'The Catholic Priesthood' in M. Hill (ed.), *A Sociological Yearbook of Religion in Britain, 8*, London: S.C.M.

Moore, M. (1988): *A Study of Alternative Industrial Action in the Eighties*, M.B.S. dissertation, University College, Dublin.

Mosher, W. D. (1980): 'The Theory of Change and Response: An Application to Puerto Rico 1940–1970', *Population Studies*, 34: 45–58.

Moynihan, M. (ed.) (1980): *Speeches and Statements by Eamonn de Valera*, Dublin: Gill and Macmillan.

Müller, W. (1990): 'Social Mobility in Industrial Nations' in J. Clark *et al.* (eds).

Munnell, A. H. (1982): *The Economics of Private Pensions*, Washington D. C.: The Brookings Institution.

Murphy, D. (1984): 'The Impact of State Taxes and Benefits on Irish Household Incomes', *Journal of the Statistical and Social Inquiry Society of Ireland*, 25: 55–120.

Murphy, J. A. (1975): *Ireland in the Twentieth Century*, Dublin: Gill and Macmillan.

Murphy, T. (ed.) (1987/1989): *Industrial Relations in Ireland: Contemporary Trends and Developments*, Dublin: Department of Industrial Relations, University College Dublin.

Murray, S. (1984): *Survey of Employee Industrial Relations in Irish Private-Sector Manufacturing Industries*, Dublin: Industrial Development Authority.

Myles, J. (1984): *Old Age in the Welfare State: The Political Economy of Public Pensions*, Boston: Little Brown.

Myles, J. (1988): 'Postwar Capitalism and the Extension of Social Security into a Retirement Wage' in M. Weir, A. Orloff and T. Skocpol (eds), *The Politics of Social Security in the United States*, Princeton: Princeton University Press.

Myles, J. (1989): *Old Age in the Welfare State: The Political Economy of Public Pensions*, Lawrence, Kansas: University Press of Kansas.

Naroll, R. (1970): 'Galton's Problem' in R. Naroll and R. Cohen (eds), *A Handbook of Method in Cultural Anthropology*, New York: Natural History Press.

Neal, M. A. (1970): 'The Relation Between Religious Belief and Structural Change in Religious Orders: Developing an Effective Measuring Instrument', *Review of Religious Research*, 12: 2–16.

NESC (1982): No. 64. *A Review of Industrial Policy*, Dublin: NESC.

NESC (1982): No. 66. *Policies for Industrial Development: Conclusions and Recommendations*, Dublin: NESC.

NESC (1983): No. 67. *An Analysis of Job Losses in Irish Manufacturing Industry*, Dublin: NESC.

NESC (1986): No. 83. *A Strategy for Development, 1986–1990*, Dublin: NESC.

NESC (1989): No. 88. *Ireland in the European Community: Performance, Prospects and Strategy*, Dublin: NESC.

NESC (1991): No. 90. *The Economic and Social Implications of Emigration*, Dublin: NESC.

Nic Ghiolla Phádraig, M. (1976): 'Religion in Ireland', *Social Studies*, 5: 113–180.

Nic Ghiolla Phádraig, M. (1986): 'Religious Practice and Secularisation' in P. Clancy *et al.* (eds).

Nic Ghiolla Phádraig, M. (1988): 'Ireland: The Exception that Proves Two Rules' in T. M. Gannon (ed.), *World Catholicism in Transition*, New York: Macmillan.

Nisbet, R. A. (1969): *Social Change and History*. New York: Oxford University Press.

Nolan, B. (1981): 'Redistribution of Household Income in Ireland by Taxes and Benefits', *The Economic and Social Review*, 13: 59–88.

Nolan, B. (1991): *The Utilisation and Financing of Health Services in Ireland*, Dublin: The Economic and Social Research Institute.

Nolan, B. and Callan, T. (forthcoming): 'Cross-National Poverty Comparisons Using Relative Poverty Lines: An Application and Some Lessons', *Review of Economic Inequality*.

O'Brien, J. F. (1981): *A Study of National Wage Agreements in Ireland*, Dublin: The Economic and Social Research Institute.

O'Brien, J. F. (1987/1989): 'Pay Determination in Ireland: Retrospect and Prospects', in T. Murphy (ed.).

O'Carroll, J. P. (1987): 'Strokes, Cute Hoors and Sneaking Regarders: The Influence of Local Culture on Irish Political Style', *Irish Political Studies*, 2: 77–92.

O'Carroll, J. P. (1991): 'Bishops, Knights – and Pawns? Traditional Thought and the Irish Abortion Referendum Debate of 1983', *Irish Political Studies*, 6: 53–71.

O'Connell, P. (1982a): 'The Distribution and Redistribution of Income in the Republic of Ireland', *The Economic and Social Review*, 13: 251–278.

O'Connell, P. (1982b): 'A Sociology of Fiscal Crisis'. Paper read at Sociological Association of Ireland Conference, 1982.

O'Connor, E. (1988): *Syndicalism in Ireland: 1917–1923*, Cork: Cork University Press.

O'Connor, J. (1973): *The Fiscal Crisis of the State*, New York: St. Martin's Press.

OECD (1966). *Investment in Education*. Dublin: Stationery Office.

OECD (1978): *Public Expenditure Trends: Studies in Resource Allocation*. Paris: OECD.

OECD (1979): *Economic Survey, Ireland*, Paris: OECD.

OECD (1982): *Economic Survey, Ireland*. Paris: OECD.

OECD (1988): *Economic Survey, Australia*, Paris: OECD.

OECD (1989a): *Economic Survey, Ireland*, Paris: OECD.

OECD (1989b): *Revenue Statistics of the OECD Member Countries, 1965–88*. Paris: OECD.

OECD (1990): *Economic Survey, Australia*, Paris: OECD.

OECD (1991a): *Economic Survey, Portugal*, Paris: OECD.

OECD (1991b): *OECD in Figures*, supplement to *The OECD Observer*, June/July.

O'Farrell, P. N. (1980): 'Multinational Enterprises and Regional Development: Irish Evidence', *Regional Studies*, 14, 2, 141–50.

O'Farrell, P. N. (1984): 'Components of Manufacturing Employment Change in Ireland 1973–1981', *Urban Studies*, 21, 155–176.

O'Farrell, P. N. and Crouchley, R. (1984): 'An Industrial and Spatial Analysis of New Firm Formation in Ireland', *Regional Studies*, 18: 221–236.

Offe, C. (1985): *Disorganized Capitalism*, Cambridge: Polity Press.

O'Hagan, J. W. and O'Higgins, M. (1973): 'Are Ireland's Social Security Payments Too Small? A Comment', *The Economic and Social Review*, 5: 199–200.

O'Hearn, D. (1989): 'The Irish Case of Dependency: An Exception to the Exceptions?', *American Sociological Review*, 54: 578–96.

O'Hearn, D. (1990): 'The Road from Import-Substituting to Export-Led Industrialization in Ireland: Who Mixed the Asphalt, Who Drove the Machinery, and Who Kept Making Them Change Directions?' *Politics and Society*, 18: 1–37.

O'Higgins, M. (1990): 'The Distributive Effects of Public Expenditure and Taxation: An Agnostic View of the CSO Analysis' in C. Sandford, C. Pond and R. Walter (eds), *Taxation and Social Policy*, London: Heineman.

O'Higgins, M. and Ruggles, P. (1981): 'The Distribution of Public Expenditure and Taxes Among Households in the United Kingdom', *Review of Income and Wealth*, 27: 298–326.

O'Higgins, M. and Jenkins, S. (1989): 'Poverty in Europe', paper presented to Conference on Poverty Statistics in the European Community, Noordwijke, October.

O'Higgins, M., Schmaus, G. and Stephenson, G. (1989): 'Income Distribution and Redistribution: A Microdata Analysis for Seven Countries', *Review of Income and Wealth*, 35: 107–131.

O'Kelly, K. (1986): 'Fifty Voices: A Report from Bellinter' in S. MacRéamoinn (ed.), *Pobal: The Laity in Ireland*, Dublin: Columba Press.

O'Leary, B. (1987): 'Towards Europeanisation and Realignment? The Irish General Election, February 1987', *West European Politics*, 10: 455–465.

O'Leary, B. (1990): 'Setting the Record Straight: A Comment on Cahill's Country Report on Ireland', *Governance*, 3: 98–104.

Olson, M. (1982): *The Rise and Decline of Nations*, New Haven, Conn: Yale University Press.

O'Mahony, D. (1967): *The Irish Economy*, 2nd edition, Cork: Cork University Press.

O'Malley, E. (1989): *Industry and Economic Development: The Challenge for the Latecomer*, Dublin: Gill and Macmillan.

O'Malley, E. (1990): 'Ireland' in *The Impact of the Internal Market by the Industrial Sector, The Challenge for the Member States*, Brussels: Commission of the European Communities.

OPCS (1990a): *Abortion Statistics 1988*, London: HMSO.

OPCS (1990b): *Birth Statistics 1988*, London: HMSO.

Orridge, A., (1976): 'The Irish Labour Party' in W. E. Paterson and A. H. Thomas (eds), *Social Democratic Parties in Western Europe*, London: Croom Helm.

O'Sullivan, E. (1991): 'The 1990 Presidential Election in the Republic of Ireland', *Irish Political Studies*, 6: 85–98.

O'Toole, R. (ed.) (1989): *Sociological Studies in Roman Catholicism: Historical and Contemporary Perspectives*, Lampeter: Edwin Mellen Press.

Padao-Schioppa, T. (1987): *Efficiency, Stability and Equity: A Stragegy for the Evolution of the Economic System of the European Community*, Oxford: Oxford University Press.

Paloheimo, H. (1991): 'Between Liberalism and Corporatism: The Effect of Trade Unions and Governments on Economic Performance in Eighteen OECD Countries', in R. Brunetta and C. Dell'Aringa (eds).

Parsons, T. (1960): *Structure and Process in Modern Society*, Glencoe Ill: Free Press.

Parsons, T. (1964): 'Evolutionary Universals in Society', *American Sociological Review*, 29: 339–357.

Parsons, T. (1967): *Sociological Theory and Modern Society*, New York: Free Press.

Paukert, F. (1973): 'Income Distribution at Different Levels of Development: A Survey of Evidence', *International Labour Review*, August-September: 97–125.

Payne, C., Heath, A. and Payne, J. (1991): 'Modelling Trends in Multiway Tables' in R. Davies and A. Dale (eds) *Analysing Social and Political Change*, London: Sage.

Peillon, M. (1982): *Contemporary Irish Society: An Introduction*, Dublin: Gill and Macmillan.

Perez-Diaz, V. (1986): 'Economic Policies and Social Pacts in Spain During the Transition: The Two Faces of Neo-Corporatism', *European Sociological Review*, 2: 1–19.

Peterson, R. B. (1987): 'Swedish Collective Bargaining: A Changing Scene', *British Journal of Industrial Relations'*, 15: 31–48.

Pinto, M. (1990): 'Trade Union Action and Industrial Relations in Portugal' in C. Baglioni and C. Crouch (eds).

Ploeg, J. D. van der (1989): 'Introduction' in C. Leeuwis *Marginalisation Misunderstood*, Wageningen: Wageningen Agricultural University.

Poggi, G. (1990): *The State: Its Nature, Development and Prospects*, Cambridge: Polity Press.

Polanyi, K. (1944): *The Great Transformation*, New York: Rinehart.

Popper, K. R. (1957): *The Poverty of Historicism*, London: Routledge and Kegan Paul.

Power, R. and Roche, M. (1990): *National Farm Survey 1988*, Dublin: Teagasc.

Pro Mundi Vita (1973): 'Pluralism and Pluriformity in Religious Life: A Case Study', *Bulletin*, 47.

Przeworski, A. (1983): 'Methods of Cross-National Research, 1970–1983: An Overview', Berlin: Wissenschaftszentrum.

Przeworski, A. (1985): *Capitalism and Social Democracy*, Cambridge: Cambridge University Press.

Pyle, J. L. (1990): *The State and Women in the Economy: Lessons from Sex Discrimination in the Republic of Ireland*, Albany: State University of New York Press.

Quadagno, J. (1987): 'Theories of the Welfare State', *Annual Review of Sociology*, 13: 109–128.

Raftery, A. and Hout, M. (1990): 'Maximally Maintained Inequality: Expansion, Reform and Opportunity in Irish Education, 1921–1975', ISA Research Committee on Social Stratification and Mobility, Madrid.

Regini, M. (1984): 'The Conditions for Political Exchange: How Concertation Emerged and Collapsed in Italy and Great Britain', in J. H. Goldthorpe (ed.).

Registrar-General (1982): *Fifty-Ninth Annual Report of the Registrar-General 1980*, Belfast: HMSO.

Registrar-General Northern Ireland, DHSS (1989): *Annual Report 1987, No. 66*, Belfast: HMSO.

Rehn, G. and Viklund, B. (1990): 'Changes in the Swedish Model' in C. Baglioni and C. Crouch (eds).

Review Group on the Treatment of Households in the Social Welfare Code (1991): *Report*, Dublin: Stationery Office.

Riordan, E. J. (1920): *Modern Irish Trade and Industry*, London: Methuen.

Roca, J. (1987): 'Neo-Corporatism in Post-Franco Spain' in I. Scholten (ed.).

Roche, W. K. (1981): 'Convention and Change in Irish Industrial Relations: Comparisons and Differentials', in W. K. Roche and F. Quinn, *Trends in Irish Industrial Relations*, Dublin: College of Industrial Relations.

Roche, W. K. (1982): 'Social Partnership and Political Control: State Strategy and Industrial Relations in Ireland', in M. Kelly, L. O'Dowd and J. Wickham (eds), *Power, Conflict, and Inequality*, Dublin: Turoe Press.

Roche, W. K. (1987a/1989): 'State Strategies and the Politics of Industrial Relations in Ireland Since 1945' in T. Murphy (ed.).

Roche, W. K. (1987b): *Social Integration and Strategic Power: The Development of Militancy Among Electricity Generating Station Workers in the Republic of Ireland, 1950–1982*, D.Phil. thesis, University of Oxford.

Roche, W. K. (forthcoming): 'Organisational Dynamics and the Business Cycle:

Aspects of the Growth and Performance of British Trade Unions in the Republic of Ireland', *British Journal of Industrial Relations*.

Roche, W. and Larragy, J. (1987/1989): 'The Trend of Unionisation in the Irish Republic', in T. Murphy (ed.).

Roche, W. K. and Larragy, J. (1990): 'Cyclical and Institutional Determinants of Annual Trade Union Growth in the Republic of Ireland: Evidence from the DUES Data Series'. *European Sociological Review*, 6: 49–72.

Rose, R. (1985): 'The Significance of Public Employment', R. Rose (ed.), *Public Employment in Western Nations*, Cambridge: Cambridge University Press.

Ross, A. M. and Hartman, P. T. (1960): *Changing Patterns of Industrial Conflict*, New York: Wiley & Sons.

Ross, Miceal (1986): *Employment in the Public Domain in Recent Decades*, Dublin: The Economic and Social Research Institute.

Rottman, D. and Hannan, D. F. (1981): 'Fiscal Welfare and Inflation: Winners and Losers'. Dublin: The Economic and Social Research Institute.

Rottman, D., Hannan, D. F., Hardiman, N. and Wiley, M. (1982): *The Distribution of Income in the Republic of Ireland: A Study in Social Class and Family Cycle Inequalities*, Dublin: The Economic and Social Research Institute.

Rottman, D. and O'Connell, P. (1982): 'The Changing Social Structure of Ireland'. *Administration*, 30, 3: 63–88.

Rottman, D. and Reidy, M. (1988): *Redistribution Through State Social Expenditure in the Republic of Ireland: 1973–1980*, Dublin: National Economic and Social Council.

Ruzicka, L., Wunsch, G. and Kane, P. (eds) (1989): *Differential Mortality: Methodological Issues and Biosocial Factors*, Oxford: Clarendon Press.

Ryan, L. (1979): 'Church and Politics: The Last Twenty-Five Years', *The Furrow*, 30: 3–18.

Ryan, L. (1983): 'Faith Under Survey', *The Furrow*, 34: 3–15.

Sandford, C. and Morrissey, O. (1985): *The Irish Wealth Tax: A Case Study in Economics and Politics*, Dublin: The Economic and Social Research Institute.

Sani, G. and Sartori, G. (1983): 'Polarisation, Fragmentation and Competition in Western Democracies' in H. Daalder and P. Mair (eds), *Western European Party Systems*, London: Sage Publications.

Sardon, J. P. (1990): *Cohort Fertility in Member States of the Council of Europe*, Population Studies No. 21, Strasbourg: Council of Europe.

Sartori, G. (1968/1990): 'The Sociology of Parties: A Critical Review' in P. Mair (ed.).

Saunders, P. and Klau, F. (1985): 'The Role of the Public Sector', *OECD Economics Studies*, Special Issue, No. 4 Spring.

Scharpf, F. W. (1981): 'The Political Economy of Inflation and Unemployment in Western Europe: An Outline', Berlin: Wissenschaftszentrum.

Scharpf, F. W. (1984): 'Economic and Institutional Constraints of Full-Employment Strategies: Sweden, Austria, and West Germany: 1973–1982' in J. H. Goldthorpe (ed.).

Scharpf, F. W. (1991): *Crisis and Choice in European Social Democracy*, Ithaca, New York and London: Cornell University Press.

Schattschneider, E. E. (1960): *The Semi-Sovereign People*, New York: Holt, Reinhart and Winston.

Schmidt, M. G. (1982): 'Does Corporatism Matter? Economic Crisis, Politics and Rates of Unemployment in Capitalist Democracies in the 1970s' in G. Lehmbruch and P. C. Schmitter (eds), *Patterns of Corporatist Policy-Making*, London and Beverly Hills: Sage.

Schmidt, M. G. (1988): 'The Politics of Labour Market Policy: Structural and Political Determinants of Rates of Unemployment in Industrial Nations' in F. G. Castles *et al.*(eds), *Managing Mixed Economies*, Berlin: de Gruyter.

Schmitter, P. C. (1979): 'Still the Century of Corporatism?', in P. C. Schmitter and G. Lehmbruch (eds).

Schmitter, P. C. (1981): 'Interest Intermediation and Regime Governability' in S. Berger (ed.) *Organizing Interests in Western Europe*, Cambridge: Cambridge University Press.

Schmitter, P. C. (1991): 'Sectors in Modern Capitalism: Modes of Governance and Variations in Performance', in R. Brunetta and C. Dell'Aringa (eds).

Schmitter, P. C. and Lehmbruch, G. (eds) (1979): *Trends Towards Corporatist Intermediation*, London and Beverly Hills: Sage.

Scholten, I. (ed.) (1987): *Political Stability and Neo-Corporatism*, London and Beverly Hills: Sage.

Schwerin, D. S. (1980): *Corporatism and Protest: Organisational Politics in the Norwegian Trade Union Movement*, Kent, Ohio: Kent Popular Press.

Scitovsky, T. (1978): 'Market Power and Inflation', *Economica*, 45: 221–233.

Scitovsky, T. (1980): 'Can Capitalism survive – an Old Question in a New Setting', *American Economic Review*, 70, *Proceedings and Papers*.

Scully, J. T. (1971): *Agriculture in the West of Ireland*, Dublin: Department of Agriculture.

Sexton, J. J. (1982): 'Sectoral Changes in the Labour Force Over the Period 1961–1980', *Quarterly Economic Commentary*, August, Dublin: The Economic and Social Research Institute.

Sexton, J. J., Walsh, B. M., Hannan, D. F. and McMahon, D. (1991): *The Economic and Social Implications of Emigration*, Dublin: National Economic and Social Council.

Shalev, M. (1983a): 'The Social Democratic Model and Beyond: Two "Generations" of Comparative Research on the Welfare State'. *Comparative Social Research*, 6: 315–351.

Shalev, M. (1983b): 'Class Politics and the Western State' in S. E. Spiro and E. Yuchtman-Yarr (eds), *Evaluating the Welfare State: Social and Political Perspectives*, New York: Academic Press.

Sharratt, B. (1977): 'English Catholicism in the 1960s' in A. Hastings (ed.), *Bishops and Writers: Aspects of the Evolution of Modern English Catholicism*, Wheathampstead: Anthony Clarke.

Shavit, Y. and Blossfeld, H. P. (eds) (1992): *Persistent Inequality: Changing Educational Stratification in Thirteen Countries*, Boulder, Col.: Westview Press.

Siegel, B. J. (1970): 'Defensive Structuring and Environmental Stress', *American Journal of Sociology*, 76: 11.

Simons, J. (1986): 'Culture, Economy and Reproduction in Contemporary Europe' in D. A. Coleman and R. S. Schofield (eds), *The State of Population Theory: Forward from Malthus*, Oxford: Basil Blackwell.

Sinnott, R. (1978): 'The Electorate' in H. R. Penniman (ed.), *Ireland at the Polls: The Dáil Election of 1977*, Washington DC: AEI Press.

Sinnott, R. (1984): 'Interpretations of the Irish Party System', *European Journal of Political Research*, 12: 289–307.

Skocpol, T. (1981): 'Political Response to Capitalist Crisis: Neo-Marxist Theories of the State and the Case of the New Deal'. *Politics and Society*, 10: 155–201.

Skocpol, T. (1985): 'Bringing the State Back In: Strategies of Analysis in Current Research' in T. Skocpol, D. Rueschemeyer and P. Evans (eds), *Bringing the State Back In*, Cambridge: Cambridge University Press.

Skocpol, T. and Amenta, E. (1986): 'States and Social Policies', *Annual Review of Sociology*, 12: 131–157.

Slichter, S. H., Healy, J. J. and Livernash, E. R. (1960): *The Impact of Collective Bargaining on Management*, Washington D.C.: Brookings Institution.

Smeeding, T. (1982): 'An Anti-Poverty Effect of In-Kind Transfers: A "Good Idea" Gone Too Far?', *Policy Studies Journal*. 10: 499–522.

Smeeding, T. and Schmaus, G. (1990): 'The LIS Database: Technical and Methodological Aspects' in T. Smeeding, M. O'Higgins and L. Rainwater (eds), *Poverty, Income Inequality and Income Distribution in Comparative Perspective*, Hemel Hempstead: Harvester/Wheatsheaf.

Soskice, D. (1990): 'Wage Determination: The Changing Role of Institutions in Advanced Industrialized Countries', *Oxford Review of Economic Policy*, 8: 36–61.

Soskice, D. (1991): 'Reinterpreting Corporatism and Explaining Unemployment: Co-ordinated and Non-co-ordinated Market Economies', in R. Brunetta and C. Dell'Aringa (eds).

Sperber, J. (1984): *Popular Catholicism in Nineteenth Century Germany*, Princeton N.J.: Princeton University Press.

Steinmetz, G. and Wright, E. O. (1989): 'The Fall and Rise of the Petty Bourgeoisie: Changing Patterns of Self-Employment in the Postwar United States', *American Journal of Sociology*, 94: 973–1018.

Steinmetz, G. and Wright, E. O. (1990): 'Reply to Linder and Houghton', *American Journal of Sociology*, 96: 736–740.

Stepan, A. (1978): *The State and Society: Peru in Comparative Perspective*, Princeton N.J.: Princeton University Press.

Stephens, J. (1979): *The Transition from Capitalism to Socialism*, London: Macmillan.

Stinchcombe, A. L. (1968): *Constructing Social Theories*, New York: Harcourt Brace and World.

Stolnitz, G. J. (1956): 'A Century of International Mortality Trends: 2', *Population Studies*, 10: 17–42.

Strauss, G. (1951): *Irish Nationalism and British Democracy*, London: Batsford.

Streeck, W. (1990): 'The Uncertainties of Management in the Management of Uncertainty: Employers, Labor Relations and Industrial Adjustment in the 1980s', *Work, Employment, and Society*, 1: 281–305.

Sturmthal, A. (1951): 'Comments on Selig Perlman', *Industrial and Labour Relations Review*, 14: 483–496.

Summers, R. and Heston, A. (1988): 'A New Set of International Comparisons of Real Product and Prices for 130 Countries, 1950–1985', *Review of Income and Wealth*, 1–26.

Szuchewycz, B. (1989): '"The Growth is in the Silence": The Meanings of Silence in the Irish Charismatic Movement' in C. Curtin and T. M. Wilson (eds).

Taylor, L. J. (1989): 'The Mission: An Anthropological View of an Irish Religious Occasion' in C. Curtin and T. M. Wilson (eds).

Taylor, L. J. (1990a): 'The Healing Mass: Fields and Regimes of Irish Catholicism', *Archives des Sciences Sociales des Religions*, 71: 93–111.

Taylor, L. J. (1990b): 'Stories of Power, Powerful Stories: the Drunken Priest in Donegal' in E. Badone (ed.).

Teitelbaum, M. S. (1984): *The British Fertility Decline: Demographic Transition in the Crucible of the Industrial Revolution*, Princeton N.J.: Princeton University Press.

Telesis Consultancy Group (1982): *A Review of Industrial Policy*, Dublin: National Economic and Social Council.

Therborn, G. (1986): *Why Some Peoples Are More Unemployed Than Others*, London: Verso.

Third Programme (1969): *Economic and Social Development 1969–1972*, Dublin: Stationery Office.

Tomlin, B. (1966): *The Management of Irish Industry*, Dublin: Irish Management Institute.

Treiman, D. J. (1970): 'Industrialisation and Social Stratification' in E. O. Laumann (ed.), *Social Stratification: Research and Theory for the 1970s*, Indianapolis: Bobbs Merrill.

Tussing, A. D. (1978): *Irish Educational Expenditures – Past, Present and Future*, Dublin: The Economic and Social Research Institute.

Van de Kaa, D. J. (1987): 'Europe's Second Demographic Transition', *Population Bulletin Volume 42*, No. 1, Washington D.C.: Population Reference Bureau Inc.

Vernon, R. (1966): 'International Investment and International Trade in the Product Cycle', *Quarterly Journal of Economics*, 80: 190–207.

Visser, J. (1987): *In Search of Inclusive Unionism: A Comparative Analysis*, Ph.D. Thesis, University of Amsterdam.

Visser, J. (1990): 'Continuity and Change in Dutch Industrial Relations' in C. Baglioni and C. Crouch (eds).

Wallace, J. (1981): *Industrial Relations in Limerick City and Environs*, Limerick: National Institute for Higher Education.

Wallace, J. and O'Shea, F. (1987): *A Study of Unofficial Strikes in Ireland: Final Report*, Dublin: Stationery Office.

Walsh, B. (1968): *Some Irish Population Problems Reconsidered*, Dublin: The Economic and Social Research Institute.

Walsh, B. M. (1972): 'Ireland's Demographic Transformation 1958–70', *Economic and Social Review*, 3: 251–275.

Walsh, B. M. (1974): 'Income Maintenance Payments in Ireland', *The Economic and Social Review*, 5: 213–225.

Walsh, P. (1991): 'Industrial Relations and Personnel Policies Under the State Sector Act', in J. Boston *et al.* (eds), *Reshaping the State: New Zealand's Bureaucratic Revolution*, Oxford: Oxford University Press.

Weafer, J. A. (1986a): 'The Irish Laity: Some Findings of the 1984 National Survey', *Doctrine and Life*, 36: 247–253.

Weafer, J. A. (1986b): 'Change and Continuity in Irish Religion, 1974–1984', *Doctrine and Life*, 36: 507–517.

Weafer, J. A. (1988): 'Vocations - A Review of National and International Trends', *The Furrow*, August.

Weafer, J. A. (1990): 'Vocations in Ireland: Annual Report 1989', *Briefing*, 20: 219–220.

Weber, M. (1904/1958): *The Protestant Ethic and the Spirit of Capitalism*, New York: Charles Scribner.

Western, B. (1991): 'A Comparative Study of Corporatist Development', *American Sociological Review*, 56: 283–94.

Whelan, C. T. (ed.) (forthcoming): *Values and Social Change in the Republic of Ireland*, Dublin: Gill and Macmillan.

Whelan, C. T., Hannan, D. F. and Creighton, S. (1991): *Unemployment, Poverty and Psychological Distress*, Dublin: The Economic and Social Research Institute.

Whelan, C. T. and Whelan, B. J. (1984): *Social Mobility in the Republic of Ireland: A Comparative Perspective*, Dublin: The Economic and Social Research Institute.

Whelan, C. T. and Whelan, B. (1988): *The Transition to Retirement*, Dublin: The Economic and Social Research Institute.

Whitwell, J. (1990): 'The Rogernomics Monetarist Experiment', in M. Holland and J. Boston (eds), *The Fourth Labour Government: Politics and Policy in New Zealand*, Oxford: Oxford University Press.

Whyte, J. H. (1974): 'Ireland: Politics Without Social Bases' in R. Rose (ed.), *Electoral Behaviour: A Comparative Handbook*, New York: The Free Press.

Whyte, J. H. (1980): *Church and State in Modern Ireland 1923–1979*, Dublin: Gill and Macmillan.

Wilensky, H. (1975): *The Welfare State and Equality*, Berkeley: University of California Press.

Wilensky, H. A. and Lebeaux, C. (1958): *Industrial Society and Social Welfare*, New York: Russell Sage Foundation.

Wilkinson, B. (1991): 'The Irish Industrial Relations Act 1990 – Corporatism and Conflict Control', *Industrial Law Journal*, 21: 21–37.

Wilson, B. (1966): *Religion in Secular Society: A Sociological Comment*, London: Watts.

Wilson, B. (1979): *Contemporary Transformations of Religion*, Oxford: Oxford University Press.

Wilson, B. (1982): *Religion in Sociological Perspective*, Oxford: Oxford University Press.

Wilson-Davis, K. (1982): 'Fertility and Family Planning in the Irish Republic', *Journal of Biosocial Science*, 14: 343–358.

Winter, M. M. (1973): *Mission or Maintenance: A Study in New Pastoral Structures*, London: Darton, Longman and Todd.

World Bank (1990): *World Development Report*, Oxford: Oxford University Press.

Wrigley, E. A. (1972): 'The Process of Modernization and the Industrial Revolution in England', *Journal of Interdisciplinary History*, 3: 225–259.

Wrigley, E. A. and Schofield, R. S. (1981): *The Population History of England 1541–1871: A Reconstruction*, London: Edward Arnold.

Wuthnow, R. (1988): *The Restructuring of American Religion: Society and Faith Since World War II*, Princeton, N.J.: Princeton University Press.

Index